The World Come of Age

The World Come of Age

An Intellectual History of Liberation Theology

LILIAN CALLES BARGER

OXFORD
UNIVERSITY PRESS

OXFORD
UNIVERSITY PRESS

Oxford University Press is a department of the University of Oxford. It furthers
the University's objective of excellence in research, scholarship, and education
by publishing worldwide. Oxford is a registered trade mark of Oxford University
Press in the UK and certain other countries.

Published in the United States of America by Oxford University Press
198 Madison Avenue, New York, NY 10016, United States of America.

© Oxford University Press 2018

All rights reserved. No part of this publication may be reproduced, stored in
a retrieval system, or transmitted, in any form or by any means, without the
prior permission in writing of Oxford University Press, or as expressly permitted
by law, by license, or under terms agreed with the appropriate reproduction
rights organization. Inquiries concerning reproduction outside the scope of the
above should be sent to the Rights Department, Oxford University Press, at the
address above.

You must not circulate this work in any other form
and you must impose this same condition on any acquirer.

Library of Congress Cataloging-in-Publication Data
Names: Barger, Lilian Calles, 1955– author.
Title: The world come of age : an intellectual history of liberation theology / Lilian Calles Barger.
Description: New York : Oxford University Press, 2018. | Includes bibliographical references and index.
Identifiers: LCCN 2017052753 (print) | LCCN 2018021201 (ebook) | ISBN 9780190695408 (updf) |
ISBN 9780190695415 (epub) | ISBN 9780190695422 (online content) | ISBN 9780190695392 (cloth)
Subjects: LCSH: Liberation theology.
Classification: LCC BT83.57 (ebook) | LCC BT83.57 .B3655 2018 (print) | DDC 230/.0464—dc23
LC record available at https://lccn.loc.gov/2017052753

1 3 5 7 9 8 6 4 2
Printed by Sheridan Books, Inc., United States of America

En memoria de mi madre
Nieves Esther Zapettini de Calles
Y
los condenados de la tierra cuya historia nunca se contó

Contents

Acknowledgments   ix

Introduction   1

PART I *Origins*

1. Religion and Cultural Crisis   13
2. The Political Is the Total   35
3. The Irony of America   50

PART II *Reconstructions*

4. Liberatory Sensibilities   69
5. New Foundations   87
6. The Vitalism of Religion   105

PART III *Elaborations*

7. A Salvific Social Order   131
8. Secularizing Religion   152
9. The Feminine Principle   174
10. A Culture of Solidarity   193

PART IV *Reverberations*

11. A Tenuous Consensus — 219
12. A New Orthodoxy — 237
Epilogue — 256

Notes — 265
Bibliography — 315
Index — 363

Acknowledgments

THIS BOOK IS the fruit of many life-long experiences, from Latin American shantytowns to feminist religious gatherings in the United States and the support of countless people of faith, hope, and love too numerous to name. Recently, the University of Texas at Dallas and its faculty, to which I am indebted, supported the research for this project, including Charles Hatfield, Michelle Nickerson, Stephen G. Rabe, and Michael Wilson. A special thank you to Daniel Wickberg for his encouragement. Joerg Rieger, then at the Perkins School of Theology, read my early draft and provided a valuable theological perspective. The Hispanic Scholarship Fund was a source of early support and the American Association of University Women funded a year of writing.

Works of history are not possible without librarians and archivists. I am thankful to them as they helped me track down little-known texts. I received significant assistance from the staff at Instituto Bartolomé de las Casas, Lima, Perú; David M. Rubenstein Rare Book & Manuscript Library at Duke University; Burke Library at Columbia University; Princeton Theological Seminary Library, and Schomburg Center for Research in Black Culture; Bridwell Library at Perkins School of Theology; McDermott Library at the University of Texas at Dallas; and the University of New Mexico – Taos.

Access to the people who made history is invaluable, and I was fortunate to have the opportunity to speak with a gracious James Cone, Rosemary Radford Ruether, and Dr. Kristin Herzog, widow of Frederick Herzog, who extended hospitality. All gave me first-hand accounts of the early years of liberation theology.

As part of my studies and research, I spent a semester at Princeton Theological Seminary enriching my understanding of the task of theology. I am thankful for the faculty and graduate students I met who gave me their time as I learned to see my project from a theologian's point of view. I am particularly appreciative of the intellectual generosity shown to me by Mark Lewis Taylor, Bruce McCormack, Derek Woodard-Lehman, Melanie G.M. Webb, Matthew A. Bruce, and the opportunity to discuss this project with Cornel West, then at Princeton University.

Throughout the research and writing phase, I presented portions of this work at conferences, discussion groups, and blogs, and had many informal conversations with generous scholars. I am thankful for being included in presenting, or writing, for the Society for U.S. Intellectual History, with a special thanks to Andrew Hartman and Robert Greene; the African American Intellectual History Society, with a special thanks to Christopher Cameron; the American Society for Church History, the Latin American Studies Association, the Dallas Area Social Historian discussion group, the Religion in American History blog, and Cynthia R. Krkoska-Nielsen's theology and philosophy blog *Per Caritatem*. It was a privilege to participate in the 2016 National Endowment for the Humanities Institute "Problems in the Study of Religion" at the University of Virginia, led by Charles Mathewes and Kurtis Schaeffer, giving me the opportunity to test my own thinking against an outstanding group of religion scholars.

Along the way, I shared portions of my draft and received excellent feedback from Mark Edwards, Paul Crouse, Tim Lacy, and Trevor Burrows, and had informal yet helpful discussions with many fine scholars including Ray Haberski, Gary Dorrien, David Hollinger, Karen Baker-Fletcher, J. Kameron Carter, Edward Blum, Richard King, Mark Noll, Molly Worthen, Ruben Flores, Celucien Joseph, Anthony Chaney, and Stanley Hauerwas. Victoria Beliveau gave me invaluable assistance in clarifying my prose. At Oxford University Press my editor Theo Calderara, Drew Anderla, and the excellent production team supported the publication of the book, and the comments of two anonymous readers helped me refine my arguments.

Finally, I am grateful for many friends, old and new, my family, and the natural beauty of New Mexico, which gave me reprieves from the work and sustained me through the years, and a warm embrace for my husband David N. Barger for enduring patience and love through many years of chasing my dreams.

Introduction

ON SEPTEMBER 11, 2013, the 85-year-old Dominican priest Gustavo Gutiérrez found himself in a private audience with the newly elected pope. Gutiérrez, known as the father of liberation theology, had a long but strained relationship with the Vatican. Many in the Church hierarchy saw him as an advocate of melding of Christianity with Marxism. Now, however, there was a new man at the top of that hierarchy—Pope Francis, formerly Archbishop Bergoglio of Argentina, the first Latin American pope. The two men met at the insistence of Archbishop Gerhard L. Müller, head of the Vatican's office in charge of doctrine, who had worked with Gutiérrez in Peru and had become a good friend and supporter. Word of the meeting sent the Catholic press into a flurry of speculation. The Catholic News Agency reported that "behind closed doors," the pope was distancing himself from Gutiérrez's liberation theology. When they met again in May 2015 it seemed to suggest the opposite, and many believed that the Vatican was turning the page on a divisive chapter of its history. By then the speculation over the pope's position on liberation theology had gone global, picked up by the *New York Times, The Guardian,* and *Al Jazeera*.[1]

Since the 1960s, Gutiérrez had been advocating for a new theological method, one that would take as its starting point the perspective of the poor and the marginalized. Born in Lima, Peru, a *mestizo* raised in the Monserrat barrio and afflicted with childhood polio, Gutiérrez joined the cause of combating widespread poverty in Latin America. Strategically deploying Marxist analysis, his book *Teología de la liberación* (1971) and those of his like-minded peers set off decades of controversy. Liberation theology was embraced by revolutionaries and in turn criticized by the Vatican and persecuted by right-wing governments. By the 1990s, many saw liberation theology as a passing fad, the unfortunate product of the revolutionary enthusiasm of the 1960s. Now, in 2013, for the first time it appeared that under the new pope, liberation theology was gaining legitimacy in the eyes of faithful Catholics. For some, such as the Brazilian liberation theologian Leonardo Boff, who had experienced Church censorship in the 1980s, the prospective change came as a welcome reprieve: "Francis is one of us." For others, who cited Pope Francis' history of opposition to liberation theology, that assumption was "foolish speculation." The positive gestures of the pope, some asserted, were just that, a simple pastoral sign of his long-standing concern for the poor and for halting the discord over how best to advocate for social justice.[2]

As archbishop of Buenos Aires, the future pope had worked tirelessly for the poor while rejecting liberation theology. His skeptical opponents accused Archbishop Bergoglio of having collaborated with the Argentine right-wing governments in the 1970s. The pope himself took up the subject in his first apostolic exhortation, *Evangelii Gaudium*, later in 2013, in which he condemned global capitalism, consumerism, and the blight of poverty, writing, "I want a Church which is poor and for the poor." He affirmed a "preferential option for the poor," a core tenet of liberation theology. This document, combined with the invitation to Gutiérrez, brought criticism from many on the right (both Catholic and non-Catholic), who heard the pope as advancing liberalism at best and communism at worst. United States observers such as Rush Limbaugh, the conservative talk show host, called the exhortation "pure Marxism." The public intellectual and religious skeptic George Will wrote disdainfully, "Pope Francis embodies sanctity but comes trailing clouds of sanctimony. With a convert's indiscriminate zeal, he embraces ideas impeccably fashionable, demonstrably false, and deeply reactionary." Catholic columnist Pat Buchanan accused the pope of spreading "moral confusion." In sum, conservative critics agreed that the pope and the Church should stick to questions of individual salvation and private moral guidance rather than naively engaging in politics.[3]

There was as much evidence for the claim that Pope Francis had embraced liberation theology as there was for the claim that he was leading a revitalization of traditional Catholic social teaching, one in which the poor are the center of God's attention—a position that thrilled many progressive Catholics and non-Catholics alike. The difference between Catholic orthodoxy and liberation theology lay in the contested phrase "preferential option for the poor." For liberationists, the option for the poor went beyond an ethical charitable stance; it required a conversion by joining the poor, applying the perspective of the poor as a hermeneutic lens in the reading of scripture, and praxis—a process of action and reflection that did not avoid politics. Pope Francis affirmed the perspective of the poor as a hermeneutic tool, and his criticisms of the global economic system sounded like an endorsement of liberation theology.[4]

Adding to the murkiness surrounding Pope Francis and Gutiérrez were media reports in which liberation theology was ill defined—as a vague ideological distortion of Christianity or a straightforward expression of Catholic values. The public, and media observers, displayed a thin understanding of the origins and key ideas of this theo-political movement. Seen solely as the product of Latin America, cultural observers easily characterized it as a renegade Catholic theology and reduced it to a simplistic Marxist-inspired concern for the poor.

Neither was there awareness of the affinities and common origins of Latin American and North American liberation theologies. Five years earlier, during the 2008 US presidential campaign, candidate Barack Obama came under fierce criticism for his personal association with the black liberationist pastor Jeremiah Wright. Not only was Obama asked to answer for Wright's public statements, but also was asked on numerous occasions to explain why he had attended a church associated with liberation theology. Wright's scathing condemnation of US imperialism ("Not 'God Bless America'; God damn America!") and the perception that he blamed the United States for the catastrophe of 9/11 ("America's chickens are coming home to roost") drew the black liberation theologian James Cone, the movement's foremost proponent in the 1970s, back into the public spotlight. Cone, a Protestant, broke ground for black liberation theology with his book *Black Theology & Black Power* (1969), which advocated for theologians to join black people in the struggle for liberation in a racist society. The media flurry surrounding Wright's controversial statements seemed to confirm what pundits had long suspected: liberation theology was an anti-American fanaticism founded on inverse racism and aimed at inciting violence.[5]

The ink spilled in critiquing liberation theology has produced little historical insight. Part of the reason for the faint understanding reflected in these two very public incidents is a history entangled with the fate of failed radical movements of the 1960s. It seemed that after wreaking havoc on the sedate religious and political status quo that characterized post–World War II intellectual life, by the 1990s liberation theology had suffered an almost complete repudiation. It became passé among social thinkers, only to survive in obscure corners of the academy. In the new millennium liberation theology returned with a roar, alarming its critics and mystifying most of the public.

Appreciating the passionate reactions that liberation theology continues to foment requires tracing the historical origins of multiple streams of liberationist thought that emerged across the American hemisphere in the 1960s and 1970s. Above all, the first generation of liberation theologians offered a theology unwilling to engage in the modern division of religion and politics. Mass demands for justice and freedom brought into question the understanding of the relationship between God and the world. Those participating in Latin American revolutionary movements, Black Power, and women's liberation came to view religion as a justification for exclusion rather than freedom. The American states, led by the imperial power of the United States and with the blessing of religion, could no longer defend a society based on racist, classist, and sexist myths. Modern theologians struggling to rationalize the division between divine justice and social justice could not ignore the reality of human suffering. The oppressed, those constrained in their freedom due to unjust ideologies represented in social and political institutions, recognizing the degree of their "unfreedom" because of poverty, racism, and sexism became restless under the religious status quo. In response, liberationists took up the cause of the oppressed and sought an effective answer to political and religious alienation.

The liberation theologians of the 1960s and 1970s—a diverse group of radicalized religious intellectuals—prepared to bring a fresh critical stance to their discipline. Joining a common discourse that gripped radicals, they entered the opening created by a fraying post–World War II political consensus and engaged in a thoroughgoing critique of the status quo. Emboldened by tensions within the liberal theological establishment and the possibilities Vatican II offered Catholics, they challenged the truce that made theological criticism impotent in political debate. Gutiérrez, Cone, and the feminists Mary Daly and Rosemary Radford Ruether—separately, yet simultaneously and along with numerous peers—initiated movements that shared major features of a new theological method. Through a proliferation of books, journal articles, and ecumenical gatherings, they debated how to speak about God in a world in which the masses of humanity remained outside the power structures. During a few short years, Latin Americans and North Americans, Catholics and Protestants, black and white men and women participated in an intense discussion among themselves and with their detractors about how theology was to facilitate the immediate struggle for human liberation. What they shared in their trans-American conversation was a set of grievances against the theological establishment, which was dominated by white North American and European men, on behalf of the oppressed in the Americas. The liberationists' project to bring the world's marginalized into freedom shook the religious establishment and challenged the division of the world between the religious and the political, the sacred and the profane. Across the Americas, liberation theologians inspired by the Cuban Revolution and Third World anti-colonial movements embraced the declaration of German theologian Dietrich Bonhoeffer that the world had "come of age."

A Protestant dissident under the Third Reich, Bonhoeffer wrote letters from a Nazi prison reflecting on the relationship between religion and an enlightened world. He saw the modern world, having achieved autonomy from metaphysical thinking, as moving from a religious consciousness to a world consciousness. Through science, technology, and humanistic inquiry, he wrote, the world was gaining mastery over previous mysteries and no longer needed the "working hypothesis" called "God." This new world of human mastery reflected "a world come of age," responsible for itself without recourse to a God far removed from the world. What the world needed, Bonhoeffer proposed, was a crucified God who identified with its suffering. It needed a religion that came not from the hubris of power, from above, but from the suppressed truth emerging from below—a religion of God's transcendent presence in the immanent suffering of the world. For Gutiérrez, Bonhoeffer's world come of age required "worldliness" in religion that identified with the outcast, the suffering, and the oppressed. By exercising their political reason and asserting their freedom, black people, the poor, women, and other excluded groups were undergoing a profound change in their understanding of the divine relationship to the world. Liberation theologians announced the coming of age of the subordinated and prepared to offer a theological perspective and method suitable for the times.[6]

This book is a history of a theological transformation in a world come of age. It explores how the first generation of liberation theologians built their ideas and recast the relationship between politics and religion. I make three interlocking arguments. First, by turning toward culture and the history of oppressed people and by deploying social theory, liberationists argued that values rooted in the idea of divine transcendence (the classic purview of theology) could be brought to bear in the political sphere. Second, by looking across national boundaries and over a long period, I highlight how the deep contradiction between freedom and oppression within the history of the Americas led to the emergence of liberation theology. Third, I argue that liberation theology marked the end of the modern attempt to maintain the perilous and unproductive myth of a separation between the secular and the religious. By challenging the sacred/secular divide of modernity, liberationists reshaped the terms of engagement and opened the floodgates for a full-throttled entry of religious claims into the political sphere. Understanding the role liberationists played in redefining the relationship between religion and politics sheds light on subsequent history.

Ties That Bind

To understand why liberation theologians saw a need to refine the relationship between religion and politics, it is best to begin with the long relationships between the United States and the subjugated peoples within its borders and between the United States and Latin America. The American republics that arose from centuries of conquest and colonization shared many features: expansive and fertile land inhabited by indigenous people, an extensive slave trade, an ideology of racial stratification, an assigned place for women, visions of a social order underwritten by religion, and a class of educated elites receptive to liberal ideas reverberating from the European Enlightenment. The American nations also differed in ways that shaped their future relationship. Nineteenth-century Latin America was a largely Catholic continent with widespread syncretism and native cosmologies, a large percentage of its people of indigenous origins, and a social order based in traditional communities and Catholic corporatism. The largely Protestant United States placed great emphasis on the rhetoric of individual liberty and equality, and a belief in a divine national mission before an expansive frontier.

The United States sought continental expansion and economic opportunities in the Spanish-American territories. In turn, Spanish-American revolutionary leaders courted the support of the United States, tying their continental destiny to the North and following its constitutional model. Expressing a republican vision for the Americas, US recognition of the new Latin American nations brought with it the Monroe Doctrine (1823), a unilateral policy warning European imperial powers not to interfere in the affairs of the Western hemisphere. Over the course of the nineteenth century, and as a founding statement of US policy toward its Southern neighbors, the Monroe Doctrine combined with the idea of manifest destiny—an expression of white racial pride, belief in the virtue of the Anglo-American people and their institutions as exceptional, and a divine sense of mission to Christianize "uncivilized" people. By the end of the nineteenth century, justified by biblical injunctions and a theology of self-evident truths, the United States was emerging as a new kind of imperial power achieved through Indian removal, filibustering in Latin America, the Spanish-American war, and growing economic might.[7]

The United States had developed a clear ideological understanding, underwritten by religion, of its role in the world. The historian Michael H. Hunt outlined three core ideas in the United States' outlook toward the world: national greatness in the promotion of liberty abroad, namely the American mission; the placement of foreign people in a racial hierarchy with the Anglo-Saxon race at the top; and a conservative attitude toward revolutions other than its own. Anglo-American values were Christian values, universal values, and came with the responsibility to spread them throughout the Americas and the world. Within the context of these ideas, Latin America and its largely Catholic people were viewed as backward, corrupt, underdeveloped, and in need of a strong moral guide to modernization.

The United States entered the twentieth century emboldened by a sense of divine mission. Theodore Roosevelt and Woodrow Wilson set the course for the American century by espousing an assertive, interventionist foreign policy. In the wake of World War I, Wilson proclaimed a cosmopolitan future featuring new freedom at home and liberal internationalism abroad. Americans saw themselves as having a divine duty to extend freedom and democracy, particularly in its own backyard. World War II and the Cold War intensified the often-bloody US influence in Latin America, as Americans attempted to contain communism and defend freedom through a policy of Third World development and modernization. The rise of the United States as an imperial power, with Latin America under its thumb, drew the lines of the international order and sparked new grievances across the Americas and the world.[8]

After World War II there arose an international liberal faith in scientific expertise and its potential to eliminate inequality, free individuals from illegitimate authority, and replace outdated traditional societies. Through a mixed economy with capitalism at its core, and with modernization bringing lagging nations into the technological age, liberalism would triumph over the economic, political, and individual unfreedom that threatened most of the world. Against the challenge of communism's global spread, Arthur M. Schlesinger Jr. affirmed Wilson's earlier vision: "History has thrust a world destiny on the United States." For the sake of freedom—a freedom defined by the individualism of capitalist economics—theologians and religious leaders relinquished their critical moral voice and joined others against Godless communism. By the 1960s, many religious and secular thinkers no longer believed the rhetoric that divided the world between the free and the unfree, the modern and the underdeveloped, religion and politics.[9]

Disillusioned intellectuals in the United States and Latin America thought liberalism was failing on multiple fronts—politically, economically, socially, and existentially—sowing the seeds of a hemispheric New Left. For advocates of human liberation, the long history of the Americas revealed a contradiction between professed religious values and liberal notions of freedom on the one hand, and the state of unfreedom experienced by African Americans, indigenous people, the rural and urban poor, and women on the other. In the Americas it was possible to proclaim spiritual freedom and equality while underwriting political bondage and social exclusion. The unrealized promise of democratic inclusion, set against the newly heightened expectations of marginalized people, highlighted a contradiction. It was a contradiction residing at the core of American theology.

Against the gospel of individualism, the restless progressives and impatient radicals of the 1960s shared in a new awareness of the deeply embedded nature of social practices and relationships. In the midst of economic plenty and scientific advancement, stalled democracy in the United States and failed development abroad, and the hardening of attitudes on race, class, and gender, these thinkers called for a self-reflective examination of modern society. Religion and its institutions came under intense scrutiny. Social upheaval cast doubt on the assumptions of post-Enlightenment theology: a sacred/secular split, a universal humanity, a private religious self, and ideological autonomy. Understanding the breakup of the cultural cohesion of the Cold War in the 1960s, and leading to what became the "age of fracture" of the 1990s, requires consideration of the change in the religious landscape, the ramifications of which extended throughout the American hemisphere. Liberation theologians, Catholic and Protestant, fought for a new political-religious arrangement that would replace the post-war period's self-assured liberalism.[10]

In 1970, when liberation theology was emerging, the historian Sydney E. Ahlstrom noted the radical turn in religion. The decline of the US Protestant establishment and a fundamental shift in religious attitudes was producing what he described as a "*crise de la conscience* of unprecedented depth." Ahlstrom was too early to completely see, but not too early to sense, the coming of a new theo-political arrangement.[11]

Scope and Themes

This book offers a cultural history of liberationist ideas. I consider a complex of migrating ideas—trends in thought moving both temporally and spatially within a *longue durée*. The emphasis is on a web of interconnected and circulating ideas rather than direct lineage to antecedent thinkers, social networks, or personal biography. Nor do I provide the kind of institutional or social movement history that is available elsewhere. Rather, I illuminate liberationist innovations within larger intellectual trends. I regard religious ideas not as segregated or contained within a special category but as part of the overall frame of social thought. Within an expansive frame, one can see a persistent religious liberatory sensibility and examine how this sensibility converged with numerous intellectual and social movements. Instead of viewing liberation theology as a spontaneous break or aberration, taking a long view allows one to see historical continuity marked by moments of critical recalibration. A cultural history of thought demonstrates how liberationists responded to the confluence of ideas, some of them seemingly contradictory and with earlier origins.[12]

Modern religious thought developed in two parallel streams: formal academic and ecclesial theology and popular expressions. The view of theology as a scholastic and fixed discipline of religious elites fails to take into account its adaptive nature and the many ways and places it is constructed. Such a view also disregards the creation of religious meaning by ordinary people. Religious thought as a process of meaning formation has consequences beyond professed or private belief, involving rituals of inclusion and belonging, daily practice, public engagement, and aspirations for self and society. Historically, the informal theologies expressed by religious dissenters, subordinated people, and unschooled charismatic leaders were often at odds with the formal theology of ecclesial leaders and institutions. Instead of setting religion aside for a strictly political interpretation of liberationist movements, my aim is to show the import and ubiquity of religious ideas in modernity. Both popular and formal theologies have social and political ramifications. My focus is on the cultural conversation among trained theologians and religious thinkers and how they made a significant move to recognize the stream of religious protest historically expressed by subordinated people. By recognizing an alternative theological stream of thought, liberationists challenged the view that religious knowledge emerging "from below" proceeded from irrational enthusiasm.

Liberationists as a group were not systematizers, nor overly concerned with theoretical precision. Expressing the romantic mood of the 1960s, they were more interested in evoking a particular image of God to spur political action than in restating moribund dogma. Engaging in theological poetics, they were comfortable with paradox and contradiction, making analysis a tentative affair. However, broad themes continually show up in liberationist arguments—including the tensions between freedom and oppression, immanence and transcendence, and the universal and the particular, as well as the power of ideology to obscure reality. I have chosen to focus on those themes I found the most compelling at the nexus of political and theological history.

Due to differing political locations and internal conflicts that emerged in the movement's early days, black, Latin American, and feminist liberation theologies continue to be viewed as separate phenomena, overlooking so much of what they share. There is a scarcity of historical (rather than theological) studies of the affinities among these three streams of liberation theology. Latin American liberation theology has received the greatest attention, coming to stand for "liberation theology" in general. But the black and feminist liberation theologies that US thinkers developed were not an import of Latin American theology. Rather, liberation theologians were intellectual siblings born of a shared revolutionary history.[13]

Since the 1970s, liberation theology (or theologies) has spread globally, taking on multiple meanings in popular movements and in public conversation. For many observers, liberation theology has failed as a political or religious movement. Liberation theologians founded no institution, proposed no *singular* program for change, and established no school—the key features of a recognized movement. Its social expression in disparate communities has been too diverse to coalesce into mass action. Nevertheless, its sensibility continues to inspire multiple social movements and political initiatives throughout the world. Looking beyond its blurred boundaries, we can see how liberationist thought reconfigured the theo-political ground across the ideological spectrum. By illuminating the historical origins of a set of ideas, the significance and influence of liberation theology for the late twentieth century and beyond becomes clearer.

Because this book crosses multiple boundaries of identities, interests, and expressions of religious and social thought, I am cognizant of the risk of ascribing more historical coherence than is warranted. The ever-present danger in undertaking a history of ideas is in constructing a facile abstraction that obscures the self-understanding and particularity of one's subjects. Nevertheless, in attempts to hear and understand the most salient features of liberationists' arguments, I have discerned shared patterns of thinking. The bulk of my examination focuses on affinities rather than on internal debates. These affinities and initial feelings of solidarity nonetheless contained the seeds that eventually made it all but impossible for an effective social movement to cohere and deliver on its promise of freedom for oppressed people. Ultimately, deep contradictions were evident among liberationists—a weakness that plagues most radical movements.

Sharing with liberationists the impulse to engage in moral inquiry of modern theology and society, I give my subjects the benefit of the doubt in their commitment to human freedom. I regard liberationist thought as neither an attempt to obscure a hidden political agenda nor an exercise in religious mystification. Rather than rejecting failed religion and theological reasoning, they remained both liberally minded and theist because they believed in the rightness of their cause. My intention is to approach my subjects and their ideas with both sympathy and a historian's critical eye.

This is the story of how, through a process of adaptation and cross-pollination, religious, social, and political ideas deemed irreconcilable moved toward a convergence in which liberation theology emerged. As politically committed intellectuals, liberationists embraced modern reasoning and put forth a simultaneous critique. Reconciled to a secularized world come of age, liberation theologians ushered in a de-privatized religion as a socially energizing force and made a singular American contribution to change in the theo-political conversation.

PART I
Origins

I
Religion and Cultural Crisis

"GOD IS BLACK," "Jesus Christ is Che Guevara," and assertions that "if God is male, the male is God" were the bold declarations that disrupted the staid theological world of the 1960s. These were the conclusions reached by liberation theologians as they faced an immediate theo-political crisis. The theological shift they expressed shocked many in an unsettling recognition that American religion was experiencing a political realignment across liberal and conservative lines and lacked an adequate response to the unrest sweeping the Americas. The heart of the crisis was a heightened awareness of religion's role in perpetuating inequality. The hallowed walls of religious institutions no longer ensconced God ready to sanctify the North American way of life. Under pressing political demands, God's dwelling place had moved to urban slums, consciousness-raising groups, and revolutionary strategy meetings.[1]

The end of the 1960s presented a theological crisis rarely seen in American history. Religious intellectuals, like their secular peers, grappled with the reverberation of the Cuban Revolution, militancy among blacks, and the radicalization of women. The failing liberal consensus of mid-century was ill fitted for the emerging new consciousness. The Cold War order splitting the world between the free and unfree nations appeared increasingly to be the machinations of empire. The easy mid-century accommodation between the political interests of those in power and the professed values of justice and equality showed signs of strain. This chapter explores how, across the Americas, the first generation of liberation theologians, working in particular contexts, faced the cultural crisis and emerged as an intellectual movement with an overlapping set of immediate concerns.

Daring to Be Black

African Americans had long understood the tension between the theological and the political, and their connection to the global struggle for freedom. Their history was one of confronting two seemingly irreconcilable truths: the biblical promise of freedom and equality and the reality of political bondage. The nineteenth-century commitment to securing property in persons contradicted liberalism's promise of freedom and equality with the inadvertent, or explicit, underwriting by religion. The abolition of chattel slavery brought new forms of exclusion, leading to a Jim Crow society. At the end of World War II, returning African American men who had fought for freedom abroad found their freedom denied at home, contributing to a growing Civil Rights movement in Southern black churches. Against the few black voices that railed against the white man's religion, the history of the black freedom movement remained tied to Christianity. Finding a renewed affinity with oppressed people beyond the borders of the United States reinforced African American resolve to secure freedom.

At mid-twentieth century, the Civil Rights movement continued to display both a global awareness of oppression and its religious roots. Toward the end of his life, Martin Luther King Jr. expressed the belief that the fate of the American Negro was tied to "the world house," writing in 1967, "Equality with whites will not solve the problems of either whites or Negroes if it means equality in a world society stricken by poverty . . ." Reiterating the ideas of the 1963 "Letter from Birmingham Jail," he saw the desire for freedom as a phenomenon among the masses of disinherited in a worldwide movement. King's message reached the far corners of Latin America through religious journals such as *Cristianismo y Sociedad* and *Cristianismo y Revolución,* connecting civil rights with emancipation movements beyond US borders.[2]

King identified a lag between the material and scientific promise of the age, and moral and spiritual ends. Key to understanding the unrest among the colored people of the world was racism and economic exploitation, along with rising expectations of equality. Turning his attention toward the Third World, he noted the neocolonial grip on Latin America that strangled its economic lifeblood through US foreign policy, business cartels, and corrupt local elites. Recognizing that economic disparity had instigated a "world-wide freedom revolution," King called for a massive redistribution of the world's wealth. Awakened to Western technological possibilities by the expanding reach of media and inspired by religion, "oppressed people cannot remain oppressed forever." Heightened hope set against the reality of those left behind brought a sense of increasing crisis.[3]

King expressed the need for a resolving synthesis through a revolution in values that went beyond capitalism or communism. This synthesis was a socially conscious democracy that recognized the individual embedded in a community, yet infused with a new ecumenical spirit to overcome the pride of class, tribe, nation, or race. King proposed a universal vision empowered by the love ethic of the great world religions—*agape*. This was not passive love, but rather a sacrificial, relentless pursuit of love's object, which was justice. Active love involved the Niebuhrian principle of coercive power wedded to Gandhian nonviolence against a recalcitrant pride of group. The choice for King was between the global chaos of unfulfilled expectations and the justice of a new communitarian spirit.[4]

The de-Christianization of a significant segment of black radicalism contradicted King's evocation of religious sentiment. He was cognizant of the growing crisis among black intellectuals and attempted to revitalize within the conservative Negro church the religious fervor that could instigate social action. Nevertheless, while King led local pastors and laypeople, many of them young, in street marches singing "We Shall Not Be Moved," national religious organizations offered only cool support. In the "Letter from Birmingham Jail," noting the disillusionment he saw, he asked, "Is organized religion too inextricably bound to the status quo to save our nation and the world?" The widening gap between the conservatism of the churches and social unrest pointed to a brewing theological crisis.[5]

For radicals, who abandoned liberalism to demand economic equality and self-determination for black people, King's religiously laden appeal was too little, too late. The history of the freedom movement from the abolitionists to Black Power had been an attack on institutional racism. Except for nationalist strains that emerged from time to time, the movement had been largely integrationist and a protest against exclusion. From its inception, the black freedom movement found in the Christian faith the bias for justice and equality obscured by white theological interpretations. Having received the faith from white missionaries, many slaves, and freemen, accepted Christianity as their own, either as a haven from daily pain or as a way to inspire resistance. The collapse of Reconstruction, Northern migration into crowded industrial cities, and the establishment and persistence of Jim Crow exclusion fomented in black intellectuals a growing disillusionment with the acquiescence of African American churches to white notions of respectability.

Twentieth-century black writers such as Richard Wright, Langston Hughes, and James Baldwin expressed disenchantment with Christianity and the ability of the African American churches to resist oppression. Could a religion that had brought black people into slavery ever provide a solution and hope for freedom? Richard Wright's 1954 book *Black Power: A Record of Reactions in a Land of Pathos*, offering his observations on Pan-Africanism, cast Christianity as having produced in the African an eroded sense of self. Black protest poetry often carried conflicted religious feelings in which Christ was sometimes a white oppressor and at other times a black liberator who suffers with his people. In over sixty poems, Hughes carried this religious and racial conflict. His 1931 poem "Christ in

Alabama," written in response to the unjust rape conviction of nine black boys in Scottsboro, is a startling critique of white Christianity:

> *Christ is a nigger,*
> *Beaten and black:*
> *Oh, bare your back!*
>
> *Mary is His mother:*
> *Mammy of the South,*
> *Silence your mouth.*
>
> *God is His father:*
> *White Master above*
> *Grant Him your love.*
>
> *Most holy bastard*
> *Of the bleeding mouth,*
>   *Nigger Christ*
>   *On the cross*
>   *Of the South.*

By casting Christ as a nigger, beaten and crucified, and equating his suffering with the experience of black people in the South and portraying God as a white master, Hughes stretched the boundaries of acceptable American Christianity. A strong reaction from a white audience to his first public reading at the University of North Carolina brought threats of violence. As Hughes saw it, for white people, "It's bad enough to call Christ a bastard . . . but to call Him a nigger—that's too much!"[6]

In the 1960s, James Baldwin concluded that rather than admonitions to love one another, only the fear of retaliation appeared to be effective enough to change white behavior. Baldwin had grown up in urban storefront churches hearing the message from black preachers of reconciling oneself to suffering here and now to gain a crown in heaven. The message that the black race was under the curse of Ham, forever doomed to serve white brothers, carried political consequences. In *The Fire Next Time* (1963), Baldwin acknowledged the failure of a "white God" and the growing persuasiveness of Malcolm X's message that "God is black." He finally saw the truth that the Christian church had functioned as a colonizing power with "unmitigated arrogance and cruelty." Increasingly in the twentieth century, radicals and intellectuals saw black preachers as the errand boys for their white masters and Christianity as the opiate of the black masses.[7]

The fissure between the African American church and radicals accelerated the rise of the Nation of Islam. Malcolm X, its chief spokesman, engaged in a scathing indictment of African American churches and white liberals. He said what other radicals had concluded: "white man's religion" was the most effective ideological means of subjugating black people. The deepest violation inflicted by the "white devil" was to take away the black man's God in exchange for a "blond-haired, blue-eyed Jesus!"— a God who looked like the slave master and acted like one. Under this God, the black man stood under a curse, sentenced to life on his knees, bowing to and pleading with the white man, sustained by promises that for his good behavior he would gain a "pie in the sky" reward. What the Negro believed about God constructed the cruelest of mental prisons—an ideology of racist submission. Malcolm X's message on the international stage reached the black middle class and sensitized them to the accommodating messages in Christian sermons. Rather than join the Nation of Islam, they questioned the terms of white-defined religion within their own churches.[8]

The prophetic stance taken by King and Malcolm X radicalized a new generation of black intellectuals, contributing to an inevitable break between integrationist and nationalist factions. The Civil Rights movement favored by moderates gained significant concessions of equality before the law, but militants noted little change in the daily economic reality of most black people. In their minds, there was a need for an existential revolt to break the mental dependence and powerlessness. For angry urban youth impatient with King's nonviolent conciliatory stance, Malcolm X became the iconic figure of Black Power and black nationhood.

King's assassination in 1968 solidified the Black Power movement, whose main political tactic was confronting power structures on the local level through economic development, community control, and the validation of black culture. Instead of integration with whites, blacks would actualize their freedom by gaining control over their history and future. Black Power called for a new consciousness that rejected white normative values, reoriented black experience as a source of values, and provided a sense of "collective manhood."[9]

Impatient with the pace of domestic politics, Black Power leaders found common cause with Third World people who were resisting US power abroad. In *Black Power: The Politics of Liberation in America* (1967), Stokely Carmichael and Charles V. Hamilton cast Black Power as part of an international struggle for liberation, and US blacks as a colonized part of the Third World. The world consciousness evident in the history of the freedom movement remained at the center of Black Power ideology.[10]

The call to remake black cultural life and politics called for a black nationalist religion. In the 1950s, Detroit United Church of Christ pastor Albert Cleage, inspired by William H. Johnson's 1935 painting depicting a crucified black Jesus, popularized the black Messiah at the Shrine of the Black Madonna. He was following a long tradition of a black Messiah that included that of black nationalist Henry McNeal Turner's 1898 declaration, "God is a Negro." Cleage was one of the few ministers who embraced Black Power and viewed Christianity as being in need of decolonization from white influence by recognizing not only the need for love, but also the need for power that sometimes necessitated violence. Cleage's *The Black Messiah* (1968) depicts a black Jesus as a revolutionary and a necessary image to free black people. Only a religion that emphasized God's chosen people as a black Israel and recognized Jesus as black was a suitable Black Power religion. Yet, the religion of Black Power was still not a full-orbed theology. As a forerunner, Cleage combined black nationalism, racial pride, and chosenness, identifying the religious impulse within Black Power.[11]

At the time, historian Vincent Harding, a collaborator with King, observed that the freedom movement had gone beyond singing, preaching, and nonviolent action. Although strong elements in Black Power viewed religion as a part of the exploitation of black people, there was also, for Harding, a "strong and causative link between Black Power and American Christianity." Concluding, "nothing kills a nigger like too much love," Black Power turned King's theme of love for the white neighbor to a necessary search for the "beloved black community" disdained by the "genteel, oh-so-white Jesus." Harding saw the movement's religious pulse in a "perennial tension between salvation ... and a day of destruction demanded by a just God." In a strike against the parochialism of "Judeo-Christian" sentiment, Harding saw a new universalism, which, in the words of Julius Lester, identified with the world's suffering people: "The Indians of Peru, the miner in Bolivia, the African and the freedom fighters of Vietnam" were all fighting for "the right to govern his own life." The religious mooring of Black Power and the call for self-love placed it in direct opposition to African American churchmen who showed no propensity to break with an integrationist strategy or with white institutions. Nevertheless, Harding noted that young people were forging a black religion that matched their political commitment.[12]

The emergence of Black Power, with its cultural revolt and militant politics, reverberated throughout the old ranks of the civil rights and national church organizations. A group of prominent African American clergy in majority white denominations felt compelled by their own anxious discomfort to issue a statement on Black Power as the National Committee of Negro Churchmen (NCNC). In a statement published simultaneously in April 1966 in the *New York Times* and the *Los Angeles Times*, the NCNC sought to correct the distorted view of Black Power among American leaders. The conditions of economic inequality keeping Negroes trapped in ghettos, uneducated and powerless—rather than Black Power—was the source of racial unrest. Formal equality under the law did not hide the vast and growing economic inequality between whites and blacks. They charged that white men never justified their claim to power as they went about "aping God." Black men unable to implement the demands of justice became a "race of beggars." Deploying an implicit Niebuhrian principle, the NCNC asserted that the concern for power was legitimate because ultimate power belonged to God, and no group could justly hold an inordinate amount of power over another. The inequality in power was the root of injustice in American society.[13]

The NCNC called on white churches to move from integrationist efforts to black participation in institutional power. They called on Negro citizens to recognize that America had asked them to fight for opportunities as individuals and yet, except for a chosen few, they experienced group oppression. The demands of justice required that African American churches and civic organizations neither fear power nor retreat into "otherworldly" divine power. They called for instituting justice and racial reconciliation in the here and now, while warning of the corrupting influence of seeking power as an end in itself. The group went on to become the National Committee of Black Churchmen (NCBC) and to press for change in national Protestant and Catholic Church bodies and the National Council of Churches. The Black Power statement of NCNC, even with its conciliatory tone, demonstrated that radical ideas had infiltrated the center of the liberal religious establishment.[14]

The NCBC was able to establish a Black Power beachhead in predominantly white institutions without the support of independent black Baptists and African Methodists, who remained fundamentally conservative in their outlook. Through interlocking leadership in national organizations, the NCBC participated in the April 1969 Detroit conference on National Black Economic Development. At this event, James Forman, former international affairs director of the Student Nonviolent Coordinating Committee (SNCC) and self-professed atheist, managed to pass a Black Manifesto, which was the most radical statement to date. The following month, Forman disrupted the Sunday morning service at the historic Riverside Church in New York City and read the manifesto from the altar to a stunned congregation.[15]

The manifesto was a significant indictment of religious institutions for their participation in legitimizing racism and economic exploitation. Placing blacks in the context of "colonized people," it asserted that white churches and synagogues had aided the exploitation of "colored people around the world." The manifesto demanded reparation for slavery of $500,000,000 from white churches and synagogues, a first step toward government reparations, for the purchase of land and for building separate communications, educational, and organizational networks by and for black people. In a declaration of war against the establishment, it called on black people to make their demands known and to seize control of church offices until conditions were met. In solidarity with African, Latin American, and Asian people against US imperialism, the manifesto declared a willingness to use armed resistance against churches that had established themselves through imperial power. It called on white Christians to practice the patient forbearance and nonviolence that they had for centuries advised to black people. The only other option for white people was to "kill us." The message was clear: Christianity, despite the Negro who still clung to it in faith, was an instrument of subjugation. Nevertheless, Gayraud S. Wilmore, a participant in the NCBC, noted that Forman's willingness to confront the churches displayed a ray of hope in religion among disaffected young blacks. It resounded as a cry for assurance that God was not a racist.[16]

The claims of Black Power went to the heart of Christian theology. The manifesto served as the final impetus for finding a theological stance that considered the black experience seriously. In 1967 the NCBC had raised the question of the possibility of a useful theology for social change as it entered into dialogue with conservative African American clergy, liberal whites, and Black Power leaders. An adequate response needed to go beyond the redemptive suffering motif, the universal love ethic of King, and the idea that blacks had no authentic theology of their own. It had to respond to the charge by Malcolm X that the entire Christian religion and its theological construction was the product of, and the tool of, white racism. Black leaders were looking for a way to justify their Christian faith in the face of growing religious alienation—an approach to the biblical text independent of a white inherited hermeneutic. The risk was losing a whole generation of young people demanding a God of justice.

The Black Power controversy reached a young scholar, James H. Cone, going through his own existential crisis of faith. Cone grew up in Bearden, Arkansas, amid the racial segregation of the 1940s and 1950s, the son of a man who offered a continual example of defying white privilege, refusing to allow his wife to work in white people's homes. Overcoming a deficient education and encountering institutional racism, Cone excelled and in 1963 received his Ph.D. in systematic theology from Garrett Seminary at Northwestern University. His dissertation was on the work of the neo-orthodox theologian Karl Barth. During graduate school in Evanston, Illinois, Cone, surrounded by the upheaval of the Civil Rights movement, struggled between theological studies that appeared increasingly irrelevant and the march for freedom outside the library walls. It was in his teaching position at Philander Smith College in Little Rock where he faced the irrelevancy of so much of the European theology he had learned. The black students at Philander came from the cotton fields, seeking a future in a society that Cone saw increasingly as defining black as "nonbeing." Observing the nationwide urban unrest and hearing the challenge of Malcolm X's denunciation of

Christianity brought Cone to see his situation as one of "theological bankruptcy." The classic theology he had learned left him at a loss to explain the meaning of the biblical text in the midst of a Black Power revolution. Cone wondered why, in his entire seminary education, he had not read one text of black historical experience, and why his theological teachers seldom talked about the race problem in America. It was as though slavery, Jim Crow, and lynching had never happened. The erasure of black history from American theology made it irrelevant to the black struggle.[17]

Inspired by Black Power and NCBC's call to find a suitable theology, in 1968 Cone wrote an essay, "Christianity and Black Power," published in *Is Anybody Listening to Black America?* edited by C. Eric Lincoln. The essay was his first articulation of a liberating theology for and about black people. He argued that Black Power was not the antithesis of Christianity, "rather, it is Christ's central message to twentieth-century America." What appeared as an irrational demand, Cone asserted, reflected the willingness of black people to die rather than live without freedom. After three hundred years of suppression and accommodation, the black man "will protest, violently, if need be, on behalf of absolute and immediate emancipation." Black Power was not alien to the black church, because the movement was the very essence of Christianity—freedom for the captives. As a "prophetic" community the black church was to demand a complete restructuring of society as "nothing less than *immediate* and *total* emancipation" for all people. Cone, in adopting the language of protest, violence, and emancipation, had acquired the militancy of Black Power.[18]

The next year, Cone expanded his essay in *Black Theology and Black Power* (1969), deploying classic theological categories combined with the history of black resistance. For him, Black Power was an attempt to express Paul Tillich's mid-century existential theology through the "courage to be." Defining the struggle in taken-for-granted masculinist terms, Cone declared that no longer did the "black man" plead for integration but rather he forcefully seized his own humanity. He agreed with Malcolm X that the dream of integration meant acceptance of "white man['s]" values, religion, and culture—an offer black people must refuse. The black man's experience was a battle against "demonic forces" expressed in the structures of American society. Cone viewed an awakened black consciousness as the key to the black man's emancipation. As for white people, they had been warned: "if whites do not get off the back of blacks they must expect that blacks will literally throw them off by whatever means are at their disposal. This is the meaning of Black Power." He charged that Black Power was antithetical to the white liberal who "wants change without risk, victory without blood." The white liberal, able to intellectualize the racial problem eloquently, found that he could do "nothing" short of risking his life. The black man "is free when he determines the limits of his own existence." Cone assumed that the struggle was between white and black men. The black man was leading not only in a political struggle, but also in challenging the very understanding of God.[19]

Seeking to recover the vitality of a black revolutionary religion, Cone argued that the independent black church was the historical base for slave rebellions and escape into freedom, and a pulpit for proclaiming justice and equality. Historically, black churchmen did not accept the belief that God had "ordained slavery for them." Rather, they bore witness to the apostasy of white Christianity's attempt to justify slavery. He noted that after the Civil War, the black churches began to lose their independence from white institutions. In the process, they underwrote Jim Crow and new rationalizations for black subjugation. In the hope of full equality, black preachers, as "devoted 'Uncle Tom[s],'" began to preach accommodation to white values and resignation to suffering. No longer in legal slavery, Cone argued, black people entered a more pernicious slavery of the soul. Going beyond the conciliatory stance of the NCBC, Cone's first book was nothing short of a declaration of war on the theological establishment. He directed his message to blacks and whites and to both sides of the liberal and conservative theological divide. The entirety of American theology had offered a God of accommodation and acquiescence.[20]

Black Theology and Black Power launched Cone onto the national stage, where he met the activist Stokely Carmichael, the writer LeRoi Jones, and other radicals, who noted his critique of the churches and with whom he found common cause in black liberation. One the one hand, Cone was dismayed at Black Power leaders' vehement dismissal of the black church. Black radicals did not seem to notice that they were following white liberals by embracing the critique of black religion as otherworldly escapism. Cone, on the other hand, was attempting to forward a history of the black church as a foundation for resistance. Offered a position at the prestigious Union Theological Seminary, Cone welcomed the opportunity to place his developing black theology among respected theological minds.[21]

Cone went on to write *A Black Theology of Liberation* (1970), in which he offered a theology that began with the reality of black oppression. Cone viewed the white glossing of theological categories such as obedience and providence as constructs that sanctioned genocide of the Amerindians and enslavement of the Africans. He argued that "God is black" because black liberation was a divine goal that identified with the oppressed, the poor, and the humiliated. Blackness was a symbol of oppression with which God empathized in solidarity. Otherwise, a colorless and impartial "God is a God of racism" rendered black people invisible. Blackness was not only an identifying mark in racist society but also an ontological condition shared by all who dared to "become black with God." His first two books, written as if in the heat of passion, left many ideas ill defined as he worked through an intellectual and personal religious struggle to define a God responsive to black people. In the subsequent *God of the Oppressed* (1975), Cone offered a sophisticated analysis of the role of racist ideology in the construction of theology and developed more fully the meaning of liberation as God's historical project.[22]

Cone had become a leader among black theologians including J. Deotis Roberts, who had earned his Ph.D. from the University of Edinburg in 1957, and the Presbyterian minister and scholar Gayraud S. Wilmore, who proposed the black experience as a beginning point for interpreting the biblical text. Cone and the first generation of black liberationists undertook a debate among themselves of the possibility of black theology and its relationship with the rest of Christian tradition. They drew from a European and American theological and philosophical heritage and the history of black people to build the foundations of a black liberation theology, a theology that would not evade politics in the name of peaceful coexistence with whites.

Few white theologians found Cone's caustic approach compelling; however, an exception was the German American and Duke Divinity School theologian Frederick Herzog. Having spent part of his life in Germany, his experience under the Third Reich deeply marked his thought. After the war and studying under Barth, Herzog confronted the racist nature of the Jewish Holocaust. Returning to the United States with a heightened awareness of racism, he became active in the Southern Civil Rights and labor movements. In the winter of 1970, only months before the publication of Cone's *A Black Theology of Liberation*, Herzog published an essay in *Continuum* titled "Theology of Liberation." Unaware of Cone's brewing theology of liberation, or similar movements occurring in Latin America, Herzog was the first in North America to use the term *liberation theology*. He charged that liberal theology was increasingly irrelevant in its attempt to adjust itself to the secular mind, glorifying pluralism and relativism without coming to terms with the power dilemmas in North American society. The unequal distribution of power between black and white, between poor and rich, was the political organizing principle of society. Herzog called for liberal theology to give way to a "theology of liberation" that would "de-honkify Christ."[23]

Herzog went on to recognize the affinities between emerging Latin American and black liberation theologies. In dialogue with both, he wrote *Liberation Theology: Liberation in the Light of the Fourth Gospel* (1972), a rebuke of liberal theology in which he called for whites to abandon their "private religious dreams" and "morass of subjectivity" and identify with the "wretched of the earth." He called for theologians to reject the privatized "Gnostic self" for a communal self in a revolution of consciousness that sided with the oppressed. He joined the new breed of black theologians and the few white disaffected liberals who set out to dismantle what they viewed as a failed theological heritage.[24]

A Permanent Cultural Revolution

As North American blacks experienced radicalization through participation in the Civil Rights and Black Power movements, the 1959 Cuban Revolution reverberated across the Americas. The revolution was self-consciously anti-imperialist, dedicated to the systematic demolition of old structures of the exploiting class. Emerging from the countryside, its leader Fidel Castro and his group of revolutionary guerrillas rolled tanks into Havana, overthrowing the US-backed dictator Fulgencio Batista. Castro and his revolutionary vanguard, including its leading theorist, the Argentine Ernesto "Che" Guevara, had spent most of the 1950s organizing and planning insurrection among students, workers, and peasants. Castro embodied the resentment of many Cubans toward US dominance on the island. The Spanish-American War had enabled Cuba to secure independence from Spain in 1898 and led to the imposition of the Platt Amendment to its constitution, giving the United States the right to intervene in its domestic politics. The island became a de facto colony of the United States. By 1959 the influence of US military, economic, and cultural power was both overwhelming and inescapable. The island was awash in US money, tourists, mob activity, and a military presence that accrued to the benefit of an elite minority. Peasants, who represented 40 percent of the population of mostly Afro-Cubans, worked on sugar plantations where poverty, illiteracy, and lack of health care prevailed. A year after the overthrowing Batista, and obstructed by a negative US response, Castro proclaimed his Marxist commitment and vowed to break the chains of dependence, build a truly independent Cuba, and address economic and racial inequality. As Castro turned to the Soviet Union for support, the United States viewed the revolution as a threat to national security and an unprecedented loss of control over the direction of Latin America, turning the region into a bloody field, and Cuba became a focus of Cold War politics.[25]

For disaffected Latin Americans and North American radicals constituting the New Left, Cuba became a symbol of new possibilities and a sign of anti-colonial resistance by nations of the "Third World." Coined by the French economic historian Alfred Sauvy, the term *Third World* drew from the idea of a third estate, or those who made up the lowest ranks of the French revolution. The concept unified African, Asian, and Latin American nations, becoming a rallying point against the exclusionary economic order and a way to succinctly express cultural relations with the West. The Cuban Revolution, regarded as a product of the Third World, was a tangible opportunity to connect North American black freedom struggles with larger global movements. Under the auspices of the Fair Play for Cuba Committee, radicals such as LeRoi Jones, Robert F. Williams, and Stokely Carmichael flocked to Cuba to see for themselves the possibilities of a post-racist society and a model for cultural self-determination. The Cuban Revolution served as a catalytic event, tying black radicals and the New Left to Latin American movements, and led to a feeling of solidarity among those sharing political grievances against the United States.[26]

Guevara's call for the immediate extension of the revolution to the entire western hemisphere reshaped Latin American politics and culture. At the conference of the Organization of American States in 1961, Guevara cast the revolution as representing not only Cuban people but all the "dispossessed of the world." The revolution, in solidarity with the oppressed of the Third World, intended what Marx had proposed in "Theses on Feuerbach" (1845)—not to merely interpret the world but to transform it. The goal was "a new man and a new woman" built on new material foundations, and a new consciousness was in process of overturning the alienated individual of capitalist societies. Guevara attacked Western theology by arguing that capitalist ideology, supported by appeals to the "theory of divine origin" or justified by promises of otherworldly rewards, led to a belief that a class society was God-ordained. As a Marxist he viewed religion as part and parcel of an ideology of power. Guevara also believed that "when Christians dare to give an integral revolutionary testimony, the Latin American revolution will be invincible." The challenge was how to harness the vitalism of religion for a socialist revolution.[27]

Fidelismo, the call for an immediate socialist revolution, spread like wildfire in Latin America, inciting a sense of a shared destiny. Weak civilian governments across the continent recoiled under the destabilizing effects of revolutionary-inspired action and demands for reform. Student unrest, involvement by previously politically inactive indigenous groups, urban labor strikes, and guerilla activity in the countryside contributed to the hot cauldron of uncertainty and instability. The revolution revitalized various factions of the previously moribund Latin American left, and pro- and anti-Castro factions struggled for control over the future of the region. The revolution struck a blow to US dominance in the Americas, and efforts to prop up faltering right-wing governments reinforced the anti-Yankee mood.[28]

The Catholic Church reeled from the shock waves of Castro's Cuba, where it played no positive role in the overthrow of the Batista dictatorship. The Church became a haven for conservatives who feared the implementation of the revolutionary goals spreading throughout the continent. Against rising popular sentiment, the Church faced becoming even more isolated and irrelevant, or changing. The failure to support a popular revolution raised questions about its role in legitimizing economic disparity. Clerical and lay groups pressed for responsive action. Catholic pastoral workers and university students left their elite institutions to join the restless masses of the poor, radicalizing their own perspective. Conservative Christian Democratic parties appealed to the urgent need for socioeconomic and political change and proposed a revolution of aggressive reform that bypassed Marxism. While the Church encouraged responsible social action on the part of faithful Catholics, it continued a formal stance of neutrality in politics. The Cuban Revolution had damaged previous ways of thinking about the social and political order, and the Church hierarchy found itself with a legacy of political accommodation and a loss of confidence among the laity.[29]

By the end of the 1960s, with the death of Che Guevara and the evident contradictions of the Cuban Revolution that had failed to deliver a socialist paradise, Latin American intellectuals found themselves in a political and inspirational vacuum. Cuba had not fulfilled its promise for the continent—economic and racial equality. Under crushing poverty, the mass of Latin Americans continued to hold conservative notions of deference to landowners and political elites. For religious intellectuals, the looming threat of reactionary governments accentuated the need for a way to awaken the people to their plight by appealing to the religious imagination. Only a change in consciousness would arouse the people to demand justice.

The Second Vatican Council, after centuries of an official apolitical stance, provided a break for some Catholics to advocate a more radical position concerning structural change in Latin America. Vatican II, as a major liberalizing move, allowed more Catholics to engage positively with modern society and its problems by encouraging a spirit of collaboration, local initiative, pluralism, less authoritarian models of leadership, and a renewed commitment to the poor. For Latin American bishops returning from the council in Rome, the Vatican's call to engage the modern world looked very different from the perspective of the Third World, which was gripped by widespread poverty and revolutionary fervor. Engaging with the world in Latin America meant confronting vast inequality. It was in this new spirit that the Latin American Bishops Conference (CELAM), first formed in 1955, recognized its role in mediating change on the continent. There was now room for Latin American bishops to avail themselves of the expertise of social science in addressing systemic problems and to reemphasize aspects of long-neglected Catholic social teaching. Encouraged by the changes, progressive theologians pursued theological innovation.

After Vatican II, a revolutionary mood infected the clergy working among the poor. By 1965, Camillo Torres, a Catholic priest and sociologist, had turned away from his work as a university chaplain and his research on poverty, political violence, and democracy to become fully engaged in the Colombian guerilla action. He had concluded, "as a Colombian, as a sociologist, and as a Christian, and as a priest, I am a revolutionary." Giving up the "duties and privileges of the clergy" and conventional progressive politics, he was persuaded that "the Revolution is not only permissible but obligatory for Christians." As the founder of the United Front of the Colombian People, Torres organized disillusioned liberals, disaffected young intellectuals, militant Catholics, labor activists, and communists to advocate for radical land reform, including the expropriation of church property, the nationalization of industries, and free mass education. Rejecting charges of communism, he nevertheless joined communists to work for common goals. The lack of change, Torres asserted, was not due to insufficient knowledge but by the unwillingness on the part of the minority ruling class to give up power except by force. He shared with King the view that the essence of the Christian faith was *agape*, self-giving love of neighbor. Under crushing oppression, love required revolutionary action. Roman Catholics could not hide behind religious piety but faced an imperative to bring about the conditions to feed, clothe, and house the majority of the people. Although the Church had to remain unaligned from any political system, it had to join others in history to bring about embodied love in this world. Torres' 1966 death while engaged in guerilla warfare led Latin American youth and many of his clerical peers to regard him as a Christian martyr.[30]

The Cuban Revolution and the opening presented by Vatican II provided the main impetus for the radicalization of Latin American theology. There remained for Torres, as for Black Power advocates in the United States, insufficient religious justification for social change beyond appeals to justice and the persuasive power of love. Across the continent, religion seemed to be less a positive force for change and more a mere salve for oppressed groups and justification for the oppressors. Progressive Catholic and Protestant theologians, engaged in a similar project, sought a meaningful response to vast inequity and turmoil. They concluded that the problem was how theology was constructed on an ideological approach to the biblical text. A change in ideological position promised to provide a change in theology.

The 1968 meeting of CELAM in Medellin, Columbia brought previously isolated national bishops together to address common problems; survey the economic, political, and cultural situation of the continent; and consider the available responses. A minority group of theologians and social scientists armed with economic and sociological studies were prepared to assist the bishops in drafting a number of significant statements; the documents, a mixture of traditional and reformist elements, established the first articulation of a liberationist theme. The classic meaning of "liberation" as a spiritual release from sin began to change in Catholic circles in the 1950s, acquiring a political nuance influenced by Third World independence movements. The Medellin statements, frequently evoking liberation as a positive humanizing process, noted the marginality experienced by many on the continent, growing frustration in the midst of heightened expectations, and the insensitivity and unjust exercise of power among privileged groups. The final documents directed to the people of Latin America called for addressing the "oppressive structures" that kept a large mass of people poor and on the edge of slavery.[31]

The slavery under which the mass of Latin American people lived was not only economic but also physical, cultural, and spiritual. Two failing systems, liberal capitalism and a conservative state socialism, caught the continent in a neocolonial situation of dependency. No longer could the bishops avoid considering the internal and external sources of "human wretchedness" and the great evil of poverty. An effective theology required understanding the "economy of salvation" as an "action of integral human development and liberation" that did not separate the temporal from the spiritual. The meeting at Medellin catalyzed a new theological development in which concerns for this world appeared to supersede the pristine doctrine of spiritual salvation that had been standing for centuries.[32]

A key theological advisor at the conference, Gustavo Gutiérrez, had already begun to conceptualize a "theology of liberation." In his youthful studies he had aspirations of becoming a psychiatrist, and involved himself in militant campus politics and the student movement *Acción Católica*. In the 1950s, many promising Latin Americans went to Europe for their education. Gutiérrez studied at Louvain University in Belgium, where he specialized in philosophy and psychology and became a close friend of Camillo Torres. After writing his thesis, "The Psychic Conflict in Freud," he went on to study theology in Lyon, France, and returned to Peru to serve as a chaplain to university students involved in sociopolitical activities.

Confronted with the situation in Peru, Gutiérrez, like Cone, came to the realization that his European theological education failed to address the country's crushing poverty and began to see poverty as destructive, structural, and class centered, something that required an uprooting rather than charity. In 1962 he joined the new Department of Theology and Social Science at the Catholic Pontifical University in Lima, facing before his students the same dilemma of theological irrelevancy as Cone. Throughout the 1960s he continued to be active in various forms of Catholic social action, presenting papers on a newly developing method for constructing theology. One of these early occasions, in 1964, was at a pastoral conference organized by the priest and critic of the West, Ivan Illich, in Petropolis, Brazil, where he asserted that theological interpretations should be based on real-world engagement. Gutiérrez's radicalization resulted not only from a theological rereading but also from an alternative reading of Latin American history.[33]

Gutiérrez went on to write *Teología de la liberación* in 1971, with the English-language edition in 1973 published as *A Theology of Liberation*, which stressed the reality of poverty as the organizing principle of theology. Poverty was not only the evil of material want, but also included voluntary poverty that rejected an oppressive system and embraced solidarity with the poor. Gutiérrez argued that lack of food, shelter, health care, and education condemned a vast number of people to the margins of humanity, as "poverty means death." For many of the world's poor, poverty meant a literal, not just a social death. He saw deficiencies in casting the problems of the Third World, shared by minorities within rich nations, as merely problems of economic underdevelopment. Liberation from all forms of oppression required a liberating praxis—the reflective moral action of a "preferential option for the poor." As a liberating praxis, theology offered the possibility of "a new way to be human, a *permanent cultural revolution.*" Only re-visioning the theological task was sufficient to rectify the gap between the present crisis and the possibility of an emerging "new humanity."[34]

Gutiérrez explicitly drew from the thoughts of French Catholic philosopher Maurice Blondel and his 1893 book *L'Action* by proposing reading the "signs of the times" through critical reflection. The evident sign of the times was the global "irruption of the poor" as they became active historical agents. In this situation, the true theological task was "orthopraxis," "to do the truth" rather than a mere proclamation of a pristine truth applied to the world. An encounter with the world, rather than tradition or revelation, was the starting point. Theology as critical reflection refused to legitimate the existing order through idealist or spiritualist approaches: "To conceive of history as a process of human liberation is to consider freedom as a historical conquest; it is to understand that the step from an abstract to a real freedom is not taken without a struggle against all the forces that oppose humankind." Engaged with the historical events of human struggle, the theologian emerged as a new type of Gramscian "organic intellectual." Gutiérrez's theological beginning point of social reality, rather than church teaching, was a clear and radical departure from the standing Catholic theology. Gutiérrez's Catholic peers, including the Uruguayan Juan Luis Segundo and the Brazilian Hugo Assmann, repeated and enhanced his first formal articulation of Latin American theology of liberation.[35]

Catholics were not alone in calling for a new theology. At Vatican II and Medellín, Protestants had participated as observers and were formulating their own theological solutions to the Latin American crisis. Protestants' contribution in the construction of a liberation theology grew out of a history of minority status. Tied to North American mainline and missionary efforts, they were often viewed as cultural agents for US imperialism. In the twentieth century, through a series of continental gatherings, Protestants sought a new religious identity freed from foreign influence. In 1961, Church and Society in Latin America (ISAL) organized in Peru and began to explore the means of positive political engagement. The move toward cultural autonomy from Europe and North America, and revolutionary solidarity, provided the means by which Protestants joined Catholics in articulating a contextual theology suitable for the continent. Despite differences, together they signaled the creation of an opposing intellectual block against US and European political and theological hegemony.[36]

In 1963, ISAL began publishing the leftward-leaning journal *Cristianismo y Sociedad,* adopting Richard Shaull's call for a theology that supported revolutionary change. Shaull, a New Left radical, missionary, and Princeton Theological Seminary professor, was the foremost Protestant theologian on the continent. He warned a North American audience in his 1955 book *Encounter with Revolution* of the political and theological crisis emerging in Latin America. It was in the pages of *Cristianismo y Sociedad* that two of his students, Brazilian Presbyterian Rubem Alves and Argentine Methodist Jose Miguez Bonino, called for a Protestant theology, going beyond Shaull's revolution to liberation. Bonino and Alves, having earned PhDs from Union and Princeton Theological Seminaries, respectively, found themselves sharing a "messianic–prophetic" vision with Catholics and experiencing marginalization within their official church structures. In revolution and liberation, radical Protestant and Catholic theologians found common cause.[37]

Alves' Brazilian origins and North American ties placed him in a crucial juncture in the development of liberation theology. Under Shaull's supervision, he completed his controversial 1968 Princeton dissertation, "Toward a Theology of Liberation." The book, published a year later as *A Theology of Human Hope,* was on the cusp with Cone, Herzog, and Gutiérrez in putting forward a theology of liberation. Alves, drawing from the German theologian Jürgen Moltmann, Herbert Marcuse's critical theory, and North American pragmatism, provided a definition of truth as action in history. He defined a liberating "messianic humanism" as the historical activity of God responding to the demands of the "political humanism" emerging among Third World people. The "world proletariat," as a new consciousness, included radicalized students raised in abundance and the North American black man systematically made poor, both becoming aware of their unfreedom. Alves, Bonino, and their mentor, Shaull, provided an early ecumenical bridge between theologians in the Americas. Appearing frequently in the 1970s in the pages of *Christianity and Crisis* and *Cristanismo y Sociedad*, they contributed key ideas regarding revolution and history that became foundational in the liberationist movement.[38]

Beyond God the Father

While men advocated for liberation from race and class oppression, women, sharing in the liberatory sensibilities sweeping the Americas, found the new theology's appeal to black manhood and a "new humanity" to be suspiciously rendering them invisible. The first generation of black and Latin American liberation theologians were decisively masculinist in their orientation, eliding the role of gender in theological thought. Cone acknowledged years later that he had begun with the idea that women's liberation was a joke and a distraction from the real issue of race. After all, white women had historically charged black men with rape, instigating lynching, while society ignored the rape of black women by white men. Cone viewed Black Power's assertive black manhood as foundational, ignoring the sexism within the black community.[39]

For Latin Americans seeking a unifying identity, class circumvented the divisive issues of race and sex. Class provided a way to unite the largest segment of heterogeneous Latin Americans under pressing economic problems. Gutiérrez initially acknowledged the double oppression under which poor women lived, but it was poverty rather than gender that defined his basis for a theology of liberation. Argentine liberationist philosopher Enrique Dussel identified the crux of the Latin American problem as political oppression of the world's periphery by the center. Political oppression featured "pedagogical domination" that controlled the "analytical horizon" through mass media, and "erotic domination" represented by the sexual subordination of indigenous women. While noting the role of sexism in oppression, Dussel explicitly chose not to include an analysis of women's exclusion in his 500-year historical survey of the Latin American Church. Through the 1970s, male liberationists ignored sex-based subordination while women continually appealed to the new theology as illuminating their own situation. Gender asymmetry remained in the first stages of liberationist thought.[40]

It would be up to women radicalized by the feminist movement to articulate their own theology of liberation by bringing attention to the interconnected nature of race, class, and sex. Engagement with the civil rights movement opened the way for women to question their own position in society. Beyond liberal expansion of political rights, the women's liberation wing of the movement viewed women as victims of patriarchy—a total social system that exerted control over women's bodies, lives, and imaginative horizon. Religious institutions, as part of that system, did not escape the ramifications of the far-reaching women's movement, and neither could the movement deny its religious roots. Many women participating in consciousness-raising groups and activism began to identify sexism in their faith communities and to recover their own distinct religious narrative. An example is Pauli Murray, who participated in the Civil Rights movement working with King, was a founding member of the National Organization for Women, and was the first African American woman Episcopal priest. In her life and thought, racism, sexism, and religion were interlinked. Murray's biography is representative of religious feminist activists and the multiple barriers they encountered.[41]

Women participating in New Left movements identified cultural and social barriers not remedied by law. When the personal became political, radicalized women saw religious ideas as the ultimate support for sexism and sought, as theologians and clergy, to break through the impenetrable sexist veil of religious institutions. The emerging feminist theologians caught a rising tide of suspicion and discontentment with tradition among many laywomen who filled the pews. The struggle for full participation in all areas of society included confronting the theology and exclusionary religious practices rather than abandoning religion.

Mary Daly and Rosemary Radford Ruether, as feminists and Catholic theologians, challenged religious language, the interpretation of sacred texts and symbols, and the ecclesial hierarchy that underwrote women's subordination. Coming from the progressive wing of the Catholic tradition, they drew from the historical stream of women's religiosity. They looked to their foremothers for inspiration, including Protestants Elizabeth Cady Stanton and Lucretia Mott. As women in the 1960s made claims to the public sphere, Daly and Ruether, along with other Catholic and Protestant women who joined them, found the theological language needed to recover a lost female self—one hidden by the force of custom and tradition. They began a deep questioning of modern theology as key to understanding women's subordination in society and uncovered a rhetoric of privatized religion that hid its political and masculinist underpinnings.[42]

Raised in a Catholic family, Daly went on to earned two PhDs, one from St. Mary's College in religion and another in theology and philosophy at the University of Fribourg in Switzerland. Returning to the United States, she joined the faculty of the Jesuit-run Boston College in 1967. Inspired by Vatican II's explicit affirmation of women's equality before God and the existential philosophy of Simone de Beauvoir, in 1968 Daly wrote *The Church and the Second Sex*. Bringing together ideas from two discordant sources and with her ethical and philosophical questioning, Daly drew attention to the subordinated status of women in the Catholic Church through its practice of male-only hierarchy and teachings on sexuality; she proposed wholesale feminist reforms. Her book was a catalyst for the ensuing conflict between the demands of feminism and long-held practices of religious institutions. Subsequently, in *Beyond God the Father* (1973), judging the possibilities for escaping misogyny within Christian theology, Daly considered the black theology of James Cone. She concluded that his "fiercely patriarchal" mindset turned religious resignation among black people into a "cry for vengeance." Cone had turned the crutch of religion into a weapon and offered women no hope for escaping sexism. Women, she surmised, needed to look beyond the confines of the Church to escape misogyny.[43]

Beyond God the Father was Daly's last radical negotiation with Christianity. She concluded that Christian theology was an unredeemable sexist ideology providing the justification for the patriarchy through the "mystification of roles" in which "if God in 'his' heaven is a father ruling 'his' people, then it is in the 'nature' of things and according to divine plan and the order of the universe that society be male dominated." Breaking out of the straitjacket of sexism and misogyny required recognizing the male idols internalized by women and the intimate link between racism and sexism. *Beyond God the Father* was Daly's final break with all forms of monotheistic and patriarchal religion to a divine and elemental female Self.[44]

Unlike Daly, Ruether did not leave the Catholic Church or Christianity; she stayed to remake them from within. The daughter of a Catholic mother and an Episcopal father, she grew up in a humanistic and ecumenical household. After earning a doctorate in the history of Christian thought at Claremont School of Theology, she went on to teach at the predominantly black Howard University's School of Religion in 1966. As a white feminist at Howard, she began to read the emerging black theology and participated in the antiwar and Civil Rights movements. She set forth her ethic for change in *The Radical Kingdom: The Western Experience of Messianic Hope* (1970). Trained in the Western classics, Ruether drew from the broad history of thought to write a collection of essays published as *Liberation Theology: Human Hope Confronts Christian History and American Power* in 1972 and *New Woman New Earth: Sexist Ideologies and Human Liberation* in 1975. A prolific writer, her work appeared frequently on the pages of journals such as *Christianity and Crisis, Christian Century*, and *Commonweal*, providing her a ready platform to spread her ideas.

During the 1960s and 1970s Ruether developed her theological criticism. She called for an abandonment of all forms of "apocalyptic dualism" founded on Gnostic body–soul dichotomies and the subjective–objective "Cartesian" dualism of modern science. A split view of reality infested every area of life and impeded the development of a true liberation theology that could address alienation from the body, the community, and the earth. In the triad of racism, classism, and sexism engendered by dualism, the oppression of women was "undoubtedly the oldest form" in human history and the basis for all other forms of oppression. As a caste within every race and class, women made up the "first and final proletariat." Addressing sexism was the key to solving the problems of both class and race.⁴⁵

The battles over race and class that divided the women's movement were migrating to feminist theology. Ruether attempted to stave off a reprise by noting that sexism and racism were historically linked with the white male ruling class, pitting blacks against women in a strategy of divide and conquer. White feminists, argued Ruether, did not understand the underwriting of racism by the "feminine mystique" and the "cult of the ornamental 'white lady.'" Black women, in their intersectionality, were in the position to illuminate the relationship between race, class, and sex, and challenge the tendency among liberationists to emphasize polarity, pitting one oppressed group against another. Turning toward Torres' and Gutiérrez's case against class oppression, she saw an emerging cosmopolitan vision in which Latin America provided a key interpretation of the Christian faith and revolutionary struggle. The oppressed were perceiving the ideological content of "Constantinianism" that simply "baptizes the empire." Ruether called on feminists in the developed world to engage in creating the socioeconomic conditions for the liberation of all women; otherwise, liberal feminism remained a movement of white privilege.⁴⁶

The contributions of feminist theologians like Daly and Ruether and those who joined them completed the triad of race, class, and sex that challenged the standing theo-political status quo. As a loose intellectual movement, liberation theologians speaking for distinct groups expressed solidarity in thought responding to the cultural and political crisis in the Americas. As modern intellectuals they understood the political efficacy of evoking God and the history of engaging the religious imagination for social change. Their project to recover lost religious vibrancy at the end of the 1960s sought an authentic world-shaping faith and a theology emerging from the perspective of the subordinated. Faced with an unprecedented crisis of faith and culture, liberation theologians were set to rewrite centuries of theo-political history.

2

The Political Is the Total

THE DISRUPTIVE ISSUES of race, class, and sex that burst on the scene in the 1960s brought with them a critique of the established relationship between religion and politics. Beyond the immediate crisis, liberation theologians took on a set of intransigent problems within their discipline: a commitment to the private and existential needs of the individual, and ineffectiveness in addressing social questions. Centuries earlier the Protestant Reformation had cemented a perennial political problem within theology that was again presenting itself in mid-century America. The brief history presented in this chapter, in which by necessity I am blurring the lines between Protestant and Catholic thought, illuminates how theology came to view itself and the unresolved political questions that were again nipping at its heels. The theo-political negotiation that began in sixteenth-century Europe, the reverberations of the Enlightenment, and the Romantic interiorization of heart religion remained as a residue within postwar theology.

Challenging the splitting of politics and religion, both Catholics and Protestant liberationists voiced the attitude of the radical wing of the Reformation, an influential minority appealed to by many subsequent dissenters. In many ways Catholics liberationists, steeped in modern European theology and working independently of church hierarchy, took up the older Protestant move of an oppositional popular religion. In their refusal to bypass politics in addressing social questions, liberationists strengthened the theological significance of the political, going against well-established religious thought.

The Autonomy of Theology

Americans had long held politics and religion to be inextricable even while professing the necessity of formal state/church separation. In Catholic Latin

America and Protestant North America, the relationship between these two spheres was mutually influential, often featuring an uneasy accommodation for the sake of social cohesion. Liberal politics and religion strained to maintain their boundaries without giving up their alternative visions for society. Religious thought recognized this coexistence. Beyond the Catholic and Protestant sectarian conflict inherited from the Reformation, nineteenth-century theologians divided along broader lines. They either held to liberal notions of a universal religious experience while negotiating with modernity, or espoused conservative propositional objectivism unable to escape the tide of rationalism. The blurred lines between these two tendencies were evident all along the liberal–conservative continuum. In any case, post-Enlightenment theology shared in modernity's search for epistemological certainty and a sustainable society.

Christian theology's self-understanding is as a formal hermeneutical practice of systematic and rational study of the biblical text, primarily addressed to a particular believing community. For most of Christian history, theologians attempted to discern the will of God by engagement with the text. In times of political or cultural challenge, they built rational and defensive arguments, *apologias*, for the unpersuaded. Post-Enlightenment theology sought to reconcile faith and biblical interpretation with modern skepticism while claiming autonomy in thought. As theologians attempted to satisfy new epistemological demands, much of social and political life escaped their critical examination. Theology consequently negotiated itself into a position of irrelevancy among the critical disciplines.

Nonetheless, the biblical text was not solely in the purview of elites' reading and interpretation. Religious thought arising from the everyday perceptions and responses of common people to the divine easily extend beyond the boundaries of normative Christianity. How ordinary people read or heard scripture and conceptualized God carried political and social ramifications and presented a threat to both political and ecclesial authority—a problem that especially plagued fractious Protestants. Recognizing that religious thought exceeded the bounds set by church authority or formal theology, liberationists moved to recognize the alternative stream of the religious thought of the marginalized.

Liberationists began by questioning theology's assumed intellectual and political autonomy. Appeals to the biblical text, faith, reason, and tradition had provided a bulwark from outside challenges. Liberationists expressed suspicion of biblical interpretations that ignored the self-interest of the theologian and methods of exegesis that presumed to extract eternal truths without awareness of the world. James Cone asserted that "theology is not what theologians claim it to be"—universal language about the divine—rather, "it is *interested* language" emerging from a particular time and place. As "subjective speech about God," Cone concurred with Ludwig Feuerbach, "theology is anthropology."

Liberationists, understanding theology as historically and politically contingent rather than fixed for all time, refused to give it an autonomous existence. Politics, they concluded, constituted all theology. The claims of the marginalized coming to bear on religion and politics called for redefining the relationship between the text, the reader, and the world.[1]

Liberationists, understanding the theologian as always reading the text from an ideological position, reconceived the interpretive practice. Their arguments involved method, point of view, and, more importantly, the sociopolitical currency of any reading. By approaching the text in a new way, examined in subsequent chapters, they expanded the boundaries of who was considered fit for engaging in the construction of theology, and from what perspective. This invited the charge that liberationists actually engaged little with the text itself and peddled nothing less than an ideology. However, liberationists, who never claimed autonomy or impartiality, justified their approach precisely on ideological terms. They called peers to task for viewing themselves as dealing with pristine categories of thought, but also for sidestepping the relationship between religion and politics. Theologians, who viewed themselves as above the fray, resisted being dragged into what they perceived as ideological battles.

The Great Separation

Theology's resistance to a direct address of the political was deep-seated, the result of a theo-political truce. Centuries before our current understanding of "the secular" as a sphere of society devoid of any appeals to divine authority or transcendent meaning, European reformers were laying down the essential elements of the modern relationship between religion and politics. The Reformation's mark on that relationship left the question of the ultimate authority in society unanswered. Did the state or the church ultimately dictate the terms of the social order? In the twentieth century, theology again encountered the same questions: How could the two domains, both asserting autonomy and ultimate authority, make claims to a unified social vision without negating each other? Were societal arrangements of power determined by the will of God, always contested, or agreed upon by a tentative political contract? Different expressions of Christianity answered these questions in diverse ways, for example, the long-running Catholic refusal to acknowledge the autonomy of the state and the rejection of its jurisdiction by radical Protestant sects.

Modernity responded to these questions through the creation of the secular state and recognition of a semi-autonomous and separate religious sphere in society. Liberation theologians, while not questioning the legitimacy of the modern state, nevertheless questioned what they judged to be an ideological subordination of religious values to politics. They were seeking to negotiate a critical place for theology within politics. As they championed the claims of the oppressed, it appeared to threaten a severing of the *cordon sanitaire* between theology and political philosophy, which evoked hostile responses from both secular and religious thinkers.

The concern was with the erosion of what the liberal political scientist and historian Mark Lilla characterizes as the "Great Separation." The Great Separation constituting politics emerged from the cauldron of the Reformation, resulting in an uneasy truce between the church and the nascent modern state. While the state established its claim over this world, the church provided assurances for the next. The separation of the spiritual and the secular as two domains evoked the Augustinian model of two cities—the earthly and the heavenly. Martin Luther's theology accepted the doctrine of the two realms or kingdoms, the secular and spiritual, leaving unanswered the question regarding their relationship. Luther saw the political realm as concerned with the material world and the maintenance of order. He viewed the spiritual realm, under the purview of the church, as concerned with the condition of the inner person. The assumed separation left unresolved the conflict of authority and jurisdiction in determining the lived values of an emerging modern society.[2]

The dichotomy between the theological and the political broke with the medieval unified world to create a fragmented human experience, forming the foundation for much modern-era thinking. One could hold to religious values in the private realm and exercise effective, and often contradictory, political rights in society, for example, holding that all things belong to God while hallowing private property. The political expression of faith often resulted in a tendency toward religious quietism on one hand and divinely sanctioned nationalism on the other. Luther attempted to avoid the subordination of the spiritual to the secular, while arguing against the radical Anabaptist refusal to acknowledge the coercive power of the state. In the name of law and order, Luther and the magisterial reformers deployed the power of kings to carry out their reforms and underwrote the state/church alliance that had preeminence in the eighteenth century.[3]

To Luther's consternation, his doctrine of Christian freedom and moral equality did not remain within the church walls, but rather the theo-political quality of his ideas inspired revolutionaries among the peasantry. The publication of *Memmingen Articles*, written by the Lutheran pastor Sebastian Lotzer and the journeyman furrier Christoph Schappeler, instigated the peasant uprisings of 1525. The articles, sounding much like the works of twentieth-century revolutionaries, summarized the grievances of the German peasantry, demanding, among other things, release from serfdom, free access to natural resources, and the return of expropriated common fields. The authors insisted that their demands for justice and equity in the political sphere sprang from divine justice. In a time of economic and political upheaval, as petty civil and ecclesial lords attempted to extend their jurisdiction, radical groups of peasants in different locales began to align themselves based on divine law that superseded differences in German common law. Civil law and religious visions for society were on a collision course, moving Luther to side with the political order of kings by calling for the suppression of peasant uprisings.[4]

Chief among the peasant leaders was Thomas Müntzer, an early supporter of Luther turned antagonist, who believed that poverty was detrimental to faith. In Zwickau, installed as a pastor, he noted that a majority of the population was impoverished and a few were particularly rich. Nevertheless, the mystical Müntzer believed that the poor without instruction arrived at a sound faith through the immediate effect of the Spirit. This was a theology from below, free of institutional restraints having social and political consequences. Through inflammatory rhetoric, he espoused a millennial reign of Christ brought about through revolutionary violence against the godless. Whether Catholics or Lutherans, those who opposed the realization of the kingdom of God on earth were doomed to destruction. Drawing from the Old Testament prophets, Müntzer viewed history as an unfolding in which God's elect, the common man, would slay the godless and usher in the rule of justice—a total social revolution. He dedicated his own manifesto to the church of the poor.[5]

In the nineteenth century, after Frederick Engels tagged Müntzer as a pre-Marxist revolutionary, German socialists championed him. As a celebrated leader of the Peasants' War, Müntzer came to represent the downtrodden and was seen as a harbinger of modern communism. The class nature of the Peasants' War provided fertile ground for an interpretation of the Reformation as an early attempt by the bourgeois to overthrow feudal structures and signal the revolutionary future for the peasants. In the *Peasant War in Germany* (1850), Engels delivered a full Marxist interpretation of Müntzer. He examined Müntzer's political significance based on a materialist conception of history, and interpreted his religious fervor as an unfortunate illusion about where the real historical forces lay. In the Marxist interpretation, his theology appears as a trope for the real idea: to establish a classless society without private property. In the twentieth century among leftist circles, the tragic figure of Müntzer represented the original revolutionary.[6]

Marxist interpretations of Müntzer multiplied exponentially. The German utopian Marxist Ernst Bloch rediscovered him for the twentieth century in his influential study, *Thomas Münzer als Theologe der Revolution* (1921). Müntzer and his radical followers provided a useable past for both political revolutionaries and radical religious thinkers. His egalitarianism, his demand for immediate justice in this world, and his stance against the state-established churches and Luther presented a different reading of Christianity. The demands of the peasantry for economic justice appealing to the laws of God, rather than political jurisdiction, offered a model for an alternative path to revolution.

The Luther/Müntzer opposition is the original story in an oft-repeated history of the conflict within religious thought that was again erupting among American radicals of the 1960s. Christian theology since the Reformation recognized the egalitarian nature of the faith and the central theme of justice claimed by many social and political movements. Through the modern era, the demands of justice and equality inspired popular revolutionaries to emphasize the imminent righting of the world against the conservatism of the established churches. Drawing from that history, Rosemary Radford Ruether's *The Radical Kingdom: The Western Experience of Messianic Hope* (1970) laid out a continual historical link between Müntzer "anarchic communism," American religious utopianism, and the New Left of the 1960s. What remained an obstacle was that lacking specific means by which to establish a new social order, utopian thinkers quickly sought to escape the world they wanted to save.[7]

The practical means of implementing a social project based on the demands of equality and justice appeared to elude religious thought. Luther solved this problem by abandoning the attempt to establish God's kingdom on earth, leaving it to a future act of God alone, and instead spiritualized the role of the church. Justified by faith and morally equal within the spiritualized church, one remained politically unequal in this world, creating numerous disputes regarding the position of slaves, women, workers, and the poor. Both Protestantism and Catholicism left governing the affairs of this world to the emerging modern state, whose primary role was to secure personal liberty and property and maintain law and order rather than to establish broadly defined social justice. The post-Reformation churches devoted themselves to cultivating civic virtue, subjection to secular authority, and feelings of benevolence toward others among their members. Consequently, sermons, hymns, and devotional tracts were devoid (except among dissenters) of political critique even as they often remained politically serviceable for the purposes of the state. The historical concession of theology to modern politics gave occasion for the charge by liberationists that theology acted as a conservative force rather than a revolutionary world-building one.[8]

In the Americas, the separation between religion and politics was never fully complete. The legacy of the Great Separation created as many problems as it solved, and the spiritualization of justice and freedom diluted the claims of subordinated people within both the church and the new American states. The theo-political entanglement raised immediate questions: Did the Christian faith admonish slaves and the lower classes to obey those above them, or did it do away with status distinction among men? How could the order of society resolve these questions? Additionally, implementing church–state separation was fraught with difficulty, as clergymen sought to influence the political sphere through a formal or *de facto* national church and access to state apparatus. Often they sought to actualize, if in circumscribed form, Luther's liberty of conscience and justice within a rising modern state. Yet, religious claims worked two ways—with liberty of conscience and Christian freedom available to justify slave holding and pecuniary interest.

In the realm of nineteenth-century popular religiosity, various visions for society vied for influence. Radical abolitionists, social reformers, and indigenous and women's rights advocates were often politically at odds with church teaching that justified the standing social order with calls to obedience. Attempts by Christianized slaves to reconcile their faith with their political bondage often resulted in resistance. In Latin America, the Catholic Church found itself competing with politically active folk religion in the countryside, or outbreaks of zealous social action. Faith, understood as being oriented toward God's justice, could underwrite renunciation or spur periodic eruptions of protest and defiance. Multifarious resistance flourished in the gap between positive liberal and religious visions and political reality, and neither the church nor the state could claim the whole meaning of human life within its purview. The tension between freedom and obedience contributed to recurring crises among women, blacks, indigenous people, and workers, as they attempted to assert religious values to gain political rights.

Through this history, theology demonstrated its political constitution, yet its self-understanding as a disinterested discipline avoided a direct challenge to the political order. Not that politics totally escaped the minds of theologians. The twentieth century brought a resurgence of various political theologies attempting to provide a biblically based political ethic. Theologians, understanding politics as being primarily about maximizing power arrangements for the ordering of society, attempted to resolve the ongoing conflict between the divine–human relationship and social power arrangements, such as equal before God, unequal in society. Splitting the difference, they contextualized Christian ethics for a particular situation while presenting justification for the state. The North American tradition of the social gospel, Reinhold Niebuhr's public theology of Christian realism, and Martin Luther King's nonviolent resistance are examples of theological ethics applied to the political situation. Except for dissenters who emerged from time to time, Protestant theology's accommodation to liberalism never questioned the autonomy of the political realm itself, but rather sought to provide reasons for moral influence.

Similarly, a reluctant Catholic Church found itself compelled into a truce regarding effective social authority by the rise of the liberal state. Nineteenth-century changes left Catholicism with a measure of sociopolitical influence as it recognized at least a semi-autonomous state. The church/state truce in Latin America was fraught with conservative resistance against the extension of the secular state into all areas of life (not the least birth, marriage, and family) and continued into the mid-twentieth century, when the idea of a new Christendom forwarded by the Catholic philosopher Jacques Maritain flourished. I offer a more detailed discussion of Maritain's political theology and new Christendom in Chapter 7. The new paradigm forwarded by Maritain viewed the state and church as occupying different but interlocking domains in a "distinction of planes," offering a new direction for lay people's political involvement. This view of interlocking domains held that the church and state fully recognized each other's legitimacy and provided justification for liberal Catholic social action.

As the United States sought to guarantee religious freedom through disestablishment and attempted to erect a solid wall between church and state, Latin American states established a recognized domain of the Catholic Church with limited freedom for dissenting groups. The authority of the Church extended to prescribing the private morals of its members yet within the limits of state law. Throughout the Americas the contentious lines between the public and private needs, politics and religion, remained contested, generating multiple battles over social values and morality. The bifurcation of the political and theological realms in both Protestant and Catholic thought presented itself to liberationists as hindering an effective critique of society. Gustavo Gutiérrez argued that in Latin America the "distinction of planes" under the ideas of new Christendom resulted in the "dysfunctional" safeguarding of the Church's interest through political maneuvering and support of a conservative social vision. The inadvertent theological tendency was to spiritualize social problems out of existence and avoid a confrontation with the standing order of society.[9]

Heart Religion

Liberationists encountered an additional obstacle to a faith-inspired political conscience: the eighteenth-century turn toward subjective religious knowledge reinforced by enlightened ideas. Whether it was Jean-Jacques Rousseau's assertion in *Emile* that true understanding comes through personal experience or Immanuel Kant's rational faith expressed in *Religion within the Limits of Reason Alone*, the Enlightenment approached religion in the way it approached all other questions, with a fundamental belief in one's capability to know and experience the essence of the faith. Creeds, reinterpreted in practical ways, served to aid a person's growth toward self-fulfillment. The turn toward individual reason or experience as the authority in religion diminished the role of the spiritual community.

The new enlightened attitude joined currents within theology. The seventeenth-century father of pietism, the German Lutheran Philipp Jakob Spener had asserted that "our entire Christianity consists in the inner or new man, and its soul is faith." With pietism as a "system of feeling," contrasted with orthodox reasoning and flowing with Romantic currents, the historic understanding of obedience based on faith in an objective revelation, the dogmatic statements of church tradition, was significantly weakened and replaced by the heart religion that subsequently ran through many transatlantic revivals. For revivalist John Wesley, "Feelings are the divine consolations" and the proof of faith. The religion of the heart, with its emphasis on the personal religious experience, found outward expression primarily in a private moralism. And, even if at times it expressed deep sympathy for slaves and the deserving poor, it remained uncritical toward the political arrangements of power. Faced with the new historical criticism grounded in enlightened reason and influenced by pietism, theologians defended the Christian faith on grounds of the unique nature of the religious experience.[10]

Under modern reasoning, theology had to demonstrate its logic to a mind able to give assent and serve as the final judge of the trustworthiness of any proposition. Theologians began to retreat from asserting absolute knowledge derived from the biblical text and moved toward claiming personal experience as the standard of authority for the truth of religion. With a self-authenticating experience poised to serve the needs of the individual, the Bible became a text of mythical poetic expression, instigating a search for the essence of its message—the true meaning beyond the form. Demythologization, stripping the biblical text of its supernatural claims, and personal experience presented a new basis for the certainty of religious knowledge outside dogmatic orthodoxy.[11]

The Romantic theologian Friedrich Schleiermacher, the father of liberal theology, and the literary philosopher Samuel Taylor Coleridge provided the most creative solutions to the problem of religious knowledge in a turn toward existential truth. Coleridge, who influenced American Transcendentalism's idealist faith in finding God within, set religious knowledge within the vital experience of spiritual truth available through the faculty of "reason," defined as the "organ of the supersensuous." Reason, the human faculty for sensing spiritual truth, offered the means for self-transcendence. The authority of the biblical text, accessible through reason, lay in "its fitness to our nature and needs," not in any supposed objective truth. The interaction between the text and the reader's experience of faith created religious truth. For Schleiermacher, religion was neither objective moral knowing nor action, but rather something that lay in the realm of subjective feeling, a "sense and taste for the Infinite." The religious feeling, or intuition, for Schleiermacher was an immediate self-consciousness of total dependence. In

On Religion: Speeches to Its Cultured Despisers (1799), he attempted to uncover the essence of religion concealed by metaphysical rationalization. Schleiermacher's subjective definition of religion, which eschewed the need for external authority, colored the understanding of Protestant Christianity throughout the nineteenth century.[12]

Schleiermacher did not wholly atomize the individual; neither did he see salvation as otherworldly. The awareness of interdependency was situated in the here and now. "If there is religion at all, it must be social, for that is the nature of man," he wrote. In his self-reflective *Monologues* (1800), written at the height of his involvement with Berlin's Romantic circle, he grappled with the conflict between the inner world of freedom and the constraints of society. Under false social prescriptions, the individual experienced either pain or superficial satiety, leading to spiritual slavery. Schleiermacher's social ethics of individuality, in which society both constituted and constrained the individual, set the course for the future of Protestant theology in which the religious subject's willing and choosing was the point of departure.[13]

While Schleiermacher was concerned primarily with the nature of religious feeling as a form of contemplation of the self and the world, he made two foundational moves critical for liberationists. One was to validate the subjective religious experience as a source of truth, and the other was to place religious feeling within culture and history and not outside it. Liberationists drew from both contributions. On the one hand, they rejected a reified middle-class experience as a standard for religious truth. On the other, they embraced a historically situated religious experience placing the oppressed, rather than the middle class, at the center of the theological project.[14]

Schleiermacher had insisted on the moral individual as thoroughly related to the community in an act of self-constitution. With Søren Kierkegaard, mid-nineteenth-century Protestant existentialism reached a peak in articulating the primacy of the individual, in his assertion "Truth is subjectivity." Revolting against the cultural Christianity and idealism of his age, the Kierkegaardian individual gained the absolutism that Hegel had assigned to the state. True Christianity, as an existential ethic for action, provided the means by which the individual gained freedom from the oppressive society and false religion by transcending it. Rubem Alves observed that in Kierkegaard's divided world, "He cannot take history seriously . . . he inveighs against all the structures—philosophical, political, religious—which had absolved man from the central demand of 'salvation,' namely the task of becoming an individual." Alves, like his liberationist peers, questioned an existential freedom that de-historized the individual, leaving open the question of how one standing against history could change it. Kierkegaard's existentialism had a significant influence on twentieth-century German theology that sought to critique the Christianity of liberal bourgeois culture. The theological pull remained toward the willing and acting individual and defining *his* place in society.[15]

Under the sway of revivalism and expanding liberalism, nineteenth-century North American theology continued with a reformulated Calvinism augmented by Scottish moral philosophy, with the project of self-mastery at the center. Unitarian theology, featuring a solitary God, provided the foundation for William Channing's social thought in "Self-Culture" (1838). The reification of the individual in Channing's thought gave birth to the transcendental self-deification of Ralph Waldo Emerson, who, in his repudiation of society as a hindrance to the individual, sought an oceanic union with nature. Incorporating the sociability of religion, Horace Bushnell's *Discourses on Christian Nurture* (1847) proposed the raising of children in ways that would foster Christian virtue within the family and church. Bushnell remained focused on the social constitution and moral nurturance of the individual, yet made a move toward considering the social conditions in the development of a religious consciousness. Among the evangelical revivalists such as Charles Finney, the emphasis on a spiritual conversion and self-discipline independent of religious communities followed in the same vein of individual transformation. Evangelical Protestant theology, with its diverse expression and centered on the individual's development, supported a liberal political and economic system. It also had within it, as we shall see, the seeds of reform and the future social gospel.[16]

Protestantism was not alone in constructing a private religious experience able to engender social sympathy within a minimalist state. Catholic dogmatic unity did not escape heart religion, notably in the Tubingen School theologian Johann von Drey, who, while eschewing Protestant subjectivism endemic to modernity, shared an affinity with Schleiermacher's natural religion rooted in a personal mystical sense of the divine. He wrote, "man becomes aware of God, as he becomes aware of himself." The Catholic middle classes and local clergy of the nineteenth century—becoming aware of themselves and the surrounding social need brought on by industrial capitalism, and moved by religious feeling—found ways to engage in social amelioration independent of church hierarchy, through a personal reinterpretation of the Catholic faith. The Magisterium's rejectionist stance toward enlightened philosophy and the liberal economic order proved an insufficient guide for sympathetic modern laypeople.[17]

Compelled by increased social unrest and the anxiety of laypeople, Leo XIII's 1891 encyclical *Rerum novarum* attempted to provide a moral guide for industrial reform against the rising threat of socialism among workers. The allies of the church, the anti-socialist moderate liberals, sought a bourgeois adaptation of classic Christian civilization. The strategy of Leo XIII included the promotion of an organic hierarchical ordering of society and Christian democracy, supporting moderate social welfare policies and the creation of parallel institutions. The encyclical described the parameters for robust Catholic social engagement that continued among the middle classes through Vatican II. The social teachings of Leo XIII supported a reformist bourgeois stance, leaving the socially marginal and subordinated at the mercy of the charitable inclinations of the empowered classes.[18]

Post-Enlightenment Christianity centered on the middle-class drive for self-knowledge and self-improvement by which society was to progress toward human betterment. There is no doubt that religious-inspired sympathies motivated many middle-class reformers to emphasize public charity, but there was no categorical theological or political dictum to share or relinquish power. Social change was dependent on personal conviction and sympathy. The emphasis on personal feelings and voluntary action, and de-emphasis on communal belonging and obligation, had political implications by absolutizing the minimalist state as the rightful agent of the social order, establishing the aspirational values of the middle class, and reifying the individual.

The twentieth century brought a backlash to the strain of Schleiermacher's theology spearheaded by the intense criticism of the Swiss theologian Karl Barth and of H. Richard Niebuhr. Schleiermacher was increasingly seen as a cultural accommodationist who, in order to argue for "truth in religion" to his liberal and enlightened contemporaries, betrayed theology's critical function. The church was to remain a pure spiritual society that nurtured self-consciousness untangled from political interest. Barth, on the way to becoming the foremost theologian of the twentieth century, charged that Schleiermacher's theology elided the political by focusing on personal piety and by asserting the autonomy of religious feeling from other forms of knowledge. As a politically active liberal supporting economic equality and social welfare, Schleiermacher provided no avenue for these goals except the cultivation of religious sympathy. The individual's feelings of interconnectedness and dependence were to burst forth as goodwill toward all humankind. Private religion left the laboring and enslaved classes at the mercy of the benevolent feelings of those having social and political power.[19]

A Critical Theology

Post-Enlightenment theology was ill prepared to withstand the tragedy-fraught twentieth century and began the first phase of critical self-questioning within the discipline. The cataclysmic events of World War I and the subsequent critique of Schleiermacher instigated a move toward a critical theology. The German church struggle of World War II, compromising both the Protestant and the

Catholic churches by the encroachment of National Socialism, exposed the fatal fault lines in the truce between religion and politics. Barth charged that the *Kulturprotestantismus*, Protestantism resigned to the needs of modern culture and built on the legacy of Schleiermacher, had contributed to the *völkisch* ideology of the Nazi state. The German church struggle and Barth's work brought into question the church–state consensus of the age and introduced a significant critical feature to theology, questioning both humanistic revolutionary projects and conservative legitimation.

Barth developed his political theology as an active socialist pastor in the 1910s and in his early work, *Romans II* (1922) and then *Ethics*, a series of lectures given in 1928. Known as the "red pastor" he saw congruence between the Christian gospel and the historical movement toward social justice, and advocated the end of capitalism, solidarity with the poor, and rejection of the individual-centered religion of imperial Germany. His dialectic theology sought to reestablish the otherness of God against a humanistic, feeling-based religion that made the individual the center. He viewed the utter transcendence of God as having political ramifications, as it stood both *against* and *for* the world in a "theology of permanent revolution," an idea picked up by Gutiérrez and a useful concept for liberation theology.[20]

In the aftermath of the Holocaust, theologians influenced by Barth and critical social theories sought to reexamine not only the nature of evil but also how theology, as part of the societal superstructure, was implicated in an unjust political order. Two Germans, Catholic Johann Baptist Metz and Protestant Jürgen Moltmann, sought a basis for a new political theology, questioning the bourgeois religion that combined nationalism with a state sponsorship of religion. They viewed bourgeois religion as contributing to the rise of National Socialism, and built their thought on an eschatological vision of hope grounded, not in the hereafter, but in human history. Moltmann and Metz, along with Barth, and later Wolfhart Pannenberg in the 1960s, provided key terms for liberationists. I will examine these theologies in later chapters.

Reflecting on the theology they had inherited, liberationists concurred with Juan Luis Segundo that "every theology is political." In a series of course lectures delivered at Harvard Divinity School and published as *The Liberation of Theology* (1976), Segundo argued that theology emerged from a priori "commitments to change and improve the world" and did not escape the "ideological mechanism of established society." He had arrived at this stance as a Jesuit priest in a journey that began in the 1950s. Having earned a doctorate from the Sorbonne and writing two theses—one on philosophy and the other on theology—exposed him to the evolutionary thought of Jesuit philosopher Pierre Teilhard de Chardin and the creation-centered spirituality of the Christian existentialist Nikolai

Berdyaev. These thinkers contributed to his rejection of mid-century theology with its marked individualism and dualism. Segundo's intellectual pursuits, like those of many of his peers, were driven by a personal quest to identify the source of contradiction between the ethical values of Christianity and crushing poverty in Latin America.[21]

Liberationists building a new critical theology extrapolated the earlier critique of Schleiermacher's legacy and applied it to the whole of theology. Frederick Herzog noted that Schleiermacher never asked why there were "countless multitudes who do not have the time and the freedom to reflect on their precious, private white selves." A modern intellectual framework defined the essential human experience as "a private self," without critical reflection on one's interests. The result, Herzog charged, was a definition of religious experience as "an untroubled leisure of peaceful solitude" possible only for a certain class. Liberationists viewed earlier critiques of Schleiermacher as insufficient in bridging the gulf between the political and the theological, perpetuating a "platonic" strain. James Cone argued that in America, theology was the product of an exclusively white experience and amounted to "a bourgeois exercise in intellectual masturbation." Similar to Marx's argument regarding the connection between material interest and ideology, Cone charged, "Unfortunately, American theologians from Cotton Mather and Jonathan Edwards to Reinhold Niebuhr and Schubert Ogden, including radicals and conservatives, have interpreted the gospel according to the cultural and political interests of white people." He noted how enlightened "white theology" made it possible that "Jonathan Edwards, often called America's most outstanding theologian, could preach and write theological treatises on total depravity . . . without the slightest hint of how these issues related to human bondage." He charged that American theology in mid-century amounted to an abstraction ignoring the historical experience black people. The key criticism was that post-war critical theologies continued to feature unyielding notions of God's transcendence, always in danger of escaping history, a persistent hope in an eschatological horizon that faded into an unspecified future, and a silencing of the theological voice of the oppressed. America theology remained too removed from a suffering world.[22]

The Brazilian Hugo Assmann concluded that the idealistic "progressive" theology of the affluent nations was a "parasite" in need of eradication from the mind of the colonized. The Latin American mind shaped by European thought and influenced by North American power had to go through a "detoxification" before one could take political action. Liberationists throughout the Americas charged that Western theology served the rich and powerful because the powerful found in the Bible a personal source of truth, which validated their political power. By asserting the "primacy of the political sphere" as the "most important element of human activity," liberationists attempted to break through theology's self-understanding as politically autonomous.²³

The argument that the political had primacy over the theological was not new at the end of the 1960s. In the 1920s, the controversial German political theorist Carl Schmitt forwarded the idea that theology could not escape the political. Schmitt reintroduced the long-buried term *political theology* and defined all politics as groups making the distinction between friend and enemy. A political community came into being when people were willing to join others in making the distinction of who was in and who was out. The result was the creation of marginal groups. Schmitt argued that the liberal state operated from a notion that all conflicts could be resolved through reason, technology, or social organization, and did not recognize a bearer of ultimate sovereignty as residing in any one person. In this scenario, groups created by a common identity of mutual interest remained in constant competition with one another in appealing to the monopoly power of the state. In the liberal state, "the political is the total," rendering all claims political and propagating ideology. Schmitt argued that the notion that something is outside the political is in itself a political decision, including the claims of theology. By the mid-century, the idea that the political is the total had ramifications for the newly identified claims of the Third World and the marginalized within affluent nations. The subordinated, bound together by common interest, found that a theology claiming neutrality supported their ideological enemies. Recognizing the political role of theology required breaking through the façade of the Great Separation and the rhetoric of private religion.²⁴

For the emerging liberation theologians, the social upheaval calling for an effective response was at odds with their theological legacy. Theology's attempt to bypass politics had produced a socially exhausted discipline and an impotent religion unable to deal with cultural change. The alternative was not a return to the medieval order—an overlapping church and state—but rather the adoption of a critical stance. Liberation theologians set out to reawaken a political consciousness in the very heart of their discipline. They had a rich, if buried, history to draw from, as currents from the Reformation and the Enlightenment repeatedly met a religiously inspired resistance among excluded groups. Joining the legacy of protest and resistance, liberationists expressed not only the revolutionary impulse of the radical Reformation but also their preparation to reenact the theo-political history of the Americas.

3
The Irony of America

THE UPSURGE IN resistance by excluded groups at mid-twentieth century revived the historical fits and starts toward freedom that had long taken place in the Americas. A recurring dialectic of freedom and oppression was once again at play. Many Latin American intellectuals reconsidering modernization's promise of economic and political self-determination reached the conclusion that it only brought perpetual underdevelopment enriching the United States and Europe. Under a new form of imperial power, the colonial domination of the continent remained. Radicalized blacks, frustrated with the exhausted means for full inclusion in American democracy, found freedom illusory as long as the definition of *black* was unfreedom. Women who had embraced feminism and enjoying hard-won rights, sensed that sex-based inequalities embodied in a total patriarchal culture were beyond the remedy of liberal reform. Liberationists encountered a pernicious reproduction of oppression not fully addressed by religion or politics.

The history of revolutionary Americas examined in this chapter exhibited the paradox of enormous expectations of freedom and an unfathomable level of human misery. Under republican governments, and with the aid of enlightened reason and orderly religion, optimistic nation builders were hopeful of actualizing new utopian societies of material abundance and freedom. The subordinated multitudes of slaves, women, and the indigenous faced less clear prospects. The effects of intertwined religion and politics produced for them the push and pull of domination and submission, order and disorder, acquiescence and rebellion—a seedbed for new religious ideas. The historical contest over the actualization of freedom engaging elites and subordinated people provided liberationists with a useable past for locating an alternative theology of resistance and helped forge a common intellectual project across the Americas.

Utopian Possibilities

Ideas migrating from the Spanish and Scottish Enlightenments of the eighteenth century and taking root in the Americas, plus the influence of dissenting religion, created the gestational environment in which multiple forms of utopianism flourished. The values of human brotherhood, mutuality, and charity provided by religion often overlapped and coexisted with liberal ideas of freedom, equality, reason, and tolerance. At other times, the religious values of obedience, authority, and social hierarchy appeared irreconcilable with liberal ideals. For those privileged by race or social rank, America was an opportunity to launch religiously inspired utopian projects. From the early Puritans seeking to build their City on a Hill and the Jesuit communally organized settlements in Spanish America to numerous nineteenth-century utopian movements, the Americas offered the possibility of realizing the kingdom of God through human agency. Religion was not the only source of utopian thought. Liberals expressed the hope of universal equality and freedom through the establishment of modern states, natural law, the goodness of men, and the possibility of progress. Coexisting religious and liberal ideas of how to order new societies came to define the Americas.[1]

A transatlantic print culture brought new ideas about freedom and equality debated in European academies and salons. Throughout the Americas, such ideas necessarily fomented debates about the role of religion. Enlightened elites promoted a foundation for society based on the application of useful knowledge and the self-constraint of virtue and honor. Reformers sought to build legal, economic, and political institutions based on observation and empirical evidence, freed from metaphysical presuppositions. Human reason and the pursuit of liberty, tempered by the moral guide of religion, promised to subdue the wildness of the hemisphere. Under the sway of enlightened reason and missionary zeal, the barbarism of virgin lands would yield to civilization.[2]

As eighteenth century colonials began to see themselves as distinct from Europeans, the idea of an American hemisphere emerged. The prospects for a community of nations free from European domination promised to be what Thomas Jefferson regarded as the "grandest spectacle of nature." The whole complex of enlightened thinking revolved around the Americas as set apart geographically, politically, and culturally from the rest of the world, representing an unparalleled opportunity in world history. Americanism found enthused adherents across the western hemisphere. As Hegel's "land of the future," the new nations offered the possibility that the "burden of the world's history" to actualized freedom could reach fruition. How a deeply entrenched and often opposing religion was to fit within this liberal scheme remained unclear.[3]

Persuaded by the belief in a divine plan for society, or seeking to establish a viable liberal order, nation builders reproduced oppression rather than utopia. Subjugation coexisted with visions of a flourishing society only experienced by a few. For Africans and indigenous people uprooted from their lands and communities, America was where the meaning of freedom became a live idea. For white women, the experience in the new nations was remarkably like that of the old world left behind. Excluded groups rallied from time to time to assert economic and political independence or inclusion into the new states through persuasion or violence. Breathing the common air of enlightened ideas and motivated by religious fervor, subjugated people defined a holistic freedom—an expansive freedom more inclusive than political liberty or spiritual liberation.[4]

Enlightened thought provided some clues for the positive role of religion. Radical thinkers shared a belief in human reason and sought a natural religion freed from archaic institutions. Hume, Voltaire, and Diderot expressed a wholesale anti-religious sentiment in which religion was mere superstition—an impediment to progress. Religion made men slavish and aroused prejudice of every kind. Confronted with religion, man had to choose: freedom and knowledge, or slavery and ignorance. Only the most radical expressed this complete refutation of religion. For the largest segment of enlightened thinkers, the disdain for metaphysical abstraction did not result in a rejection of religion; rather, their thought struggled toward a religious and political synthesis. Regardless of its need for reform, true religion was useful for the ordering of society. Moderate Enlightenment texts, from John Locke's *A Letter Concerning Toleration* (1689) to Immanuel Kant's *Religion within the Limits of Reason Alone* (1793), forwarded a more positive account of religious sentiment and provided a foundation for a natural religion considered necessary for social order.[5]

Religious intellectuals, active at the center of the European Enlightenment, advocated change for both theology and political philosophy. They addressed questions left unresolved by the Reformation regarding the relationship between human freedom, nature, and God's sovereignty, and between reason and revelation. With new knowledge provided by science, alleviating suffering through the application of reason became possible. Protestant, Jewish, and Catholic thinkers grappled to find a middle way that balanced faith and reason. They sought the means to embraced science and toleration as embodied in the emerging modern state while retaining an effective faith, having a profound effect on theology. The Swiss theologian Jacob Vernet, and others, advocated a "purified, reasonable, and tolerant theology." For the religious Enlightenment, faith without knowledge roused dogmatic and enthusiastic religion. Asserting religion as a necessity for "regulating men's lives according to virtue and piety," theologians argued that reason without faith produced immoral skepticism. From the beginning, theologians remained close to new currents of thought and the requisite political philosophy influencing the course of American nations.⁶

In the Spanish American colonies, liberal political thought settled among a ready audience of *letrados*, the administrative class of Creole men of letters. While a network of universities remained under the control of conservative religious orders, new ideas spread quickly through private libraries, economic and scientific societies, and print culture. Sons of elite Spanish American families continued to study in Europe and returned radicalized—the germinating seed for future claims to independence. Like their Anglo-American counterparts, Creoles quickly accessed new political thought. The ideological content of Locke's *An Essay Concerning Human Understanding* (1690), Jean-Jacques Rousseau's *Discourse on the Origin of Inequality* (1754), and Adam Smith's *The Wealth of Nations* (1776) did not escape discontented Spanish Americans. The 1794 private Spanish translation of the French *Declaration of the Rights of Man* by Antonio Nariño supplied key justification for resistance to Spanish control, while the empire retained a tight rein on the majority heterogeneous population. The *Declaration* articulated the demands of the bourgeois against the nobility, with no intent of creating an egalitarian society with those below. In Spanish America, as in Anglo America, the desire not to disturb the acquiescence of slaves and indigenous people tempered the spread and reception of the ideas of liberty and equality.⁷

The possibility of enlightenment in Spanish America appeared to contradict established religion among the populace. *Letrados*, many of them priests, embraced the ideals of liberty, equality, and brotherhood, and sought to separate institutionally bound religion from statecraft and to promote the eradication of superstition among the lower classes. Religious devotion not founded on reason appeared to be a hindrance to establishing liberal republics. The Mexican José María Luis Mora, a republican and priest, railed against ecclesiastical wealth and attacked monastic education that did not prepare the populace for mental independence. In the 1844 essay "*Sociabilidad Chilena*," the Chilean Francisco Bilbao, highly critical of the remaining colonial institutions, declared, "Let us leave that [Spanish] past" of ignorance, despotism, and degradation. He presented a clear choice in the political realm as being between Catholicism and republicanism. The people of the continent had to choose either blind obedience to dogma or the liberty of free thought.⁸

Revolutionary Spanish American thinkers strained to find an alternative source of values with which to moderate disruptions to the social order. Regardless of diatribes against ecclesiastical and clerical power, an "enlightened" religion offered a necessary service in the purpose of nation building. In *Dogma socialista* (1846), the Argentine Esteban Echeverría, offering a positive assessment, cast Christianity as the true "natural religion . . . of human brotherhood" that could flourish only under toleration and separation of church and state. The Argentine Juan Bautista Alberdi proposed in 1853 that necessary religion had to be brought into the realm of reason and toleration; the Catholic faith was to be protected "as the first need of our social and political order" and as the binding agent of the new Latin American nations. The leaders of independence movements viewed religion, divested of its excesses, as crucial to moral progress, public honor, and a common American future. This view they shared with their revolutionary and liberal cohorts in North America.[9]

Religion, bound up with what constituted the nation, produced in the former British colonies the unlikely marriage of republican this-world rationality and otherworld-oriented piety. Religion was both a threat and an aid in establishing liberty. Thomas Paine's attack on dogma in *The Age of Reason* (1794) cast organized religions as "no other than human inventions, set up to terrify and enslave mankind, and monopolize power and profit." While the founders of the United States were deists and unitarians holding to heterodox ideas, evangelical religion appeared to be necessary to shape the virtuous citizens required by republicanism. As Amanda Porterfield argues, libertarian politics and evangelical religion were "codependent" rather than antagonistic. Each appealed to the other's projects to forward its own interest. John Adams, Benjamin Rush, and Jefferson viewed the values of the Christian religion, cultivated through education, as indispensable to the republic. Religion "divested of the rags" imposed by the clergy and the excessive enthusiasms of the common man, and finding a new base in reason, could bind the nation together. Protestants, Roman Catholics, and the tiny Jewish community embraced a republican vision that both betrayed some of their most valued beliefs regarding human fallenness and need for divine aid and excluded a vast number of people from the definition of freedom. Belief in a divinely sanctioned social order and the sway of republicanism produced a distinct political theology, forging an exclusionary white nation and an "Americanized Christ." While the enlightened mind cast a negative shadow on religious dogma, the Christian religion still offered the possibility of national unity through the promise of brotherhood. The task that remained was how to integrate distinct groups of slaves, women, the indigenous, and landless labor, perceived as unable to exercise true freedom and thus inferior, into the vision of universal brotherhood.[10]

The Common Man

The promise of brotherhood and new political thought did not adequately address the problem of the "unenlightened" masses growing in both strength and number. The challenge for nation builders was how to prepare heterogeneous groups for progress while maintaining social control. Unrestrained equality and free thought threatened social cohesion. Modern thinkers were generally in agreement with Voltaire that philosophy was not for the common man, whose daily life was physical work, or for women tied to bodily needs. One's particular social position limited the possibility of knowledge; reaching beyond one's station was pretentious for those ill-suited for ruling. Too much education of the lower classes made them restless and apt to question authority, whereas too little impeded social progress.

The notion of a popular enlightenment debated by modern social reformers sought the elimination of superstition and promoted rational work habits, thrift, and self-discipline. Debates centered on whether literacy made slaves or peasants more disciplined and productive or merely sowed discontent. Proposals to alleviate human suffering through apolitical reform and pedagogical projects rarely entailed the more expansive notion of freedom. In both Europe and the Americas, new ideas quickly spread among the lower classes through oral transmission and an expanding print culture. Peasants, indigenous people, slaves, wage laborers, and women found the essential ideas supporting their immediate economic and political demands. By the nineteenth century, reformers had lost control over the dissemination and adaptation of the ideas they had unleashed, often resulting in localized revolts demanding more than relief.[11]

Popular enlightenment became part of the American vision for well-ordered and free nations. In Latin America, from the beginning of independence (the period between 1810 and 1826), national leaders understood that they had brought about a limited political revolution rather than a social one. The wars of independence fought by ordinary men, slaves, and indigenous people in hopes of freedom did not result in social equality. The founders of American nations on both continents, fearing an irrational Hobbesian war of all against all, designed governments that not only checked the power of unencumbered political ambition but also offered controls over propertyless, unfit races, and women. Governments throughout the Americas were set up to mitigate conflict rather than foster inclusion, which made future reform a protracted process.[12]

Seeking to follow the republican experiment of the United States, Latin American nation builders viewed the newly independent continent as a mental colony—a people under tutelage. They sought a complete break from the vestiges of Spanish colonial institutions that were keeping the mass of the people trapped in a feudal past. In the search for cultural autonomy for themselves, and preparation of their people for enlightened freedom, *letrados* turned to the romantic socialism of Henri de Saint-Simon, the Scottish school, and utilitarianism. Social thinkers such as the Mexican Ignacio Ramírez, Chilean José Victorino Lastarria, and Cuban Enrique José Varona embraced Auguste Comte's positivism with its motto "order and progress." Positivism, as the main intellectual movement of the nineteenth century, ensured a new type of Latin American, free from superstition and emulating the practical Anglo-American mind.[13]

Positivism in education, as "a great equalizer," was to prepare a population for self-rule. Popular education promoted by Simón Rodríguez and Domingo Faustino Sarmiento did not necessarily free the minds of the mass of the people. The Uruguayan theorist Ángel Rama noted that nineteenth-century education, instead of producing an informed republican citizen, resulted in reinforcement of an unequal social order by instilling deference to controlling Creole elites. The need to maintain a stable social order contradicted the desire for liberty, progress, and democracy, and displayed liberalism's perennial ambivalence toward the extension of freedom. The revolutionary implications of popular education, examined in Chapter 4, remained a key issue in political mobilization for liberationists at mid-twentieth century.[14]

Despite the marked differences among nations, what bound American elites in the nineteenth century was the unifying ideology of race, tied up with class and gender, as a means of social ordering. Despite the rhetoric of universal brotherhood and equality, social markers determined the degree of freedom to which one aspired. The supposed ability for self-government set the limits of freedom. In the United States, the presence of race-based chattel slavery, the systematic removal of Indian people from communal lands, and the understood self-evident incapacity of women for liberty demonstrated a fundamental inequality. In Latin America, the remains of a Spanish colonial system of *castas*— a racially, socially, and economically stratified system of classification, with women remaining a hidden caste within it—was an impediment to creating an enlightened society. Blind imposition of ideas of progress on those regarded as *gente sin razón*, people without reason, struggling to preserve their communal folkways, resulted in political chaos and despotism. The need to check the propensity of lesser men to impose themselves in the political order limited the ideals of liberalism.[15]

As the United States was in threat of dissolving the union over the place of slavery within its borders, Latin American thinkers looked to the "natural" and essential constitution of their people and the land to explain their failed political projects. Seeking solutions to chaos that threatened the social fabric, statesmen such as Sarmiento and Alberdi turned to United States as a model. The United States, which was itself on the verge of civil war, nevertheless provided an example of segregating its inferior races and avoiding miscegenation. Racial segregation and subordination, being at the foundation of society and regarded as necessary for building an orderly civilization, constrained the expansion of liberal freedom.[16]

Harbingers of Resistance

Three options remained for people on the margins of elite political projects. A select few aspired to join the enlightened classes against great social and economic odds, through appeals for inclusion and attempts at cultural whitening; others could acquiesce and remain dependent on the *noblesse oblige*; or, at risk of death, they could rebel to make their own claim to freedom and equality. Elite white women offered reasoned arguments for political inclusion drawing on the struggle of racialized others. As black and indigenous people joined in the revolutionary spirit of the age, charismatic leaders appealing to both enlightened reason and religious sentiment led waves of resistance across the Americas.

In Spanish America, the cross-pollination of religion and new political thought and the presence of communal ties spread revolutionary ideas in the Andean highlands. The seditious Iroquois text *Apocalypse de Chiokoyhikoy*, first published in Canada in 1777, called on Indians in Canada and Spanish America to revolt against European rule. An early Creole critic of colonial rule, José Baquijano y Carrillo, as editor of the journal *El Mercurio Peruano,* circulated the ideas of the radical French priest Guillaume Thomas Raynal and his censored *Histoire Philosophique des Deux Indes* (1770). Raynal depicted the conquest as tyrannical and predicted the bloody revolt of indigenous people. The *Histoire* rearticulated the Black Legend of Spanish conquests and cruelty, advancing a major ideological cult in the radical wing of the European Enlightenment—the anti-colonial cause of the American Indian. The polemics of the Black Legend drew from the sixteenth-century priest Bartolomé de Las Casas and his chilling descriptions of Spanish conquest in *Brevísima relación de la destrucción de las Indias* (1552). De Las Casas further illustrated the deep American irony of thinking about freedom. He initially advocated for indigenous people's rights to self-determination while proposing the importation of African slave labor.[17]

After 1760, a number of large-scale rebellions broke out among previously quiescent indigenous people. The claim to self-rule was often associated with the rejection of Catholic authority for a reclaimed indigenous religion. In other cases, Indians deployed Catholicism as a means of gaining control over their own lives and justification for an alternative to the colonial order. The Great Rebellion that began in 1780, led by José Gabriel Túpac Amaru, II and his wife Micaela Bastidas Puyucahua, in the region of Cuzco, went beyond the typical village riot. The imposition of Bourbon reforms in the 1770s resulted in higher taxes, restricted trade, and imposing Spanish public education aimed at eliminating the use of native languages. The leadership of Indian society, mestizos, and Creoles disaffected from the metropole instigated the greatest revolt against colonial rule in early modern times. Túpac Amaru II, an Indian noble and community governor, called for the reconquest of indigenous lands. Well connected to elite Creoles, educated by Jesuits, and supported by local priests, he proclaimed his devotion to the Catholic religion while appealing to the cult of the Inca to advocate self-rule. He invoked images of himself as the biblical David who would free his people from the rule of Goliath in a messianic vision. The Great Rebellion's demand for self-rule included a racial egalitarianism consisting of indigenous people, mestizos, zambos, and Creoles for the creation of a Peruvian nation. Túpac Amaru's vision for communal justice called for the end to bonded Indian labor, emancipation of slaves, and bureaucratic reforms of economic and political institutions. His millenarian view of history had a distinct Christian cast that called upon divine providence to bring about the return of the Inca. Túpac Amaru combined enlightenment notions of freedom with a religious vision.[18]

Historian Steve Stern argues that rather than attempting to return to an idyllic time, Túpac Amaru appealed to peasant notions of an inclusive Andean proto-nationalism, which resulted in an exclusive Creole nationalism in the following century. Seen as part of emancipation currents running through the revolutionary Atlantic, indigenous revolts in the latter half of the eighteenth century set the stage for national independence. After independence, Latin American nations continued to experience proto-nationalist projects, often involving local priests, arising among discontented peasants who identified their cause of social justice with appeals to God. Whether religion was deployed by elites to maintain orderly societies or appealed to by popular leaders to instigate rebellion, it was impossible to escape its political ramifications.[19]

The appeals to freedom and God as the final authority ran through the revolutionary Americas, bringing global attention to the hemisphere. Between the Anglo-American and Spanish American wars of independence, the majority slave population of French Saint-Domingue, inspired by the revolution in the metropole, undertook a claim to universal freedom. The French Revolution's *Declaration of the Rights of Man* (1789) quickly blurred the boundaries of its conception as a claim by elite white Frenchmen and became a claim asserted by the colored and black slave populations at the periphery of the empire. C.L.R. James's *The Black Jacobins* (1938) offered what became an influential historical depiction of the emancipated slave Toussaint L'Ouverture reading Raynal's *Histoire* and seeing himself as the "black Spartacus" who would avenge his people. A devout Catholic who received a liberal European education, L'Ouverture drew on both religion and enlightened thought to proclaim his project to establish liberty and equality among Saint-Domingue's enslaved population. As the emergent leader of the revolt, he experienced what Jonathan Israel called the essence of the Enlightenment and the first step to freedom, "a revolution of the mind."[20]

The revolution of the mind for enslaved people included a reimagining of God adapted to immediate needs. Plantations provided the environment for African religions to meld with Catholicism, creating a free political space. The early leaders of the Saint-Domingue slave revolt not only relied on organization across scattered plantations, but also, through religious practice, awakened the imagination to political possibilities. On the eve of revolt, Dutty Boukman, a key religious leader, led his co-conspirators in a Voodoo ceremony rejecting the "god of whites" for a god that would listen to the cries for liberty and order revenge on crimes against the oppressed. Religious practices throughout the duration of the insurrection offered a necessary inspiration, binding people together and unleashing violent retribution. The struggle was not only a political process by which the new Haitian nation launched its own "empire of liberty," but also a spiritual and mental process of emancipation. Religion as a source of political energy remained a distinct characteristic of American black thought.[21]

The tragedy-fraught revolution on Saint-Domingue sounded an alarm throughout the world of how far the ideals of freedom could go. As Susan Buck-Morss argues, slavery as a trope of unfreedom in the midst of real global slavery could not have escaped Rousseau's notice as he declared, "Man is born free, and everywhere he is in chains." Neither could the self-liberation of slaves on Saint-Domingue escape Hegel's notice as he explicated the slave/master dialectic as a struggle for freedom in world history. It most certainly did not escape Mary Wollstonecraft, who had taken up the British anti-slavery cause to cast women's social position in *A Vindication of the Rights of Woman* (1792) as one akin to slavery, "which chains the very soul of woman, keeping her for ever under the bondage of ignorance." Freedom was not understood except against slavery, the state of absolute subjection of one being to another. In the aftermath of the Saint-Domingue's revolution, the ubiquitous presence of slavery haunted the nascent modern American mind.[22]

As Haiti became the first republic established by the self-emancipated, slavery as the primary form of labor was entrenched in the growing capitalist economies of the Atlantic trade. Nevertheless, the acceptance of slavery as an unchanging order of things was showing signs of cracking under economic and religious pressure and increased slave resistance. The Americas, the global first in ending colonial rule with proclamations of liberty, became the focus of attention for the international abolitionist movement. Increasing dissonance between a rationalized system of slavery and a moral sensibility inspired abolitionist preachers. Through a millenarian message, Quakers, Methodists, and Baptist itinerant preachers proclaimed a jubilee of freedom and justice and countered centuries of biblically based justifications for slavery. Asserting an intuitive moral argument grounded in evangelical piety, they turned to both natural law and new methods of biblical exegesis. The reverberations of abolitionist preaching, appealing to the authority of God, threatened to overturn the existing social order through a radical egalitarianism.[23]

Blacks in the revolutionary Atlantic gravitated toward the biblical theme of justice, fusing spiritual salvation with aspirations for political freedom. Abolitionist thought offered an opportunity to reinterpret the biblical text in this-world terms. Phillis Wheatley, an enslaved woman whose intellect impressed her white elite audience, pointed out "the strange Absurdity ... of Modern Egyptians," who cried liberty but exercised oppressive power over others. Olaudah Equiano, a former slave and denizen of the Atlantic world, told the persuasive and intertwined stories of gaining both spiritual freedom and material freedom. As an enslaved sailor aboard the *Aetna*, he learned to read the Bible with help from his shipmates, and "I began to raise my fear from man to him [God] alone ... with prayers anxiously to God for my liberty." He asked his reader to understand slavery as keeping men in a state of both spiritual ignorance and bareness of mind. In an expression of "double consciousness" and as a spiritual insider in Christianity and a political outsider of Ibgo origins, Equiano read the biblical text by placing himself at the center of the biblical story of liberation. Identifying with outsiders, such as Moses and the prophets, Equiano forwarded God's advocacy on behalf of the oppressed. Appealing to his audience's desire to display true Christian piety, he set his conversion experience against the inauthentic religiosity and illegitimate political authority of the slaveholders. Equiano's rhetoric linked the justice of God with both political and spiritual freedom.[24]

The revolutionary winds had also persuaded the North American colonists to revolt against what they saw as the encroachment of enslavement under British rule. Paine, a disheveled economic refugee from the London slums and unlikely self-educated leader, rallied ordinary men for the revolutionary cause. In *Common Sense* (1776), Paine used the plain language of revivalist fervor and Lockean liberalism to instigate political action. By evoking natural rights endowed by the "Almighty," he railed against the illegitimate rule of monarchs that "at last cheated [the colonies] into slavery." Paine's millennial vision did not benefit only the British colonies, or only men of a certain class, but rather made America "the cause of all mankind" having the power to "begin the world again." Paine's appeal to the common man did not include Indians, blacks, or women. However, his argument for political and religious liberty drew allies from among the dissenting Protestants. The repeated trope of slavery deployed in Paine's rhetoric made the presence of actual slavery conspicuous, contributing to a full assault on the institution.[25]

In the aftermath of the Revolution, the rhetoric of universal freedom did not escape the attention of slaves, freemen, women, and the emerging class of propertyless wage laborers; they read political freedom through a religious liberatory sensibility. The ubiquitous Pauline injunction, "there is neither Jew nor Gentile, neither slave nor free, nor is there male and female, for you are all one in Christ Jesus" reinforced the religious impulse toward freedom. Slavery seen as contrary to both natural law and religion persuaded the preachers Richard Allen and Absalom Jones to found the Free African Society in 1787, which produced some of the first black religion-inspired anti-slavery texts. Unlike Paine, who abandoned Christianity for a rationalist faith, blacks did not forsake the religion that had sustained them in slavery and tenuous freedom to make their case. Yet, the attempt to persuade a cruel white society of the rightness of black people's cause by appealing to the Christian religion and principles of liberty was not enough. Gaining freedom, black leaders concluded, required the emancipation of the black mind.[26]

David Walker, a faithful member of Allen's anti-slavery African Methodist Episcopal Church and founder of the first black newspaper in the United States, *Freedom's Journal*, proposed outright revolt against the racial oppression that kept blacks in not only physical but mental chains. His cause was in arousing the consciousness of slaves and changing the freeman's conception of himself that limited his aspirations from being the "most degraded, wretched, and abject set of beings that ever lived since the world began." Walker's *Appeal to the Coloured Citizens of the World* (1829), replete with evangelical language, denounced the white Christianity that had enthroned itself in God's place and made a clear distinction between the "God of the blacks" and the God of the oppressors. Evoking Haiti as an example of "the glory of blacks and the terror of tyrants," he argued that blacks could enter into freedom by asserting their will through action—but first the mind had to be delivered from the negative images of blackness. As a work of political theology, his *Appeal* drew on founding texts of the American nation and biblical Israel.[27]

Walker perceived that Jefferson's theories of black inferiority had hardened into an accepted ideology that reproduced itself in the minds of both whites and blacks. Highlighting the essential bond of exploited blacks around the world, enlightening the black mind was the first step toward "entire emancipation of your enslaved brethren all over the world." Securing the freeman's position required them, through education and religion, to "go to work and enlighten your brethren! Let the Lord see you doing what you can to rescue them and yourselves from degradation." The *Appeal* was widely distributed, often covertly in the South, and read out loud in the tradition of black preaching, serving as an instrument for forming a consciousness among blacks as an oppressed and chosen people.[28]

White and black women were also challenging political exclusion, often appealing to the Christian religion and their ability to reason. Wollstonecraft articulated a universalist argument that tied enlightened reason to discerning and obeying the will of God. Drawing from religious and romantic texts, she argued that through illumination of the mind women gained "the dignity of a rational will that only bows to God." Wollstonecraft tied freedom to education, and her influence persuaded women throughout the Americas, such as Judith Sargent Murray, to pursue self-education. Consequently, they hoped to establish their mental capacity and legitimate their participation in political and theological debates and to advocate forcefully on their own behalf. [29]

Excluded from the revolutionary slogan "liberty, equality and fraternity," women inspired by religion drew parallels between their own emancipation with that of slaves and indigenous people. In Latin American *tertulias*, or literary salons, reading and writing about the plight of the Indians and peasants provided an avenue through which Creole women highlighted their own political position. The radical socialist Flora Tristán, the daughter of a French mother and an elite Peruvian father, tied women's emancipation to equality before God. In the Spanish text *La emancipación de la mujer [Emancipation of Women]* (1846) she described the position of women in relation to man, "The most oppressed man finds a being to oppress, his wife: she is the proletarian of the proletarian." As a female messiah, she addressed her message "especially to the women, to deliver them from the superstitions that overwhelm their souls and shrink their hearts, and with an aim to deliver them from the priests by giving them a lively faith and a burning charity to sustain them in the struggle!" Tristán, like the abolitionists Lucretia Mott and Sarah Grimké, found a religious motivation for a biblically based refutation of women's subordinated position in society standing against the claims of clergymen and religious institutions. Sarah Grimké's *Letters on the Equality of the Sexes* (1838) harkened back to the Reformation to make her case asserting the individual conscience, saying: "Here I plant myself. God created us equal; —he created us free agents: —he is our Lawgiver, our King and our Judge and to him alone is woman bound to be in subjection, to him alone is she accountable for use of those talents which her heavenly Father has entrusted her. One is her Master even Christ." She closed her letter with, "Thine for the oppressed in the bonds of womanhood." [30]

While Grimké's *Letters* alluded to slavery and solidarity with the oppressed, black women carried the double burden of race and sex, and a real threat of bodily enslavement. As speakers and writers, freewomen learned to use both the lectern and the press to assert their moral feminine authority. Sojourner Truth, Jarena Lee, and Julia A.J. Foote took to public preaching and writing as a liberatory action on behalf of "racial uplift." They grounded their public arguments in the prophetic tradition enabling Sojourner Truth to declare, "The Lord has made me a sign unto this nation, an' I go round a'testifyin' an' showin' on 'em their sins agin my people." For women, religiously laden writing and speaking demonstrated both knowledge and authority as an act of self-definition against overwhelming social odds. A nascent feminist political theology was germinating in the tense gap between religious and political freedom in which women lived.[31]

Women, slaves, and indigenous people found in religion the rhetorical means and inspiration to challenge their exclusion. Among the elite and advancing classes, an occupation with church and state entanglement and with determining the limits of religious toleration continued to different degrees. Yet throughout the nineteenth century, in the mind of the unrepresented and unprotected, in which the state interests contradicted their own, inseparable religion and politics held the key to freedom. The subordinated articulated an unrecognized alternative theological stream of thought that had no need to speculate about separating the religious from the secular because the God of the oppressed, James Cone noted, was the "God of history" rather than a spiritual abstraction. The inequality that remained in the aftermath of abolition and the granting of universal male franchise made separating religion and politics impossible.[32]

The subterranean theo-political stream running through the history of the Americas was again rising to the surface in the 1960s in renewed claims for justice. Liberation theologians, as participants in marginalized communities, sought to legitimate that unrecognized voice. Increasingly it was the militant voice of an alternative theological stream standing against the dominant view of God and God's will that was being heard in Latin American shantytowns, black organization meetings, and women's consciousness-raising groups. As the historically muffled voices resurfaced and liberationists responded, it served to bind them together in the solidarity of a common theo-political project.

For black liberationists, the history of black people—their survival and their resistance—from the founding of the American nation was a direct source for constructing a new political theology. Cone asserted,

> Contrary to what whites say in *their* history books, black power is not new. It began when black mothers decided to kill their babies rather than have them grow up as slaves. Black Power is Nat Turner, Denmark Vesey, and Gabriel Prosser planning a slave revolt. It is slaves poisoning their masters, and Frederick Douglass delivering an abolitionist speech. This is the history that black theology must take seriously . . . because divine activity is inseparable from black history.

The theology of Allen and Walker was black clergy's refusal "to accept the racist white church as consistent with the gospel of God." A religious community serving as both the spiritual and political center of life gave birth to black theology.[33]

In Latin America, the history of colonialism and neocolonial oppression called for a theology of emancipation. Enrique Dussel noted that Latin American history began with domination by a handful of Spanish elites with their "instruments of civilization" and "national messianism." Instead of a "utopia," the continual struggle for justice gave birth to a distinctively political theology expressed by "a small but never interrupted stream of prophetic protest" taken up by dissenting priests and revolutionaries. At the very heart of the continent's history remained an "eschatological promise" of unfolding freedom carried not by the official Church, alienated from the people, but by the "*avant-garde* Church" among the poor. The history of oppressed people registered a refusal of the distinction between the religious and the political, and it was in their religious expression that liberationists found God speaking.[34]

Feminist theologians also turned to their radical foremothers. They drew on the long history of struggle for gender equality beginning with the first-century Jesus movement to the radical wing of the Reformation. By breaking what Mary Daly called the "Great Silence" of women's history, they found neglected visionaries Hildegard of Bingen, the mystic Julian of Norwich, and the Quaker co-founder Margaret Fell Fox, appealing to the work of the Spirit as the source of their authority, as examples of a nascent feminist theology. In American history they found Anne Hutchinson, Lucretia Mott, the Grimké sisters, and Elizabeth Cady Stanton in their struggle against the collusion of political and ecclesial power. Oppression and the possibilities of liberation found at the center and edge of the social world vis-à-vis the patriarchy sowed the seeds of a woman-centered theology. In unearthing women's past, Catholic theologian Elisabeth Schüssler Fiorenza noted finding "our strength, historical agency, pain, and struggle within our common historical experience as women." Feminist theologians tapped neglected religious thought that remained outside the frame of male-centered theologies. This alternative woman-centered theological stream offered a rich source with which to construct a full-orbed feminist theology and challenge masculinist assumptions about the nature of the divine.[35]

Representing distinct group claims within a historical American struggle for freedom, liberationists recognized oppressed people as crossing multiple boundaries of Enlightenment thought, utopian aspirations, prophetic impulses, and political reality. Liberationists' use of and relationship to this past was selective and meta-historical, more concerned with the nature and meaning of history and the driving force of historical change than with offering empirical evidence for God's liberatory purpose. Breaking with Rankean realist historiography, which dominated theological scholarship at mid-century, and moving to a *history for*, they reinterpreted the meaning of the past and rearticulated perennial ideas about freedom, equality, and the purposes of God.

The recovery of the past provided legitimation for liberationists; they were moving with history instead of against it in a progressive motion toward unfolding freedom. Stalled universal freedom required reawaking the lost emancipatory role of religion. They charged that Christian salvation, historically understood by subordinated people as a holistic freedom, had solidified into an ahistorical and otherworldly goal emptied of political significance. Reawakening the religious liberatory sensibility for world-changing action at mid-twentieth century called for deconstructing and redefining the meaning of Christian salvation in politically potent terms.

PART II
Reconstructions

4

Liberatory Sensibilities

RELIGIOUS AND LIBERAL ideas, growing in American soil, generated a dynamism that by the 1960s opened the way to redefine Christian salvation and relocate it within history. This chapter examines how, as a fully actualized salvation, liberation contained the spiritual, economic, political, social, and bodily realms of existence. Furthermore, liberationists sought to exchange the salve of otherworldly hope offered to subjugated people for a historical struggle toward freedom undertaken by the oppressed themselves. Men often described liberation as a Hegelian-like confrontation between slave and master. Feminists viewed women, confined within the dynamics of sexism, as struggling between the self and the internalized oppressor in unleashing psychic energy. Fundamentally, the idea of liberation was of a communal process rather than based on the individual, for only in solidarity with others was freedom possible. Awakening the political potential of solidarity among oppressed people called for the advocacy of the committed placing themselves at the nexus of prophetic denunciation and revolutionary change.

The Meaning of Freedom

Liberationists built their idea of *salvation as liberation* on modern definitions of freedom as a categorical imperative, an unconditional moral obligation, while recognizing the limits on the individual within society. Freedom, as set forth by Jean-Jacques Rousseau and Immanuel Kant, defined the relationship between the individual and the modern world. The measure of a good society was the degree of freedom, as self-determination and self-actualization, enjoyed by individuals. Rousseau's *The Social Contract* (1762) presented freedom as basic to human nature: "to renounce freedom is to renounce one's humanity." To be human was to be free. Freedom, as the autonomy of the solitary individual, was the first good by which to measure all other goods. Natural freedom stood between desire and power, which, in a state of nature, was an anarchic freedom unconstrained by political rule, law, or any superior and encompassed natural, civil, and moral aspects, placing individual desires and the needs of society continually at odds. His philosophy, based on an ahistorical theory of an unknowable state of nature, set the foundation of all modern revolutionary movements. How to define the attributes of Rousseau's freedom, and how to situate the individual within a society both restraining freedom and essential for its preservation, engrossed modern thinkers.[1]

Kant looked beyond the realm of nature to locate freedom in moral autonomy. In answering, "What is enlightenment?" Kant viewed man as emerging from a moral immaturity in which he had been unable to use his own understanding without the guidance of established authority. Human enlightenment was breaking free from moral and mental tutelage. In the 1785 *Groundwork for the Metaphysics of Morals*, Kant made autonomy his a priori proposition, and the essential condition for making moral judgments. Moral autonomy was not self-government but rather depended on the universality of the categorical imperative, the sound judgments of the highest good at which reason would by necessity arrive. Rather than no law, a higher law restrained reason, which it found by exercising its critical function. Kant assumed a shared universal moral consciousness as the final test of the good, offering a rational limit to freedom.[2]

Kant's view of human nature as rational and morally autonomous severed the individual from a social context. His model of autonomy presumed detachment from the world as the first condition necessary for freedom, requiring courage to break from self-imposed dependence. The individual's subjugated condition within a web of social relations had no bearing on his moral autonomy, as he remained an end in himself. He had a duty to remain non-servile. Moral maturity required overcoming bodily needs and desires that continually kept one subject to necessity, and true freedom meant remaining unimpeded by sympathy, sensual love, or pain. Viewed from the position of an individual attached to a particular community with ethical demands, Kant's freedom was unworkable. However, the assertion of moral autonomy under the constraint of the categorical imperative served as a justification for subsequent revolutionaries. As Jean Bethke Elshtain argued, Kant's foundation for freedom as moral autonomy becomes, against his social conservatism, the necessary opening by which subordinated people asserted self-determination. In modern history the subordinated, in a self-liberatory move, presented a claim against their social conditions based on the demands of a universal humanity. All good reason had to concede that the subordinated, like all others, had a claim to recognition as equals.[3]

Within the stream of enlightened thought, Christian theology's definition of freedom as God's salvation remained an article of faith. Salvation was a radical and universal freedom from sin and evil moving toward the final triumph of God in a future perfected world. History was a struggle between the Christian notion of sin, as estrangement from God and neighbor, and the future reconciled world coming into being. Ultimately, only God could fulfill the coming of a new world into historical and universal fruition even as believers undertook a limited task of bringing it about. The question remained of how to live in an alienated world, in the process of becoming, without premature flight into the next. In preserving the utopian vision of a God-initiated salvation, life in a world full of woe became secondary to an ultimate world. This was the first target of liberationist critique. They charged that the distinction made between the world of struggle and an idyllic not-yet-world transferred human hope for freedom (salvation) to something beyond history, allowing human suffering to exist without effective protest. The theological sticking point supporting this "pie-in-the-sky" thinking and troubling liberationists was the speculative understanding of God's transcendence.[4]

Liberationists engaged in a full assault on the spatial and temporal location of salvation by challenging the understanding of God's transcendence and the sacred/profane binary of modernity. At stake was whether a God removed from the world sympathized with those who suffered in the present. Historically, the willingness of religious believers to engage in political activism depended on where the emphasis fell between God's absolute otherness and God's presence in the world serving as a guarantee of effective action. Rubem Alves argued in *A Theology of Human Hope* (1969) that the dominant language of transcendence, in which the Nietzschean God "is the end of history . . . 'the Unmoved and the Sated and the Permanent,'" rendered the world "unreal," thus devoid of meaning and forsaken. If God was "wholly other," then the world was wholly profane, bereft of the divine. Since Kant had posited religion as standing outside speculative reason, thus dividing the world, and Schleiermacher had attempted to ground it in human experience, theological thought swung between emphasizing God's transcendence and God's immanence. Much of the tension between liberal and conservative theology revolved around this point. The debate continued in the twentieth century, with social Christianity moving toward God's presence in the world, only to have neo-orthodoxy reassert God as wholly other. Alves viewed the assertion of an absolute transcendence as forcing a choice: either God was the cause, in that everything happened for an inscrutable reason, or suffering had a meta-historical reward. Neither of these choices effectively addressed alleviating suffering in a "profane" world.[5]

Liberationists challenged absolute transcendence by locating salvation in the present and joining secularizing currents in post-war theology away from metaphysics to humanity as an agent of history creating its own future. God's transcendence rightly understood, Hugo Assmann asserted, "consists in the fact that he stands before us on the frontier of the future. God is *pro*-active—he calls us forward." Gustavo Gutiérrez, advocating the abandonment of an "otherworldly" disposition that distinguished between "the natural and supernatural," argued that a theology responding to the contemporary crisis had to concede that human history was the theater in which we encounter God. Even as alienation pervaded the world, so did a latent salvation, and thus, "We can no longer speak properly of a profane world." José Miguez Bonino noted that in the struggle for freedom, "transcendence ... can only be found within praxis, never as a super-added, disembodied x." Black people's experience of transcendence, James Cone argued, was confronting oppression by stepping into the divine future through stories and songs of liberation. "Liberation as a future event is not simply *other*worldly but is the divine future that breaks into their social existence," thus enabling resistance in the present. Transcendence standing outside the world served as "an opiate" of resignation to suffering. Only in the light of finding transcendence within the immanent did the promise of God's liberation of his people have any political significance.[6]

A distant God, Alves charged, accompanied the idea of a universal humanity obscuring the situation of oppressed people. One spoke of loving humanity in general while ignoring specific oppression. A worldwide "proletarian consciousness" was rejecting salvation of a universal and disembodied humanity that hid particular suffering. Nietzsche's existential move to "kill God" was a modern attempt to deal with the problem of suffering. Nietzsche concluded that human liberation was possible only in abolishing that which underwrote suffering—that which made it acceptable—religion. Seeking to energize religion for creative social change, Alves situated divine transcendence in the present: "the future is mediated into history through the present ... where the future is being formed. History is thus the medium in and through which God creates for the world, man, and himself, a future that does not exist." Instead of God's salvation being outside and above suffering, it was displayed in the wretched moments of history and the particularity of suffering.[7]

Exhibiting an affinity with Kant's categorical imperative liberation, under a relocated transcendence, became an a priori theological commitment. It was the good by which to measure all theological ideas. Going beyond idealism, liberationists rejected the universalizing of humanity and salvation that failed to account for and alleviate human suffering. Moving toward a new theological method to locate divine transcendence in history, with all its political and social significance, liberationists prepared to radically redefine the meaning of Christian salvation and relocate it from the next world to the present one.

An Integral Liberation

The politically laden language of liberation reworked the meaning of Christian salvation. Liberation was neither abstracted Lockean liberty nor mere Kantian moral freedom, but situated within a dynamic and all-encompassing historical and social process. Salvation, as an "integral liberation," included all the realms of existence in one shared human history and destiny. Noting Herbert Marcuse's *Eros and Civilization* (1955), Gutiérrez argued that Latin America's situation of dependency called for not only an exterior liberation from the conditions of class but also an interior liberation from Freudian-defined psychological repression. "Repression," rather than being merely the experience of isolated individuals, was a total societal condition of inner and outer reality. It was in the "transformation and fulfillment of the present life" in all its aspects, Gutiérrez asserted, that "the absolute value of salvation—far from devaluing this world—gives it its authentic meaning and its own autonomy." Thus, salvation, which "embraces all human reality," healed the breach between the self, God, and others that defined the very nature of sin—alienation.[8]

Alves proposed that liberation also involved recovering a "Dionysian erotic sense of life." It was through the body that one loved, worked, and realized one's solidarity with others. True liberation negated the suffering under hunger, violence, and threat of death that made the erotic sense of life impossible for a large number of the world's people. Because "the Messiah, the power of liberating freedom, is 'flesh,'" true human liberation rejected dualism to affirm the body and free it from what made it unfree for the world. Uniting inner and outer notions of salvation in an integral liberation, Latin Americans committed to radically change the concrete conditions under which the oppressed lived.[9]

Cone, adapting the thought of Albert Camus, described liberation as the striving toward escaping the "the absurdity of being black in a white racist world." "Metaphysical rebellion," Camus proposed, was the means "by which man protests against his condition and against the whole of creation." Liberation, Cone asserted, is the denial of slavery as the essential condition of black existence, and "freedom means the affirmation of blackness." It required recognizing that "freedom is an existential reality" and involved a metaphysical rebellion that exchanged a distant white God for a God who suffered with his people. This was a communal struggle, meaning that there was no isolated individual: "To be in sin means to deny the community." Viewed as solidarity, liberation was an attempt to redefine freedom away from the nexus of power and desire displayed in acquisitive individualism that eroded communal bonds. Solidarity in the liberation struggle stood as a bulwark against what Alves described as the "violence of the private forms of good."[10]

Rosemary Radford Ruether also redefined salvation within an immanent frame. For women, liberation involved confronting the fundamental sexist and hierarchical nature of all forms of domination. She charged that while the *philosophes* imagined the possibility of liberation for the bourgeoisie, workers, and peasants, the subjugation of women remained "an unalterable necessity of nature." For enlightened thinkers, "The ascendancy of Reason meant the ascendancy of the intellect over the passion, and this must ever imply the subjugation of women." Women, seen as shackled by a petty, sensual, and trite female mind, were unable to exercise autonomous reason. Only as women claimed the "human capacities of intellect, will, and autonomous creative consciousness" while not denying their association with the culturally despised body and nature, Ruether argued, did humanity move toward an integral liberation.[11]

Reaching back to the history of early Christianity, Ruether attributed sexist subordination to an infestation of the moral, epistemological, and ontological perceptions by a Gnostic body/soul dualism. Ruether shared with Alves a concern for the dualism that produced the "prurient/puritan" syndrome reducing women to sexual objects. The dualism of male/female was the original model of alienation in which the male carried ideas associated with "intellect, transcendent spirit, and autonomous will" and the female with "the body, sensuality, and subjugation." Ruether noted that even as white middle-class women gained political rights, they did so by emulating male behavior of impersonal rationality in the public sphere. The freedom sought by elite women presented itself as a repudiation of those things associated with the female role in marriage and motherhood. Neither had the sexual revolution, a revolt against the "bourgeois family," released women from the virgin/whore dualism. The sexual revolution remained another means of male access to women's bodies. Liberation, as a "psychic revolution" for everyone, demanded a true synthesis of opposites that dissolved marginalizing dualisms and produced a "transformation of values" able to challenge the systems of authority, identity, and social relations. The challenge for the liberation of women was capturing female autonomy while not losing the sense of communal personhood that invited men into a new cultural paradigm.[12]

Liberationists displayed confidence that a Hegelian march toward an integral liberation was well underway, and time was ripe for the community of the oppressed to claim their freedom. Mistakenly by attempting to "de-historize(d) man" and unmooring the individual from a community, modern existentialism sought to release humanity into freedom. Under liberationists' proposals, only the community of the oppressed was in a position to open up a new way of freedom for the world. Through a common awareness of a divine birthright of freedom and conscious action, the oppressed entered into history and germinated the future. For Alves, "history is the medium in and through which God creates . . . a future that does not yet exist . . . the present is broken open—really open—toward the new." Viewing freedom as a historical unfolding and progressive left a great deal of unexplored slippage between the divine liberatory will and the reality of unfreedom experienced by so many. The oppressed as the harbingers of liberation elided the reality of what Thomas Hobbes described as the life of most men as plagued by "continual fear . . . solitary, poor, nasty, brutish, and short." If history was the medium by which God, presumed as unlimited in love and power, created the future, then inescapable suffering presented the danger of ascribing to God the history liberationists rejected as unjust.[13]

Black and Latin American theologians, in evoking history, faced opposite directions in relating to the past. Latin Americans followed an intellectual tradition of repudiating the past. Seeing the continent at the periphery of the First World, torn by revolutions, and still struggling to gain its historical agency, escaping the shadow of the past constituted freedom. A future pregnant with expectations rather than appeals to a problematic past provided the impetus for change in Latin America. Bonino asserted, "God is . . . the freedom which intervenes in history in order to prevent the past from determining the future." Motivated by a "protest born of the suffering present," gaining a future orientation made action possible, allowing the poor to liberate themselves. Latin Americans sought liberation as a "discontinuous possibility," a break from the "given" conditions of the past.[14]

Black liberationists, in contrast, looked to a black past to reclaim God's liberatory action on their behalf. Frantz Fanon, the psychiatrist and colonial theorist, had prescribed reclaiming the past as a trigger for change in the "psycho-affective equilibrium" of the colonized. Out of an ideology of white Manifest Destiny, liberationists wrenched a black American Israel as the crux of historical salvation. The biblical story of Israel's deliverance from slavery and the prophets' call for justice was one with the history of black people's struggle for freedom. Looking back to "the auction block and slave drivers," Cone looked for signs of divine favor and asserted that for black people God was not a Cartesian "metaphysical idea" under debate, and morality was not reducible to "Kant's categorical imperative"; rather, God was the source of hope for survival at the "level of concrete history." In the stories of survival passed down through generations, black people recognized that "They were created for liberation—for fellowship with God and the projection of the self into the future, grounded in historical possibilities . . . laying claim to that which rightfully belongs to humanity." Remembering God's action on behalf of the black community offered the raw material for constructing a black theology of liberation.[15]

An Emancipated Mind

Defining salvation as a holistic freedom and locating it within history, rather than in a place or time beyond, still did not provide the means for its actualization. Liberation remained abstract and theoretical. Making emancipation of the oppressed a political reality called for a mind-altering education. In 1930s, the Marxist Antonio Gramsci had emphasized breaking the cultural hegemony of the bourgeoisie and the dependency of laboring classes by educating them for revolution based on the aspirations of workers. At mid-century, liberating Latin America would take more than a new political program; it called for what Paulo Freire, the Brazilian philosopher of critical education, described in *Pedagogy of the Oppressed* (1970) as *conscientization*, or consciousness-raising, by which the oppressed learn to perceive their situation and take action. Drawing from Marxist and Christian thought, he viewed human beings as having the ability to re-create themselves by shaping the social and material world. Education in the Americas, he charged, had been a hegemonic project producing well-behaved citizens and not free people. Rather than replicating existing social structures, freeing the mind involved a break from the "miseducation" of "banking" methodologies that simply reproduced oppression. Instead of teaching Third World people to accept the norms of modern society, dialogical education recognized people's ability to reason and develop an independent political consciousness. Similarly to John Dewey, as expressed in *Democracy and Education* (1916), Freire proposed a critical and democratic view of education that included a participatory theory of knowledge. Through a critical education, excluded groups "cut the umbilical cord of magic and myth that binds them to the world of oppression." From the perspective of Freire's method, the subordinated were bound to the systems of oppression because they believed in them, and a critical education provided the necessary demystification.[16]

Freire's influence was both deep and broad. During the 1960s and 1970s, Freire maintained relationships with educators, intellectuals, and theologians throughout the Americas. The 1968 Latin American Bishops Conference endorsed the process of *conscientization* as indispensable for pastoral action, encouraging political education in lay-led base ecclesial communities (BECs). The independent black education movement in the United States incorporated Freire's methods. Women's liberationists made women-only consciousness-raising groups key in movement recruitment and mobilization. Among the New Left, radical education was key to instigating political resistance.[17]

The adoption of Freire's educational method throughout Latin America encouraged adult literacy and worked as a solidarity-building project useful in thousands of BECs. Beginning in the late 1950s, Latin American bishops responded to the critical shortage of priests by authorizing BECs as para-Church institutions. They invited foreign clergy to Latin America to forestall the advance of evangelical Protestant and leftist groups, and BECs among the poor served as a major drive for Catholic lay mobilization and renewal. As grass-roots gatherings often meeting in homes, they followed the organic patterns of Protestant evangelization. Radicalized pastoral workers and priests applying Freire's pedagogy encouraged the poor to read the biblical stories afresh by drawing from their own experiences, making connections to daily life and seeing themselves within the gospel stories. Participants acquired both reading and critical thinking skills by which they recognized that poverty was not the will of God but the result of exploitation. Under a new reading, for example, the Good Samaritan narrative instead of being a story of charity to neighbor becomes one of violent exploitation by the powerful and an example of solidarity inspiring action. Liberationists saw a theology from below, arising from the awakened the political consciousness of the poor. Praxis, involving both reflection and action in the environment of BECs, became part of the construction of a new liberationist hermeneutic method.[18]

In the United States, the struggle to free the black mind was a long one. Stokely Carmichael and Charles V. Hamilton, advocates of Black Power, viewed the basis of subjugation as bound up in Hans Morgenthau's definition of political power as "psychological control over the minds of men." Under conditions of oppression, the task was to decolonize the mind, a project of the mid-1960s with SNCC's (the Student Nonviolent Coordinating Committee's) schools in the South. As a supplement to the perceived miseducation in public schools, so-called freedom schools exposed black youth to radical ideas and practical methods that transformed them into self-directed activists. Freedom schools followed a long tradition in which the mind was the first battlefield for black freedom.[19]

From David Walker's 1829 *Appeal* to the 1960s, freeing the black mind was the opening move for escaping the reproduction of oppression. Walker had recognized that ignorance was "a mist, low down into the very dark and almost impenetrable abyss," reducing blacks to abject submission, servility, and wretchedness. The educator Carter G. Woodson proposed in *The Mis-education of the Negro* (1933) that blacks were educated in ways that supported the dominant culture of European Americans, producing dependent beings unable to think for themselves. In an effort to correct black self-hatred and the emulation of white people, he advocated a new educational curriculum that brought attention to black folklore, history, and writers. Woodson heavily implicated the "Negro church" in the political role of education, as both conserving the racist regime and being a catalyst for racial uplift. Many others, like W.E.B. Du Bois, viewed education as key to black freedom. In *The Wretched of the Earth* (1961), a text that exerted wide American influence, Fanon went further, advocating a radical mind-awakening education that placed the struggle for freedom in the hands of the oppressed. It was, as the anti-colonial writer Aimé Césaire proposed, a political education intended "to invent the souls of men."[20]

There was a long tradition in black thought that tied political freedom to religion, but revitalizing the revolutionary potential of black religion required a mind free to reject a Christianity serving the interest of white people. In *Narrative of the Life of Frederick Douglass* (1845), Douglass narrates the revelation that the ignorance of the black man was the source of the white man's power. Thus, knowledge became the pathway to freedom. Douglass saw slaves kept in a state of ignorance and superstitious and made to believe God willed their enslavement. Dismayed that many believed that slavery was God ordained, he strove to reconcile black suffering with a just God. Emancipating his mind and gaining sufficient knowledge of the Bible, Douglass found the limit of his criticism of religion:

> "I mean strictly to apply to the *slaveholding religion* of this land, and with no possible reference to Christianity proper; for, between the Christianity of this land, and the Christianity of Christ, I recognize the widest possible difference—so wide, that to receive the one as good, pure, and holy, is of necessity to reject the other as bad, corrupt, and wicked."

In America, two Christianities existed side by side—one false, engendering ignorance and passivity, and the other true, requiring human action. Douglass frequently repeated the theme that American Christianity was a corrupt false religion at odds with Jesus's proclamation of justice and freedom for the captive and the poor.[21]

Douglass's mental emancipation allowed him to read the biblical text through his own experience and thus become what theologian Reginald F. Davis identifies as a precursor of liberation theology. Through his abolitionist writing and speeches, Douglass took on the entire ecclesiastical structure, black and white, refusing to settle for an eschatological meaning of liberation that left the here and now unchanged. Douglass's theological stance, asserting both the justice of God and the necessity of human action, was part of an alternative stream of religious thought. Cone saw in his predecessors a theology emerging from a self-liberated mind, asserting the black experience as the defining lens through which to judge all theological claims. Black people did not simply receive the language of God given to them by whites; historically they had constructed their own theology necessary for freedom.[22]

Cone saw the historical connection between a free black mind, the repudiation of white-defined Christianity, and the revolutionary potential of African American religion. Unlike Latin American liberationists who found an immediate point of engagement in the foment of radicalized BECs, Cone and other black liberationists followed Woodson and Martin Luther King Jr.'s example by seeking to reawaken the standing black churches. They viewed African American churches as places where a black consciousness and a black theology could take root and recover a revolutionary religion.

A Spiral of Violence

A consciousness of oppression and an emancipated mind able to discern God's will against the prevalent political order necessarily led to conflict. A political theology in which freedom in history was the will of God could not avoid the language of revolutionary struggle. Both Cone and Gutiérrez drew from Hegel's master/slave dialectic in *The Phenomenology of Mind*, in which the struggle for freedom required risking one's life. Fanon argued in *The Wretched of the Earth* that the process of decolonization was an unconditional demand for recognition and an absolute change in the order of the world. The ensuing violence, a medium for creating new men and nations, was the product of a "Manichaean world, of a compartmentalized world. . . . It's them or us." The only way out of the Manichaean world in which "the 'thing' colonized becomes a man" was violence. Fanon's emphasis on the essential violent, racist, and systematic nature of colonialism found a corollary in the relationship of the United States to blacks within its borders and Latin America at the periphery. The closed nature of the colonial system maintained through violence called for virulent resistance.[23]

The assumption of foundational violence and the master/slave metaphor that undergirds the history of Western and Third World political discourse provided a ready-made analysis of the situation. Liberation was the abolition of the master, also in need of liberation, by the slave. When the slave asserted his freedom, the master forfeited all his claims. For Gutiérrez, theology had to respond to Albert Camus' question in *The Rebel* by deciding whether freedom and life were worth striving for to the point of death. Having gained awareness, Gutiérrez asserted, "freedom [is] a historical conquest; it is to understand that the step from an abstract to a real freedom is not taken without a struggle against all the forces that oppress humankind." The goal was a "continuous creation, never ending, of a new way to be human." The Latin American situation of despair in which millions had little to lose lowered the cost of violence for the "permanent cultural revolution" that Gutiérrez evoked.[24]

The violent struggle for recognition created a political community. In rebellion, Camus asserted, the oppressed found solidarity—"I rebel, therefore we exist." Liberation was the process of going from "nonbeing to being," and the creation of a historical people. For Cone, becoming a community of struggle was the very nature of Black Power's demand for recognition. Freedom involved the potent creative act of forging a new community of revolution, "a radical black encounter with the structure of white racism, with the full intention of destroying its menacing power." A political theology announcing a liberating message and seeking to affect real world conditions was easily embroiled in conflict.[25]

A ready political metaphor was the Exodus narrative, in which a divine mandate compelled Israel to become a free and chosen people. Liberationists followed a long tradition of viewing the Exodus as the quintessential story of liberation, having material, political, and spiritual meaning. It had been useful for Puritans as they began their "errand into the wilderness," it inspired and saturated black sermons and spirituals, and it was alluded to by Karl Marx. Told as a this-world historical account, with its themes of oppression and corruption, it captured the revolutionary thrust of Western thought. For Israelites, unawakened to their freedom destiny, the known present in bondage appeared more secure than the unknown future. Only as they were "forced to be free," Alves concluded, did they enter the promised land. Liberationists interpreted the Exodus as a divine mandate that constituted Israel as a political community moving toward a free future.[26]

Oppressed people in the Americas found themselves in the same historical position as the biblical Israelites, witnessing God's revolutionary initiative on their behalf forging a new political community of solidarity. Through the motif of the Exodus, Cone read historical acts of black rebellion as the manifestation of God's commitment to human freedom. For Cone, "revelation is a black event— it is what blacks are doing about their liberation" in which the oppressed saw themselves as "persons-in-community" rather than as autonomous individuals. A liberated community as a divine and teleological goal called for confronting all opposing forces.[27]

In *Liberation and Reconciliation* (1971), J. Deotis Roberts, attempting to go beyond Cone's language of violent confrontation, looked for a revolution with reconciliation between equals as the final goal. Freedom and ultimate reconciliation required moving from object to subject; from a relationship defined by the slave/master to one that the Jewish philosopher Martin Buber called the I–Thou relationship. Instead of integration into American society, which assumes subordination to the dominant power, the I–Thou relationship allowed reconciliation between equals. For Roberts, neither "law and order without justice" nor black nationalism dealt effectively with the reality of American society. He saw the goal of replacing the slave/master relationship with love as necessary to overcome estrangement. However, explicitly drawing from a Niebuhrian Christian realism, he believed that love was not sentimentality that overlooked wrongs. Rather, Roberts argued, "love is always being crucified in history and thus the need for the pushing and shoving of justice." Because "equality is a higher social goal than peace," Niebuhr had asserted in *Moral Man and Immoral Society* (1932), only coercive force, in which violence might be the sole means, could break the self-interest of those in power. Only in the aftermath would the church, black and white, be the reconciling force in a racist society.[28]

Both Roberts and Cone viewed Christian social action as going beyond the use of "truth force," or moral power, as modeled by Martin Luther King Jr. History demonstrated that modern societies did not function, as Carmichael noted, "by morality, love, or nonviolence, but by power." The "conscienceless power" of white America did not respond to moral arguments. To arrive at mutual recognition, the process of liberation had to pass through what Roberts called the "manly art" of conflict, requiring courage and risking violence. Roberts could not escape Cone's argument that the nature of black religion was *resistance* and the knowledge that "he who would be free must strike the first blow." In the new black theology of liberation, emphasizing the confrontation and resistance advocated by Cone, overshadowed the theme of reconciliation Roberts suggested.[29]

Violence was not merely metaphorical or categorically excluded as a live option. The 1968 Medellin meeting of the Latin American Bishops Conference (CELAM) had charged that Latin America was in a "sinful situation" of "institutionalized violence" in which conflict was a concrete reality. Liberationists justified their willingness to consider violent means as taking place within an already violent system where poverty crushed millions. They saw institutionalized violence as intimately tied to "institutionalized hypocrisy," which spoke of peace but continued to produce oppression. Radical change called for immediate forceful action.[30]

America, "born in violent revolution" Cone noted, had never been a nonviolent nation, and Black Power delivered a commensurate response. Slogans of "law and order" and "the American way of life" camouflaged the systemic violence sustained by laws that sanctioned force against subjugated people and blessed by moralists. The arguments against violence served as a smokescreen for injustice. "We cannot let white rhetoric about nonviolence and Jesus distort our vision of violence committed against black people," Cone asserted. The "obscene questions" regarding violence asked of those initiating their own freedom, instead of those who used violence to safeguard their own power, exposed the hypocrisy. For Cone, whites displayed a concern for violence wrapped in the language of Christian love only when they saw themselves as the possible victims, not when blacks were beaten and shot in the streets. Millions of willing Christian men killed in the nation's wars yet found armed revolutionaries objectionable to their Christian conscience. The question was *whose* violence one was willing to endorse.[31]

Carmichael's 1966 essay "What We Want" prescribed the use of violence as determined by the black community on a case-by-case basis as it encountered white racism. He built his argument on Robert F. Williams' call in the early 1960s for black people to "meet violence with violence" in armed self-defense. Black men had a duty to defend their homes and families against white aggression, and nonviolent resistance became impossible. Carmichael charged that white liberals, afraid of being recipients of violence, tried to pacify black people and buy acquiescence through reform proposals. For Black Power advocates, white self-righteous polemics against violence were a ruse for power. Cone concurred. Only the community of victims of injustice, in dialogue with their own tradition of resistance and the biblical text, was in the position to judge the ethics and limits of violence. In an already violent system, where thousands died daily due to the lack of life's necessities, categorical rejection of violence was not an option. Cone argued, with Black Power leaders, "no one can be nonviolent in an unjust society."[32]

Latin American revolutionary violence had gone beyond mere rhetoric, bringing to the surface an unresolvable theological problem. Juan Luis Segundo, writing in *Christianity and Crisis,* viewed the Gospel message as essentially anti-Manichaean, rejecting the friend/enemy binary, thus making Christians poor revolutionaries when it came to violence. On the other hand, Bonino noted that Christian pacifism might nevertheless be self-justification for acquiescence. Appeals to peace and reconciliation became a heretical appropriation of Christian teaching by a capitalist system in order to conceal class exploitation. The inability of those in power to make decisions against their interests had compelled Camillo Torres to take up "revolutionary liberating violence." Bonino conceded that justified violence presented the danger of a counter-revolutionary act that substitutes one form of oppression for another. Institutional violence meeting counter-violence quickly escalated to what Brazilian bishop Hélder Câmara, an advocate of the poor, called a "spiral of violence." Liberationists remained in an ambiguous relationship with violence in which they saw neither absolute violence nor pacifism as congruent with the reality of a revolutionary situation. Rhetoric that refused to categorically renounce violence was a point pursued by their detractors, who questioned the Christian legitimacy of liberationists' theology, which became an unfortunate and enduring characterization.[33]

The language of violent confrontation was gendered and masculinist language. Men viewed the struggle within a framework of man-against-man opposition that overcame the passivity and receptivity long associated with women. Men had historically resorted to violent revolt to lay claim to freedom. In the narrative of his life, Douglass offered an account of how a slave becomes a man. Douglass recounted how his violent confrontation with the slave breaker Edward Covey had "kindled in my breast the smoldering embers of freedom, and revived within me a sense of my own manhood." Crushed intellectually and spiritually, "transformed into a brute," and despairing of the goodness of God, he believed the subsequent feeling of triumph in having defeated Covey was worth the possibility of death. From the tomb of slavery to the resurrection of freedom, "my long-crushed spirit rose, cowardice departed, bold defiance took its place." In the abolition of the master, a new man emerged. Violence served as what Fanon identified as a "cleansing force" in the colonized mind, ridding the subordinated man of an inferiority complex and passivity. What emerged was a new *man*, self-reliant and independent. Douglass expressed the struggle to recover black manhood, a struggle that remained within the Black Power movement.[34]

In defining the search for freedom as a violent struggle, women had a distinct disadvantage. Short of the women's self-defense movement few advocated taking up arms, making the espousal of violence a less certain liberating strategy. Consequently, women turned to existential and psychic means in overcoming oppression. While men appealed to struggling historical communities based on class or race standing against an external power, women as a group did not constitute a separate historical community. Women, embedded in particular communities, found themselves within a personal politics of intimate relationships with those that benefited from their oppression. Black women were exposed to double jeopardy, being unable to exercise violence within their own communities or against a dominant society, an exercise which only men could take up. Violence being a relatively unrealistic option, for women liberation meant a greater interrogation of the relationship between the self and the community.

Ruether objected to casting liberation as a battle between the oppressed and the oppressor, relocating the struggle within the self. Oppression was never merely a matter of violent imposition requiring the expulsion of the other. The chief form of enslavement for women was through psychological and cultural conditioning under the terms of the patriarchy, a situation in which the "woman's chief enemy is herself." Ruether, following the 1960s feminist currents of post-Freudian appropriations, charged that psychoanalysis had become the chief tool, replacing patriarchal religion, to rationalize the subordination of women. Nevertheless, psychoanalysis, freed from the sexist perversion of its theory, had potential as a tool for guiding women to "psychic health." The process of psychic liberation was the work of the vital virtues of anger and pride that "exorcize the demons of self-hatred and self-destruction," and moves toward the "resurrection of autonomy and self-esteem."

The process of liberation, often taking place in women-only consciousness-raising groups, was an angry revolt against an oppressive system. Pride, instead of being a deadly sin, recovered an authentic and good humanity through the assertion of the self. Ruether was restating the earlier argument of theologian Valerie Saiving Goldstein that women suffering from a lack of self-pride fell into the sin of self-negation. Instead of being a struggle between two opposing powers, the recovery of pride, anger, and self-assertion experienced through consciousness-raising could be described according to Freire: "Liberation is thus a childbirth, and a painful one," by which a new woman gives birth to herself. Giving birth to the self became the means by which women joined men as equals in human solidarity.[35]

Ruether saw other dangers in characterizing liberation as the struggle between good and evil forces. It fostered projecting all negativity onto an alien community, and merely reversing the relationships of power dehumanized both the oppressor and oneself. Revolt by victims "tends to rush forward to murder and self-aggrandizement," as the victims fall headlong onto the same path of power as their oppressors. Oppressors, seeing the negative side of their own self-righteousness reflected in the revolt of "evil ones," reinforced their moral position as "God's elect." In a dualistic world, both sides suffered from an inability to self-critique. Only when the protest and the response remained in dialogue, calling both to an authentic humanity, could true liberation occur. Human solidarity was available on the other side of an inner revolt by the subjugated and repentance by those holding unjust power. Without casting off "apocalyptic dualism" to fight the battle within the self, all theologies of liberation failed. Ruether called for a transformation of values that went beyond dualism and opposition, to mutual human flourishing.[36]

A Prophetic Minority

Viewing the liberation of the oppressed as the crux of salvation history changed the locus of action from the centers of power to the periphery. Instead of addressing sympathetic liberal reformers to instigate political change the theological message was now directed to those at the bottom seeking freedom. Liberationists viewed those in power, enslaved by megalomania, as incapable of initiating liberation for the masses of people, for they were the chief beneficiaries of unjust relationships; without the oppressed, they failed to exist. The church of poor people, and blacks as a community of struggle, were "artisans of [their] own destiny." Roberts called on the black church to become "a gestalt, a structure of mass power of black people," and to launch an assault on white power in all its manifestations. True solidarity was not self-deferential sympathy displayed by whites or a commitment to an idealist universal humanity, but participation in the "struggles of the wretched of the earth."[37]

The work of the faith community, according to Gutiérrez, was engaging in "prophetic denunciation" in society and "conscienticizing evangelization" among the poor. The prophetic denunciation was also Cone's angry "word to Whitey" to aid in the destruction of America's racist ideology. Prophetic denunciation recognized that no privileged group had ever given up power without pressure from below, and it served as a warning in the manner in which Jesus addressed the religious authorities of his time. Evangelization aimed at raising political awareness directly addressed to the oppressed and urged them to become historical protagonists. There would be no more pleading at the doors of power; rather, there would be a seizure of power.[38]

The call for the oppressed to engage in their own struggle for freedom, and the role of the theologian in raising awareness of God's liberatory action, created a question as to who was to initiate the process. There was a contradiction between a theology arising from a critical reading of the text from below, and the role of a prophetic minority acting on behalf of the oppressed. In *The Secular City* (1965), American theologian Harvey Cox described the avant-garde of God as those "whose ties to particular political and cultural arrangements are sufficiently tenuous that it is always ready to move to the next stage in history." These were the ones Ruether described as the "alienated intelligentsia," a "prophetic element," able to mediate between the revolt of the oppressed and the prevailing society. The committed theologian as the *avant-garde* of God, ambivalent toward ecclesiastical structures, was in a position to awaken the subjugated to their historical role and to join them in its actualization.[39]

Liberationists judged the situation of oppressed people, persecuted by the demands of survival and kept passive by religious fatalism, as rendering the struggle for freedom a "heroic" act that only a minority could bear. Enrique Dussel argued, "Being a prophet is not child's play. It is violent work; it is subversive; it is pedagogy." A prophetic minority, made up of both the theologian and leaders arising from among the people, leveraged liberation on behalf of the many. The problem of who would instigate liberation brought to the surface the tension between subordinated people and cultural elites. To place at the forefront of the struggle an enlightened minority of priests, theologians, and social activists who perceived the necessity of the situation placed the oppressed at the mercy of elite action. Ruether noted the danger to the prophetic figure engaged in a "parasitic identification with the oppressed . . . viewed as 'suffering saviors.'" Motivated by utopian visions, guilt, and self-hatred, the prophet became ineffective and rejected by those he or she sought to "help."[40]

On the other hand, liberationists asked, how could those in the grip of inertia and without the means of perceiving the complexity of the system be expected to initiate liberation for themselves? Drawing from Lenin's argument in *What Is to Be Done?* (1902) that the oppressed will fail to turn spontaneously revolutionary, Segundo sought to eliminate the opposition between the elites and the people. Segundo noted that *conscientization* was a never-ending process that complicated life, making it a high-cost endeavor. In an "economy of energy," and acting out along "the lines of least resistance," the immediacy of experience is a condition found in every social class. All people therefore are, in different spheres of life, part of the people and the opposing minority. For Segundo, no social change was possible without the effort of a minority committed to distancing itself from mechanized thinking. Theologians, pastoral workers, and organic lay leaders emerging among the people embodied the prophetic minority, the necessary avant-garde. Liberationists as elite thinkers remained at odds between their critical "prophetic denunciation" and advancing the role of subordinated people in constructing theology from below.[41]

The history of revolution and resistance in the Americas demonstrated that to be human was to be free, and freedom required a struggle. Liberationists concluded that instead of waiting for freedom to materialize, a prophetic minority would lead subordinated people to become historical protagonists. Blacks would break with a theology that refused to deal with racism. Latin Americans would challenge a theology that eluded class struggle. Women would take on the dualism and sexual hierarchy that permeated theological thought. Instead of rearticulating "timeless truths," a new theology looked to the experience of the oppressed as a beginning point in the historical process of liberation. Instead of avoiding the conflict of human history by focusing on the private religious experience, it fulfilled a prophetic role by joining the political struggle. Constructing a liberating theology for revolutionary action required understanding the material and ideological conditions of oppression and building on a new foundation for religious knowledge. The social sciences, rather than idealist speculation, as a handmaiden for theology promised liberationists the needed tools for their project.

5
New Foundations

NINETEENTH-CENTURY THINKERS GRAPPLED with the methodological conflict between theology and the emerging social science—a difference that drove the search for a resolution in both disciplines. Both social scientists and theologians invested their attention in identifying, by different means, the values necessary for a viable modern society. In accounting for the formation of values, social science found an unexplained gap between empirical evidence and accepted religious notions of what ought to be. Theology's insistence on a fixed source of values standing outside history left it without a practical means by which to deal with prodigious change. The question of whether science would replace religion in determining the lived values of a society occupied social thinkers. Finding common ground required traversing the gulf between facts and values.

In the course of the twentieth century, social sciences and theology moved closer together. The effects on theology of historicism, social theory, and pragmatism resulted in conceding greater realms of knowledge to science and allowed robust cross-disciplinary dialogue. Epistemological questions gave way to ethical ones. The question of right action replaced the question of what was true. Developments of social theory recognizing a plurality of knowledge allowed religious and social scientific claims to move closer to, if not reconciliation, a mutual recognition.

By the 1960s, theologians and social theorists, instead of continuing to reify the opposition between scientific facts and religious values, increasingly shared an understanding in the relationship between the individual, society, and the social function of religious faith. Situating theology within these changes brings into focus antecedent ideas that came to constitute the liberationist theological method, one that began with the world rather than with abstract truth applied to the world—a radical change from classic theology. This and the following chapter will examine how these changes came about and set a new foundation for liberationist thought.

The sociologist Werner Stark exemplified the mid-century nexus of theology and social theory. A Jewish convert to Catholicism, Stark wrote a collection of essays entitled *Social Theory and Christian Thought: A Study of Some Points of Contact* (1958), which explored the "border country between sociology and theology," an explicit values-directed approach that marginalized him within the field. His examination began with Augustine's socio-theological reflection on the *civitas divana* and the *civitas terrena*, and the body of Christ as a metaphor for society as an organic whole animated by the love of God. Stark viewed Augustine as providing an elaboration of an "organological sociology" combined with a progressive view of history, establishing a foundation for a social quasi-organic integration. Consequently, he saw in modern social theory, as exemplified by Kant, Hegel, and Marx, a secular version of Augustinian socio-theology. Stark exemplified the perennial endeavor within sociology to find an organic basis for society and identify the religious features seemingly unexplained by science.[1]

The Science of Society

How theology and social science came to share key presuppositions begins with a set of originating concerns. Before the rise of modernity, a person's position in a stable hierarchy determined by his or her birth made neither the serf nor the lord free in any modern sense. New ideas reverberating from the Reformation and the Enlightenment eroded the previous assumption of an organic unity between the individual and society. The view of the human person as belonging in a "great chain of being," a hierarchal cosmic system with God at the top with every one subject to obligations and responsibilities, faded.[2]

The German Reformation was a decisive moment in the transition. Martin Luther's emphasis on personal faith for salvation, and the sweeping away of priestly and institutional mediation, laid the groundwork for what became the modern individual. In *Treatise on Christian Liberty* (1520), Luther reiterated the apostle Paul by characterizing the nature of Christian liberty this way: "a Christian man is a perfectly free lord of all, subject to none. A Christian man is a perfectly dutiful servant to all, subject to all." Luther's believer, once released from obligations to society, reentered voluntarily. His doctrine, setting the individual alone before God, had profound political, social, and theological implications. The salvation of the individual and nurturance of the interior life, rather than participation in the spiritual community, became a significant focus of subsequent Christian theology particularly among Protestants.[3]

Luther's Christian freedom of the individual complemented enlightened freedom, as the liberalism of Thomas Hobbes and John Locke, with its social contract theory, placed an economically striving and rational individual at the center of the modern political project. Leaving the question of virtue to the individual, thus to a private religion, the early modern state committed itself to the facilitation of markets and unconstrained scientific inquiry. The striving for enlightened freedom created tension in balancing the needs of the individual and the needs of social and political life. The interest of the self, seeking emancipation from the constraints of tradition and custom, appeared in opposition to the interests of society.[4]

By the late eighteenth century, the autonomous individual appeared to hinder both freedom and human happiness and presented the need in the minds of many to reestablish society on a more comprehensive basis. Laissez-faire liberalism, with its denigrated labor dislodged from the context of family and guild, and new property relations drew the ire of both conservatives and radicals, who noted the alienating nature of modern life and attempted to recover some sense of social unity. With the old social relationships in shambles and within the Enlightenment itself, there emerged the new "science of man," defining society as a collection of historically contingent individuals. The science of man attempted to reassert the mutual constitutive element of the individual and society and identify both a universal human nature and the cause of its diversity.[5]

Among conservative thinkers, the reasserting of community placed the human person within a reconstituted social hierarchy. Hegel reflected a conservative view of society as a *"communitas communitatum"* instead of a collection of directly sovereign individuals. For Edmund Burke, who longed for the reestablishment of old social bonds, integral participation in a community had a moral, if not religious, base. The sociologist Steven Seidman argued that religious and cosmological assumptions supported the "communitarian ideal" and noted how "The principles of philosophical conservatism entered into the very center of sociological theory," evident in the continual interest in, among other things, the moral order and hierarchy.[6]

The radical Romantic critique focused on the dualist nature of enlightened thought that placed freedom/determinism, mind/body, and spirit/matter in opposition. Unhappy with the internally divided self and fragmented society, radicals sought harmony through a fundamental restructuring. They proposed a community of fully developed individuals animated by spirit and free from tradition and authority. The individual was to be in harmony with himself and the community. Subsequently, among left-wing Hegelians, Marx saw the actualization of individual freedom and a reconstituted community in the solidarity of the working class. Both conservatives and Romantic radicals, in seeking a new basis for their communitarian ideal, contributed to the persistent themes of alienation in social theory. Among sociologists, from Auguste Comte to Max Weber, community was set against the relations of competition and contract in a rationalized society.[7]

Post-Enlightenment social theory, infused with a mythical and religious flavor, placed the function and form of religion as central in the development of social science. In the 1966 book *The Sociological Tradition,* sociologist Robert S. Nisbet identified community, authority, status, the sacred, and alienation as perennial concepts in sociology. These concepts, also central concerns in theology, provided a common language between the disciplines, making the steady move toward convergence unsurprising. The culturally turbulent 1960s politically charged these concepts, fueling the rhetoric of the New Left and Third World liberation movements. New self-identified communities engaged in asserting their status, challenging established authority, expressed the disaffection from the status quo and redefined the meaning of the sacred. As social movements, they were forming at the nexus of the long-standing concerns of social science and theology.[8]

From its inception, social science ventured to solve the riddle of religion. In *The Course of Positive Philosophy* (1830), the socially conservative Auguste Comte, influenced by the utopian Henri de Saint-Simon, proceeded to establish a positive science of society having primacy over both metaphysics and theology. Positivism established the natural sciences, with their reliance on observation, general laws, and value neutrality, as the standard by which to study society. Nevertheless, Comte envisioned a religious organization that he believed was fundamental to social well-being. Comte's *System of Positive Polity, or Treatise on Sociology Instituting the Religion of Humanity* (1851) proposed the "Religion of Humanity" as a scientific religion, adopting the pattern of Catholicism with its own catechism, rituals, and saints. Diverse thinkers such as John Stuart Mill, Elizabeth Cady Stanton, and Brazilian emperor Dom Pedro II briefly embraced the Religion of Humanity. Comte and those who followed him viewed religion as providing the necessary inspiration for social cohesion while rejecting the particular dogma of Christianity.[9]

Comte's scientific positivism had widespread influence in the Americas. Positivism presented the greatest challenge to prevailing Catholic culture in Latin America, as intellectuals looked for scientific principles by which to address "diseases of the social organism." The fascination with positivist science as a chief tool for nation building, along with Herbert Spencer's naturalism and Mill's utilitarianism, contributed toward an anti-metaphysical stance in Latin American thought. The priority of empirical science remained dominant among intellectuals until the early twentieth century, when *modernismo,* in an anti-positivism backlash, reintroduced humanistic values rooted in the classical age and Christian ethics to Latin American intellectual life.[10]

In the Protestant ethos of North America, Comte's influence was less marked but notable in Lester F. Ward's work *Dynamic Sociology* (1883). Seeking a replacement for religious faith bringing meaning to people's lives, Ward proposed "sociocracy," a government resting on social science and opposing irrational religion. Across the Americas, positivist social science appeared useful for ordering society and offered a new basis for values as a replacement for dogmatic religion.[11]

Moving with social science, Catholic and Protestant theologians sought to recapture the spiritual essence of an organic social whole that had disintegrated with modernity. A key strategy was validating the individual's religious knowledge and affirming the social nature of religion, two projects seemingly at odds. Following Friedrich Schleiermacher's existentialism and Hegel's idealism, theologians attempted to both establish religious sentiment as a form of autonomous knowledge and place it within history, rather as a divine given, hoping to thus reconstitute an organic community. Johann Sebastian von Drey, desiring Catholic theological renewal, addressed the historical criticism posed by enlightened Protestants by appropriating a social and organic vision of history. Guided by the idea of historical continuity in Christianity, he sought to recapture the Catholic faith in his 1819 essay "On the Spirit and Essence of Catholicism," as Catholicism's corporatism drew Protestant converts seeking a more thorough restoration of an organic community. The sway of religious sentiment necessarily placed the private experience of the believer, rather than a historically situated community, at the center. Nevertheless, the historicism taking hold formed a significant first step toward explaining the social nature of belief.[12]

For the emerging social science, the fact/value distinction served as a built-in limitation in the study of religion in that there remained an element of values formation unaccounted for by the facts. The fact/value dichotomy appeared as an unbridgeable gap between empirical facts gathered from the world and different value judgments asserted by religion. Among the theorists setting the direction of the discipline, the mechanism of value formation became a prime area of study. While Marx's historical materialism rejected the fact/value dichotomy as based on idealism, both Emile Durkheim and Weber took the split for granted and sought to resolve it by the objectification of values. Observed as objective and connected to other social structures, moral absolutes limited the individual, thus compliance appeared equivalent to group conformity. Weber, emphasizing the irreducible nature of competing values, left no rational way to determine the primacy of one over another. The only way to measure any value was how it inspired effective social action, not by an illusive self-authenticating experience. The resulting action, rather than what was believed to be true was the measure of the validity of any expressed value.[13]

A New Basis for Values

From the inception of the interdisciplinary relationship, both theologians and sociologists found the others' discipline encroaching on their field of inquiry. Appeals to moral absolutes were seemingly at odds with science's search to find a social origin. Theologians had to deal with the causal explanations for belief, and sociologists had to account for values not reducible to positivist explanations. Under the challenge of social theory, theology found itself responding to the claim that religious practice and belief were expressions of social, political, and economic structures rather than divinely given. Theologians felt compelled not only to respond to philosophical objections but also to explain the social origin of belief. Increasingly, they took on the language of social science to account for and affirm ideas about God, sin, and salvation. On the other hand, sociologists' attempts to study religious phenomena quickly ran into the constraints of the fact/value distinction, and looked toward religion for guidance. As social science attempted to explain the origins of belief, theologians offered the counter-argument that an explanation of origins did not demonstrate that a belief was false. It was at this nexus of facts and values that theology and social science converged and found expression in liberation theology.[14]

Because theology defined itself as a discipline deploying both faith and reason, ample room remained for incorporating social science, a process that liberationist Hugo Assman called the "sociologization of theology." Rosemary Radford Ruether also argued for expanding the parameters of theological practice: "Only with such a multi-disciplinary integration of human sciences can we begin to speak on the basis for a theology of liberation." In their appropriation of social science, liberationists recognized that it did not merely report facts but also developed theories as to the underlying nature of social relations. Social theories adopted either a functionalist view, in which conflict was resolved within the existing system, or a dialectical view of continual conflict and change. The social theory providing the best explanation for the sources of oppression, empirically or theoretically, and identifying a means for its alleviation was tentatively adopted in the newly developing biblical hermeneutic. By availing itself of the whole range of knowledge, Ruether noted, "theology is losing its confinement as an exclusive ecclesiastical science, but only because it is finding its place in a reintegrated view of the human community . . ." thus "sketching the horizon of human liberation in its fully redemptive context." The objective was to find a social theory to aid in unmasking the race-based, class-based, and sex-based ideological components of existing theologies. In this move, liberationists joined many of their mid-century secular peers who were reevaluating the commodification of life eclipsing not only the individual, but also the community.[15]

Gustavo Gutiérrez identified the 1968 meeting of CELAM as the first recognition that social science, tied to Marxist analysis, provided tools for understanding the conditions of class oppression, writing, "Medellin marks the beginning of a new relationship between theological and pastoral language on the one hand and the social sciences which seek to interpret this reality on the other." Gutiérrez regarded Marx's theoretical attention to historical forces and a commitment to transforming the world as the most instructive elements for the development of "orthopraxis" by theologians. In *God of the Oppressed* (1975), James Cone asserted the important role of social science in illuminating the link between black lived experience in a racist society and theology. Referring to Ludwig Feuerbach and Marx, Cone reiterated Marx's argument of a connection between the "ruling material force of society" and "ruling intellectual force." He joined in looking to political and social theory as a key component of a theological method. The common goal among liberationists was to eliminate the perceived breach between Christian values of freedom and justice and the actual order of society and to create the possibility of critically informed human action. Social science and theology appeared as destined allies.[16]

Latin America's social and religious intellectuals throughout the continent possessed significant experience with social science. Beginning in the 1950s the concern with the structural sources of poverty led to the establishment of Catholic-sponsored social science research centers staffed by foreign-trained researchers. Theologians, clergy, and social scientists spent a significant amount of time becoming familiar with the conditions of extreme poverty. By the late 1960s, research centers linked in a continent-wide network were active in almost every country. New data and theories for the witnessed inequality swept religious circles and raised questions regarding the role of religion in justifying or alleviating suffering.[17]

Juan Luis Segundo engaged in the most critical conceptualization of the relationship of theology with social science. Founding Montevideo's Peter Faber Center of Theological and Social Studies in 1965, Segundo turned to the sociology of religion to answer the social questions of his day. By the 1970s, his work brought him opportunities to teach at prestigious academic centers, including the Chicago Divinity School, and his writing appeared on the pages of *Christianity and Crisis*. He argued in *The Liberation of Theology* (1976) that a useful and necessary sociology had to break with the positivist, or behaviorist, approach coming from the United States and rampant in Latin America, to viewing society as a whole system. This was a spreading critique of the moribund nature of social science at mid-century. C. Wright Mills argued in *The Sociological Imagination* (1959) that sociology had to move away from its "bureaucratic ethos" wedded to technique, high-formalized theory, and small-scale milieu to understand why a more rational society did not yield more freedom. Mills, viewing individuals as primarily embedded in society, proposed understanding modern unease through the "public issues of social structures." Segundo drew from similar currents in Latin America and the work of Argentine sociologist Eliseo Verón, who argued in his 1971 essay "Ideology and Communication of the Masses: The Systematization of Political Violence" that the breakup of analysis into smaller and smaller subfields obscured ideology. Verón asserted that sociologists were more concerned with how many people went to mass, a measure of social conformity, than how religion shaped their political attitudes. Quantitative sociology and social psychology had displayed an interest in religion as another sphere of adaptation. It was therefore necessary, Segundo argued, that a useful sociology recover the ground claimed by Marx in *The German Ideology* by illuminating "the religious mechanisms that help to impose cultural traits on the one hand, and the possible deformation of religion resulting from cultural adaptation on the other hand." It was at this intersection that sociology and social theory became significant partners in a liberating theology.[18]

Everything Is Tottering!

Having begun with Kantian reason, Schleiermacher's religious consciousness, and Hegel's historical idealism, and under the sway of social science, theology moved away from epistemological certainty and a private believer toward a historically and socially situated knower. The theologian Johann Gottfried von Herder's historicism and Charles Darwin's evolutionary theory had a sustained influence on recasting theological ethics. Increasingly, religious thinkers, observing the developing structures of modernity and seeking to show the non-contradiction of science and values, viewed human beings as situated within a plural context of meaning toward some unknown teleological end. An emphasis on ethics over epistemology reformulated the theological task. Understanding the ethical effects of religious knowledge rather than its "truth" promised to build a bridge between the individual's faith experience and society.

The German theologians Albrecht Ritschl and Ernst Troeltsch profoundly influenced Americans during the progressive era. Ritschl and Troeltsch recast the theological task away from metaphysics and individual experience toward the social and historical. Identifying the nature of the good required the historical investigation of the Christian community rather than arguments based in metaphysics. Ritschl attempted to establish a new base for religious knowledge free of the world-denying metaphysics underlying Lutheran dogmatism and pietism. By turning from the Romantic move in Schleiermacher and emphasizing Kant's moral reasoning, he validated ethics ahead of objective or subjective knowledge as a basis for religious faith. Nevertheless, as Ritschl and Troeltsch turned toward establishing the credibility of Christianity by demonstrating its ability to facilitate an ethical social order, they left Schleiermacher's religious subject largely intact. The question became not how we know anything about God, but how we live out human reconciliation toward the kingdom of God—a key contributing idea to the social Christianity of the progressive era.

Science, Ritschl argued in *The Christian Doctrine of Justification and Reconciliation* (1870), began with judgments on the worth of objective observation yielding certain facts about the world. While scientific facts focused on separate and distinct natural phenomena, in the social world, "All perceptions of moral ends or moral hindrances are independent value-judgments, in so far as they excite moral pleasure or pain." Every religion was the exercise of an "independent value-judgment" to resolve the contractions of life. In Christianity, he argued, "Knowledge of God can be demonstrated as religious knowledge only when He [God] is conceived as securing to the believer such a position in the world as more than counterbalances its restrictions." The truth of any belief was in living and acting out what one reckoned to be true against the contradiction of the world. True religious knowledge resolved the difference between the *ought* and the *is* of life—the value/fact distinction. Ritschl maintained a socially situated individual as the primary producer of values, and the role of religion was to provide society the moral tutoring necessary for applying scientific knowledge. The *ought* of religion and the *is* of society were thought to be ultimately reconcilable. His concern for finding a positive connection between religiously derived values and society assumed the ultimate virtue of the German social order in which he lived. In the twentieth century, Karl Barth viewed Ritschl as "the very epitome of the national liberal German bourgeois of the age of Bismarck ... the perfected Enlightenment." The Christian faith supporting the interest and values of middle-class society appeared to leave no room for a theologically informed critique of politics or culture.[19]

Troeltsch, a student of Ritschl, disrupted an 1896 German gathering of theologians concerned with advancing secularization by declaring, "Gentlemen! Everything is tottering!" The collapse of absolute propositions under the new philosophical ground cleared by Marx and Darwin necessitated a new foundation for religious knowledge. As a member of the newly established History of Religion School at Göttingen University, Troeltsch engaged in the comparative and scientific study of religious values. Historical scientific thinking dominated his theology. His book *The History of the Social Teaching of the Churches* (1912) expressed the intellectual anxiety of the age and a historical consciousness of the place of ethical practice in the constitution of society. Influenced by his friendship with Weber, Troeltsch deployed a historical sociological approach to ethics, identifying two key concepts in its development: the advent of the state that had alienated social groups from one another, and subsequently from the state, and the political economy that defined modern society. Thus, the social problem was fundamentally political. Harmony was Troeltsch's normative criterion for the relationship between Christianity and society while allowing for religion's self-generating vitalism. Thus like Ritschl, rather than holding to an absolute source of values, his historicism relativized Christian ethics to its milieu and held to its ultimate instantiation in German society—a point of view that then quickly disintegrates into the position that what is, is right. [20]

Along with the German influence in the increased concern for social ethics, no philosophy had more influence on American theology than the pragmatism advanced by Charles Peirce, William James, and John Dewey. Peirce was a deep, if unorthodox, religious thinker, believing that his philosophy would eventually reconcile science and religion. Peirce considered religion a communal process of proposing potential ethical and universal truths—truths that could only be finally judged by experience. He noted that pragmatism was the culmination of the principles laid down by Jesus: "by their fruits you will know them." Throughout his writing, he called for a scientific theology and for regarding theologians as "scientific men" discovering new knowledge rather than dogmaticians. Peirce's epistemological idealism gave way to James and Dewey's radical empiricism, what the theologian Gary Dorrien has referred to as holding "the key to making theology truly modern."[21]

James rejected as abstraction the dualism of fact/value and thought/action, preferring "a pragmatic method" in approaching the world. Human beings as historically constituted and ideas as products of history left room for religion. Religion, James asserted, was "man's total reaction upon life," a distinct expression of moral freedom. As such, pragmatism had "no *a priori* prejudice against theology... If theological ideas prove to have a value for concrete life, they will be true... for how much they are true, will depend entirely on their relations to other truths that also have to be acknowledged." In the essay "Pragmatism's Conception of Truth" (1907), James argued, "truth happens to an idea, it becomes true, is made true by events." The test of truth, including religious truths, was always practical, and "its validity was the process of valid-*ation*." A pragmatist, he proposed, "turns away from abstraction and insufficiency, from verbal solutions, from bad a priori reasons, from fixed principles, closed systems, and pretended absolutes and origins. He turns towards concreteness and adequacy, towards facts, towards action, and towards power." By the 1960s James' description of a pragmatist, concerned with action and power, fit many religious radicals attending to the social and political consequences of their ideas.[22]

With religion as "man's total reaction upon life," James was concerned with the effective fruits of mysticism, even with its tendency toward fanaticism, to unleash human initiative and encourage social transformation. He drew from Jonathan Edwards' *Treatise on Religious Affection* as an authority in measuring the effectiveness of religious experience in producing practical change: quoting Edwards, "The degree to which our experience is productive of practice shows the degree in which our experience is spiritual and divine." Yet long after Edwards, and before James gave pragmatic action priority, a bearer of the Quaker inner light, radical abolitionist Lucretia Mott, had rattled her audience with "Let our fruits test the purity of our profession." It was this attitude of making religious truths tangible that energized American projects of self-mastery and social reform.[23]

As James emphasized the religious psychology of "men in their solitude," Dewey expressed pragmatism in a vision of social democracy in which the religious imagination played no small part. In *A Common Faith* (1934), Dewey, who had a mutually influential relationship with the Chicago theologian Edward Scribner Ames, sought to ground "the religious" not in formal historical religion, but as a mode of experience. He explicated how values derived through a radical historicism found the individual within a web of social relations. Historic religions as products of evolution in their social environment called for their reconstruction to serve current needs. The religious experience was not contained within formal structures, and its emancipation from religion allowed a new faith to emerge in the pursuit of human welfare. Dewey sought to reorient the vitalism of religious ideals toward the construction of a social democracy, giving secular ends transcendent meaning. His move to extricate the religious feeling from religion and its institutions paralleled theological developments that sought to free an authentic world-shaping faith from dogma. In the midst of wide historicism, religion continued to fall on intellectual hard times as a superfluous institution.[24]

The founding of the Chicago Divinity School in 1890 initiated the greatest influence of pragmatism on religious thought and left a distinct mark on American theology. The pragmatism of the University of Chicago philosophy department, with its luminary figures Dewey, James Tufts, and George Mead, came to bear on the theologians including Ames, Shirley Jackson Case, George Burman Foster, Shailer Mathews, and its alumnus the Yale theologian Douglas C. Macintosh. The Chicago theologians, building on Ritschl and Troeltsch, took on sociohistorical methods for understanding the religious experience, committing themselves to both scientific inquiry and moral reasoning that would encourage social sympathy. Acutely aware of the rapid secularization of the academy, they moved to reconstruct Christian theology on a scientific basis. The "Chicago School" had inherited New England Calvinism from its predecessor, the Baptist Union Theological Seminary in Morgan Park, Illinois; by 1900 and virtually overnight, it had replaced it. Like Peirce and his "metaphysical club," this group of theologians had grown up under the shadow memory of what Mark Noll has called the "theological crisis" of the Civil War. Dogma, the certainty of truth, and moral absolutes all appeared ill suited to avert war or social crisis. The Chicago theologians, far from the nation's Eastern power centers, made their presence known at the height of progressive reform. It was for them to reformulate an empirical theology suitable for new times and initiate the twentieth century's secularization of theology.[25]

Mathews, a historian and dean, defined the socio-historical method that gave the school its signature and applied it to the development of systematic theology or dogma. He argued in *The Growth of the Idea of God* (1931) that theologies, like any other set of ideas, were attempts to resolve particular social problems of their age. Case followed in 1943 with his book *The Christian Philosophy of History*, writing, "history can be said to make religion" to be re-created by each generation for its own time. As a historical product of the social mind, what was "true" in one era was inadequate for another. Thoroughly immersed in a progressive and advancing view of history, the Chicago School embraced the promise of ever-increasing levels of moral achievement.[26]

Participating in the advancing science, the Chicago School offered empirical methods for arriving at a universal and individual moral ethic and reconciling values with social facts. These scholars moved Schleiermacher's religious consciousness into a fuller "relationality of experience," focusing on religious knowledge as a reflection of social experience. Theology, like philosophy, would follow the course set by Dewey in the *Reconstruction of Philosophy* (1920), in which the discipline would be rooted not in metaphysics or dogma but in experience. Ames, who shared in Dewey's religious naturalism, articulated a new understanding of God as the representation of the ideals of the community rather than as a transcendent being. Seeking the realization of Christian ethics by arguments based in science and human experience rather than on divine mandate, Chicago theologians both recognized the limits of life and committed to the possibility of transcending human experience. With no less evangelical fervor, they promoted a theology based in the history of the believing community and offered a theology open to the contingency and dynamism of the world, not only to their intellectual peers but also to laypeople caught in the flurry of the social gospel.[27]

In "Can Pragmatism Furnish a Philosophical Basis for Theology?" (1910) Macintosh argued that the claim of pragmatism—"that indeed all true judgments about reality are actually or potentially useful, so that usefulness of a belief indicates with more or less probability of its truth"—provided a useful basis for a scientific theology. Macintosh took up the Jamesian challenge in *Theology as an Empirical Science* (1919). He continued in *The Problem of Religious Knowledge* (1940), in which revelation was the ethical discernment of the good that begins with the existence of God as a working hypothesis. He argued that belief "can be transformed into a categorical knowledge only by empirical verification." By mid-century, the original fervor of Chicago's pragmatic theology had suffered the same fate as the philosophy that had given it birth. Its empirical methods came under questioning as a failure to evaluate the moral standards embedded in the "neutral" scientific method itself. Nevertheless, through the wide-reaching influence of the Chicago School, pragmatism remained a subterranean strain running through American theology as it gave up its claim to epistemological autonomy.[28]

From its North American origins, quick translation and intellectual exchange carried the ideas of pragmatism broadly throughout the Americas and Europe. Largely neglected by scholars until recently, the philosopher Gregory F. Pappas demonstrated the historical crosscurrents between Latin American thought and North American pragmatism. The writings of Peirce, James, and Dewey reached their widest circulation during World War II. Spanish philosophers having influence in Latin America including Miguel de Unamuno, José Ortega y Gasset, and Eugenio d'Ors, self-identifying as a pragmatist, referred to key features of pragmatic thought. Latin Americans, having inherited the scientism of the positivist tradition, shared with pragmatism an interest in the connections between thought, action, and social structures. Among Latin American progressive reformers, Dewey had the most influence as a philosopher of education. The hemispheric circulations of pragmatism's approach to arriving at tentative truth made ready an intellectual environment for conceptualizing liberation theology.[29]

Yet with multiple affinities between Latin American thought and pragmatism, Catholic liberationists traversed a wider theological gulf than their Protestant cohorts as pragmatism met greater ecclesial resistance. It is easy to propose that pragmatism was born out of a Protestant attitude, ready to break with tradition and willing to reform its conclusions, and thus already alien to Catholic thought. Neither did the virulent distaste of Peirce, James, and Dewey for Catholicism nor their methods for arriving at truth make pragmatism palatable to the orthodoxy of the Magisterium. Pope Pius X in 1907 charged that modernist theologians within Catholicism had adopted "the principle of the Americanists, that the active virtues are more important than the passive, both in the estimation in which they must be held and in the exercise of them." In the modernist crisis of the early twentieth century, the epistemological disruption of pragmatism was the "synthesis of all heresies." Nevertheless, the French philosopher Maurice Blondel, a faithful Catholic caught in the modernist crossfire, took up pragmatism in his idea of truth as "critical reflection on action," and his thought found its way into the liberation theology of Gutiérrez. (I examine this connection in the next chapter.) Latin American liberationists were set to resolve the antagonism between the Catholic faith and its presumed historicity and the rejection of its dogmatism by pragmatic thought.[30]

In the twentieth century, theology continued through periods of innovation and correction. The effort to harmonize the Christian faith with history, science, and modern society, and the outbreak of World War I, brought sustained criticism of Ritschl and Troeltsch's socio-historical methods. Against the progressive sense that divinity was found in the world, there was a growing countercurrent of neo-orthodoxy. Barth's early "theology of crisis" responded to a theology that had become anthropocentric, and reasserted an inscrutable God known through a transcendent revelation rather than through human initiative. His characteristic dialectic theology embraced paradox and mystery and provided no means for recognizing religious knowledge as unique among other forms of human knowing. In order to free God from the culture-bound assumptions, Barth, a political radical, intervened by presenting a wholly transcendent God beyond history, demanding justice and instantiating human freedom. In the wake of the Great War's vast devastation, neo-orthodoxy's negative stance toward a progressive view of history gained adherents seeking to absolve God of the consequence of human moral failure.[31]

America felt these critical theological currents. The brothers H. Richard Niebuhr and Reinhold Niebuhr argued that the liberal theological search to discern ultimate reality through a progressive view of history and science was hopelessly misguided. Holding to a neo-orthodox God who was wholly other, yet who demanded justice in the world, called for a pragmatic approach to workable social ethics. This Nieburhian theological mix of a transcendent God and political pragmatism split reality in two and forged Christian realism. At its core, Christian realism held to an irreconcilable antagonism between political expediency and privately held morality, and represented a reassertion of the distinction between divine transcendence and human history.

In *Christ and Culture* (1951), H. Richard Niebuhr noted that the attempt to identify Christian ethics with American culture was the religion of the "once-born," those at home in the world. It made no demands on its middle-class adherents in which a meek Christ "enters into their homes and all associations as the gracious presence which adds an aura of infinite meaning to all temporal tasks." A misguided genteel tradition, blind to actual ethical contradictions, attempted to fully reconcile the demands of Christian ethics with their morally bankrupt culture. The result was a validation of the middle-class way of life. Reinhold Niebuhr went further by asserting the impossibility of exercising private ethics in the political realm. While religion provided the "religious man with a reinforcement of his moral will and a restraint upon his will-to-power," it also resulted in "absolutising of the self," making it politically unworkable. For liberationists at mid-century, Christian realism with its private ethics and political pragmatism was impotent in confronting the standing arrangements of power.[32]

By the 1960s, theology had undergone multiple permutations and was fragmenting under new pressures. Political unrest, the increased recognition of the social constraints on the individual, and theories unmasking the ideological underpinnings of society raised questions for theology. The autonomous individual whose religion was a private self-authenticating experience was wounded but still alive, with his champions seeking to restore him to a respectable position against groupthink and mass society. To those seeking a radical reordering of society on communitarian ideals, the modern individual appeared increasingly white, male, and privileged, supported by an ideology in which religion played no small part. In its appeal to the individual and his milieu and in attempting to validate modern society, theology had failed to account for the perspective of the excluded.

While historicism, social science, and pragmatism laid a new theological foundation for building a politically responsive theology, it remained insufficient for confronting the unjust status quo. The liberal attempt to harmonize religious ethics with society by adopting historicism had reinforced, rather than challenged, middle-class exclusionary values. Neo-orthodoxy's repudiation of liberal theology and reasserting divine transcendence had only produced a politically distant God, inattentive to present suffering, for expediency. The definition and application of religious values, as a sign of moral or political virtue, continued to be subject to the whims of those in power. Theology, whether in its liberal or conservative flavors, Cone noted, remained uncritical toward the "American way of life." Failing to confront structural racism in the church and society, the whole continuum of American theology shared a common guilt in white supremacy.[33]

First Step

Liberation theologians inherited a salient set of ideas with which to address the contemporary crisis, and a new theological dynamism was possible. With new possibilities, liberationists deployed the ideas that trumped the sharp dualism of thought/action and sacred/profane and moved to free theology from any remainder of an ahistorical and extra-contextual reality. More concerned with who determined the theological presuppositions, they concluded that the first principle and chief error of modern theology was the preservation of the bourgeois individual in a divinely sanctioned hierarchy of power. Instead of accepting social inequality as a given, the founding principle of a new hermeneutic method became the categorical demand for liberation of the oppressed.

The first step in biblical interpretation was a moral judgment on the real conditions under which the oppressed lived. Social science, with its quantitative methods and theoretical reflection, convinced many religious radicals that they could no longer approach the text in a disinterested manner. Classic theology, Segundo noted, "does not assert its independence from the past," having appropriated the history of the world, philology, and cultures in its understanding of scripture. However, resisting available knowledge, "theology does implicitly or explicitly assert its independence from the sciences that deal with the present." Understanding the mechanisms of deep structural inequality, the "connection between the past and the present," Segundo asserted, provided the necessary real-world illumination for a liberating interpretation of scripture.[34]

That being the case, liberationists began not with scripture, as hermetically isolated, but with an encounter with the world and a socio-political commitment. The willingness to incorporate social science as the first step did not come from a naïve regard for science as ideologically neutral. Rather, it came from the conviction that the theologian always and already held a set of presuppositions about the world before encountering the biblical text. The theologian had no choice, Segundo asserted, but to approach the text "from a pretheological commitment to change and improve the world." Otherwise, he risked producing a theology that, in the name of doctrinal purity, dissolved into a false universal that rendered it politically mute. Rather than orthodoxy, "orthopraxis"—deeds and action in solidarity with the oppressed—confirmed the reality of the kingdom of God. Gutiérrez pragmatically argued, "only by doing the truth will our faith be 'verified.'" What was to be done in any specific situation was not deducible from the certainty of faith independent of context. Thus, the social sciences provided important knowledge about the world by which faith could act in a critical world-changing way. Every theological question, Segundo argued, "begins with the human situation . . . only on the basis of this contextual option does theology begin to have any meaning at all." Liberationists sought a remedy for the whole of human suffering even as they recognized it as provisional. The evaluative tools of social science replaced the abstraction of philosophy as the critical partner for theology.[35]

The second theological step was to respond to suffering in light of the working hypothesis of God's action for human liberation. Segundo argued that the interplay between the past and present reality, the world and the text, in an adaptation of Martin Heidegger's philosophical "hermeneutic circle," offered the means by which to continually reinterpret scriptures based on present needs. The hermeneutic circle rendered theology contingent rather than static and rendered the biblical text open and responsive. A dynamic theology required approaching the world with ideological suspicion and approaching the scripture with an exegetical suspicion. Otherwise, theology remained a reified conservative way of thinking that lacked the "here-and-now" criteria necessary for social change. Beginning with present reality freed theology from universalizing language to become "a serviceable tool for orthopraxis, for a social praxis that is liberative." Continual interplay between the world and reflection on the text became the critical means by which theology injected renewed values into society.[36]

As Latin American liberation theology applied a social scientific understanding of reality to biblical interpretation, the early stirrings of black liberationists displayed a less direct approach to a new theological method. Cone's understanding of theology as beginning with a social reality was not his initial position, as expressed in his 1970 book *A Black Theology of Liberation*. Unfamiliar with theological developments in Latin America, Cone added only black experience as an essential component of understanding the biblical text. He still understood the theological task as primarily one of rational study beginning with the text. Black experience, in addition to the classic categories of tradition, reason, and revelation, served as an interpretive lens. Cone assumed the classic theological stance of asserting the primacy of revelation as received knowledge rather than having the realities of the world shape one's theological formulations. Criticized by his peers for overdependence on white theological methods, Cone, in his subsequent engagement with the historical black resistance in *The Spirituals and the Blues* (1972), established a stronger basis in black history as providing both the context and the content of theology. Marxist theory, the sociology of knowledge, and race analysis increasingly facilitated identification of the connection between the experience of black people and the biblical text.[37]

By 1975, in *God of the Oppressed*, Cone expressed that theology "must emerge consciously from an investigation of the socioreligious experience of black people" as a starting point. He observed how historically the theologically untrained began their understanding of God through their experience of oppression, turning to the biblical text for the motifs that overturned white theology and affirmed their life. He argued that if theologians had read the biblical text through the eyes of the black slaves, they would have found a different notion of God's purpose in history: "truth in this sense is black truth." Since the Reformation, white theologians presuming to know God's will for oppressed people "were ethically wrong because they were wrong theologically." Their theological error was a method that attempted to derive ethics abstracted from the world. This idea was echoed among feminists and expressed by Ruether as "Our criterion for what is truthful is, finally, what is most ethically redemptive." Similar to Dewey in his charge against philosophy, Cone called on theology to drop its preoccupation with speculation, which failed to address current suffering. Liberationists speaking across multiple groups and historical experiences asserted theological truth as having no independent validity outside the experience of the oppressed. They expressed a deep suspicion of the possibility or desirability of universal and neutral theological language.[38]

In the wake of the new black theology, *Prophesy Deliverance!* (1982) by the philosopher Cornel West identified American pragmatism as a major component of black prophetic tradition, rejecting the search for certainty and unmovable foundations. True knowledge for slaves, as Cone argued, was the result of testing and evaluating the white master's claims rather than something based on preconceived foundational truths. Pragmatism had broken the "Cartesian individualism" of private religion for a broader "framework of intersubjective communal inquiry" in keeping with black history. While pragmatism had neglected class struggle and venerated scientific knowledge, it had also overthrown epistemology for ethics and "the desirable and realizable historical possibilities in the present." West identified the pragmatic historicism that ran through black religion and that was articulated in liberationist thought.[39]

Asserting that theology was never neutral or autonomous, liberationists concurred with the radical critics of religion. While the confidence in the positivist case against religious belief eroded and theology made greater concessions to the historical determination of religious truth, what remained was the most arduous critique against religion—it functioned as an ideological mechanism that maintained the status quo and was therefore detrimental to social change. Responding to this charge in innovative ways allowed liberationists to be both political radicals and theists. Religion as a Jamesian total reaction to life could not avoid the political. How liberationists asserted the ideological nature of religious thought and retained a critical and positive role for faith is the subject of the next chapter.

6

The Vitalism of Religion

DIVERSE THINKERS SINCE the eighteenth century had brought a charge against religion as detrimental to social progress, and yet by the mid-twentieth century the criticism seemed less essential to modernity than it initially appeared. Other social thinkers drew on religious ideas useful for multiple, and often radical, political and social projects. The appeal to religion was not merely a rhetorical tool of persuasion or a manifestation of cultural lag, but an inescapable reference. The secular/religious opposition set up by modernity appeared, at best, to be ambivalent. The instability of the secular/religious divide examined in this chapter was an opportunity for liberationists to assume a critical stance toward religion as ideology while retaining a positive utopian function for faith. Furthermore, a new understanding of the many ways individuals were inescapably embedded in society and the sociology of knowledge rendered the struggle for freedom as confronting a total system of domination, of which religion was only a part.[1]

The challenge to religion as ideology initiated by Jean-Jacques Rousseau, Ludwig Feuerbach, and Karl Marx set the course for subsequent social theorists to consider the possibilities and limits of religion as a revolutionary force. How did religion work for or against social change? In the search for the tools of human liberation, liberationists turned to the concept of ideology as a way to critique theology and its political implications. Joining other mid-century intellectuals for whom the concept of utopia, with its religious and political connotations, was once again a live idea, liberationists reasserted the world-changing and world-building power of religion. This recuperation of utopia served to overcome the secular/religious divide.

Religion as Ideology

Facing the loss of faith within radical movements compelled liberationists to interrogate the ideological role of religion as a conserving force. The critique was as old as modernity itself, beginning with the historical criticism questioning the basis of religious knowledge and moving on to the scrutiny of its social mechanism. In *A Discourse on Inequality* (1754) and *Emile* (1762), Rousseau, considered one of the founders of social theory, argued that the Christian religion had two detrimental effects. First, religion was part of the social contrivance that placed some men over others, keeping the latter in a condition of subjection. The source of inequality was neither nature nor God, but rather a human maneuver and a historical product by which some men enjoyed greater riches and comfort, and the deference of others. Social institutions and their hierarchies were the result of the vanity and manipulation of those in power. The clerical hierarchy held men in a state of terror, and the fear of losing one's soul destroyed the possibility of freedom. Rousseau saw dogmatic religion and its institutional structures as perpetuating inequality and dependence on others.

Second, Christianity had politically corrosive effects. In *The Social Contract* (1762), Rousseau presented Jesus' teaching "my kingdom is not of this world" as launching an indifference to the world, shattering the unity of the state and making impossible the civil religion necessary for social cohesion. Rejecting the idea of original sin as the source of social alienation, he regarded man's problem as situated in the power arrangements of society, requiring a political solution. For Rousseau, the primacy of the political, rather than the subjective or theological, transformed the problem of theodicy into politics. At a fundamental level, Rousseau perceived the Christian faith as a refusal to be absorbed into the body politic by denying the absolute claims of the state.[2]

Rousseau intended not to do away with religion but rather to reformulate it in a politically positive form. Despite its negative effects, some form of religion was necessary for political and psychic wholeness, providing comfort for the suffering and oppressed. He viewed with suspicion those attempting to free themselves from all religion, as they were devising the means to displace the authority ascribed only to God with their own. By relativizing human authority, religion served human freedom. Rousseau proposed a new natural religion of morality, a civil religion based on "inner sentiment," replacing both enlightened reason and divine revelation. How religion, Christian or otherwise, could escape ideology remained to be explained.[3]

Feuerbach went beyond the Enlightenment's historical criticism and continued with Rousseauian ideas by attending to the ways that religion constructed human consciousness and served as an ideological cover for inequality. In *The Essence of Christianity* (1841), Feuerbach located religion wholly within the human realm and redefined God as a projection of an alienated self. The aim was to demythologize God so that humanity could be fully in possession of its true and concrete self: "The Divine Being is the subjective human being in his absolute freedom and unlimitedness." The individualistic nature of Christianity, underwritten by the doctrine of immortality and the definition of God as a being-for-himself, produced an absolutized self against the real world. Feuerbach regarded theology as essentially anthropology—man's attempt to understand himself. Under the Hegelian dialectic of history, religion was man struggling to enter into freedom, and theological dogma became a form of bad faith—a false ideology. Religious language, rather than being meaningless, expressed the essence of Christianity: "man is the God of man." Denying any reality outside history, the only truly achievable goal was what man himself brought about.[4]

Marx viewed Feuerbach's religious man as an abstract product of a bourgeois society and considered his theory of religious projection to be part of a materially based social process. In Marx's search for an integral unity, he attempted to overcome the dualism by asserting the dynamic relationship between ideas and material conditions. Combining a scientific materialism with dynamic historical idealism offered the most useful and unified social theory. His study placed social theory at the service of material reality—the means of sustaining life. Historical materialism identified economic relations as the basis for society and the source of inequality. Capitalism, as a necessary historical stage in world development toward freedom, unleashed progressive forces that rationalized the socioeconomic order. However, it simultaneously contributed to new forms of enslavement through the reification of class division, subjecting individuals to inescapable economic and social forces. In Marx's dialectic, capitalism produced within itself the revolutionary seeds, the working classes, of its own collapse. The unequal material base of society, founded on private property, proliferated a superstructure of ideological institutions justifying inequality, of which religion was just one.[5]

Religion as ideology was, in Marx and Friedrich Engels' *The German Ideology* (1845), a process of mystification justifying social arrangements. Society, driven by material forces, produced a self-generating and self-justifying system of thought as ideology—a set of beliefs, attitudes, and assumptions about the world obscuring the very nature of material reality. The assumed givenness of the social world deflected any possible criticism of inequality and naturalized it. Marx regarded any form of ideology as a false consciousness—a distortion of reality in the social mind. The only way to unmask false consciousness was by exposing the material conditions through an empirical science. Marx's negative assessment of ideology became a basis for a more thorough critique of religion. Any accessible truth of Christianity was irrelevant. What mattered was how Christianity functioned in justifying and maintaining inequality.[6]

Religion as foundational in an unjust society left no possibility of its reform. Marx's essay "Critique of Hegel's Philosophy of Right" (1844) summed up Christianity as "Man makes religion." As the yearning of the oppressed masses, religion, "the opium of the people," had only one real function: to provide comfort against real suffering. In order to give up religion and its illusory happiness, people needed to be relieved of the real cause of suffering—material deprivation. The mechanism that gave rise to the particularity of religious ideology was still unexplained.[7]

Twentieth-century social theorists continue to grapple with the persistent nature of religious belief. Contrary to Feuerbach's and Marx's critique of religion as an illusory mental projection, French sociologist Emile Durkheim presumed that the sociology of religion rested on the idea that no human institution is viable under a false premise, but rather is evidence of the reality of religious experience. Durkheim attempted to examine religion based on its own terms. In *Elementary Forms of the Religious Life* (1912), he offered the modern definition of religion as a social phenomenon centered on the idea of the totem, a complex of beliefs and practices that segregate the world between that which is essentially sacred and that which is profane, "Profane things are those things to which such prohibitions apply and which must keep their distance from what is sacred." The sacred totem arose from the creative effervescence of the communal gathering, by which society constitutes itself out of human self-consciousness. Durkheim considered religion a real phenomenon, rather than an illusion, serving the needs of social integration and cohesion.[8]

Max Weber demonstrated both the creative and the legitimating role of religion in *The Protestant Ethic and the Spirit of Capitalism* (1904), in which religious ideas were the foundation for a capitalist economic order. According to Weber, Protestantism provided the operational ideas, such as the Calvinist concept of "calling" supporting the work ethic, for constructing the rational and disenchanted world necessary for capital accumulation. The sacred/profane elements Durkheim had identified and Weber's concept of operating ideas described the process of legitimation but did not explain why some ideas were more efficacious than others. Marxists' view of religion as ideology and its reevaluation as a social force by Durkheim and Weber were useful concepts for both critiquing and recovering the positive role of religion.[9]

Marxist thought provided Latin American liberationists with a significant framework for analyzing inequality and responding to the charges against religion. The goal of social justice based on a structural understanding of society, rather than on individual choice, appeared congruent with the prophetic tradition and served as an opening for Marxist–Christian dialogue throughout the twentieth century. Notwithstanding, Juan Luis Segundo viewed Marx as inconsistent in his application of the concept of ideology. It seemed as though Marx viewed religion "as *nothing but* an error . . . requiring suppression" and as something ultimately "destroyed" by science, while holding art, philosophy, music, and politics as destined to serve the social revolution. Segundo argued against regarding economic factors as the sole determining factor in the superstructure. Material relations did frame various structures including religion; nevertheless, they also enjoyed a real autonomy from the economic infrastructure. With respect to religion, he viewed Marx as offering "its abolition as a *precondition* for the revolution rather than an *effect* of the revolution." Along with Segundo and many radicals before him, liberationists contended *for* the positive role of religion to bring about a social revolution.[10]

Segundo saw in Weber's *The Protestant Ethic* a useful and effective model of "analogy" between a set of beliefs and economic attitudes, allowing a relative autonomy of the superstructure. The identification of analogies allowed religion an ideological role in social change. Ideologies were relatively good or bad, Segundo argued, providing a necessary "system of goals and means" facilitating human action. The theological task was "de-ideologizing" the mind by exposing the true or false nature of any ideology. Accordingly, neither a quantitative nor a pure Marxist sociology that denied the relative autonomy of the superstructure was sufficient for building a theology of social change.

Karl Mannheim's *Ideology and Utopia* (1929) served as a needed bridge between Marxism and a critical theology by defining a sociology of knowledge that combined Hegel's historical idealism with Marx's refusal to accept ideas as generated independently of the conditions of production. The social had primacy over the individual, and one's position in society provided the predetermined thinking that reflected the "collective unconscious" of the group. Mannheim differentiated the sociology of knowledge, with its total conception of ideology, from a Marxist theory of ideology. Marxist theory assumed individuals intentionally avoided the truth due to material self-interest. In the sociology of knowledge, ideology encompassed the *total* system of historically situated thought to which all were subject, not merely the politically motivated. Mannheim attempted to define a total theory of knowledge that recognized the social position of the individual while leaving room for the possibility of socially unattached intellectuals. The sociology of knowledge still did not explain the formation of new values but only existing ones.[11]

By 1944, in *Diagnosis of Our Time,* Mannheim had concluded that analysis alone did not provide a value system suitable for a post-war social order of democratic freedom beyond laissez-faire or totalitarianism. He proposed "planning for freedom," requiring cooperation between sociologists and theologians in recasting the "paradigm" of values and defining the spiritual experience necessary for social change. The partnership of theology and sociology could construct new values rather than merely providing an explanation of already existing norms.[12]

Deploying Mannheim's sociology of knowledge and in response to the Marxist claim that religion functioned as ideology in a pejorative sense, Segundo asserted that faith, as a belief in an "objectively absolute value," was the basis for all ideologies and inescapable in political thought. Faith, as cast by Segundo, was an irreducible element distinct from religion. In contrast, religion bound men to the world through law and ritual. While religion was scientifically verifiable, faith was outside the boundaries of empirical inquiry. This modern distinction between religion and faith allowed liberationists to critique religion while retaining its core vitalism. Yet faith, Segundo asserted, was bound to a necessary ideology in order to find expression. Faith did not tell one what to do in a particular situation; it simply functioned as the grounds for making a choice, providing "freedom for history" with ideology filling the gap, "an empty space" between faith and history. Faith required an always "partial and provisional" ideological form in order to be active in the world. Bringing a charge against the antipathetic ideology embedded in modern theology, liberationists acknowledged that this did not necessarily mean that a scientifically informed ideology had no role to play—"*political impartiality*" was impossible. The theological problem was grounding political ethics in a set of abstract absolutes and claiming their neutrality rather than addressing an ever-changing historical situation. The setting aside of the positive role of faith, as an irreducible remainder, allowed the critique of ideologically bound religion.[13]

Ideological analysis, Gustavo Gutiérrez argued, acted as a critical reflection that safeguarded against considering as permanent elements in the nature of reality what were only contingent. He saw an all-pervasive dogmatism masking reality running through politics, science, and religion. In Latin America he viewed the denial of a link between a privatized religion and the political order as evidence of a Church beholden to dominant groups. Theology as an ever-changing reflection on a dynamic reality played the reverse role of ideologies that justified a given social order. Thus, a critical theology worked against the establishment of cultural idols, namely power exerted through false ideologies.[14]

The long resistance to Marxist thought in the United States shaped the initial expression of black theology. James Cone's earliest work did not engage in sustained Marx-inspired analysis but was wholly interested in challenging the ideology of whiteness. His race analysis assumed the foundational soundness of U.S. political economy, which lacked only the inclusion of black people. In *God of the Oppressed*, Cone formulated a theory of white power through the sociology of knowledge that viewed consciousness as a social product of "reciprocity between ideas and social reality." Drawing from Feuerbach, Marx, and Mannheim, and following the example of theologian H. Richard Niebuhr, he viewed all ideology negatively as "deformed thought," a function of the "subjective interest of an individual or group." Cone differentiated between the "social determination" of thought and ideology. Theologians needed to recognize the relative nature of apprehending God's self-disclosure, or revelation, in culture and the "social *a priori*" of all thought. Racist ideology distorted the experience of an authentic faith of both blacks and whites.[15]

Niebuhr's work earlier in the century offered the possibility of linking social analysis and theology. *The Social Sources of Denominationalism* (1929) was a model for understanding the class-bound origins of Christian denominations in the United States, and the religious difference between the churches of the disinherited blacks and poor and the churches of the middle class. Niebuhr argued that faith, a vital spiritual force, remained smothered by middle-class institutional trappings, producing a lukewarm religiosity. Christianity was as much a victim of capitalist acquisitiveness as of irreligious communism; each was a fundamentally secular ethos denying a transcendent source of values. The assertion by Niebuhr that middle-class religion emphasized individual (white) salvation joined a host of criticisms of late progressivism. In a series of books, and deploying George Herbert Mead's social theory, Niebuhr explored the limits and possibilities of the relationship between society, the self, and the Christian faith. Never reducing faith to social forces or values to mere preferences, Niebuhr showed the social conditions that shaped American Christianity and modeled the use of social analysis for both North American and Latin American theologians later in the century.[16]

Following Niebuhr's analysis of the conflict between faith and culture, Cone noted the obvious dialectic of thought and experience in white theology. Unable to break with the slave/master stance, he contended that contemporary theology, such as that of the conservative Billy Graham or the liberal Paul Tillich, was an ideological distortion of the gospel, making liberation of oppressed people a peripheral theme and a trope for white liberation. While religious liberals had relativized faith in regard to history, they never did proceed to the "problem of the color line." The eliding of race was the "demonic" legacy of the Enlightenment, denying the humanity of oppressed people and justifying their enslavement. Cone charged that despite the work of Martin Luther King that tied love to social justice, white theologians continued with the usual abstract arguments about the love of God. Frederick Herzog concurred with Cone. Having experienced the compromising of theology by German National Socialism, Herzog asserted that American theology had taken "immediate flights into the ultimate," evading the reality of the social and bodily suffering of black people. The eliding of race was symptomatic of a deeply rooted ideology of whiteness that distorted theological thought.[17]

The concept of ideology recognized the detrimental effects on the thinking of not just the middle classes but also of oppressed people. In 1939, the black sociologist W.T. Fontaine observed that while a new generation of black scholars questioned the "democratic–liberal–scientific" worldview, the "American Negro is a supreme example of a *situationally determined* knowledge," allowing him to embrace an ideal of American democratic utopia against the reality of his true situation. Cone concurred that black people in America fell victim to racist ideology, forgetting that God was for them and resigning themselves to oppression. Ideology, he observed, "is telling the biblical story in light of the economic and social interest of a few" and denying its a priori social narrative form. Under the contention that "biblical thinking is liberated thought" and history manifested God's liberatory action, Cone asserted that a theology that did not emerge from the black struggle for freedom was ideology and "*ipso facto* invalid and thus heretical."[18]

Cone's assertion that God was for the oppressed and against slave masters was not a validation of the entirety of black culture, as he noted that black people were also prone to error and distortion. The errors of triumphalism and resignation in black religion required a reassertion of the difference between God's perspective and our own. Biblical stories, Christian tradition, and the living history of black people forced one to move out of one's own subjectivity, providing a check on distorted thinking. The problem was how to differentiate God's self-disclosure in black history and the historical context in which theology was articulated. What was God's action and what was merely contextual apprehension? The theologian's task was to decipher the dialectic in which God enters into the social context, appropriating the experiences of the oppressed as God's own. Ultimately, Cone conceded, we are bound to finite and socially situated knowledge. Never assured of escaping ideological distortion, "We are creatures of history, not divine beings. I cannot claim infinite knowledge." The theologian, as he told the story of God's action on behalf of black people, could "never assume he had spoken the last word."[19]

The nascent feminist theology presented a more radical notion of religious ideology, going beyond interpretation and context to question the biblical text itself. Women saw not only classism and racism, but also sexism as distorted thinking about God. While male liberationists continued to view the biblical text in a positive interpretive light, feminists began with a hermeneutic suspicion of the source, not just the context or method of its interpretation. They followed the path of Elizabeth Cady Stanton, the theorist of the nineteenth-century women's movement, who, as an evangelical reformer in abolition, equated women's position with that of slaves. Stanton, following Romantic currents, set the individual woman enclosed within the "solitude of the self" in opposition to an oppressive society. By 1886, a politically exasperated Stanton concluded that the failure to obtain equal rights was rooted in religion and the Bible, written by men who "never saw or spoke to God," and she set out to rewrite scriptures and a radical commentary in *The Woman's Bible* (1898). For Stanton, a plain and literal reading of the Bible, rather than the metaphorical one that was the standard of theology, supported divinely ordained women's subjugation. A long list of biblical arguments denied woman her individuality, intellectual capacities, and rights to her own body. Instead of a wholesale rejection of religion, Stanton called for a new rational religion providing equality between the sexes and the application of science for social change. Only a religion that encompassed science with the goal of women's emancipation was suitable for a new age of human flourishing. Stanton's thematic criticisms served as a precursor to a full-orbed feminist theology that questioned the biblical text as the product of the male's drive for domination.[20]

Religion and Sexism (1974), a collection of essays by emerging feminist Christian and Jewish theologians, examined images of women ranging from Old Testament portrayals to the theology of Barth and Tillich. In the preface, Rosemary Radford Ruether reiterates that despite material or psychological explanations of misogyny, "religion has been the ideological reflection of this sexual domination and subjugation" and the "cultural sanctioner." Through the language and images of a patriarchal God, the "Judeo-Christian tradition" provided divine sanction for sexism. In *New Woman, New Earth* (1975), Ruether, drawing from Engels' study *The Origin of the Family* (1884), charged that foundational sexist ideologies rooted in the "war against the mother" required that liberation include the massive restructuring of the socioeconomic relations between work and domestic life. She observed that "language is the prime reflection of the power of the ruling group to define reality in its own terms," and theological language was part of the superstructure of systematic male power in society, validating the male experience of the sacred as the only truly human one. "Sexist ideologies" naturalized female subordination and viewed men as the sole bearers of the *imago dei*, the image of God. Ruether went on to argue in her major work *Sexism and God-Talk* (1983) that feminist theology, which recognized sexism as foundational in all Western thought, made the "sociology of theological knowledge visible." Attentive to all sexist elements, women were to seek out the most "useful tradition" from scripture to post-Christian criticism to construct a truly liberating theology.[21]

Social theory had the raw material with which theologians could interrogate the ideological nature of religion and addressed inequality. In Latin America, where economic deprivation occurred in a situation of blatant class differences, Marx's analysis of class structure proved useful. Never providing a fully defined political program, liberationists attempted to justify a critical role for faith that went beyond the alleviation of social ills that circumvented structural change. For blacks and women, social theory explained an unyielding racism and sexism that failed to respond to legal remedies and moral suasion. Modern social theory gave an account of religious ideology and explained why the principle of equality before God and Christian reform not only failed to liberate but also reproduced oppression. Incorporating social theory, liberation theologians represented a cumulative shift from the previous existential focus on the individual that had dominated modern theology, to the ideological formation of the political and social order.

Between Social Theory and Theology

Liberationists' deployment of social theory followed wide social thought that reconfigured religious ideas in support of radical visions. In the twentieth century, social radicals, speaking on behalf of black people, women, workers, and the politically disenfranchised, did not engage in a wholesale rejection of religion but found within it the ideas correlating to socioeconomic liberation. Throughout the Americas, Marx-inspired social theory provided the language for an alternative articulation of Christianity that attempted to bridge the divide between fact and moral action. With historical materialism and a reevaluation of religion as a starting point, José Carlos Mariátegui, W.E.B. Du Bois, and Charlotte Perkins Gilman refused to surrender religion as a vital force for social change. These radical thinkers, usually treated in scholarship as secular, retained a distinct religious impulse. As theological innovators, they illuminated the connection between social conditions and what people believed about the divine. They reflected continuity in the attempt to bridge the gulf between religious-inspired action and political realities.

Waves of European immigrants and the emergence of urban workers' parties in the late nineteenth century brought Marxist ideas to Latin America. The twentieth century saw repeated attempts to adapt socialism to a heterogeneous culture, alternating between asserting a Latin American exceptionalism ruled by its own "Indo-American historical space–time" and making an attempt at a wholesale appropriation of modern development patterns into an essentially agrarian society. In the 1920s and 1930s Mariátegui, a Peruvian journalist and self-styled political philosopher, proposed a reformulated Marxism. A suitable Marxism required taking into account the history and present reality of Peru and its indigenous majority. As a *mestizo* of lower economic class, outside the elite intellectual circles, Mariátegui spent time in the Latin Quarter of Paris (1919–1923), coming under the influence of Henri Barbusse, a leading figure in the French Communist party. He returned radicalized with the conviction that socialism was the next step for Peru and convinced of his own heroic role.[22]

In his project to address the race- and class-based political and economic exclusion of the indigenous and *mestizo* populations, Mariátegui promoted the recognition of native cultural elements, land reform, and the adoption of modern industrial methods built on the legacy of Incaic communalism. He viewed the liberal doctrines of private property and abstracted individual liberty as standing against the communal heritage of Inca society. For Mariátegui, Latin America had not progressed in the anticipated Marxist pattern largely due to the continent's small bourgeoisie beholden to outside imperialist power and lacking a progressive national sensibility. A socialist revolution undertaken by indigenous peasants and bypassing a viable bourgeois not only encompassed Peru but also extended to colonialized people throughout the world.[23]

The young *indigenistas*, a literary and political movement in which Mariátegui participated, put aside the anti-religious liberalism of the prior generation of intellectuals. A new perspective on religion joined a political populism among an emerging alliance of lower and middle classes. Mariátegui's significant contribution to the *indigenista* movement attempted to combine the universal in historical materialism with the particular religious–mythical orientation of Latin America. Akin to Túpac Amaru in the eighteenth century, Mariátegui, a lifelong Catholic, appealed to an Inca cultic past to promote a social revolution. He held a critical view of organized religion with its corrupt priests and institutional abuses. The vanguard journal *Amauta* and the novels of his fellow *indigenistas* portrayed Catholic clergy as greedy, lustful, and hypocritical. The *indigenistas*' valuation of the Peruvian past and the application of sociological analysis led from a rejection of institutional religion to a positive assessment of the religious sensitivities of the Peruvian people as a source of political energy. The folk religion of the people was set against official Catholicism as useful for social change. In 1927, on the pages of *La Sierra*, a major *indigenista* journal, the Peruvian social scientist Emilio Romero articulated the hope for a politically viable religion by examining what he viewed as a syncretism of Catholicism and Inca cultic elements resulting in a "sensual mysticism." Romero predicted that the mysticism of the Peruvian highlands would give birth to a new religion of social justice. A reconstructed religion would transform Latin America.[24]

Mariátegui's most famous work, *Seven Interpretive Essays on Peruvian Reality* (1928), was a Romantic effort at a dialectic materialist explanation of Peru's history. His essay "The Religious Factor" drew from Waldo Frank's understanding of the role of Protestantism in America capitalism, James G. Frazer's *The Golden Bough* (1890), and the existentialist Spanish philosopher Miguel de Unamuno. Unamuno had insisted that the message of Christianity was historically distorted, and believed that only through heroic struggle did humanity gain self-awareness and ultimate salvation. From Unamuno's *The Agony of Christianity* (1925), Mariátegui drew a dialectic relationship between religion and politics, elevating politics to a spiritual plane. Mariátegui asserted, "The Inca people knew no separation between church and state"—the political and the religious represented a unified vision of the world and inseparable in their social ends. Leaving the anti-religious prejudice behind, he refused to reduce Marxism to a mere historical materialism. Seeking a scientific theory of society, Mariátegui did not believe that Marxism subsumed the religious impulse. For him "a revolution is always religious" and "communism was essentially religious" in that significant social change required the deepest commitment of the self. Mariátegui's ideas reflected the communal theocracy of the ancient Incas and the impossibility of separating religion and politics for subordinated people.[25]

Mariátegui, in turning to the Incas as an inspirational source, engaged in a major appropriation of the concept of myth. He combined a Marxist revolutionary drive with the religious–mythical elements essential for constructing the idea of a Latin American utopia. Drawing from the French social theorist Georges Sorel, who regarded the spiritual and moral aspects of Marxism as key in understanding what motivated people toward action, Mariátegui viewed myth as encompassing faith in and commitment to a liberatory vision that engendered heroic struggle. In his 1925 essay "Man and Myth," he offered the recuperation of myth as essential to social change. Under scientism and rationalism, "bourgeois civilization suffered from lack of myth, of faith, of hope." As a spiritual force, "myth moves man in history," vitalizing the will toward action. A strict materialist interpretation of social forces did not account for the thrust of revolutionary change. Neither reason nor science, providing humanity with a sense of its own power, gave meaning to existence. Bringing spirit within an immanent frame of history, "religious motives have been displaced from the heavens to the earth. They are not divine; they are human, social." He insisted that because every political act is dependent on faith and heroic willpower, only a matter of semantics separated the Marxist from the religious man.[26]

Mariátegui's contextual reading of Marx that regarded religion as having a generative power became a significant contribution to Latin American thought and a bridge by which liberationists connected a socialist revolution and the Christian faith. Gutiérrez regarded Mariátegui as a forerunner in the search for an "indigenous socialism" that applied Marxist principles without dogmatism to a "unique historical reality." The blending of the emancipatory impulse in Christianity and Marxism made possible the recuperation of utopia within Latin American theology as a necessary element in social change.[27]

In the United States Du Bois was part of the early formation of black sociology encountering a unique set of problems presented by the intertwined political and religious life of the black church. The sociologists who emerged in the late nineteenth century examined the black experience and the conflict between segregation and assimilation. They sought to resolve the tension between the individual and the community, in which the black church played a central role within a racist society. Speaking from the margins of intellectual life, black sociologists addressed the conditions of life in the era of urbanization and Jim Crow and sought out remedies for the low social status of black people. In the aftermath of chattel slavery, a strictly empirical approach was insufficient. Their sociological and moral analysis endeavored to reinforce the status of black people as full human beings. For black sociologists, social integration was a conflicted issue in which the black man had to choose between losing his particularity in exchange for inclusion or preserving it through exclusion. The role religion played in the process of black integration was inescapable.[28]

Du Bois' *The Philadelphia Negro* (1899), the first comprehensive sociological community study in America, marked the beginning of the golden age of black sociology. Trained by William James, Weber, and George Santayana, Du Bois in his writings reflects strains of Hegel's historical idealism with a concern for the actualization of freedom, the emergence of self-conscious manhood, and heroic vitalism. Combining James' emphasis on contingency and voluntary ethics with Hegel's idealism, applied to the particularities of black life, provided a way toward a politically committed social science. Eventually Du Bois plotted a logical path to Marx as both necessary for a critique of religion and the best path to realizing Christian values.[29]

In the *Varieties of Religious Experience* (1902), James had offered an empirical historical investigation of religious phenomena stripped of metaphysical formulation. As a philosopher and psychologist, he was concerned with the effects of belief on the individual's move toward self-expanding social connection. The social efficacy of the "will to believe," or faith, measured its positive force. James judged the fitness of any theology as resting on its congruence with the psychological needs of religious individuals. The historically contingent nature of religion, he argued, demonstrated that "The gods we stand by are the gods we need and can use, the gods whose demands on us are reinforcements of our demands on ourselves and on one another." His analysis of socially efficacious religious sentiment was concerned with exceptional individuals, saints, and religious geniuses, often standing outside religious institutions. In this way, James followed the existential theological currents of his day that situated the meaning of the religious experience in the choosing and willing individual.[30]

Du Bois, using James' view of the historical contingency of belief, went beyond the individual to examine the social nature of religion by documenting black religious life, first in *The Negro Church* (1903), in subsequent writing including *Souls of Black Folk* (1903) and *Darkwater: Voices from Within the Veil* (1920), and in numerous speeches. He focused on both the role of religion in providing a field of agency for political awakening and its role as a conservative force in maintaining the color line in the form of white Christianity. Du Bois' social analysis concluded, "a nation's religion is its life and as such white Christianity is a miserable failure," with scarcely any attempting to live by the democratic ethics of Jesus. American Christianity was "Jim Crowed from top to bottom." He charged that the white religious establishment had resisted every social reform, from labor to the women's movement, and served as the bulwark of slavery. As the historian Edward Blum has demonstrated, in the mind of Du Bois, American society reflected religious categories of clean and unclean, man and beast, sacred and profane, in which white people were regarded as closer to God. Racism reflecting Durkheim's categories of the sacred and profane emanating from religion constituted the whole of society. The search for the social and ideological roots of racism led Du Bois to engage in a scathing critique of American religion.[31]

Casting Du Bois as an irreligious thinker who died an agnostic obscures his deeply religious sensibilities, evident throughout his life and writings. In *W.E.B. Du Bois: American Prophet* (2007), Blum constructs an alternative profile of a complex religious and moral thinker who was not simply deploying religious language as a rhetorical strategy. Du Bois' rejection of the dominant expressions of religion did not indicate a rejection of the Christian faith; rather, a hope that true religion would prevail propelled his cool-headed social criticism. Like the writings of his critical predecessors David Walker and Frederick Douglass, *Souls* and *Darkwater* are replete with biblical language delivered in a prophetic mode. In *Souls,* Du Bois narrates a spiritual history of black people's attempt to come to self-consciousness of freedom, placing himself within the veil of social exclusion. The veil, an allusion to a biblical image that segregated the sacred from the profane and a recurring theme in Du Bois' work, not only was a separation within society but also placed black people behind the veil in the realm of the holy. While he criticized the black church for betraying its own people, he portrayed black people with their "sorrow songs," their charismatic religious leaders, and the emotional effervescence of their gatherings as spiritually attuned to the true nature of Christianity. He set the spiritual experience of black people against the false and immoral Christianity of white America. When distorted by lessons of passive submission and a justification for exploitation, the true religion of universal brotherhood produced a spiritual and psychological "wage of whiteness." The "double-consciousness" of black people went all the way down to two conflicting religious visions: cursing God and dying, or remaining with hope in an unfulfilled divine promise of freedom.[32]

Du Bois continued to tie the American racial struggle with global movements. In the introduction to the 1953 edition of *Souls*, he proposed that the global color line was the instrument for maintaining economic privilege over colonized people. His writings on Pan-Africanism portrayed Africa as the cradle of the human race, the crucible of suffering, and the place for the ultimate battle between good and evil. The black race's privileged perspective of "second sight" would usher in the salvation of the world's civilization. Du Bois' messianic Pan-African project attempted to redeem the entire history of the black race distorted by white philosophy and theology and tied the African American struggle to the world.[33]

When viewed from an alternative theological stream of black religious resistance, Du Bois's heterodoxy appears as a deeply engaged theological reflection. As the first race theorist and American sociologist of religion, Du Bois linked race and class with religious ideology. The transformation of the world required a combination of science and religion, in which religion acquired a this-world orientation, and science gained guiding moral principles. To the end of his life, Du Bois attempted to combine politically useful social science and the vitalism of faith. To do so, he repudiated the white religious establishment while valuing black religious experience and thus prepared a way for a black theology of liberation. Cone saw in Du Bois a "protest against the silence of [a white] God" in the face of black suffering. Cone, like Du Bois, asserted the epistemological privileged position of black people. As a perceptive thinker, Du Bois was able to critique religion without negating its vitalist role and thus contributed to the confluence of social theory and theology.[34]

Gilman, following her predecessors Lucretia Mott, Stanton, and Matilda Joslyn Gage in the nineteenth century, articulated her own remaking of religion. As a progressive-era feminist reformer and best known for her woman-centered fiction and social economics, she advocated a radical restructuring of all aspects of society that required a new religion based on maternal values. Gilman's *Women and Economics* (1898) attempted to make visible women's reproductive work in the creation of social capital, and this was fully envisioned in her utopian novel *Herland* (1915). Unlike Stanton with her liberal individualism, Gilman considered the actualization of personal freedom as available only when one realized one's self as part of a social whole. Rather than abolishing religion, she viewed society as an organic web of relations in a process of social evolution in which religion served as a cohesive element.

Less known is her work *His Religion and Hers* (1923), in which she draws from the sociologist Lester Ward's gynocentric theory of female superiority to celebrate maternal ethics as a life-giving religion for society. She wrote that religion as "a lever to move the world" gave men both the will to die for a spiritual ideal and the ideological power necessary for the subjugation of women. The distortion of Christianity into a "death-based" religion in which "its main appeal is that the believer may be 'saved' in the 'other life'" was inadequate for a new society. Having departed from the socially beneficial teachings of Jesus, who taught "thy kingdom come on earth" and spoke of "God in man," a birth-centered ethic offered a reformulation of Christianity. The new religion based in science rather than unfounded beliefs would be committed to improve the human race in the here and now. Gilman combined her radical social theory with a new and more fitting theology.[35]

Gilman signaled a forward movement toward a feminist theology by transforming the idea of the divine from a God above-and-beyond to a female-centered ethic of a God within, serving the needs of humanity on earth. Her nascent feminist theology continued in Ruether's project to rehabilitate maternal values and feminine images of the divine. Both Gilman and Ruether began with historical materialism in understanding women's social position. Both attempted to articulate a new ethic transforming women's status, an ethic in which religion was to play a role in the creation of a new society. Even as Gilman offered a vision of a feminist utopia in the novel *Herland*, Ruether articulated a similar communitarian socialism in her 1975 essay "New Woman and New Earth: Women, Ecology, and Social Revolution," as she asserted the practical nature of human solidarity that recognized mutual interdependence. Under the purview of a feminine life-giving ethic, Gilman's "sublime force" of religion would usher in a new social economy expressing compassionate connections. By joining social science and a reformulated religion, a new society was possible.[36]

The social thought of Mariátegui, Du Bois, and Gilman offered a scientific basis for a new society while continuing to view religion as an indispensable source of morals and cohesion. As socio-politically motivated thinkers advocating for subordinated people, these writers transgressed the divide that kept religion and science, facts and values apart. They attempted to overturn dominant religious thought for a more authentic articulation of religion. By modifying historical materialism, they allowed for the relative autonomy of religion in constituting values. They sought an actualization of human liberation by blending social theory and religious–mythical sensibilities into a possible utopia. Mariátegui, Du Bois, and Gilman represent a range of American social thinkers who followed a similar path and helped to bring about the recognition of the liberatory implications of religion in the twentieth century. Liberation theologians, in continuity with these predecessors, engaged in a scathing critique of dominant theological currents, embraced modern social theory, and asserted a vitalist political role for religion. Additionally, the post–World War II period saw new all-encompassing theories of culture and society that further explained the position of subordinated people.

A Total Theory of Culture

Post-war intellectuals, social theorists, and theologians sought to understand the threat to human freedom posed by the spread of totalitarianism and the individual caught in the net of mass society. The failure of enlightened reason to further human flourishing, and religion's inability to resist the rise of totalitarianism, raised questions for both social theory and theology. In an unexpected move among intellectuals, the broad recognition of modernity's failure to stand against despotism led toward recovering religion as a moral guide and inspiration. This was religion unmoored from ecclesial institutions, a defused and unspecific religious sensibility. As early as 1943, American philosopher Sidney Hook sensed a turn from science to religion, a "transcendental consolation," and characterized it as a "failure of nerve" on the part of intellectuals. By 1950, the *Partisan Review* was declaring a full-blown "change in convictions" regarding religion as "more creditable." The *Review* called on John Dewey, Hannah Arendt, Jacques Maritain, Paul Tillich, and others to evaluate the intellectual shift.[37]

The turn toward religion was evident in the German Institute for Social Research (ISR). Since 1920, ISR had been engaged in an attempt to rescue rational scientific thought from what it diagnosed as the irrationality of industrial society. In *The Dialectic of Enlightenment* (1944), Theodor W. Adorno and Max Horkheimer deployed a Freudian–Marxist critique of enlightened reason for its instrumentality. They viewed the Enlightenment as having produced an irrational ordering of the world evident in advanced capitalism, with its features of mass manipulation, bureaucratic control, and the barbarism of National Socialism. The deemed instruments of liberation and the myth of facts now enslaved enlightened men.

In facing the reified logic of the market and technological dominance, critical theorists attempted to define the mechanisms of social control in mass society. Interdisciplinary analysis synthesized Freudian psychoanalysis, Marxist theory, and historical idealism to critique what Weber identified as the "iron cage," the modern rationalization of social life. Critical theorists departed from an orthodox interpretation of moribund Marxism to move toward a broader and ever-changing total theory of culture to explain the failure of a revolution to emerge among the working class. Economics alone failed to adequately explain political behavior. The search for a total theory of culture encompassing all elements of human experience was an attempt to explain the whole of reality by transgressing disciplinary boundaries and challenging concepts considered to provide the "last word."[38]

Participants in the ISR (which was becoming known as the Frankfurt School), including Eric Fromm, Adorno, and Horkheimer, engaged in sustained dialogue with theology in their search for religion's emancipatory possibilities. The Frankfurt School represented a conscious effort at incorporating religion into social theory by interacting with prominent theologians, including the Catholic Johann Baptist Metz and the Protestants Jürgen Moltmann and Tillich. Frankfurt theorists viewed religion as intersecting with many levels of human experience, both systemic and subjective, and as providing necessary language of hope and despair, freedom and submission. Religion was not only a means for pacification and social integration but also the basis for authority, power, and critique of society. The Frankfurt School's attention to religion was not an anti-religious project but a means of deploying religion's critical element and reasserting subjective freedom. Religion offered a possible key to unlocking the total system of unfreedom that had subsumed the modern individual.[39]

In the 1930s, the theorists of the Frankfurt School crossed the Atlantic to live in exile and establish the New School for Social Research in New York City, revitalizing social philosophy in American sociology. A leading figure of the 1930s Frankfurt School exiles, the Hegel scholar Herbert Marcuse was by the 1960s the acclaimed father of the New Left and gained influence throughout the Americas. Marcuse's books *Eros and Civilization* (1955), *One-Dimensional Man* (1964), and *An Essay on Liberation* (1969) evaluated the culture and ideology of advanced industrial society as new forms of total social control. He combined his teacher Martin Heidegger's idea of Marxist revolutionary action with individual authenticity as a response to the "crisis of Marxism." The Cold War, the consumer capitalism of a complacent middle class, and Third World nationalist movements reflected an incomplete Marxist project. Marcuse stressed the unity of theory and practice in his central concern for human emancipation. Within a totalizing theory of society, he attempted to recapture the existential human experience subsumed by overpowering social forces.[40]

Marcuse's critique of both capitalist and communist industrial society began with attention to the systemic basis of oppression in the form of poverty, racism, and imperialism. He focused his criticism on the individual absorbed in a one-dimensional world that operated through voluntary compliance, turning workers into "sublimated slaves." The slavery in modern society was more pernicious because it enclosed both slave and master in an inescapable "corporate machine." Individuals were bound to the system of production and consumption by the creation of false needs. The promise of technology for a better world was now subsuming man. Religion, along with art, philosophy, and politics as part of mass culture, had taken on the "commodity form," losing its protest potential. The entire societal system eliminated any possible critical opposition, resulting in the individual's experiencing a closed one-dimensional world. In the modern search for the integration of the individual and society, rationality had produced new chains for human enslavement.[41]

Marcuse's hope for escaping the industrial vise required a "Great Refusal" in a heroic act of "*moral* rebellion against the blasphemous religion of this society" to bring about a total revolution. Marcuse assumed a modern individual with a drive for self-determination and freedom against an objectified world. Nothing short of an "absolute refusal" could challenge the totalizing system. In *One-Dimensional Man*, Marcuse's hopes for a total socialist revolution looked to a substratum of outcasts and outsiders, those who lived in the liminal spaces of society. The revolt of the subordinated people was by its very nature revolutionary because it opposed the system from without. The opposition of the dispossessed, the poor, the persecuted races seen in the global foment of unrest marked the "beginning of the end." While Marcuse attempted to locate the social revolt of oppressed groups, the Great Refusal against bourgeois society remained an exercise of the avant-garde individual struggle for freedom. The anticipated surge of radicalized masses of the subordinated failed to materialize, and in *An Essay on Liberation*, Marcuse set out to find the revolutionary subject in the global New Left. He saw revolutionary potential in Black Power, the worldwide student movement, and Third World struggles in weakening the grip of capitalism. Lacking a concrete proposal for change and aiming his argument toward fueling any latent unrest, critical theory for Marcuse remained a negative practice that "wants to remain loyal to those who, without hope, have given and give their lives for the Great Refusal."[42]

A New Utopia

The utopian quality of Marcuse's thought, in which emancipatory possibilities remained present in the substratum of society, carried the influence of the Marxist philosopher and utopian Ernst Bloch. Mentored by the sociologist Georg Simmel and tangentially associated with members of the ISR, Bloch, in his famous work *The Principle of Hope* (1959), attempted to recover the positive aspects of social thought and culture dismissed by ideological critique. He viewed religion, philosophy, and art as having the potential to produce the subjective conditions necessary for revolutionary change. Bloch began his investigation of revolutionary potential in the *Spirit of Utopia* (1918), exploring the subversive chiliasm of biblical religion; in 1921, he studied the Reformation radical Thomas Müntzer. Bloch's more nuanced view of ideology saw within it both techniques for domination and a utopian seed useful for social change. He argued that in the ideologies of the ruling classes, emancipatory potential existed within repressive elements. Marxist analysis was more than a mere unmasking of the oppressive elements; it recovered the residue of emancipatory hope buried within ideology. Viewing the past as containing live options and the present as unrealized potential, Bloch's process for social change required excavating latent possibilities in the present illuminated by the past. Hope, filling the gap between theory and praxis and expressed in utopia, acted as an opposition to existing reality. To realize their full potential, human beings needed to overcome the social–historical forces through a revolutionary struggle.[43]

Bloch rejected the view of religion as simple delusion and an instrument of mystification for bourgeois culture. Religion was useful for inspiring a social revolution. Dreams, visions, and myths were necessary expressions of human beings driven by hunger and longing for something more than the current situation—a utopia. By freeing the critical utopian kernel from the shell of ideology, Bloch saw in Christian eschatology, a branch of theology concerned with the final destiny of the world, an "anticipatory consciousness," a utopian core by which to build a philosophy of hope. At the heart of Christianity, as expressed in the life of Müntzer, was a not-yet-socialist utopia that had not acquired the scientific tools for its actualization. By appropriation of the religious impulse toward the future, Bloch infused Marxism with religious dynamism. In reinterpreting religious ideas within the domain of Marxism, he secularized the eschatological perspective of the Christian faith.[44]

As Bloch developed his theory of a necessary utopia encased within ideology, Mannheim in *Ideology and Utopia* (1929) moved to connect social groups with their particular interests to specific modes of thought. Particular segments of society expressed ideologies, trans-individual systems of ideas maintaining the status quo, or utopias that strove to change it. Both ideology and utopian thinking in some way distorted reality, and the difference lay in how they related to the world. Drawing from Bloch's work on Müntzer, Mannheim located the beginning of utopian mentality as arising from the oppressed strata of society longing to realize otherworldly visions contrary to the established order. The Peasant Wars represented the "spiritualization of politics" and the birth of modern politics as the lower strata recognized their social and political significance. Mannheim did not see the emergence of the peasant chiliastic mind as driven by rational ideas; rather, he saw it as emerging from myths vitalized by "ecstatic–orgiastic energies." In effect, Mannheim saw the utopianism expressed by oppressed classes as irrational. He viewed the middle classes as having an effective ideology combining visions of the sublime with existing reality in a rational "process of becoming" through a "liberal–humanitarian" ideal. The actualization of a bourgeois utopia was in the gradual historical process rather than in a sudden breakthrough into the world demanded by the subordinated.⁴⁵

Social theory's turn to a positive role for religious hope accompanied the theological search for a final reconciliation with the science of society. The view that liberatory elements remained within an oppressive society was expressed in the Christian–Marxist synthesis of the French Jesuit theologian Pierre Teilhard de Chardin. In *The Phenomenon of Man* (1955), censured by the Catholic Church and published posthumously, Teilhard espoused an ultimate unity of science and religion brought about by an evolutionary process and the religious poetic imagination. Gutiérrez saw in Teilhard the end of the faith/science conflict, an arrival at a "religion of the world" as " humankind had taken hold of the reins of evolution" and moved toward the realization of something qualitatively new. Teilhard proposed that unfinished man was in the process of becoming, and through a convergence of mental, biological, and spiritual energy was moving toward the "Omega Point," a unified and new human consciousness, a manifestation of the Cosmic Christ. The new fully socialized man, the Pauline new man, would emerge to transcend the isolation of the self. Teilhard's evolutionary theism envisioned a historical process moving toward a renewed humanity brought about by progressive and complex interactions at all levels and domains of human existence. Going beyond Marx, Teilhard asserted that the cultural and spiritual forces in history were progressing toward human solidarity and a way out of the exhausted faith/science conflict to recast Christian salvation in a holistic historical frame. Overcoming the faith/science divide, and a positive function for utopia, presented a fresh avenue for constructing a political theology.⁴⁶

The idea of utopia suffered from multiple repudiations and failed projects in which a charge of utopianism was the death knell to any social movement. Thomas More's *Utopia* (1516) portrayed the New World as a symbolic construct, a place of possible new beginnings; subsequently, the idea of utopia suffered the fortunes of failed political projects. Gutiérrez noted that More's *Utopia* reflected on the political implications of renaissance humanism in which the "common good prevails, where there is no private property, no money, or privileges"—the opposite of the situation in More's own country. Subsequently, as the "city of the future," *utopia* became synonymous with "illusion, lack of realism, and irrationality." Nevertheless, Gutiérrez contended that the recovery of utopia led to "authentic and scientific knowledge of reality and to a praxis that transforms what exists." Thus, utopia was regaining its "initial intention, its quality of being subversive to and a driving force in history." Reaching back to More, Gutiérrez redefined utopia as a "denunciation of the existing order" and the "annunciation of what is not yet," only achieved through praxis. Theology as praxis had a role in announcing a new revolutionary future.[47]

Following Bloch's idea of the necessity of a "luminous horizon," Gutiérrez reframed utopia not as an illusory wish but as a historical movement toward a future of greater harmony. While ideology masked reality by dogmatizing political action, faith, and science, utopia offered the historical dynamism for change and emerged in times of crisis when what was made possible by science was at odds with lived experience. Gutiérrez charged that equating utopia with an unrealizable ideal was a neutralizing ideological move by those in power. As the possibility of actualizing the kingdom of God, utopia was a necessary mobilizing element in history and became a live idea in those willing to throw themselves into the revolutionary struggle. He quotes the philosopher Eric Weil, "Revolutions erupt when man is discontent with his discontent." The end goal was "a new humanity in a new society of solidarity," which meant freedom from exploitation and injustice. Praxis, which remains self-critical and continually open to the future, allowed utopia to avoid becoming a "politico-religious messianism" and absolutizing any revolution.[48]

José Míguez Bonino also contended for the positive utopian character of faith, rejecting the dualist position that separated social facts from religious values. Modern theology impeded the building of the kingdom of God by reserving it for private and spiritualized significance. He asserted, "faith is not a different history but a dynamic, a motivation, . . . [an] eschatological horizon, a transforming invitation" rather than an otherworldly illusion. The kingdom of God, as an analogical image, did not deny history but served as a call to the realization of communal life. Faith had a "utopian function," having a place in history. Ultimately, the project of utopia was a human work, and faith the means by which to understand and seize the meaning of history as the product of human action. By redefining utopia and locating the kingdom of God within history, liberationists joined Bloch in secularizing Christian eschatology.[49]

Latin Americans explicitly articulated a redefinition of utopia that reclaimed its revolutionary function. Both Ruether and Cone were less explicit but also reflected the utopian impulse in American thought in their own theological poetics. While Ruether rejected any idea of a female-centered utopia that ran through some quarters of women's liberation, and attempted to distance herself from failed projects of the past, she insisted on the practical viability of a new society of human solidarity. Unmasking sexist ideologies, Ruether went on to construct a utopian vision of the communitarian restructuring of family life, work, and relations with the earth. The feminist theological task was not to return to origins, some pure moment in the past, but to construct a future "new humanity." Cone took up the path followed by Du Bois with his strong criticism of institutional religion while seeking to retain the significance of the black religious experience. Like Du Bois, Cone found in black spirituality a true and authentic core that was necessary for liberation. Black religion displayed what Tillich had identified as the "Protestant Principle," the critical and dynamic protest against the absolutist religious claims, which in America meant the racial pride of white religion. Cone, in his attack on white theology and his turn toward the emancipatory element in black religion, demonstrated Bloch's argument that under the ideological mask of racist domination and acquiescence there lay an efficacious drive toward utopia—true liberation.[50]

Modern social theory and theology shared a new recognition of the individual's embeddedness in ideological structures and the rediscovery of emancipatory possibilities. Humanistic and existential concern with a reified individual that elided the dynamics of inequality, which had occupied much of modern thought, lay exposed. A total social system of domination in which people of color, the poor, and women appeared particularly trapped came into view. As the Spanish theologian Alfredo Fierro noted in the twentieth century, universal man in search of salvation disappeared, for in science the "only thing that is real . . . are human groups, social classes, races, national or linguistic communities, historical generations, and historical epochs." Individual salvation gave way to social salvation.[51]

The recognition of religious hope as self-justifying and the secularization of Christian eschatology offered a positive world-changing role for religion. The philosophical rehabilitation of utopia, as the forward pull of future possibilities, and the recognition that within religion lay a key to human freedom supported the conviction that the theologian had a role in locating God's liberatory action. For liberationists, the recasting of religious hope as having liberatory potential and its placement within a socio-historical frame was both promising and insufficient in securing the liberation of oppressed people. A liberating theology had to go beyond the hope expressed in the "private religious dreams" of those in power. Rather its foundation was the experience of those who carried the weight of hope—the oppressed. Christian hope took on this-world significance by participating in the overturning of systems that denied human freedom. Impatient with waiting for the realization of hope in the structures of society, liberationists pressed for reflective action that seized the reins of history to bring about change rather than producing reams of unfruitful analysis Suspicious of the rationalization of hope that abandoned the oppressed to the contingencies of history, they went on to challenge all theologies that obscured the concrete meaning of hope for the wretched of the earth. The oppressed needed more than deferred hope and assurances that all would be well. In the next chapter, I will examine the social Christianity and critical post-war theologies that liberationists found useful and ultimately inadequate for challenging the social arrangements of power.[52]

PART III
Elaborations

7

A Salvific Social Order

ALONG WITH NEW philosophical and theoretical ideas migrating to theology, the twentieth century also brought practical changes as Catholic and Protestant laypeople, clergy, and activists sought a basis for applying Christian values to social ills. Throughout the American hemisphere, a socially centered Christianity took hold in a progressive-era response to the perils of modern life. The social ramifications of the ideas presented in Charles Darwin's *On the Origin of Species* (1859), the devastating effects of industrial capitalism, urbanization, and threatening unrest among new immigrants and workers brought into question the dominant operating values, an area that religion had claimed as its own. Washington Gladden's and Walter Rauschenbusch's social gospel in North America and Catholic Action and Jacques Maritain's new Christendom in Latin America proposed Christianizing society through institutional reform. By the mid-twentieth century, a languishing social Christianity was facing an inability to deal what appeared to be permanent social upheaval. Religious thinkers were once again coping with explaining how faith-based values claimed by so many made any difference in the workings of society. Having attached itself to liberalism, theology was coming under the same critique, as it appeared helpless in responding to unrest, revolutionary movements, and the pressure for inclusion by marginalized groups. The brewing theological crisis was of concern not only to religious thinkers but also to secular thinkers seeking political renewal.

In the aftermath of World War II, Hannah Arendt, the German American political thinker, participated in the effort to identify the means for renewing political life. Having received training from the theologian Rudolf Bultmann, who attempted to rescue the Christian faith from the loss of credibility through a radical demythologization of the Bible, Arendt grappled with what she regarded as a religious crisis. Like many other mid-century intellectuals, she sought to release vital faith from the bounds of religion to recover political hope. *The Human*

Condition (1958), resonating with a religious sensibility, expressed her indictment of Christianity for contributing to "world alienation" and retreat into subjectivity, thereby contributing to totalitarianism, imperialism, and anti-Semitism. Christianity, with its focus on a *vita contemplativa* and the future life, engendered a profound political indifference demeaning the *vita activa*, the necessary political action. For Arendt, Christian freedom amounted to a "freedom *from* politics, a freedom to be and remain outside the realms of secular society altogether." The human solidarity required for public life became impossible. Arendt's faith was in recapturing the necessary *amor mundi*—love of the world that would inspire political action. Nevertheless, the waning of institutional religion, which acted as a preserver of faith, threatened the survival of all vestiges of a politically necessary hope for the world. As an alternative, Arendt proposed the establishment of faith in creation rather than faith in God, and urged the recognition that care of the world expressed through political action had priority over care of the self.[1]

Subsequently, liberation theologians displayed the this-world consciousness Arendt called for and came to view the political sphere as an end in itself. Questioning the effectiveness of the reformist mode of social Christianity, liberationists argued that it continued to make a distinction between a spiritual realm and life in the world, and failed to account for the experience of God from the perspective of the oppressed. The idea of a promised heaven remained a backdoor escape from intransigent problems, abandoning oppressed people to the ravages of history. Bypassing a Christian gloss to reform projects, by the late 1960s it was possible to imagine a potentially salvific social order—one that had the power of divine–human reconciliation. This theological development, completing the break with otherworldly transcendence and the emphasis on the existential condition of the individual, gave the political realm increased urgency. In this and the next chapter, I argue that the social Christianity that dominated two-thirds of the century and the post-war political theologies did not cause or necessarily lead to liberation theology but nevertheless provided a useful set of ideas for building a theology of liberation and ultimately the secularization of religion—validating the religious essence of political action.[2]

The Autonomy of the Political

Latin American liberation theology's regard for the world as the site of salvation followed Catholicism's circuitous route in addressing the problems of modern society and confrontation with the liberal state. Catholic theologians of the late nineteenth century, as they brushed against Protestant and liberal ideas, arrived at new formulations for political engagement. By the mid-twentieth century, Catholic Action, a practical strategy for political influence, and Maritain's new

Christendom were centerpieces of Latin American reform activism and Christian Democratic parties.

Liberationists' conflict with Catholic social Christianity begins in nineteenth-century Europe, where issues confronted by the working classes became a problem not of charity but of justice. In *The Question of the Worker and Christendom* (1864), German nobleman and Catholic bishop of Mainz, Wilhelm Emmanuel von Ketteler, eschewing socialism, questioned liberalism's claim to absolute rights in property and the wage system that reduced workers to living on bare necessities. His solution depended on the elite classes becoming aware of their moral responsibility in aiding the restoration of craft guilds. His vision was not democratic; rather, it was for a return to the corporate social order of the medieval world. Ketteler's organic and paternalistic view of society became a foundation for Catholic social doctrine. At the end of his life, Ketteler had moved from taking a strong corporatist position, which viewed the alleviation of social ills as dependent on the moral response of individuals, to supporting limited liberal state reform. By the late nineteenth century, caught between morally inspired action and a looming socialist revolution, Catholic social thought increasingly displayed reformist tendencies, culminating in Pope Leo XIII's 1891 encyclical *Rerum Novarum*.[3]

Rerum Novarum was the first of several papal encyclicals leading to Vatican II that sought to apply Catholic teaching to massive wealth disparity, exploitation of workers, and the rights of the poor. The encyclical outlined the ordering of society based on two separate spheres of influence: the Church oversaw the spiritual and the state the temporal. Assuming unchangeable social inequality, it left many questions unanswered regarding labor unions and the limits of state intervention. Different interpretations of *Rerum Novarum* increasingly divided Catholics. Some attempted to reestablish a long-gone corporatist hierarchical society, some sought amelioration of conditions based in individual initiative, while still others sought the actualization of Christian democracy through liberal reform.[4]

By the early twentieth century, the Church was facing a modernist crisis challenging orthodoxy. The 1907 encyclical *Pascendi Dominici Gregis* by Pope Pius X declared that "modernist" elements in the Church threatened the "destruction of all religion," not just Catholicism. Pius X vehemently railed against an unspecific group of theologians whose flirtations with modernity threatened Catholic orthodoxy. The principal errors of theological modernism were "agnosticism" in approaching revealed truth, which ascribed the source of "religious sentiment" to the individual heart, and "historical criticism" of the Bible that assumed the "evolution of dogma." The modernist controversy hindered theological reformers who sought to break with the rigidity of Neo-Scholasticism and allow for meaningful engagement with society, deferring for decades the recasting of the Catholic faith in politically potent terms.⁵

Pius X's alarm over the implications of theological innovation extended to clerical and laypeople's free interpretation of *Rerum Novarum* in dealing with the problems of labor. A key example was the French lay *Semaine sociale* movement, which threatened social hierarchies through broadly defined democratic strategies. Founded in 1904 by Marius Gonin, the *Semaine sociale* promoted the social teaching of *Rerum Novarum* and a Christian vision of economic life. *Semaine sociale,* convening once a year, brought together laypeople to reflect on the Catholic role in society. Their initial vision, cast by Henri Lorin, a lawyer who had contributed to the writing of *Rerum Novarum*, established two guides for Christianizing society: Catholic moral teaching and the facts offered by the new science of sociology. Lorin's 1908 declaration of the *Semaine sociale* mission stressed the dignity of the human person, fraternal justice and equality, and progress toward the common good. Human work was a dynamic practice of justice moving society toward the future reign of God. The religious and the social person, he asserted, lived on a single undifferentiated plane. His interpretation of *Rerum Novarum* looked to both the means of association and legislation in securing social justice through a progressive democratic effort. By 1907, falling under the suspicion of the ecclesiastical hierarchy, Lorin and *Semaines sociale* were accused of "pernicious egalitarianism" that extolled individual autonomy and owed more to Jean-Jacques Rousseau than the Bible, circumventing divinely instituted authority. The Magisterium regarded social and theological modernism as of the same cloth as liberal Protestant tendencies.⁶

Lorin's modernist foray reflected the thought of his mentor, the French philosopher Maurice Blondel. Contributing to *Semaine sociale* from 1910 to 1947, Blondel came to its defense over charges of social modernism. Lorin's emphasis on the dynamic importance of work demonstrated Blondel's philosophy of action. Blondel, as a committed Catholic, rethought the viability of the idea of God for the modern age, asserting that the truth of faith was evident through a strictly secular understanding of human expectation and desire. His most controversial work, *L'Action* (1893), bridged the gulf between transcendence and immanence that divided rationalist philosophy and Catholic theology without denying either Christian revelation or the rights of reason. He defined an "integral realism" that united the spiritual and material dimensions of life through a phenomenological study of action encompassing its mental, practical, and moral aspects. By *action*, Blondel meant what later philosophers called *existence*. Through his dialectical understanding of action as arising from the movement of the free human will and a desire to an end beyond itself, he found traces of the transcendent present within the immanent. Human persons actualized freedom through action and recognition of their interdependence with others. The desire to move beyond oneself invested action with authentic spiritual finality and defined the relationship with others, the world, and God.[7]

Blondel's attempt to define the natural and supernatural as concurrent in human action offered a foundation for Catholic social engagement. By locating transcendence within the immanence of action, he defined religious faith and its questions as arising from concrete historical and cultural experience. Social engagement gained significance in the search for the transcendent kingdom of God in the world. Latin American liberationists drew from Blondel's privileging of human action over dogma as spiritually significant. Gustavo Gutiérrez, exposed to the thought of Blondel in his European studies in the 1950s, came to regard him as a significant inspiration for recasting theology as reflection on action: He had "characterized the human state as 'transnatural.' Devoid of supernatural life, human beings are nevertheless oriented to it by necessity." Praxis rather than dogma was the means of locating transcendence in the world and thus was the appropriate focus of theology.[8]

Moral Influence: Jacques Maritain and the Rise of Catholic Action

A desire to respond to the modern world furthered the growth of lay lead Catholic Action, an authorized strategy to influence society and part of the mandate of Pope Pius XI's 1931 encyclical *Quadragesimo Anno*. Pius XI called for the reconstruction of a just economic order that placed limits on, but did not abolish, profit and private property, and encouraged lay involvement in politics. Pius XI called for rallying faithful Catholics not by forming autonomous political parties but by exerting moral influence under strict obedience to the Church. Catholic Action, as a new defense tool against the eroding effects of liberalism and the threat of communism, was to remain apolitical and not beholden to any political party. Nevertheless, the initiative was difficult to confine within the conservative purview of the Church.[9]

Catholic Action fomented multifarious and wide responses for improving social conditions. At the beginning of the century, Latin American nations remained under the neocolonialist pact between the United States and its bourgeois oligarchy. The advancement of liberalism, positivism, and secularization increased the autonomy of all functions of society from the Church and had unprecedented influence on the political–cultural elites. The Catholic Church reluctantly accepted church–state separation after a century of political wrangling and outbreaks of violence. Urbanization, industrialization, and the arrival of politically conscious European immigrants eroded the commitment to the Church. Concurrently, new means of communication stimulated the political participation of previously excluded segments of the indigenous population. The besieged Catholic Church faced the declining influence of conservatives, its traditional core of support. It also struggled to maintain its social, if not political, power and to restrain the rising anti-clerical sentiment presented by new radical groups of socialists and Marxists.

In comparison, the minority status of U.S. Catholics offers a history of Catholic Action distinct from that of Latin Americans. Struggling to assimilate, Catholics in the United States dealt with both anti-Catholic suspicion and anti-immigrant sentiment. For most of its history, North American Catholic social thought remained conservatively cautious, committed to private devotion and mutual aid through charitable and fraternal institutions. Some ventured beyond the Church's social sphere, participating in labor union activism. *Rerum Novarum* was key in encouraging cultural assimilation and prepared Catholics to take a more active part in addressing the wider society. The aftermath of World War I energized religious orders to address a variety of urban problems. Under the leadership of John Courtney Murray in the 1930s and 1940s, the laity was encouraged toward Catholic Action and interreligious cooperation. The post–World War II period marked by the public advocacy of Dorothy Day and the Catholic Worker Movement—a model of distributive economics, personalist philosophy, and pacifism—became a militant expression of Catholic social Christianity while remaining within the bounds of the Church's orthodoxy. In need of further examination as a forerunner to liberation theology, Day and the Catholic Worker movement displayed a radicalizing of religious thought and action. For most of the twentieth century, concerned U.S. Catholics, like their Latin American counterparts, remained engaged in a variety of social aid initiatives rather than systemic change.[10]

The 1930s and 1940s, the height of Catholic Action across the hemisphere, brought Vatican emissaries to Latin America to assist in launching local social programs. Some of this activity was firmly devoted to combating liberalism and Protestantism that threatened Catholic cultural dominance. Papal social encyclicals and the neo-Thomist philosophy of Maritain galvanized Catholic Action as a new strategy toward Christian democracy. In the first half of the twentieth century, Catholic Action inspired intellectuals such as the Peruvian Victor Raul Haya de la Torre, founder of the American Popular Revolutionary Alliance, the Argentine José Ingenieros, and the Mexican José Vasconcelos to cast Catholic social teaching into viable political movements as a bridge between rapid secularization and the tradition-bound Latin American church.[11]

Catholic Action in Latin America also inspired many independent groups among students, workers, and peasants. Young Catholics desiring to remain faithful to the Church were offended by the intransigence of conservatives, alienated by the Russian Revolution–inspired communist parties, and put off by the anti-clericalism of indigenous movements and found themselves without a satisfactory channel for political expression. Groups with varying political sensibilities coalesced in the Catholic university movement. The university movement converged with other intellectual currents that eschewed positivist utilitarianism and rejected North American imperialism for a humanist Latin Americanism. The Catholic student movement, viewing universities as essential centers for solving social problems, became an incubator for the leaders of reformist Christian Democratic parties that emerged in mid-century. It was among this group of young Catholics that the papal encyclicals calling for political engagement and the philosophy of the Catholic Frenchman Jacques Maritain had the greatest influence.[12]

Maritain, disillusioned with the Western intellectual malaise of the era and the pressing social crisis, sought to recast democracy in a Catholic vein. To faithful Catholics, he provided a means of moving beyond an organic hierarchical view of society. To liberals, he attempted to provide an alternative theistic foundation for liberty. *Integral Humanism: Temporal and Spiritual Problems of a New Christendom* (1936) presents his most influential ideas, which defined an integrated view of the human person, offered a new relationship between religion and culture, and replaced the hierarchical features of Catholic social teaching with democracy and pluralism.

Maritain spent part of the war and post-war years in the United States teaching and writing, having wide influence among American intellectuals including Mortimer Adler and Walter Lippmann, and forming a deeply sympathetic friendship with the radical community organizer Saul Alinsky. After a 1936 Latin American lecture tour and becoming a corresponding member of the Academia Brasileira de Letras, his greatest political influence was in Latin America, which both embraced and reviled his Catholic liberalism. In the post-war period he became a champion of human rights, and his philosophy of the human person was significant for global movements; Christian Democratic parties in Latin America, the United Nations' 1948 Universal Declaration of Human Rights, and the Second Vatican Council all bear Maritain's imprint. By the 1960s, the presidential election of Eduardo Frei in Chile and Rafael Caldera in Venezuela showed his deep influence in Latin America. Both men adopted Maritain's political philosophy.[13]

Maritain viewed the problem of modernity as arising from an autonomous reason cut off from its transcendent source. His personalism rejected the bourgeois individual, which he attributed to the severing of human nature into mind and body as reflected in the thought of Luther, Descartes, and Rousseau. The devastating "anthropocentric humanism" of the Enlightenment had made faith merely subjective, and modern man experienced a loss of belief in a common good. Politics, having abandoned the religious sources of its humanism, had provided an arid rationalization of democracy and borne fruit in the anti-humanism of totalitarianism. Emptied of the transcendent values of justice and love, democracy became the sovereign will of the people, enshrined in the apparatus of the unresponsive bourgeois state. The accompanying capitalist economic order, marred by "a sin [that] little by little inflicts temporal death on the social body," scorned the poor as instruments of production and regarded the rich as mere consumers. The rejection of the evangelical forward thrust in history distorted the liberal rights of man, the most positive fruit of the Enlightenment.[14]

Drawing from his understanding of the holism of medieval society and Thomas Aquinas' natural law theory, Maritain cast a vision for a Catholic communitarian democracy founded on a theocentric "true humanism." The natural and spiritual intentions of the human person were inseparable from the good of the community. With a divine destiny, the person displayed both the "wound of concupiscence" and the infusion of the love of God. Based in man's freedom and experience of grace, Maritain attempted to reconstruct a social democratic ideal, which recognizes the person as enmeshed in the inescapable realm of politics. The transformation of the world required a moral rationalization and a "Christian heroism," establishing just structures of fraternal love. The recognition of an "integral humanism" offered the possibility of a "New Christendom" as a "temporal common regime whose structures bear . . . the imprint of the Christian conceptions of life." A new integral humanism recognized both man's natural grandeur and his weakness as inhabited by God, providing the inspiration for a "work of sanctification of the temporal order." Asserting the embeddedness of the human person in a political sphere with its own significance, Maritain provided no specific means for achieving his social vision.[15]

Breaking with traditional Catholic thought in which temporal activity was valued for its instrumental role in the spiritual salvation of souls, Maritain sought to provide theological justification for the autonomy of the secular realm as an end in itself. He proposed the legitimate autonomy of the secular realm to meet its own ends by establishing human freedom and actualizing human knowledge. In the age of new Christendom, science, civil society, and philosophic reason would continue to enjoy their autonomy yet be reconciled to the animating vitality of religious faith. A sanctified temporal order of a Christian democracy would care for the laboring classes, preserve freedom from totalitarian aggression, and overcome the dualism that disassociated the spiritual from the secular. Christian ethics no longer represented a mystifying universe of words and formulas with no efficacious means of realization. The spiritual realm, as the domain of the Church, was to infuse the secular with the necessary moral vitality and thus "reconcile wisdom with science" and save society from barbarism and utilitarianism.[16]

Maritain rejected the utopia of an "absolute maximum of social and political perfection" and offered no specific political program. Expressing ambivalence toward the machinery of the modern state, Maritain viewed the primary duty of the state as enforcing social justice and establishing the common good. He continued to maintain the distinction between the spiritual and temporal spheres of life, even while considering those spheres now reconciled. The possibility of Maritain's political vision necessitated that Catholics represent an active majority, which accounts for his wide influence in Latin America; however, this was a group that, in an increasingly pluralistic society, could not assert a particular claim to justice and the common good or even agree among themselves how to construct it. Yet, by recognizing the legitimacy of the secular realm with its own ends, Maritain opened new avenues for political engagement by faithful Latin American Catholics in the mid-twentieth century. Worldly politics had its own justification independent of the Church.[17]

The World Come of Age

At mid-century, the tiny Protestant minority in Latin America struggled to leave the *evangélico* ghetto and find avenues for political participation. The Protestant challenge concerned not only social distress but also that of breaking down the Catholic cultural dominance and securing independence from Anglo-American influence. Protestants first arrived in Latin America during the colonial period as tradesmen and merchants, and participated in political dissent. The missionary movements of the global Great Awakening and a tide of immigration in the early twentieth century increased the number of Protestant adherents. The movement emphasized unmediated individual conversion, pietistic motivated social work, and education, bringing a wave of modernity converging with the anti-Catholicism of liberals. Protestants advocated freedom of conscience, religious liberty, and a Christian humanism standing against both the collectivism of communism and the individualism of capitalism. Protestantism presented itself as unassimilable with Catholic society, having the potential to disrupt the religious hegemony. Their proselytizing aimed at extracting people from what they regarded as a superstitious and tradition-bound society. This stance resulted in outbreaks of persecution of them as heretics. To the Catholic hierarchy, Protestantism, with its rejection of all sacramental structures, represented a "disturbing foreign body" capable of subverting the Church–civilization synthesis.

Pressures from within Protestant churches to remain separate from Catholic society, and pressure from without in the form of political exclusion, resulted in *petit bourgeois* pietism, an opposition to the world, and ghettoization. By the 1940s, young Protestants expressed a desire to emerge from their religious ghetto and participate in social and political life through the Student Christian Movement. Sequestered in their churches, Protestants lacked a theological raison d'être for political engagement and for overcoming the opposition between their faith and the surrounding society.[18]

In the post-war period, Dietrich Bonhoeffer provided Latin American Protestants a theological foundation for political engagement, making a significant ecumenical contribution to liberation theology throughout the Americas. Bonhoeffer, executed in a Nazi concentration camp, gained immense influence after the war as a martyr who had defied totalitarianism through political resistance. He was an outspoken critic of the silence of German Christians in the face of oppression and a leader in the dissenting Confessing Church movement. Bonhoeffer's early works *Sanctorum Communio* (1927) and *Act and Being* (1931) presented a theology of sociality that held to the interrelatedness of the person, community, and God. He articulated a Christian social philosophy that emphasized ethical encounters with the other as the boundary of the self.[19]

Bonhoeffer spent 1930–1931, with the Great Depression in full swing, as a Sloane scholar at New York's Union Theological Seminary and traveled to Cuba and Mexico during his time there. He studied under Reinhold Niebuhr and became a lifelong friend of another student, the African American political activist Albert Franklin Fisher. While in New York, he visited Fisher's Harlem church, the Abyssinian Baptist Church, which was then under the leadership of Adam Clayton Powell Sr., observing black life and recognizing the theological ramifications of the "Negro question." Powell was an expounder of the black social gospel (discussed in the following chapter) that emphasized black human dignity and the social justice teachings of Jesus.[20]

Bonhoeffer's brief time in the United States shaped his still-evolving theological ethics, leading to his later confronting and connecting American racism with anti-Semitic ideology. The theologian Reggie L. Williams offers an intellectual biography of Bonhoeffer's time in Harlem and how it shaped his theological outlook. While at Union he found an optimistic liberal theology sterilized by pragmatism for utilitarian ends. Disappointed by white churches that he saw as nothing more than comfortable social and charitable clubs, Fisher introduced him to Harlem intellectuals' critique of a white Christ and a different expression of American Christianity. Crossing the color line, Bonhoeffer immersed himself in the African American community and through soulful spirituals, Powell's prophetic sermons, and Harlem's literary culture he encountered a black Jesus who suffered with black people. Rather than an analytical and spiritualized theology of the comfortable, he found an embodied "ethic of resistance." Powell's church was an altogether new experience for the young Bonhoeffer, a world away from both the German-centric theology of his education and Union, and set the trajectory of his future theology and thinking about race. From his encounter with the black Jesus emerged a deeply empathetic theology that allowed him to later identify with the persecuted Jews under the Third Reich.[21]

As a contemporary of Arendt, Bonhoeffer was, like other intellectuals of the World War II generation, reevaluating Christianity's ability to respond to the modern crisis of war-torn Europe. In the posthumously published *Letters and Papers from Prison* (1945), he also called for a "this-worldliness" in which one "[lives] fully in the midst of life's tasks, questions, successes and failures, experiences, and perplexities—then one takes seriously no longer one's own suffering but rather the suffering of God in the world." This was a move away from private religion to sociability and practical action. In the post-war period, Bonhoeffer's thought had worldwide influence as the center of theology moved from transcendence and subjectivity to the world. His ideas contributed to cutting the *cordon sanitaire* between theology and political philosophy.[22]

Called the apostle of secular Christianity, Bonhoeffer gained a broad audience through *Letters*, a series of reflections written to friends and relatives in the urgency of the great evil of Nazi Germany. He proposed that in the understanding of science, culture, and philosophy, the "world [had] come of age" and that this historical reality required a "religionless Christianity" in which one lived as though God did not exist. Bonhoeffer saw humanity as having outgrown the need for religion, a dogmatic system of beliefs and practices, as it realized the self-disclosure of God in history. Human reasoning had demonstrated the superficiality of reducing God to a deus ex machina as a ready answer to the imponderable questions of life. His declaration of the end of religion was a theological estimation, not a sociological observation, expressing the need to bring faith down to earth. Influenced by Williams James' definition of truth as made true by events, Bonhoeffer's *Ethics* (posthumously published in 1949) approached the world with an immediate moral judgment on reality and attempt to overcome a system of timeless ethical values. Surmising the will of God in the immediacy of the moment was not a claim of certainty, but rather called on human responsibility for the world.[23]

Bonhoeffer defined historically conditioned "religion" as the worship of a God above and remote from human suffering. Religion was a system of unworkable metaphysics, private sentiment, and privilege—a form of ideology in which to hide. In the development of human autonomy that displaced God, the Enlightenment had produced a Christianity that had retreated into the realm of the inner person, abandoning the suffering of the world. The retreat of faith from an effective politic was displayed in national Lutheranism, which was unable to respond against the rise of Nazism. The revaluing of the secular by Bonhoeffer was not a sweeping-aside of the failures of history with a progressive triumphalism; rather, the fits and starts of human experience were part of the bargain in gaining human autonomy. A "religionless" Christianity delivered from both Catholic institutionalism and Protestant biblicalism brought God's self-disclosure to a suffering world. The modern situation required a reassessment: Instead of God being evoked at the boundaries of human knowledge and suffering, God, and thus theology, had to be situated in the warp and woof of life.[24]

Christianity, Bonhoeffer proposed, needed to break with pietistic mysticism to become "worldly" in order to know the true aid of a suffering God. Human emancipation from religion allowed the recognition of the presence of a God who suffered *with* humanity. Humanity could then see "history from below, from the perspective of the outcast, the suspect, the maltreated, the powerless, the oppressed and reviled, in short, from the perspective of suffering." Freed from metaphysical tutelage, one recognized the presence of God liberated from the institutional bounds of religion. Bonhoeffer's prison reflections flowed with the efforts of others to find a theological basis for validating the world as a field of action. The unsystematic nature of Bonhoeffer's *Letters* allowed for multiple readings, and subsequently both liberal and conservative theologians claim him as their own.[25]

Bonhoeffer's political theology entered Latin America through the *Cuadernos Teológicos* (1954), a publication of Union Theological Seminary in Buenos Aires. In the 1950s, Bonhoeffer's *Letters*, promoted by the American missionary Richard Shaull, gained a wide audience among Protestant students. Shaull went to Colombia in 1942, and later to Brazil as a professor at the conservative Campinas Presbyterian Seminary as part of the mid-century effort by Protestant missionaries and Maryknoll priests to evangelize Latin America. The living conditions of the people shocked and radicalized many foreign missionaries. In Colombia and Brazil, Shaull found extreme poverty in urban shantytowns and an almost complete lack of response from Protestant groups, who saw the problem as one of individual salvation. His experience living among the people inspired in him a turn toward structural social change then offered only by Marxist groups.

Working with the Student Christian Movement, Shaull became concerned with moving Protestants out of their isolated world; he arranged dialogues between Protestant students, Marxists, and Catholics. The future liberation theologians Rubem Alves, José Miguez Bonino, and Julio de Santa Ana were among his young students. Throughout the 1950s, his influence grew in ecumenical circles. Working with the World Council of Churches (WCC), he contributed guidelines on the social responsibility of Christians in Latin America. The WCC endorsement of the ethics of a responsible society opposed both laissez-faire capitalism and communism and upheld the state's responsibility for a just distribution of wealth, guaranteeing individual freedom, and accountability to citizens. The WCC represented the international post-war consensus of liberal Christian thought.[26]

Shaull was also engaged in warning a North American audience of a coming crisis in Latin America. Initially in *O Cristianismo e a revolução social* (1953), Shaull addressed the challenge of Marxism posed to Christians in Brazil. Later, in *Encounter with Revolution* (1955), written to awaken a North American audience, he described the worldwide upheaval among the world's millions of "disinherited." He warned that crushing poverty, along with growing awareness of the possibilities of new technology showcased by the spectacle of American films, was fomenting restlessness among the world's poor. They were demanding not only bread but also power, making the privileged classes increasingly uncomfortable. Neither Marxism, with its absolutism, nor liberal democracy beholden to elites was adequate to address the revolutionary mood. The need was for a contextual theology that recognized that God was active in history as a basis for social action. In subsequent years, Shaull came to view Marxism as the only alternative left standing that could provide his increasingly radicalized students with political direction.[27]

In a 1966 speech titled "The Revolutionary Challenge to Church and Theology," offered at the Geneva conference of the WCC and published in *The Princeton Seminary Bulletin* and the Argentine journal *Cristianismo y Revolución*, Shaull argued for a theology that took the revolutionary situation on its own terms. The systemic nature of social, political, and economic oppression called for joining the revolutionary upheaval instead of trying to Christianize it. Only by casting aside "ahistorical" metaphysical thinking and reclaiming the "iconoclastic and transfiguring power" of Christianity against an otherwise impossible system of total domination could theology contribute to the global revolution. In the revolutionary thought of those who had undergone "radical historicizing" was "the possibility that the future is really open, that hope can be victorious over established power, and that meaning and fulfillment are possible in life lived in an intense revolutionary struggle." Without absolutes and illusory utopias, theology's principal task was to provide the resources for "transcendence and transgression," releasing the revolutionary into an open future.[28]

Drawing from Herbert Marcuse's *One-Dimensional Man*, Shaull viewed the totalizing order "as so rational in its rationality that those who oppose it can easily be portrayed as lacking in judgment and common sense." Overturning this "one-dimensional existence" required a new political strategy and an "ethic for revolution." The model for political action was the revolutionary "guerilla" engaged in small, but not insignificant, strategic assaults to bring change to the entire system. Recognizing the precariousness of social structures, in which "violence seems to be impossible" without bringing wide devastation, did not rule out the judicious use of violence at strategic points of the system. Shaull's concept of revolution appeared to move from an object of Christian concern in his early work, to a rhetorical device for imagining political and social engagement, to a final coalescing of theology with revolutionary aims. The ambiguity of his final language, whether analogous or actual, presented an erasure of the line between Christian engagement and revolution. It offered an opening for guerilla tactics and violence as a viable means for change. Shaull's thought represented a theological transition from the desire to provide a Christian influence in the midst of social upheaval to the embracing of a revolution on its own terms.[29]

Shaull's call for a theology of revolution reverberated throughout the theological world of the 1960s. Some castigated him for an irresponsible promotion of revolution; others, for not going far enough in providing concrete and historicized language. A contextualized theology, which set aside all a priori demands of the Christian faith for the needs of a revolution, still needed to be able to determine the ethical limits and effective features of any political project. He had failed to provide a viable ethic for revolution. After the Geneva conference, Shaull continued to articulate a theology of revolution in which the social and political context was the chief source of theological reflection.[30]

After 1966, Shaull, then a professor at Princeton Theological Seminary, participated in the New Left, devoting himself to the Civil Rights movement and working with Students for a Democratic Society, in which he saw the same revolutionary principles evident in Latin America. As a member of the editorial boards of the journals *Christianity and Crisis* and *Cristianismo y Sociedad*, he was a frequent contributor, advocating theological engagement with revolutionary change. Both journals served as a platform for the hemispheric Christian New Left, with frequent debates about the possibility of social democracy in Latin America and its connections to the Civil Rights movement. During his time at Princeton he directed the dissertation of Rubem Alves, a significant early contributor to Latin American liberation theology.[31]

The influence of Bonhoeffer's ideas and Shaull's leadership inspired the creation of the Protestant ISAL (Church and Society in Latin America) student movement in 1961. ISAL, with its roots in the earlier campus organizations formed to promote social engagement among an isolated Protestant community, served as an incubator for future liberationists. In 1976 the Uruguayan liberationist Julio de Santa Ana cited Bonhoeffer as exerting more influence than any other theologian on the development of Protestant liberation theology.

He offered key ideas for social action and overcoming of the church/world dualism, recognizing the process of secularization in Latin America and making the connection between religion and ideologies. Bonhoeffer had no easy answers. His participation in a conspiracy to assassinate Hitler and his death at the hands of the Nazis clarified the limits and messiness of Christian political commitment. Nevertheless, Bonhoeffer's life was an example of bold confrontation and proved instructive for addressing the Latin American situation.[32]

The choice for Latin American Protestants in the 1960s was to retain a socially ineffective faith or enter the suffering of the world in order to meet God there. *Letters* emphasized the coming of age of the secular world, and Protestants recognized that institutional dogmas were crumbling around them in a society demanding answers; their only option appeared to be joining the world through cultural, economic, and political action. However, Latin America was not the mature world that Bonhoeffer had described in Germany, requiring Latin Americans make a commitment to promote the continental march toward "a world come of age." In Latin America, the call for a religionless Christianity meant a rejection of the petit bourgeois pietism that had kept Protestants sequestered in their churches. The exit from a religious ghetto meant praxis in the world through a commitment to liberation of the oppressed. Recognizing the ideological elements in Protestantism that served an individualist capitalist ethos, they embraced ecumenism. These Protestants began to see like-minded Catholics as fellow sojourners in the political struggle. The church walls no longer imprisoned the Protestant faith.[33]

By the late 1960s with revolutionary currents running throughout the continent, it was clear to ISAL participants that political commitments expressed among intellectual circles fell short; they must join the people in their struggle for liberation. The nascent liberation theologians in ISAL developed ambivalence toward Shaull's theology of revolution. He had introduced them to the paradigm-shifting thought of Bonhoeffer and provided theological training for many of them. Shaull had acknowledged the contextual and ideological nature of all theology. Yet, they remained troubled by his continued measure of old-style transcendence that escaped the demands of history. His language of revolution appeared to be a rhetorical tool to impress North American radicals rather than having emerged from Latin American soil. It also relied heavily on the perspective of a revolutionary vanguard. Shaull's theology spoke for the people; the people did not speak for themselves. By the late 1960s, among his students, the language of liberation was replacing that of revolution. Nevertheless, Shaull's involvement in the creation of the ISAL, with its ecumenical and Marxist dialogue, and his theology of revolution were instrumental in the thought of a generation of liberation theologians.[34]

History Is One

Changes were happening among Catholics as they continued with the idea of a new Christendom as the primary guide for political engagement through the early 1960s. The post–World War II period saw the emergence of Christian Democrats, non-confessional ecumenical parties, drawing from a broad base of the middle classes seeking to apply religious values to the social–political situation. Christian Democrats eschewed both individualist capitalism and collectivism for a broad democratic communitarianism. They advocated social welfare, pluralism, democracy, and progressive reform. With roots in the Catholic Action movements of the 1930, Christian Democrats grew alongside new indigenous socialist and Marxist parties such as the Peruvian *Aprista* and Venezuelan *Acción Democrática*. The anti-clerical indigenous movements advocated a break from European- and U.S.-inspired economics and politics; they promoted a stance that reflected the popular *indigenismo* sentiment of Latin American society. Christian Democratic parties were part of a larger search for *tercerismo*, a third way between capitalism and socialism.[35]

Christian Democrats experienced a period of ascendancy in the 1950s, culminating with the Chilean 1964 election of the liberal reformer Eduardo Frei. Displaying Maritainian influence, Frei ran under the banner "revolution with liberty." Rafael Caldera, elected president of Venezuela in 1968, called for a nonviolent social revolution to realize the Christian concept of man and avoid a threatening violent and materialist revolution. In the 1960s, Christian Democratic parties became identified with the failing U.S.-sponsored Alliance for Progress and increasingly lost their Catholic distinctiveness through their broad ecumenism. Internal differences between the liberal and radical elements in the parties grew. The Cuban revolution, dependency theory, and the radicalization of university groups intensified ideological battles among Christian Democrats, making way for Marxist-inspired splinter groups such as Camilo Torres' United Front in Colombia and the Brazilian *Acao Popular*. The centrist position taken by Christian Democrats appeared increasingly unstable to the disaffected and either devolved into Marxist militancy or was disregarded as irrelevant in the face of continual societal distress.[36]

Students involved with Catholic Action and exposed to new European political theologies and revolutionary movements underwent radicalization and began calling for a deeper political commitment to address the structural roots of poverty. Students, along with laypeople and clergy, left their comfortable positions to join the struggles of the poor in the urban shantytowns and the countryside. Coming to terms with human misery, activists rejected the slow reform of progressive politics and turned to radical strategies. Among radicals, the

Maritainian theological assumption of the distinction between the spiritual and temporal spheres of life, each having its own proper ends, appeared untenable. The distressed situation and the failure of Christian Democrats to deliver meaningful reform presented a sea change demanding a new faith-centered ethic and shaped the increasingly militant theo-political thought of Gustavo Gutiérrez.[37]

Gutiérrez addressed a situation where the ideas about the relationship between religion and politics were under intense questioning. Gutiérrez argued that Maritain's Church/world distinction, fruitful in Europe, had no effect on the thoroughgoing identification of the Latin American Church with the interests of the bourgeois oligarchy. In *A Theology of Liberation*, Gutiérrez used a considerable amount of space to reject the stance of new Christendom that bifurcated the political and the spiritual. Claiming the autonomy of politics in Catholic progressivism was "contradicted by the strong bonds which consciously or unconsciously tied the Church to the existing social order." It helped maintain rather than challenge a misunderstood "common good." The world, having reached maturity, rendered all human activity including religion as political, and "human reason has become political reason ... an orientation to power." As the oppressed experienced a political awakening and attempted to overthrow their current world for something altogether new, the distinction between the secular and the sacred appeared to tie the hands of those committed to realizing God's justice on earth.[38]

For Gutiérrez, theological change necessitated admitting that the world, in asserting its secularity, had transformed human understanding of itself from a cosmological vision to a historical one. Oppressed humanity, gaining a political consciousness and freeing itself from the "tutelage of an alienating religion which tends to support the status quo," envisioned itself as an agent of history able to shape its own future. Latin America, participating in its own distinct and uneven process of secularization, was experiencing what appeared as a sudden rupture from tradition. This being the case, Gutiérrez viewed "worldliness" as a necessary understanding of the relationship between God and humanity.[39]

Along with Blondel's orientation of finding transcendence in the immanence of the present, Gutiérrez turned to the French theologian Henri de Lubac and the *nouvelle theologie* for the concept of a unified reality. In his controversial *Le Surnaturel* (1946), de Lubac argued that the malaise of Catholic theology lay in the distinction between natural and supernatural, or grace, that cut off the divine from the human. He argued the issue through a conceptual genealogy of the "supernatural" in Thomism. The supernatural, de Lubac maintained, was not the miraculous but the natural infused with desire for a divine destiny. The desire for God was the very essence of human nature and thus did not exist devoid of grace. Rather, the integral unity of nature and grace rendered the historical world part of divine destiny. The implications for liberation theology were evident, as the subordinated moving to actualize freedom displayed a desire that had a divine origin and promise of fulfillment. Adding Wolfhart Pannenberg's concept of universal history, which asserted the historicity of divine self-disclosure, Gutiérrez argued that no longer was it persuasive to speak of "two histories, one profane and one sacred, 'juxtaposed' or 'closely linked.'" Rather "history is one," and within it was the call to salvation, actualizing liberation. Gutiérrez argued against defining the world against the religious criteria of the sacred; rather, the profane, the temporal, defined religion and thus the meaning of salvation.[40]

Gutiérrez's thought was also moving with the secularizing theologies expressed by the resurgence of political theology in Europe. The primary articulators of the new political theology in the 1960s, the Lutheran Jürgen Moltmann and the Roman Catholic Johann Baptist Metz, broke the post-war theological silence on the meaning of the Holocaust and human suffering. Inattentive to the present, what continued as formal theology lacked any meaningful response to the Cold War threat of nuclear destruction, the reverberations of the Cuban and Third World revolutions, and the Civil Rights movement in the United States. The ongoing Christian–Marxist dialogue, grappling with Ernst Bloch's revitalization of hope through the recovery of eschatology, dialogue with Frankfurt School theorists, and Vatican II reinvigorated the intellectual environment. The new political theology identified the transcendental and existential orientation of modern theology that reified the individual as the chief culprit of its irrelevancy. The modern experience, judged as profoundly political, required a movement toward a de-privatized religion. Addressing the secular man required acknowledging the Kantian understanding of enlightenment as the public use of reason. Moltmann and Metz reasserted the political message of the Hebraic prophets and the public crucifixion of Jesus by locating the center of the Christian faith not in the private realm but in the public "profanum of the world." Theology could face the crumbling walls of private religion or lose all remaining relevancy.[41]

Both Moltmann and Metz attempted to acknowledge rather than overlook the world's suffering. Following Bloch's *Principle of Hope*, Moltmann provided a theological articulation in *Theology of Hope* (1964). He was concerned with how hope survived in the midst of real suffering and looked to the suffering, death, and resurrection of Jesus as the nexus of Christian hope. The Christian faith as revolutionary hope, and moving toward the future, transformed the present. Instead of the Greek transcendental definition of God's revelation as the "epiphany of the eternal present," Moltmann defined the self-disclosure of God as the promised future. The principle of hope, the future of possibilities, disclosed the "divine promise *against* suffering." Thus, Moltmann offered a change in the location of transcendence from above and beyond the world to the future: "to know God is to suffer God," and suffering in history anticipated future relief through hope. In *The Crucified God* (1972), Moltmann continued to present God as being in solidarity with human beings in their suffering. Instead of understanding God as impassible, unmoved by human anguish, Moltmann asserted God's response to and participation in human suffering.[42]

In *Theology of the World* (1968), Metz expressed the conviction that theology needed to deal with the memory of human suffering by affirming the secularization of the world. Influenced by his dialogue with the Frankfurt School to "enlighten the Enlightenment" rather than reject it, Metz offered a theology in which secularization was a freeing of humanity and "an originally Christian event." As a force in history, secularization had arisen not "against Christianity but through it." To Christianize an alienated world was to "bring it into its own" and affirm it by joining in its move toward the future of freedom. Modernity, having established the political as the realm in which to pursue freedom, resulted in a post-Enlightenment theology that sequestered the "religious consciousness" in "the intimate, the private, and the apolitical sphere." Consequently, charity situated in the realm of I–thou relations was devoid of political relevance. Instead, Metz argued that the new political theology as a corrective "emphasizes that Christian salvation is intrinsically concerned with the world, not in a natural-cosmological sense, but in socio-political sense," allowing faith to fulfill its transformative potential. Affirming secularization and releasing faith from private religion was a double strategy for addressing human suffering.[43]

While Gutiérrez affirmed secularization and de-privatization of religion, the political theologies of Metz and Moltmann still remained abstracted and removed from the experiences of Third World people. In *A Theology of Liberation*, Gutiérrez argued that the difficulty with Moltmann's redefinition of God's self-disclosure as hope in a promised future was that without being rooted in historical praxis, it elided the exploitive present. The liberatory function of hope "will be [realized] only if hope in the future seeks roots in the present." Placing God's self-disclosure in the temporal future meant it remained an illusion and an evasion of the present struggle. God's self-disclosure, thus transcendence, had to be situated in the present reality of oppressed people. The assumption of the political as the realm of human freedom was still a bourgeois dream and overlooked the reality of "dependency, injustice, and exploitation in which most of humanity finds itself." A new political theology needed to articulate the perspective of those at the bottom. The critical function given to a de-privatized religion did not provide sufficient historical praxis for the liberation of the oppressed; de-privatizing bourgeois religion in Latin America served only to embolden the political power of the status quo.[44]

As Latin America was taking responsibility for its own history, only a theology from below proved effective. For Gutiérrez the theological challenge was "not how we are to talk about God in a world come of age" that affirms secularity, a move theology had already made, "but how we are to tell people who are scarcely human that God is love." These are the "nonpersons, the humans who are not considered human by the dominant social order—the poor, the exploited classes, and the marginalized races, all the despised cultures" left out of the definition of freedom. The resources for the liberationist project were within the religious experience of subordinated people. While popular religion contained some oppressive elements of the dominant ideology, it also carried "subterranean streams" of protest and resistance. Gutiérrez asserted that liberation theology therefore began "with the hopes of the poor, expressed in their own words from within their own worlds." Without the poor as the subjects of history, a theology of hope remained an elite academic exercise and an abstraction.[45]

Latin American liberationists who joined Gutiérrez integrated the secular and the sacred, immanence and transcendence, theology and theory toward an understanding of salvation as a latent historical reality. The unity of history rendered the transformation of the world and building a just society through the political struggle a "salvific process."[46] Recognizing the universality of salvation and situating the social order within the "salvific horizon," one could no longer speak of a profane world. Gutiérrez asserted that the movement toward "the historical political liberating event *is* the growth of the Kingdom and *is* a salvific event." Declaring "history is one," making no distinction between the sacred and the profane, and viewing human liberation as the "historical realization of the Kingdom," he left an unresolved remainder by adding, "it is not *the* coming of the Kingdom." The fissure allowed by Gutiérrez between temporal progress and ultimate salvation remained a distinction without a meaningful difference. While he attempted to maintain an ultimate difference for salvation not encompassed by the political and social order, his failure to articulate the content of that difference renders it invisible and without effect in his theology. This theological strategy gave a new urgency to political projects seen as the coming of the kingdom of God. Gutiérrez recognized the danger of "any absolutizing of revolution," yet without offering a political criterion beyond the goal to liberate the oppressed, one could not determine the long-term efficacy of any project, giving to liberation theology a continual critical and pragmatic stance.[47]

The recognition by theologians of the autonomous and grace-filled nature of the political increased its significance as the medium for freedom. As they redefined politics and culture as independent of any transcendent authority, yet remaining within divine destiny, competition intensified between established religion and politics for the allegiance of expectant multitudes. Would religion or politics deliver the promised freedom to the huddled masses yearning to breathe free? The standing religion had shown its inability to provide better earthly prospects even when it had the best of intentions. In a world run through with revolution, liberationists offered a complete redefinition of the political that retained a religious vitalism within it. Latin American theological relocation of divine action within the sphere of politics resulted in a secularization of religion, ascribing a religious essence to political action, and paralleled the intellectual movements in North America.

8

Secularizing Religion

MODERNITY IN AMERICA was a project not only to free politics from religion, but also involved actualizing a religiously inspired vision within expanding liberalism. In the course of the nineteenth century, North American religious thought began a thoroughgoing reorientation toward this world expressed by reformers and reached a high point in the social gospel of the early twentieth century. Continued societal stress under aggressive capitalism and the rising demands of labor, women, and minorities, plus the thrashing devastation of two world wars, accelerated this-world thinking, generating multiple theological responses. The Cold War rhetoric of the 1950s brought into stark relief the disparity between the promises of liberal democracy and the reality of life among the unrepresented. By the mid-1960s, with a heightened awareness of their abstract distance from suffering people, theologians turned to secularity and a "theology of hope," seeking a new paradigm for political relevance. This chapter demonstrates how drawing from the social gospel and post-war political theologies, North American liberationists, like their Latin American counterparts, responded by moving to a full secularization of religion, giving politics new theological import.

In the post-war era, the Christian realism of Reinhold Niebuhr and the existential theology of German émigré Paul Tillich occupied the borderland between a waning social Christianity and the rising radical theologies of the 1960s. Both Niebuhr and Tillich renegotiated the meaning of social Christianity, providing an intellectual bridge for liberationists. At the invitation of Niebuhr, Tillich joined the faculty of Union Theological Seminary in 1933. Beyond his systematic work, Tillich, as a public theologian, reached a broad audience with *The Courage to Be* (1952), *Dynamics of Faith* (1956), and *Theology of Culture* (1959). As Doug Rossinow has demonstrated, Tillich's call for authenticity and courageous action helped ignite the youth rebellion of the 1960s. The need to address the existential situation by demanding a decision toward action, expressed by Tillich, captured the restless mood spreading in the American hemisphere. His concept of sin as an all-encompassing alienation rather than a merely personal moral failure was also a key idea. Offering a theology of culture, Tillich attempted to bridge the gap between the sacred and the secular and to address middle-class disquietude.[1]

Tillich reasserted that religion as a separate realm was a cultural construct, explaining, "religion is the substance of culture, culture is the form of religion," and identified religion as evidence of humanity's estrangement from itself. Tillich's view of religion as the expression of an all-encompassing "ultimate concern" meant there is "no place besides the divine, there is no possible atheism, there is no wall between the religious and the nonreligious. The holy embraces both itself and the secular." The dissolving of religion into the secular was not an embrace of secular*ism,* denying the possibility of self-transcendence; rather, it was an acknowledgment that humanity, in an act of faith, engaged in pursuit of the "unconditional, infinite, ultimate concern"—the holy.

With no ultimate reality standing over against a separate secular sphere, what appeared in its place was a "theonomy." Tillich defined a theonomy as "a culture in which the ultimate meaning of existence shines through all finite forms of thought and action; the culture is transparent, and its creations are vessels of a spiritual content." The "Protestant principle" demanded theonomy and expressed the conquest of religion by the "Spiritual Presence" in culture: "it is Protestant, because it protests against the tragic-demonic self-elevation of religion and liberates religion from itself for the other functions of the human spirit." Across time, space, and culture, the incognito "latent church," rather than the particularity of Protestantism, was the true medium for the iconoclasm bringing about a theonomy.[2]

At the nexus of the old and the new, Tillich stood at the edge of something novel, and his influence was evident in James Cone's, Mary Daly's and Rosemary Radford Ruether's early liberation theology. Tillich considered himself a "boundary man" standing between theory and practice, between the sacred and the profane, and between an impossible utopia and the possibility of politics. In a sense he was right—his existentialist theology of culture marked the borderland between the privatized religious sentiment that fueled social Christianity and a religious experience offered by liberation theology that was wholly situated within the political.[3]

The Social Gospel

The stagnant, yet never completely supplanted, social Christianity that Tillich addressed in the 1950s had a long gestation with multiple contributions and expressions. Beginning in the late nineteenth century, America faced new questions about the place of the beleaguered individual in industrial society. In the 1865 founding of the American Social Science Association, many religious thinkers assumed the compatibility of social sciences and their interest in Christianizing society. G. Stanley Hall, Charles A. Ellwood, and Richard Ely regarded their sociological work as harmonizing with enlightened Christianity. Ely's *Social Aspects of Christianity* (1889) sought to rouse those who sat in the pews and expressed concern for the increased alienation of the worker from the church, a phenomenon he viewed as understandable owing to the middle class, who spoke of love but did not, in effect, love the poor. He charged that Protestant preachers spoke of keeping the Sabbath while the worker toiled seven days a week. They preached against the errors of socialism and labor unrest while ignoring the corruption that robbed the worker of just wages and imposed high interest on the poor. "All false systems of religion exalt the love of God above the love due our fellow-men, and tell us that we may serve God by injuring our fellows." The Christian mission was "to bring to pass the kingdom of righteousness . . . and redeem all social relations," yet the search for the kingdom had been divided into two parts, theology and the science of society. Ely proposed that practical Christian love required intense study of social science, the "human science of happiness," as a partner to theology in order to fulfill the "golden rule." Ely was part of a progressive social gospel movement that included a wide spectrum of political and theological traditions motivated to reform society according to Christian ideals.[4]

From its earliest beginnings, religion in America has been a conflict-fraught movement toward secularization—actualizing a religious vision within society while building a modern nation based on scientific reason, tolerance, and liberty. From what Mark Noll calls the "Puritan canopy," a covenantal and comprehensive theological, social, and political system, which fell under the sway of republicanism to the abolition and moral reform movements of the nineteenth century, many sought to actualize a religious vision. White and black abolitionists caught up in the moral fervor of revivalism, such as William Lloyd Garrison, Lucretia Mott, and Maria W. Stewart, focused their attention on the negative moral influence of slavery on the individual, both slave and master. New social relations were to spring from awakened individual sympathy and virtue. By the end of the century, the American social gospel was emerging concurrently with a transatlantic movement and the crisis brought on by industrial society.[5]

Washington Gladden, traumatized by his first ministerial experience in urban Brooklyn, became the recognized father of the American social gospel. In 1880 he broke with the sympathetic disposition of evangelical religion centered on individual salvation that left social arrangements unchallenged. In *Social Salvation* (1902), a series of lectures given at Yale Divinity School, Gladden took on the "social question," which, for him, presumed the interdependent features of society. Gladden addressed a variety of urban problems—crime, immigration, the influx of "ne'er-do-wells," and the problems of labor, political corruption, and poverty—with a biblical vision of "the city that ought to be: the regenerated, purified, redeemed city; we must see it, and believe in it, and be ready to work and suffer to bring it down to earth." This vision required that the urban multitudes of immigrants, poor, and labor be "Christianized" through education of their moral conscience and character for social cooperation. Christianity, middle-class morality, civilization, and progress was of one cloth in Gladden's mind. These assumptions built the social gospel.[6]

With a view that held to God's immanence in history, Gladden embraced Horace Bushnell's idea of Christian nurture by extending it to society along with the New Theology expounded by Theodore T. Munger that recognized a new relationship with science. Darwinian science prompted a progressive view of the world, and the New Theology replaced an excessive concern for individual salvation with the recognition of communal life. Congruent with an organic view of society, Gladden and most social gospel adherents came to embrace some form of socialism, ranging in intensity from an attitude of sympathetic solidarity to scientific socialism. The social gospel spread under the conviction that the problems of industrial America required evolutionary transformation of institutions and the inculcation of American (Christian) values in the urban underclass rather than radical restructuring.[7]

Subsequently, Walter Rauschenbusch became the effective spokesman for the new social gospel movement. The genesis of his theology was the eleven-year pastoral encounter with the miserable conditions of impoverished congregants in his Hell's Kitchen church. Presiding over the funerals of children who died from hunger and disease, he realized that the piety of his youth was wholly inadequate to address the situation of his immigrant congregants. He concluded that politics and economics, rather than individual moral failure, were at the root of their suffering. A sabbatical in Germany reading the work of Karl Marx, Leo Tolstoy, and the German theologians began to shape his emerging social gospel. Reading Henry George's *Progress and Poverty* (1879), the first critical analysis of the economic underbelly of the gilded age, which called for a militant Christian protest, converted Rauschenbusch into the most influential and widely recognized proponent of social salvation.[8]

Rauschenbusch's *Christianity and the Social Crisis* (1907), dedicated to his Hell's Kitchen congregation, became an American classic. By drawing on the message of the Hebraic prophets and the moral teachings of Jesus, and by conflating America with biblical Israel, he argued that the chief sin of selfishness fostered the evils of capitalism. Capitalism, with its emphasis on private property and control, contributed to the major ills of society, including gross wealth inequality, poverty, indecent housing, child labor, illness, militarism, and war. The influence of capitalism had silenced the Christian pulpits against the excesses of the wealthy. In response, Rauschenbusch proposed that the Christian mission was establishing the reign of God on earth through a renewal of all human relationships by asserting, "Whoever uncouples the religious and the social life has not understood Jesus." Jesus' message of the kingdom established the principle of justice standing against the plague of individualism. As the religious correlative to evolutionary progress, the establishment of the kingdom of God was Rauschenbusch's primary theo-political vision, sidestepping the presumed division between religion and politics. For Rauschenbusch the kingdom of God, always coming yet never quite actualized, was to encompass the whole of society.[9]

Subsequently, in *A Theology for the Social Gospel* (1917), Rauschenbusch offered an expansive and comprehensive theology to reflect the change brought on by the renewal of the Christian conscience. No longer prophetic, he declared that the "social gospel has become orthodox," as was evident among evangelical churches. They had become a constructive force in American politics, he observed, by coming to understand the collective nature of sin and salvation His theology pointed to the solidaristic nature of Freidrich Schleiermacher's God-consciousness, resident in the individual, and the historical understanding of salvation of Albrecht Ritschl. Ritschl had emphasized the practical aspects of the faith over dogma, and the kingdom of God as the ideal good. Nevertheless, under an inadequate inherited theology, Rauschenbusch noted, "we are told that environment has no saving power," remaining silent on social salvation. Theology had failed to recognize sin as selfishness with its social consequences, and instead considered it an individual transaction with God. The social gospel represented the enlargement of Christian salvation and the realization that the individual was subject to "super-personal forces of evil" in social structures that bred selfishness and its consequences. Salvation included converting the super-personal forces bound by capitalism into a cooperative commonwealth. Thus, the individual experienced a conversion from selfishness to solidarity with others.[10]

Rauschenbusch viewed the establishment of the kingdom of God and reforming the social order as a "saving act." In Christianizing society, the role of the state was the promotion of the common good through active application of religious values to the economic and political system. Thus, "the greatest future awaits religion in the public life of humanity." The significant role of the state in securing social justice moved Samuel Zane Batten, a proponent of Christian democracy, to ask whether the state was the medium by which to seek the kingdom of God. The idea of the kingdom of God brought to earth had deep political implications and assumed the continuation of an already declining de facto Protestant establishment.[11]

Addressing a middle-class white audience on economic inequality, social gospel leaders failed to notice the ubiquity and structural nature of racism. In 1914, Rauschenbusch had expressed the belief that racism was largely a problem of the South lagging behind the nation, perhaps one reflected in a small minority. The "Christian way out," he admonished, was "to take our belated black brother by the hand and urge him along the road of steady and intelligent labor, of property rights, of family fidelity, of hope and self-confidence." Some, like Josiah Strong, believed that the white race was the superior race, destined by God to assert its influence. Others, failing to see the systemic nature of the "Negro problem," believed that evolving liberal progress and democracy would inevitably bring a remedy to the race issues. Gladden expressed sympathy for the Negro, but it was upon meeting W.E.B. Du Bois that he recognized the political nature of the problem. Reading *The Souls of Black Folk* (1903) changed the way Gladden saw the race problem in America. Instead of regarding it as a failure of individual ethics, represented by lynching by whites and lack of education for Negroes, he recognized the oppression of blacks as a class. The blindness to race, and unquestioned assumptions about the character of the poor, was the outgrowth of those who remained the subject of social justice—the white middle class. The social gospel vision relied on middle-class morality and initiative working against the sin of selfishness on behalf of the downtrodden. Expected to rely on the good graces of middle-class paternalism, the marginal lower classes still did not speak for themselves.[12]

As a theology the social gospel was supremely practical—it did not present a challenge to dogmatic categories. Biblical hermeneutics and concepts of God, the world, and humanity remained largely within the broad boundaries of classic Christian thought. The individual's religious experience and sense of moral obligation were its energizing forces. As a secularization of religion, the point was a more rigorous application of religious values to society and to break the social irrelevancy of the churches. Its theological contribution was in appropriating the sociological concept of social structures in the language of "social salvation" beginning the reformulation of the relationship between religion and politics.

The immediate influence of the social gospel was in providing a religious justification and inspiration to the progressive movement. Its leaders largely sought reform as pastors, labor, and community organizers rather than as theologians eschewing revolution for slow-paced reform toward social democracy. Fundamentally nationalistic and considering the American political structures to be fundamentally sound and God given, they saw the possibility of reasserting the waning influence of Protestantism in a pluralistic society. At various points, the belief in action for the betterment of society united unlikely allies such as the fundamentalist William Jennings Bryan and the socialist historian William D.P. Bliss. The social gospel's lack of political sophistication subsequently brought it scathing criticism. Looking back a century later, the theologian Gary Dorrien reflected a general negative response among social thinkers when he noted that the social gospel was "sentimental, moralistic, idealistic, and politically naïve. It preached the gospel of cultural optimism and the Jesus of middle-class idealism. . . . it was culturally chauvinistic, spoke the language of triumphal missionary religion, baptized the Anglo-Saxon ideology of Manifest Destiny, and rationalized American exceptionalism." Nevertheless, throughout the twentieth century, reformers continued to look to the social gospel as a model of progressive and religious achievement in need of revitalization.[13]

An Alternative Stream

The limited history of social gospel leaders as mostly white, middle-class, and male clergy who addressed the larger public through their pulpits, writing, and activism, hides the contributions of those on the margins. African Americans and women not only were participants but also contributed to the meaning of social Christianity. Long excluded from formal theological discourse, women and African Americans had practiced a theologically unrecognized form of social Christianity since the nation's founding. Engaged in experimental reading of the Bible and practical reform, they had been constructing a particular social understanding of God. When seen through the reflective action of women and African Americans, elements of liberation theology are evident in the social gospel.[14]

Women such as Wellesley professor Vida Scudder, one of the few women within the circle of male leaders, promoted socialism and critiqued the extreme individualism in American Christianity. Her book *Socialism and Character* (1912) proposed the consistency of socialism with Christian values. She wrote widely, including social gospel novels such as *A Listener in Babel*, featuring a beautiful but morally shallow heroine, locating a critical tension between social justice and social expectations. The novel offered women an opportunity to articulate a socially concerned theology through narrative—a feature of the future feminist theology. Scudder's Christian socialism carried the conviction that the tradition of noblesse oblige, with its philanthropy and reform, was "a sedative to the public conscience." Converting greedy capitalists to Christian charitable values was insufficient—the economic system needed complete restructuring to include the voices of the worker and the destitute. Scudder believed that the demands of workers themselves had done more to change industrial conditions than enlightened reformers. Scudder's gender-consciousness theology went beyond writing to engage in sustained reflective action through support of the settlement house movement and the Women's Trade Union League. Christian socialism provided the best opportunity for women to exercise their skills of cooperation and sense of solidarity, both of which were considered Christian and feminine values, in the public sphere.[15]

Jane Addams, among the best known of social gospel adherents, also contributed to theological change as the founder of the experimental Hull House. Addams secularized Christianity by escaping the confines of the church and ecclesial authority and moving to the community of Hull House. The social good and divine intent became equivalent as Addams, in refusing to uphold the secular/sacred duality, considered the practice of democracy and sympathetic cooperation to be within the realm of Christian ethics. She noted, "Jesus had no set of truths labeled religious . . . all truth is one and that appropriation of it is freedom." In association with John Dewey and in close collaboration with Graham Taylor, a theo-sociologist at Chicago Theological Seminary, Addams combined pragmatism, in which "action is the only medium man has for receiving and appropriating truth," with a religious commitment to human dignity and equality. In her religious pragmatism, she argued that Jesus and primitive Christians did not mark off truth from action; rather, action revealed the nature of truth—a life of love toward neighbor. Private and public spaces, theology and pragmatism, and thought and action coalesced in Addams' Hull House project.[16]

Addams and Scudder demonstrate how the social gospel validated women's theological reflection, which had long emerged from day-to-day life. Rather than formal theological discourse, reflective action provided women spiritual authority. Women's religious reflection, viewed as being bound to the care of bodies and maintenance of communal ties, already bore the marks of a God who was at hand. They followed the impulse of earlier women who, without full political or ecclesial participation, found the means for spiritual influence by applying themselves to social housekeeping. Embodying the privileging of practice and experience over dogmatic assertions, Scudder and Addams served as models for regarding the present world as the place in which to establish the kingdom of God. Within the social gospel movement, white women remained within the accepted parameters of their gender and exercised spiritual authority. Instead of a display of individual piety, the movement recognized women's social housekeeping as having theological import.

While many white women found a natural place at the center of the social gospel movement through their relationships and collaboration with men, African Americans' articulation of social Christianity did not fall near the center of the movement but rather appeared as a concurrent alternative stream. The end of Reconstruction and the 1890s brought the end to the home missions movement in the South that had provided education for social uplift, proved

African colonization a cruel hoax, and increased questioning and denial of the franchise. Laws supporting "separate but equal" and the resultant Jim Crow society obscured the ideal of racial equity. The white social gospel displayed a static view of the American social order, regarding it as fundamentally good and merely in need of reclaiming its Christian roots. For African American men and women who regarded their history as a political and theological exodus, the movement was a continuation of a dynamic historical process toward freedom and the means to create a black public stage on which to advocate that the Christian faith required racial justice. Through a black social gospel, they acted as subjects of change rather than merely the object of white sympathy and carried forward the political resistance residing in black religion.[17]

Reverdy C. Ransom exemplified the black social gospel. Born a free man in 1861 and raised in the conservative African Methodist Episcopal (AME) Church, Ransom became an urban minister and ultimately a bishop despite his radical politics. His early urban ministry placed him in contact with wide and deep despair brought on by poverty, low wages, and unsafe and squalid housing. In 1900, he founded the Institutional Church and Social Settlement in Chicago. Ransom, awakened to the need for social salvation, considered the debased condition of the black race the result of an unhealthy environment. Critical of churches, he charged that the sermons of black ministers offering individual hope of escape from the world failed to deal with the reality of African American life outside the church walls. His disillusionment with the black church dovetailed with his encounter with the social gospel of white promoters.[18]

In 1893, Ransom heard speeches by Gladden and other social gospel leaders including George Herron, the radical Christian socialist, and became a close friend of the sympathetic Jane Addams. Ransom, like his white counterparts, believed that America was a Christian nation founded on liberty, equality, and brotherhood, concepts he regarded as foundational in the teachings of Jesus. The treatment of blacks in America served as a test of white Christianity's veracity. Ransom embraced socialism as a systemic restructuring of the society and focused on bringing to light the racism in both industry and the labor movement. As editor of the *AME Review* between 1912 and 1924, he wrote on a variety of race-related issues, including lynching, unequal justice, discrimination, and disenfranchisement. He charged white Christians with hypocrisy on race matters as they acquiesced to segregation, economic exclusion, and violence. Becoming associated with W.E.B. Du Bois and the Niagara Movement, he opposed Booker T. Washington's ethos of accommodation, promoted racial pride, and joined Ida B. Wells' anti-lynching crusade. Through his writing, speaking, and activism, Ransom offered a contemporaneous critique of both the conservative African American church and the white social gospel.[19]

Ransom and his peers such as Adam Clayton Powell Sr., and many before them, looked to the spiritual giftedness of blacks, not whites, to revitalize American Christianity. Unwilling to overlook the machinations of racial power, Ransom viewed the elimination of racism as foundational for justice. Social salvation for blacks was not a matter of moral persuasion that appealed to white sympathy, or of self-help among blacks, but of power embodied in black people asserting their rights in the social, economic, and political structures of America. In a 1930 speech, Ransom carried forward the protest element in black religion that was later rearticulated by Malcolm X and James Cone, charging that "the white man yields nothing, even to his own poor laboring masses, through sympathy or love. He yields not to the persuasion of logic or the sanctity of religious creeds. He only yields or compromises in the face of aggressive, determined, uncompromising power." The black social gospel grounded its theological outlook not in a religious idealism but in the experience of black people in American society.[20]

Ransom's focus on power, rather than a sympathetic and thorough application of Christian values in society, was also the basis for Reinhold Niebuhr's critique of his fellow progressives in *Moral Man and Immoral Society* (1932). Niebuhr shared in the vision for social democracy but concluded that political power, rather than a more conscientious application of Christian values, could bring it about. He charged the progressivism of his age with an idealism that failed to recognize that "individualistic ethics" based on the teachings of Jesus was not a foundation for dealing with the realities of society. Niebuhr argued that groups were less moral than individuals, and that pride rather than selfishness was the nature of sin. The power that produced group cohesion was the same power that produced pride of group. Self-interest, magnified through the group, led to greed, racial injustice, and inequality. Thus, the most horrendous sins were social—based on pride of clan, family, community, or nation asserting its primacy. Groups derived their primacy partly from the possession of coercive power, "economic or martial," that is, the ability to force other groups to live by their terms. The problem of the Negro and labor was a lack of group solidarity. Lacking faith in voluntary cooperation, Niebuhr argued that the Negro was without hope if he waited for white people to offer a moral response to his plight. Regardless of benevolent feelings, unless coerced into equality whites were not inclined to yield.[21]

Niebuhr proposed that the only way to equalize power in society was by using the opposing political power of self-assertion, resistance, and coercion. By virtue of the overwhelmingly negative odds of success, violent resistance was futile for a group in the minority. The risk of unleashing revolutionary violence by subordinated groups and because "equality is a higher social goal than peace," it was the coercive power of the state, he asserted, that must break the self-interest of groups. Niebuhr established his interest in the social realm and an enduring conviction that coercion by the state, and by implication the possibility of violence, might at times be necessary in the political realm for the goal of justice.[22]

The implication of Niebuhr's theology was offering an inspiring moral vision, but one with no practical role for religion, assumed as a private individual affair, in breaking the grip of social problems. His theology of Christian realism posited that Jesus' love ethic had nothing to offer in the way of social efficacy and remained a possibility only in the private sphere of interpersonal relations. Niebuhr charged that love demanded more than justice, and moralists were making unrealistic sentimental demands on politics. Religious idealism "from a political perspective is quite impossible," he asserted. Expressing a neo-orthodox sensibility, he argued that God alone would bring the kingdom to fruition at the end of history. The function of the kingdom of God in the present was as a "principle of judgment" and hope against the uneasy conscience of man. Rejecting the social gospel's political quest for the kingdom of God, he concluded, "the full force of religious faith will never be available for the building of a just society, because its highest visions are those which proceed from the insights of a sensitive individual conscience." The secular/sacred and private/public split in the ethics of Christian realism required finding pragmatic solutions that "accepted a frank dualism in morals." Under Sidney Hook's critical eye, "Niebuhr's theology has a grand irrelevance to the specific patterns and problems of social life," and supported a "myth of a private and mysterious absolute." After the energy of the social gospel, the effect of Niebuhr's dualism in morals emptied mid-century Protestantism of its political vitality, and American religion entered a period of social retreat. This did not impede the post-war American penchant either for religious revivalism, in which individual salvation remained the center, or for equating piety with patriotism.[23]

The charges against the social gospel made by Niebuhr struck a chord because he was making a critique from within the political left. In subsequent decades, as Christian realism came to stand for the ideological consensus as a left/right collusion against communism, the social gospel became a term of derision among theologians and intellectuals. Unlike the white social gospel, which had lost its appeal among cultural elites, the black social gospel that took the dynamics of power seriously continued strong into the 1970s. It offered African Americans continued hope for change in the racist structures of society. It also remained alive among other radicals such as those within the labor movements led by the pacifist A.J. Muste, whose work began during the progressive era and continued to his death in 1967. Through a worker education program, Muste promoted a social gospel springing not from the middle classes but from the emerging class-consciousness of the workingman and woman. The timeliness of Muste's concern with raising the consciousness of the working class and organizing them to advocate for themselves made him a bridge from the social gospel to the development of liberation theology later in the century.[24]

Nevertheless, for liberationists, Niebuhr's Christian realism provided key ideas regarding the nature of power and the pride of group that constituted the American political landscape. In his clear assessment, Niebuhr had refused the use of Christian values as a smokescreen for the true nature of power. He provided a corrective to American liberal theology's confidence in human nature and benevolence. In *A Black Theology of Liberation,* Cone saw Niebuhr moving in the "direction of blackness" with a willingness to admit the necessity of meeting power with countervailing power. Nevertheless, Niebuhr's pragmatic theological ethics was enmeshed in the white American way of life in which race was largely tangential to larger social problems. Seen from Cone's perspective, Niebuhr was right—white theology built on group pride was not available to solve the social problem of racism in America.[25]

Both the social gospel and Christian realism had gendered implications for a revitalized feminist movement. Rosemary Radford Ruether saw in Niebuhr's arguments a reified dichotomy between the private religious values situated in the home and considered the domain of women, and the masculinist execution of public justice freed from those values. Thus, she observed, "morality is privatized, sentimentalized, and identified with the 'feminine' in a way that both conceals the essential immorality of sexism and rationalizes a value-free public world." She charged that justice in Niebuhr's analysis was a coercive "balancing of competitive egoism" leaving no room for the ethics of love and mutuality. Contrary to Niebuhr, in *The Radical Kingdom* (1970), Ruether sought to recover the social gospel as a positive theological development toward Immanuel Kant's idea that "the Kingdom of God is come unto us." By demythologizing the kingdom of God and bringing it down to earth, the social gospel moved toward eliminating that chasm between religious vision and social reality. Ruether asserted that in arguing for the autonomy of politics from an ethic of love, Niebuhr surrendered justice to the operating principle of power. For her, Niebuhr was the public theologian for "bourgeois society," which relegated the ethics of love to women in the home and masculinized the public sphere. Divorcing private virtue from the public good not only pushed cooperative and religious values out of the public domain, but pushed women out, too. A social revolution required a political theology in which the values of reciprocity and solidarity replaced those of domination and submission. While she recognized the "paternalistic and sentimental" attitude still resident in the social gospel's identification with middle-class culture, Ruether, unlike Cone, rejected Niebuhr's countervailing power as an effective response to inequality.[26]

Although the social gospel and Christian realism lacked sufficient awareness of the recalcitrant nature of racism and sexism in the structures of society, they offered useful ideas. The social gospel proposed the actualization of the kingdom of God on earth as a way to address the inequities of modern society for a more just social order. God's justice was to become a reality on earth. Christian realism illuminated the dynamics of group power in American politics and refused to hide behind pietistic pretense. In the decades of the 1960s and 1970s, both of these political theologies bequeathed useful ideas to religious radicals.

Living in the Secular City

The social gospel's fading influence, replaced by mid-century Niebuhrian Christian realism and Tillich's theology culture and the new political theologies articulated by Jürgen Moltmann and Johann Baptist Metz, prepared the religious field for a radical change in its stance toward the world and politics. In the midst of unease regarding the role of religion in addressing social unrest, there was also an increasing sense of power and hope as religious intellectuals viewed humanity awakening to its divine destiny. By the mid-1960s, theologians had arrived at a tipping point and had acquired the necessary language for the full secularization of religion—a practice of a politically situated self-transcendence.

The Baptist theologian Harvey Cox, completing his doctoral dissertation at Harvard University and teaching at Andover Theological Seminary, popularized the idea that secularization coincided with the Christian view of human destiny. Spending a year in Berlin reading the work of Dietrich Bonhoeffer, Cox picked up the theme of the "world come of age" in his best-selling *The Secular City* (1965). The book, situated in an almost giddy progressivism and the assumption of unending abundance of 1960s America, proposed that the process of secularization, breaking down the wall between religion and other spheres of society, freed humanity to take responsibility for the world. Intended for the narrow audience of the National Student Christian Federation, the book soon found its way to a broader popular and intellectual audience with Cox featured in the pages of *Time* magazine. Cox's provocatively stated, if not original, argument reverberated among social scientists and religious thinkers significantly enough to produce, in the following year, *The Secular City Debate* (1966) edited by Daniel Callahan. Critics and proponents from the pages of *Christianity Today, Christian Century, Christianity and Crisis*, and *Commonweal* all weighed in, registering a sense that *The Secular City,* for good or ill, marked a critical moment in American theology.[27]

Cox's book resonated not only among Protestants but also among Catholics who were freshly reconsidering their approach to social questions encouraged by the Vatican II document *Gaudium et Spes*. Quickly translated into Spanish as *La Ciudad Secular*, among the emerging Latin American liberationists Cox's book was a point of contention against North American theology. Liberationists charged that North American theology in its irrelevant stance toward the Third World, was busy justifying itself ad nauseam before the modern non-believer in which the *Secular City* was an example. Latin Americans saw their task as not in offering an apologia in the face of secularism but in justifying God's preferential advocacy for those considered non-persons. Nevertheless they found agreement with Cox, in that secularization appeared to be dissolving the walls between the separate spheres of society, and joined him in looking to Bonhoeffer's idea of religionless Christianity to assert a necessary "worldliness" that addressed the distress of poor multitudes.[28]

Cox called on German Friedrich Gogarten, an early collaborator with Karl Barth in formulating a dialectical theology, who proposed a "secular theology" in *The Reality of Faith: The Problem of Subjectivism in Theology* (1959). Secularization, Gogarten argued, was the fruit of the relativizing function of the Christian faith, giving humanity responsibility for the world rather than keeping it under the forces of mysterious nature. Cox presented three aspects of the biblical faith that opened the world to secularization: "the *disenchantment of nature* begins with the Creation, the *desacralization of politics* with the Exodus, and the *deconsecration of values* with the Sinai Covenant, especially with its prohibition of idols." Nature as "disenchanted" was a creation of God, separate from humanity and no longer a source of mystery and subject to scientific inquiry. The rule of Yahweh relativized all politics and abolished the privileges of divine right and "sacral politics." Like ancient idols, which functioned as Emile Durkheim's "representation collective" totem and were forbidden by Yahweh, modern man understood values as a product of his own creation, thus rejecting the absolutism of any value. Cox argued that the secularized view of nature, politics, and values was the legitimate outcome of biblical religion.[29]

Urban civilization and the collapse of religion were concurrent phenomena representing the fruit of the biblical vision. The city as a "technopolis" was Cox's symbol of secularization. Deploying social theory from Karl Marx to Albert Camus and drawing from Lewis Mumford's *The City in History: Its Origins, Its Transformations, and Its Prospects* (1961), Cox identified the secular city, with its anonymity, mobility, bureaucracy, and mass organization, as the positive means by which humanity was establishing its independence from the tutoring of religion. What for many modern theologians and social theorists was the bane of modernity, Cox celebrated. Under his archetype of the human city, that had often served as a symbol of estrangement from God and self—the technopolis—became a place of self-actualization and reflected "man's coming of age." The secular city did not depend on gods and myths but rather on the responsible exercise of power. It was a place where the language of politics replaced the language of metaphysics. In the secular city, the God of history banished the God of metaphysics.[30]

By recovering some of the language of the social gospel, Cox broke with the consensus of Cold War Christian realism and called for a "theology of revolutionary social change." He reasserted the concept of the kingdom of God as a possible historical reality coming about through the mechanism of society. The secular city, characterized by its reciprocity and interdependence, allowed its identification with the kingdom of God. Even as the kingdom of God required renunciation of the old order, so too did the secular city demand a new way of being, "a conversion" from a passing age to the realization of a new reality. An adequate theology for the new reality was to act as both "catalyst" and "catharsis" for action. Through a new theology, the church was to function as the "avant-garde of God" and a "cultural exorcist" driving out the "demons" of poverty, racism, and war. The avant-garde of God called men out of their "adolescent illusion" of religion and metaphysics to a "new regime" of secularity that would embrace responsibility for society.[31]

Cox was a religious intellectual fully reconciled to the modern world in which God's intent and the progressive project of modernity converged. In a series of lectures published in *God's Revolution and Man's Responsibility* (1965), he proposed that in a "world-in-revolution," one undergoing radical change, neither nature nor the supernatural disclosed God but rather the liberating acts of history. He noted the revolutionary mood in Cuba and Latin America as a case wherein the old theology had no effective means of responding. The tension between theology's validation of a particular political order and denying the political any divine significance needed resolution. God was more interested in the unfolding of scientific, secular, and anti-colonial revolutions liberating the world than in religion. An obsolete religion, contradicting the secular as having salvific meaning, denied God's continual self-disclosure in history. Through a "despiritualized" reading, the Bible gained its political immediacy toward freedom. Cox's argument, in which God's action and historical social change became indistinguishable, presumed knowledge of divine intent, giving political projects a salvific character. The assumption was that immanent change displayed a progressive and direct step toward the good.[32]

Like many other liberals of the time, Cox was active in the Civil Rights movement, working with Martin Luther King Jr. as a member of the Southern Leadership Conference. Acknowledging the negative urban experience of the Negro, he viewed it as a cultural residue of the past to be solved by the social mobility and centralization of the city, rather than as a fundamental structural problem. Astonishingly, this allowed him to minimize the racist experience of urban environments, a fact he later regretted. The Watts race riots in August 1965, a few months after the publication of the *Secular City*, demonstrated that instead of a sparkling place of possibilities for social mobility and freedom, American cities were places of "sophisticated humiliation" for blacks, In these early years Cox, encouraged by the dismantling of Jim Crow laws, displayed a certain blindness of American theology with respect to the structural nature of racism. Rising social awareness would shortly demand that theology face both race and poverty. The source of human wretchedness in modern society needed interrogation rather than elision by liberal optimism. By the end of the 1960s, as a frequent contributor to ongoing debates in *Christianity and Crisis*, Cox had embraced the counterculture to become an early advocate of, and one of the few white theologians to advocate for, the emerging liberation theology.[33]

Liberal theology's upbeat mood toward social change and the promise of a secularized religion marked by *The Secular City* was challenged by an alternative and largely urban stream of black revolt against the status quo. King had called the Watts riots the "rumbling of discontent from the 'have nots' within the midst of an affluent society." Against euphoric optimism and liberal faith in science and technology, King provided a contemporaneous antidote by combining a dose of a liberal world-consciousness, Niebuhrian realism, and black prophetic religion to confront the racial problem in America. King inherited a black social gospel from his father and grandfather, both Baptist preachers, in a mix of impassioned conservative preaching with community activism. He was among the generation of African American theologians who came into their own in the 1930s and '40s, earning advanced degrees and undertaking the formal study of black religion. Men like Howard Thurman, Mordecai W. Johnson, and Benjamin E. Mays asserted the dignity of the human person, attacked the sin of segregation, and advocated nonviolent action against Jim Crow. They all traveled to India to meet Mahatma Gandhi and study nonviolent resistance, and connected the black struggle in America with global anti-colonial movements. Throughout King's education, beginning at Morehouse College under the mentorship of Mays and continuing to his graduate studies, the protest elements of black religion combined with the growing world-consciousness of liberal theology.[34]

King's social gospel emphasized the historical realization of the kingdom of God and the personalism of Edgar S. Brightman, placing a high value on the interdependence of the individual and the community. Standing against Niebuhr's assertion that *agape* did not offer the basis for a just society, King nevertheless corrected Rauschenbusch's naïveté on the recalcitrant nature of social evil. Niebuhr's writings and the history of the black freedom struggle gave him a heightened understanding of the workings of political power. Instead of waiting for America to live up to its creed, he unflinchingly pushed the margins of the "theistic dilemma" for black people, who asked, if God is good, why do black people suffer? Rejecting revolutionary Marxism and the long-suffering negotiations of liberalism, black freedom required the coercion of "truth-force" in nonviolent resistance. The goal was the "beloved community," a colorblind society of human brotherhood. The beloved community—built on solidarity, human dignity, and the impartiality of God—permeated King's thought. Rather than passively waiting for the manifestation of the kingdom of God, he believed, free individuals actively collaborating with the demands of divine justice could bring about its realization.[35]

In 1967, reflecting on the progress of the Civil Rights movement in *Where Do We Go from Here: Chaos or Community?* King saw the movement experiencing a counterrevolution of white resistance and despair among its ranks. Desegregation, voting rights, and the dismantling of Jim Crow had cost white people little, uncovering a more pernicious racism. Whites and blacks held divergent expectations for equality, and economic inequality remained unyielding, denying black people and the poor decent jobs and adequate housing. The continual indoctrination of inferiority was breeding a radical response in Black Power. In an America built on individual rights, overcoming oppression required more than the solitary individual, King asserted "We have been oppressed as a group and we must overcome that oppression as a group." Negros needed to join forces with the rest of America's poor and use their marginal freedom to attack the "structures of evil . . . by the day-to-day assault of battering rams of justice." Rather than wait for the workings of structural power, only active engagement in some form of coercive power could break the resistance of white racism. The alternative was despair.[36]

A Secular Theology

King's assassination brought what the historian Gayraud Wilmore called "a hardening . . . a terrible silence" over the black community as anger turned to hopelessness. Among those newly radicalized by Black Power, King had conceded too much in his appeal to universal justice and brotherhood, under the assumption that whites could be shamed into doing the right thing. Cone charged that although the white power establishment had first seen King as a radical for his strategy of civil disobedience, ultimately it embraced him because he did not represent a threat to the system. Moral suasion, nonviolent resistance, and legal remedies often embraced by liberals did not solve intransigent racism. Only by addressing the underlying problem of white theology, the ultimate cosmic shelter for white people, was the elimination of racism even a possibility, and black theology had to go further than proclaiming universal justice. It had to do away with a white God. "The white God is an idol created by racists, and we blacks must perform the iconoclastic task of smashing false images," Cone argued. The impartial and universal God of the powerful needed to be overthrown for a particular God who was *partial* to the oppressed, to black people, "because the Kingdom belongs to the poor *alone*." The white God provided a racist society with the moral justification for their sense of superiority and produced acquiescence among blacks.[37]

As religious intellectuals were debating the significance of secularity, Cone asserted the long-standing secularity of black religion against the still prevalent "white lie" in black churches that Christian salvation was primarily concerned with "otherworldly reality." Selling pie-in-the-sky salvation to black people had allowed white theology to ignore their current plight. While many black people had accepted white men's pernicious definition of a circumscribed salvation, the protest element in black religion was returning as a reminder that black salvation was liberation from economic, political, and social oppression. In Cone's use of history, the prophetic strain of black religion had always been a secular one, not requiring any otherworldly justification or promise of heavenly reward: "the idea of heaven is irrelevant in Black theology." Since revolutionary America, he argued, black preachers such as Richard Allen, Nat Turner, and Nathaniel Paul had understood political liberation as God's salvation in the here and now. While white preachers talked about freedom from personal sins, leaving social arrangements unchanged, black preachers continually turned to the Exodus of Israel as the promise for freedom from political bondage, never accepting the separation of the sacred from the secular, spiritual salvation from social salvation. Being both secular and political was essential to black theology.[38]

Cone charged that white theologians had recently discovered "hope theology," and Moltmann had "surprisingly caught the spirit of black slave preachers" in addressing human suffering. Yet by ignoring the "actual bearers of hope," he wrote, hope theology inevitably became another "'abstract' talk geared to the ideological justification of the status quo." Long before, as black people had encountered a "Crucified and Risen Lord in the context of American slavery," antebellum black preachers made the "politics of hope" central in their sermons. The double meaning of Negro spirituals and prayers contradicted white missionaries' delayed hope of heaven and offered a protest against an intolerable present. Having encountered God in the midst of real suffering, hope, Cone insisted, was not "an intellectual idea; rather it is the praxis of freedom in the oppressed community." The black God was not a set of comfortable ideals nor an absolute ethical principle by which to organize society. Because God acts on behalf of the oppressed, "There can be no Christian theology that is not social and political."

Consequently, the political project of freedom for black people was the very meaning of God's salvific act.[39]

The political feature of black theology made all the difference in the world for the oppressed, because it addressed the social rather than the individual source of their suffering. Cone drew upon Bonhoeffer's understanding that divine presence was found only among the suffering, and in America that meant "in the ghetto" and among those "enslaved and trampled underfoot" by racism. A black theology had to go further than personal salvation and empowerment; as Cox argued, it needed to become a "theology of revolution" against white racism. J. Deotis Roberts concurred: "We are in need of social salvation as well as personal." A "bootstrap philosophy" or "personal piety" was insufficient to address the psycho-cultural nature of evil and suffering in American society. A black political theology, a "gospel of power," was a message of non-appeasement and action against white-controlled institutions. In a secular world come of age, in which oppressed people were awakening to their plight, quietism and otherworldly projections that denied God's present salvation were no longer available as a psychic salve for suffering. For black liberationists, the theology of secularity and hope that was in vogue among white theologians, along with enduring resistance and a deep understanding of the machinations of power, had long been resident within black religion.[40]

As black theologians and Latin Americans claimed a new nexus for political and social salvation, Ruether identified a sexist strain in a private/public dichotomy that escaped male liberationists. Ruether, like her male colleagues, considered salvation fully situated within the political and social realm, and additionally she deemed the private domain of the home as political. At the place where the personal became political is where the secular theology failed women. Cox's championing of the city as the place of public freedom, validating human power against both nature and the constraints of communal bonds, devalued the private realm associated with women. His writing had celebrated a masculinist ideal by asserting that the "defamilialization of work" in urban society had cut the "umbilical cord" to the economy of the home, "making it possible for man to increase his range of freedom and responsibility." He followed previous American thought regarding the private sphere, denying it political significance in which freedom meant men escaping it confines. Ruether's criticism drew from the nineteenth-century culture of domesticity which valued the home as the place for actualizing "I–Thou" relationships, unbearable among the urban crowd, tempering ambition and pecuniary interest and binding men to place. The virtues of private religion and sympathy were the domain of women, leaving the public sphere as an unfettered field of manly action and competition. Privatization had political consequences for religion as clergymen became increasingly associated with the private world of (passive) women sitting in their pews, and the validation of the market as the manly sphere of action eroded ecclesial political influence. While Cox chipped at the wall between religion and politics and de-privatized religion, Ruether noticed that he retained the wall between women, sequestered in the emptied private sphere, and the masculine public world of the city.[41]

Ruether called for a more thorough theological secularity and for dissolving the last frontier for liberation, the private/public dichotomy reflected in the "urban-suburban ecology" of the professional man and suburban housewife. Actualizing a new humanity depended upon breaking the conflict between religion and the secular but also between work and family, private and public life, which denied women full autonomy. Under the standing capitalist system, valuing competition and power, she noted that escaping the "cult of True Womanhood" was impossible, requiring a move toward revolutionary communitarian socialism. Like Charlotte Perkins Gilman, she proposed that such a society "would communalize the home," with the primary community making the basic decisions of daily life. While her male counterparts neglected the home in their theologizing, Ruether saw it as key in a whole sphere of salvation for both women and men. Breaking with individual salvation toward a communitarian ideal meant that a religious "conversion, therefore, cannot be fulfilled in a private inward way, it must move outward toward the transformation of reality" having political import.[42]

Overcoming the polarity between private religious sympathy and political pragmatism called for secularizing religion and recovering its political vitalism. In *The Radical Kingdom* (1967) and a *Commonweal* essay, "Schism of Consciousness" (1968), Ruether noted the fissures within Catholicism and called for the recognition of the "free church," which, having escaped institutional religion, was "dissolving the boundaries" of that "magic circle of the sacred." The free church of religious revolutionaries, rather than simply reforming an existing institution was abandoning sacred spaces and joining the world and its struggle, she wrote: "The theology of the free church, then, I would suggest is a secular theology, that worldly interpretation of the gospel toward which Bonhoeffer was groping during his last days in prison." Rather than a passing fad, secular theology carried messianic and revolutionary hope giving theological significance to the present world. Rather than the closed system of dogmatic "secularism" that denied the possibility of transcendence, secular theology found self-transcendence within the dynamism of the historical "community of man." There was a danger of conflating the "free church" and secular theology, she conceded, with an affirmation of the present power structures of society. This had already occurred in Christendom as the church and society had coalesced into one mutually supporting hierarchical system. A new Spirit of freedom was unfolding in which the "dialectic of man's existence forces him to stand out against the powers and principalities in his own history and move in a constant élan of self-transcendence." Seeking to reawaken the political efficacy of religion, she noted that it was radicals throughout American history that had kept the light of prophetic religion lit. Prophetic religion was found wherever the community of the true church expressed faith in the possibility of transcending and overcoming the present hierarchical order.[43]

Seeking a useable past, Ruether argued that every social movement in America had succeeded only when it had availed itself of the Christian language of liberation, standing in critical discontinuity with the prevailing social order. The authentic Spirit of the free church expressed in radical religion had struggled both against slavery and for women's emancipation. Its decline followed the identification of Christianity with the American way of life, depriving religion of its prophetic function and lulling its fervency for justice. Ruether saw the resources for social renewal within the Christian faith in which the public execution of Jesus by political and religious authorities had public rather than personal import. The public nature of the crucifixion, which tried and executed Jesus as a criminal, stood as the historical and elemental critique by the Christian faith against the ruling powers. Through continual renewal, the communitarian left recovered a prophetic faith maintaining its critical function and committing to the "penultimate amelioration" of injustice, thereby existing for the "salvation of the world."[44]

By locating salvation in the political, Cone and Ruether carried the idea of the kingdom of God and social salvation to its radical end. They shared many features with their theological forbearers. The proponents of social Christianity and liberationists sought to address inequality in modern society. Both theological outlooks emerged in a time of crisis and deployed the tools of social science. Both validated the political sphere as the location for faith-inspired action in addressing human suffering. The shift recast the kingdom of God from an otherworldly ideal to one realizable through the change mechanisms of society.

The social Christianity and liberation theology that ran through the American hemisphere and sharing the language of social justice often appear as one and the same, with only a change in actors. However, their differences in interpreting the nature of power from above to below made them irreconcilable. Along with continuities, there were major breaks between liberationists and the social Christianity of liberal proponents. Social Christianity began with unchanging biblical values applied by reformers to a dynamic world and proved at times to be quite militant. Liberationists began with the lived reality of oppressed people, knowledge from below, as the first step in biblical interpretation and in formulating action. While social Christianity assumed the soundness of the political order and sought evolutionary change concurrent with liberal notions of progress, liberationists were ready to consider the necessity of a radical revolution. Instead of appealing to the middle classes to instigate reform, liberationists looked to blacks, women, and the poor as the agents of change. Liberationists abandoned the secular/sacred split to fully locate divine action in the historical struggle for freedom. Relinquishing appeals to an otherworldly transcendence, history was the location of God's action. Unafraid of social disruption that optimistically led to a new humanity, liberation theologians were eager to provide a theological basis for radical praxis. They recognized the interdependence of political ideology and religion and were unwilling to trust the Christianization of the liberal social order, with its classist, racist, and sexist foundations, as sufficient for change.

Liberation theology's full embrace of secularity marked the great distance traversed by religious thought since its encounter with modernity, from another world to this world. The Reformation's "disenchantment of the world," moving toward a rationalized religion purged of its belief in magic and the immanent forces of the supernatural, had arrived at a full secularity. Modernity's attempt to place religion strictly within the confines of pure reason was in full bloom. As theology moved toward secularization in the twentieth century, it met the alternative stream of religious thought arising from the concrete experiences of oppressed people awakened to the political implications of God's immediate presence. A theology free of otherworldly transcendence did not abolish God but asserted a holism ascribing religious meaning to the political sphere.

The prospective consequences were stark. In a world in which the political is the total, and theology is ideologically committed, maintaining the critical stance liberationists promoted was untenable. With God near at hand and acting in history, what *was* with all its injustice and contingency could easily be read as divinely given. Liberationists carried with them a reticent assumption of modern social progress, never engaging in a direct address to the state. Even though they maintained a measure of distinction in their own minds between the ideal of the kingdom of God and any particular political program, in the ravines of culture the distinction did not hold. Radical politics and the utopian ideals of the kingdom of God converged. How to differentiate and explain the difference between the present ruled by power and deemed unjust, and God's liberatory and preferential action in history, remained unsettled.[45]

By finding a public ethic in a secular theology, the political action of the subordinated was no longer at best a plea for inclusion, or at worst an act of rebellion, but rather an act of God in history. Leaving the enclosure of the churches, a secularized religion would have its influence felt in a freshly validated political sphere. What remained a challenge was the rhetoric of a universal humanity that pervaded both politics and religion, hiding the particular nature of multiple and interlocking oppressions. As specific group claims emerged, universal humanity needed to give way to the specifics of race, class, and sex as a basis for group solidarity. Liberationists had all the foundational ideas to offer a solution.

9
The Feminine Principle

CALLING MARGINALIZED GROUPS to political action required not only a new view of God's relationship to the world but also a shared story. The rise of social history with marginalized groups at the center circulated a new awareness of oppression. With the aid of a secularized theology, the particular stories previously untold and borne by blacks, ethnic minorities, the poor, and women their struggle for freedom gained the perspective of a divine initiative. This chapter and the next demonstrate how liberationists across the hemisphere turned to narrative in the naming of oppression and in constructing a politically effective group identity. Under the sway of identity politics, the desire to validate a group's solidarity—defined as neither sympathy nor feelings of social belonging but rather shared struggle against particular suffering—and redefining a universal new humanity appeared at odds. In the search for a narrative that took into account both the particular and the universal, women were no different from other marginalized groups.

The recognition of women as an oppressed group and the possibility of a liberating theo-politic depended on a great number of ideas and historical changes converging. White women, embedded within a community with dominant men and assumed as being without an independent history, complicated viewing them as an oppressed group. The new field of women's history became a necessary first step. Otherwise, race and class privilege and the view of woman as a derivative of man threatened to make white women's subjugation invisible. Women still needed a sacred story of their own.

Feminist liberation theology hinged on recognizing women vis-à-vis men, identifying them as the "Other," and making a claim to equality—a historically tenuous position. Advocates in the nineteenth century had asserted the equality of men and women "before God" as a key teaching of Christianity. However, a long-held belief in difference as part of the divine order of creation made reaching functional equality arduous. The valuation of differences in a hierarchy of values served modern societal and capitalist goals.

Into the twentieth century, accelerated changes in women's political, economic, and social status rewrote the narrative for women's lives. Strides in science, social theory, and historiography began to loosen the cultural straitjacket, and the private place of women opened to recognize their political coming of age. A critical mass of newly educated women theologians moved with what Nancy Cott identified as the key claims of modern feminism: opposition to sex hierarchy, assumption of the social construction of woman's subordination, and the identification of women as a social group—proposals that became radicalized in the women's liberation movement. These societal and attitudinal shifts emboldened many to challenge one of the last remaining barriers in theological abstraction—sexism.[1]

Sisterhood

The period between World War II and the 1970s exposed the foundations for a feminist theology and praxis. The French existentialist philosopher Simone de Beauvoir's *The Second Sex* (1949), with the English translation available in 1953, provided a historical, philosophical, literary, and anthropological excavation of the status of modern women from childhood to old age. De Beauvoir began with an autobiographical question that turned to the "irritating" philosophical one, "what is woman?" Her book was a full-throttle attempt to answer the eternal woman question by addressing the existential question, "what is man?" She observed that while acquiring basic political rights in Western society, women remained marginalized in every other aspect. Her argument hung on the notion that as man came to represent transcendence through his mental and political activity, woman became the "Other," forced into immanence by attending to the everyday. The entirety of Western patriarchal tradition was based on woman as "'the sex'... defined and differentiated with reference to man and not he with reference to her; she is the incidental, the inessential as opposed to the essential. He is the Subject, he is the Absolute—she is the Other." Society, not biological fact, produced woman as an inconsequential being. In asserting, "One is not born, but rather becomes, a woman," de Beauvoir drew the parameters of the sex/gender system and set the theoretical foundation for understanding women's oppression.[2]

De Beauvoir took the modern critique of religion and added the question of sex and gender, a feature that few enlightened men had considered. De Beauvoir's analysis indicted the Christian religion by charging that in dividing the soul from the body, it considered the flesh the enemy of the soul: "the flesh that is for the

Christian the hostile *Other* is precisely the woman." In a scathing critic of monotheism, she noted two reasons that religion was ideologically effective in the subordination of woman: God being male gave men divine endorsement of his sovereignty over woman, and the "fear of God" repressed any motivation toward female revolt. She likened the position of women to the plight of the Jew and the Negro, arguing that the ingenious formulation of "equality in difference" had produced something akin to the Jim Crow "separate but equal" rhetoric. The association of woman with the flesh and as a source of man's sin undermined the Christian claim of equality.[3]

As a bestseller, *The Second Sex* created a ruckus among conservative critics with its key sections on sexual initiation, lesbianism, and obligatory motherhood. Censored by the Catholic Church, in the 1950s the book faded into the margins of intellectual discussion and was read only by the dedicated few. However, propelled by the 1965 second edition of Alfred C. Kinsey's *Sexual Behavior in the Human Female*, which cited de Beauvoir, North American feminists rediscovered *The Second Sex*, resulting in a flood of books and articles furthering de Beauvoir's theory of woman's oppression. De Beauvoir, who in the late 1940s believed that feminism was practically over, fueled an emergent feminist theory in the 1960s. Radical theorists Kate Millett and Shulamith Firestone, among others, elaborated on the idea of woman as "Other," the sex–gender system, and patriarchy. Among feminist thinkers, her work was not without controversy. Some viewed her ideas as based on a hierarchical dualism of same/other and transcendence/immanence, and calling women to enter the male world of freedom. De Beauvoir displayed a certain phallocentric argument for why society rendered woman the Other, stating, "For it is not in giving life but in risking life that man is raised above an animal." De Beauvoir signaled the coming philosophical battle over sex and gender.[4]

De Beauvoir's existential stance, her socialism, and her analysis of women's situation as social entrapment produced in the rising women's liberation movement a politics of self-fashioning that aimed at transcending the existing codes of femininity. Her vision was of an androgynous society in which biology was no longer destiny, thus liberating women from femininity and its confines. She articulated an intellectually fecund theory of intersubjectivity and in her subsequent autobiographies, *Memoirs of a Dutiful Daughter* (1958), *The Prime of Life* (1960), and *The Coming of Age* (1970), popular in the revitalized feminist movement, she modeled a woman thinker who had lived out a life of sexual freedom, eschewing the cage of monogamy and the ties of motherhood. *The Second Sex* and its critical reception carried the inherent tensions and hopes within feminism and shaped the intellectual climate for American women theologians.[5]

Through the twentieth century, women raised an intellectual challenge in all arenas of thought and culture. Early in the century, as suffragettes claimed the franchise and achieved protective legislation based on women's special nature, women social scientists, including Elsie Clews Parson and Helen Thompson, questioned the assumption of "woman's nature." These women secured their place by working among sympathetic men and set the foundation for understanding sex differences as socially conditioned. In the post-war period, amid a resurgence of the cult of domesticity, Margaret Mead sought an empirical basis for sex role differentiation, and rather than ease change in gender norms her theory rooted in biology unwittingly reinforced them. Women intellectuals were moving on other fronts. Mary Ritter Beard's first feminist intervention in history, *Woman as Force in History* (1946), proposed that long-neglected women had made key contributions to social developments and were worthy of study. In 1964 the sociologist Alice Rossi published "Equality Between the Sexes: An Immodest Proposal." She offered a "socially androgynous conception of the role of men and women" and a way to revitalize a moribund feminist movement "undermined by the conservatism in psychology and sociology." By 1967, Gerda Lerner had picked up Beard's project to legitimize women's history as a field of study and uncovered a lost history with her first book, *The Grimké Sisters from South Carolina: Rebels against Slavery*. While women fought for equal status and recognition, difference continued to serve a political purpose. The tension between difference and equality remained, and rather than avoid the dilemma of equality/difference, feminists of the 1960s waded deeply into the quagmire to establish new political ground. These cumulative challenges supplied the ideas and a narrative for an intellectual revival of modern feminism and for constructing a politically charged group identity.[6]

The sociologist Helen Mayer Hacker had proposed in 1951 that women, similarly to blacks, Jews, and immigrants, constituted a minority group within American society. Minority status was not a statistical concept but was, rather, dependent on the presence of unequal treatment solely due to physical or cultural characteristics. It also carried with it "feelings" of a lower status. She proposed that members of such a group may not be aware of their group identity and may even reject identification or engage in self-hatred by accepting the dominant characterization. Women were no exception. Hacker went on to assert that, as was the case with American Negroes, women's unequal economic, educational, social, and political position produced a caste-like women's " subculture" at odds with their class. Women had group-specific language and interests, and gender-specific jobs, while identifying with the dominant world of men. Hacker's description of a "woman's world" in which its participants were unaware of participation and inequality implicitly pointed to the need for consciousness-raising. Hacker, along with others, was deconstructing sexually assigned roles and inadvertently identifying a common experience useful for group identity in the 1960s and 1970s.[7]

As women social scientists, historians, and theoreticians broke new ground, religious women slowly gained access to theological training and inclusion in ecclesial leadership. Since the nineteenth century, women had built informal theologies out of their daily experience, evident in creative writing and political essays, yet lacked sufficient access to address the center of dominant theological thought. After a protracted process of pursuing church leadership and theological education, a few achieved ordination (for example, Antoinette Brown Blackwell, who in 1851 was ordained in the Congregational church). Some women with sufficient theological knowledge joined Elizabeth Cady Stanton's 1895 heterodox rewriting of the Bible. The Chicago Theological Seminary, a center for the social gospel, awarded its first undergraduate divinity degree to Florence Fensham in 1902. The continued pressure for full inclusion began to bear substantial fruit when in 1954 Harvard Divinity School, an old bastion of American liberal religion, admitted the first women to its M. Div. program. Letty M. Russell, one of the first women at the Divinity School, went on to become a first-generation feminist theologian. In 1956 the Methodist Episcopal Church and the Presbyterian Church, USA, two major Protestant bodies, accepted women's ordination. Women could finally see institutional possibilities ahead.

The trend continued, and by the late 1960s women's caucuses within the major denominations pursued reform in everything from sexism in Sunday school curricula to representation in church leadership. In the 1970s a trickle became a flood as women rushed to seminaries and formed a network of theologically trained women. Initial ecumenical conferences at Alverno College in 1971, and subsequently at the Grailville Community in Loveland, Ohio, in 1972, drew from the growing mass of women ready to recast theology in light of their own experience. They set out to be more than women doing theology or providing a feminine gloss to biblical interpretation. Rather, they sought to reformulate the discipline. Many of the newly trained theologians remained in a reformist mode, reconsidering the tradition and reinterpreting the biblical text by finding a feminine "canon within the canon." Others, moving in an alternative and radical theological stream such as that of Quaker Margaret Fell in the seventeenth century, moved outside the text to find a continually evolving disclosure of the divine unbound by the text. Religious women's participation in a concurrent broad-based feminist movement and liberal theology's long-standing openness to innovation created the ideal conditions for the emergence of feminist liberation theology.[8]

In 1960, Valerie Saiving Goldstein had given the first signal that an opportune moment for a fully articulated theology from the perspective of women was imminent. Goldstein's theological education began in the 1940s at Bates College; she went on to doctoral work at the University of Chicago Divinity School. After a family hiatus, she finished her doctorate at Union Theological Seminary. Her focus was the process philosophy of Alfred North Whitehead, a major influence in late twentieth-century theology. Whitehead reasoned that God experienced the world as it came into being. The understanding of God as *experiencing* rather than *creating* the world *ex nihilo* by going before it gave significance to the human experience. Goldstein's 1960 essay, "The Human Situation: A Feminine View," written as a graduate student and published in the *Journal of Religion,* expressed how her female experience affected her theological views: "It is my contention that there are significant differences between masculine and feminine experiences and that the feminine experience reveals in a more emphatic fashion certain aspects of the human situation which are present but less obvious in the experience of men." She charged that sexual difference and the presentation of the male point of view as universal had a profound effect on understanding the human condition.[9]

As a theologian and a woman, Goldstein was no longer convinced that when theologians spoke of "man" it was a generic term. Since theology was almost exclusively a male domain, the temptation to identify male experience with the universal truth was too great. She aimed her critique toward the theology exemplified by Reinhold Niebuhr, which saw the human condition primarily as estrangement, conflict, and anxiety, giving rise to the first sin of pride and self-assertion. This way of thinking, she charged, was a product of the modern era's "hypermasculine" drive for power, as expressed in capitalism, imperialism, and technology. Theology from this "male standpoint" set the primary sin of pride, against love, equated with selflessness and sacrifice. She proposed that the "feminine experience" was not primarily one of estrangement and anxiety; rather, woman's problem was the negation of the self.[10]

Goldstein observed that modernity was giving way to a society in which "the characteristic traits inherent in femininity are being increasingly emphasized, encouraged, and absolutized." These were the values that Lionel Trilling called the "cooperative virtues." Women were learning through education and new experiences to "transcend the boundaries of a purely feminine identity." They were not seeking to do away with femininity; rather, they sought "a higher unity . . . they want, in other words, to be both women *and* full human beings." For Goldstein, this called for a theology more in keeping with the new social experience.[11]

Goldstein's proposal drew heavily from Mead's cultural anthropology and the post-war change in social science's thinking about sex differences. Social science moved from a strict social constructivist view to a modified view that considered the role of biology. Mead exemplified this change. In a critique of American society, *Sex and Temperament in Three Primitive Societies* (1935), Mead concluded that human nature was malleable and there existed no link between sex and behavior. Fourteen years later, with the publication of *Male and Female: A Study of the Sexes in a Changing World* (1949), Mead conceded that biology, including women's reproductive role, provided a yet-undetermined substratum of orientation in culture. Goldstein asserted, "We must begin with the central fact about sexual difference: that in every society it is women—and only women—who bear children." Motherhood imposed a requirement to put the needs of the child before one's own in the indispensable and absorbing "I–Thou" relationship. The temptations of woman were quite different from those of man, rooted in the biological facts of embodiment and its social meaning. Thus a woman, even one who believed in the equality of the sexes, learned to give too much of herself, to become "without value to herself ... perhaps even God." Woman's sin, Goldstein concluded, becomes the "underdevelopment or negation of the self," looking to others for self-definition, mistrust of her own reason, and "sentimentality." Contrary to Niebuhr's universalist and masculinist thesis, woman's sin was not pride but selflessness.[12]

The theological establishment ignored Goldstein's essay, but it made its way in mimeograph form through the informal feminist networks in divinity schools and religion departments during the 1960s. At the time of publication, the essay was provocative enough for *Time* magazine to publish an article titled "Religion: Male and Female Theology." Otherwise, Goldstein's ideas did not garner serious consideration until the 1970s, when her argument was useful for casting Niebuhr as a symbol of liberal male chauvinism. The decade also continued a counter-trend in feminist thought challenging biological determinism and essentialism, begun earlier by Karen Horney's and Clara Thompson's critique of Freud. Nancy Chodorow proposed *The Reproduction of Mothering* (1978) for a psychoanalytic approach, recognizing that societal values rather than nature constructed gender identity and behavior. Nevertheless, Goldstein's essay became part of the feminist canon, decried for its implied essentialism but praised for the validation of women's experience. Her theology remained a feminine theology, one that captured women's perspective, falling short of the full-orbed feminist political theology that followed. Subsequent battles within feminist theology echoed Goldstein's early theological intuition and the threshold of essentialism it threatened to cross.[13]

Feminist intellectuals sought a popular audience, and mainline churchwomen gave a welcome reception to the 1963 publication of Betty Freidan's *The Feminine Mystique*. Freidan, drawing from de Beauvoir, argued that women were in crisis due to "a stunting or evasion of growth" of an independent identity. The "feminine mystique," a false ideology that held to women's natural role as wife and mother, kept them unresponsive to the depth of their dissatisfaction. Citing the psychologist Erik H. Erikson's concept of identity crisis, she noted that social theorists recognized the need for an independent identity in males, displayed in autonomy and self-realization, yet failed to acknowledge such a need in women. She saw women as having "forfeited their own existence" by living through husbands and children. The feminine mystique, which considered a forfeited female self to be normal, was "burying millions of American women alive." Contrary to Goldstein, Friedan pointed to Mead, aided by Freudian psychology, as one of the chief collaborators in granting scientific sanction to the inevitability of "woman's role." While Mead, Friedan noted, was a model of a woman thinker who was establishing women as unique human beings, not simply misbegotten men, she ultimately betrayed women by tying them to bodily functions. Friedan's liberal feminism revolted against an essential female identity and opted for forging an autonomous self. *The Feminine Mystique* was widely circulated through church reading groups and required for the leadership of United Methodist Women, providing a grassroots base for a liberal political movement.[14]

Friedan's subsequent founding of the National Organization for Women (NOW) and the passage of Title VII of the 1964 Civil Rights Act launched a movement seeking inclusion of women in all areas of society. The historian Ann Braude has shown that the founding of NOW featured a religious impulse within its ranks. The Catholic sister Joel Read, and Pauli Murray, the first African American woman ordained in the Episcopal Church, were among its founders. On NOW's agenda was the reform of religious institutions, reflected in establishing the Women and Religion Task Force to spread the message of women's equality in liberal denominations. The reforming strategy of NOW depended on working within the existing economic, political, and social institutions; not alienating men; and making a mass appeal to equity. NOW was not the only expression of a politically revitalized feminism and a concomitant religious impulse. Other women were moving toward a break from liberal feminism.[15]

The mid-1960s saw college-aged women participating in the New Left through involvement in the Student Nonviolent Coordinating Committee (SNCC), Students for a Democratic Society (SDS), and anti-war groups. They soon became aware of their second-class status within a movement proclaiming its commitment to equality. The New Left had appeared as a herald of a radical democratic revolution against racism, war, and economic exploitation, but women found that the revolution did not include changes in their status. They found themselves playing the role of secretaries and housewives within movement organizations. Disillusioned with the New Left and NOW's reformist strategy, women turned toward radical forms of feminism and came to view women's emancipation as the first step for all other liberatory strategies.

A clear signal of discontent among radical women came in 1965. Casey Hayden and Mary King, women within the leadership circle of the New Left, wrote "a kind of memo" addressing the problems of women in the movement, which they attributed to the overarching "common-law caste system" of sexual subordination that permeated every aspect of women's life—work, personal relationships, and institutions. What made the caste system menacing was its imposition not by law but rather by custom and tradition based on assumed biological differences. This made withdrawal by women virtually impossible. The system was "forcing [women] to work around or outside hierarchical structures of power which may exclude them." The "memo" expressed a deep frustration with men in the movement and their seeming unwillingness to acknowledge and discuss sexual caste.[16]

Hayden and King derived their ideas from experiences in the New Left and by reading de Beauvoir's *The Second Sex*. The awakening of Hayden's social consciousness occurred when she was a student participating in the Austin-based Christian Faith and Life Community, a seedbed for the New Left. King, the daughter of a southern Methodist minister, first became involved in civil rights through the YWCA. Hayden and King drew a parallel between the treatment of Negroes and the treatment of women, arguing that in the acknowledgment of the racial caste system, the "sexual caste system" remained invisible. The idea of coerced participation in sexual caste supplied the organizing principle of solidarity for women's liberation.

Radical feminists viewed every institution, including marriage, the church, and the state, as needing a complete overhaul—if not abolishment. As liberal and socialist feminists assumed the separation of public and private life, radicals asserted, "the personal is political." Women's lives enclosed within an all-embracing sexual caste system kept them in perpetual bondage and in a subordinated political position. Drawing from de Beauvoir's theory of intersubjectivity, all interpersonal encounters between men and women, including intimate ones, reflected the gender power dynamic of society. Neither political reform programs nor a socialist revolution was sufficiently effective in changing the long-standing position of women. While radicals claimed that men and women were fundamentally the same and championed androgyny, they organized based on the social experience ascribed to females. Through thousands of consciousness-raising groups, many held in churches and divinity schools, women discovered a shared oppression and the affinity of "sisterhood." Sisterhood expressed a willingness to challenge any social institution that denied women freedom and equality. As differences among women emerged due to class, race, and ethnicity and the eschewing of essentialism threatened the concept of a universal sisterhood, the strategic necessity of group cohesion kept the idea alive.[17]

Toward the Great Mother

While Protestants were creating a strategic mass of theologically trained women, Catholics launched the first strikes toward a feminist theology. They crossed a greater distance between the dogma of the Catholic Church and feminism than did their Protestant cohorts. In 1968 when Mary Daly, then a professor of theology at Boston College, published *The Church and the Second Sex,* the feminist movement was in full swing. Daly, who was a member of the increasingly splintered NOW and going through her own radicalization, drew from de Beauvoir to engage in a critique from within the Catholic Church. Without adopting de Beauvoir's atheism, she concurred with her on nearly all points regarding the function of religion in the subordination of women. Woman was the "Other" forced into false humility and dependence by a total ecclesial and theological system.

Daly took on the daring role of revamping the ideological superstructure of Catholic theology. She saw a hopeful opportunity to extend the work begun by Vatican II by challenging the "anti-feminism" in Christian tradition. She argued that the "eternal feminine," an idea that reached beyond theologians to philosophers and psychoanalysts, supplied the foundation for religious anti-feminism. She found traces of the idea of the eternal feminine in thinkers as diverse as William James and Pierre Teilhard de Chardin. The "school of the eternal feminine is radically opposed to female emancipation," striving to keep women in bondage by the maintenance of a pedestal constructed from the most anachronistic and anti-scientific thought and the "lulling effect of habit and custom." Woman's effort to escape the confines of the pedestal, and to become a self-defined human being, opened her to charges of "masculinization" with dire social consequences. The "Eternal Woman" was self-less, "shrouded in 'mystery,'" always a mother embodied in the Virgin Mary as the model of obedience and submissiveness. The Virgin Mary, "domesticated and enchained," was an inversion of the ancient Great Mother.[18]

Daly insisted on the necessary destruction of theology founded on anti-feminism by root and branch. A hierarchical view of humanity and the rhetoric of "God's plan," considered evident through natural law, maintained the myth of the eternal feminine. The assumption of God's masculinity, even though no one had ever asserted that God was literally male, along with the divine attributes of immutability and omnipotence, reflected an alienating distortion. The presumed changelessness of the world and God's self-disclosure as fulfilled and closed did not allow a fresh encounter with the modern world. Through the process described by Harvey Cox in *The Secular City*, Daly called for an "exorcism" of anti-feminist myths and the "demon of sexual prejudice" that stunted and mutilated women's lives.[19]

Daly wrote *The Church and the Second Sex* in a reformist frame of mind, igniting a flurry of controversy and fanning the flames of the nascent feminist theology. Subsequently, Daly became disillusioned with the possibility of reform within Christianity. In a 1971 sermon delivered at the Harvard Memorial Chapel, she announced that Christianity was unredeemable, and she called for women and men to form an "exodus community" escaping Christianity. Thus began Daly's journey to a post-Christian religion in her 1973 book *Beyond God the Father: Toward a Philosophy of Women's Liberation*, which called for the destruction of the sexual caste system and patriarchy and the embrace of a revolutionary "sisterhood as antichurch." Only a Nietzschean "transvaluation of values" that unmasked both the eternal feminine and the eternal masculine could free humanity from the dualism of sexual caste and move toward universal androgyny. The self-liberation of women through bonding in the "sisterhood of man," a phrase intended to challenge the masculine universal, was the most effective action toward human liberation. Daly proposed, in highly colorful language, the reclaiming of women's right to name self, God, and the world, and "castrating" the language of a "He-God" built on a "phallocentric" ethic. Daly repudiated patriarchal monotheism and led an exodus to the counterculture's rising goddess spirituality.[20]

Daly's highly quotable critique of theological language as a system of domination and her public defiance of monotheism had a significant influence on feminists seeking to reconstruct Christianity from within. Daly had spoken the theologically unspeakable. Additionally, the broad political realignment then taking place across religious traditions, one that privileged action over dogma, was an opportunity for a feminist theological movement to gain a critical mass of adherents and to coalesce among both Catholics and Protestants. Rosemary Radford Ruether, Elisabeth Schüssler Fiorenza (also a Catholic), and the Protestants Letty Russell and lay activist Sheila D. Collins, among others, were ready to provide the feminist movement with a suitable Christian theology.

In 1975, Fiorenza, a professor at the University of Notre Dame, described the new field of feminist theology as emerging from women's liberation, which had "uncovered the sexist structures and myths of our culture" and was dismantling them. Quoting Paulo Freire, Fiorenza compared women's situation with that of blacks: "Any situation in which 'A' objectively exploits 'B' or hinders his [*sic*] pursuit of self-affirmation as a responsible person is one of oppression." The androcentric theology of the "old boys' club" assuming objectivity and "white middle-class male" privilege needed to be replaced by a "partisan" theology that recognized the "feminine mystique" in the oppression of women. Male liberation theologians had done only slightly better. Having brought attention to the imperialistic white theology, they had failed to consider that "the 'maleness' and 'sexism' of theology is much more pervasive than the race and class issue." Thus far, a masculinist theology had prolonged women's internalization of the passive virtues of self-sacrifice and self-denying love, discouraging women's autonomy.[21]

Noting that earlier suffragettes had sought political integration into the nation, feminists, Fiorenza asserted, recognized that in every area of thought and culture, "We are the 'other,' socialized into helpmates of men or sex objects for their desire." Inclusion through "equal rights" was insufficient, and token acceptance into male-dominated divinity schools and seminaries fell well short of gaining women full equality. The need was for a "humanization" of all societal institutions and a theological revamping congruent with the change in women's new consciousness.[22]

Fiorenza drew the parameters of feminist theology within the Frankfurt School's critical theory and women's liberation. Constructing a "critical theology" required integrating the "so-called male-female areas, the intellectual-public, and the personal-emotional" of human experience and taking on centuries of misogyny not only as an intellectual project but also as a practice. Feminist theology looked to the experience of consciousness-raising, the narrative of "sisterhood," and rooting the discipline in "emancipatory praxis and solidarity." The fruits of theological innovation were quickly evident in new women-centered liturgies, celebrating women's experiences and blurring the boundaries between the sacred and the profane of daily life. By the end of the decade, Fiorenza had co-founded the radical movement "women-church," a network of alternative spiritual communities standing against "kyriarchal" ecclesial structures and promoting a "discipleship of equals." Beginning as a Catholic movement, the women-church soon welcomed Protestants, minority women, lesbians, and leaders of the larger women's movement, including Gloria Steinem.[23]

What kept the new theology uneasily within the confines of Christianity was its appeal to the biblical text and symbols, albeit reinterpreted, and the ethics of freedom and equality. In *A Different Heaven and Earth* (1974), Collins summarized the features of a feminist theology. She began her book project as a reporter for the Joint Strategy and Action Committee, an ecumenical church agency, and not as an academic theologian. Frustrated by difficulty in conveying the new feminist theology in traditional language and categories, she encountered a writing block. The breakthrough came through a personal feminist awakening: "I had been struggling to exorcise the patriarchal demon for *myself*!" Crossing the threshold of feminist realization, she was no longer a disinterested reporter but had become one with her subject, desiring to uncover her own religious history. She described her situation as rising from a new consciousness of the "death of old authorities" and recognizing that "the places where the transcendent is being met are being reconstituted." This was happening not only among the "silent majority of women," she noted, but also among blacks, Hispanics, American Indians, and Asians. Collins is an apt example of how feminist theology placed the laywoman's experience at the center of the thinking about God. It marked the revival of religious writing by ordinary women bringing an alternative theological stream to the fore.[24]

Collins asserted that experience, rather than dogma, was the "crucible of theology." The content of theology was biography, made up of the concrete experiences of daily life, uniting women who had the courage to overcome their position as a "subordinated Other." All oppressed people must write their own history, and for women it must become "herstory," a concept already part of the nomenclature of women's liberation. Collins noted the significant tension for women who through the centuries had had to choose between yielding to authority and tenaciously asserting their own path. She looked to medieval women such as St. Teresa of Avila, but also the alternative theological stream of the Puritan Anne Hutchinson, the Grimké sisters, and Mary Baker Eddy, women whose experience defied the prevailing orthodoxy.[25]

Feminist theology, Collins asserted, required what the sociologist Peter Berger had offered in *The Sacred Canopy* (1967), recognizing that the most important task of society was "nomization" or the naming of the world. Religion served as a system of naming and a legitimating sacred canopy against the threat of social chaos. Collins charged that the Judeo-Christian tradition had, through positing a transcendent power beyond experience, provided the authorization of patriarchy. The task was not to undertake the liberal demythologizing of the biblical text, which failed to deconstruct its patriarchal underpinnings, but to "*re*mythologize" women's experience by recovering ancient stories and imagining new myths. An alternative theology that spoke from the experience of women was by its very nature "partisan" and could not presume a universal human experience. The solidarity of sisterhood and the writing of herstory allowed a breakthrough in naming the source of human alienation—the ancient "patriarchal revolution."[26]

New stories articulated the "feminine principle" as a particular "set of responses to the 'givenness' of raw experience." Collins drew her definition of the feminine principle from the depth psychology of Carl Jung, the comparative mythology of Joseph Campbell, the archeology of Johann Bachofen, and the history of antiquity of E.O. James, using these sources as evidence of an alternative and hidden history. She noted that modern scholarship had discovered the presence of an ancient and revered "Great Mother" that elevated feminine power, subsequently overthrown by the Yahwist cult. Every known culture, Collins asserted, had organized around certain inescapable sexual dualities: the masculine principle stood for aggressiveness, competition, and intellectuality; the feminine principle stood for receptivity, intuitiveness, and inclusiveness. Modern feminists had rightly suspected that references to the universal stood in for the dominance of the masculine. While radicals sought to erase all sexual difference in order to challenge the false universal, Collins asserted that a positive valuation of the feminine principle served as a useful frame of reference for constructing new androgynous universals that valued the masculine/feminine duality rather than abolishing it. Collins mirrored a long line of thought, from Margaret Fuller's feminine principle in the nineteenth century to Charlotte Perkins Gilman's maternal ethics in the early twentieth, seeking to assert both equality and the significance of difference.[27]

With woman's ever-changing experience as the guiding principle, Collins declared the possibility of the end of theology as a systematized and never-changing body of knowledge about God. "Perhaps for the future there can be no theology—that is, no systematized body of knowledge about God—but only *theologizing*, that dialectical process of action/reflection which generates new questions," she wrote. The end of the theologian sequestered in an ivory tower with its stained-glass windows made way for many particular communities to articulate their experience of God. Theologizing by women did not begin with someone else's text but with retelling, reliving, and remembering their own lives serving as a "revelatory" act disclosing God.[28]

In feminist theologizing, God the noun became God the verb, "to God," an idea first proposed by Daly in *Beyond God the Father*. Collins noted that modern culture was going through a process of assigning names to God more congruent with the contemporary experience, but this naming was provisional, open to continual redefinition. Reifying God in the process of naming was ultimately "the projection of anthropomorphism onto a sacred deity" and "idolatrous." God as a verb capturing the process of becoming was more in harmony with the dynamic of experience and reflection. "To God" was the act by which the religious self journeyed from the "Other," entrapped by otherworldly transcendence and exclusion, to the subjectivity of "I am." Escaping from dogma, authority, and tradition, women were renaming God and the world in a constant dialogue of divine experience. Asserting the uniqueness of women's experience, while attempting to arrive at equality in difference, found Collins and her cohorts struggling with the undertow of essentialism. Subjective experience, rather than unchanging truth, as the foundation for theology expressed by Collins was the key feature of feminist theologizing, embraced by adherents and decried by critics.[29]

Against the essentialism that threatened to suffocate the tender root of feminist theology were strong strands of humanistic resistance. As early as 1970, Ruether expressed reluctance to replace the brotherhood of man with sisterhood, which she regarded as a continuation of Western dualism. The idea of sisterhood raised the question of whether women constituted a people, similar to a racial or ethnic group—a concern expressed at the 1972 Grailville conference. James Cone had asserted that women as such were not "a people," thus placing them outside the rubric of liberation. Race subsumed gender as the site of struggle. Ruether asserted the fundamental nature of sexism as the root of all forms of exclusion; however, she viewed sisterhood as having a limited function as a "therapeutic community" to arrive at consciousness of oppression. Solidarity, thus the liberation of humanity, meant women had to go beyond sisterhood.[30]

Ruether viewed feminism as a venture into a *terra incognita* to create an integrated "new humanity" free from patriarchal power. It presented a deeper critique of the sharp dualism in Western thought, providing the key to the dialectic of liberation. She noted that since the Renaissance, modernity had struggled to overcome the dualism and hierarchy of traditional society. Unfulfilled possibilities within the Enlightenment resulted in the continuation of sexual complementarity. Even the radical St. Simonians, who called for the liberation of women, "were primarily concerned with the liberation of the repressed, 'feminine side' of men in a way that reinforced the stereotypic differences between male and female 'nature'." Ruether saw again in the rhetoric of the liberation of women the continual threat posed by essentialist notions.[31]

Essentialism had serious repercussions for authentic freedom. Women and other subordinated groups, Ruether argued, did not experience themselves except through the perspective of dominant men who defined the terms of their rebellion. Seeking an authentic freedom through a cultural rebellion, women, blacks, and colonized people were in danger of reinscribing the false identities they sought to escape. Ruether noted that blacks caught between assimilation or embracing the traditional and unworkable "identity of a slave" served as a parallel to women. The self-assertion of a new black identity, evident in the defiance of the Black Panthers, threatened to re-create the angry black man of the white imagination. For women, the journey of revolutionary struggle resulted in either emulating men by engaging in "self-hatred," or embracing the societal definitions of womanhood. Radical sisterhood could simply read as acting out the "male dread of unleashed feminine power." It was not surprising, to Ruether, that one militant group called itself WITCH: Women's International Terrorist Conspiracy from Hell. Sisterhood, like black manhood, remained inadequate as a representative of a full humanity, for "there can be no salvation for one which is not the salvation of all." A new ethos of a "community of reconciliation" required overcoming sexism as men and women sought reintegration into a new humanity. This was the meaning of biblical salvation—the overcoming of alienation. Quoting the apostle Paul, "there is neither male nor female, slave nor free, Jew nor Greek," Ruether, considering herself a radical liberal, appealed to a spiritual androgyny and human solidarity rather than an essential woman's experience and sisterhood.[32]

A New Narrative

Building solidarity called for a narrative, a common story of struggle. At the cusp of an emergent narrative theology, liberationists found a compatible theological tool for the experience of the oppressed. Both concrete and malleable, narrative as theology was an opportunity to challenge the received story and construct a new and inclusive one. As James Cone asserted, "white theologians built logical systems; black folks told tales," and it was in the telling of tales that divine action in history could be known.[33]

A theological turn toward narrative served as a corrective to the dominance of abstract reason and individualism. Historical criticism had undermined the foundations for a literal reading of the Bible, resulting in varied responses among theologians. Conservatives, under a modern rubric of reason, insisted on the necessary historical accuracy of the text by which they maintained orthodoxy. Liberal theologians, however, seeking to accommodate the historical criticisms, turned to a hermeneutic that separated the historical veracity of the narrative, a secondary consideration, from its "true" essential meaning. The biblical narrative, viewed as myth, was increasingly subject to abstraction by those attempting to extract its deeper meaning. Proliferating complex interpretations had rendered the narrative superfluous, as theology moved away from the concreteness of the text. Neo-orthodoxy's critique of liberal theology began a recovery of the narrative hidden under multiple layers of theological interpretation. In *The Meaning of Revelation* (1941), H. Richard Niebuhr called for closer attention to the narrative features of the Bible and the individual's experience arising out of a shared communal life eclipsed by abstract arguments. The individual entered the tradition through embracing Christian truth expressed in stories, memories, and recollections. A shared narrative bound the individual to the spiritual community.

While Niebuhr argued for a return to the narrative, the necessary methodological tools arose out of mid-century literary criticism and Ludwig Wittgenstein's philosophy of language. The 1971 essay by religious scholar Stephen Crites, "The Narrative Quality of Experience," marked a watershed moment for narrative theology, taking up where Niebuhr had left off. Crites noted that outside a narrative frame, the human experience was not understandable. Narrative took the forms of sacred stories that functioned as overarching unifying structures, the mundane stories of daily life, and the temporal forms of experience itself. Narrative expressed "coherence through time" by organizing inchoate experience. Humans lived within sacred stories as communal worldviews, creating their sense of self and the world. Sacred stories, Crites argued, were nevertheless changeable, if not consciously so. Sallie McFague, a feminist theologian and former student of H. Richard Niebuhr, followed by arguing in *Speaking in Parables* (1975) that the narrative structure of the biblical text, as parable and metaphor, modeled the imaginative language necessary to speak of divine activity in history. Parables as extended metaphors were the way by which the transcendent "comes to ordinary reality and disrupts it." McFague sought to construct theology away from abstraction to connect with the narrative frame held by ordinary people. Narrative in the form of poetry, fiction, and biography was set to change theology in ways more congruent with how ordinary people arrived at their understanding of God.[34]

Narrative provided the tool for capturing women's experiences and giving them religious meaning. The first task for feminists was in recovering, rereading, and reimaging the women of the Bible, particularly Mary and Eve, who as archetypes had served to either oppress women or liberate them. Other biblical women, such as Hagar, Sarah, Jezebel, and Mary Magdalene, were open to feminist readings. Ruether looked to ancient Middle Eastern myths to unveil a suppressed story of the Great Mother hidden under the creation of Eve story. Drawing from the work of psychoanalyst Karen Horney and her theory of the male castration complex, Ruether reimagined the story of Eve's creation from the rib of Adam as an attempt to cast woman as "totally dependent on the male for her *raison d'etre*." Nevertheless, as Collins asserted, the story of Eve reaching for the forbidden fruit of the knowledge of good and evil could read as a revolutionary act of self-assertion against a patriarchal God. Feminists took up the ritual eating of the apple as a narrative reenactment in which women asserted an independent identity. Mary, carrying the weighty problem of the "virginal mother," was a more complex figure. At times, feminist theologians saw Mary as countering the myth of woman as the source of sin and providing a symbol of feminine authority. At other times, as a symbol of subordination and perpetual motherhood, Mary became hopelessly unredeemable. Feminist theology thus began a process of recovering the women of the Bible who had been lost under a patriarchal text and masculinist interpretations.[35]

Feminist theologians looked beyond the biblical text and women's history to literature—poetry, novels, and short stories—as sources for understanding women as embodied subjects and for naming the movements of the divine. The literary work of Adrienne Rich, Charlotte Perkins Gilman, Kate Chopin, Anne Sexton, and Doris Lessing expressed the struggle to regain a lost female self. These writings offered a story of struggle for self-actualization, life, and freedom uniting women across the ages. Feminist theologians delved into the whole of women's literature and history to connect women's lived experience with the movement of God expressed in poetic and imaginative language. Women's stories served as alternative sacred narratives. The move beyond the biblical text marked a dividing line between those who would remain within the Christian religion and those who would go on to establish a feminist spirituality freed from that tradition.[36]

As white middle-class women offered challenges to religious tradition through their own experience, black women continued to consider race to be the first line of struggle. Feminist scholarship and politics remained split along racial lines. Intellectuals, who were critical to the functioning of historical freedom movements, were waging a distinct battle to speak for black women forming their own radical feminist organizations, including the Third World Women's Alliance. The "Black Woman's Manifesto," published in 1970 by the Alliance, argued that black women should be suspicious of any claim to "common oppression" coming from white women whose chief complaint was "boredom, genteel repression, and dishpan hands." The rhetoric of common oppression among women hid economic and racial injustice. In 1970, Maxine Williams and Pamela Newman called for black women to go beyond the nationalism of Black Power and the irrelevancy of white feminism to develop their own feminist consciousness. They argued for Third World women to take action against oppression and assert rights over their own bodies, exploited through denigrating work and involuntary sexual labor. Some black women joined forces with white women, seeing sex as a sufficient basis for solidarity. The activist Florynce "Flo" Kennedy, involved in both NOW and the Black Power movement, concluded in 1973 that "whether you're fighting for Women's Liberation or . . . Black Liberation, you are fighting the same enemies." [37]

Black Power set the foundation for the emergence of "womanist" black feminist theology in the 1980s and 1990s when the entry of black women into the theological academy reached a critical mass. Challenging her mentor Cone, Jacquelyn Grant's 1979 essay "Black Theology and the Black Woman" called for the inclusion of black women in liberation theology. The 1980s found black women turning to the writings of Anna Julia Cooper, Zora Neale Hurston, Ida B. Wells, and Alice Walker—who coined the term "womanist" in her 1983 book *In Search of Our Mothers' Garden*—for the stories that defined their lived experience. Walker's definition of a womanist as "a black feminist who is audacious, willful and serious; loves and prefers women, but also who may love men; is committed to the survival and wholeness of entire people, and is universalist, capable, all loving, and deep" offered a radically embodied and communal path for theology. Women taking up a womanist theology in the 1990s, including Delores S. Williams with her book *Sisters in the Wilderness: The Challenge of Womanist God-Talk* (1993) and Emilie Maureen Townes' *Womanist Justice, Womanist Hope* (1993), among others, connected the struggle of black women in the African diaspora with that of women of color throughout the world. They challenged the privilege of white feminists and overreliance on abstract theory and an oppositional stance, and underscored the connection of black womanhood with the sanctity of the black family and community. In a commitment to *action,* womanist theology "talked back" to both white feminist and black male theologians from the lived experience of black women against a universalizing and masculinist ethos. What feminist-inspired theologies arising in multiple communities shared was a commitment to the experience of women as oppressed and the retelling of their stories as the starting point for any theological reflection.[38]

The first generation of feminist theologians were involved in a critical and creative project that brought together divergent strands of religion and modern thought. Their public battles to gain ordination and entry into male-dominated ecclesial institutions dominates their known history. Through a more radical project that went beyond inclusion in ecclesial hierarchy, they reimagined the entire Christian tradition and theological foundations. They sought a new inclusive definition of humanity by uncovering the lost feminine principle buried under layers of masculinist philosophy and theology. Appealing freely to solidarity with other oppressed groups, ancient myths, "herstory," and pragmatically derived ethics, they were always in threat of playing into the sexist ideas they sought to overturn. More fully actualizing Schleiermacher's romantic definition of the religious feeling as an immediate self-consciousness of the infinite and a validation of the individual woman's experience made lasting solidarity difficult. The subjective nature of the religious experience came to its fullest expression in feminist theologizing: a theology fully situated in the experience of women and freed from a transcendent source of values or tradition.

Through narrative, feminist theologians readily saw affinities between race and class on one hand, and sex on the other, allowing them to identify women's struggle with racialized minorities and Third World people. Neither black nor Latin American male liberationists offered reciprocity to women as women. The intersectionality of black women offers the clearest illustration. At the birth of liberation theology, black women were in a double bind, at the margins of both the white feminist and masculinist black theologies. Neither theology provided a full accounting of their situation. White women speaking from within the dominant group displayed a certain racial and class blindness. Marginalized men sought to escape the lower-status association with women; thus, in the struggle for recognition, women within their ranks did not represent an asset. Male liberationists' self-assertion as historical agents could not identify with the understood self-negation of women—a negation that served the needs of the "race" or the "people." Male liberationists illustrated Ruether's argument that enlightened men could imagine peasants and slaves asserting their freedom, yet viewed women hidden within these groups as perpetually bound to nature and subsumed within a universal (male) humanity. The modern pursuit of freedom remained a decidedly male venture.[39]

10

A Culture of Solidarity

RETURNING TO THE United States from observing the 1955 Bandung Conference of non-aligned nations, Richard Wright noted the deeply organic nature of the new nationalism on display. He listened as Third World leaders espoused self-determination through "ideological disarmament and moral re-armament" while making universal humanist appeals against racism, political subjugation, and economic exploitation. The goal was modernization allowing their nations to catch up with Western progress while renewing native culture and religion. Wright sensed the unleashing of "two of the most powerful and irrational forces in human nature," race and religion, into one "system of identification" against all forms of colonialism that went beyond the choice between liberal democracy and Marxism. As a secular humanist, he considered the path to modernization to be on a collision course with religiously underwritten archaic particularities of race and culture. Wright viewed the Third World, making its last appeal to the "moral conscience of the West," as caught between the desire for inclusion and the search for recognition of its independent and unique cultures.[1]

Wright's astute observation of the convergence of politics, cultural identity, and religion did not anticipate the adoption of the language of anti-colonialism by members of the New Left. For radicals, promises of modernization in Latin America and liberal inclusion for black people in North America were forms of colonialism underwritten by false universal values suspected of promoting US imperial power. Anti-colonial movements supplied an alternative universalizing narrative for those on the margins of the liberal project, as the drive for recognition turned the sources of exclusion—race, class, and sex—into the means of forging a new culture of solidarity.

The demand for recognition was an echo from the Enlightenment. The philosopher Charles Taylor noted in his 1992 essay "The Politics of Recognition" how late-twentieth-century politics turned on the demand for recognition among subaltern groups, including women, blacks, and colonized people. The collapse of the fixed hierarchies of the *ancien régime* wrought in modernity a "politics of equal recognition" of human dignity first articulated by Rousseau. Going further, Hegel established mutual recognition between master and slave as the first premise toward freedom. Severed from traditional communities of place and kin, the modern individual was on a quest to find a new basis for identity through common experiences or shared values. Identity, linked to recognition, was a self-understanding shaped in a dialogical and often distorting social process. Misrecognition, or nonrecognition, signified a form of oppression and injustice.[2]

The 1960s embrace of group identity through a "politics of difference" challenged the rhetoric of a homogenizing universalism. Advocates for excluded groups argued that the dominant society imposed a homogenizing cultural ideal upon those deemed as lacking. Exclusion marked their difference. An internalized sense of inferiority reproduced inequality in minority groups, women, and the colonized. The language of difference and recognition offered a way for liberationists to redefine God and humanity away from the universal, suspected of hiding domination, toward acknowledging the particular experience of groups. This chapter explores how Latin American and black theologians advanced their liberatory theology by joining the anti-colonial demand for recognition.[3]

Latin American Reality

The search for a unique and unifying identity has a long history in Latin American thought, and here I offer the barest outline of that history leading to liberationists' intervention. After the wars of independence, nineteenth-century elites embarked on nation-building projects determined to overcome the continental patchwork of race, language, and cultural distinctions. The reverberation of the new enlightened political philosophy valorized a set of universalizing ideals about the meaning and goals of modern nations. The necessity of national cohesion raised questions: What was the essence of being Peruvian or Cuban? What was the logic of Latin American nations? No longer under kings or empires, citizens of new nations needed a common purpose and means of identification.[4]

Latin America sank its roots into the idea of *mestizaje*, a racial and cultural admixture of people under colonization who were neither European nor Indian. Modern civilization stressed racial purity, deeming *mestizos* both culturally and racially inferior. Increasingly *mestizaje* moved away from marking biological race to defining the search for "*lo Americano*," both as a unique cultural identity and as an obstacle to progress. The historian Leopoldo Zea noted that unlike much of Western thought, Latin Americans' concern with identity went beyond the standard philosophical questions of Being. Arguments often reflected the parochial viewpoint of a concrete man and were thus alien to the truly universal. The challenge for elites attempting to build modern nations was in locating a cultural distinction independent of Europe while maintaining some recourse to the universal. An enlightened universal threatened an impossible erasure of distinct cultural identities among resistant native people. Assuming a racially impure *mestizaje,* nation builders inadvertently contributed to images of Latin America as backward and lacking the ability to be truly modern.[5]

The first strategy of liberal republicans was to establish enlightened modernity by destroying all vestiges of Spanish colonial culture. As the sons of independence, they proclaimed a mission to bring non-Iberian European civilization to the continent. Domingo F. Sarmiento's, who in 1864 became the Argentine ambassador to the United States foundational work *Facundo: Civilización y Barbarie* [Civilization and Barbarism] (1845) attempted to set an international course for Argentina. He posited an opposition between the civilization of the urban people of European extraction residing in Buenos Aires and the heirs of a backward Spanish colonialism, the indigenous and mixed-race people of the countryside. For Sarmiento and his allies, the future of Argentina was in identifying with and emulating European and Anglo-American culture. Consequently, Latin American identity and its future were continually embroiled in a dialogical colonizing process.

Failing to break patterns of despotic rule or find congruency with a Catholic social order, in 1853 the Argentine political theorist Juan Bautista Alberdi observed, "The republic is not a reality in South America because the people are not prepared to rule themselves." The continent still appeared as a derivative of bygone feudal Europe, and independence as "nothing more than dismemberment of European power." Everything, whether the Christian religion, the system of laws, or the organization of South America's cities and governments, was an import, and "the indigenous person does not figure in or make up the world of our political and civil society." Indigenous rural people loyal to traditional communities and the rule of *caudillos,* and "backward" Africans, appeared as obstacles in nations' attempts to achieve modernity.[6]

Liberal men of letters in the second half of the century, among them the Chileans Francisco Bilbao and José Victorino Lastaría and the Peruvian Javier Prado, made an incomplete turn from foreign models of nationhood by combining enlightened universal principles with the particular experience of their countries. They sought to define the Latin American difference as rooted in race, understood as the essential constitution of the people, the culture-shaping natural environment, or as the result of archaic scholastic education. Viable republics required an American philosophy based on the experience and epoch of each country, rather than an abstract philosophy incongruent with the continent. Advocating the necessity of mental emancipation through an autochthonous philosophy, politic, science, and literature, Lastarria asserted, "we must be original." By embracing scientific positivism, these intellectuals hoped to locate an authentic culture and envision a utopian future. The crisis of identity created by the rhetorical opposition of modernity to an autochthonous reality remained at the heart of Latin American thought. Frustrated intellectuals saw their nations as both modern and not yet modern.[7]

José Martí, the intellectual leader of Cuban independence, ushered in the twentieth-century search for cultural independence. He broke with Eurocentric ideas by defining a wholly native source of identity. Martí, exiled from Cuba, spent years in Europe and the Americas, including his most productive, 1880–1895, in New York City. His observations of the North American scene, addressed to a Latin American audience, warned of the imminent threat of U.S. imperial domination. Martí's erudition, and death as a Cuban revolutionary, established him as a central figure among intellectuals.

Although Martí's focus was in securing an independent Cuba, he constructed a continental vision anchored in a common purpose and spiritual values transcending the discrete geographic borders of its nations. Martí's essay "*Nuestra América*" (1891), published in New York and Mexico City, offered a foundation for continental identity by contrasting a *mestizo* "Our America"—natural, diverse, and creative—with the expansionistic and aggressive "Other America"—the United States. Martí sought to escape US-centric Pan-Americanism, "excessive importation of foreign ideas and formulas," and to define a unique native experience.[8]

Martí also attempted to negate the significance of race by declaring, "there are no races." Unlike the U.S. citizens who believed in the "incontroversial superiority of the Anglo-Saxon race over the Latin race," he believed that to be Cuban meant more than being white, mulatto, or Negro. He proposed embracing an identity springing from indigenous roots, and abandoning foreign ways that produced a derivative and inauthentic culture. The continent needed to cultivate its own leaders and institutions, recover its Inca history, and a "common cause had to be made with the oppressed." The Cuban nation, and by extension Latin America, could unite under shared values and history. Martí, and many who followed, attempted to overcome heterogeneity and produce a unifying *mestizo* identity: a constructed cultural essentialism that hid the assumption of racial and ethnic differences that remained.[9]

After Martí, attempts at cultural self-definition turned to either some notion of an indigenous past, unadulterated Christian–European values, or a pessimistic attention to national peculiarities. *Modernista* writers rejecting positivism continued to assert Latin American uniqueness. Facing U.S. ascendancy, the Uruguayan José Enrique Rodó warned in *Ariel* (1900) against imitating a foreign model while "sacrificing irreplaceable uniqueness" and falling into "nordomania," an unhealthy fascination with North America. Combining Christian idealism and classic Greek humanism, and drawing an analogy from Shakespeare's *The Tempest*, Rodó set Latin America's spiritual idealism, Ariel, against the vulgar pragmatism of the North American, Caliban. Rodó plotted a path for a continental identity based not on an indigenous past but on a classic European heritage to overcome the utilitarianism and "egalitarian barbarity" of North America. Rodó's vision of Latin America as a paragon of classic European civilization elided its indigenous and colonial past.[10]

Rather than erase the heterogeneous nature of the continent, *La Raza Cósmica*, written by the Mexican José Vasconcelos in 1925, celebrated the racial fusion of *mestizaje* yielding a "cosmic race" whose mission was to forge a universal humanity. The Dominican Pedro Henríquez Ureña also proposed a utopian vision of a new universal man in *La Utopia America* (1925). Through the strength of its various racial contributions, Vasconcelos envisioned a cosmic race bringing about a spiritual era directed by love and joy rather than necessity. The "divine mission" of America was "fusing all peoples ethnically and spiritually" to arrive at an integral race capable of true brotherhood. In envisioning a singular continental future, made up of the fusion of diverse cultural and racial elements, utopian thinking was never far away.[11]

Throughout the twentieth century, Latin America's sense of itself was continually entangled with modernity and the past. The writer Samuel Ramos brought attention to what he deemed to be the essential psychology of the Mexican people. *Profile of Man and Culture in Mexico* (1934) drew from the psychology of Carl Jung and Alfred Adler to cast the Mexican national character as "compensating for an unconscious sense of inferiority." Conquest, colonization, and incomplete mental independence produced a profound sense of lack and impeded the nation's sense of its own *mestizo* identity. Ramos portrayed a clash between two cultures: pagan Amerindian and Spanish Catholic. Seeking to establish a foundation for a national culture and reform, Ramos exemplified the tension between the particularity of the region and the desire to identify with the universal and recognize its European heritage.[12]

Intellectuals were unable to shake the underlying unease that the continent's reality was incongruent with dominant European and North American models of society. Through the 1950s, many viewed Latin America's lost identity as a self-inflicted wound due to what Argentine essayist Hector A. Murena described as the "original sin of America," an incomplete rejection of Europe that had left it without a history of its own. Among the diverse cultures and peoples, coalescing effective national identities proved impossible. The continent needed to look away from both external models and particularity of culture or race and find a new narrative for self-definition.

Complex cultural dynamics and history, but also its political and economic challenges, shaped the continent's sense of self. In the first half of the twentieth century, Latin America experienced a new awareness of the political ramifications of a population not easily assimilated into a monoculture. Longtime acquiescence by indigenous people turned into a demand for increased participation. Populist and Marxist-inspired labor movements questioned a political and economic system beholden to elites and foreign interests. The post–World War II period brought a brief revival of the traditional left, communist and socialist, only to retreat, splintered and divided. The traditional left faced problems in organizing workers, a weak and petty bourgeoisie, and an overwhelming number of peasants. The Catholic Church's resistance to Marxism, along with U.S. Cold War interventions, reverberated throughout the continent. The 1950s made evident to many observers the continent's ensnarement in both an ideological and a global political and economic system.[13]

The reverberations of anti-colonial movements brought the conviction that the historical difference suffered by Latin America was what Frantz Fanon called the particularity of the "colonial wound." Literary theorist Walter D. Mignolo characterized the colonial wound of the continent as one imposed by the "colonial difference" marked by modernity. It was neither race, culture, nor environment that plagued the continent but its relationship to imperial power. Under the pressure to be truly modern, Europe and the U.S. societies had loomed large as the standard of measure. Latin America needed a new post-colonial story to make sense of the perpetual problem of underdevelopment.[14]

The Cuban Revolution clarified the nature of Latin America's political and economic relations with the rest of the world, galvanizing intellectuals and popular movements. Overthrowing the U.S.-backed dictator Fulgencio Batista, a band of revolutionaries demonstrated that a small country could successfully break with the ideological and economic control of the United States. Peasant guerillas took up arms without the participation of the old Communist party. Che Guevara asserted that underdevelopment was an economic distortion created by imperialism and supported by a co-opted national bourgeoisie. The result of foreign exploitation was mass unemployment, low wages, poverty, hunger, and oppression. Frequently evoking Martí, Guevara cast the revolution as continental in character—"Cuba's battle is the battle of all Latin America"—and a fight against U.S. economic monopoly, requiring a unified strategy. As the "vanguard of America," Cuba served as a model for a socialist revolution, standing in solidarity with all the world's oppressed people. The Revolution evoked the idea of forging a Latin American identity beyond race and nation through the development of an autochthonous socialism.[15]

A revitalized New Left broke with the weak and ineffective orthodox Marxism and labor movements. The New Left asserted that it was unnecessary for Latin America to go through the anticipated Marxist revolutionary stages, and it could not hope to do so with a small bourgeoisie beholden to the United States. Cuba had demonstrated that an immediate armed revolution from below could force the hand of history. The Revolution inspired the formation of guerilla groups in the early 1960s, beginning in rural areas and moving into cities by the end of the decade. U.S. intervention, whether shoring up weak civilian governments or assisting in military coups, added fuel to the revolutionary fire. Nevertheless, repression, structural change, and strategic errors among revolutionary groups failed to establish a Cuba-style revolution on the continent.[16]

The initial enthusiasm for Cuba waned by the late 1960s as the hope for a continental revolution failed to materialize. The peasantry, the imagined vanguard of a socialist revolution, was abandoning the countryside en masse and moving into the urban areas, drawn by the elusive prospect of jobs. For workers, unorganized and participating in an informal urban economy, the impoverished shantytowns, rather than unions, became the focus of political organizing. In an informal economy, the salient issue was not controlling the means of production but the means of state, which determined the basic conditions of life. The state, rather than the employer, was the target of mobilization. With the presence of radicalized priest and pastoral workers, the density and misery of cities turned tens of thousands of lay-led BECs (base ecclesial communities), among the poor into a seedbed for the emergent liberation theology and political mobilization.[17]

Social scientists were also gathering vast amounts of new data and reexamining the reasons for the distressed situation of underdevelopment. The imported modernization theory of the 1950s promised a way for the continent to catch up in terms of development and to contain communism. Modernization theory encouraged free markets and scientific forms of production while discouraging traditional religious–cultural values at odds with a liberal capitalism. By opening up their nations to the global capitalist system, and through an evolutionary process, Latin American nations were to follow the pattern of Anglo-American development from feudalism to industrialization.

By the 1960s, social scientists had rejected modernization theory and were articulating an alternative explanation: dependency theory. They rejected the linear model of development by insisting that Latin America had never been truly feudal. Since colonization the continent had been part of the worldwide capitalist system, and its political economy had been defined by the dominant powers. In *Dependency and Development in Latin America* (1967), the Brazilian F.H.

Cardoso and the Chilean Enzo Faletto, both sociologists, noted that "structural dependency" relationships condemned the continent to perpetual underdevelopment. The situation was not correctly described with the terms *underdeveloped nations* and *advanced nations*, but rather *exploited* and *exploiter*. Despite structural determination, change was possible through intervention and resistance in collaboration with social movements. Dependency theory offered a scientific explanation and overarching narrative for the historical experience of the continent. Rather than race, autochthonous culture, or national character, it was Latin America's position in the "world-system" that shaped its reality and identity.[18]

Liberationists, with their commitment to social science, quickly grasped dependency theory to make sense of massive injustice. Dependency theory identified all that ailed the continent and served as a unifying narrative. Under the sway of dependency theory, *liberation* as a word of "confrontation and conflict" replaced the passivity of *development*. The term *liberation*, Hugo Assmann noted, was itself a "dislocation of the semantic axis of the word 'liberty' . . . a concrete example of ideological and semantic domination." The liberationist commitment to dependency theory was not a neutral step; rather, it was the language of liberation theology. Dependency, not merely an external structure, "must be seen as an overall conditioning factor in our history, molding us into what we have become culturally, socially, economically, and politically." Dependency also produced religious distortions through the importation of a "dependent Christianity" weighted down by a "theological absolutism." What all Latin American nations shared was a dependency-bred identity supported by religion. An integral liberation demanded a truly autochthonous theology—a theology from below.[19]

Dependency theory and the after-effects of the Cuban Revolution produced a consensus among young radicals. José Míguez Bonino observed that young people were finding it impossible to understand the Christian faith without reference to Guevara's revolutionary ideals. For them, Guevara represented the world they lived in, one in which revolution and liberation were legitimate transcriptions of the Christian gospel. It was with ease that they answered the question "Who, then, is Jesus Christ?" with "Jesus Christ is Che Guevara." "Guevara Christians" saw dependency as the salient feature of their reality. They did not view North America's advanced society and prosperity as the result of higher moral character or the principles of free enterprise, democracy, or education. Rather, they saw it as feeding off a systematic subjugation of its southern neighbor. Slogans of "freedom and democracy" were opportunities for the United States to pillage the continent while protected by escalating internal repression. The economic reality had distorted Latin American religion.[20]

Radicals regarded Christianity in Latin America as bound by two historical experiences. The first was conquest and colonization, tying a Catholic Church alienated from the people to the colonial structures of domination. In the second, Christianity had been co-opted by Protestant-inspired liberalism and neo-colonialism cloaked in the "hoax of democracy." Both projects, the colonialism and liberal capitalism, plundered the continent for the enrichment of external empires. Both conservative and liberal forms of religion had betrayed the people by surrendering them to imperial power and the resultant poverty, malnutrition, illiteracy, exploitation, and death. What underlay ideologically bound religion was theology—the derivative nature of thinking about God that was propagated among the people.[21]

The Narrative of the Poor

The Cuban Revolution generated a consolidation of cultural identity and inspired genre innovation in a generation of writers. The Latin American boom of the 1960s brought the traditional intellectual class of literary writers to the world stage for the first time. The vanguard of the movement, such as the Colombian Gabriel García Márquez and Cuban Alejo Carpentier, reimagined the history of the continent from below through localized stories challenging the accepted history. García Márquez's prize-winning novel of magical realism, *One Hundred Years of Solitude* (1967), attempted to rewrite a fictionalized sweep of the continent's history. Through the Edenic town of Macondo and the Buendia family and by combining fact and utopian myth, he challenged the official story centered on elites. The cycle of repression, violence, and economic exploitation marking the continent's history served as the raw material for García Márquez's novel. Carpentier's historical novel *El Siglo de las Luces*, literally translated as "the century of lights," retells the story of the Caribbean in the shadow of the French and Haitian revolutions. Carpentier places blacks as agents in the creation of the modern enlightened world, thus challenging the dominant narrative. In an attempt to write a revisionist history of the continent from the bottom up, Uruguayan journalist Eduardo Galeano in 1970 wrote *The Open Veins of Latin America*, casting the continent as a victim of five centuries of pillage and exploitation. Galeano's rewriting served as a political project, in which the future lay in the hands of the emerging rebellious masses of "dispossessed, the humiliated, the accursed." The proliferation of politically inspired writing, aided by international publishing and acclaim, announced to the world that Latin America was ready to write its own history. The theme of a shared history and the inclusion of the subordinated constructed a mobilizing narrative for new social movements.[22]

For traditionally Catholic people, any political shift required a religious change through an appeal to a higher authority. An ecclesial opening for a new theology appeared in the Vatican Second Council's *Gaudium et Spes* (1965), a hastily written document concluding that without economic justice, world peace was unattainable. Reflecting the influence of Jacques Maritain, the Council recognized that "we are witnesses of the birth of a new humanism, one in which man is defined first of all by this responsibility to his brothers and to history." The document called for a "truly universal economic order" that addressed the injustice of "undue dependence" experienced by the poor. In addressing the distress of the poor, the Council affirmed, "if one is in extreme necessity, he has the right to procure for himself what he needs out of the riches of others." While the participating bishops split on many doctrinal and liturgical issues, they agreed on the issue of social justice, with no consensus on how far the prophetic challenge should go. Did extreme necessity justify violence? Religious radicals interpreted the document as an opening for a militant advocacy for social justice.[23]

However, failing to include Third World bishops along with 600 Latin Americans in the writing of the document, *Gaudium et Spes* remained a product of a First World perspective based on a Western model of development tied to the values of dignity, freedom, and participation. The document appealed to affluent individuals and governments to remember the poor, and gave no practical moral guidelines on how the poor communities were to meet their own needs and the moral terms of coercion. The key difference between relying on the charity of the powerful toward the weak and empowering the poor to alleviate their own situation is critical in distinguishing liberation theology from the main currents of Catholic social thought. Nevertheless, the Council's charge in *Gaudium et Spes* expressed a new openness to considering socio-historical forces by recognizing the responsibility to scrutinize "the signs of the times and [to interpret] them in the light of the Gospel." In the ambiguity of the document, emergent liberation theologians scrutinizing the signs of the times viewed the continental situation as marked by oppression and unrest, requiring a rereading of the Gospel from the perspective of the poor. *Gaudium et Spes* allowed liberationists room to claim the mainstream of Catholic social thought as their own.[24]

By the end of the 1960s, liberation theologians had the resources to respond to Gutiérrez call for "critical reflection on historical praxis" that "penetrate the present reality." The Cuban Revolution energized and unified a variety of social movements; a scientific dependency theory explained the historical problem of Latin America, providing a basis for solidarity beyond race and culture; Vatican II invited the consideration of economic injustice and societal distress. Broad and long-term theological changes allowed the emerging liberationists to view God's self-disclosure in the immanence of human history. Armed with these changes, the Bishops at Medellín in 1968 called on the faithful to "transform and perfect the world in solidarity" beyond the exhausted means of liberal capitalism and Marxist systems. They noted that "dependence on inhuman economic systems... for many... borders on slavery," producing an "internal colonization" with the elite classes deploying repressive force. The continent also experienced an external "neo-colonialism," making it beholden to an international capitalist system. The result was misery and injustice that "cries to the heavens."[25]

The bishops at Medellín declared their commitment to denouncing the conditions that kept people in poverty and joined the poor in solidarity through simple living and working among them. Committed to a grassroots process of *concientización* and mobilization, they called on the Church to transform the world through a "profound conversion" of people and unjust structures. The hoped-for result was a "new humanity," a new self-understanding for Latin Americans as "artisans of [their] own destiny" arising among the people.[26]

Base ecclesial communities as an on-the-ground venue for revolutionary ideas to spread worked in two ways. These groups provided the social context for liberationist reflection on praxis and for articulating a narrative of oppression and liberation. In turn, a new contextualized theology invigorated participants by giving them a religious justification for political action. An early model was the Solentiname Community in Nicaragua. As a newly ordained priest and poet, Ernesto Cardenal founded Solentiname in 1965 in the remote archipelago of Lake Nicaragua as an intentional community among poor *campesinos*. Serving as an incubator for revolution through consciousness raising, the community attracted intellectuals and artists. An inspiring 1970 trip to Cuba convinced Cardenal that the Christian "Gospel is essentially political or else it is nothing." His poetry and narratives expressed outrage with corruption, poverty among the peasants, and U.S. dominance. Through prophetic poetry as a political praxis, Cardenal located the kingdom of God within revolutionary movements. Following the example of the martyred Camilo Torres, he considered his priestly role to be a revolutionary one. By the 1970s, the Solentiname islands became a guerilla training ground, attracting the attention of the brutal right-wing dictator Anastasio Somoza, who ordered the bombing of the community's chapel. Cardenal became the chief international spokesman for the 1979 Sandinista revolution and was noted by European political theologians Johann Baptist Metz and Jürgen Moltmann for his theo-political poetry and praxis.[27]

Cardenal's record of his dialogue with the people of Solentiname demonstrated a commitment to a narrative theology arising from the history of the land and its people. His collection of poems, *Salmos* (1963), a reinterpretation of the biblical Psalms, reflects the struggle for social and political liberation. Contemporized, *Salmos* allowed him to show God's solidarity with the weak, the poor, the oppressed, and the social castoffs. *Salmos* portrays the oppression of the people by wicked dictators, the gangsters, and government bureaucracy. In a dramatic narrative, the oppressors are set against the oppressed in a Manichaean struggle between good and evil.

Subsequently *The Gospel in Solentiname* (1975), a compilation of the daily discussions that took place in the 1960s, illustrates *campesinos* interacting with the biblical narrative, offering their own interpretation of the text. A political reading of the Gospels equated the U.S.-backed Somoza with biblical Herod, who slaughtered the innocent, and Sandinista guerillas with Christ. The narrative emerging in Solentiname, and in other radicalized BECs, supplied not only the revolutionary context but also the content of liberation theology. As the poor told their story and supplied the interpretation of the biblical text, they constructed a theology from below as the central feature of liberation theology. Liberation theologians as committed intellectuals took on the task of recognizing and legitimizing what they deemed as God's voice among the people.[28]

Gustavo Gutiérrez's *A Theology of Liberation* was the culmination not only of long-term intellectual change within theology, as I have already shown, but also of cultural and political experience. Persuaded that theologians could no longer ignore poverty, dependency, and neo-colonialism, and needed to open their eyes to radical resistance and suppression, Gutiérrez viewed the challenge of overcoming the colonial mentality as one of the great theological tasks. His theological decolonization drew from the critical tradition of the sixteenth-century priest Bartolomé de Las Casas; from the *avant-garde* poet Cesar Vallejo, whom he quotes as having protested, "my God, if you had been a man, you would know how to be God"; from José Carlos Mariategui's indigenous and mystical socialism; and from contemporaneous philosophical currents. The clues for the content of a new theology were already resident in the culture.[29]

Enrique Dussel, an ally of Gutiérrez and at the forefront of a philosophy of liberation in his book *Filosofía de la liberación* (1977), challenged the dominant ideology espoused from Hegel to Marcuse for a philosophy "rising from the periphery, from the oppressed, from the shadow that the light of Being has not been able to illuminate. Our thoughts set out from non-Being, nothingness, othernesss, exteriority, and the mystery of non-sense. It is, then, a 'barbarian' philosophy." He offered the necessity of decolonizing the mind of the oppressed through an epistemic relocation from the center of Europe to the marginal, yet critical, insight of Latin America. Decolonizing was process of dismantling cultural practices and patterns of thought and belief that continually reinforce inequality. The Third World, in a privileged epistemic position, he asserted, was challenging all forms of oppression generated by modernity. Joining Dussel, Gutiérrez found an oppositional way of knowing among the oppressed and for decolonizing what Dussel described as "fetishist religion," the totalizing religion of modern thought.[30]

José Maria Arguedas, a Marxist and Gutiérrez's contemporary, had an immediate influence by providing a literary model of knowledge from below. Arguedas, a Peruvian ethnologist, folklorist, and novelist, attempted to capture the social and existential location of the *mestizo* caught between two worlds. He followed the legacy of Mariategui's *indigenismo,* taking up his spirit of social criticism and moving beyond him to find in the *mestizo,* rather than the indigenous, the future of the nation. Arguedas' initial attempts at fiction were in Quechua, the language of his childhood; however, no literary market existed for such writing. Turning to Spanish, he found that his Quechua self and the Spanish language were at odds with his attempt at authenticity. His literary works attempted to forge a new cultural identity by placing the wisdom of the indigenous people at the heart of a Peruvian *mestizaje*, changing both the indigenous and the dominant Creole culture. In a desire to adequately portray the Quechua's cosmological vision in narrative, Arguedas attempted to translate the values and syntax of the language into Spanish. The result was a literary innovation of "transculturation," defined by the literary critic Angel Rama as the process of creating something new by the convergence of seemingly opposing cultures while maintaining the best of both worlds.[31]

Throughout this oeuvre, much of it drawn from his own upbringing among the indigenous Quechua, Arguedas presented Peruvian culture as a struggle between two opposing views of the world. One was the Western worldview, with its scientific rationality and individualistic stance in which religion served as a tool for oppression. The other was the worldview of the Quechua, with its communitarian vision and religious–mythical sensibility. His best-known novels, *Yawar Fiesta* (1941) and the autobiographical *Deep Rivers* (1958), portray the clash of worldviews and the resulting oppression and social unrest. The effect of Arguedas' novels was what the Venezuelan liberation theologian Pedro Trigo called a "narrative theology" in which the subaltern become historical subjects, reflecting their understanding of God.[32]

Shortly before Gutiérrez began writing *A Theology of Liberation*, he and Arguedas became friends and found a mutual interest in the social problems of Peru. In Arguedas' act of literary transculturation, Gutiérrez found a source of inspiration to engage in a transculturation of theology. Only transculturation offered a bridge between the God of the poor and the God of the powerful, and between the European theology of his education and the spontaneous theology that emerged from the people. Gutiérrez dedicated his work to Arguedas, introducing his book within the narrative frame of Arguedas' novel *All the Bloods* (1964). The passage quoted by Gutiérrez describes a scene situated in a parish church. A reluctant *mestizo* sacristan engages in conversation with a visiting priest, who views the *mestizo* as being of higher quality than the previously assigned ignorant Indian sacristan. The dialogue for the scene expresses the deep divide between the God of the powerful represented by the priest, who sends suffering without consolation, and the God who is among the Indian people, a God of hope. Gutiérrez saw Arguedas as representing powerless people who gain agency to act in history and construct a theology from their everyday lives.[33]

Reading the narratives of Arguedas served as a step toward Gutiérrez's "spiritual decolonization" in which the revolutionary "Other" found their historical agency. In this way, liberation theology recovered the religious sensibilities and language of the people in a new narrative. It was a story of God's partiality to the downtrodden, the poor, and the marginal, and against the powerful—and it offered a bridge to religiously alienated intellectuals such as Arguedas through affirming a unique Latin American experience.

Latin American liberation theology, as a narrative arising from below, was the culmination of the continent's long search for a politically effective and unifying identity and an attempt at decolonization. It sprung from a long history of subjugation and marginalization of the majority of its people. Liberation theologians sought a new epistemological location, a way of knowing neglected by modern theology, to empower the lowest classes to assert their knowledge of God and their call to freedom. As children of the "colonial process," Latin Americans sought to decolonize epistemology, breaking the psychic and economic power of European-centered modernity and North American domination that kept its people in perpetual dependence.[34]

A Colonial Situation

Gayraud S. Wilmore, professor of social ethics at Boston University's School of Theology, proposed in a 1972 address, "Ethnic Identities and Christian Theology," that the worldwide identity crisis among people of color could not avoid having theological implications. Western theology emphasized "at least in theory" the universality of the faith and the unity of all mankind. It relied on that "liberal shibboleth 'The Brotherhood of Man and the Fatherhood of God.'" The social gospel, Protestant evangelicalism, and early American sociology, Wilmore asserted, agreed that the individual rather than the group was key in social regeneration. Seeking to make itself acceptable to the modern individual and counting ethnicity as irrelevant, American theology left out subjugated people in articulating its concept of God. The belief in the *"via theologia"* toward the integration of self-determined individuals into the American melting pot denied racial and cultural differences. Trusting in the construction of a *"new* race" of faith, people of color were to rely on the natural process of assimilation to render them more universally white. Wilmore demonstrated how theology supported a liberal ethos and promoted the "middle-class American way of life" designed to foreclose the development of countervailing power by minorities.[35]

Wilmore noted that people of color were beginning to discover the group power available through ethnic solidarity. He observed that, fatigued by oppression and motivated by a desire for liberation, ethnic people were "plumbing the depths of the adopted religion for symbols of independency and resistance." He saw parallels between people of color in the United States and the oppressed people of Latin America, who were uncovering the religious underpinnings of "spiritual emasculation." Facing the disorientation of unprecedented societal change and the homogenization of differences, they were discovering that oppression was the result of a "world culture stamped with the *imprimatur*, thought-forms and values of Europe and America." Incapable of addressing the source of social injustice and dehumanization, the theology of white men and "great white churches" was giving way to new ethnic theologies of liberation. Theologically, Wilmore asserted, liberation required recovering the meaning of *Pentecost*, in which each person hears the Word of God in "his own tongue." Tying North American blacks with the world's oppressed people in a shared spiritual awakening, Wilmore signaled the arrival of American theology in its circuitous route to recognize race and ethnic particularity in the 1970s.[36]

The foundation for a theology that affirmed both black racial pride and acknowledged the political position of African Americans was arduous and long in coming. Since emancipation, black thought, attended by religion, had grappled with defining the place of the Negro in society, recognizing both his or her particular identity and Americanness. Nationalist and integrationist impulses coexisted, often in the same thinker, moving along a continuum based on the degree to which whites displayed a disposition to expand black participation. The political thought of Martin Delany, Alexander Crummell, Henry McNeal Turner, and Marcus Garvey, as a varied and religiously infused black nationalism, expressed the conviction that central to black freedom, and its denial, were race and racial oppression. A multifarious black nationalism, accentuated by religion, encompassed movements calling for land set-asides within the continental United States; exodus to regions outside America, usually Africa; or political, economic, and cultural separatism within national borders. Short of acquiring land and the establishment of a separate state, a spiritual and cultural nationalism nonetheless gained currency. Cultural nationalism called for a return to authentic black values and a spiritual and existential liberation. Advocates held that only as the race established its identity and power as a group could it hope to negotiate on an equal basis for non-oppressive coexistence within U.S. borders.[37]

Du Bois' *The Souls of Black Folk* (1903) inaugurated the twentieth-century search for reconciliation of ethnic distinctions with national belonging. As Latin

American intellectuals sought a unique national identity rooted in *mestizaje,* Du Bois advanced an ambiguous concept of Negro identity as a basis for group cohesion. He described the history of slavery and segregation as producing a "double consciousness" and the psychic toll of being an "American, a Negro; two souls, two thoughts, two unreconciled strivings; two warring ideals in one dark body." Reconciling this "twoness" for a singularity of thought required that the Negro neither give up his distinctiveness nor assert an absolute difference, forever excluding him from the American nation. Resisting both segregation and the erasure of assimilation, Du Bois moved toward advancing a cultural black nationalism, a moral and intellectual autonomy that would secure blacks an effective place in national life.[38]

Finding a race-affirming place within American democracy played a role in the politically attenuated social thought of the inter-war period of black artists and writers. They were part of what Du Bois called the "Talented Tenth," propagating the image of Alain Locke's racially assertive "New Negro" demanding equal opportunity in American society and a distinct black identity. The creative production of the ideologically diffused 1920s Harlem Renaissance attempted a shame-free black self-image through individual freedom of expression. Black artists and writers seeking recognition of black culture deployed an aesthetic of ethnic realism, drawing from the common folk and ghetto life for their subject matter. Under the gaze of white purveyors of culture, their venture into an African-inspired romantic primitivism threatened to reify what whites already believed about black people as the possessors of a vital and vulgar emotional hedonism. Addressing black and white audiences, writers such as Langston Hughes, Zora Neale Hurston, and Claude McKay sought integration into the white-dominated literary establishment while espousing a distinct black identity. The economic effects of the Great Depression on urban blacks brought home the reality that the nation was not ready to embrace racial enlightenment. As the bravado of the Harlem Renaissance faded, attempts at inclusion turned from culture toward social and class struggle.[39]

By 1934, a despondent Du Bois had resigned from the NAACP and called on Negroes to build on their economic strength and develop a "nation within a nation," a race-based solidarity alternative to liberal individualism. After decades of advocating for integration, he concluded that whites had no plans for the survival of colored people if it involved "self-assertive modern manhood." He believed that U.S. political life was composed of a plurality of groups, and only as blacks constituted a recognizable group would they gain entrance into the democratic process. Regardless of the social reality, the liberal tide of democratic individualism was moving against Du Bois' desire for politically effective recognition of black ethnicity.[40]

Despite Du Bois' attempts to instill racial pride, many African Americans were lulled into quiescence by the promise of universal brotherhood. The historian Richard H. King has shown how post-war social thought established a universal understanding of humanity that deemed racial and ethnic differences as nonessential. The assumption of equal natural capacities, legal–political integration, and a consensus in "Judeo–Christian" values ensured the rights of the individual over the group. Gunnar Myrdal's social analysis in *An American Dilemma* (1944) expresses the optimism of the new consensus in which racial prejudice gave way to individual liberty and equality of the "American Creed." The reactive pathology of black culture was to dissolve into assimilation. A suspiciously Western universal human type replaced the previous essentialist views of race and culture. The American creed required that blacks regard themselves as simply American in a nation denying them an ethnic identity allowed to other groups. Black intellectuals attempted to bridge the gap between a socially ascribed Negro identity, which served as a means of social exclusion, and a claim to the universal that held the nation together.[41]

Black writers at mid-century addressing a white audience displayed different notions of the individual's assimilation into national culture. Richard Wright's Marxist-inspired *Native Son* (1940) protested against the brutalizing oppression of racial caste among black lower classes, for which violence was the only alternative to cultural assimilation. Focusing on an atomized and dehumanized central character, Wright rendered invisible the protective effects of cultural institutions, including the black church, sustaining the self-respect of a large segment of black people. Ralph Ellison's modern epic *The Invisible Man* (1952) rejected the sociopolitical understanding of the black experience. Ellison's novel portrayed an existential search for freedom and depicted the Negro's psychological experience of living as a "phantom" and as a figment of whites' imagination. Ellison called for recognition of the black man as an individual set against overcoming a socially inscribed identity. In *The Fire Next Time* (1963), a religiously alienated James Baldwin deployed Christian-laden language to persuade his white audience that "color is not a human or personal reality; it is a political reality." Baldwin espoused the goal of racial amalgamation while critiquing white normative values. His last attempt at moral pleading ended with a biblical allusion warning that the failure to end the racial nightmare was set to bring "fire next time." Baldwin was anticipating his own rage and the militant currents of the 1960s, which would eclipse his strategy of critical moral suasion. Subsequently a revitalized black nationalism rejected Baldwin's pleading and desire for amalgamation as a form of emasculated self-hatred.[42]

Several strands of thought came together in the new black nationalism of the 1960s, rejecting both all forms of integration and the progressivism of Myrdal's

"American Creed" to positively assert the distinctions of black cultural cohesion. The fear of losing distinctiveness in the constraints of mass society and the assessment of black culture as pathological drove a counter-current toward particularism. Harold Cruse argued in *The Crisis of the Negro Intellectual* (1967) that while individualism was the American ideal, the nation was composed of groups vying for power. The insidious "individualist–integrationist" drive, pervasive among all sectors of black thought, led to "cultural negation." Without "economic autonomy" and independent institutions, the Negro could not make his distinct cultural claim and identify with America as a whole. Cruse viewed the racial solidarity of black cultural nationalism as necessary for participation in pluralistic America.[43]

Cruse wrote within the context of a revival of black cultural nationalism and global decolonization movements. Black radicals looking beyond the Civil Rights movement for a political strategy found an answer in linking Third World anti-colonialism and U.S. imperialism to racism at home. Writing for *The Liberator* in 1963, Cruse, as a disaffected Marxist, charged that the Negroes in America "exist in essentially the same relationship to American capitalism as other colonials." Racism institutionalized in New Deal policies and the subsequent violent unrest in urban ghettoes ignited the view of U.S. blacks as an internal colony. People trapped in a spatial apartheid, lacking jobs and adequate housing and shut out of the economic system, appeared increasingly like other subjugated people throughout the world. By 1966 Martin Luther King Jr. was also referring to northern ghettos as a "system of internal colonialism." Anti-colonial ideas offered a ready-made explanation of the position of blacks in America.[44]

Anti-imperialism gained adherents among black nationalists such as Malcolm X, Stokely Carmichael, LeRoi Jones, and Huey P. Newton, who connected the destiny of the domestic freedom movement with the fate of the Third World, particularly Africa, and to the promise of the Cuban Revolution. Carmichael and his co-author, political scientist Charles V. Hamilton, argued in *Black Power: The Politics of Liberation in America* (1967) that black people suffered as a group rather than merely as individuals. The solution was group action. The inescapable reality of "institutional racism," standing in stark contrast to the claim of "color blindness," rendered the United States a "colonial situation" in which the black man was forced to live in his own "country of color." Carmichael and other black intellectuals acknowledged that colonialism was not a perfect analogy, but it was the nature of the relationship, not land or legal status, that mattered. Changing a colonial relationship required both consciousness raising and action for community control. The unity that came from a black cultural nationalism required a shared history, and Malcolm X offered a useful primal story.[45]

The Autobiography of Malcolm X (1964) was more than one man's heroic rise from the ashes of racial oppression. Malcolm X articulated a collective biography of black struggle and redemption. While modernity assumed the individual power of self-creation, Malcolm X explored how racist thinking foreclosed autonomy and thus shaped the history of black people. As Malcolm Little, he grew up around integration-seeking petty bourgeoisie aspiring to white respectability by "breaking their backs to imitate white people." The murder of his Garveyite father by white reactionaries left his family economically and emotionally devastated. Little's contempt for Negro accommodation drove him to find company among those he regarded as more honest, the street hustlers of Harlem who displayed the "vivid *lived* dissent" characteristic of "oppressed men." Caught in the criminal justice system, Little found himself in prison full of self-hatred, addicted to drugs, and angry with God. In the crucible of prison realizing that he had believed and lived a lie about God and about himself, Malcolm Little died and Malcolm X was born. In a religious conversion to the Nation of Islam and revolted by the new awareness that he had "sinned" by accepting the white man's story, Malcolm X began to reconstruct his own history and that of black people.[46]

Undoing the white man's story meant rejecting his history and religion. Casting Christianity as the final justification for racism, his message to accommodating "house" Negroes was "My black brothers and sisters—no one will know who we are . . . until we know where we are!" An authentic identity required the rejection of the name of *Negro* and an embrace of their heritage as Black people. The Nation of Islam, as "the natural religion for the black man," provided an alternative mystical story of racial origins in which the first man was black. Having built an advanced civilization in Africa, black people enslaved by the "devil white man" forgot their "glorious history." Brainwashed to see themselves as heathen savages, only deserving of what the white man dished out, they had acquired a false identity. For Malcolm X, it was "no more humbling ourselves . . . trying to unite with the slave master" through a false religion. The struggle for black liberation took place on many fronts, but the one Malcolm X took on was to awaken black self-consciousness through an alternative theo-political narrative of separatism.[47]

While the Nation of Islam, with its separatism and alternative history, never captured the religious imagination of a significant number of African Americans, the assassination of Malcolm X in 1965 brought a resurgence of black national identity. Imamu Amiri Baraka, who as LeRoi Jones had experienced an "identity transformation" with his 1960 visit to Cuba, displayed the refashioning of the self among the leadership of Black Power. The artists he met in Cuba modeled the possibility of politically committed art, challenging him to join Third World intellectuals pledged to changing the world. Cuba, he wrote, was "a turning point in my life," one that sparked a psychological Negro-to-Black conversion—a dual process of rejecting white values and asserting distinct particularities toward building Black Power's notion of identity. A new black arts movement with new symbols, distinct values drawn from black experience, and a defiantly hypermasculine "collective manhood" expressed this new awareness. Recognizing the ethnic basis of U.S. politics, Black Power, with its radical black aesthetic, called for embracing a collective self-assertive identity as a means of gaining an effective share of power in society.[48]

Black Power's conception of black identity owed a great deal to Frantz Fanon's theory of decolonization, which addressed the double challenge for colonized people. *The Wretched of the Earth*, focused on political action for liberation, became available in English in 1963. Black Panthers leader Eldridge Cleaver called it the "Bible" of black liberation. Fanon's earlier work *Black Skin, White Masks* (1952), published in English in 1967, examined the psychological features of a fragmented black consciousness and the battle for recognition. He drew from Jacques Lacan's idea that mental disorders had a social cause, and Jean-Paul Sartre's existentialism. Fanon proposed that the binary of race, and all the attending ideas, was a social construct in which each of us is "locked into our own particularity" with the "white man . . . sealed in his whiteness and the black man in his blackness."[49]

The binary of race occurred in a double process: first, economic domination of black people; second, an internalization of white projections in which blackness was associated with sin, evil, and the dark side of the soul. The result was a sense of inferiority. As the scapegoat of white society, the black man represented all that was opposed to progress, liberalism, and enlightenment. Attempting to strip himself of the fictitious category of race through cultural and linguistic whitening, the black man became alienated from himself. The only answer was for the black man to assert his humanity and fight to decolonize the mind, not for the sake of a romanticized slave past, a Marxist ideal, or a nonexistent Negro, but for himself. The individual must enter "the zone of nonbeing," stripped of the race on which his identity was based, to emerge in a Hegelian moment of self-consciousness to exist for himself. It was insufficient for the black man to be regarded as a person and given his freedom by the master; he had to fight for absolute and "reciprocal recognition" in his particularity as a being-for-itself without reference to the master's false universal. Fanon's move toward a "new humanism" concluded that the only duty of any man was to not renounce his freedom and to recognize that "there is no Negro mission; there is no white burden."[50]

Black intellectuals made an incomplete appropriation of Fanon's thought. On the one hand, they embraced his analysis of a white-defined identity and the need to dismantle it through a struggle. On the other, they did not fully consider

Fanon's revolutionary nationalism as rejecting a unique black essence or history. Fanon, as a psychiatrist concerned with the individual's existential freedom, left limited theoretical resources for the construction of ethnic solidarity in the Americas. Nevertheless, Fanon made an important contribution in the construction of black identity.[51]

Peoplehood

The milieu of a new cultural nationalism presented all the necessary elements to assert the narrative of a black God. Malcolm X's theo-political challenge to the integration-seeking Negro church, the call to decolonize the black mind of all vestiges of racist ideologies proposed by Fanon, and the search by the National Committee of Black Churchmen for a response to religiously alienated Black Power all formed the impetus for a new theological perspective. Additionally, the 1960s had produced a critical mass of black intellectuals and artists engaged in race critique and cultural creation, and a significant number of theologically trained thinkers were offering the possibility of challenging the white theological establishment.

James Cone cast black theology as affirming Jones' understanding that "Black Power is the Power first to be Black," and to be Black was a culture, a way of being in the world, independent of white ways and ideas. Even as Jones depicted black people's struggle for self-definition in the *Dutchman*, a racially and psycho-sexually charged play about black manhood, black theology confronted white society as the "racist Antichrist." It was this attitude of defiance that separated black theology from liberal theology. The revolutionary consciousness of Black Power yielded a black theology overturning the theologies produced at white seminaries. The task was to "kill gods that do not belong to the black community" and assert "I am black because God is black." Black theology was therefore iconoclastic in bringing down all abstract definitions and interpretations of the biblical God not congruent with black liberation. The search for a black identity, Cone asserted, was the search for the God of black struggle. In declaring, "Sin, then, for blacks is loss of identity," black theology was also moving with feminist description of women's sin as self-negation, making a claim to theological recognition.[52]

Along with recovering an authentic black way of being, Cone argued that antebellum black religion had produced an unrecognized and distinct theology through stories, asserting, "the theme of liberation expressed in story form is the essence of black religion." Black history was the story of black people, "saying no to every act of white brutality" through acts of resistance. Black theology acknowledged the daily encounters with the "white insanity" of racism, and the experience of loving oneself because one is black, not in spite of it. It opposed the individual "navel-gazing" of white religion by coming together in solidarity. Only a concurrent reading of the biblical narrative and black history could, Cone argued, produce an adequate theology of divine activity on behalf of black people. Conveyed through story, black theology offered both a communal identity and a sense of belonging.[53]

Cone turned to slave spirituals, and their secularized form in the blues, for the narrative content of black theology. The turn to the spirituals paralleled the black arts movement's emphasis on vernacular language, which produced plays and poetry accessible to a mass audience and evoked the effervescence of the religious gathering. In his third book, *The Spirituals and the Blues: An Interpretation* (1972), Cone regarded the slaves' songs of survival as an essential affirmation of black humanity, laden with theological meaning. The myth that spirituals represented religious escapism, he noted, went along with the idea that slaves were docile and contented in their enslavement. He noted how Du Bois saw in the spirituals his own struggle to gain self-conscious manhood and how he had interspersed phrases from the "sorrow songs" throughout *The Souls of Black Folk*, calling them "the rhythmic cry of the slave"; the "voice of exile" expressing "a faith in the ultimate justice of things." Black music, as a narrative of black people, was both social and political. Following the functionalism of African music, spirituals were never merely creative works for their own sake; rather, they served as a record of devastation and of overcoming. Redefining the meaning of God, Jesus, heaven and hell, sin and redemption, life and death, spirituals reflected the experience of oppression and the hope of earthly liberation. While spirituals affirmed a universal dimension of the human spirit, Cone argued, "no attempt was made to transcend the faith of the community by assuming a universal stance common to 'all' people." As an act of reconstruction, spirituals emphasized what Howard Thurman had noted in 1947 as the "somebodiness" of black people, with the frequent invocation of "I" as a child of God. The troubled context of their creation resisted any universalizing of spirituals' meaning.[54]

The claim that God was black, read by some as a reverse form of racism, presented the problem of the particular and the universal. Cone mostly spoke concretely of the black race, yet at times he situated blackness in the realm of ontology; to be black meant to identify with the oppressed regardless of skin color. The issue of universality, he asserted, was a ruse of white people, who thought of themselves as "universal people" and who believed that their experience and history were the standard, regarding their "*white* tools" as the only right way to do theology. As "interested language," theology reflected the perspective of those engaged and filtered all ideas about the divine through a particular human experience. Any useful universal had to go through the particularity of black history and experience.[55]

J. Deotis Roberts, seeking to resolve the dilemma, noted that the brilliance of the Christian religion was that it was "at once particular and universal, personal and social." Both the universal and the particular were necessary. The image of the black Messiah, he contended, was the symbolic means by which black people overcame their identity crisis—a problem of a "false identity." Roberts rejected Albert B. Cleage's notion that Christ was literally black, but saw the symbolic image as standing against what Vincent Harding had identified as the universalized "Americanized Christ," a WASP alien to black people. The particularity of the black Messiah, identifying with the disinherited, liberated the black man from his false identity, allowing him to "be left alone with Christ" and to find himself in the symbol. The "universal Christ" reconciled the black person to a humanity by which he reached beyond himself and his situation. Theology had to give expression to black experience while not rejecting the universal nature of the faith.

Roberts viewed the corrective focus on ethnicity as bringing to light the white nature of the "brotherhood of man" and contesting the liberal view that ethnicity was parochial. Rejecting the notion that a tradition-bound community enclosed itself in particularity, he defined ethnicity as a necessary feeling of "peoplehood." Roberts concurred with Wilmore's charge that theology no longer hide under the "fatherhood of God and the brotherhood of man" to avoid the nascent power of ethnic groups in the name of the individual. Only when blacks, along with whites, affirmed their authentic peoplehood was the reconciliation of a "new humanity" possible. The political theology of black liberation, concerned with ethnic identity and peoplehood, provided a religiously infused narrative that vindicated the legitimacy of Black Power in American society.[56]

Through black peoplehood, Latin American native identity, and women's sisterhood, liberation theologians across the hemisphere found a shared narrative of oppression and solidarity not only in the Americas but also throughout the world. Women's liberation, Latin American revolutionary movements, and Black Power were forging solidarity by claiming distinct identities and shared suffering. Feminist theologians identified women's struggle with that of blacks and Third World people; Latin Americans and black theologians saw their groups linked to global anti-imperialist movements. By harnessing the religious impulse running through radical and Third World movements, they challenged a homogenizing and exclusive universalism of white theology and joined the wretched of the earth in their struggles. In committing to particular political projects, the problem of which events or mobilizing initiatives disclosed divine intent remained. Discerning divine intent and the political efficacy of any movement was possible only after one had made a commitment—what Paul Tillich called the inescapable "risk of faith." In this risk, the committed theologian had a role as a herald of solidarity and locator of a new inclusive humanity.[57]

By rejecting a universalized image of humanity, liberationists brought the particular story of oppressed groups with their political claims to the attention of the theological establishment. Reflecting the worldwide "groaning for freedom" and the demand for recognition among subordinate people, they asserted a reimagined God as partial, rather than impartial and uninterested, and reread the biblical stories in a narrative of oppression and liberation. Nevertheless, the appeals to a common experience denied the differences that were quickly evident among them. Oppression did not fall evenly or in the same way across groups. Some groups were more oppressed than others. Against the brewing external criticism and growing internal debates, examined in the next chapter, liberation theologians needed to either resolve their differences or find that the hope for a culture of solidarity eluded their theology.[58]

PART IV

Reverberations

11

A Tenuous Consensus

THUS FAR THIS has been a story of confluence, in which politics, theology, and culture brought the oppressed and their advocates together in a common cause. The hopes for the excluded were high. Yet, realization of the solidarity across marginalized groups initially imagined by liberationists did not come easy. Differences within liberationists' ranks, and counter-challenges from a consensus theology in its last throes, tested the coherency of liberation theology. As the new Latin American theology challenged the U.S. empire, black and feminist theologians within its borders found an institutional space in which to incubate a new orthodoxy. Latin America, historically an object of North American missionary and political expansion, quickly drew the bulk of the relevant attention, casting the entire enterprise of liberation theology as a Latin American product and a problem for U.S. regional political and cultural dominance—a historical characterization that has endured. This chapter and the next examine the debates among liberationists that threatened an enduring solidarity and the mixed reception of the movement by an increasingly fragmented theological establishment.

Liberationists entered a religious environment lacking self-criticism even as it increasingly espoused a progressive social vision. C. Wright Mills' critique vividly captured the political state of religion and theology as it entered the 1960s. His 1958 essay "A Pagan Sermon to the Christian Clergy" drew attention to the moribund state of Cold War theology and religion. Considering himself "religiously illiterate and unfeeling," Mills gave a blistering indictment of the "moral insensibility" evident in North American Christianity, writing, "the morality of war now dominates the curious spiritual life of the fortunate people of Christendom." Claims to necessity and realism supported an ethos of "total war" justified by the "metaphysics of militarism." With its failure, religion had joined mass culture in its dulling effect and had become a "subordinated part of overdeveloped society." He charged that religion as a dependent variable "does not originate;

it reacts. It does not denounce; it adapts. It does not set forth new models of conduct and sensibility; it imitates. Its rhetoric is without deep appeal . . . religion has generally become part of the false consciousness of the world and of the self." The moral bankruptcy, Mills argued, was not inherent in Christianity, as its history had shown both its revolutionary and its reactionary potential. While modern politics had become the "locale of morality; it is the locale both of evil and of good," Christianity's claim to "stay out of politics" betrayed its moral conscience for political accommodation. Having moved the production site of social values to politics, Mills nevertheless displayed an unwillingness to engage in wholesale rejection of religion and invited its revitalization as a positive political force. Mills' indictment gained the attention of the Protestant press, which both commended the call for moral action and objected to the one-sided appraisal. More than a decade after Mills, liberationists were advancing a full-orbed response in what José Miguez Bonino called "a qualitative leap" to a politically committed theology.[1]

Cracks in the Establishment

Liberationists offered a challenge to a set of key ideas embodied in a group of related institutions representing the North American Protestant establishment and its international reach. These institutions included the ecumenical National Council of Churches, the Riverside Church, and Union Theological Seminary. Together with the journals *The Christian Century* and *Christianity and Crisis*, founded by Reinhold Niebuhr, they formed the recognized voice of mainline Protestantism. Generally, this Protestant establishment supported a wide range of social democratic ideals and anti-communism. As the liberal wing of Christianity in the United States, it emerged out of the Modernist/Fundamentalist conflicts of the 1920s and promoted a civil religion of America's God-given responsibility among a community of nations.

The global challenge of the Great Depression and the ruin resulting from World War II had a broad influence in establishing Christian realism as the dominant political theology among Western democracies. Under Christian realism's anti-utopian strain, pacifism gave way to anti-totalitarianism, justifying the deployment of U.S. economic and military power. Domestically, social democracy relented under what Mills had identified as the ideological formula of "mixed economy plus the welfare state plus prosperity" embodied in New Deal policies. The Protestant establishment saw its role as providing a moral compass for society, checking U.S. power against the excesses of human pride and standing with the World Council of Churches' responsible society ethic. Through the 1950s into the mid-1960s, Protestantism slid into ideological complacency, espousing

Christian realism that was suspicious of the machinations of human pride; at the same time, it paradoxically lost the ability to effectively critique U.S. power and itself.[2]

Multiple issues wore down liberal unanimity and uncovered the enduring pacifist and social gospel roots. Liberals in the post-war period espoused the abolishment of segregation and racism through the slow mechanism of pluralism and group politics. Martin Luther King's morally inspired action moved them to revitalize a role for social activism. Debates over how to respond sympathetically to the Civil Rights movement in the early 1960s served as training for entering the fray over the Vietnam War. By 1965, as the war escalated, Protestantism was struggling with U.S. foreign policy and confronting internal differences on the morality of the war. The conflicts over Vietnam and Cold War policy began a quick erosion of the unified political commitments of the theological establishment.[3]

The historian Mark Hulsether has demonstrated how in the 1960s and the early 1970s, the pages of *Christianity and Crisis* reflected a sea change in orientation among religious intellectuals. Addressing a small but highly influential audience, the journal brought many leading religious and secular writers to its pages, including Hannah Arendt, Margaret Mead, and Peter Berger. What began as disagreements over the Civil Rights movement continued in discussions over the cultural context of theology and new radical ideas. Debates took up the possibility of situational ethics and just war theory, sexual morality and feminism, and secularization and pluralism. The cultural turbulence created by social movements questioning every societal standard and institution, polarized theologians over civil disobedience and the counter-culture.

Mainline Protestantism entered the 1970s with a leftward turn among its ranks, and a greater openness to the claims made by women, blacks, Third World people, and others demanding political recognition. American religion was experiencing what the sociologist Robert Wuthnow described as a "major restructuring" under the pressure of vast social change. Theologians continued to maintain that God was above race, class, gender, and nationality, and assert that they spoke to universal needs and desires within particular contexts. Encountering an intellectual arena that had lost the conviction of its previous Christian realism, and experiencing change in what Wuthnow identified as the "symbolic boundaries" of religious identification, feminist and black liberationists had an opportunity to forward a theology more congruent with the new social landscape.[4]

Changes within the World Council of Churches (WCC) also shaped the reception of liberation theology. The increasing presence of Third World churches within the WCC and their accompanying anti-Americanism embroiled the Protestant press in frequent debates on issues that were international in scope.

Many viewed the 1966 Geneva Conference, where Richard Shaull delivered his speech "The Revolutionary Challenge to Church and Theology" as, in the words of John C. Bennett, a "climactic event" bringing to the fore issues of global economic disparity, the spread of war, and racial injustice. Debates over U.S. imperialism, development, and revolutionary nationalism eroded confidence in an international liberal center. As Hulsether has shown, the pages of *Christianity and Crisis* were replete with articles drawing attention to the Third World; three issues in 1973 were devoted to Latin America. The debate over revolutionary movements, which were increasingly supported by the Protestant left, and U.S.-sponsored repression damaged the existing confidence in development and provided the milieu for the reception of Latin American liberation theology; it also brought theological attention to the complaints of domestic minorities.[5]

The position of blacks, women, and Latin Americans relative to those in power in the United States also shaped the reception and the ensuing debates over liberation theologies. The North American response was split among the mea culpa of a chastened liberalism, rising neo-conservatism, and reassertion of Christian realism. Critics focused on Latin American theology, noting its utopianism, its Marxist analysis, its openness to violence, its significance for U.S. relationships with the Third World, and its usefulness for promoting social change at home. While Latin Americans challenged U.S. dominance in the region, homegrown liberation theologies resounded as a plea for inclusion and were regarded as another step toward the full integration of women and minority groups into democracy. In Latin America, the movement became a specific target for U.S.-sponsored state repression and incurred a backlash from within the Catholic hierarchy. The crisis perpetuated by U.S. dominance abroad and the unfinished democratic project at home defined the reception of liberation theology in intellectual circles. Friends and foes divided along political lines.

Uneasy Fulcrum

The exuberance of the 1960s experienced by the Latin American New Left, with its project of direct democracy, anti-authoritarianism, and social equality, gave way to stifled hopes in the 1970s. *The Rockefeller Report on the Americas* (1969), referring to the Medellín bishops, warned U.S. policy leaders of the Catholic Church's vulnerability to "subversive" and "revolutionary" penetration. The U.S.-backed national security state, spread via multiple military coups, reinforced dictatorships and suppression of groups deemed revolutionary, making victims of thousands of civilians. The 1970 election of socialist Salvador Allende in Chile and the subsequent U.S.-backed overthrow in 1973 shattered the initial elation. Hopes of breaking the continent's dependent status dwindled. The decade brought political persecution to hundreds of dissident bishops, priests, and nuns, who suffered arrest, torture, and death. Repressive regimes forced some liberationists into exile, including the Argentine Enrique Dussel, the Brazilian Hugo Assmann, and the Chilean Sergio Torres, fueling the sense that they were indeed a threat to the dominant ideology.[6]

Under increased repression, religious–political realignment across Latin America eclipsed the idea of new Christendom as a practical consensus. The Catholic Church was in flux, experiencing a weakening of its cultural dominance and divided between independent action in base ecclesial communities and the hierarchy. The Church was also negotiating its position in confronting state-sponsored violence that targeted churches as havens for subversives. In a post-Medellin Church, the assumption of the historical role of religion in legitimizing the standing regime no longer held. Repression brought an uneven response; national churches split along lines of acquiescence and vigorous protest. Ecclesial leadership defended Argentina's "Dirty War" targeting those that threatened Christian civilization. Yet the religiously inspired Mothers of the Plaza de Mayo defied their priests by taking up the public challenge to the regime. In Brazil and Chile, where laypeople and clergy experienced victimization, church authorities spoke up against human rights abuses with different degrees of effectiveness. Between revolutionary movements and state repression, the loyalty of Latin American Catholics appeared increasingly divided.[7]

Political realignment complicated what it meant to be a Protestant minority within the weakened Catholic-dominated culture. This was a new environment, where traditional Protestants also attempted to define a theological identity independent of North America and Europe. Many crossed a historical Protestant/Catholic divide and joined forces in confronting religious conservatives and repressive states. In Chile, Protestants split between those who joined Catholics against Augusto Pinochet's regime, and a still lingering anti-Catholic, anti-communist fundamentalist faction supporting the dictatorship. In Argentina, a vocal minority joined dissenting Catholics organizing against the dictatorship in the Ecumenical Movement for Human Rights. A contest within religion that had previously sanctioned political power, or retreated into quietism, redrew the boundaries between Catholics and Protestants.[8]

Latin American liberationists were elaborating on their theology in a situation of political siege. They debated among themselves the limits of Marxist theory, the definitions of democracy and human rights, the means of exercising political power, the efficacy of violence, and the possible extent of *concientización* in a popular church historically bound to a fatalistic view of life. The diffusion of the language of liberation theology among politically awakened laypeople made it into a symbol of the basic aspirations of wider and more complex popular religious movements that were often less radical and more in keeping with progressive social Christianity. Through the 1970s, liberationists continued their involvement with base ecclesial communities, listening to the people and addressing their critics. Ironically, opposition resulted in the broader dissemination of their ideas, as previously uncommitted Catholics and Protestants joined liberationists.[9]

Latin American liberationists were also dealing with a mix reception in the United States. Frederick Herzog's early engagement with liberation theology positioned him as a mediating figure between U.S. liberals and liberationists. Herzog, convinced of the inescapability of liberation theology, developed early relationships with liberationists who were participating in multiple small gatherings that brought black and white theologians together. While at Duke University, he corresponded extensively with James Cone, and wrote the introduction to the English translation of Assmann's book *Theology for a Nomad Church* (1975). Ahead of his theological peers in recognizing the unprecedented change brought by liberation theology, Herzog addressed what he viewed as a theological crisis requiring a fundamental reorientation.

Herzog charged that American theology engaged in several avoidance strategies, such as making liberation theology a Third World problem obscuring the unjust situation within the United States. The self-congratulatory leftward turn of his liberal cohorts was insufficient in addressing domestic structural racism and classism. In the debates over Latin American liberation theology and its critique of U.S. relationships with the Third World, liberals avoided dealing with the local black–white confrontation. "Liberation theology for us begins with 'our black brothers at home,'" he wrote. While black voices had been given ample room for self-expression, "white theologians have not yet begun a concerted effort of self-examination." Theologians displayed an "allergy" to seeing their own thought as a form of ideology. Herzog also observed how some theologians were attempting to repackage Latin American liberation theology for a very different North American context, or they were spinning myths about its origins and staying power. Additionally, their preoccupation with a universal "false image of man," enthrallment with secularized society, and obsession with demythologizing the biblical text for "cultural despisers" avoided confronting real suffering. American theology needed to turn away from alleviating the anxieties of the "white middle-class self," a self built on acquisitiveness, and turn in solidarity with those who suffered. While some pondered the death of God, an apolitical and uninteresting question, the more important question was whether God was white or black. It was the nature of the "self's solidarity with the oppressed" and the character of God—as an exalter of the mighty or as one who suffered with the lowly—that was contested.[10]

Herzog's concern for maintaining an appeal to a universal ethos and the desire to differentiate between divine and human agency tempered his strong sympathetic response to liberationists. It was essential to building community, he warned, that a theology of liberation not represent a mere "folk theology" concerned only with one's own group. A "unitary view of history," while provisionally appropriate in Latin America, in the United States rendered "America as God's chosen people, leading a straight line of self-interest-logic to the notion of Manifest Destiny." In proposing that the revolution was God's rather than man's, he delineated a needed distinction "between the history we humans make and the reality of God as a mover of all history." God was not committed to unjust history, and a purely secular (unitary) approach to history, popular in Latin America, tied to a theistic worldview compromised God's justice. It was too easy to identify U.S. nationalist self-interested history as "redemptive" and sanctioned by God. Herzog proposed that in North America, sex, class, and race conflicts required that theology go "through history," by rethinking the socioeconomic context in a process of praxis/reflection, rather than identifying it as sacred or circumventing it. Herzog set out to develop an all-encompassing liberation theology for North America that went beyond the particularity of groups and escaped the "'religiosification' of the American Empire."[11]

Meanwhile, a "shaken" John C. Bennett of Union Seminary, carrying Niebuhr's legacy of Christian realism, represented the chastened liberal response. Noting the significance of black and feminist theologies in the United States, he nevertheless turned the bulk of his critical attention to Latin America. Bennett considered liberation theology to be signaling a religious transformation within Catholicism. The Church was attending to the unprecedented rising voices of the oppressed demanding justice, which had implications for the exercise of U.S. power abroad. He viewed Gutiérrez as attuned to extreme forms of poverty that escaped most Western thinkers. Bennett expressed both the sympathy and the discomfort of his peers with the specifics of liberation theology. Acknowledging the just claims made by blacks, women, and the poor of Latin America, he nevertheless warned against disregarding the real differences between men and women, viewing racism in monolithic and unchanging terms, and espousing violence for the sake of bringing about a vague utopian future. In the whirlwind of new theologies, he countered, "there was nothing new about the influence of experience on theological method." This was true from Luther to Barth, he noted, underscoring the point of liberationists that theology expressed the experience of elite white men. Unruffled by Gutiérrez's deployment of Marxism, he nevertheless viewed it as marking "a return of naïve utopianism with a tendency to absolutize the results of a Marxist revolution." A failure, such as the overthrow of Allende in Chile, brought "temptations to despair." In realist fashion, Bennett confronted the social and theological crisis while remaining skeptical of any idealistic approach to problems.[12]

Bennett offered a constructive response in his book *The Radical Imperative: From Theology to Social Ethics* (1975), a recovery of the social gospel ethos he had expressed 40 years earlier in *Social Salvation* (1935). He viewed the multiple expressions of liberation theology as a revitalization of Walter Rauschenbusch's social gospel, "a theology of liberation for the industrial workers," and as having affinities with Niebuhr's *Moral Man and Immoral Society*. Caught between a sense of guilt and the desire to exculpate himself from "bland acceptance" of U.S. domestic and foreign policy, he conceded that the social gospel never regarded race or sex as a theological issue. The new global attention to suffering brought on by racism, poverty, and sexism was bound to raise questions about the morality of identifying with the power of privileged white men. He saw a convergence in Protestant and Catholic liberation theologies as a "radical Christian social ethic" recovering the significance of the kingdom of God and illuminating the distortions caused by "individualism and privatism." Bennett's chastened liberal response proposed a revitalization of social justice, embodied in the social gospel's vision of the kingdom of God, as a political imperative.[13]

Lutheran theologian Richard J. Neuhaus—who, by 1975, along with the Catholic theologian Michael Novak, broke with his liberal friends to embrace neo-conservatism—was less sanguine about reconciling the kingdom of God with a political project. In a review of Gutiérrez's *A Theology of Liberation*, noting its wide and justifiable acclaim, he expressed the danger he saw in regarding any revolution as concomitant with the kingdom of God. Such an assumption overrode the "critical distance" Gutiérrez espoused. Neuhaus charged that in constructing a politicized theology in which history was "Christo-finalized," Gutiérrez had simply changed ideological sides. In announcing "a new man in a new society," he had failed to adequately define the means for achieving it, thus was close to providing a "carte blanche legitimation for joining almost any allegedly revolutionary struggle to replace almost any allegedly repressive regime." Neuhaus readily admitted that religion did easily become captive to all manner of ideology, but we "ought not to glory in our parochialisms," inescapable as they are. He insisted in neo-orthodox fashion that the Christian faith "must always say no" to both the prevailing order and those who seek to overthrow it. This was not neutrality, but "a clear choice against evil" and a modest refusal to choose any absolute alternative to the kingdom of God. For Neuhaus, the kingdom of God remained a transcendent reality, and the theological task was in addressing a different plane of experience not accessible through the political. Ideology was no replacement for theology.[14]

Neuhaus viewed both Latin American and black liberation theology as "wrestling with tension between what is indigenous and what is catholic." He conceded the liberationist point that in seeking the universal, Jesus became a set of abstract propositions stripped of human flesh—what the liberationist José Comblin called the "iconization" of Jesus. Yet "identifying with Jesus as 'one of us,'" a claim anyone could make, rendered Jesus a "cultural captive" to the conceit of the day. Neuhaus presented the concerns of many of his peers. Historically, the universality of the faith yielded to contextualized expressions in the belief that "the finite can contain the infinite," yet they feared that starting with the particular quickly descended into essentialist chauvinism.[15]

Two dangers that beset the reception of liberation theology were noted by Neuhaus: a Western romanticized condescension that celebrated the proposition that "salvation comes from the Third World," and the attempt to parrot in North America a theology born out of a dramatically different context. U.S. radicals were nurturing an "anti-Americanism" that even the anti-war activist Daniel Berrigan had rejected. Neuhaus proposed that the North American antidote to liberation theology was a renewal of the nation's tradition of "accountability to the poor," "empathy," and "covenant responsibility." Pressing the call for radical empathy, he missed the liberationist assertion that the oppressed were growing impatient waiting for the largesse of the privileged and that they were the agents of their own liberation rather than recipients of charity. Neuhaus, cognizant of social injustice, provided no clear means for the actualization of specific Christian social values outside the goodwill of individual action within the confines of an assumed liberal state.[16]

The Christian realist Thomas Sanders, in a *Christianity and Crisis* exchange with Rubem A. Alves, forcefully articulated the charge against utopianism. Sanders, who had spent a decade in Latin America, asserted that the presupposition of liberation theology was a "moralistic ideology" in the form of what Niebuhr called a "soft utopianism." A moralistic ideology viewed the world in clear "good and bad categories," as "oppressors and oppressed," with no room for "moral ambiguity." History, Sanders wrote, "is not a progressive unfolding of moral aspirations but a permanent dialectic between the hopes of mankind and the contradictions that undermined them." Setting "capitalist" against "socialist" prevented understanding of the complexities of the Latin American experience. Since no political program corresponded with the kingdom of God, decision makers had to pragmatically choose among a complex number of options to work toward the best achievable balance. Sanders observed that the meanings of *revolution*, *socialism*, and *liberation* were continually shifting, being "co-opted" by every political operator. Over time, liberationists' utopianism was destined to generate increased disillusionment with the limits of social projects evoking liberation.[17]

Sanders believed that favorable reception of Latin American liberation theology was due to the "strangeness of trying to understand" the beleaguered continent and the ramifications of the U.S's own loss of confidence. Displaying the long-held attitude that Latin America was essentially lacking, he proposed that rather than focusing on the continent's constant state of crisis, observers needed to understand it for what it was—better off than the rest of the Third World. Failed programs were not the result of impositions from outside but were due to its own "political underdevelopment." Catholic Christianity needed to recover the "pragmatism or 'realism' of the Thomist political tradition" rather than offering a utopia "beyond the possibilities of Latin America."[18]

Alves' response, titled "Christian Realism: Ideology of the Establishment," expressed irritation with Sanders' condescending attitude that characterized liberation theology as parochial and that assumed intellectual sophistication on the part of North Americans. He objected to the portrayal of Latin Americans as "adolescent" and "highly emotional types" still mired in immature utopian illusion. He argued that Christian realism held to a set of hidden presuppositions similar to Marx's critique of utopianism as a form of false consciousness, in which "the utopian dreamer ignores the iron determinism of economic reality." Positive science considered the social process to be independent of the imagination and the scientist to be the model of a man who confronts reality. Thus realism held that "the limits of the future are determined by the structure of the present," leaving no room for the imagination. Christian realism viewed all forms of utopian thinking as not only mistaken but an expression of sinful desire for an absolute or impossible moral purity. In such a manner, realism gave preference to the social order that existed, its own concrete absolute.[19]

Drawing from Paul Tillich's "Protestant Principle," Alves responded that Christian utopianism "is not a belief in the possibility of a perfect society but rather a belief in the nonnecessity of *this* imperfect order." All "reality" was a provisional human construction and open to remaking. He charged that those committed to an existing social order disparagingly use the term *utopian* for others who wish for change. To view the social order as fixed, subject only to small adjustments here and there, was "idolatry"—a reification of ideology. The pragmatism of Christian realism denied the possibility of fundamental change made possible by God's transcendent action. He wrote, "History ... can never be seen as self-enclosed," a statement that slightly evaded the liberationists unitary view of history. Speaking for his cohorts, Alves cast liberation theology as having global and ecumenical implications that challenged North American theological "cultural imperialism."[20]

Latin American liberationists were also receiving criticism from European theologians. Jürgen Moltmann, who provided liberationists with many useful ideas, charged that Latin Americans, in an attempt to cast off imperialism and construct an "indigenous theology," were in danger of provincialism rather than a new "world-theology." As a group, Moltmann observed, Latin Americans engaged in a scathing critique of European ideas but failed to acknowledge their indebtedness to the Western history of freedom. They borrowed heavily from Rousseau, Kant, Hegel, Marx, and Engels, treating them like their own discoveries and neglecting their own thinkers. Even the attempt at critiquing the theology of Moltmann and Johann Metz indirectly affirmed the positions they so vigorously rejected. Gutiérrez, he gibed, "has written an invaluable contribution to European theology." The second set of problems was Latin Americans' shorthand use of Marxism that lacked a radical turn toward a class analysis, neglected liberal democracy, and failed to demonstrate a "peculiarly Latin American way to socialism." Without a "revolutionary subject," namely the exploited themselves, intellectuals and university students were insufficient to spark revolution. The assertion of a "revolutionary situation" was a self-reference to "elite circles gathered ceremoniously to confirm themselves." Moltmann's criticism displayed a particular imperial blindness to on-the-ground situations and small-scale political projects in tens of thousands of BECs, and the adaptive features of liberation theology.[21]

The apparent contradiction between using European-dependent theological categories and attempting an indigenous theology appeared unresolvable. The criticism that liberationists remained unspecific, utopian, theoretical, and alienated from their own people was an unfair assessment in view of the situation in which the burgeoning theology was developing. Nevertheless, their intellectual project was deeply dependent on inherited ideas that attempted to move beyond the divide that existed between the reality of the social situation and the abstraction of their discipline. Under the critique that their theology was insufficiently rooted in the experience of the mass of Latin American people, liberationists in the 1970s were quickly adapting to the situation of deferred hope, as well as repression. Gutiérrez's 1979 book *The Power of the Poor in History* moved beyond a theoretical model and articulated a "people's theology." Against the charges of critics, the liberationists' theological method, rejecting dogmatism and requiring continual reflection on praxis, proved itself highly resilient and open to innovation.

Theodicy

As Latin America received the bulk of the critical attention, black and feminist liberationists experienced their halcyon days. The New Left as an agglomeration of loosely organized local and national groups with their anti-imperialist, anti-capitalist, and universalist ethos had all but disappeared. The social movements of the 1960s dissipated into the "multicultural left" of splintering minority groups exploring the possibility of coalition politics. Political and social gains made by the various movements brought opportunities in academic institutions. Black studies and women's studies programs, affirmative action and legislative victories, visible black and women leaders, and appropriations by popular culture of images of lived dissent diminished the initial radicalism of Black Power and women's liberation. Black and feminist theologians rising in the institutional ranks were working out their ideas within the relative affluence and expansion of social liberalism. Taking advantage of hiring initiatives, women and blacks entered divinity schools and religion departments in unprecedented, albeit yet small, numbers. The cultural and institutional openings presented an opportune moment for liberationists to establish enclaves within the academy.[22]

The reception of black theology was taking place within a religious establishment reconciling itself to Black Power as a positive movement toward a post-racial society. As the intellectual leader of black theology, Cone and his early caustic rhetoric dampened an effective critical and public response from intimidated white liberals. Relatively free from the distraction of addressing white critics, black theologians and religion scholars had time to develop their theologies and engage in internal debates about the direction and nature of black religion.

The vigorous debate within black intellectual circles was widely disseminated through the Protestant and academic press. Cone's first books, *Black Theology and Black Power* (1969) and *A Black Theology of Liberation* (1970), began a tidal wave of scholarship in the 1970s and 1980s. Differences arose on the prospects for reconciliation with whites, minority group violence as a viable strategy, the necessity of white theological categories, the assumption of Christianity as a starting point, the origin of conservatism in the black church, experience as a source of theology, and the potentially devastating problem of theodicy that marked black thought from inception. As Cone received the bulk of the attention, with his ideas appearing as a monolithic expression of black religious thought, the deep differences among black theologians reflecting historical divisions were not evident to all.[23]

Some black religionists, such as the Civil Rights activist Julius Lester, doubted that there was such a thing as a black theology since "blackness is not a spiritual value but a psycho-political attitude." In reviewing C. Eric Lincoln's edited collection of essays *The Black Experience in Religion* (1974), Lester saw little more than "political polemics in religious language" designed to "shock white liberals." It was a theology dependent on white definitions of blackness. He surmised "there cannot be a viable black theology until the problem of suffering is confronted courageously," and confronted in a way that did not make black people into victims of white society. As victims, black people were denied a "theological existence" out of the reach of racism—an unmediated relationship with God that allowed the renewal of whole persons in the midst of hardship. The regenerative faith of black people that circumvents the master's religious "bloodletting system" appeared to have escaped black theology. Lester ended his essay with the scathing indictment that theologians' uncertainty about their identity as blacks and as Christians resulted in "a cry of despair masked as the bark of militancy."[24]

The question of why blacks suffered had a long history and had implications for a theology that claimed to speak for marginalized people. Theodicy, first conceived in 1710 by the philosopher G.W. Leibniz, offered a rational and theistic explanation for evil. The concept became key in the sociological understanding of religion as providing the means to integrate chaotic and disrupting events into socially ordered meaning. A viable theology that responded to the history of oppression had to answer the long-standing theodicy question, the persistence of suffering against the promised justice embedded in religious social visions.[25]

The religion scholar Anthony B. Pinn has examined the enduring question of theodicy in black religion. Black believers had attempted to explain the evil of slavery and the origin of human suffering while maintaining faith in the goodness and justice of God. Slaves and freemen combined pedagogical and punitive justification for suffering with a sense of chosenness. From Absalom Jones, David Walker, and Maria W. Stewart in the nineteenth century to W.E.B. Du Bois, Reverdy Ransom, and Martin Luther King Jr. in the twentieth, there was an understanding of suffering as redemptive, by which God works out divine purposes for a greater and future good. King had held to the notion of black people as "suffering servants" whose undeserved suffering worked toward bringing about the Beloved Community. However, appeals to chosenness, providence, and mystery failed to satisfy the question posed by Du Bois: "Why did God make me an outcast and a stranger in mine own house?" The nagging question of why black people suffered disproportionately and persistently, and how this fit into the divine plan for liberation, reemerged in full force in black theological debates. The Black God who suffered with those on the slaughter-bench of history was no match for the God who undergirded the master's system of domination.[26]

William R. Jones, a philosopher of religion, aggressively took up the question of theodicy in a 1971 *Harvard Theological Review* article, "Theodicy and Methodology in Black Theology: A Critique of Washington, Cone and Cleage," and subsequently expanded his argument in *Is God a White Racist?* (1973). Drawing from the reflections on Jewish suffering and Jean-Paul Sartre's existential philosophy, Jones' logical analysis sought to uncover the presupposition and weakness in Cone's theistic premise. Jones drew attention to "the perennial issue of black religion: What is the meaning, the cause and the 'why' of black suffering?" He considered the "unsavory" question of theodicy as the controlling question in all black theology—liberation presumed suffering, which called for an account. Reviewing *A Black Theology of Liberation*, he noted Cone's rejection of classic theodicy that held that suffering was punishment, served a pedagogical role, or was mitigated by future compensation. In the book, Cone rejected the idea that blacks are chosen to suffer on behalf of others. Rather, Cone claimed that it was *because* blacks experienced oppression that God had chosen to identify with them. In an explanation of black suffering, Cone pointed to white racism as the cause that evidently a sovereign God either could not, or would not, stop. In Christian theology, Jones noted, suffering was a sign of either divine favor or disfavor, and black theologians had not shown evidentially that black people were favored. The innocent suffered because they were not in fact innocent, or because they were to receive some recompense in a distant future—an idea rejected by black theologians. Neither could black theologians hide under the vague notion that God's ways were inscrutable. The "manifest[ed] scandal of particularity," that is, that black people suffered disproportionately and over a long history, raised the "*question* of divine racism."[27]

The theological commitment to black liberation in history, as a first principle, demanded a this-world response to human suffering. Jones argued that the assertion that black liberation was essential to God's nature denied the historical reality of centuries of slavery and the dominance of white people. Cone's selective use of history had failed to offer empirical evidence of God acting on behalf of black people. In the absence of a liberatory event, such as in the Exodus narrative, blacks could not know whether God was for them or not. The logic of theism either cast black people as victims of divine racism, or required a return to the quietism of pie-in-the-sky compensatory theology. There was no answer for this-world suffering in black theology. Jones proposed that black religion adopt "humanocentric theism" as an explanatory principle, doing away with a sovereign God outside human choice and action and eliminating the idea of divine racism or quietism. A theism that featured the "functional ultimacy of man" provided a higher view of human freedom as a "codetermining power." Human beings were the source of and relief for suffering.[28]

Cone's response sympathetically recognized the significance of the problem of explaining black suffering. Historically, some slaves had rejected the Christian faith as a cruel ruse; more recently, Black Power had expressed anti-religious anger. In *God of the Oppressed* (1975), Cone devoted an entire chapter to considering the question of divine racism as "absurd," in light of the biblical narrative in which God is committed to liberation. He wrote, "It is a violation of black faith to weaken either divine love or divine power." The "crux" of the issue was not the "*origin* of evil" but what God had done about it. Cone appealed to the historical Christ-event, the crucifixion, as the once-and-for-all liberatory action that identified with black people and gave them the necessary horizon to "suffer for freedom." Black faith was not passive endurance but an active praxis of resistance. Jones, Cone charged, had engaged in an unfair internal critique without regard for the presupposition of black religion—the suffering of Jesus Christ as God's self-disclosure in solidarity with the oppressed. Conceding that his Christological position was sure not to satisfy Jones and his black humanist peers, Cone ultimately placed liberation in an outside transcendent reality and reasserted the historical vitalism of religious faith in the actualization of freedom. The theodicy question brought out the contentious nature of defining the particularity of black religion, and the problem of bridging the claims of faith and secular freedom.[29]

While white males were reticent in evaluating black and feminist theology, Rosemary Radford Ruether took on the task of critiquing the weaknesses of her black liberationist peers. Before Cone had published his first book in 1969, Ruether had responded to the call for a black theology. She asked to what extent such theology was possible without being a form of parochial "racial propaganda." She reasoned that a contextual black theology, in the tradition of King, had the potential to be "reconciling rather than alienating" and "universal yet at the same time particular" to the situation of blacks' encounter with the alienating Caucasian Christ. Instead, she saw an emerging theology estranged from the people it professed to represent. She noted in 1971 that Cone, as the foremost black theologian, was "on the agenda of every radical theological panel in the country" and represented the rise of "Negro intelligentsia . . . alienated from the living context of the black community." Functioning within a male white power base addressing white people, Cone's theology, she asserted, was not "truly 'black' in a cultural sense." It appeared that black caucuses, within white institutions willing to allow a few minority elites visibility, simply slid into bourgeois respectability dressed in militant language and abandoned the poor unchurched black masses. Black elites, through an intensely theoretical approach, were struggling to identify with their own communities where they no longer belonged.[30]

Ruether viewed Cone's theory of race and the association of whiteness with oppression and blackness with liberation as straining metaphors into an unworkable "contextual absolute." He had failed to differentiate between "many kinds and levels of oppression," or to make clear that oppression's manifestation was not intrinsic to a racial identity. Blackness as a metaphor for universal humanity and an uncritical claim to virtue in oppression was wedded to "identification of whiteness with demonic power." However, not only did Cone reify racial categories, he failed to produce a theology that viewed black people as more than merely oppressed.[31]

Besides the reification of race and alienation from the black community, Ruether identified a clear crisis developing between the black line of a "super-male-chauvinist tradition" and feminist theology. Segregated within their respective enclaves, the white male-dominated academy pitted them against each other. The complexity of the relationship between black and feminist theology was evident in the position of black women and in the broader debates within feminism. One of Cone's graduate students addressed the theological invisibility of and the double burden carried by black women. Jacquelyn Grant's 1979 essay "Black Theology and the Black Woman" called for the inclusion of black women in theology and charged that black men had accepted the patriarchal structures of white society, making the call for liberation "inauthentic." In subsequent decades Cone, as a result of dialogue with feminists and growing Third World contact, displayed greater awareness of women's oppression and repudiated his earlier male-centered theological myopia.[32]

Many-headed Monster

Ruether also discerned problems within the newly established feminist theology. The 1970s' intense deconstruction by feminists took place with little opposition; regarded as a fad rather than a profound upending of classic theological categories. In 1972, Margaret Mead and Ruether became the first two women in thirty years to serve on the editorial board of *Christianity and Crisis*, and their influence brought many feminists to its pages. Ruether noted that feminists were creating their own separate "social encapsulation" within elite male-dominated universities that remained largely out of touch with ordinary women. Her critique of the developing feminist theology was similar to critiques of black and Latin American theologians as being insufficiently rooted in the people they claimed to speak for. The new group of elite women tended to be white, middle-class, childless, and career focused, obscuring class and race in woman's oppression. Their theology "tended also to be alienated from the *experience* of most women." She saw clear evidence in the denigration of motherhood, with *abortion* the only word associated with it, which she saw as arising from the subversion of childbearing in the adopting of male career patterns. Ruether, who supported abortion rights, held that using maternity against women was at the root of female oppression, representing the "one power men do not have." Feminists' inability to recapture motherhood as a positive experience accepted what Mary Daly had called "phallic morality." Ruether called for women theologians to unmask the false consciousness that produced misogyny even among feminists.[33]

Besides the issues of class and race, feminist theology was splintering along changing definitions of feminism and debates over the features of a suitable religion for women. The theologian Carol P. Christ, a leader in what Mary Daly had called the exodus community, in 1977 reviewed the state of feminist theology, in which deep and irreconcilable differences were evident. She observed that the feminist challenge to the core symbols and language of Western theology made it both "emotionally threatening" and incongruous with mainstream religious thought. Valerie Saiving and Daly represented the revival among religious "reformists and revolutionaries" within feminist thought. Following Elizabeth Cady Stanton, feminists had uncovered the anti-woman attitude permeating the whole of Christian tradition. In response, they had opted for either reform, believing in a redeemable "essential core" of Christian faith, or revolutionary reconstruction, concluding that the negative power of religious symbols made them irredeemable. Christ argued that the core symbols of the Christian faith were sufficiently psychological and socially powerful to shape, negatively, the experience of women. Ruether, as a radical reformer who advocated the "transformation of the symbols of oppression," had not shown how the liberation of women was congruent with male images of divinity. Christ pointed out that it was not only the male symbols that were problematic, but also the underlying core values of omnipotence, absolute transcendence, and hierarchy that underwrote what Daly had called the "Most Unholy Trinity" of rape, genocide, and war, and that made them incompatible with women's liberation. The fundamental question Christ asked concerned the extent to which feminist Christian theology remained either Christian or feminist. Christ announced that the negative experience with patriarchal religion was producing a vital spirituality movement of revolutionaries embracing the Goddess, and creating new rituals independent of Judeo-Christian religion.[34]

By the mid-1970s, the initial period of theological deconstruction in a reformist mode had led some into a revolutionary reconstruction, producing multiple ruptures within feminist theology. The publication of *Womanspirit Rising* (1979), edited by Christ and the Jewish theologian Judith Plaskow, brought together in dialogue reformers such as Elisabeth Schüssler Fiorenza, Sheila Collins, and Phyllis Trible and revolutionaries who rejected monotheism such as Naomi R. Goldenberg, Starhawk, and Zsuzsanna E. Budapest. Agreeing with Freud and Marx that religion "kept people dependent on authority," they nevertheless asserted that it offered women necessary meaning. Women's experience, as a key idea, engendered disagreement among these contributors. Which elements constituted an "authentic" female experience, and what was the result of an imposition and "alienated? " What was the basic experience that led to liberation? Was it the revaluing of bodily experiences associated with traditional marriage and motherhood in a holistic feminist vision, or the experience of confronting sexist culture that presupposed an existing feminist awareness? Other disagreements remained regarding the extent to which feminist theology could remake Western religion, the degree of association between women and nature, freedom's relationship to the limits of nature, the liberatory potential of the erotic and sexuality, and whether the goal was equality or female ascendancy. In all these questions, the lines of difference were difficult to draw, but those taking on the feminist theological project agreed that "patriarchy is a many-headed monster" requiring diverse approaches on multiple fronts. The decade of the 1970s exposed the multifarious nature of women's experience as a shifting and unstable concept that eroded the power of the previously evoked sisterhood. After rejecting the inherited theology, the possibility of finding a workable feminist theology that spoke to all women or even all feminists was uncertain.[35]

The U.S. reception of liberation theology defined the extent to which liberationists had the opportunity to redraw the boundaries of their discipline. Religious elites used their diminished influence on avoiding conflict at home and responding to innovations coming from Latin America that threatened U.S. dominance. Latin American liberationists, although experiencing internal differences, maintained a unified front as they confronted state repression, dealt with ecclesial backlash, and engendered political and religious realignment on the continent. Their theology showed great adaptability to a quickly changing situation. First-generation black and feminist theologians taking advantage of new opportunities dealt with contentious issues among their ranks and established enclaves within ambivalent liberal institutions. There they had the space to develop the long-term intellectual and political viability of their projects. Together, blacks, feminists, and Latin Americans were filling the vacuum left by post-war theology's ineffective response to a changing cultural situation. The future effectiveness of liberationists to forge a new permanent consensus required not only a critique but also a constructive theology that addressed the relative difference and position of groups within U.S. pluralism and imperial reach.

12

A New Orthodoxy

DESPITE HISTORICAL AND intellectual affinities that offered hope for cross-group solidarity, personal contact among liberationists magnified their differences. The first direct meeting between black and Latin American liberationists was on the international stage of the 1973 World Council of Churches (WCC) symposium in Geneva. The symposium, an attempt to promote the new liberation theologies to an ecumenical European and North American audience, turned into four days of heated debate. Archie LeMone, a sympathetic WCC staff member writing for *Christianity and Crisis*, noted that liberationists did not follow the expected script of railing against suffering; "There was no Latin American cabaret-style 'revolution,' and there were no more 'auction blocks' showing off 'bad mothers' exuding militant rhetoric, crying 'many thousands gone.'" As a united front at the "cross point of history: ecumenical history," liberationists were defining the terms of the discussion and generating "structural convulsions" for Western theology. LeMone sensed that the initial response among those who "control the means of the production of power" was an impulse to either divide and conquer the shaky ground of Third World solidarity, or plead for reconciliation.[1]

Differences threatened the "frail alliance" displayed by Third World representatives, including James Cone, Hugo Assmann, and Paulo Freire. After straining to address a "woefully disarmed" audience, which had retreated into "stunned silence," Assmann surmised that in a situation of "incommunication" it was best to direct his attention toward the representatives of black theology—a relationship more crucial for coalition building. As a fair-skinned Brazilian of German descent, Assmann expressed regret over his European education and unease with his "gringo" face, which alienated him from the black and indigenous people of his continent. However, neither did he consider himself a Westerner, as he still searched for a Latin American identity. The need was, he surmised, for a bridge between a colonized theological language and the indigenous, "a grass-roots language ... a third language" that truly met Latin American people on their own terms. Tempted to read the North American black experience in Marxist terms rather than in racial terms, he nevertheless saw possibilities for dialogue, conceding that race presented a deep contradiction in the Latin American experience not explained by class alone.[2]

Cone, whom Freire described as "a Third World man ... born in the world of dependence—exploitation—within the First World," responded coolly to Assmann's overture. He emphasized that the context of theological language and the differing historical experiences of a slave and a master, evident in Assmann's elite racial status, made constructive communication between them problematic. They both agreed that this inability to communicate across different worlds applied particularly to the chasm separating Third World from First World. In committing to dialogue irrespective of difficulties, Latin Americans and North American blacks faced differences arising from each group's relationship to the history of the hemisphere.[3]

Establishing the global solidarity of oppressed people would not come easily. The problematic historical relationship between the United States and Latin America complicated the possibility of bridge building. Class, race, and gender differences produced further estrangement. The attempts by Latin Americans to redefine their relationship with the United States were at odds with multiple groups negotiating their position within it. Each group's relative power position to the United States was decisive in shaping its view of the others. Nevertheless, within a broad intellectual movement grappling with both internal differences and mounting liberal and conservative criticism, a significant new theo-political space was forming. The splintering of North American theology along political lines, and the weakened Latin American Catholic cultural hegemony, offered an opportunity for liberationists across the hemisphere to reroute the political-religious discourse. Together they acted as a wedge for asserting an alternative theo-political vision demanding the reconfiguration of social power. This chapter demonstrates the inextricable differences and the broader implications for the future of theology and the realignment of religious commitments.

Detroit 1975

The debates that began in theological journals and continued in Geneva reached a climax at the 1975 Theology in the Americas conference in Detroit, a gathering of liberationists from across the Americas. The legacy of the 1960s pervaded the conference planning. The echo of C. Wright Mills' 1960 *Harper's* essay, "Listen, Yankee: The Cuban case against the United States," addressed to a North American audience and disseminated in Latin America, captured the angry tone for the decade. Inspired by visits to Latin America, Mills viewed Cuba as an agent for an international New Left. Cuba represented the voice of the "hungry-nation bloc," composed of Asia, Africa, and Latin America, responding to U.S. imperialism. Using the voice of a fictional revolutionary, Mills expressed solidarity with the Latin American grievances against U.S. Cold War policy and offered an ideological bridge for radicals across the hemisphere. Long after the New Left launched its critique and the promise of Cuba had dissipated, early planning for the Detroit conference retained an expectation that the gathering would finally bring to fruition the vision of the New Left by confronting U.S. power and forging effective political ties among the aggrieved.[4]

The Sacred Heart Seminary, situated within Detroit's black ghetto, where unemployment was high and shuttered stores abounded, was an apt symbol for inequality. Organized by the exiled Chilean priest Sergio Torres and sponsored by the U.S. Catholic Conference and the National Council of Churches, the Theology in the Americas conference was the first ecumenical hemispheric gathering of two hundred theologians, social scientists, and activists. Its initial objective was to promote dialogue between oppressed groups and to produce an all-encompassing liberation theology for a receptive North America. Latin Americans clearly controlled the agenda from the outset. Initially they were to share their method and experience with a North American audience. A distinguished group gathered, including the Latin Americans Hugo Assmann, Gustavo Gutiérrez, José Miguez Bonino, and Enrique Dussel; black theologians James Cone, J. Deotis Roberts, Herbert Edwards, and Preston Williams; and feminists Sheila Collins, Rosemary Radford Ruether, and Beverly Harrison. Social scientists from both continents came ready with analysis of the interlocked system of race, sex, and class oppression. Whites, who made up the largest percentage of participants, included the sympathizers Frederick Herzog, the Presbyterian minister and theologian Robert McAfee Brown, and the Canadian Catholic Gregory Baum, the editor of *The Ecumenist*. Their presence made the absence of other invited members of the old Protestant establishment noticeable. The preliminary proposals for a new theological consensus were a mix of appeals for the North Americans to recommit to a tradition of civil religion, with its values and symbols of the nation, and demands for a radical break.

There was a sense in which liberation theology, perceived as a Latin American import, became shorthand for a great many socio-political grievances. Global oppression tied to systems of domination within the United States worked as an overarching theme. The situation in the United States existed in a dialectical process with Latin America and the Third World. Change, the organizers believed, "demands the dismantling of the center" that dominated the American hemisphere through its political, economic, and cultural power. Latin Americans hoped to present their theology, often an abstraction in the North American debate, and challenge U.S. theologians to address oppression within their own borders. North American advocates spoke of "unmasking the demonic structures of autonomous power" obscured by the ideology of efficient markets and the "military–industrial complex." They observed that the United States was experiencing increasing inequality within its borders and exploiting foreign people for the advantage of an elite class. Only as a compliant middle class gained consciousness of the systems of domination and acquired a "view from below" could they join the oppressed and realize their full humanity. The agenda addressed the need to awaken the religious imagination of the middle classes, which provided the bulk of legitimation to an oppressive social order.[5]

The initial problem-defining statement, "The American Empire," was a critical review of the historical imperial expansion of the United States expressed in the Monroe Doctrine and Manifest Destiny as well as the commercial–military hegemony of "neocolonial penetration." The statement, infected with the anti-American mood, noted that the triumphant history of the United States was unraveling, a result of shifting economic, political, and cultural forces within the empire itself. The United States was experiencing a flight of capital from the metropole to the periphery, increasing the misery of its own lower classes, weakening the security of the middle, and producing a consolidation of power at the top. International and domestic strains were bringing into question the viability of the "American dream" and the image of the United States as "divinely chosen." The viability and legitimacy of the American empire were in question.[6]

Christianity had been involved both in the creation of the empire and in radical challenges to it. First, Protestantism offered the legitimating vision of the United States as a "messianic extension of the kingdom of God." Later, Catholicism, fully incorporated into the nation, joined the legitimating process, giving the United States ideological strength in Latin America. Nevertheless, North American religion had produced communities of resistance evident in black religion, Mexican American Christianity under Our Lady of Guadalupe, and the social gospel's alliance with socialism. The critical movements of resistance had subsided under post–World War II prosperity obscuring the structural problems within the United States. The statement went on to assert that through employing social science, specifically Marxist analysis; reflective reading of the biblical text; and praxis, Latin American liberation theology offered a starting point for addressing the experience of subordinated people within the United States.[7]

The consistent feedback to the initial statement was that the view of the United States as an "evil empire" exaggerated its power and hid a complex global system. Ruether responded with much chagrin, stating, "in effect, the

Latin Americans are to provide the 'theology' and the Americans the 'Devil.'" Although she viewed the statement as a partly correct assessment of the situation, the initial proposal for the conference, she charged, carried a judgmental attitude that cast all who lived within the borders of the United States as culpable, making it ultimately unpalatable to the American people. Others deemed the statement too "Third Worldish," not sufficiently situated in the history and people of the United States, and highly dependent on critical theory. Some pressed the view that the racial, ethnic, and gender struggles in the United States were more significant than class. The strong separation of church and state within a strong tradition of civil religion, and utopian elements within populist religion, rendered imported Latin American liberation theology as ill-suited for adoption. An effective North American liberation theology, Ruether asserted, would draw from the positive elements of "messianic language" running through the Puritan and Enlightenment traditions, the reform movements of the nineteenth century, and the social gospel. The conference planners adapted to the criticism by emphasizing the history, traditions, and experience of oppression within the United States and sought to avoid the imported "consumer good" mentality of the European–North American theological market.[8]

From the planning to the actual gathering in those few hot August days, defining *the* North American experience was more complex than originally assumed. Blacks and other minorities, angered by their exclusion from the early planning, challenged the assumption that white theology stood for the whole of religious reflection in the United States, with Latin Americans having more to say about the domestic context than they did. Demanding recognition, those considering themselves "colonized people"—Chicanos, Native Americans, Puerto Ricans, Asian Americans, and Appalachians as a small contingent, expressed concern that blacks and white women dominated the minority response in the plenary sessions. The Catholic Sister Jeanne Rollins, speaking for Native Americans as the marginal within the marginalized, described her community as one dispossessed of its lands and finding itself in a no-exit situation. Native people were caught between a reservation system preserving the "last signs of self-pride" and urban assimilation that was sure to destroy any remainder of their community. Chicanos spoke as a *mestizo* people, *la raza*, "Exiles-in-Their-Own-Land," forgotten by a Catholic Church "dominated by the WASP mentality." Chicanos contended that the binary of white oppressors and black oppressed made other minority groups invisible. Chicanos had come to the conference in the hope of sharing a common struggle, but found that the representatives of Latin America appeared as well-educated offspring of successful people, remarkably different from themselves. Ultimately, Chicanos concluded that their struggle for recognition was their own, and Latin Americans did not speak for them.[9]

Rather than addressing the sins of the empire, minority-group participants wanted to address the unjust welfare system, unfair housing, racism in education, sexism, economic inequality, a broken judicial system, and capital punishment. They agreed that the struggle for liberation was fertile ground for theological reconstruction. Yet, as the conference week progressed, recognition grew that "there is no overarching theology of liberation." Participants complained that subordinated groups forced to compete with one another weakened their critique of the dominant ideology. It became clear there was "no single North American experience" on which to build solidarity. Nevertheless, the conference began as a search for a synthesis of disparate experiences and interests.[10]

Addressing the stated objective of finding an all-encompassing liberation theology congruent with the history of the United States, the Jesuit theologian John A. Coleman proposed American civil religion as a beginning point. The idea of civil religion, emanating from Rousseau's natural religion of the state and Puritan covenant theology, had, since the publication of sociologist Robert Bellah's 1967 essay "Civil Religion in America," been a topic of discussion among social scientists and religion scholars. Bellah's 1975 book, *The Broken Covenant: American Civil Religion in Time of Trial*, went further by attempting to address the legitimate claims of racial minorities, competitive individualism, and unrestrained capitalism that was producing a deep "cultural crisis" and feelings of spiritual alienation. He sought to wrest out of the "empty and broken shell of civil religion" a historic communitarian ethic that could possibly restore "republican virtue" to American political life.

Drawing heavily from Bellah, Coleman viewed civil religion as embodying the universal values of liberty, justice, and equality congruent with Christian faith. He proposed that the high tradition of civil religion espoused by a long list of national figures including Thomas Jefferson, John Winthrop, Susan B. Anthony, and Martin Luther King Jr., associated with either national or group liberation, provided a "usable past." As the religion of the state, it did not supplant but rather complemented particular religions in a pluralistic society, binding the nation together through transcendent values, ritual, and a sense of belonging. Embracing civil religion required "avoiding the cynical view which sees every legitimacy system for political realms as, in all respects, a false ideology." Having failed in its promise owing to corruption, jingoism, and ambiguity, civil religion nevertheless carried the seed of a North American liberation theology that appealed to the broadest sectors of the mainstream.[11]

Coleman presented civil religion's shared affinities with Latin American liberation theology. Both were political theologies stressing the historical experience of the community and akin to pragmatism, being future oriented and testing any theoretical position against praxis. Both held the values of equality, distrusted elitism and pretensions of power, embraced the common person, and provided a place for the church in the realm controlled by the state. Coleman concluded that liberation theology was an attempt by Latin Americans to create a civil religion in which a Marxist–Christian utopianism functioned as a referent and a point of contact among disparate groups seeking social justice. North America's useable past and civil religion "constitute the key area of 'conscientization'" in the domestic liberation struggle. Coleman called for a reemphasizing of the progressive American "exodus experiences of liberation," evident in the Pilgrim's flight from persecution to the black Civil Rights movement, siding with the oppressed people of the world.[12]

The suggestion offered by Coleman that civil religion functioned as an appropriate North American liberation theology received a mixed reception. Ruether conceded that civil religion, featuring the national language and symbols of liberty and justice, could possibly, without "*being less critical of America!*" offer the resources for responding to Latin American criticism. American people needed some hope, some recourse to a positive past, over the accusation of self-serving imperialism.

In his pre-conference paper, Herzog offered a strong criticism to the idea that civil religion, which he saw as based on "phony covenant," could serve as a liberation theology. While admirable qualities in civil religion had helped in America's self-understanding, he objected to Bellah's basic premise of Americans as "covenant people" as a false notion. There was no basis for understanding God's historic covenant with Israel as transferable to the American nation. The idea of civil religion as a "higher religion," too, was incomprehensible for Christian theology, dulling the sharp criticism of oppression in the founding of the United States In recovering the integrity of Christian theology, he asserted, the task was to critique all ideologies that masked God's liberatory work in history and absolutized the nation.[13]

Herzog argued that a bankrupt American theology needed to grasp the significance of the universal "Divine Mandate" for freedom at home and abroad. The interdependence between North America and Latin America, the religious underwriting of "pecuniary success," and the need to recover the liberation tradition were pressing for attention. The United States had a liberation tradition evident in Shays' Rebellion, abolitionism, the social gospel, and the women's movement. An effective response to the social crisis required that theology recognize the dialectical process between the world and the United States, bringing about a new relationship between Protestants and Catholics in the hemisphere. Furthermore, "Global issues are congealing also as local issues," Herzog wrote, having reached the American South in the black struggle, with rising possibilities among women, American Indians, and Chicanos. Through "radical repentance" and "consciousness-altering," the nation had to free itself from its white political and economic institutions. Realizing global interdependence, Herzog asserted, demanded the transformation of national myths grounded in "blind self-interest" to a consciousness that recognized the necessity of "creative self-limitation."[14]

The appeals to an American liberation tradition, the promotion of civil religion, and the plea for solidarity among oppressed people fell badly on the ears of the black delegation. Having arrived angry over a program designed by whites and Latin Americans, Herbert Edwards, from Duke University Divinity School and speaking for blacks, noted, "Racism has been the only ecumenical faith that America has subscribed to." It mattered little whether one evoked Adam Smith, Marx, socialism, or the myth of civil religion. All these ideologies coexisted with racism. Reviewing black history, Edwards charged that racism was the "overall and informing principle of action" in America. He asserted that while Latin Americans, feminists, and black theologians shared grievances against a common enemy, there were compelling reasons for the coalition not to adhere. Women and Latin Americans "were more acceptable to the enemy," since they were primarily white and spoke out of shared white power denied to blacks. While elite women and Latin Americans were *speaking for* the powerless by "assuming identification with the struggle," the experience of black theologians was personal as "their blackness makes them one with the despised whether they will it or no." The willingness of white theologians in the United States to listen to and learn from Latin Americans was due to the "ease by which one entered into a common universal language" of racist exclusion. It was easier for North American theology to look beyond its borders than listen to the black voices from within.[15]

The tensions seen in Geneva between Latin Americans and black theologians were once again evident in Detroit. The groups split on the significance of race and their relative relationship to the U.S. empire; thus, how to define the universal nature of the faith and degrees of oppression between groups complicated the encounter. With regard to the North American and Latin American theology profiled at the gathering, Edwards had clearly stated, "I do not find my experience [as a black person] reflected there; I do not find any awareness of me being a person." The planners had placed too much weight on class analysis, obscuring race in the United States, with Cone charging that it reflected the betrayal of black people by the North American religious left. Secure in his position at Union Theological Seminary, Cone commented that he was not interested in talking about liberation, a word already tainted by white appropriations, "in this setting, in Detroit, U.S.A., I see people I've been fighting against. Here I don't talk about liberation; I've got to talk about black." He acknowledged his unwillingness to concede many points in the presence of people he suspected had not experienced concrete suffering. Yes, he acknowledged, "once you have your things together you gradually get together with other oppressed people in order to deal with the ever-growing oppressive structures. Without that, I don't think we have any hope." Conversely, Latin Americans, presenting their case in a full day of conference proceedings, continued to press the significance of class in a global struggle and charged that black theology, as a North American product, represented a plea for blacks to become full members of the oppressor class of the empire. As one participant asked, "Are free blacks to be part of an imperial nation that is the oppressor of other nations?" The greatest tension was over whether race, class, or identification with empire primarily established privilege.[16]

While male theologians were debating class and race and their position vis-à-vis the dominant theology, members of the "women's caucus," as one-third of the participants, were experiencing unease among themselves. The shadow of differences and solidarity among women that characterized 1975 as the UN's International Women's Year hung over Detroit. Minority women, making claims on multiple fronts, expressed public dissatisfaction with the exclusion of their concerns from the agenda. Nevertheless, women attempted to present a unified front by vehemently protesting the planning process, which they felt produced an elitist, hierarchical conference showcasing the Latin American "clerical class" with a notable absence of grassroots voices. They suspected that Latin American theology, with its emphasis on class analysis, and black theology, with its grounding in race, did not sufficiently address the realities of sexism. The delegation, dominated by middle-class white women, distanced themselves from a liberal women's movement they viewed as interested only in securing their own access to political power. Rather, this group carrying the ethos of radical feminism saw women's oppression as distinct and fundamental to understanding an interlocking system of multiple oppressions.[17]

Beverly Harrison, a professor at Union Theological Seminary, expressed gratitude for the methods provided by Latin American theologians that allowed women to make their own claims against the dominant paradigms. Nevertheless, Latin American theology and its use of Marxist analysis was still too "objectivist," moving toward an "absolute dualism." Dualism, buried in class struggle, made women "invisible" in theology. She noted that theologians continued with the attitude that began in the nineteenth century, as radical feminism was "domesticated," "pushed out," and "killed chiefly by the churches," with its adherents accused of having "trouble with their femininity." Once again women found themselves struggling because "the enemy we are trying to expel from within ourselves is the idea that we are simply 'other'—whatever 'the other' happens to be—to man, to male." Beatriz Melano Couch, author of *La mujer y Iglesia* (1973) and the only Latin American woman present, considering herself to be in solidarity with her male colleagues rather than a feminist theologian, nevertheless agreed that racism and sexism in the ideology of *machismo* deserved attention in the construction of liberation theology. For women represented at the gathering, attending to class and race alone did not alleviate the *sui generis* sexual oppression interwoven into the very fabric of theology.[18]

In the final session, Coleman reflected on the gathering, concluding that there was no universal language of liberation available, thus, "all pretense to speak *the* universal language stems from either obfuscation or domination." Noting that "every language is tribal," Coleman asserted that Rawlsian speech about universal justice ran into a host of contradictions in the particularity of meaning. Several times participants made claims that their position was the last word in explaining oppression. "There was a shadow side to every liberation language" that hid the "ambiguity" of differences within groups, making a pure definition of liberation impossible. Coleman saw the "ghost of the Enlightenment," with its claim to analytic scientific reason as the only shared language. He believed the weakness of liberation theology lay in assuming a liberatory goal for history that jumped immediately to politics without any ethical criteria for discriminating among alternative political projects. Critical reflection on praxis needed an "ethical norm about the substantively good society" that was not reducible to politics or economics. Short of an ethical norm, Coleman asserted, civil religion, with its "common law, civil rights, and civil libertarianism language," while flawed, remained an indispensable tool for North America.[19]

Having begun to establish mutuality and solidarity, Brown noted that the conference agenda had "quickly gravitated into 'special interest groups,'" with even white males, "feeling the most threatened," forming their own caucuses. All the groups found that in any given situation they were oppressors. Nevertheless, Brown viewed the conference as setting a new theological direction. Theology was now an "open-ended, corporate, self-correcting, engaged process," undertaken not by isolated individual minds but in a shared struggle. No longer viewed as the articulation of "timeless" and "universal" truths, it was being viewed for what it had always truly been, a reflection of a particular time and a particular community. Brown saw multiple dangers for liberation theology; it could be easily dismissed as a naïve fad, criticized as utopianism, or misrepresented in emotionally laden terms such as *communist*. The word *liberation* co-opted in popular discourse or interpreted as a privatized "inner liberation" emptied it of its revolutionary potential. Liberation theology needed to keep the dialectic alive between the particular and the global, and remain grounded in a community of struggle.[20]

The turn to the particular identities of marginalized people, and the breakdown of appeals to the universal, made finding a new orthodoxy at Detroit unlikely. Theologians compelled to reflect the diversity within the American hemisphere were recognizing an alternative theological discourse—organic, particular, and arising from below. They agreed that race, class, and sex were interlocking global systems of oppression, but finding a necessary common foundation escaped them. The meaning derived from group history appeared irreconcilable with a congruent theology. Although no clear consensus emerged, participants shared the conviction that the world was open to change and that theology, as a critical discipline, could play a part in that change. The nature and the means of change and a common language for God remained elusive, and the implications reverberated beyond Detroit.

Cognitive Dissonance

The Theology in the Americas conference marked a seismic shift in religious thought from the accumulated pressure of intellectual and cultural change. The religious sociologist Peter Berger, in a 1967 essay "A Sociological View of the Secularization of Theology," forwarded arguments made in his book *The Sacred Canopy* (1967). He observed that having begun with Friedrich Schleiermacher, theology's move from transcendence to immanence and from an objective view of religious reality to the subjective experience was sowing the seeds of its own demise. Earlier, in 1961, Berger decried the subversion of transcendence necessary for existential freedom by a therapeutic gospel that worked to ensure middle-class compliance. Continuing with his concern for transcendence, Berger characterized modern theology as having adopted the grammar of philosophical rationalism and the tools of social science, casting the entire Christian tradition as a "mythological world" with no objective encounter with a divine other. This move "replicates to an amazing degree, in form if not in content, [Ludwig] Feuerbach's famous program of reducing theology to anthropology," he wrote. Theologians were accepting a "secularized consciousness" as an "unquestioned standard of cognitive validity" and abandoning the proposal that "modern consciousness be *re*mythologized." Surprisingly, having left the necessary premise of the discipline, secular theologians "continue to operate as theologians."[21]

Berger viewed the "pluralization of social worlds" in modernity as turning belief into a set of politically loaded and shifting "religious preferences." Ceasing to refer to a transcendent God, the Christian belief in divine intervention in history had become one of many political perspectives. Theology had only two choices. It could defend itself by asserting an objective reality, within an increasingly ghettoized context, or surrender to a modernity in which the particularity of religious claims faded into extinction. Berger feared that failing to maintain a role for divine transcendence neutralized the social role of religion in providing meaning and coherence.[22]

In the 1970s, the loss of transcendence remained a significant issue for Berger. He continued his argument that religion provided a necessary "transcendent plausibility" for the social order through an overarching "sacred canopy." Transcendence, which in the early 1960s Berger regarded as necessary for existential *freedom* and for spurring opposition to a total system, became, in the cultural crisis of the 1970s, significant for maintaining social *order*—two seemingly opposed functions. He sensed that the abandonment of transcendence and objective religious truth placed the search for individual freedom within the immediately political. Berger had not yet discerned that the idea of divine transcendence was not disappearing but merely relocating from above-and-beyond to the political sphere. Not recognized was that what appeared as the end of a theology of transcendence, and thus the secularization of religion from within, was actually the beginning of militant political–religious claims rather than the neutralization of religion's cultural power.[23]

Social and religious shifts noted by cultural observers had theologians pondering the future of their discipline. There was a new discourse, and the boundaries of theology were blurring and shifting. A 1975 *Christianity and Crisis* symposium titled "Whatever Happened to Theology?" attempted to assess the extent to which social, economic, and political issues had eclipsed the concern for divine transcendence that had always been the mark of theological thought. The difference in the opinions expressed demonstrated how each participant viewed the relationship between theology and modernity. Respondents included those committed to continuing the multifarious liberal projects, and the liberationists Ruether, Bonino, Herzog, and Carol P. Christ as the voices of an encroaching new orthodoxy. The opinions ranged from bewilderment at the "chronic ill health" of theology to celebration of the birth of a new paradigm.[24]

Those critical of the situation pointed to a deteriorating process over a period of two hundred years that had institutionalized the theologian in the academy. Van A. Harvey, professor of religion at the University of Pennsylvania, surmised that the theologian unmoored from an organic religious community felt pressed to "harmonize the cognitive dissonance between the Christian faith and new knowledge" in the natural and social sciences in which he appeared as an "amateur." Compelled to defend his case on what biblical criticism considered dubious historical claims, the theologian had moved on to cultural criticism, what Wallace M. Alson Jr., a Presbyterian minister and college president, described as various faddish forms of "social relevance" falling under the "tyranny of immediate religious experience." Theology, having cast its lot with modernity, was not immune from the anxiety of the age. It was experiencing the shaking of the foundations occurring across academic disciplines questioning imperialism, racism, and sexism. The result was a plethora of new theologies providing what

Gordon D. Kaufman, professor at Harvard Divinity School, described as "a kind of decoration for and legitimation of almost any partisan position in the culture." Theology, critics asserted, was now a "common prostitute" and a "pawn in the socio-cultural process," merely reflecting culture rather than providing critical norms. The jargon of liberation, oppression, and revolution had emptied theology of drama and meaning. Those lamenting the state of affairs called for reconnecting the theologian to the religious community and building a new and unspecified foundation for the discipline.[25]

Liberationists welcomed the new landscape that exposed the ideological distortion of modern theology. Bonino argued that the only theology that was collapsing was that of "Western bourgeois culture" with its belief in an "autonomous realm of spiritual life." A "new postbourgeois" Christianity, perceived as deviant and strange in the metropole, was emerging among subordinated people who were repossessing the faith and "cleansing" it of ideological distortion. Proponents argued that liberation theologies were dismantling the ideology of domination, with its dependency on Western scientific rationality and the idea of a God-above that had underwritten modernity. The "return of the repressed," Ruether asserted, was bringing into question notions of progress built on the conquest of people below. In the debate over the state of the discipline, what an establishment in shambles viewed as the loss of the necessary language of transcendence, liberationists saw as bringing into view the experience of the oppressed hidden by abstraction. Liberals, neo-conservatives, and liberationists all held to the necessity of a critical autonomy for their discipline and, playing experience against rationality, each saw the other side as too dependent on modern thought.[26]

The Last Appeal

The same year, a concerned Berger joined Richard Neuhaus and other neo-conservative theologians in the publication of "An Appeal for Theological Affirmation." The document, signed by an ecumenical group and first published in *Worldview* and reprinted in *Theology Today*, navigated the divide between the new secularizing theologies and what one signer called the "madness of fundamentalist fad" by reasserting the autonomy of the discipline from cultural encroachment. Although they did not name their target, liberation theology was clearly on the minds of the signers. The appeal repudiated making religious claims subject to modern thought that equated "reason with scientific rationality." Modern rationality placed religious claims in the realm of subjectivity, thus rendering theology a pure expression of human experience, "God being humanity's noblest creation." Liberationists had clearly placed the experience of the oppressed at the center. Thus religion, critics charged, appeared as nothing more than human projections deployed for the sole purpose of "individual self-realization and human community." The signers argued against making social, political, and economic programs, whether they promoted the "American way of life," socialism, or "raising human consciousness," the criteria for theological truth. The denigration of transcendence undermined the awareness of the "enormity of evil" and an ultimate source of values that served as an effective motivation against all "dehumanizing structures." Transcendent values were a necessary and unmovable reference point in the pursuit of justice. While affirming the need to address injustice in all forms, the signers charged that the "modern pursuit of liberation from all social and historical restraints is finally dehumanizing." The appeal, evoking the limits set by tradition and inherited institutions, upheld the necessity of an objective reality outside human experience, and asserted theology's autonomy from modern thought and politics—an untenable and eroded position. History and liberationists' arguments had shown how culture profoundly shaped theology rather than existing as an autonomous discipline.[27]

The appeal provoked an intense rebuttal. In the roundtable discussion published in *Theology Today*, Letty M. Russell, a professor at the Yale Divinity School, called the appeal a "broadside" that denounced unspecified "enemies" and that it failed to address what was at issue—orthopraxis. The issue at play was not orthodoxy, or the loss of transcendence to secularization, but how to respond to the "crushed ones" who were groaning for liberation. Richard Shaull, noting, "our theological world is falling apart," advised that the correct response to the failure of tired concepts to meet the needs of a new cultural situation was not restating them in a "louder voice." For liberationists, the appeal had sidestepped the critical issue. It had failed to identify the existing systems in need of confrontation or to offer the means for arriving at a just social order, leaving abstracted religious values unrealizable in a world of political choices. The new social landscape demanded that theology make a political choice rather continue the pretense of neutrality.[28]

Meanwhile in Latin America, liberationists were the target of vehement opposition from both the ecclesial hierarchy and a rising popular conservative movement. The early challenges came from the Belgian Jesuit missionary Roger Vekemans and Colombian Bishop Alfonso López Trujillo. In the 1960s, Vekemans established a school of scientific sociology at the Universidad Católica de Chile to advance a U.S.-sponsored anti-communist development and democratic models. After the 1970 election of Salvador Allende in Chile, Vekemans, financed by numerous U.S. and European sources, launched a vigorous campaign against liberation theology. Vekemans' books *Caesar and God: The Priesthood and Politics* (1972) and *Theology of Liberation and Christians for Socialism*

(1976), and the journal *Tierra Nueva* provided a socially aware alternative to liberation theology. Vekemans and Trujillo set out to reverse the radicalization trend in the Latin American Episcopal Conference, initiated at Medellín. Together they secured the 1972 election of Trujillo as secretary-general, shutting out liberationists from access to formal institutional structures through the 1970s. The key points of criticism were the deployment of Marxist theory and strategies viewed as incompatible with Catholic thought, the threat of a popular church unaccountable to the hierarchy found in base ecclesial communities, and violence as a facile solution. They objected to the politicization of Catholic social teaching that addressed the needs of the poor as a distortion of the spirit of Medellín, and attempted to reverse the trend by calling for a depoliticization of liberation.[29]

The theological and political turbulence in Latin America was great enough for Pope Paul VI to address the meaning of liberation in the Apostolic Exhortation *Evangelii Nuntiandi* (1975). The word *liberación* had become ubiquitous among intellectuals, activists, and laypeople, carrying multiple meanings. Seeking to dispel ambiguity and assert its proper meaning, Pope Paul affirmed the liberation of man as a holistic salvation that included the concrete social, political, and economic situation, but moved beyond the immanent to a transcendent salvation—a gift of God alone. Pope Paul attempted to extract liberation from the restricted concept of revolution and reappropriate it within a framework of traditional Catholic social teaching. He rejected any definition of liberation reduced to "temporal" aspects of life and asserted that it must include openness to the "divine Absolute." In seeking liberation for all humanity, an integral approach to evangelization included social action on behalf of justice. Nevertheless, the role of the Church was not simply to provide political mobilization through the invocation of religious symbols.[30]

In *Evangelii Nuntiandi,* the means by which to seek justice remained vague. The exhortation displayed more concern for the Marxist appropriations of theology and revolutionary violence than for the ideological justification for state repression ravaging Latin America in the name of Christian order. Like his predecessors, Pope Paul appealed to the "conversion of the heart," and the means of realizing liberation in history remained undefined. Inadvertently, the Pope, in attempting to reconcile an immanent and transcendent understanding of liberation, had proceeded to do what liberationists were protesting: legitimize the standing social order by placing a critical aspect of liberation outside history. The effort to reestablish the spiritual meaning of liberation continued with the 1979 election of Pope John Paul II, who viewed liberation theology as part of larger and detrimental secularizing forces, and demonstrated how far liberationists had gone in redefining the terms of a global theo-political debate.[31]

Trujillo, the Vatican's chief spokesman in Latin America, responding to liberationists, concurred in *Liberation or Revolution?* (1975) that Marxist analysis was incongruent with a Christian worldview. Trujillo, reflecting the sensibility of the crumbled ethos of new Christendom noted that desperate people restless and hungry for freedom were "easy prey of vindictive men of violent inclinations." Liberation, having become "fashionable," was in danger of losing its theological meaning and becoming equated with a false revolution. The view of politics as the total of human life, and the demand that the Church choose the revolution, was a notion of change that eliminated pluralist opposition. Striving for "political neutrality" in theology was not indifference, or legitimation, but a necessary condition for autonomy of the religious sphere in the service of its spiritual mission and the common good. Faith, unbound by relative options, was open to different political commitments. Responding to the exigencies of public life, faith did, as Juan Luis Segundo had argued and Trujillo conceded, produce different political commitments. In the midst of political turmoil, a theology issuing from the ecclesial hierarchy with the pretense of neutral guidance, as Trujillo maintained, remained unpersuasive and suspect for many faithful Catholics making ethically laden choices.[32]

Latin American liberationists were also encountering an on-the-ground conservative backlash. After the euphoric mood of the Medellín Bishops' conference in 1968, grassroots opposition began to build among the middle classes. State repression and opposition within the Catholic Church tended to embolden conservative adversaries. Oppositional response took the form of regrouping in such initiatives as the Society for the Defense of Tradition, Family, and Property in Chile, standing against all systemic reform. The Peruvian *Sodalitium Vitae*, explicitly organized to combat liberation theology, viewed it as challenging not only to Church authority but also the social order. *Sodalitium Vitae* began in 1973 as an orthodox Catholic group called "God and Country," first appearing at the Catholic University of Peru and supported by influential bishops. Connecting liberation theology with violent revolutionary movements, and under a banner of an alternative "theology of reconciliation," *Sodalitium Vitae* attempted to defuse political activism through nonviolent conflict resolution and reassertion of social Christianity. The spread of liberation theology awakened previously politically inactive conservative sectors of Latin American society that had assumed a truce between a Catholic social order and modern politics.[33]

Mobilization among conservatives was a hemispheric phenomenon and an offshoot of liberationists reasserting the significance of the political. In the U.S., the entrance of liberation theology into the vacuum created by the breakup of the theological consensus over American power helped rally the New Christian Right. The mobilization of women and minorities, and the belief that U.S. global power was in decline, became by the mid-1970s a cultural crisis for conservatives. For many, liberation theology signaled the apostasy of the Protestant mainline and the bankruptcy of the theological establishment. A broad fundamentalist–evangelical and Catholic coalition joined forces with a growing secular neoconservative movement. The Christian Right viewed the cultural crisis as a spiritual battle for the soul of America, and its politic grew out of a concern with the spread of Godless communism, the pervasiveness of secular humanism, racial unrest, and the loosening of sexual mores associated with feminism. Since the 1920s, fundamentalists and new evangelicals to different degrees had placed their hope for national renewal in individual salvation and limited cultural engagement that assumed the soundness of American political life. Cultural change eroded the trust in the preserving power of American institutions and in the slow hand of providence to bring about heart renewal.[34]

The rise of the Christian Right was not merely a reactionary political response to the culture wars; it signaled internal theological change among conservative thinkers that calls for examination. Carl F.H. Henry, regarded by the emergent Christian Right as the theological father of the movement, spent the 1960s rejecting systemic reform as a strategy. He placed priority on personal conversion and acts of piety as the means to renew society, leaving a limited yet significant role for a "God-ordained" state. In *Uneasy Conscience of Modern Fundamentalism* (1947), he had encouraged a conservative form of personal social engagement while rejecting the means of state for advancing the kingdom of God. In the 1970s, Henry, critiquing liberation theology for its Marxist exegesis and redefinition of salvation, called for an alternative and engaged evangelical vision for society going beyond individual action. Counting the nation's foundations as Christian, Henry sought a biblical and "realistically possible" vision for a "new social organism" availing itself of the "sociological tools at our disposal." His ambitious vision was no facile application of biblically derived values but a pragmatic and politically laden one, displaying a tension between justifying an all-encompassing program for transforming society and maintaining the long-held priority of individual salvation. Henry demonstrated the extent of theological change that had occurred since early in the century as it turned toward historicism, social science, and pragmatism. Across the left/right spectrum, theology was validating the religious and spiritual significance of the political.[35]

For conservatives, the cultural crisis and a change in theological focus, from personal salvation to social renewal, compelled a loosening of the boundaries between the public realm of the political and the private realm of religion and morality. The Baptist preacher Jerry Falwell, who founded the Moral Majority, a key organization of the emerging Christian Right, had earlier expressed a repudiation of political activism. His 1965 sermon entitled "Ministers and Marches" questioned the Christian sincerity of Martin L. King Jr. and James Farmer with their "left-wing" associations and declared "Nowhere are we commissioned [by the Bible] to reform the externals ... Our ministry is not reformation but transformation," meaning the salvation of souls. By the mid-1970s, Falwell signaled an essential change in political and theological disposition and became the chief grassroots organizer and spokesman for conservative Christian activism. Organizing its social power and inspired by a persistent millenarianism, the New Christian Right turned from the volunteerism of the evangelical religion, with individual action as the centerpiece, to the means of state to preserve God's moral order. Virtuous leaders and just law would renew society. Understanding the change in disposition within the grassroots of evangelicalism—from the sectarian and non-activist stance of the post-war period to broad-based mobilization—requires an accounting of the realignment of conservative theology and its relationship to political society. For a movement whose ultimate priority was the salvation of the individual in the hereafter, public engagement that accepts the political realm as spiritually significant requires justification that links the salvation of souls with the social and cultural milieu. Conservative evangelicals, situated across denominational lines and often pitted against their more liberal church leadership and seminaries, found a theologically tenable politic serving as an opposition against the provocation of leftward liberationist incursion. With God on their side, they could lead in the redemption of American culture and the salvation of their children.[36]

As seen in the regrouping of religious conservatives across the hemisphere, the change in theology brought about by liberationists gave rise to broad social engagement outside their ranks. The redrawn parameters of the theo-political space fomented a public religious–political contest that included liberals, radicals, and newly mobilized conservatives in redefining the coming new social order. Sydney E. Ahlstrom observed in 1970 that the modern mind, infected with a suspicion of religious doctrine and awareness of the contradiction between the ideal and the actual, and losing faith in institutions, was changing the social landscape through a shift in moral and religious values. He argued that the widely sown seeds of radical Protestantism had come to fruition in secularizing theologies that combined "strenuous moral precisionism" with "evangelical experientialism" and a determination to use the means of state for asserting moral claims. What Ahlstrom saw as the purview of 1960s radicals on the left became a broader shift as groups on the right ventured out of a privatized religion. Religious conservatives were like other groups experiencing disenchantment with institutions, expressing moral outrage, and developing a willingness to avail themselves of the state apparatus to actualize their social vision.[37]

The crisis within the Protestant establishment and liberationists inroads had unleashed a torrent of passion across the hemisphere. In North America, religion that in the post-war period had shown the restraint of either liberal Christian realism or fundamentalist–evangelical separatist tendencies experienced political realignment and increased activism. In Latin America, liberation theology, filling the vacuum left by a discredited new Christendom, accelerated the erosion of the cultural hegemony of the Catholic Church and stimulated political pluralism. The monistic–corporatist tradition in Latin America, which sought to hierarchically harmonize the different components of society for the common good, was seriously weakened. The proliferation of popular expressions of the Catholic faith independent of the ecclesial hierarchy, and Protestant growth among the disenfranchised, provided a base for religion-inspired mobilization. Liberationists found that they were no longer alone, and their call for a politically committed theology emboldened others to forward alternative visions for the social order under the authority of God.[38]

Liberation theology signaled the late-twentieth-century understanding of the individual as being subject to social forces, thus defining her experience by the political. Modern politics was no longer a place of proximate truth and negotiation but a place to make ultimate claims to justice and the social order. Post-Enlightenment theology, having attended to the existential and personal experience of believers, moved to validate the political stage of individual actualization. Theology, as a referent for transcendent situated values, and political philosophy, rooted in the exercise of secular power, moved toward convergence. As liberation theologians asserted claims on behalf of blacks, women, and the poor, they were the avant-garde entering a newly defined theo-political space and unleashing previously quiet religious passions they did not anticipate.

Epilogue

IN THE FINAL decades of the twentieth century, liberation theologies expanded and diversified. The transnational conversation begun in Geneva and Detroit continued through the Ecumenical Association of Third World Theologians (EATWOT), organized in 1976. EATWOT became the main international body for advocating global justice through a contextual theology from the perspective of the world's oppressed people. In multiple gatherings, blacks, women, and Latin Americans continued their dialogue to strengthen their solidarity and resolve their differences. As opponents attempted to discredit liberation theologies, the core ideas were spreading in other regions of the world. The promulgation of liberation theology had uncovered new forms of oppression. Theologians speaking for multiple ethnic groups—Asians, Africans, the disabled, and the sexually marginalized—entered the conversation. Any place Christian missions had touched was susceptible to liberationist inroads. Theology was no longer a static set of principles supplied by First World theologians and applied to diverse contexts. Rather, the understanding of God emerged from the experience and reflection of the world's marginalized in whom the universal and the particular, religious values and political demands, converged. The first generation of American liberationists brought the compelling story of oppressed people into the center of elite theological discourse, with global and often unexpected reverberations.[1]

Joining the Multitudes

The revolutionary currents that ran through liberation theology in turn galvanized Latin American grassroots movements, with many arising from the tens of thousands of base ecclesial communities. Among them were the Brazilian Landless Workers Movement of the 1970; the 1979 Sandinista revolution in

Nicaragua overthrowing the ruthless dictator Anastasio Somoza Garcia, which drew much of its political strength from liberationist-inspired base ecclesial communities; the revitalized Columbian Quintín Lame Movement of peasants in defense of communal lands in the 1980s; and Mexico's *Las Abejas* (the Bees) Maya community in Chiapas in the 1990s, a movement in sympathy with the revolutionary Zapatistas that demonstrated the inspiration of liberation theology in resistance to state terror and the denial of human rights. What these people's movements had in common was ethnic solidarity, shared poverty, and a deep sense of alignment with divine justice.[2]

The Catholic Church continued to experience deep divisions within its ranks and among the laity as liberation theology spread globally. A number of Bishops embraced liberation theology, including the Mexican Samuel Ruiz Garcia working on behalf of indigenous people in Chiapas and the Brazilian José Ivo Lorscheiter. In turn, the Vatican attempted to hold back the tide by reinforcing its social and political teaching and disciplining renegade priests, which only furthered the spread of liberationists' ideas. Multiple events kept liberation theology at the forefront as the Church divided against itself. The Archbishop Oscar Romero of El Salvador, gunned down in 1980 by a right-wing death squad in his defense of the poor and human rights, did not consider himself a liberationist, nevertheless he was counted as a martyr for their cause by many. The 1985 controversy over the ecclesial censure of the Brazilian theologian Leonard Boff for his critique of the Church's "monarchic and pyramidic" structure; the leftward turn of the continent, marked by the 1999 election of the socialist Hugo Chavez as president of Venezuela; the 2005 election of Cardinal Joseph Ratzinger, who, as Pope Benedict XVI, vehemently opposed liberation theology; and, to the dismay of the Church, the 2008 election of liberationist Bishop Fernando Lugo, known as "Bishop of the Poor," as president of Paraguay fueled turmoil. It was the election of Jorge Mario Bergoglio as Pope Francis in 2013, with his conciliatory tone, which offered a sign of breaking the impasse.[3]

From 1980 to the early decades of the new millennium, Black and feminist theology produced a second and third generation of politically committed theologians and extended the reach of their ideas by applying their theological method to new situations. On the heels of the Christian Right, the Reverend Jesse Jackson's multiracial Rainbow Coalition and his 1984 presidential candidacy offered a moral critique in the age of Reagan. The campaign, displaying the characteristics of a black religious revival and a "rainbow theology," gained unprecedented support from black clergy. As Reverend Benjamin F. Chavis of the United Church of Christ explained it, "Jackson's theology is a theology of liberation, informed by the black church's religious experience and in dialogue with the religious and political experiences of the world community, particularly the Third World." Feminist theology highlighted its broad appeal to women at the first of a series of Re-Imagining Conferences in 1993. The Presbyterian Church (U.S.A.) and the World Council of Churches sponsored the Minneapolis event of over 2,200 theologian, clergy, and laywomen from over forty denominations. Evoking the divine Sophia, the gathering brought together feminist theologians, clergy, and laypeople "to do the theological work born out of women's experience" and mobilize to "tell the truth" and "trouble the waters" of the patriarchy. The ensuing uproar over what some viewed as the promotion of lesbianism and goddess worship resulted in Re-Imagining being noted in 1994 as a top story of Christian politics according to *The Christian Century*.[4]

The 1990s marked a counter-trend by the expansion of neoliberalism's promise of economic prosperity. Social movements languished and were in need of revitalization provoking broad theological attention to wealth inequality. A new generation of liberation theologians and their sympathizers turned to critique global capitalism with its consumerism, technological efficiency, and the commodification of all life. The 2010s brought a new surge of socio-political resistance. The Occupy Wall Street movement spread globally, protesting against the social and economic inequality represented by the top 1% of world's wealth holders. Among the ranks of Occupy were Protestants and Catholic clergy, theologians, and lay activists roused to action by liberation theology.[5]

The Black Lives Matter movement (BLM), founded by Alicia Garza, Patrisse Cullors, and Opal Tometi, burst on the scene in 2013 as a response to the fatal police shooting of unarmed Trayvon Martin and a pattern of extrajudicial violence against black people. As a revitalization of liberation movements, its affirmation, "When Black people get free, everybody gets free," expressed the intersectionality experienced by many. The apparent lack of connection between BLM and the black church raised questions of whether religion held any remaining influence in secularized black political life. Black theologians and religious observers pointed out that the lack of clergy in the BLM did not translate into the death of the black church. Rather, the scholar of African American religion Terrence J. Johnson argued that the black church, having suffered the physical erasure of urban gentrification and economic displacement, remained "a counterpublic, a reference point in and through which many people define justice and what it means to be human." BLM as an organic outgrowth of the political history of the black church undergoing a religious transformation displayed the political "vocabulary and hermeneutical moves" of liberation theology— a refusal to divide the spiritual from political in a theology from below. Similarly to the role Black Power played in the emergence of black liberation theology, some viewed BLM as calling the black churches to their mission of social justice. Reading the signs of the times,

Occupy Wall Street and BLM provided opportunities for liberation theologians to join the multitudes and offer constructive contextualized theologies. They viewed movements for social justice as displaying the immanent work of God on behalf of the oppressed at the nexus of the political and the theological.[6]

A Broken Cordon Sanitaire

As multifarious movements across the Americas felt the socio-political reverberations of liberation theology, there is a deeper and wider change in American societies. Centuries of religious resistance and accommodation, and critical theological and intellectual changes, converged in liberation theology, placing religion and politics in a shared ideational field. A set of immediate cultural factors also contributed to its emergence. A critical mass of religious intellectuals, sufficiently detached from formal ecclesial structures and trained in the critical tools of the modern academy and who saw themselves as a prophetic minority aligned with radical movements, provided the necessary distance for their critique. Global communication networks ensured the wide dissemination of ideas. Social and political unrest throughout the Americas, Third World consciousness sustained by anti-colonial sentiment, and the fragmentation of post-war liberal international consensus offered the opportunity to intervene. The unresolved and below-the-surface tensions between religion and politics, and the contradictions evident in the hemispheric history of freedom, pressed for resolution. Modern theology's turn toward this-world and new social theories by which to critique racism, classism, and sexism supplied the intellectual means for reconnecting political expectations with religious hope.

Liberation theology expressed a mid-century shift toward recovering religion as a positive political force for change after a period of dormancy. Instead of addressing private concerns and pietistic values in a political vacuum, liberationists exposed the ideological constitution of all theology. The questions shared by theology and social theory regarding the relationship between the individual and society, status and authority, freedom and oppression, and the need to account for the construction and realization of societal values was an opportunity for disciplinary confluence. Through a theistic social theory, liberationists redefined the meaning of salvation and validated the political sphere as the place to actualize human freedom. Incorporating resistance from below into formal theological categories, they addressed the abyss of despair between divine justice and political reality into which the oppressed fell. They recovered the political vitalism of religion and attempted to build an integrated conceptual bridge between the political and the theological.

Nevertheless, liberationists speaking truth to power were unable to realize the just social order they imagined. Neither did oppressed people become harbingers of a new humanity. At the end of the twentieth century, liberationists had to adapt to several social and political changes: the end of the Cold War, the quieting of radicalism, the fall of dictatorships in Latin America, the rise of neoliberalism, minority gains in the academy, and the strength of the religious right. Globalization exposed an empire that was everywhere and nowhere, and the idea of Third World opposition against the First World became less persuasive. Despite an expanding economy, democratic initiatives, and promising grassroots movements, the mass of Latin American people and significant numbers of North Americans continued to experience crushing poverty and marginalization. Women and minorities continued to encounter entrenched institutional sexism and racism. The solidarity needed to confront oppression on multiple fronts did not coalesce. Emerging at a critical point for radical movements, liberationists suffered the fate they had sought to avoid—fomenting the production of reams of theoretical analysis and fueling popular debate rather than structural change. Prophetic protest was easier than actualizing a new politic. Without a sustainable political program, theological reflection on the experience of the oppressed appeared to sympathetic critics as acquiescence to a surging neoliberalism. By the mid-1990s other observers, seeing the inability of liberationists to articulate a political strategy or build cross-group coalitions and watching the eclipsing of radical movements, declared liberation theologies dead—an intellectual curiosity piece of the late twentieth century—only to see it reasserted in the new millennium.[7]

From a historical perspective, the success or failure of any intellectual movement in meeting its stated goals is not a measure of its achievements. The tendency to breed ideological excesses, or short-term victories, are inadequate to ascertain a movement's influence. Nor does inner coherence or contradictions of arguments offer assurance of a movement's credibility. The power of a movement in ideas is its ability to transform the assumptions of the cultural conversation. The articulation of previously implicit thought, slight shifts in the ideological positions of critics, and changes in the cultural language are the most salient features of its influence. Often, what intellectual movements accomplish lies outside the vision of their proponents, as it moves throughout the ideational field of society and taking on unexpected new social forms. The success of liberation theology lay in challenging the long-held explicit methods and goals of theology, redefining the relationship between religion and politics in a new theo-political space, and altering the expectations for the role of religion in social change rather than legitimation.

In a more diffused manner, liberationists contributed to changes in popular religious attitudes. The new attention given to the demands of the poor and the marginalized contributed to a recovery of the language of social justice and the growth of the prosperity gospel—two seemly opposed ethics. In the last two decades of the twentieth century and into the new millennium, a reenergized turn toward social justice, which had a definition as elusive as that of *liberation*, was evident across the religious spectrum. Social justice could simply mean a renewed personal commitment to helping the poor, a taking up of the cause of saving the unborn, or a motivation to advocate for gay people. Claims to social justice could encourage economic activism for indigenous and labor rights, or school choice. The language of social justice, a central feature of social Christianity muffled in the mid-twentieth century, was again ubiquitous among the political and religious mainstream, often with vastly different goals.

Alongside the resurgence of social justice, the prosperity gospel that was quickly spreading throughout the Americas also marked a religious turn toward this world. Charismatic preachers promoted spiritual liberation of the mind, an idea akin to consciousness-raising, rather than a revolution in social structures, to free people from poverty. Through faith declarations that promised to unlock abundance here and now, and by casting out the demons of poverty and oppression, the poor could experience emancipation into wealth and health in *this* world. Social justice and the gospel of prosperity, holding different sensibilities, demonstrated a broad awakening of the plight of the poor and marginalized that could easily circumvent structural change in a neoliberal age.[8]

Liberation theology has longer implications. The sociologist José Casanova, in *Public Religions in the Modern World* (1994), examined five cases of massive upsurge in religious activism in Western societies, including the liberationist-inspired churches in Brazil, the New Christian Right, and Catholicism in the United States. Casanova noted the societal trends that had thrust religion into a public contest over values as religious activists engaged in political tumbles. He proposed that what was transpiring in the refusal of activists to accept a marginal role was a "deprivatization" of religion and thereby redrawing the boundaries between religion and political life. Casanova called for reconsideration of the relationship between religion and modernity, and a worn-out theory of secularization that failed to explain what was happening.[9]

Modernity's move toward secularization meant transferring the creation of shared values from religion to a nonreligious public sphere. Since the nineteenth century, social theorists had held that the triumph of reason and science would eventually render all religion untenable, and it would cease to play a significant role in societies. Religion, if it remained at all, would serve the needs of self-actualization and self-expression of individuals. The ramifications of modernity in the Americas, where religious devotion was culturally entrenched, would follow the way of a presumed secularized Europe. However, this secularization thesis, which held sway for most of the twentieth century, began to look like a myth of elite intellectuals as religious activism erupted in the 1980s. A wide religious–political reawaking mandated a rethinking of the long-held theory of secularization.

The full force of religion reasserting itself into the public square in increasingly militant terms raised the question of how to reconcile competing values in pluralistic societies, breaking the *cordon sanitaire*. Private/public distinctions were increasingly debated, contesting the boundaries between political pragmatism and religious values. Liberal, radical, and conservative political theologians entered the debate along with social scientists and political philosophers, focusing on how to arrive at a set of shared values through negotiation and what the philosopher John Rawls called "public reason." The assertion of religious values in the public sphere escalated the debate over what constituted public reason. Social scientists and political philosophers could no longer view religion as a premodern residue, because it featured a distinct attribute of modernity—the theological validation of political society.[10]

At the end of the twentieth century Peter Berger, who had worried about the loss of the sacred canopy provided by religion and underwriting the social order, had reversed himself and was declaring the theory of secularization a myth. The relationship between modernity and religion was more complicated than originally presumed. Nevertheless, he viewed the rise of public religion, specifically of the conservative type, as a reactionary movement against secular encroachment. Berger saw in popular religious sentiments a revolt against the undermining of religious certainty and the influence of global secular elites. The trend appeared to be a desecularization of society, as religious groups pushed against marginalization by asserting a religious vision.[11]

Viewing desecularization as a reactionary response to modernity fails to account for the changes *within* religious thought regarding the relationship between God and the world. What was not anticipated was that changes in religious attitudes displayed the effects of liberal monism, the demand for a single political language and one source of social authority, and would be significant enough to muddle the presumed modern split between the sacred and the secular. Instead of disappearing, religious intellectuals began to challenge the assumption of a Great Separation and uncovered the precarious nature of the truce required for modern politics. The desecularization of society prompted by increased religious inroads into the public sphere was not a reaction against modernity, but rather its product. What appears as desecularization of society from one perspective appears as the secularization or deprivatization of religion from another.[12]

Liberation theology acted as a catalyst for the secularization and deprivatization of religion. By forwarding the idea that the construction of the world mattered, and advancing the possibility of locating divine action in history, they underwrote the entry of militant religious claims, left and right, into the political process. Breaking down the difference between this world and the next, and locating transcendence in the immanent, liberation theology opened up the political arena to divine initiative. In a liberal society, turning the focus from private values to socially situated ones necessarily meant the embrace of the political. Compelled into a political choice, religious faith, as liberationists argued, could not escape ideology.

Pressing for the recognition of the particularities of race, class, and sex in theology, which had long held to a universal humanity and truth, liberation theologians inaugurated a widespread transformation in religious attitudes. They stimulated rethinking of the inextricable relationship between politics and religion even as the results were not necessarily congruent with their goals. They increased awareness of how theology, in its collusion with the liberal political project with its universalism and idealism, failed to respond to the experience of the mass of people in the Americas, and reasserted the revolutionary history of the hemisphere. Reintroducing questions about the goals of political life and the relationship between religious values and their actualization in history, liberationists helped forestall the predicted demise of religious influence in the political sphere.

Notes

INTRODUCTION

1. Francis X. Rocca, "Under Pope Francis, Liberation Theology Comes of Age," *Catholic News Service* (September 13, 2013), http://www.catholicnews.com/services/englishnews/2013/under-pope-francis-liberation-theology-comes-of-age.cfm; "Vatican Analyst: Pope Distances Himself from Liberation Theology," *Catholic News Agency* (September 17, 2013), http://www.catholicnewsagency.com/news/vatican-analyst-pope-distanced-himself-from-liberation-theology/; Jim Yardley and Simon Romero, "Pope's Focus on the Poor Revives Scorned Theology," *New York Times* (May 24, 2015): A1; "Catholic Church Warms to Liberation Theology as Founder Heads to Vatican," *The Guardian* (May 11, 2015), https://www.theguardian.com/world/2015/may/11/vatican-new-chapter-liberation-theology-founder-gustavo-Gutiérrez; Paul Vallely, "Pope Embraces Liberation Theology," *Al Jazeera America* (September 22, 2015), http://america.aljazeera.com/articles/2015/9/22/pope-embraces-liberation-theology.html (accessed December 1, 2017).
2. Stephan Farrar, "Liberation Theology Activist: Pope Francis Is One of Us," *Church Militant* (December 27, 2016), http://www.churchmilitant.com/news/article/liberation-theology-activist-pope-francis-is-one-of-us; Francis Phillips, "Pope Francis Was All Too Familiar with Liberation Theology, That's Why He Opposed It," *Catholic Herald* (June 14, 2013), http://www.catholicherald.co.uk/commentandblogs/2013/06/14/pope-francis-was-all-too-familiar-with-liberation-theology-thats-why-he-opposed-it/.
3. Pope Francis, *Apostolic Exhortation Evangelii Gaudium* (Rome: The Vatican, 2013), https://w2.vatican.va/content/francesco/en/apost_exhortations/documents/papa-francesco_esortazione-ap_20131124_evangelii-gaudium.html; quotes in Jeet Heer, "Conservatives to Pope Francis; Stick with Salvation. We'll Handle the Politics," *The New Republic* (September 22, 2015), https://newrepublic.com/article/122889/pope-franciss-conservative-critics-just-dont-his-politics; Ed Stourton, "Is the Pope a Communist?" *British Broadcasting Company* (June 7, 2015), http://www.bbc.com/news/magazine-33024951.

4. Rohan M. Curnow, "Which Preferential Option for the Poor? A History of the Doctrine's Bifurcation," *Modern Theology* 31, no. 1 (January 2015): 27–59; Brian Hamilton, "Pope Francis and Liberation Theology," *The Immanent Frame* (May 19, 2014), http://blogs.ssrc.org/tif/2014/05/09/pope-francis-and-liberation-theology/.
5. "Obama Pastor's Theology: Destroy 'The White Enemy,'" *WorldNet Daily* (March 17, 2008), http://www.wnd.com/2008/03/59230/; Daniel Nasaw, "Controversial Comments Made by Rev. Jeremiah Wright," *The Guardian* (March 18, 2008), https://www.theguardian.com/world/2008/mar/18/barackobama.uselections20083; David A. Graham, "Jeremiah Wright Is Still Angry at Barack Obama," *The Atlantic* (September 26, 2015), https://www.theatlantic.com/politics/archive/2015/09/what-ever-happened-to-jeremiah-wright/406522/; James Cone, *Black Theology & Black Power* (San Francisco, CA: Harper & Row, 1989).
6. Dietrick Bonhoeffer, "June 8, 1944" & "July 16, 1944," in *Letters and Papers from Prison* (Minneapolis: Fortress Press, 2010), 479; Larry Rasmussen, "Bonhoeffer and the Anthropocene," *NGTT DEEL 55*, Supplementum 1 (2014): 941–954; Gustavo Gutiérrez, *A Theology of Liberation* (Maryknoll, NY: Orbis Books, 1973), 42.
7. Anders Stephanson, *Manifest Destiny: American Expansionism and the Empire of Right* (New York: Hill and Wang, 1995); Robert Walter Johannsen, Sam W. Haynes, and Christopher Morris, *Manifest Destiny and Empire: American Antebellum Expansionism* (College Station, TX: Published for the University of Texas at Arlington by Texas A&M University Press, 1997); Reginald Horsman, *Race and Manifest Destiny: The Origins of American Racial Anglo-Saxonism* (Cambridge, MA: Harvard University Press, 2006); Thomas F. O'Brien, *Making the Americas The United States and Latin America from the Age of Revolutions to the Era of Globalization* (Albuquerque, NM: University of New Mexico Press, 2007); Stewart Brewer, *Borders and Bridges: A History of U.S.-Latin American Relations* (Westport, CT: Praeger Security International, 2006).
8. Michael H. Hunt, *Ideology and U.S. Foreign Policy* (New Haven, CT: Yale University Press, 1987); Lester D. Langley, *America and the Americas: The United States in the Western Hemisphere* (Athens, GA: University of Georgia Press, 1989); William Inboden, *Religion and American Foreign Policy, 1945–1960: The Soul of Containment* (Cambridge, MA: Cambridge University Press, 2008); Nicole Guétin, *Religious Ideology in American Politics: A History* (Jefferson, NC: McFarland & Co, 2009).
9. Arthur M. Schlesinger Jr., *The Vital Center: The Politics of Freedom* (New York, NY: De Capo Press, 1988), 219.
10. Howard Brick, *The Age of Contradiction: American Thought and Culture in the 1960s* (Ithaca, NY: Cornell University Press, 1998); David Steigerwald, *The Sixties and the End of Modern America* (New York, NY: St. Martin's Press, 1995); Daniel T. Rodgers, *The Age of Fracture* (Cambridge, MA: Belknap Press of Harvard University Press, 2011); David Lehmann, "The Religious Field in Latin America: Autonomy and Fragmentation," in *Latin America 1810–2010: Dreams and Legacies*, eds. Claude

Auroi and Aline Heig (London: Imperial College Press, 2012); Diana Sorensen, *A Turbulent Decade Remembered: Scenes from the Latin American Sixties* (Stanford, CA: Stanford University Press, 2007).

11. Sydney E. Ahlstrom, "The Radical Turn in Theology and Ethics: Why It Occurred in the 1960's," *Annals of the American Academy of Political and Social Science* 387 (January 1970): 2.
12. Daniel Wickberg, "In the Environment of Ideas: Arthur Lovejoy and the History of Ideas as a Form of Cultural History," *Modern Intellectual History* 11, no. 2 (2014): 439–464; "Intellectual History vs. the Social History of Intellectuals," *Rethinking History* 5, no. 3 (2001): 383–395; "What Is the History of Sensibilities? On Cultural Histories, Old and New," *American Historical Review* (June 2007): 661–684; David Armitage and Jo Guldi, *The History Manifesto* (Cambridge: Cambridge University Press, 2014).
13. Christian Smith, *The Emergence of Liberation Theology: Radical Religion and Social Movement Theory* (Chicago, IL: Chicago University Press, 1991) brought attention to Latin American liberation theology as a developing social movement. Mark Hulsether, *Building a Protestant Left: Christianity and Crisis Magazine, 1941–1993* (Knoxville, TN: University of Tennesse Press, 1999) provides a detailed, if circumscribed, examination of the reception of liberation theology by ambivalent liberals; Gary Dorrien, *The Making of American Liberal Theology, Vol III* (Louisville, KY: Westminster John Knox Press, 2001–2006) places black and feminist liberation theologies within a trajectory of theological ethics.

CHAPTER 1

1. James Cone, *A Black Theology of Liberation* (Maryknoll, NY: Orbis Books, 2008), 75; Jose Miquez Bonino, *Doing Theology in a Revolutionary Situation* (Philadelphia, PA: Fortress Press, 1975), 2; Mary Daly, *Beyond God the Father* (Boston, MA: Beacon Press, 1973), 19.
2. Martin Luther King, Jr., *Where Do We Go From Here: Chaos or Community* (Boston, MA: Beacon Press, 2010), 167; Thomas E. Jackson, *From Civil Rights to Human Rights: Martin Luther King, Jr., and the Struggle for Economic Justice* (Philadelphia, PA: University of Pennsylvania Press, 2007).
3. King, *Where Do We Go From Here*, 169–170; see "Mas allay de Vietnam," *Cristianismo y Sociedad* Vol. VI, No. 16–17, 1968.
4. King, *Where Do We Go From Here*, 190.
5. Martin Luther King, Jr., "Letter from Birmingham Jail," Martin Luther King Papers, www.kingpapers.org; Gayraud S. Wilmore, *Black Religion and Black Radicalism* (Maryknoll, NY: Orbis Books, 2006), 196.
6. Steven Gould Axelrod, Thomas J. Travisano, and Camille Roman, *The New Anthology of American Poetry* (New Brunswick, NJ: Rutgers University Press, 2003), 704–705; quoted by Mary Beth Culp, "Religion in the Poetry of Langston

Hughes," *Phylon* 48, no. 3 (3rd Qtr., 1987): 240–245; Michael Thurston, "Black Christ, Red Flag: Langston Hughes on Scottsboro," *College Literature* 22, no. 3 (October 1995): 33.

7. Richard H. King, *Race, Culture and the Intellectuals: 1940–1970* (Baltimore, MD: Johns Hopkins Press, 2004), 206; James Baldwin, *The Fire Next Time* (New York, NY: Dial Press, 1963), 71, 59; Wilmore, *Black Religion*, 201.
8. Malcolm X and Alex Haley, *The Autobiography of Malcolm X* (New York, NY: Random House, 1964), 246, 224, 166.
9. Wilmore, *Black Religion*, 226; William L. Van Deburg, *The New Day in Babylon: The Black Power Movement in American Culture, 1965–1975* (Chicago, IL: University of Chicago Press, 1992), 52.
10. Stokely Carmichael and Charles V. Hamilton, *Black Power: The Politics of Liberation in America* (New York, NY: Random House, 1967), Introduction, xi.
11. Van Deburg, *The New Day in Babylon*, 112, 237–241; Henry McNeal Turner and Edwin S. Redkey, *Respect Black: The Writings and Speeches of Henry McNeal Turner* (New York, NY: Arno Press at *The New York Times*, 1971), 176.
12. Vincent Harding, "The Religion of Black Power," in *The Religious Situation*, ed. Donald R. Cutler (Boston: Beacon Press, 1968), 4–11; Vincent Harding, "Black Power and the American Christ," *The Christian Century* (January 4, 1967): 10–13.
13. "Black Power Statement, July 31, 1966" by National Conference of Black Churchmen, in *Afro-American Religious History: A Documentary Witness*, ed. Milton C. Sernett (Durham, NC: Duke University Press, 1985), 466.
14. Wilmore, *Black Religion and Black Radicalism*, 232.
15. Wilmore, *Black Religion and Black Radicalism*, 234. See also *New York Times*, May 10, 1969: 1.
16. James Forman, "The Black Manifesto," The Archives of the Episcopal Church, http://www.episcopalarchives.org/Afro-Anglican_history/exhibit/pdf/blackmanifesto.pdf; Wilmore, *Black Religion and Black Radicalism*, 246.
17. James Cone, *My Soul Looks Back* (Nashville, TN: Abingdon Press, 1982), 19–36. Personal interview with James Cone, New York, NY, November 16, 2011; James Cone, *God of the Oppressed* (San Francisco, CA: Harper & Row, 1975), 5–6.
18. James Cone, "Christianity and Black Power," in *Is Anybody Listening to Black America*, ed. Eric Lincoln (New York, NY: Seabury Press, 1968), 4–7.
19. James Cone, *Black Theology & Black Power* (San Francisco, CA: Harper & Row, 1989), 7, 40, 22, 27, 28.
20. Cone, *Black Theology & Black Power*, 93, 105.
21. Cone, *My Soul Looks Back*, 56.
22. Cone, *Black Theology*, 4, 63–65.
23. Frederick Herzog, "Theology of Liberation," in *Theology from the Belly of the Whale: A Frederick Herzog Reader*, ed. Joerg Rieger (Harrisburg: Trinity Press International, 1999), 90. Personal interview with Dr. Kristin Herzog, Durham,

NC, January 9, 2012; letter to Patrick Stawski from Kristin Herzog dated April 13, 2012. Correspondence by Herzog to James Cone, March 8, 1970. Herzog Papers Archive, Duke University.

24. Frederick Herzog, *Liberation Theology: Liberation in Light of the Fourth Gospel* (New York, NY: Seabury Press, 1972), Preface and 2.

25. Samuel Faber, *Origins of the Cuban Revolution* (Chapel Hill, NC: University of North Carolina Press, 2006); Ramon Eduardo Ruiz, *Cuba: The Making of a Revolution* (New York, NY: W.W. Norton, 1970); Steven G. Rabe, *The Killing Zone: The United States Wages Cold War in Latin America* (New York, NY: Oxford University Press, 2012), 59–65.

26. B.R. Tomlinson, "What Was the Third World?" *Journal of Contemporary History* 38, no. 2 (April 2003): 309; Cynthia Young, *Soul Power: Culture, Radicalism, and the Making of a U.S. Third World Left* (Durham, NC: Duke University Press, 2006), 20; LeRoi Jones, "Cuba Libre," *Evergreen Review* 4, no. 15 (November–December, 1960): 346–353.

27. Che Guevara, "The OAS Conference at Punta del Este, August 8, 1961," in *Che Guevara Reader: Writings on Politics and Revolution*, ed. David Deutschmann (Melbourne, Australia: Ocean Press, 2003), 251; Guevara, "Socialism and Man in Cuba, 1965," in *Che Guevara Reader*, 246; Guevara quoted in "Both Marx and Jesus," *Time Magazine* (June 5, 1972): 57.

28. Thomas C. Wright, *Latin American in the Era of the Cuban Revolution* (Westport: Praeger, 2001).

29. Phillip Berryman, *Liberation Theology: The Essential Facts About the Revolutionary Movement in Latin America and Beyond* (New York, NY: Pantheon Books, 1987), 13; Christian Smith, *The Emergence of Liberation Theology: Radical Religion and Social Movement Theory* (Chicago, IL: University of Chicago Press, 1991), 92–93.

30. Camilo Torres, *Revolutionary Writings* (New York: Harper & Row, 1972), 7, 242, 306, 269.

31. Smith, *The Emergence of Liberation Theology*, 83; Second General Conference of Latin American Bishops, *The Church in the Present-Day Transformation of Latin America in the Light of the Council: II Conclusions* (Washington, DC: Division for Latin America, USCC, 1973), 36; Donal Dorr, *Option for the Poor: A Hundred Years of Catholic Social Teaching* (Maryknoll, NY: Orbis Books, 2003), 209.

32. Second General Conference, 42–48.

33. Robert McAfee Brown, *Gustavo Gutiérrez* (Atlanta, GA: John Knox Press, 1980), 20–25.

34. Gustavo Gutiérrez, *A Theology of Liberation* (Maryknoll, NY: Orbis Books, 1988), 21, 81; Dorr, *Option for the Poor*, 209.

35. Gutiérrez, *A Theology of Liberation*, 21, 10.

36. Carlos Mondragón, *Like Leaven in the Dough: Protestant Social Thought in Latin America, 1920–1950* (Madison, WI: Fairleigh Dickinson University Press, 2011).

37. Smith, *The Emergence of Liberation Theology*, 116–117; Rubem Alves, "Protestantism in Latin America: Its Ideological Function and Utopian Possibilities," *The Ecumenical Review* 22, no. 1 (January 1970): 14.
38. Rubem Alves, *Theology of Human Hope* (Washington, DC: Corpus Books, 1969), 97, 5.
39. Cone, *My Soul Looks Back*, 116.
40. Enrique Dussel, *A History of the Church in Latin America: Colonialism to Liberation, 1492–1979* (Grand Rapids, MI: William B. Eerdmans, 1981), 5.
41. Rita Gross, *Feminism & Religion* (Boston, MA: Beacon Press, 1996), 39; Douglas C. Rossinow, *The Politics of Authenticity: Liberalism, Christianity, and the New Left in America* (New York, NY: Columbia University Press, 1998); Pauli Murray. *Pauli Murray: The Autobiography of a Black Activist, Feminist, Lawyer, Priest, and Poet* (Knoxville, TN: University of Tennessee Press, 1989).
42. Ann Braude, ed., "Introduction," in *Transforming the Faith of Our Fathers: Women Who Changed American Religion* (New York, NY: Palgrave/Macmillan, 2004), 2.
43. Ann Braude, Jon Butler, and Harry S. Stout, eds., *Women and American Religion* (New York, NY: Oxford University Press, 2000), 113; Mary Daly, *Beyond God the Father* (Boston, MA: Beacon Press, 1973), 25.
44. Daly, *Beyond God the Father*, 13; Mary Daly, *Gyn/Ecology The Metaethics of Radical Feminism* (Boston: Beacon Press, 1978).
45. Rosemary Radford Ruether, "Foundations for a Theology of Liberation," in *Liberation Theology: Human Hope Confronts Christian History and American Power* (New York, NY: Paulist Press, 1972), 16–17; Ruether, "Is Christianity Misogynist? The Failure of the Women's Liberation Movement in the Church," in *Liberation Theology*, 95; Ruether, *New Woman New Earth* (New York, NY: Seabury Press, 1975), 162.
46. Ruether, *New Woman, New Earth*, 121; Ruether, *Liberation Theology*, 132, 180.

CHAPTER 2

1. James Cone, *God of the Oppressed* (San Francisco, CA: Harper & Row, 1975), 39–40.
2. Mark Lilla, *The Stillborn God* (New York, NY: Alfred A. Knopf, 2007), 55.
3. Michael Kirwan, *Political Theology: An Introduction* (Minneapolis, MN: Fortress Press, 2009), 74.
4. Steven F. Ozment, *The Age of Reform 1250–1550, An Intellectual and Religious History of Late Medieval and Reformation Europe* (New Haven, CT: Yale University Press, 1980), 273–277; George Huntson Williams, *The Radical Reformation* (Philadelphia, PA: Westminster Press, 1952), 63.
5. Roland H. Baiton, "Thomas Muntzer, Revolutionary Firebrand of the Reformation," *The Sixteenth Century Journal* 13, no. 2 (1982): 7; Abraham Friesen, *Reformation and Utopia: The Marxist Interpretation of the Reformation and Its Antecedents* (Wiesbaden: F. Steiner, 1974), 39.

6. Abraham Friesen, "Thomas Muntzer in Marxist Thought," *Church History* 34 (1965): 308–309.
7. Rosemary Radford Ruether, *The Radical Kingdom: The Western Experience of Messianic Hope* (New York, NY: Harper & Row, 1970), 31.
8. Friesen, *Reformation and Utopia*, 32–36.
9. William T. Cavanaugh and Peter Scott, eds., *The Blackwell Companion to Political Theology* (Malden, MA: Blackwell, 2004), Introduction; Gustavo Gutiérrez, *A Theology of Liberation* (Maryknoll, NY: Orbis Books, 1973), 34–37.
10. Quoted in Claude Welch, *Protestant Thought in the Nineteenth Century, Vol. 1* (Eugene, OR: Wipf & Stock, 1972), 23, 27; John Wesley, *Explanatory Notes Upon the New Testament* (London: John Mason, 1831), 389.
11. Welch, *Protestant Thought*, Vol. 1, 30; David Sorkin, *The Religious Enlightenment: Protestant, Jews and Catholics From London to Vienna* (Princeton, NJ: Princeton University Press, 2008).
12. Samuel Taylor Coleridge, *The Complete Works of Samuel Taylor Coleridge* (New York, NY: Harper & Brothers, 1863), 145; Coleridge, *Confessions of an Inquiring Spirit* (London: Edward Moxon, 1853), 86; Welch, *Protestant Thought*, Vol. 1, 91; Friedrich Schleiermacher and John Oman, *On Religion: Speeches to its Cultural Despisers* (Louisville, KY: Westminster/John Knox Press, 1994), 39.
13. Brent W. Sockness, "Schleiermacher and the Ethics of Authenticity: The 'Monologen' of 1800," *Journal of Religious Ethics* 32, no. 3 (Winter, 2004): 477–517; Steven Lukes, "The Meaning of Individualism," *Journal of the History of Ideas* 32, no. 1 (January–March, 1971): 45–66; Welch, *Protestant Thought*, Vol. 1, 52–53.
14. Schleiermacher, *On Religion*, 148; James M. Byrne, "Schleiermacher," in *The Encyclopedia of Christianity*, ed. John Bowden (Oxford: Oxford University Press, 2005), 1083–1085.
15. Søren Kierkegaard, *Concluding Unscientific Postscript to Philosophical Fragments* (Princeton, NJ: Princeton University Press, 1992), 189; Welch, *Protestant Thought*, Vol. 1, 292–314; Herbert Marcuse, *Reason and Revolution: Hegel and the Rise of Social Theory* (Boston, MA: Beacon Press, 1960), 263–267; Rubem Alves, *A Theology of Hope* (Washington, DC: Corpus Books, 1969), 34–43.
16. Gary Dorrien, *The Making of American Liberal Theology: Imagining Progressive Religion, 1805–1900* (Louisville, KY: Westminster John Knox Press, 2001), 127–140; Daniel Walker Howe, *Making the American Self* (New York, NY: Oxford University Press, 2009).
17. Quoted in James C. Livingston, *Modern Christian Thought: The Enlightenment and the Nineteenth Century* (Minneapolis, MN: Fortress Press, 2006): 188–189; Roger Aubert and David A. Boileau, *Catholic Social Teaching: A Historical Perspective*, 1st ed. (Milwaukee, WI: Marquette University Press, 2003), 136; Joe Holland, *Modern Catholic Social Teaching: The Popes Confront the Industrial Age 1740–1958* (New York, NY: Paulist Press, 2003).

18. Donal Dorr, *Option for the Poor: A Hundred Years of Catholic Social Teaching* (Maryknoll, NY: Orbis Books, 2003), 13–34.
19. Frederick Herzog, *Liberation Theology in Light of the Fourth Gospel* (New York, NY: Seabury Press, 1972), Preface, 2; Karl Barth, *Protestant Theology in the Nineteenth Century* (London: SCM Press, 1972), 425; Theodore Vial, "Schleiermacher and the State," in *Cambridge Companion to Frederick Schleiermacher*, ed. Jacqueline Marina (Cambridge: Cambridge University Press, 2005), 269.
20. Paul L. Lehmann, "Karl Barth, Theologian of Permanent Revolution," *Union Seminary Quarterly Review* 28, no. 1 (Fall 1972): 68.
21. Juan L. Segundo, *The Liberation of Theology* (Eugene, OR: Wipf and Stock, 1976), 39; Thomas C. Fox, "Liberation Theology Founder Dead at 70," *National Catholic Reporter* (February 2, 1996): 2.
22. Frederick Herzog, *Liberation Theology: Liberation in the Light of the Fourth Gospel* (New York, NY: Seabury Press, 1972), 11–14; Cone, *God of the Oppressed*, 45–47, 127. The critique of Schleiermacher was picked up by H. Richard Niebuhr in *Christ and Culture* (New York, NY: Harper and Row, 1951), and Yorick Spiegel in *Bourgeoisies and the Christian Religion: Problems of Accommodation in the Theology of Schleiermacher* (Munich: Chr. Kaiser Verlag, 1968); Richard Crouter challenges this interpretation in *Friedrich Schleiermacher: Between Enlightenment and Romanticism* (Cambridge: Cambridge University Press, 2008) by noting Schleiermacher's political activism. Michael Kirwan, *Political Theology* (Minneapolis, MN: Fortress Press, 2009).
23. Hugo Assman, *Theology for a Nomad Church* (Maryknoll, NY: Orbis Books, 1975), 56, 94.
24. Carl Schmitt, *Political Theology: Four Chapters on the Concept of Sovereignty* (Chicago, IL: University of Chicago Press, 2005), 2. Schmitt is an extremely controversial thinker, a Catholic whose political theology supported the German Third Reich. Considered an anti-liberal fascist by many, his ideas nevertheless survived his reputation to influence political theology and philosophy in the twentieth century; Heinrich Meier, *The Lesson of Carl Schmitt: Four Chapters on the Distinction between Political Theology and Political Philosophy* (Chicago, IL: University of Chicago Press, 1998).

CHAPTER 3

1. Daniel T. Reff, "The Jesuits Mission Frontier in Comparative Perspective," in *Contested Ground: Comparative Frontiers on the Northern and Southern Edges of the Spanish Empire*, eds. Donna J. Guy and Thomas E. Sheridan (Tucson, AZ: University of Arizona Press, 1998), 16–31; James Holstun, *A Rational Millennium: Puritan Utopias of Seventeenth-Century England and America* (Oxford: Oxford University Press, 1987); David Yount, *America's Spiritual Utopias: The Quest for Heaven on Earth* (Westport, CT: Praeger, 2008); Max Savelle, *Empires to Nations: Expansion*

in America, 1713–1824 (Minneapolis, MN: University of Minnesota Press, 1974); Lester D. Langley, *The Americas in the Age of Revolution 1750–1850* (New Haven, CT: Yale University Press, 1996).

2. Thomas Munck, *The Enlightenment: A Comparative Social History 1721–1794* (London: Oxford University Press, 2000); Henry F. May, *The Enlightenment in America* (New York, NY; Oxford University Press, 1976); Arthur P. Whitaker, ed., *Latin America and the Enlightenment* (New York, NY: D. Appleton-Century, 1942).

3. Harry Berstein, "Some Inter-American Aspects of the Enlightenment," in *Latin America and the Enlightenment*, ed. Arthur Preston Whitaker (Ithaca, NY: Great Seal Books, 1961), 54; Arthur P. Whitaker, *The Western Hemisphere Idea: Its Rise and Decline* (Ithaca, NY: Cornell University Press, 1954), 16, Jefferson quote 28, 70; G.W.F. Hegel, *Philosophy of History* (New York, NY: Wiley, 1944), 81, 86.

4. Ernesto LaClau, *Emancipations* (London: Verso, 1996), Fn2, 18. Eric Foner, *The Story of American Freedom* (New York, NY: W.W. Norton, 1998); Miguel Jorrin and John D. Martz, *Latin American Political Thought and Ideology* (Chapel Hill, NC: University of North Carolina Press, 1970).

5. Ernst Cassirer, *The Philosophy of the Enlightenment* (Boston, MA: Beacon Press, 1951), 134.

6. Michael Allen Gillespie, *The Theological Origins of Modernity* (Chicago, IL: University of Chicago Press, 2008); Jacob Vernet quoted in David Sorkin, *The Religious Enlightenment: Protestant, Jews, Catholics from London to Vienna* (Princeton, NJ: Princeton University Press, 2008), 76; John Locke, *A Letter Concerning Toleration* (Buffalo, NY: Prometheus Books, 1990), 13.

7. Rama, *The Lettered City*, 40; Jonathan Israel, *Radical Enlightenment: Philosophy and the Making of Modernity, 1650–1750* (Oxford: Oxford University Press, 2001), 517.

8. John Frederick Schwaller, *The History of the Catholic Church in Latin America* (New York, NY: New York University Press, 2011), Chapter 6, "The Church and Clergy at Independence"; Leapoldo Zea, *The Latin American Mind* (Norman, OK: University of Oklahoma Press, 1963), 54, 50; José Maria Luis Mora, "On Ecclesiastical Wealth (1831)," in *Nineteenth Century Nation Building and the Latin American Intellectual Tradition*, eds. Janet Burke and Ted Humphrey (Indianapolis, IN: Hackett, 2007), 37–50; Francisco Bilbao, "Chilean Sociability (1844)," in *Nineteenth-Century Nation Building and the Latin American Intellectual Tradition*, 102–107.

9. Juan Bautista Alberdi, "Foundations and Points of Departure for the Political Organization of the Republic of Argentina (1853)," in *Nineteenth-Century Nation Building and the Latin American Intellectual Tradition*, 199.

10. Thomas Paine, *The Age of Reason: Being an Investigation of True and Fabulous Theology* (New York, NY: G.P. Putnam's Sons, 1896), 22; http://www.gutenberg.org/ebooks/3743; Amanda Porterfield, *Conceived in Doubt: Religion and Politics in the New America Nation* (Chicago, IL: University of Chicago Press, 2012); quoting Thomas Jefferson, Mark A. Noll, *America's God: From Jonathan Edwards to Abraham Lincoln* (New York, NY: Oxford University Press, 2002), 63–64, 204;

Vincent Harding quoted in J. Deotis Roberts, *Liberation and Reconciliation: A Black Theology* (Philadelphia, PA: Westminster Press, 1971), 71; Edward J. Blum, *Reforging the White Republic: Race, Religion, and American Nationalism, 1865–1898* (Baton Rouge, LA: Louisiana State University Press, 2005).

11. Jonathan B. Knudsen, "On Enlightenment for the Common Man," in *What Is Enlightenment? Eighteenth-Century Answers and Twentieth-Century Questions*, ed. James Schmidt (Berkeley, CA: University of California Press, 1996), 274–283.
12. Frank M. Coleman, *Hobbes and America: Exploring the Constitutional Foundations* (Toronto: University of Toronto Press, 1977).
13. Zea, *The Latin American Mind*, 9–30; Harold Eugene Davis, *Latin American Thought: A Historical Introduction* (New York: Free Press, 1972).
14. Angel Rama and John Charles Chasteen, *The Lettered City* (Durham, NC: Duke University Press, 1996), 46–47.
15. Gary B. Nash, *Race and Revolution* (Lanham, MD: Rowman & Littlefield, 1990); Marixa Lasso, *Myths of Harmony: Race and Republicanism during the Age of Revolution, Colombia, 1795–1831* (Pittsburgh, PA: University of Pittsburgh Press, 2007).
16. Ofelia Schutte, *Cultural Identity and Social Liberation in the Latin American Thought* (New York, NY: State University of New York Press, 1993), 121. Zea, *The Latin American Mind*, 83; E. Bradford Burns, *The Poverty of Progress: Latin American in the Nineteenth Century* (Berkley, CA: University of California Press, 1980), 23–24.
17. Whitacker, *Latin America and the Enlightenment*, 13; Jonathan I. Israel, *Democratic Enlightenment: Philosophy, Revolution and Human Rights 1750–1790* (Oxford: Oxford University Press, 2011), 500–502.
18. Anthony McFarlane, "Rebellions in Late Colonial Spanish America: A Comparative Perspective," *Bulletin of Latin American Research* 14, no. 3 (September 1995): 329; Leon G. Campbell, "Ideology and Factionalism during the Great Rebellion, 1780–1782," in *Resistance, Rebellion, and Consciousness in the Andean Peasant World, 18th to 20th Centuries*, ed. Steve J. Stern (Madison, WI: University of Wisconsin Press, 1987), 134; Sinclair Thomson, *We Alone Will Rule* (Madison, WI: University of Wisconsin Press, 2002), 167–179; Charles F. Walker, *The Túpac Amaru II Rebellion* (Cambridge, MA: Harvard University Press, 2014).
19. Steve Stern, "The Age of Andean Insurrection, 1742–1782," in *Resistance, Rebellion, and Consciousness in the Andean Peasant World*, 76; J. Samuel Escobar, "Religion and Social Change at the Grass Roots in Latin America," *Annals of the American Academy of Political and Social Science* 554 (November 1997): 81–103; Jefferey L. Klaiber, *Religion and Revolution in Peru, 1924–1976* (Notre Dame, IN: University of Notre Dame Press, 1977), 5; Enrique Dussel, *A History of the Church in Latin America: Colonialism to Liberation* (Grand Rapids, MI: W.B. Eerdmans, 1981), 90.
20. Lester D. Langley, *The Americas in the Age of Revolution 1750–1850* (New Haven, CT: Yale University Press, 1996); C.L.R. James, *The Black Jacobins* (New York,

NY: Vintage Books, 1963), 171; David Scott, *Conscripts of Modernity: The Tragedy of the Colonial Enlightenment* (Durham, NC: Duke University Press, 2004); Jonathan Israel, *A Revolution of the Mind: Radical Enlightenment and the Intellectual Origins of Modern Democracy* (Princeton, NJ: Princeton University Press, 2010).

21. Laurent DuBois, *Avengers of the New World: The Story of the Haitian Revolution* (Cambridge, MA: Belknap Press, 2004), 100–101; James, *The Black Jacobins*, 88; "The Haitian Declaration of Independence," in *The Declaration of Independence: A Global History*, ed. David Armitage (Cambridge: Harvard University Press, 2007), 193.

22. Susan Buck-Morss, *Hegel, Haiti and Universal History* (Pittsburgh, PA: Pittsburgh University Press, 2009), 32, 48; Mary Wollstonecraft and Carol H. Poston, *A Vindication of the Rights of Woman* (New York, NY: W.W. Norton, 1975), 144; James Alexander Dun, *Dangerous Neighbors: Making the Haitian Revolution in Early America* (Philadelphia, PA: University of Pennsylvania Press, 2016).

23. David Brion Davis, *The Problem of Slavery in the Age of Revolution, 1770–1823* (Oxford: Oxford University Press, 1999), Chapter 11, 523–556; Franklin W. Knight, "Slavery in the Americas," in *A Companion to Latin American History*, ed. Thomas H. Holloway (Malden, MA: Blackwell, 2008), 146–161.

24. Wheatley quoted in Arlette Frund, "Phillis Wheatley, a Public Intellectual," in *Toward an Intellectual History of Black Women*, ed. Mia Bay et al. (Chapel Hill, NC: University of North Carolina Press, 2015), 43; Sylvia R. Frey, *Water from the Rock: Black Resistance in a Revolutionary Age* (Princeton, NJ: Princeton University Press, 1991), 305; Frey, "The American Revolution and the Creation of a Global African World," in *From Toussanit to Túpac: The Black International since the Age of Revolution*, ed. Michael O. West (Chapel Hill, NC: University of North Carolina Press, 2009), 51; Paul Gilroy, *The Black Atlantic: Modernity and Double Consciousness* (Cambridge, MA: Harvard University Press, 1993); Olaudah Equiano, *The Interesting Narrative and Other Writings* (New York, NY: Penguin Books, 2003), 88, 111; Eileen Razzari Elrod, "Moses and the Egyptian: Religious Authority in Olaudah Equinao's Interesting Narrative," *African American Review* 35, no. 3 (Autumn 2001): 409–425.

25. Thomas Paine, *Common Sense*, at http://www.gutenberg.org/ebooks/147.

26. Dan McKanan, *Prophetic Encounters: Religion and the American Radical Tradition* (Boston, MA: Beacon Press, 2011); *The Bible*, Galatians 3:28; Manning Marable, Nishani Frazier, and John Campbell McMillian, *Freedom on My Mind: The Columbia Documentary History of the African American Experience* (New York, NY: Columbia University Press, 2003).

27. David Walker and Peter P. Hinks, *David Walker's Appeal to the Coloured Citizens of the World* (University Park, PA: Pennsylvania State University Press, 2000), 23.

28. Peter Hinks, *To Awaken My Afflicted Brethren: David Walker and the Problem of Antebellum Slave Resistance* (University Park, PA: Pennsylvania State University

Press, 1997), 242; Rufus Burrow Jr., *God and Human Responsibility: David Walker and Ethical Prophecy* (Macon, GA: Mercer University Press, 2003).

29. Mary Wollenstonecraft, *A Vindication of the Rights of Woman*, ed. Carol H. Poston (New York, NY: W.W. Norton, 1976), 36; Barbara Taylor, "The Religious Foundations of Mary Wollstonecraft's Feminism," in *Cambridge Companion to Mary Wollestoncraft*, ed. Claudia L. Johnson (New York, NY: Cambridge University Press, 2002), 99; Sheila L. Skemp, *First Lady of Letters: Judith Sargent Murray and the Struggle for Female Independence* (Philadelphia, PA: University of Pennsylvania Press, 2009).

30. Leona S. Martin, "Nation Building: International Travel, and the Construction of the Nineteenth-Century Pan-Hispanic Women's Network," *Hispania* 87, no. 3 (September 2004): 439–446; Elsa M. Chaney, "Old and New Feminists in Latin America: The Case of Peru and Chile," *Journal of Marriage and Family* 35, no. 2 (May 1973): 331–443; Flora Tristán, *La emancipación de la mujer; o, El testamento de la paria* (Lima: Editorial P.T.C.M., 1948), 85; Domingue Desanti, "Flora Tristán: Rebel Daughter of the Revolution," in *Rebel Daughters: Women and the French Revolution,* eds. Sara E. Melzer and Leslie Wahl Rabine (New York, NY: Oxford University Press, 1993), 272–288; Lucretia Mott, "Not Christianity, but Priestcraft," at http://www.historyisaweapon.com/defcon1/mottnotchristianitybutpriestcraft.html; Sarah Grimké and Elizabeth Ann Bartlett, *Letters on the Equality of the Sexes and Other Essays* (New Haven, CT: Yale University Press, 1988), 34.

31. Richard J. Douglass-Chin, *Preacher Woman Sings the Blues: The Autobiographies of Nineteenth Century African-American Evangelists* (Columbia, MO: University of Missouri Press, 2001); Chanta M. Hayood, *Prophesying Daughters: Black Women Preachers and the Word, 1823–1913* (Columbia, MO: University of Missouri Press, 2003); Carla L. Peterson, *"Doers of the Word": African-American Women Speakers and Writers in the North, 1830–1880* (New York, NY: Oxford University Press, 1995); Olive Gilbert, Sojourner Truth, and Nell Irvin Painter, *Narrative of Sojourner Truth: A Bondswoman of Olden Time, with a History of Her Labors and Correspondence Drawn from Her Book of Life* (New York, NY: Penguin Books, 1998).

32. Cone, *God of the Oppressed*, 55.

33. James Cone, *A Black Theology of Liberation* (Maryknoll, NY: Orbis Books, 2008), 26.

34. Dussel, *A History of the Church in Latin America*, 27; Assmann, *Theology for the Nomad Church*, 134; Bonino, *Doing Theology in a Revolutionary Situation*, 6.

35. Daly, *Beyond God the Father*, 93; Elizabeth Schüssler Fiorenza, *Bread Not Stone* (Boston, MA: Beacon Press, 1983), 110.

CHAPTER 4

1. Jean-Jacques Rousseau, *The Social Contract* (New York, NY: Penguin Books, 1968), 55; David E. Cullen, *Freedom in Rousseau's Political Philosophy* (DeKalb, IL: Northern Illinois University Press, 1993).

2. Immanuel Kant, "An Answer to the Question: What is Enlightenment? (1784)," in *What Is Enlightenment? Eighteenth-Century Answers and Twentieth-Century Questions*, ed. James Schmidt (Berkeley, CA: University of California Press, 1996), 58; Philip Rossi, "The Foundation of the Philosophical Concept of Autonomy by Kant and its Historical Consequences," in *The Ethics of Liberation—The Liberation of Ethics*, eds. Dietmar Mieth and Jacques Pohier (Edinburg: T & T Clark, 1984), 5–7; Bernard Carnois, *The Coherence of Kant's Doctrine of Freedom* (Chicago, IL: University of Chicago, 1973), 48.
3. Jean Bethke Elshtain, "Kant, Politics, and Persons: The Implications of His Moral Philosophy," *Polity* 14, no. 2 (Winter 1981): 205–221.
4. James H. Cone, *For My People: Black Theology and the Black Church* (Maryknoll, NY: Orbis Books, 1994), 84.
5. Rubem Alves, *A Theology of Human Hope* (Washington, DC: Corpus Books, 1969), quoting Nietzsche 32, 37, 164. Alves was bringing up an unresolved issue— the degree to which transcendence was understood in a Kierkegaardian sense as an "infinite qualitative difference between time and eternity." Stanley J. Grenz and Roger E. Olson, *20th Century Theology: God and the World in a Transitional Age* (Downers Grove, IL: Intervarsity Press, 1992).
6. Hugo Assman, *A Theology for the Nomad Church* (Maryknoll, NY: Orbis Books, 1975), 35; Gutiérrez, *A Theology of Liberation*, 42–46, 84–85; José Miquez Bonino, *Doing Theology in a Revolutionary Situation* (Philadelphia, PA: Fortress Books, 1975), 66; Cone, *God of the Oppressed*, 159, 161.
7. Alves, *Theology of Human Hope*, 31, 97.
8. Gutiérrez, *A Theology of Liberation*, 20, 85.
9. Alves, *Theology of Human Hope*, 146, 149.
10. Albert Camus, *The Rebel* (New York, NY: Vintage International, 1991), 23; James Cone, *A Black Theology of Liberation* (Maryknoll, NY: Orbis Books, 2008), 99, 101, 104; James Cone, *Black Theology Black Power* (San Francisco, CA: Harper & Row, 1989), 134; Alves, *Theology of Human Hope*, 113.
11. Rosemary Radford Ruether, *Liberation Theology: Human Hope Confronts Christian History and America Power* (New York, NY: Paulist Press, 1972), 117, 124.
12. Ruether, *Liberation Theology*, 19, 116, 22; Ruether, "Sexism and the Theology of Liberation," *The Christian Century* (December 12, 1973): 1226.
13. Gutiérrez, *A Theology of Liberation*, 19; Alves, *Theology of Human Hope*, 40, 97–98; Paul Franco, *Hegel's Philosophy of Freedom* (New Haven, CT: Yale University Press, 1999).
14. Bonino, *Doing Theology in a Revolutionary Situation*, 76.
15. Franz Fanon, *The Wretched of the Earth* (New York, NY: New Grove Press, 2004), 148; Cone, *God of the Oppressed*, 54–55, 156, 209.
16. Gutiérrez, *A Theology of Liberation*, 57; Paulo Freire, *Pedagogy of the Oppressed* (New York, NY: Penguin Books, 1996) 139, 53, 156; Joseph Betz, "John Dewey and Paulo Freire," *Transactions of the Charles S. Pierce Society* 28, no. 1 (Winter 1992): 107–126.

17. The intellectual and social connections are evident in Richard Shaull, the North American missionary to Latin America who wrote the forward to *Pedagogy of the Oppressed*. Freire wrote the forward to Cone's 1986 edition of *A Black Theology of Liberation*.
18. Phillip Berryman, *Liberation Theology: The Essential Facts about the Revolutionary Movement in Latin America and Beyond* (New York, NY: Pantheon Books, 1987), 64; Christian Smith, *The Emergence of Liberation Theology: Radical Religion and Social Movement Theory* (Chicago, IL: University Press of Chicago, 1991), 107; Samuel Escobar, "Christian Base Communities: A Historical Perspective," *Transformations* 3, no. 3 (1986): 1–4. Christopher Rowland and Mark Corner, *Liberating Exegesis: The Challenge of Liberation Theology to Biblical Studies* (Louisville, KY: Westminster/John Knox Press, 1989).
19. Stokely Carmichael, *Black Power: The Politics of Liberation in America* (New York, NY: Random House, 1967), 35; Daniel Perlstein, "Teaching Freedom: SNCC and the Creation of the Mississippi Freedom Schools," *History of Education Quarterly* 30, no. 3 (Autumn 1990): 297–324; William Sturkey, "'I want to become part of history': Freedom Summer, Freedom Schools, and The Freedom School," *Journal of African American History* 95, nos. 3–4 (Summer–Fall 2010): 348–368; Russell Rickford, *We Are an African People: Independent Education, Black Power, and the Radical Imagination* (New York, NY: Oxford University Press, 2016).
20. David Walker, *Appeal to the Colored Citizens of the World* (University Park, PA: Pennsylvania State University Press, 2000), 20; Victor Oguejiofor Okafor, "A Reevaluation of African Education: Woodson Revisted," *Journal of Black Studies* 22, no. 4 (June 1992), 580; quoting Césaire, Fanon, *Wretched of the Earth*, 138.
21. Frederick Douglass, *Narrative of the Life of Frederick Douglass, an American Slave, Written by Himself*, ed. David W. Blight (Boston, MA: Bedford/St. Martin's, 1993), 64, 120.
22. Reginald F. Davis, *Frederick Douglass: A Precursor of Liberation Theology* (Macon, GA: Mercer University Press, 2005), 30.
23. Fanon, *Wretched of the Earth*, 2, 43–44; Richard H. King, *Race, Culture and the Intellectuals, 1940–1970* (Washington, DC: Woodrow Wilson Center Press, 2004).
24. Stephen Houlgate, *Freedom, Truth and History* (New York: Routledge, 1991), 87, 228; Gutiérrez, *A Theology of Liberation*, 21.
25. Camus, *The Rebel*, 22; Cone, *Black Theology Black Power*, 134, 136.
26. Michael Walzer, *Exodus and Revolution* (New York, NY: Basic Books, 1985); Alves, *Theology of Human Hope*, 89.
27. Cone, *A Black Theology of Liberation*, 30; J. Deotis Roberts, *A Black Political Theology* (Louisville, KY: Westminster/John Knox Press, 1974), 91.
28. J. Deotis Roberts, *Liberation and Reconciliation: A Black Theology* (Maryknoll, NY: Orbis Books, 1971), 9, 90; Reinhold Niebuhr, *Moral Man, Immoral Society* (New York, NY: Scribner, 1960), 235; Cone, in *God of the Oppressed*, challenged Roberts' attempt to make reconciliation the central theme of black theology, 239.

29. Stokely Carmichael, "What We Want," *New York Review of Books* (September 1966); Roberts, *A Black Political Theology*, 200, 140, 62.
30. Assmann, *Theology for a Nomad Church*, 65; Gutiérrez, *A Theology of Liberation*, 63–64, 154.
31. Cone, *God of the Oppressed*, 217–218, 195–196.
32. Stokely Carmichael, "What We Want"; Timothy B. Tyson, "Robert F. Williams, 'Black Power' and the Roots of the African American Freedom Struggle," *Journal of American History* 85, no. 2 (September 1998): 557; Stokely Carmichael, *Stokely Speaks* (New York, NY: Random House, 1971), 166; Cone, *God of the Oppressed*, 215–219; Robert F. Williams, *Negroes with Guns* (New York, NY: Marzani & Munsell, 1962); Timothy B. Tyson, *Radio Free Dixie: Robert F. Williams and the Roots of Black Power* (Chapel Hill, NC: University of North Carolina Press, 1999).
33. Camilo Torres, *Father Camilo Torres Revolutionary Writings* (New York, NY: Harper & Row, 1969), 46. Bonino, *Doing Theology in a Revolutionary Situation*, 121–127, and "Christianity and Violence in Latin America," *Christianity and Crisis* (March 4, 1968): 31–34; Hélder Câmara, *Spiral of Violence* (London: Sheed and Ward, 1971); Daniel H. Levine and Alexander W. Wilde, "The Catholic Church, 'Politics' and Violence: The Colombian Case," *Review of Politics* 39, no. 2 (April 1977): 220–249.
34. Douglass, *Narrative of the Life of Frederick Douglass*, 89, 83; Fanon, *Wretched of the Earth*, 51.
35. Rosemary Radford Ruether, "Women's Liberation in Historical and Theological Perspective," *Soundings* 43, no. 4 (Winter 1970): 369; Ruether, "The Psychoanalytic Revolution," in *New Woman New Earth*, 137; Ruether, *Liberation Theology*, 12; Valerie Saiving Goldstein, "The Human Situation: A Feminine View," *The Journal of Religion* 40, no. 2 (April 1960): 100; Freire, *Pedagogy of the Oppressed*, 31; Mari Jo Buhle, *Feminism and its Discontents: A Century of Struggle with Psychoanalysis* (Cambridge, MA: Harvard University Press, 1998); Sheila Ruth, "A Serious Look at Consciousness-Raising," *Social Theory and Practice* 2, no. 3 (Spring 1973): 289–300.
36. Ruether, *Liberation Theology*, 13, 16.
37. Cone, *A Black Theology of Liberation*, 103: Gutiérrez, *A Theology of Liberation*, 56; Roberts, *Liberation and Reconciliation*, 34.
38. Gutiérrez, *A Theology of Liberation*, 68–69; Cone, *Black Theology & Black Power*, 3.
39. Cone, *A Black Theology of Liberation*, 88; Juan Luis Segundo, *Liberation of Theology*, Chapter 8, 208–240; Harvey Cox, *The Secular City* (New York, NY: MacMillan, 1965), 125; Ruether, *Liberation Theology*, 14; Hugo Assmann, *A Theology for a Nomad Church*, 131.
40. Segundo, *Liberation of Theology*, 208; Enrique Dussel, *A History of the Church in Latin America: Colonialism to Liberation* (Grand Rapids, MI: W.B. Eerdmans, 1981), 243; Ruether, *Liberation Theology*, 14–15.
41. Segundo, *Liberation of Theology*, 210, 225, 226.

CHAPTER 5

1. Robin R. Das, "The Place of Werner Stark in American Sociology: A Study in Marginality" (January 1, 2008), *ETD Collection for Fordham University*, Paper AAI3301435; Werner Stark, *Social Theory and Christian Thought* (London: Routledge & Kegan Paul, 1958) 14, 29; John Milbank, *Theology and Social Theory: Beyond Secular Reason* (Malden, MA: Blackwell Publishing, 1990).
2. Arthur O. Lovejoy, *The Great Chain of Being: A Study of the History of an Idea* (New Brunswick, NJ: Transaction Publishers, 2009).
3. Martin Luther, *Treatise on Christian Liberty* (Philadelphia, PA: Fortress Press, 1957), 3; John W. Shepard, "The European Background of American Freedom," *Journal of Church and State* 50, no. 4 (Autumn 2008): 647–659.
4. Roy F. Baumeister, "How the Self Became a Problem: A Psychological Review of the Historical Research," *Journal of Personality and Social Psychology* 52, no. 1 (1987): 163–176; Charles Taylor, *Sources of the Self: The Making of Modern Identity* (Cambridge, MA: Harvard University Press, 1989).
5. Robert A. Nisbet, *The Sociological Tradition* (New York, NY: Basic Books, 1966), 21; Steven Seidman, *Liberalism and the Origins of European Social Theory* (Berkeley, CA: University of California Press, 1983), 48–51, 29; Bruce Mazlish, *A New Science: The Breakdown of Connections and the Birth of Sociology* (New York, NY: Oxford University Press, 1989); Steven Anthony Giddens, "Classical Social Theory and the Origins of Modern Sociology," *American Journal of Sociology* 81, no. 4 (January 1976): 703–729.
6. Nisbet, *The Sociological Tradition*, 47–55; Seidman, *Liberalism and the Origins of European Social Theory*, 48–55.
7. Seidman, *Liberalism and the Origins of European Social Theory*, 55–59.
8. Nisbet, *The Sociological Tradition*, 6.
9. Georg G. Iggers, *The Doctrine of Saint-Simon: An Exposition; First Year, 1828–1829* (Boston, MA: Beacon Press, 1958); L.L. Bernard, "The Significance of Comte," *Social Forces* 21, no. 1 (October 1942), 8–14; Charles D. Cashdollar, *The Transformation of Theology, 1830–1890: Positivism and Protestant Thought in Britain and America* (Princeton, NY: Princeton University Press, 1989).
10. Miquel Jorrin and John D. Martz, *Latin American Thought and Ideology*, 152; Arturo Ardao, "Assimilation and Transformation of Positivism in Latin America," *Journal of the History of Ideas* 24, no. 4 (October–December 1963): 515–522; Leopoldo Zea, *Positivism in Mexico* (Austin, TX: University of Texas Press, 1974).
11. Gillis J. Harp, "Lester Ward: Comtean Whig," *Historical Reflections* 15, no. 3 (Fall 1988): 525; Wilfred M. McClay, *The Masterless; Self and Society in Modern America* (Chapel Hill, NC: University of North Carolina Press, 1993), 120–133.
12. Bernard Reardon, *Religion in the Age of Romanticism* (Cambridge, MA: Cambridge University Press, 1985); quote in James C. Livingston, *Modern Christian Thought: The Enlightenment and the Nineteenth Century*, 188–189.

13. Irina Davydova and Wes Sharrock, "The Rise and Fall of the Fact/Value Distinction," *The Sociological Review* 51, no. 3 (August, 2003): 358–360.
14. Kerry Edwards, "Sociological and Theological Method," in *Religion and the Sociology of Knowledge*, ed. Barbara Hargrove (New York, NY: Edwin Mellen Press, 1984), 79–98.
15. Assmann, *Theology for a Nomad Church*, 63; Rosemary Radford Ruether, *Liberation Theology: Human Hope Confronts Christian History and American Power* (New York, NY: Paulist Press, 1972), 2.
16. Gutiérrez, *A Theology of Liberation*, 74, 8; John R. Pottenger, *The Political Theory of Liberation Theology: Toward a Reconvergence of Social Values and Social Science* (Albany, NY: State University of New York Press, 1989); Rufus Burrow, Jr., *James H. Cone and Black Liberation Theology* (Jefferson, NC: McFarland & Company, 1994), 38; Cone, *God of the Oppressed*, 41.
17. Christian Smith, *The Emergence of Liberation Theology*, 143.
18. Derek Michaud, ed., "Juan Luis Segundo, 1925–1996," *Boston Collaborative Encyclopedia of Western Theology*, http://people.bu.edu/wwildman/bce/segundo.htm; Segundo, *The Liberation of Theology* (Eugene, OR: Wipf & Stock, 1976), 48, 53; C. Wright Mills, *The Sociological Imagination* (New York, NY: Oxford University Press, 1959), 8; Eliseo Verón, *Lenguaje y Comunicación Social* (Buenos Aires: Ediciones Nueva Visión, 1969).
19. Albrecht Ritschl, H.R. Mackintosh, and A.B. Macaulay, *The Christian Doctrine of Justification and Reconciliation; The Positive Development of the Doctrine* (Memphis, TN: General Books, 2010), 205; Darrell Jodock, *Ritschl in Retrospect: History, Community, and Science* (Minneapolis, MN: Fortress Press, 1995); Claude Welch, *Protestant Thought in the Nineteenth Century, Vol. 2*, 1–30 (Eugene, OR: Wipf Stock, 1985); Karl Barth, *Protestant Theology in the Nineteenth Century* (London: SCM Press, 2001), 642.
20. Gary J. Dorrien, *Kantian Reason and Hegelian Spirit: The Idealistic Logic of Modern Theology* (Chichester: Wiley-Blackwell, 2015), 349; Mark D. Chapman, *Ernst Troeltsch and Liberal Theology: Religion and Cultural Synthesis in Wilhelmine Germany* (Oxford: Oxford University Press, 2001).
21. Charles Peirce, "Pragmatism," in *The Essential Peirce* Nathan Houser, editor (Bloomington, IN: Indiana University Press, 2001), 401. John R. Shook, "Peirce's Pragmatic Theology and Stoic Religious Ethics," *Journal of Religious Ethics* 39, no. 2 (2011): 346; John P. Diggins, *The Promise of Pragmatism: Modernism and the Crisis of Knowledge and Authority* (Chicago, IL: University of Chicago Press, 1994); Gary Dorrien, *The Making of American Liberal Theology: Idealism, Realism, and Modernity, 1900–1950* (Louisville, KY: Westminster/John Knox Press, 2003), 218.
22. William James, *William James: Pragmatism and Other Writings* (New York: Penguin Books, 2000), 36, 88, 27.
23. William James, *Varieties of Religious Experience: A Study in Human Nature* (New York, NY: Modern Library, 2002), 40, 24; Quoted in Carol Faulkner,

Lucretia Mott's Heresy: Abolition and Women's Rights in Nineteenth Century America (Philadelphia, PA: Pennsylvania University Press, 2011), 112.

24. James, *Varieties of Religious Experience*, 36; John Dewey, *A Common Faith* (New Haven, CT: Yale University Press, 2013); John R. Shook "John Dewey and Edward Scribner Ames: Partners in Religious Naturalism," *American Journal of Theology and Philosophy* 8, no. 2 (May 2007): 178–207.

25. Mark Noll, *The Civil War as Theological Crisis* (Chapel Hill, NC: University of North Carolina Press, 2006); W. Creighton Peden, *Empirical Tradition in American Religious Thought, 1860–1960* (New York, NY: Peter Lang, 2010); Charles Harvey Arnold, *Near the Edge of Battle: A Short History of the Divinity School and the "Chicago School of Theology" 1866–1966* (Chicago, IL: The Divinity School Association, 1966).

26. Shailer Mathews, *The Growth of the Idea of God* (New York, NY: MacMillan, 1931); Shirley Jackson Case, *The Christian Philosophy of History* (Chicago, IL: University of Chicago Press, 1943), 164.

27. Gary Dorrien, *The Making of American Liberal Theology*, 216–217; Victor Anderson, "Pragmatic Theology and the Natural Sciences at the Intersection of Human Interest," *Zygon: Journal of Religion and Science* 37, no. 1 (March 2002): 161–172; Edward Scribner Ames, "The Validity of the Idea of God," *The Journal of Religion* 1, no. 5 (1921): 462–481.

28. Douglas C. Macintosh, "Can Pragmatism Furnish A Philosophical Basis for Theology?" *The Harvard Theological Review* 3, no. 1 (January 1910), 126; Douglas C. MacIntosh, *Problem of Religious Knowledge* (New York, NY: Harper & Brothers, 1940), 372.

29. Jaime Nubiola, "The Reception of William James in Continental Europe" *European Journal of Pragmatism and American Philosophy* 3, no.1 (2011): 73–85; Anto Donos, "John Dewey in Spain and Spanish America," *International Philosophical Quarterly*, 3 (September 2001): 163; Gregory Fernando Pappas, *Pragmatism in the Americas* (New York, NY: Fordham University Press 2011). See also Ruben Flores, *Backroads Pragmatists: Mexico's Melting Pot and Civil Rights in the United States* (Philadelphia, PA: University of Pennsylvania Press, 2014) for the influence of pragmatism in Latin America.

30. Pius X, *Pascendi Dominici Gregis* (September 8, 1907), http://w2.vatican.va/content/pius-x/en/encyclicals/index.html#encyclicals; Michael L. Raposa, "Pragmatism, Democracy, and the Future of Catholic Theology," *American Journal of Theology & Philosophy* 30, no. 3 (September 2009), 288–302.

31. George Hunsinger, *How to Read Karl Barth: The Shape of His Theology* (Oxford: Oxford University Press, 1993); J. Gresham Machen, "Karl Barth and 'The Theology of Crisis'" *Westminster Theological Journal* 53 (1991): 197–207; Karl Barth, *The Epistle to the Romans*, trans. Edwyn C. Hoskyns (Oxford: Oxford University Press, 1933). Barth's theology developed, and his post-WWII work

reasserted a God who co-suffers with humanity, articulated in his 1956 essay *The Humanity of God* (Richmond, VA: John Knox Press, 1960), became useful for liberationists.
32. H. Richard Neibuhr, *Christ and Culture* (New York, NY: Harper & Row, 1951), 93; Reinhold Neibuhr, *Moral Man and Immoral Society: A Study in Ethics and Politics* (Louisville, KY: Westminster/John Knox Press, 2001), 54, 63, 81.
33. Cone, *A Black Theology of Liberation*, 107.
34. Segundo, *Liberation of Theology*, 7–8.
35. Segundo, *Liberation of Theology* 39, 76–79; Gutiérrez, *A Theology of Liberation*, 8.
36. Gutiérrez, *A Theology of Liberation*, 8, 9; Segundo, *Liberation of Theology*, 39. See also Karl Jasper and Rudolf Bultmann, *Myth and Christianity; An Inquiry into the Possibility of Religion Without Myth* (New York, NY: Noonday Press, 1958).
37. Rufus Burrow, Jr., *James H. Cone and Black Liberation Theology* (Jefferson, NC: McFarland & Company, 1994), 27, 71.
38. Cone, *God of the Oppressed*, 16–18, 200. Also, Rosemary Radford Ruether, "Imago Dei, Christian Tradition and Feminist Hermenutics," in K.E. Borresen, ed. *Image of God and Gender Models* (Oslo: Solum Forlag, 1991), 277.
39. Cornel West, *Prophesy Deliverance!* (Louisville, KY: Westminster John Knox Press, 2002), 16–21; Sheila Greeve Davaney, *Pragmatic Historicism: A Theology for the Twenty-First Century* (Albany, NY: State University of New York Press, 2000).

CHAPTER 6

1. Juan Luis Segundo, *Liberation of Theology* (Eugene, OR: Wipf and Stock, 2002), 65–66.
2. Jean-Jacques Rousseau, *The Social Contract* (New York, NY: Penguin Books, 1968), 178; Lucio Colletti, *From Rousseau to Lenin: Studies in Ideology and Society* (New York, NY: Monthly Review Press, 1972), 145; Steven Seidman, *Liberalism and the Origins of European Social Theory* (Berkeley, CA: University of California Press, 1983).
3. Jean-Jacques Rousseau, *Emile, or On Education* (New York, NY: Basic Books, 1979), 382; Authur M. Melzer, "The Origins of the Counter-Enlightenment: Rousseau and the New Religion of Sincerity," *American Political Science Review* 90, no. 2 (June 1996): 351–352.
4. Ludwig Feuerbach, *The Essence of Christianity* (New York, NY: Cosimo, 2008), 184, 47; Hans W. Frei, "Feuerbach and Theology," *Journal of the American Academy of Religion* 35, no. 3 (September 1967): 250–256; James A. Massey, "Feuerbach and Religious Individualism," *Journal of Religion* 56, no. 4 (October 1976): 379.
5. Steven Seidman, *Liberalism and the Origins of European Social Theory* (Berkeley, CA: University of California Press, 1983), 99; Karl Marx and Friedrich Engels, *Capital: A Critique of Political Economy* (New York, NY: International Publishers, 1967).

6. Ken Morrison, *Marx, Durkheim, and Weber: Formations of Modern Social Thought* (London: Sage Publications, 2006); Karl Marx and Frederich Engels, *The German Ideology* (New York, NY: International Publishers, 1972).
7. Karl Marx and Joseph J. O'Malley, *Critique of Hegel's Philosophy of Right* (Cambridge: Cambridge University Press, 1977), 127.
8. Emile Durkheim, *The Elemental Forms of Religious Life* (Oxford: Oxford University Press, 2001), 40.
9. Max Weber, *The Protestant Ethic and the Spirit of Capitalism* (New York, NY: Scribner, 1958).
10. Segundo, *Liberation of Theology*, 59–60; José Porfirio Miranda, *Marx and the Bible: A Critique of the Philosophy of Oppression* (Maryknoll, NY: Orbis Books, 1974); Denys Turner, *Marxism and Christianity* (Oxford: Basil Blackwell, 1983).
11. Segundo, *Liberation of Theology*, 102, 87; Karl Mannheim, *Ideology and Utopia* (New York, NY: Harcourt, Brace, 1949), 28; Edward Shil, "'Ideology and Utopia' by Karl Mannheim," *Daedalus* 103, no. 1 (Winter 1974): 87.
12. Karl Mannheim, *Diagnosis of Our Time* (New York, NY: Oxford University Press, 1944), 11; H.E.S. Woldring, *Karl Mannheim: The Development of His Thought: Philosophy, Sociology, and Social Ethics, with a Detailed Biography* (New York, NY: St. Martin's Press, 1987), 344–348.
13. Segundo, *Liberation of Theology*, 107–110, 125, 88. Karl Barth previously defined faith as "the awe in the presence of the divine incognito," in *The Epistle to the Romans* (London: Oxford University Press, 1968), 39.
14. Gustavo Gutiérrez, *A Theology of Liberation* (Maryknoll, NY: Orbis Books, 1973), 137.
15. Rufus Burrow, *James H. Cone and Black Liberation Theology* (Jefferson, MO: McFarland & Co, 1994), 82; James Cone, *God of the Oppressed* (San Francisco, CA: Harper & Row, 1975), 43, 91, 98, 52.
16. H. Richard Niebuhr, "The Irreligion of Communist and Capitalist," *The Christian Century* 47 (October 29, 1930): 1307; H. Richard Niebuhr, *The Social Sources of Denominationalism* (Hamden, CT: Shoe String Press, 1954). Richard W. Fox, "H. Richard Niebuhr's Divided Kingdom," *American Quarterly* 42, no. 1 (March 1990), 95; C. David Grant, *God the Center of Value: Value Theory in the Theology of H. Richard Niebuhr* (Ft. Worth, TX: Texas Christian University Press, 1984).
17. Cone, *God of the Oppressed*, 85–97, 45–46; Frederick Herzog, "Theology at the Crossroads," in *Theology from the Belly of the Whale*, ed. Joerg Rieger (Harrisburg, MS: Trinity Press International, 1999), 125.
18. W.T. Fontaine, "An Interpretation of Contemporary Negro Thought from the Standpoint of the Sociology of Knowledge," *Journal of Negro History* 25, no. 1 (January 1940): 6; Cone, *God of the Oppressed*, 93–96, 82.
19. Cone, *God of the Oppressed*, 104, 84.

20. Elizabeth Cady Stanton, "Solitude of Self: An Address before the United States Congressional Committee on the Judiciary, Monday, January 18, 1892." New York, NY: National American Woman Suffrage Association, 1910, http://www.sscnet.ucla.edu/history/dubois/classes/995/98F/doc43.html; Jeanne Stevenson-Moessner, "Elizabeth Cady Stanton. Reformer to Revolutionary: A Theological Trajectory," *Journal of the American Academy of Religion* 62, no. 3 (Autumm 1994): 673–697; Kathi Kern, *Mrs. Stanton's Bible* (Ithaca, NY: Cornell University Press, 2001); Mary D. Pellauer, *Toward a Tradition of Feminist Theology* (Brooklyn, NY: Carlson, 1991).
21. Rosemary Radford Ruether, *New Woman New Earth*, 25, xiii; Rosemary Radford Ruether, *Religion and Sexism; Images of Woman in the Jewish and Christian Traditions* (New York, NY: Simon and Schuster, 1974), 9–10, 245; Rosemary Radford Ruether, *Sexism and God-Talk: Toward a Feminist Theology* (Boston, MA: Beacon Press, 1983), 13.
22. Michael Löwy, ed., *Marxism in Latin America from 1909 to the Present* (Atlantic Highland, NJ: Humanities Press, 1992), Introduction, xiv.
23. José Carlos Mariátegui, *Seven Interpretive Essays on Peruvian Reality* (Austin, TX: University of Texas Press, 1990), 75; Löwy, *Marxism in Latin America*, Introduction, xiii–lviii.
24. Jeffrey L. Klaiber, "Religion and Revolution in Peru: 1920–1945," *The Americas* 31, no. 3 (January 1975): 292; John M. Baines, *Revolution Peru: Mariátegui and the Myth* (Tuscaloosa, AL: University of Alabama Press, 1972); Jorge Coronado, *The Andes Imagined: Indigenismo, Society and Modernity* (Pittsburg, PA: University of Pittsburg Press, 2009).
25. Michael Löwy, "Communism and Religion: José Carlos Mariátegui's Revolutionary Mysticism," *Latin American Perspectives* 35, no. 2 (March 2008): 74; Penelope Duggan, "Marxism and Romanticism in the Work of José Carlos Mariátegui," *Latin American Perspectives* 25, no. 4 (July 1998): 76–88; Mariátegui, *Seven Interpretive Essays*, 212; Jesus Chavarria, *José Carlos Mariátegui and the Rise of Modern Peru, 1890–1930* (Albuquerque, NM: University of New Mexico Press, 1979).
26. Löwy, "Communism and Religion," 72; José Carlos Mariátegui, "Man and Myth," in *The Heroic and Creative Meaning of Socialism: Selected Essays of José Carlos Mariátegui*, ed. and trans. Michael Pearlman (Atlantic Highlands, New Jersey: Humanities Press, 1996), 143.
27. Löwy, "Communism and Religion," 77–78; Gutiérrez, *A Theology of Liberation*, 56; Gary J. Dorrien, *Reconstructing the Common Good: Theology and the Social Order* (Maryknoll, NY: Orbis Books, 1990), Chapter 5, 101–126.
28. Alford A. Young Jr. and Donald R. Deskins, "Early Traditions of African-American Sociological Thought," *Annual Review of Sociology* 27 (2001): 445–477.
29. Shamoon Zamir, *Dark Voices: W.E.B. DuBois and American Thought, 1888–1903* (Chicago, IL: Chicago University Press, 1995).

30. William James, *The Varieties of Religious Experience* (Cambridge, MA: Harvard University Press, 1985), 266; Alexander W. Stehn, "Religious Binding the Imperial Self," in *Pragmatism in the Americas*, ed. Gregory Fernando Pappas (New York, NY: Fordham University Press, 2011), 300.

31. Phil Zuckerman, "The Sociology of Religion of W.E.B. Dubois," *Sociology of Religion* 63, no. 2 (2002): 246; W.E.B. Du Bois, *Darkwater: Voices from Within the Veil* (Mineola, NY: Dover Publications, 2012), 21; Phil Zuckerman, *The Social Theory of W.E.B. Dubois* (Thousand Oaks, CA: Pine Forge Press, 2004).

32. Edward Blum, *W.E.B. DuBois: American Prophet* (Philadelphia: University of Pennsylvania Press, 2007), 79–80, 103; Jonathon Samuel Kahn, *Divine Discontent: The Religious Imagination of W.E.B. Du Bois* (Oxford: Oxford University Press, 2009); Shamoon Zamir, *Dark Voice: W.E.B. Dubois and American Thought, 1888–1903* (Chicago, IL: University of Chicago Press, 1995); Manning Marable, *W.E.B. DuBois: Black Radical Democrat* (Boston, MA: Twayne, 1986).

33. Daniel Walden, "Dubois's Pan-Africanism, a Reconsideration," *Negro American Literature Forum* 8, no. 4 (Winter 1974): 261; John H. Bracey Jr. and August Meier, "Black Ideologies, Black Utopias: Afrocentricity in Historical Perspective," *Contributions in Black Studies* 12, no. 13 (1994): 111–116.

34. Blum, *American Prophet*, 183–186; Cone, *God of the Oppressed*, 185.

35. Charlotte Perkins Gilman, *His Religion and Hers* (Walnut Creek, CA: Altamira Press, 2003), 5, 226, 42. Carol Farley Kessler, *Charlotte Perkins Gilman: Her Progress Toward Utopia with Selected Writings* (New York, NY: Syracuse University Press, 1994); Sandra M. Gilbert and Susan Guber, "'Fecundate! Discriminate!' Charlotte Perkins Gilman and the Theologizing of Maternity," in *Charlotte Perkins Gilman: Optimistic Reformer*, ed. Jill Rudd and Val Gough (Iowa City, IA: University of Iowa Press, 1999), 200–216; Maureen L. Egan, "Evolutionary Theory in the Social Philosophy of Charlotte Perkins Gilman," *Hypatia* 4, no. 1 (Spring 1989): 112; Naomi B. Zauderer, "Consumption, Production, and Reproduction in the Work of Charlotte Perkins Gilman," in *Charlotte Perkins Gilman: Optimist Reformer*, eds. Jill Rudd and Val Gaugh (Iowa City, IA: University of Iowa Press, 1999), 152.

36. Brian Lloyd, "Feminism, Utopian and Scientific: Charlotte Perkins Gilman and the Prison of the Familiar," *American Studies* 39, no. 1 (Spring 1998): 93–113; Rosemary Radford Ruether, *New Woman New Earth*, 211; Charlotte Perkins Gilman, *Herland* (New York, NY: Pantheon Books, 1979), 8.

37. Wilfred M. McClay, "Totalitarianism: The Mind in Exile," in *The Masterless: Self and Society in Modern America* (Chapel Hill, NC: University of North Carolina Press, 1994), 189–225; Sidney Hook, "A New Failure of Nerve," *Partisan Review* 10, no. 1 (January–February 1943), 2–23; "Religion and the Intellectuals," *Partisan Review* 37, no. 2 (February 1950), 103–105.

38. Eduardo Mendiata, "Introduction: Religion as Critique," in *The Frankfurt School of Religion: Key Writings by Major Thinkers*, ed. Eduardo Mendieta (New York,

NY: Routledge, 2005), 1–15; Martin Jay, *The Dialectical Imagination: A History of the Frankfurt School and the Institute for Social Research, 1923–1950* (Berkeley, CA: University of California Press, 1973); Mark P. Worrell, "Authoritarianism, Critical Theory and Political Psychology: Past, Present, Future," *Social Thought & Research* 21, no. 1–2 (1998): 3–33.

39. Mendiata, "Introduction: Religion as Critique," in *The Frankfurt School of Religion: Key Writings by Major Thinkers*, 9.
40. Douglas Kellner, *Herbert Marcuse and the Crisis of Marxism* (Berkeley, CA: University of California Press, 1984), 5.
41. Herbert Marcuse, *One-Dimensional Man: Studies in the Ideology of Advanced Industrial Society* (Boston, MA: Beacon Press, 1991), 32–33, 57.
42. Herbert Marcuse, *An Essay on Liberation* (Boston, MA: Beacon Press, 1969), 62; Marcuse, *One-Dimensional Man*, 255, 256–257; Kellner, *Herbert Marcuse*, 279–289.
43. Douglas Kellner and Harry O'Hara, "Utopia and Marxism in Ernst Bloch," *The New German Critique* 9 (Autumn 1976): 11–34; Ze'ev Levy, "Utopia and Reality in the Philosophy of Ernst Bloch," *Utopian Studies* 1, no. 2 (1990): 10; Douglas Kellner, "Ernst Bloch, Utopia and Ideology Critique," *Illuminations*, at http://www.uta.edu/huma/illuminations/kell1.htm.
44. Kellner and O'Hara, "Utopia and Marxism in Ernst Bloch," 24, 16; Gerard Raulet, "Critique of Religion and Religion as Critique: The Secularized Hope of Ernst Bloch," *The New German Critique* 9 (Autumn 1976): 71.
45. Mannheim, *Ideology and Utopia*, 199–202.
46. Gutiérrez, *A Theology of Liberation*, 21–22, 101; John W. Cooper, "Teilhard, Marx, and the Worldview of Prominent Liberation Theologians," *Calvin Theological Journal* 24, no. 2 (1989): 250; Louis Caruana, *Darwin and Catholicism: The Past and Present Dynamics of a Cultural Encounter* (New York, NY: T & T Clark, 2009); Julian Huxley, "Introduction," in *The Phenomenon of Man* (New York, NY: Harper & Brothers, 1959), 11–29; Emile Rideau, *The Thought of Teilhard de Chardin* (New York, NY: Harper & Row, 1967).
47. Alfred A. Cave, "Thomas More and the New World," *Albion* 23, no. 2 (Summer 1991): 209–229; Gutiérrez, *A Theology of Liberation*, 134–137.
48. Gutiérrez, *A Theology of Liberation*, 123, 135–139; Raymond Bautista Aguas, *Relating Faith and Political Action: Utopia in the Theology of Gustavo Gutiérrez* (Notre Dame, IN: University of Notre Dame: ProQuest, UMI Dissertations Publishing, 2007).
49. José Miguez Bonino, *Doing Theology in a Revolutionary Situation* (Philadelphia, PA: Fortress Press, 1975), 138–151. John Joseph Marsden, *Marxian and Christian Utopianism: Toward a Socialist Political Theology* (New York, NY: Monthly Review Press, 1991).
50. Ruether, *New Woman New Earth*, 204–211. Paul Tillich, "The Protestant Principle and the Proletarian Situation," in *The Protestant Era* (Chicago, IL: University of Chicago Press, 1948), 163.

51. Alfredo Fierro, *The Militant Gospel*, (Maryknoll, NY: Orbis Books, 1975), 84. Post-war social thought in the Americas continued to display the concern of the individual's relationship to the social whole, including Octavio Paz, *El laberinto de la soledad* (México: Cuadernos Americanos, 1950) and David Riesman, *The Lonely Crowd* (New Haven, CT: Yale University Press, 1950).
52. Frederick Herzog, *Liberation Theology* (New York, NY: Seabury Press, 1972), ix.

CHAPTER 7

1. Hannah Arendt, *The Human Condition* (Chicago, IL: University of Chicago Press, 1998), 248, 318, 53–54; "Religion and Politics," in *Essays in Understanding, 1930–1954: Formation, Exile and Totalitarianism*, ed. Jerome Kohn (New York, NY: Schocken Books, 1994), 373. James William Bernauer, ed., *Amor Mundi: Explorations in the Faith and Thought of Hannah Arendt* (Boston, MA: M. Nijhoff, 1987).
2. R. Laurence Moore, "Secularization: Religion and the Social Sciences," in *Between the Times: The Travail of the Protestant Establishment in America, 1900–1960*, ed. William R. Hutchison (Cambridge: Cambridge University Press, 1989), 233–252; William R. Hutchison, *The Modernist Impulse in American Protestantism* (Durham, NC: Duke University Press, 1992); Darrell Jodock, ed., *Catholicism Contending with Modernity* (Cambridge: Cambridge University Press, 2000).
3. Roger Aubert and David A. Boileau, *Catholic Social Teaching: A Historical Perspective* (Milwaukee, WI: Marquette University Press, 2003), 23–25: Marvin L. Krier Mic, *Catholic Social Teaching and Movements* (Mystic, CT: Twenty-Third Publications, 2006); Rupert J. Ederer, *The Social Teachings of Wilhelm Emmanuel Von Ketteler: Bishop of Mainz, 1811–1877* (Washington, DC: University Press of America, 1981).
4. Peter Bernardi, "Social Modernism: The Case of the *Semaines Sociales*," in *Catholicism Contending with Modernity*, ed. Darrell Jodock (Cambridge: Cambridge University Press, 2000), 282. See also Richard Camp, *The Papal Ideology of Social Reform: A Study in Historical Development 1878–1967* (Leiden, Netherlands: E.J. Brill, 1969).
5. Darrel Jodock, "Introduction I: The Modernist Crisis," in *Catholicism Contending with Modernity*, ed. Darrell Jodock (Cambridge: Cambridge University Press, 2000) and http://w2.vatican.va/content/pius-x/en/encyclicals/documents.
6. Peter Bernardi, "Social Modernism: The Case of the Semaines Socials," in *Catholicism Contending with Modernity*, ed. Darrell Jodock (Cambridge: Cambridge University Press, 2000), 279–286; Bernardi, *Maurice Blondel, Social Catholicism and Action Francaise* (Washington, DC: The Catholic University Press, 2009), 10.
7. Phyllis H. Kaminsky, "Maurice Blondel: Spirituality in Praxis and Action," *Continuum* (Spring 1992) 72, 75–76; Bernardi, *Maurice Blondel*; David Grumett, "Blondel, the Philosophy of Action and Liberation Theology," *Political Theology* 11, no. 4 (2010): 502–524.

8. Phyllis H. Kamiski, "Seeking Transcendence in the Modern World," in *Catholicism Contending with Modernity*, ed. Darrell Jodock (Cambridge: Cambridge University Press, 2000) 117, 124; Gutiérrez, *A Theology of Liberation*, 44; Jean Lacroix, *Maurice Blondel: An Introduction to the Man and his Philosophy* (New York, NY: Sheed and Ward, 1968).

9. The Vatican, *Quadragesimo Anno* (1931), http://w2.vatican.va/content/pius-xi/en/encyclicals/documents; Ana Maria Bidegain, Working Paper #48, "From Catholic Action to Liberation Theology: The Historical Process of the Laity in Latin America in the Twentieth Century" (Notre Dame, IA: Kellogg Institute, 1985), 5; Jeffrey L. Klaiber, "The Catholic Lay Movement in Peru: 1867–1959," *The Americas* 40, no. 2 (October 1983):149–170.

10. Aaron I. Abell, *American Catholicism and Social Action: A Search for Social Justice, 1850–1950* (Notre Dame, IA: University of Notre Dame Press, 1963); Matthew Pehl, *The Making of Working Class Religion* (Urbana, IL: University of Illinois Press, 2016). L.R. Holben, *All the Way to Heaven: A Theological Reflection on Dorothy Day, Peter Maurin and the Catholic Worker* (Eugene, OR: Wipf & Stock, 2010).

11. Jeffrey L. Klaiber, "Prophets and Populist: Liberation Theology, 1968–1988," *The Americas* 46, no. 1 (July 1989): 5; André-J. Belanger, *The Ethics of Catholicism and the Consecration of the Intellectual* (Montreal: McGill-Queen's University Press, 1997).

12. Bidegain, Working Paper #48, 11; Harry Kantor, "Catholic Political Parties and Mass Politics in Latin America," in *Religion and Political Modernization*, ed. Donald Eugene Smith (New Haven, CT: Yale University Press, 1974), 211; Henry A. Landsberger, ed., *The Church and Social Change in Latin America* (Notre Dame, IA: University of Notre Dame Press, 1970).

13. Jacques Maritain, *Reflections in America* (New York, NY: Scribner, 1958); Bernard Doering, "Maritain and America—Friendships," in *Understanding Maritain: Philosopher and Friend*, eds. Hudson, Deal Wyatt, and Matthew J. (Macon, GA: Mercer University Press, 1987), 27–56; James V. Schall, *Jacques Maritain: The Philosopher in Society* (Lanham, MD: Rowman & Littlefield, 1998); Samuel Moyn, *Christian Human Rights* (University of Pennsylvania Press, 2015).

14. Jacques Maritain, *Range of Reason*, "Christian Humanism," University of Notre Dame Maritain Center, http://www3.nd.edu/Departments/Maritain/etext/range.htm; Jacques Maritain and Otto A. Bird, *Integral Humanism: Freedom in the Modern World* (Notre Dame, IA: University of Notre Dame Press, 1996), 114–115.

15. John Hellman, "The Humanism of Jacques Maritain," in *Understanding Maritain: Philosopher and Friend*, eds. Hudson, Deal Wyatt, and Matthew J. Mancini (Macon, GA: Mercer University Press, 1987), 121. Matthew J. Mancini, "Maritain's Democratic Vision: 'You Have no Bourgeois,'" in *Understanding Maritain*, 146. Maritain, *Integral Humanism*, 10, 111, 120, 132; Maritain, "Christian Humanism," in *The Range of Reason*, University of Notre Dame Jacques Maritian Center, http://maritain.nd.edu/jmc/etext/range14.htm.

16. Maritain, *The Range of Reason* (London: Geoffrey Bles, 1953), 204. Also, John F.X. Knasas, "Aquinas and the Liberationist Critique of Maritain's New Christendom," *Speculative Quarterly Review* 52, no. 2 (April 1988): 247–267.
17. Maritain, *Man and State* (Washington, DC: CUA Press, 1998), 20.
18. Rubem A. Alves, "Protestantism in Latin America: Its Ideological Function and Utopian Possibilities," *The Ecumenical Review* 22, no. 1 (January 1970), 6; Carlos Mondragon, *Like Leaven in the Dough: Protestant Social Thought in Latin America, 1920–1950*. (Madison, WI: Fairleigh Dickinson University Press, 2010).
19. Clifford Green, "Human Sociality and Christian Community," in *The Cambridge Companion to Dietrich Bonhoeffer*, ed. John W. de Gruchy (Cambridge: Cambridge University Press, 1999), 115.
20. Joel Lawrence, *Bonhoeffer: Guide for the Perplexed* (London, UK: Continuum International Publishing, 2010), 4; James Deotis Roberts, *Bonhoeffer and King: Speaking Truth to Power* (Louisville, KY: Westminster/John Knox Press, 2005).
21. Reggie L. Williams, *Bonhoeffer's Black Jesus: Harlem Renaissance Theology and an Ethic of Resistance* (Waco, TX: Baylor University Press, 2014).
22. Dietrich Bonhoeffer, *Letters and Papers from Prison*, ed. John W. de Grunchy et al. (Minneapolis, MN: Fortress Press, 2010), 486.
23. Bonhoeffer, *Letters*, 426, 363, 366.
24. Christian Gremmels, "Editor's Afterword," in *Letters*, 586; Klemens von Klemperer, "Beyond Luther? Dietrich Bonhoeffer and the Resistance to National Socialism," *Pro Ecclesia* 6, no. 2 (1997): 185; Peter Selby, "Christianity in the World Come of Age," in *The Cambridge Companion*, 234; Joel Lawrence, *Bonhoeffer*, 60; Tom Greggs, "Religionless Christianity and the Political Implications of Theological Speech: What Bonhoeffer's Theology Yields to the World of Fundamentalism," *International Journal of Systematic Theology* 11, no. 3 (July 2009): 293–308.
25. Bonhoffer, *Letters*, 52.
26. Angel Daniel Santiago-Vendrell, *Contextual Theology and Revolution Transformation in Latin America: The Missiology of M. Richard Shaull, 1942–2002* (Eugene, OR: Pickwick Publications, 2010).
27. Richard Shaull, *Encounter with Revolution* (New York, NY: Association Press, 1955).
28. Richard Shaull, "The Revolutionary Challenge to Church and Theology," *The Princeton Seminary Bulletin* 60, no. 1 (1966): 31, 29–30; also available at http://journals.ptsem.edu/id/PSB1966601/dmd008. Also, in Spanish, "Desafió revolucionario a la Iglesia y la Teología," *Cristianismo y Revolución* 2, no. 3 (October–November 1966).
29. Shaull, "The Revolutionary Challenge," 25–32.
30. Santiago-Vendrell, *Contextual Theology*, 129.
31. Mark Hulsether, *Building a Protestant Left: Christianity and Crisis Magazine, 1941–1993* (Knoxville, TN: University of Tennessee Press, 1999).
32. Julio de Santa Ana, "The Influence of Bonhoeffer on the Theology of Liberation," *The Ecumenical Review* 28, no. 2 (April 1976): 189.

33. José Miguez Bonino, *Doing Theology in A Revolutionary Situation* (Philadelphia, PA: Fortress Press, 1975), 168, 172; de Santa Ana, "The Influence of Bonhoeffer," 188–192.
34. Christian Smith, *The Emergence of Liberation Theology: Radical Religion and Social Movement Theory* (Chicago: University of Chicago Press, 1991), 117.
35. Kantor, "Catholic Political Parties," 221.
36. Miguel Jorrin and John D. Martz, *Latin-American Political Thought and Ideology* (Chapel Hill, NC: University of North Carolina Press, 1970), 415, 405–427. Donald E. Smith, "Patterns of Secularization in Latin America," in *Religion and Political Modernization*, ed. Donald Eugene Smith (New Haven, CT: Yale University Press, 1974), 126; Paul. E. Sigmund, "Latin American Catholicism's Opening to Left," *Review of Politics* 35, no. 1 (January 1973): 62, 67.
37. Jeffrey L. Klaiber, "Prophets and Populists: Liberation Theology, 1968–1988," *The Americas* 46, no. 1 (July 1989): 1–15.
38. Gutiérrez, *A Theology of Liberation*, 30–38.
39. Gutiérrez, *A Theology of Liberation*, 42–43.
40. Gutiérrez, *A Theology of Liberation*, 86; Henri de Lubac, David L. Schindler, and Rosemary Sheed. *The Mystery of the Supernatural* (New York, NY: Crossroad, 1998); Wolfhart Panneberg, Rolf Rendtorff, Trutz Rendtorff, and Ulrich Wilkens, *Revelation as History* (New York, NY: Macmillan, 1968).
41. Johannes B. Metz, "Religion and Society in the Light of Political Theology," *Harvard Theological Review* 61, no. 4 (October 1968): 512; Johann B. Metz, *Theology of the World* (London: Burnes & Oates, 1968).
42. Jürgen Moltmann, *Theology of Hope* (Minneapolis, MN: Fortress Press, 1993), 21, 29, 118.
43. J. Matthew Ashley, "Johann Baptist Metz," *in The Blackwell Companion to Political Theology,* ed. Peter Scott and William T. Cavanaugh (Malden, MA: Blackwell Publishing, 2004), 244; Metz, *Theology of the World,* 40, 48, 109; Metz, "Religion and Society in the Light of a Political Theology," *Harvard Theological Review* 61, no. 4 (October 1968): 509, 513.
44. Gutiérrez, *A Theology of Liberation,* 124–129.
45. Gustavo Gutiérrez, "Two Theological Perspectives: Liberation Theology and Progressive Theology," in *The Emergent Gospel: Theology from the Underside of History*, eds. Sergio Torres and Virginia Fabella (Maryknoll, NY: Orbis Books, 1978), 241, 247.
46. Gutiérrez, *A Theology of Liberation*, 91.
47. Gutiérrez, *A Theology of Liberation*, 86, 104, 139.

CHAPTER 8

1. Doug Rossinow, *The Politics of Authenticity: Liberalism, Christianity, and the New Left in America* (New York, NY: Columbia University Press, 1998).

2. Paul Tillich, *The Essential Tillich*, ed. F. Forrester Church (Chicago, IL: University of Chicago Press, 1987), 103, 72, 16, 73–88.
3. Paul Tillich, *On the Boundary: An Autobiographical Sketch* (New York, NY: Charles Scribner's Sons, 1966); Ronald H. Stone, "On the Boundary of Utopia and Politics," in *The Cambridge Companion to Paul Tillich*, ed. Russell Re Manning (Cambridge: Cambridge University Press, 2009), 208–220.
4. R. Laurence Moore, "Secularization: Religion and the Social Sciences," in *Between the Times: The Travail of the Protestant Establishment in America, 1900–1960*, ed. William R. Hutchison (Cambridge: Cambridge University Press, 1990), 233. Richard Ely, *Social Aspects of Christianity and Other Essays* (New York, NY: Thomas Y. Crowell, 1889), 5, 16. Also at http://onlinebooks.library.upenn.edu/webbin/book/lookupid?key=ha010621321.
5. Mark Noll, *America's God: From Jonathan Edwards to Abraham Lincoln* (New York, NY: Oxford University Press, 2002), 31. For the history of the social gospel see C. Howard Hopkins, *The Rise of the Social Gospel in American Protestantism* (New Haven, CT: Yale University Press, 1940); Henry May, *Protestant Churches and Industrial America* (New York, NY: Harper & Brothers, 1949); Ronald C. White and C. Howard Hopkins, *The Social Gospel: Religion and Reform in Changing America* (Philadelphia, PA: Temple University Press, 1976); Gary Scott Smith, *The Search for Social Salvation: Social Christianity in America, 1880–1925* (Boston, MA: Lexington Books, 2000); William R. Hutchison, "The Americanness of the Social Gospel: An Inquiry into Comparative History," *Church History* 44, no. 3 (September 1975): 367–381.
6. Washington Gladden, *Social Salvation* (Cambridge, MA: Riverside Press, 1902), 221.
7. Jacob H. Dorn, *Washington Gladden: A Prophet of the Social Gospel* (Columbus, OH: Ohio State University Press, 1967).
8. Henry George, *Progress and Poverty* (New York, NY: Cosimo, 2005).
9. Walter Rauschenbusch, Anthony Campolo, and Paul Rauschenbusch. *Christianity and the Social Crisis in the 21st Century: The Classic That Woke Up the Church* (San Francisco, CA: HarperSanFrancisco, 2008), 42.
10. Walter Rauschenbusch, *A Theology for the Social Gospel* (Memphis, TN: General Books, 2010), 2, 8, 69.
11. Rauschenbusch, *A Theology for the Social Gospel*, 140, 145; Samuel Zane Batten quoted in Hopkins, *The Rise of the Social Gospel*, 253.
12. Walter Rauschenbusch, "The Problem of the Black Man," *The American Missionary* 68, no. 3 (1914): 732. Ronald C. White and C. Howard Hopkins, *The Social Gospel: Religion and Reform in Changing America* (Philadelphia, PA: Temple University Press, 1976), 103–104.
13. Gary Dorrien, *Social Ethics in the Making: Interpreting an American Tradition* (New York, NY: John Wiley & Sons, 2011), 60.

14. Susan H. Lindley, "'Neglected Voices' and 'Praxis' in the Social Gospel," *Journal of Religious Ethics* 18, no. 1 (Spring 1990): 75–102.
15. Vida Dutton Scudder, *Socialism and Character* (New York, NY: Houghton Mifflin, 1912), 302; Elizabeth L. Hinson-Hasty, *Beyond the Social Maze: Exploring Vida Dutton Scudder's Theological Ethics* (New York, NY: T & T Clark, 2006).
16. Jane Addams, *Twenty Years at Hull-House* (New York, NY: Signet Classics, 1961), 80–83; Mary Jo Deegan, *Jane Addams and the Men of the Chicago School, 1892–1918* (New Brunswick, NJ: Transaction, 1988).
17. Ralph E. Luker, *The Social Gospel in Black and White* (Chapel Hill, NC: University of North Carolina Press, 1991); also see Gary J. Dorrien, *The New Abolition: W.E.B. Du Bois and the Black Social Gospel* (New Haven, CT: Yale University Press, 2015).
18. Luker, *The Social Gospel*, 173.
19. Calvin S. Morris, *Reverdy C. Ransom: Black Advocate of the Social Gospel* (Lanham, MD: University Press of America, 1990); August Meier, *Negro Thought in America, 1880–1915* (Ann Arbor, MI: University of Michigan Press, 1964); Reverdy C. Ransom, *The Pilgrimage of Harriet Ransom's Son* (Nashville, TN: A.M.E. Sunday School Union, 1949).
20. Reverdy C. Ransom, *Making the Gospel Plain: The Writing of Reverdy C. Ransom*, ed. Anthony Pinn (Harrisburg, MS: Trinity Press International, 1999), 150.
21. Reinhold Niebuhr, *Moral Man and Immoral Society* (New York, NY: Charles Scribner's Sons, 1932), 237, 252.
22. Niebuhr, *Moral Man and Immoral Society*, 235.
23. Niebuhr, *Moral Man*, 270, 81, 271; Reinhold Niebuhr, *Beyond Tragedy* (New York, NY: Charles Scribner's Sons, 1937), 282; Sidney Hook, "A Failure of Nerve," *The Partisan Review* 10, no. 1 (1943): 1–23.
24. Leilah Danielson, *American Gandhi: A.J. Muste and the History of Radicalism in the Twentieth Century* (Philadelphia, PA: University of Pennsylvania Press, 2014); Heath W. Carter, *Union Made: Working People and the Rise of the Social Gospel in Chicago* (New York, NY: Oxford University Press, 2015).
25. James Cone, *A Black Theology of Liberation* (Philadelphia, PA: Lippincott, 1970), 98, 204 Fn4.
26. Rosemary Radford Ruether, *New Woman New Earth* (New York, NY: Seabury Press, 1975), 199; Rosemary Radford Ruether, *The Radical Kingdom* (New York, NY: Harper & Row, 1970) 75–76, 87.
27. "Life in a Defatalized World," *Time Magazine* (April 2, 1965): 82.
28. Gutiérrez, *A Theology of Liberation*, 42.
29. Harvey Cox, *The Secular City* (New York, NY: Collier Books, 1990), 15; Friedrich Gogarten, *The Reality of Faith: The Problem of Subjectivism in Theology* (Philadelphia: Westminster Press, 1959). Secularization theology included the Death of God movement made popular by John A.T. Robinson, *Honest to God* (Philadelphia, PA: Westminster Press, 1963).

30. Cox, *The Secular City*, 2.
31. Benton Johnson, "Continuity and Quest in the Work of Harvey Cox," *Sociological Analysis* 45, no. 2 (1984): 79–83; Cox, *The Secular City*, 106, 136.
32. Harvey Cox, *God's Revolution and Man's Responsibility* (Valley Forge, PA: Judson Press, 1965), 29, 103.
33. Cox, *The Secular City*, "Twenty-five Years Later," xviii; Mark Hulsether, *Building a Protestant Left* (Knoxville, TN: University of Tennessee Press, 1999).
34. Martin Luther King, "Statement to the Press, August 20, 1965," The King Center, http://www.thekingcenter.org/archive/document/mlk-press-statement-regarding-riots-los-angeles; Dennis C. Dickerson, "African American Religious Intellectuals and the Theological Foundation of the Civil Rights Movement," *Church History* 74, no. 2 (June 2005): 219; Ira G. Zepp, *The Social Vision of Martin Luther King, Jr.* (Brooklyn, NY: Carlson, 1989); Clayborne Carson, "Martin Luther King, Jr. and the African-American Social Gospel," in *African-American Christianity*, ed. Paul E. Johnson (Berkeley, CA: University of California Press, 1994), 159–177; Rufus Burrow, Jr., *God and Human Dignity: The Personalism, Theology and Ethics of Martin Luther King, Jr.* (Notre Dame, IA: University of Notre Dame Press, 2006).
35. David Chappell, *A Stone of Hope: Prophetic Religion and the Death of Jim Crow* (Chapel Hill, NC: University of North Carolina Press, 2004), 48. Martin L. King, *Stride Toward Freedom* (Boston, MA: Beacon Press, 2010), 84–85. Rufus Burrow, Jr., *God and Human Dignity*, 172.
36. King, *Where do We Go From Here? Chaos Or Community?* (Boston, MA: Beacon Press, 2010), 125–128.
37. Gayroud S. Wilmore, *Black Religion and Black Radicalism* (Garden City, NY: Doubleday, 1972), 222. Cone, *A Black Theology of Liberation*, 59; James Cone, *God of the Oppressed* (San Francisco: Harper & Row, 1975), 79.
38. James Cone, *Black Theology and Black Power* (New York, NY: Seabury Press, 1969), 121, 125, 94–103; Cone, *God of the Oppressed*, 153.
39. Cone, *Black Theology & Black Power*, 101; *God of the Oppressed*, 126–129, 82.
40. Cone, *Black Theology & Black Power*, 65–66, 32; J. Deotis Roberts, *A Black Political Theology* (Louisville, KY: Westminster/John Knox Press, 1974), 15, 149.
41. Cox, *The Secular City*, 148–150.
42. Rosemary Radford Ruether, "Sexism and the Theology of Liberation," *The Christian Century* (December 1973): 1227–1228.
43. Rosemary Radford Ruether, "Schism of Consciousness," *Commonweal* (May 1968): 330.
44. Rosemary Radford Ruether, *Liberation Theology: Human Hope Confronts Christian History and American Power* (New York, NY: Paulist Press, 1972), 154–155.
45. See Alexandra Walsham, "The Reformation and 'The Disenchantment of the World' Reassessed," *The Historical Journal* 51, no. 2 (June 2008): 497–528.

CHAPTER 9

1. Nancy Cott, *The Grounding of Modern Feminism* (New Haven, CT: Yale University Press, 1987), 4–5.
2. Simone De Beauvoir, *The Second Sex* (New York, Alfred A. Knopf, 1983), xvi, 267.
3. De Beauvoir, *The Second Sex*, 167, 170, xxiii.
4. De Beauvoir, *The Second Sex*, 64.
5. Elaine Stavro, "Rethinking Identity and Coalitional Politics, Insight from Simone de Beauvoir," *Canadian Journal of Political Science* 40, no. 2 (June 2007): 439–463; Jo-Ann Pilardi, "The Changing Critical Fortunes of the Second Sex," *History and Theory* 32, no. 1 (February 1993): 51–73.
6. Rosalind Rosenberg, *Beyond Separate Spheres: Intellectual Roots of Modern Feminism* (New Haven, CT: Yale University Press, 1982); Shira Tarrant, *When Sex Became Gender* (New York, NY: Routledge, 2006); Rosalind Rosenberg, *Changing the Subject: How the Women of Columbia Shaped the Way We Think About Sex and Politics* (New York, NY: Columbia University Press, 2004); Alice S. Rossi, "Equality Between the Sexes: An Immodest Proposal," *Daedalus* 93, no. 2 (Spring 1964): 608, 611.
7. Helen Mayer Hacker, "Women as a Minority Group," *Social Forces,* 30 (1951): 60–69; http://media.pfeiffer.edu/lridener/courses/womminor.html.
8. Rosemary Radford Ruether, *Women and Redemption: A Theological History* (Minneapolis, MN: Fortress Press, 2012), 176; Sally Bentley and Claire Randall, "The Spirit Moving: A New Approach to Theologizing," *Christianity and Crisis* (February 4, 1974): 3–7; Magaret Olofson Thickstun, "Writing the Spirit: Margaret Fell's Feminist Critique of Pauline Theology," *Journal of the Academy of Religion* 63, no. 2 (Summer 1995): 269–279.
9. Valerie Saiving Goldstein, "The Human Situation: A Feminine View," *The Journal of Religion* 40, no. 2 (April 1960): 101.
10. Goldstein, "The Human Situation," 105.
11. Goldstein, "The Human Situation," 107–111.
12. Uta Gehardt, "Margaret Mead's Male and Female Revisited," *International Sociology* 10, no. 2 (1995): 197–217. Goldstein, "The Human Situation," 103–109.
13. *Time Magazine* (June 27, 1960): 76; Rebekah Miles, "Valerie Goldstein: Reconsidered," *Journal of Feminist Studies in Religion* 28, no. 1 (2012): 79; Judith Plaskow, *Sex, Sin, and Grace: Women's Experience and the Theologies of Reihold Niebuhr and Paul Tillich* (Washington, DC: University Press of America, 1980); Karen Horney, "The Flight from Womanhood," in *Feminine Psychology* (New York, NY: W.W. Norton, 1973), 54–70; Clara Thompson, "Problems of Womanhood," in M.P. Green, ed., *Interpersonal Psychoanalysis: The Selected Papers of Clara Thompson* (New York, NY: Basic Books, 1964); 274–343. Nancy Chodorow, *The Reproduction of Mothering: Psychoanalysis and the Sociology of Gender* (Berkeley, CA: University of California Press, 1978).

14. Betty Friedan, *The Feminine Mystique* (New York, NY: Dell Publishing, 1963), 77, 311, 336; Ann Braude, "A Religious Feminist—Who Can Find Her? Historiographical Challenges from the National Organization for Women," *The Journal of Religion* 84, no. 4 (October 2004): 555–572.
15. Ann Braude, "Faith, Feminism, and History," in *The Religious History of American Women*, ed. Catherine A. Brekus (Chapel Hill, NC: University of North Carolina Press, 2007), 238. See Ruth Rosen, *The World Split Open: How the Modern Women's Movement Changed America* (New York, NY: Viking, 2000), Estelle B. Freedman, *No Turning Back: A History of Feminism and the Future of Women* (New York, NY: Ballantine Books, 2002), and Christine Stansell, *The Feminist Promise: 1792 to the Present* (New York, NY: Modern Library, 2010) for a history of liberal feminism.
16. Casey Hayden and Mary King, "A kind of memo," reprinted in Sara Evans, *Personal Politics: The Roots of the Women's Liberation in the Civil Rights Movement and the New Left* (New York, NY: Vintage Books, 1979), 235; Alice Echols, *Daring to Be Bad: Radical Feminism in the America 1967–1975* (Minneapolis, MN: University of Minnesota Press, 1989); Doug Rossinow, *The Politics of Authenticity: Liberalism, Christianity, and the New Left in America* (New York, NY: Columbia University Press, 1998).
17. Carol Hanisch, "The Personal is Political," in *Notes from the Second Year Women's Liberation: Major Writings of the Radical Feminists*, eds. Shulamith Firestone and Anne Koedt (New York, NY: Radical Feminism, 1970); Evans, *Personal Politics*, 100; Robin Morgan, *Sisterhood Is Powerful: An Anthology of Writings from the Women's Liberation Movement* (New York, NY: Random House, 1970).
18. Mary Daly, *The Church and the Second Sex* (Boston, MA: Beacon Press, 1985), 105–123, 125.
19. Daly, *The Church and the Second Sex*, 127, 134.
20. Mary Daly, *Beyond God the Father: Toward a Philosophy of Women's Liberation* (Boston, MA: Beacon Press, 1973), 157, 132, 9, 18–19.
21. Elizabeth Schüssler Fiorenza, "Feminist Theology as a Critical Theology of Liberation," *Theological Studies* 36, no. 4 (December 1975): 605–608.
22. Fiorenza, "Feminist Theology," 605–615.
23. Fiorenza, "Feminist Theology," 615–616; Mary E. Hunt, "Women-Church: Feminist Concept, Religious Commitment, Women's Movement," *Journal of Feminist Studies in Religion* 25, no. 1 (Spring 2009): 85–98. See also Lilian Calles Barger, "'Pray to God, she will hear us': Women Reimaging Religion and Politics in the 1970s," in *The Religious Left in Modern America: Doorkeepers of a Radical Faith,* eds. Douglas Rossinow, Leilah Danielson, and Marian Mollin (New York, NY: Palgrave Macmillan, 2018) for the role of the women's liberation movement in the development of feminist theology.
24. Sheila D. Collins, *A Different Heaven and Earth* (Valley Forge, PA: Judson Press, 1974), "Foreword" and "Introduction." See a collection of lay women's

feminist essays and poems in Nancy J. Berneking and Pamela Carter Joern, eds., *Remember and Re-Imagining* (Cleveland, OH: Pilgrim Press, 1995). Examples of religious writing by women include Carol Lee Flinders, *At the Root of This Longing: Reconciling a Spiritual Hunger and a Feminist Thirst* (San Francisco, CA: HarperSanFrancisco, 1981) and Sue Monk Kidd, *The Dance of the Dissident Daughter: A Woman's Journey from Christian Tradition to the Sacred Feminine* (San Francisco, CA: HarperSanFrancisco, 1996).

25. Collins, *A Different Heaven and Earth*, 36, 207; "herstory" was first used by Robin Morgan in the 1970 book, *Sisterhood is Powerful*.
26. Collins, *A Different Heaven and Earth*, 54, 21, 115.
27. Collins, *A Different Heaven and Earth*, 21, 108, 99; Carol Christ and Judith Plaskow, *Womenspirit Rising* (New York, NY: Harper & Row, 1979); Cynthia Eller, *Living in the Lap of the Goddess* (Boston: Beacon Press, 1995); Margaret Fuller and Larry J. Reynolds, *Woman in the Nineteenth Century: An Authoritative Text, Backgrounds, Criticism* (New York, NY: W.W. Norton, 1998).
28. Collins, *A Different Heaven and Earth*, 191, 44.
29. Collins, *A Different Heaven and Earth*, 217–218.
30. Rosemary Radford Ruether, "Black Theology vs. Feminist Theology," *Christianity and Crisis* (April 15, 1974): 67–73.
31. Ruether, *New Woman New Earth*, 159, 162–164.
32. Ruether, "Women's Liberation in Historical and Theological Perspective," *Sounding* 43, no. 4 (Winter 1970): 371–372; Ruether, "Sexism and the Theology of Liberation," *Christian Century* (December 12, 1973): 1228.
33. James Cone, *God of the Oppressed* (San Francisco, CA: Harper & Row, 1975), 54.
34. Stephen Crites, "The Narrative Quality of Experience," *Journal of the American Academy of Religion* 39, no. 3 (September 1971): 294. Michael Goldberg, *Theology and Narrative: A Critical Introduction* (Nashville, TN: Abingdon Press, 1981), 162–163;. Sallie McFague, *Speaking in Parables* (Philadelphia, PA: Fortress Press, 1975), 4; Linda Hogan, *From Women's Experience to Feminist Theology* (Sheffield: Sheffield Academic Press, 1995); Ludwig Wittgenstein, *Philosophical Investigations* (Oxford: B. Blackwell, 1953); Stanley J. Grenz and Roger E. Olson, "Transcendence Within the Story: Narrative Theology," in *20th Century Theology: God & the World in a Transitional Age* (Downers Grove, IL: Intervarsity Press, 1992), 271–285.
35. Ruether, *New Woman New Earth*, 144; Collins, *A Different Heaven and Earth*, 207. Also, papers of "Women Exploring Theology at Grailville," Loveland, Ohio, June 18–25, 1972: Church Women United, New York, NY.
36. Roxanne Harde, "Making of Our Lives a Study: Feminist Theology and Women's Creative Writing," *Feminist Theology* 15, no. 1 (2006): 48–69.
37. Patricia Hill Collins, *Black Feminist Thought: Knowledge, Consciousness and the Politics of Empowerment* (New York, NY: Routledge, 2000); Angela Y. Davis, *Women, Race and Class* (New York, NY: Vintage Books, 1983); Kimberly Springer,

Living for the Revolution: Black Feminist Organizations, 1968–1980 (Durham, NC: Duke University Press, 2005); Maxine Williams and Pamela Williams, "Black Women's Liberation," *The Militant* (July 3, 1970 & October 30, 1970). Documents from the Women's Liberation Movement archival collection, Duke University, http://library.duke.edu/rubenstein/scriptorium/wlm/blacklib/; Sherie M. Randolph, "Women's Liberation or... Black Liberation, You're Fighting the Same Enemies," in *Want to Start A Revolution: Radical Women in the Black Freedom Struggle*, ed. Dayo F. Gore et al. (New York, NY: New York University Press, 2009), 223–247; Rhonda Y. Williams, "Black Women and Black Power," *OAH Magazine of History* 22, no. 3 (July 2008): 59–71.

38. Jacquelyn Grant, "Black Theology and the Black Woman," in *Black Theology: A Documentary History*, ed. James H. Cone and Gayraud S. Wilmore (Maryknoll, NY: Orbis Books, 1983), 323–338; Alice Walker, *In Search of Our Mothers' Garden* (San Diego, CA: Harcourt Brace Jovanovich, 1983); Cheryl T. Sanders, "Roundtable Discussion: Christian Ethics and Theology in Womanist Perspective," *Journal of Feminist Studies in Religion* 5, no. 2 (Fall 1989): 86; Delores S. Williams, "Womanist/Feminist Dialogue: Problems and Possibilities," *Journal of Feminist Studies in Religion* 9, no. 1/2 (Spring–Fall 1993): 67–73; Delores S. Williams, *Sisters in the Wilderness: The Challenge of Womanist God-Talk* (Maryknoll, NY: Orbis Books, 1993); Emilie Maureen Townes, *Womanist Justice, Womanist Hope* (Atlanta, GA: Scholars Press, 1993). Rufus Burrow, Jr., "Enter Womanist Theology and Ethic," *The Western Journal of Black Studies* 22, no. 1 (1998): 19–29; Kristin Waters and Carol B. Conaway, eds., *Black Women's Intellectual Traditions: Speaking Their Minds* (Burlington, VT: University of Vermont Press, 2007).

39. Ruether, *New Woman New Earth*, 20.

CHAPTER 10

1. Richard Wright, *The Color Curtain* (Cleveland, OH: World, 1956), 147, 140, 202; Dipesh Chakrabarty, "Legacies of Bandung: Decolonisation and the Politics of Culture," *Economic and Political Weekly* 40, no. 46 (November 12–18, 2005); Jeffrey J. Folks, "'Last Call to the West': Richard Wright's The Color Curtain," *South Atlantic Review* 59, no. 4 (November 1994): 77–88.

2. Charles Taylor, *Multiculturalism and "The Politics of Recognition,"* (Princeton, NJ: Princeton University Press, 1992), 29; Charles Taylor, *Sources of the Self: The Making of Modern Identity* (Cambridge, MA: Harvard University Press, 1989); Philip Gleason, "Identifying Identity: A Semantic History," in *Speaking of Diversity: Language and Ethnicity in Twentieth-Century America* (Baltimore, MD: John Hopkins University Press, 1992), 123–152.

3. Charles Taylor, *Multiculturalism*, 25–38.

4. Larson Brooke, *Trials of Nation Making: Liberalism, Race, and Ethnicity in the Andes, 1810–1910* (Cambridge: Cambridge University Press, 2004).

5. Leopoldo Zea, "Identity: A Latin American Philosophical Problem," *The Philosophical Forum* XX, no. 1–2 (Fall–Winter 1988–1989): 3–16; Augusto Salazar Bondy, *Existe una filosofía de nuestra América?* (México: Siglo Veintiuno Editores, 1988); Lourdes Martínez-Eschzabal, "Mestizaje and the Discourse of National/Cultural Identity in Latin America, 1845–1959," *Latin American Perspectives* 25, no. 3 (May 1998): 21–42.
6. Juan Bautista Alberdi, "Foundations and Points of Departure for the Political Organization of the Republic of Argentina," in *Nineteenth Century Nation Building and The Latin American Intellectual Tradition*, eds. Janet Burke and Ted Humphrey (Indianapolis, IN: Hackett Publishing, 2007), 201–203.
7. Leopoldo Zea, *The Latin American Mind* (Norman, OK: University of Oklahoma Press, 1963), 87–106; José Victorino Lastarria, and R. Kelly Washbourne, *Literary Memoirs* (Oxford: Oxford University Press, 2000), 81; E. Bradford Burns, *The Poverty of Progress: Latin America in the Nineteenth Century* (Berkeley, CA: University of California Press, 1980); Charles Hale, *The Transformation of Liberalism in the Late Nineteenth-Century Mexico* (Princeton, NJ: Princeton University Press, 1989).
8. José Martí, "Our America," in *José Martí: Selected Writings*, ed. Esther Allen (New York, NY: Penguin Books, 2002), 293.
9. José Martí, "Our America," "The Truth About the U.S.," "Monetary Conference of the American Republics," in *José Martí: Selected Writings*, ed. Esther Allen (New York, NY: Penguin Books, 2002), 329, 306, 292; Thomas Ward, "From Sarmiento to Martí and Hostos: Extricating the Nation from Coloniality," *European Review of Latin American and Caribbean Studies* 83 (October 2007): 83–104; Oscar Montero *José Martí: An Introduction* (Gordonville, VA: Palgrave Macmillan, 2004); Arturo Ardao, "Panamericansimo y Latinoamericanismo," in *America Latina en Sus Ideas*, ed. Leopoldo Zea (Mexico: Unesco, 1986), 157–171; Charles Hatfield, "The Limits of 'Nuestra America,'" *Revista Hispanica Moderna* 63, no. 2 (2010): 193–202.
10. Rodó, *Ariel* (Austin, TX: University of Texas, 1988), 71, 63. Cited from the Spanish.
11. José Vasconcelos, *The Cosmic Race*, 18–20; Marilyn Grace Miller, *Rise and Fall of the Cosmic Race: The Cult of Mestizaje in Latin America* (Austin, TX: University of Texas Press, 2004).
12. Samuel Ramos, *Profile of Man and Culture in Mexico* (The Texas Pan-American Series, 1973), 9; Patrick Romanell, "Samuel Ramos on the Philosophy of Mexican Culture," *Latin American Research Review* 10, no. 3 (Autumn 1975): 95; Lourdes Martínez-Echazabal, "Mestizaje and the Discourse of National/Cultural Identity in Latin America, 1845–1959," *Latin American Perspectives* 25, no. 3 (May 1998): 24.
13. For a history of U.S. Cold War intervention in Latin America see Stephen G. Rabe, *The Killing Zone: The U.S. Wages Cold War in Latin America* (New York, NY: Oxford University Press, 2012).
14. Hector A. Murena, *El Pecado Original de America* (Buenos Aires: Fondo de Cultura Economica, 2006); Walter D. Mignolo, *The Idea of Latin America* (Malden, MA: Blackwell Publishing, 2005), 8.

15. Alan Angell, "The Left in Latin America Since *c*. 1920," in *Latin America Politics and Society Since 1930*, ed. Leslie Bethell (Cambridge: Cambridge University Press, 1998), 75–144; Thomas C. Wright, *Latin American in the Era of the Cuban Revolution* (Westport, CT: Praeger, 2001); Che Guevara, "Cuba: Historical Exception or Vanguard in the Anticolonial Struggle, April 9, 1961," in *Che Guevara Reader: Writings on Politics and Revolution*, ed. David Deutschmann (New York, NY: Ocean Press, 2003), 135–136; also in the same volume, Guevara, "Political Sovereignty and Economic Independence, March 20, 1960," 102; Guevara, "The OAS Conference at Punta del Este, August 8, 1961," 251.
16. Jeffrey L. Gould, "Solidarity Under Siege: The Latin American Left, 1968," *The American Historical Review* 114, no. 2 (April 2009): 348–375.
17. Jeffrey L. Klaiber, "Prophets and Populists: Liberation Theology 1968–1988," *The Americas* 46, no. 1 (July 1989): 1–15; Susan Fitzpatrick-Behrens, *The Maryknoll Catholic Mission in Peru, 1943–1989: Transnational Faith and Transformation* (Notre Dame, IN: University of Notre Dame Press, 2012).
18. Fernando Henrique Cardoso and Enzo Faletto, *Dependency and Development in Latin America* (Berkeley, CA: University of California Press, 1979), xiv; Nils Gilman, *Mandarins of the Future: Modernization Theory in Cold War America* (Baltimore, MD: Johns Hopkins University Press, 2003); Dominador Bombogan Jr., "Liberation Theology and Dependency Theory: Tracing a Relationship," *Hapag: A Journal of Interdisciplinary Theological Research* 1 (2004): 61–91.
19. Hugo Assmann, *Theology for a Nomad Church* (Maryknoll, NY: Orbis Books, 1976), 47, 115, 134, 121; Enrique Dussel, *A History of the Church in Latin America: Colonialism to Liberation* (Grand Rapids, MI: W.B. Eerdmans, 1981), Chapter 10.
20. José Míguez Bonino, *Doing Theology in a Revolutionary Situation* (Philadelphia, PA: Fortress Press, 1975), 13.
21. Míguez Bonino, *Doing Theology in a Revolutionary Situation*, 15.
22. Eduardo Posada-Carbo, "Fiction as History: The Bananeras and Gabriel García Márquez's One Hundred Years of Solitude," *Journal of Latin American Studies* 30, no. 1 (1998): 397; Eduardo Galeano, *Open Veins of Latin America: Five Centuries of the Pillage of a Continent* (New York, NY: Monthly Review Press, 1973), 261; Diana Sorensen, *A Turbulent Decade Remembered: Scenes from the Latin American Sixties* (Stanford, CA: Stanford University Press, 2007).
23. Catholic Church, Second Vatican Council, "*Gaudium et Spes, Promulgate by Pope Paul VI, November 7, 1965*," Section 30, 55, 69, http://www.vatican.va/archive/hist_councils/ii_vatican_council/documents/.
24. Catholic Church, "*Gaudium et Spes, Promulgate*," Section 4.
25. Gustavo Gutiérrez, *A Theology of Liberation* (Maryknoll, NY: Orbis Books, 1973), 12, 56. See 1968 Medellín Documents at http://personal.stthomas.edu/gwschlabach/docs/Medellín.htm, "Justice," II.3, III.11, I.1; O. Ernesto Valiente, "The Reception of Vatican II in Latin America," *Theological Studies* 32 (2012): 795–823.

26. 1968 Medellín Documents at http://personal.stthomas.edu/gwschlabach/docs/Medellín.htm, II, 3; Gutiérrez, *A Theology of Liberation*, 56.
27. Ernesto Cardenal, *The Gospel in Solentiname* (Maryknoll, NY: Orbis Books, 1976); Ernesto Cardenal, *In Cuba* (New York, NY: New Directions, 1974), 152; Edward Elias, "Prophecy of Liberation: The Poetry of Ernesto Cardenal," in *Poetic Prophecy in Western Literature*, ed. Jan Wojcik and Raymond-Jean Frontain (London: Associated University Presses, 1984), 174–185; Reginal Gibbons, "Political Poetry and the Example of Ernesto Cardenal," *Critical Inquiry* 13, no. 3 (1987): 648–671.
28. Ernesto Cardenal, *Salmos* (Buenos Aires: Ediciones C. Lohle, 1969).
29. Quoted by Gutiérrez, *A Theology of Liberation*, 114. See also Gustavo Gutiérrez, *The Power of the Poor in History* (Maryknoll, NY: Orbis Books, 1983).
30. Enrique D. Dussel, *Filosofía de la liberación* (Mexico: Editorial Edicol, 1977), 14–15, 95–97; Margaret Kohn and Keally McBride, *Political Theories of Decolonization: Postcolonialism and the Problem of Foundations* (Oxford: Oxford University Press, 2011), 119–141; Linda Martín Alcoff and Eduardo Mendieta, eds. *Thinking from the Underside of History: Enrique Dussel's Philosophy of Liberation* (Lanham, MD: Rowman & Littlefield, 2000).
31. Angel Rama, *Writing Across Cultures: Narrative Transculturation in Latin America* (Durham, NC: Duke University Press, 2012); Carlos J. Alonso, *The Spanish American Regional Novel: Modernity and Autochthony* (Cambridge: Cambridge University Press, 1990); Nestor Garcia Canclini, *Hybrid Cultures: Strategies for Entering and Leaving Modernity* (Minneapolis, MN: University of Minneapolis Press, 1995).
32. Pedro Trigo, *Arguedas, Mito, Historia y Religion* (Lima: Centro de Estudios y Publicaciones, 1982); David Sobrevilla, "Transculturación y heterogeneidad: Avatares de los categorías literarias en América Latina," *Revista Critica Literaria Latinoamerican* 27, no. 54 (2001): 21–33.
33. Stephen B. Wall-Smith, "José Maria Arguedas: Godfather of Liberationism," *Christian Century* (November 18, 1987): 1034.
34. Angel Rama, *Writing Across Cultures: Narrative Transculturation in Latin America* (Durham, NC: Duke University Press, 2012), 10; Jennifer Marie Forsythe, "La descolonización espiritual como practica multidisciplinaria en la obra de José Maria Arguedas," *Revista de Critica Literaria LatinAmeriana* 36, no. 72 (2010): 217–231; Eugene Gogol, *The Concept of Other in Latin American Liberation* (Lanham, MD: Lexington Books, 2002).
35. Gayraud S. Wilmore, "Ethnic Identities and Christian Theology," *Nexus* XVI, no. 1 (Winter 1972): 9.
36. Wilmore, "Ethnic Identities and Christian Theology," 8–19.
37. William L. Van Deburg, *Modern Black Nationalism: From Marcus Garvey to Louis Farrakhan* (New York, NY: New York University Press, 1997); Michael C. Dawson,

Black Visions: The Roots of Contemporary African-American Political Ideologies (Chicago, IL: University of Chicago Press, 2001).
38. W.E.B. Du Bois, *The Souls of Black Folk* (New York, NY: Penguin Books, 1996), 5.
39. Du Bois, "Of Training of Black Men," in *Souls*, 87; Alain Locke and Stanley Francis Helmore, *The New Negro* (New York, NY: A. and C. Boni, 1920); Cary D. Wintz, *Black Culture and The Harlem Renaissance* (Houston, TX: Rice University Press, 1988); David L. Lewis, *When Harlem was in Vogue* (New York, NY: Knopf, 1981); Robert E. Washington, *The Ideologies of African American Literature: From the Harlem Renaissance to the Black Nationalist Revolt* (Lanham, MD: Rowman & Littlefield, 2001).
40. W.E.B. Du Bois, *The Souls of Black Folk*, (New York, NY: Penguin Book, 1996), 5. Nikhil Pal Singh, *Black is a Country: Race and the Unfinished Struggle for Democracy* (Cambridge, MA: Harvard University Press, 2004), 58–60.
41. Richard H. King, *Race, Culture and the Intellectuals, 1940–1970* (Washington, DC: Woodrow Wilson Center Press, 2004); Gunnar Myrdal, *An American Dilemma: The Negro Problem and Modern Democracy* (New York, NY: Harper & Brothers, 1944).
42. Robert E. Washington, *Ideologies of African American Literature*, 164, 207, 251–272; Ralph Ellison, *Invisible Man* (New York, NY: Random House, 1947), Prologue; James Baldwin, *The Fire Next Time*, (New York: Dial Press, 1963), 118; Eldridge Cleaver, *Soul on Ice* (New York, NY: McGraw-Hill, 1967).
43. Richard H. King, *Race, Culture*, 167; Harold Cruse, *The Crisis of the Negro Intellectual* (New York, NY: William Morrow & Co., 1967), 309, 85.
44. Harold Cruse, reprinted in *Rebellion or Revolution?* (New York, NY: Morrow, 1968), 110. Martin L. King, "My Dream," The King Center archive, *Chicago Defender* (December 19, 1966), 39, see http://www.thekingcenter.org/archive/document/chicago-defender-my-dream#; Peniel E. Joseph, *The Black Power Movement: Rethinking the Civil Rights–Black Power Era* (New York, NY: Routledge, 2006); William L. Van Deburg, *New Day in Babylon: The Black Power and American Culture, 1965–1975* (Chicago, IL: University of Chicago Press, 1992).
45. Carmichael, *Black Power*, 5, 54; Le Roi Jones, "'Black' is a Country," in *Home: Social Essays* (New York, NY: William Morrow, 1968), 85; Nikhil Pal Singh, *Black is a Country: Race and the Unfinished Struggle for Democracy* (Cambridge, MA: Harvard University Press, 2004); William L. Van Deburg, *Modern Black Nationalism: From Marcus Garvey to Louis Farrakhan* (New York, NY: New York University Press, 1997); Michael C. Dawson, *Black Visions: The Roots of Contemporary African-American Political Ideologies* (Chicago, IL: University of Chicago Press, 2001).
46. Malcolm X and Alex Haley, *The Autobiography of Malcolm X* (New York, NY: Ballantine Books, 1999), 42, 294, 167.
47. Malcolm X and Haley, *The Autobiography of Malcolm X*, 257, 165, 177, 259; Michael Eric Dyson, *Making Malcolm: The Myth and Meaning of Malcom X* (New York,

NY: Oxford University Press, 1995); Luis A. DeCaro, *Malcolm and the Cross: The Nation of Islam, Malcolm X, and Christianity* (New York, NY: New York University Press, 1998); Bashir M. El-Beshti, "The Semiotics of Salvation: Malcolm X and the Autobiographical Self," *The Journal of Negro History* 82, no. 4 (Autumn 1997): 359–367.

48. LeRoi Jones, "Cuba Libre," in *Home: Social Essays* (New York, NY: William Morrow & Co., 1966): 23–78; Komozi Woodard, *A Nation Within a Nation: Amiri Baraka (LeRoi Jones) and Black Power Politics* (Chapel Hill, NC: University of North Carolina Press, 1999); William L. Van Deburg, *New Day in Babylon: The Black Power Movement and American Culture, 1965–1975* (Chicago, IL: University of Chicago Press, 1992), 52; Simon Wendt, "They Finally Found Out that We Really Are Men: Violence, Non-Violence and Black Manhood in the Civil Rights Era," *Gender and History* 19, no. 3 (2007): 543–564; Imamu Amiri Baraka and William J. Harris, *The LeRoi Jones/Amiri Baraka Reader* (New York, NY: Thunder's Mouth Press, 2000), Introduction, xx; Imamu Amiri Baraka, *The Autobiography of LeRoi Jones* (New York, NY: Freundlich Books, 1984), 243.

49. Franz Fanon, *Black Skin White Masks* (New York, NY: Grove Press, 1967), 28, 9. Fanon refers to Jean-Paul Sartre's *Being and Nothingness: An Essay on Phenomenological Ontology* (New York, NY: Philosophical Library, 1956); Jean-Paul Sartre and George Joseph Becker, *Anti-Semite and Jew* (New York, NY: Schocken Books, 1948); Jean-Paul Sartre and Léopold Sédar Senghor, *Black Orpheus* (New York, NY: French & European Publications, 2003); Jacques Lacan, "The Mirror Stage as Formative of the *I* Function as Revealed in Psychoanalytic Experience," first delivered in 1949 at the International Psychoanalytical Association congress and published in *Ecrits,* 1966; Jacques Lacan, Héloïse Fink, and Bruce Fink, *Ecrits: The First Complete Edition in English* (New York, NY: W.W. Norton, 2006).

50. Frantz Fanon, *Black Skin White Masks* (New York, NY: Grove Press, 1967), 217–218, 7, 193, 228; Max Silverman, " Reflection on the Human Question," in *Frantz Fanon's Black Skin White Masks: New Interdisciplinary Essay*, ed. Max Silverman (Manchester: Manchester University Press, 2005).

51. Sonia Kruks, "The Politics of Recognition: Sartre, Fanon and Identity Politics," in *Retrieving Experience: Subjectivity and Recognition in Feminist Politics* (Ithaca, NY: Cornell University Press, 2001), 79–106.

52. Cone, *Black Theology & Black Power*, 135; Cone, *A Black Theology of Liberation*, 27, 74, 108. Also James H. Cone, "Christian Theology and the Afro-American Revolution," *Christianity and Crisis* (June 8, 1970): 123–125.

53. Cone, *God of the Oppressed*, 60; Cone, *A Black Theology of Liberation*, 25–26, 133.

54. Du Bois, *The Souls of Black Folk*, 204–208. James Cone, *The Spirituals and the Blues: An Interpretation*. (New York, NY: Seabury Press, 1972), 17, 54; Howard Thurman, *The Negro Spiritual Speaks of Life and Death* (New York, NY: Harper

& Row, 1947); Dwight N. Hopkins and George C.L. Cummings, *Cut Loose Your Stammering Tongue: Black Theology in the Slave Narratives* (Louisville, KY: Westminster/John Knox Press, 2003).

55. Cone, *God of the Oppressed*, 15, 39.
56. J. Deotis Roberts, *Liberation and Reconciliation* (Philadelphia, PA: Westminster Press, 1971), 68, 71; Vincent Harding, "Black Power and the American Christ," *Christian Century* (January 4, 1967): 13–14; David A. Hollinger, "How Wide the Circle of the 'We': American Intellectuals and the Problem of the Ethnos since World War II," *The American Historical Review* 98, no. 2 (April 1993): 317–337; J. Deotis Roberts, *A Black Political Theology*, (Philadelphia, PA: Westminster Press, 1974), 48.
57. Paul Tillich, "What is Faith," in *The Essential Tillich*, ed. F. Forrester Church (Chicago, IL: Chicago University Press, 1999), 23.
58. Letty Russell, *Human Liberation in a Feminist Perspective: A Theology* (Philadelphia, PA: Westminster Press, 1974), 47.

CHAPTER 11

1. C. Wright Mills, "A Pagan Sermon to the Christian Clergy," in *Politics of Truth: Selected Writings of C. Wright Mills*, ed. John H. Summers (Oxford: Oxford University Press, 2008), 163, 166; Daniel Geary, *Radical Ambition: C. Wright Mills, the Left, and American Social Thought* (Berkeley, CA: University of California Press, 2009), 201–202; Rick Tilman, *C. Wright Mills: A Native Radical and His American Intellectual Roots* (University Park, PA: Pennsylvania State University Press, 1984); Kim Sawchuk, "The Cultural Apparatus: C. Wright Mills' Unfinished Work," *The American Sociologist* 32, no. 1 (Spring 2001): 27–49; Jose Miquez Bonino, *Doing Theology in a Revolutionary Situation* (Philadelphia, PA: Fortress Press, 1975), 71.
2. C. Wright Mills, "Letter to the New Left," in *Politics of Truth: Selected Writings of C. Wright Mills*, ed. John H. Summers (Cary, NC: Oxford University Press, 2008), 257; Steve Fraser and Gary Gerstle. *The Rise and Fall of the New Deal Order, 1930–1980* (Princeton, NJ: Princeton University Press, 1989); Mark Hulsether, *Building a Protestant Left:* Christianity and Crisis *Magazine 1941–1993* (Knoxville, TN: University of Tennessee Press, 1999).
3. Hulsether, *Building a Protestant Left*, 117–125; James F. Findlay Jr., *Church People in the Struggle: The National Council of Churches and the Black Freedom Movement, 1950–1970* (New York, NY: Oxford University Press, 1993); Mitchell Hall, "CALCAV and Religious Opposition to the Vietnam War," in *Give Peace a Chance: Exploring the Vietnam Antiwar Movement*, ed. Melvin Small and William Hoover (Syracuse, NY: Syracuse University Press, 1992), 35–52; Allen J. Matusow, *The Unraveling of America: A History of Liberalism in the 1960s* (New York, NY: Harper & Row, 1984).
4. Robert Wuthnow, *The Restructuring of American Religion: Society and Faith Since World War II* (Princeton, NJ: Princeton University Press, 1988), 5, 10. Other

religious movements in opposition to war and economic inequality included the politically radical Catholic Worker movement and an emerging evangelical left. These remained within a social Christianity tradition and were for the most part theologically conservative; see Mel Piehl, *Breaking Bread: The Catholic Worker and the Origin of Catholic Radicalism in America* (Tuscaloosa, AL: University of Alabama Press, 2006), Peter Goodwin Heltzel, *Jesus and Justice: Evangelicals, Race and American Politics* (New Haven: Yale University Press, 2009), and David R. Swartz, *Moral Minority: The Evangelical Left in an Age of Conservatism* (Philadelphia, PA: University of Pennsylvania Press, 2012).

5. John C. Bennett, "The Geneva Conference of 1966 as a Climatic Event," *The Ecumenical Review* 37, no. 1 (January 1985): 26–33; Hulsether, *Building a Protestant Left*, 125–126; Jill K. Gill, *Embattled Ecumenism: The National Council of Churches, The Vietnam War and the Trials of the Protestant Left* (DeKalb, IL: Northern Illinois University Press, 2011); Robert J. McMahon, *The Cold War in the Third World* (New York, NY: Oxford University Press, 2013).

6. Jeffrey L. Gould, "Solidarity Under Siege: The Latin American Left, 1968," *The American Historical Review* 114, no. 2 (April 2009): 348–375; Nelson A. Rockefeller, *The Rockefeller Report on the Americas* (Chicago, IL: Quadrangle Books, 1969); Thomas C. Wright, *State Terrorism in Latin America: Chile, Argentina, and International Human Rights* (Lanham, MD: Rowman & Littlefield, 2007); Stephen G. Rabe, *The Killing Zone: The United States Wages Cold War in Latin America* (New York, NY: Oxford University Press, 2012).

7. Marguerite Guzmán Bouvard, *Revolutionizing Motherhood: The Mothers of the Plaza De Mayo* (Wilmington, DE: Scholarly Resources, 1994), 196; José Comblin, *The Church and the National Security State* (Maryknoll, NY: Orbis Books, 1979); Penny Lernoux "The Latin American Church," *Latin American Research Review* 15, no. 2 (1980): 201–211; Gustavo Morello, *The Catholic Church and Argentina's Dirty War* (Oxford: Oxford University Press, 2015).

8. Jeffrey L. Klaiber, *The Church, Dictatorships, and Democracy in Latin America* (Maryknoll, NY: Orbis Books, 1998).

9. Christian Smith, *The Emergence of Liberation Theology: Radical Religion and Social Movement Theory* (Chicago, IL: University of Chicago Press, 1991), 198; Charles A. Reilly, "Latin America's Religious Populist," in *Religion and Political Conflict in Latin America*, ed. Daniel H. Levine (Chapel Hill, NC: University of North Carolina Press, 1986), 42–57; Jeffrey L. Klaiber, "Prophets and Populist: Liberation Theology, 1968–1988," *The Americas* 46, no. 1 (July 1989): 1–15.

10. Frederick Herzog, "Liberation Theology Begins at Home," *Christianity and Crisis*, (May 13, 1974): 94. Frederick Herzog, "Liberation Theology," in *Theology From the Belly of the Whale: A Frederick Herzog Reader*, ed. Joerg Rieger (Harrisburg, MS: Trinity Press International, 1999), 88–89; Herzog "God: Black or White" (1970) in *Theology From the Belly of the Whale*, 59.

11. Herzog "God: Black or White," 68–69; Frederick Herzog, "Introduction: On Liberating Liberation Theology," in Hugo Assmann, *Theology for a Nomad Church* (Maryknoll, NY: Orbis Books, 1975), 1–23.
12. John C. Bennett, "Fitting the Liberation Theme in our Theological Agenda," *Christianity and Crisis* (July 18, 1977), 164–166; John C. Bennett, *Radical Imperative: From Theology to Social Ethics* (Philadelphia, PA: Westminster Press, 1975), 140–141; Gary Dorrien, "Realism in Conflict," in *Soul in Society: The Making and Renewal of Social Christianity* (Minneapolis, MN: Fortress Press, 1995), 162–220.
13. Bennett, "Fitting the Liberation Theme," 167; Bennett, *The Radical Imperative*, 105; Craig L. Nessan, *Orthopraxis or Heresy: The North American Response to Latin American Liberation Theology* (Atlanta, GA: Scholars Press, 1989).
14. Richard J. Neuhaus, "Liberation Theology and the Captivities of Jesus," *Worldview* 16, no. 6 (June 1973): 43–46.
15. Neuhaus, "Liberation Theology and the Captivities of Jesus," 43.
16. Neuhaus, "Liberation Theology and the Captivities of Jesus," 48.
17. Thomas G. Sanders, "The Theology of Liberation: Christian Utopianism," *Christianity and Crisis* 33 (September 17, 1973): 169–172.
18. Sanders, "The Theology of Liberation," 173; Dennis P. McCann, *Christian Realism and Liberation Theology* (Maryknoll, NY: Orbis Books, 1981).
19. Rubem A. Alves, "Christian Realism: Ideology of the Establishment," *Christianity and Crisis* 33 (September 17, 1973): 173.
20. Alves, "Christian Realism," 174–176; Rubem Alves, " Protestantism in Latin America: Its Ideological Function and Utopian Possibilities," *The Ecumenical Review* 22, no. 1 (January 1970): 1–15.
21. Jürgen Moltmann, "An Open Letter to José Miquez Bonino," *Christianity and Crisis* (March 29 1976): 57, 59–60.
22. Doug Rossinow, "Letting Go: Revisiting the New Left's Demise," in *The New Left Revisted*, eds. John McMillian and Paul Buhle (Philadelphia, PA: Temple University Press, 2003), 247; Stephanie Gilmore, *Feminist Coalitions: Historical Perspectives on Second-Wave Feminism in the United States* (Urbana, IL: University of Illinois Press, 2008); John David Skrentny, *The Minority Rights Revolution* (Cambridge, MA: Belknap Press of Harvard University Press, 2002).
23. John J. Carey, "Black Theology: An Appraisal of the Internal and External Issues," *Theological Studies* 33, no. 4 (December 1972): 684–697.
24. Julius Lester, "Review: The Black Experience in Religion," *Christianity and Crisis* 35 (March 31, 1975): 74–75.
25. Gottfried Wilhelm Leibniz and Austin Marsden Farrer, *Theodicy: Essays on the Goodness of God, the Freedom of Man, and the Origin of Evil (1710)* (Eugene, OR: Wipf & Stock, 2001); Max Weber, "Three Forms of Theodicy," in *From Max Weber: Essays in Sociology*, trans. H.H. Gerth and C. Wright Mills (London: Routledge, 1991), 358–362.

26. Anthony B. Pinn, *Moral Evil and Redemptive Suffering: A History of Theodicy in African-American Religious Thought* (Gainesville, FL: University Press of Florida, 2002) 7, 12; Anthony B. Pinn, *Why, Lord? Suffering and Evil in Black Theology* (New York: Continuum, 1995). W.E.B. Du Bois, "Our Spiritual Striving," in *Souls of Black Folk*, 5. For Christian thought on the problem of evil: Mark Larrimore, ed., *The Problem of Evil: A Reader* (Malden, MA: Blackwell, 2001); Marilyn McCord Adams, *Horrendous Evils and The Goodness of God* (Ithaca, NY: Cornell University Press, 1999); John Hick, *Evil and the God of Love* (New York, NY: Harper & Row, 1966); Alvin Plantinga, *God, Freedom, and Evil.* (Grand Rapids, MI: W.B. Eerdmans, 1983).

27. William R. Jones, "Theodicy and Methodology in Black Theology: A Critique of Washington, Cone and Cleage," *The Harvard Theological Review* 64, no. 4 (October 1971): 543; William R. Jones, *Is God a White Racist?* (Garden City, NY: Anchor Press/Doubleday, 1973), xx.

28. Jones, *Is God a White Racist?*, 185–187.

29. James H. Cone, *God of the Oppressed* (San Francisco, CA: Harper and Row, 1975), 163, 174, 177, 268, Fn 23; Gustavo Gutiérrez, *On Job: God-talk and the Suffering of the Innocent* (Maryknoll, NY: Orbis Books, 1987).

30. Rosemary Radford Ruether, "Black Theology and the Black Church," *America* (June 14, 1969): 684; Rosemary Radford Ruether, "The Black Theology of James Cone," *Catholic World* (October 1971) 18–20.

31. Ruether, "The Black Theology of James Cone," 19.

32. Ruether, *New Woman, New Earth*, 116. Jacquelyn Grant, "Black Theology and the Black Woman," in *Black Theology: A Documentary History*, ed. James H. Cone and Gayraud S. Wilmore (Maryknoll, NY: Orbis Books, 1983), 323–338; Rufus Burrow, Jr., *James H. Cone and Black Liberation Theology* (Jefferson, NC: McFarland, 1994), 132–139.

33. Rosemary Radford Ruether, "Crisis in Sex and Race: Black Theology vs. Feminist Theology," *Christianity and Crisis* (April 15, 1974): 72.

34. Carol Christ, "The New Feminist Theology: A Review of the Literature," *Religious Studies Review* 3, no. 4 (October 1977): 203–204.

35. Carol Christ and Judith Plaskow, *Womanspirit Rising: A Feminist Reader in Religion* (San Francisco, CA: Harper & Row, 1979), Introduction, 15.

CHAPTER 12

1. Archie LeMone, "When Traditional Theology Meets Black and Liberation Theology," *Christianity and Crisis* 33 (September 1973): 177–178.

2. LeMone, "When Traditional Theology Meets Black and Liberation Theology," 178; Paulo Freire, et al., "Black Theology and Latin American Liberation Theology" in *Black Theology: A Documentary History*, ed. James H. Cone and Gayraud S. Wilmore (Maryknoll, NY: Orbis Books, 2004), 404–408; LeMone, "When Traditional Theology Meets Black and Liberation Theology," 178.

3. Freire, "Black Theology and Latin American Liberation Theology," 404–405; LeMone, "When Traditional Theology Meets Black and Liberation Theology," 178.
4. C. Wright Mills, "Listen, Yankee: The Cuban Case Against the United States," *Harper's Magazine* (December 1960): 31–37; Mills, "On Latin America, the Left, and the U.S.," in *Politics of Truth: Selected Writings of C. Wright Mills*, ed. John H. Summers (Cary, NC: Oxford University Press, 2008), 223–233; Van Gosse, *Where the Boys Are: Cuba, Cold War America and the Making of a New Left* (London: Verso, 1993); John A. Gronbeck-Tedesco, "The Left in Transition: The Cuban Revolution in the U.S. Third World Politics," *Journal of Latin American Studies* 40, no. 4 (November 2008): 651–673; Daniel Geary, "'Becoming International Again': C. Wright Mills and the Emergence of a Global New Left, 1956–1962," *Journal of American History* (December 2008): 710–736.
5. Gregory Baum, "The Christian Left at Detroit," *The Ecumenist* (September–October, 1975) reprinted in Sergio Torres and John Eagleson, ed. *Theology in the Americas* (Marknoll, NY: Orbis Books, 1976), 406; Torres and Eagleson, ed. *Theology in the Americas*, 221; Robert McAfee Brown, "Preface and Conclusion" in *Theology in the Americas*, xxvi.
6. Torres and Eagleson, *Theology in the Americas*, 8–10; Alan McPherson, *Yankee No!: Anti-Americanism in the U.S.-Latin American Relations* (Cambridge, MA: Harvard University Press, 2003); John J. Hasset and Braulio Muñoz, ed. *Looking North: Writings from Spanish America on the US, 1800 to the present* (Tucson, AZ: University of Arizona Press, 2012).
7. Hasset and Muñoz, ed. *Looking North*, 10.
8. Rosemary Radford Ruether, "Letter of Rosemary Radford Ruether to Sergio Torres and the Planners of the Conference," in *Theology in the Americas*, 84–85, 248; José Miguez Bonino, *Doing Theology in a Revolutionary Situation* (Philadelphia, PA: Fortress Press, 1975), xix; Conrad Cherry, *God's New Israel: Religious Interpretations of American Destiny* (Chapel Hill, NC: University of North Carolina Press, 1998).
9. Sister Jeanne Rollins, "Liberation and the Native American," 202; Chicano Reflection Group, "The Chicano Struggle," 207–209; Gregory Baum, "The Christian Left at Detroit," 414, all in *Theology in the Americas*. For other liberation movements see J. Michael Clark, *A Place to Start: Toward an Unapologetic Gay Liberation Theology* (Dallas, TX: Monument Press, 1989); Vine Deloria, *God Is Red* (New York, NY: Grosset & Dunlap, 1973); Richard Cruz and Mario T. García, *Chicano Liberation Theology: The Writings and Documents of Richard Cruz and Católicos Por La Raza* (Dubuque, IA: Kendall/Hunt, 2010).
10. Gregory Baum, "The Christian Left at Detroit," 399, 426.
11. Robert N. Bellah, "Civil Religion in America," *Daedalus* 96, no. 1 (Winter 1967): 1–21. Bellah, *The Broken Covenant: American Civil Religion in Time of Trial* (New York, NY: Seabury Press, 1975), 85, 180, 142; John A. Coleman, "Civil

Religion and Liberation Theology," in *Theology in the Americas*, 126, 115. For contemporaneous discussion on civil religion, see Russell E. Richey and Donald G. Jones, *American Civil Religion* (New York, NY: Harper & Row, 1974); John A. Coleman, "Civil Religion," *Sociological Analysis* 31 (Summer 1970): 67–77; Raymond J. Harbeski, *God and War: American Civil Religion Since 1945* (New Brunswick, NJ: Rutgers University Press, 2012).

12. Coleman, "Civil Religion and Liberation Thelogy," in *Theology in the Americas*, 126.
13. Rosemary Radford Ruether, "Letter of Rosemary Ruether to Sergio Torres and the Planners of the Conference," 84–85; Frederick Herzog "Pre-Bicentennial U.S.A. in the Liberation Process," 149, both in *Theology in the Americas*, eds. Torres and Eagleson. John D. Wilsey, *American Exceptionalism and Civil Religion: Reassessing the History of an Idea*, (Downer Grove, IL: IVP Academic, 2015).
14. Frederick Herzog, "Pre-Bicentennial U.S.A. in the Liberation Process," in *Theology in the Americas*, 142–143, 156.
15. Herbert O. Edwards, "Black Theology and Liberation Theology," in *Theology in the Americas*, 186–189.
16. Torres and Eagleson, "Black Panel: Excerpts from Discussion," in *Theology in the Americas*, 352–356; James H. Cone, "From Geneva to Sao Paulo: A Dialogue Between Black Theology and Latin American Liberation Theology," in *Black Theology: A Documentary History Volume II: 1980–1992*, ed. Gayraud S. Wilmore (Maryknoll, NY: Orbis Books, 1993), 373–376.
17. Rosemary Radford Ruether, "Letter of Rosemary Ruether to Sergio Torres and the Planners of the Conference," in *Theology in the Americas*, 84; Gregory Baum, "The Christian Left at Detroit," 89–90.
18. Beverly Harrison, "Statement by Beverly Harrison," 367–369; Beatriz Melano Couch, "Statement by Beatriz Melano Couch," 374, both in *Theology in the Americas*. Beatriz Melano Couch, *La mujer y la Iglesia* [Woman and the Church] (Buenos Aires: El Escudo, 1973).
19. John Coleman, "Statement by John Coleman," in *Theology in the Americas*, 381–385.
20. Robert McAfee Brown, "A Preface and Conclusion," in *Theology in the Americas*, x, xiii, xvi; Glenn R. Bucher, "Toward a Liberation Theology of the 'Oppressor,'" *Journal of the American Academy of Religion* 44, no. 3 (September 1976), 571–534. The 1975 Detroit conference was extensively covered in the religious press including *Christianity and Crisis, Christian Century, Commonweal, America, The Ecumenist*, and *Time Magazine,* "Jesus the Liberator?" 106, no. 9 (September 1, 1975): 44.
21. Peter L. Berger, "A Sociological View of the Secularization of Theology," *Journal for the Scientific Study of Religion* 6, no.1 (Spring 1967), 3–8; Peter L. Berger, *The Noise of Solemn Assemblies: Christian Commitment and the Religious Establishment in America* (Garden City, NY: Doubleday, 1961); Peter L. Berger, *The Sacred Canopy: Elements of a Sociological Theory of Religion* (New York, NY: Anchor Books, 1967); Paul J. Fitzgerald, "Faithful Sociology: Peter Berger's Religious Project,"

Religious Studies Review 27, no. 1 (January 2001); Gary Dorrien, "Berger: Theology and Sociology," in *Peter Berger and the Study of Religion,* Linda Woodhead, ed. (New York, NY: Routledge, 2001), 26–39.
22. Berger, "Sociological View," 12–13.
23. Ralph C. Wood, "To the Unknown God: Peter Berger's Theology of Transcendence," *Perspectives in Religious Studies* 20, no. 2 (Summer 1993): 175–186.
24. Wallace M. Alston Jr. et al., "Whatever Happened to Theology," *Christianity and Crisis* 35 (May 12, 1975): 108.
25. Alston Jr. et al., "Whatever Happened to Theology," 108–109, 106, 111.
26. Alston Jr. et al., "Whatever Happened to Theology," 110–112.
27. Kenneth A. Briggs, "18 Christian Leaders Attack 'Debilitating' Secular Influences," *New York Times* (January 28, 1975): 30; Kenneth A. Briggs, "The Hartford Declaration," *Theology Today* 32, no. 1 (April 1975): 94–97.
28. Letty Russell and Richard Shaull, "Theological Table-Talk," *Theology Today* 33, no. 2 (July 1975): 187.
29. Phillip Berryman, *Liberation Theology* (New York, NY: Pantheon Books, 1987), 98. Enrique Dussell, *A History of the Church in Latin America* (Grand Rapids, MI: W.B. Eerdmans, 1981), 223. Significant gatherings of CELAM occurred in Sucra, Bolivia, 1972 and in Puebla, Mexico, 1979. Through lobbying at these gatherings, liberationists influenced the language of the documents even though they had no formal power.
30. Pope Paul VI, *Evangelii Nuntiandi, Apostolic Exhortation, 1975,* 27, http://www.vatican.va/holy_father/paul_vi/apost_exhortations/documents/hf_p-vi_exh_19751208_evangelii-nuntiandi_en.html; Donald Dorr, *Option for the Poor: A Hundred Years of Catholic Social Teaching* (Maryknoll: Orbis Books, 1983). A previous encyclical, *Populurum Progressio* (1967) by Pope Paul VI, called for a restructuring of the international economic order. Rather than a violent revolution, Pope Paul proposed a self-interested voluntary top-down approach to economic injustice.
31. Pope Paul VI, *Evangelii Nuntiandi*, 36; Cardinal Joseph Ratzinger, *Instruction on Christian Freedom and Liberation* (Washington, DC: Publishing and Promotion Services, United States Catholic Conference, 1986).
32. Alfonso López Trujillo, *Liberation or Revolution?* (Huntington, NY: Our Sunday Visitor, 1977) 11, 68–70.
33. Dussel, 228; Milagros Pena, "The *Sodalitium Vitae* Movement in Peru: A Rewriting of Liberation Theology," *Sociological Analysis* 53, no. 2 (Summer 1992): 159–173.
34. Daniel K. Williams, *God's Own Party: The Making of the Christian Right* (New York, NY: Oxford University Press, 2012); Joel A. Carpenter, *Revive Us Again: The Reawakening of American Fundamentalism* (New York, NY: Oxford University Press, 1997); Robert Wuthnow, *The Restructuring of American Religion* (Princeton, NJ: Princeton University Press, 1988); Andrew Hartman, *A War for the Soul of America: A History of the Culture Wars* (Chicago, IL: University of Chicago Press, 2015).

35. Gary Dorrien, *Social Ethics in the Making* (Malden, MA: Wiley-Blackwell, 2009), 448–460; Craig L. Nessan, *Orthodoxy or Heresy* (Atlanta, GA: Scholars Press, 1989), 299; Carl F.H. Henry, *God, Revelation and Authority*, Volume IV (Waco, TX: Word Books, 1976), 570; see also Volume VI of same multi-volume text, "Supplementary Note: The Christian and Political Duty," 436–454.
36. Matthew Avery Sutton, *Jerry Falwell and the Rise of the Religious Right: A Brief History with Documents* (Boston, MA: Bedford/St. Martin's, 2013), 57–60; James A. Speer, "The New Christian Right and its Parent Company: A Study in Political Contrasts," in *New Christian Politics*, eds. David G. Bromley and Anson Shupe (Macon, GA: Mercer University Press, 1984), 38; Kenneth W. Thompson, "The Religious Transformation of Politics and the Political Transformation of Religion," *The Review of Politics* 50, no. 4 (Autumn 1998): 545–560; Angela M. Lahr, *Millennial Dreams and Apocalyptic Nightmare: The Cold War Origins of Political Evangelicalism* (New York: Oxford University Press, 2007).
37. Sydney E. Alhstrom, "The Radical Turn in Theology and Ethics: Why It Occurred in the 1960s," *The Annals of the American Academy of Political and Social Science* 387 (January 1970): 35.
38. Christian Smith, "The Spirit and Democracy: Base Communities, Protestantism, and Democratization in Latin America," *Sociology of Religion* 55, no. 2 (Summer 1994): 119–143; Anthony J. Gill, "Rendering unto Caesar? Religious Competition and Catholic Political Strategy in Latin America, 1962–79," *American Journal of Political Science* 38, no. 2 (May, 1994): 403–425; Frances Hagopian, "Latin American Catholicism in an Age of Religious and Political Pluralism: A Framework for Analysis," *Comparative Politics* 40, no. 2 (January 2008): 149–168: Todd Hartch, *The Rebirth of Latin American Christianity* (New York, NY: Oxford University Press, 2014).

EPILOGUE

1. James Cone, "From Geneva to Sao Paulo: A Dialogue Between Black Theology and Latin American Liberation Theology," in *Black Theology: A Documentary History Vol. 2: 1980–1992*, eds. James H. Cone and Gayraud S. Wilmore (Maryknoll, NY: Orbis Books, 1993), 371–387. Examples of liberationists' proliferation include Robert Beckford, *Jesus Is Dread: Black Theology and Black Culture in Britain* (London: Darton, Longman & Todd, 1998); Xavier Irudayaraj, *Emerging Dalit Theology* (Madras, India: Jesuit Theological Secretariate, 1990); Ada María Isasi-Diaz, *Mujerista Theology: A Theology for the Twenty-First Century* (Maryknoll, NY: Orbis Books, 1996); Naim Stifan Ateek, *Justice, and Only Justice: A Palestinian Theology of Liberation* (Maryknoll, NY: Orbis Books, 1989); Richard Cleaver, *Know My Name: A Gay Liberation Theology* (Louisville, KY: Westminster/John Knox Press, 1995). New journals committed to expanding the development of liberationist studies include *Feminist Studies in Religion* (1985), *Feminist Theology* (1992), and *Black Theology: An International Journal* (2002).

2. Michael Löwy, "Socio-Religious Origins of Brazil's Landless Rural Workers Movement," *Monthly Review* 53, no. 2 (June 2001): 32–40; Camillo A. Perez-Bustillo and Karla V. Hernandez Mares, *Human Rights, Hegemony and Utopia in Latin America: Poverty, Forced Migration and Resistance in Mexico and Colombia* (Leiden: Brill, 2016), Chapter 7, 171–219, *Las Abejas*, began in a BECs embracing the indigenous theology of Chiapas Bishop Samuel Ruiz; Gonzalo Castillo-Cardenas, *Liberation Theology from Below: The Life and Thought of Manuel Quintín Lame* (Maryknoll, NY: Orbis Books, 1987). Manuel Quintín Lame was a self-educated and charismatic indigenous leader, whose deep theological thinking converged with liberationist currents later in the century. His 1939 book *The Thought of the Indian Educated in the Colombia Forrest* (Bogotá, Columbia: Organización Nacional Indígena de Colombia, 1987) is an example of an alternative popular theology among the unrepresented, and presented a messianic outrage against social and economic abuse. As moral protest it drew from both Catholic and traditional Indian cosmology.

3. Christian Smith, *The Emergence of Liberation Theology: Radical Religion and Social Movement Theory* (Chicago, IL: Chicago University Press, 1991), 222–235; Pete Hebbethwaith, "Liberation Theology and the Roman Catholic Church," in *The Cambridge Companion to Liberation Theology*, Christopher Rowland ed. (Cambridge: Cambridge University Press, 1999), 179–198; George Russell, "Cover Stories Taming the Liberation Theologians, *Time Magazine* (June 24, 2001), http://content.time.com/time/magazine/article/0,9171,141037,00.html; Alvaro de Juana, "Archbishop Romero had no interest in liberation theology, says secretary," *Catholic News Agency*, (February 21, 2015), https://www.catholicnewsagency.com/news/archbishop-romero-had-no-interest-in-liberation-theology-says-secretary-79788; Marlise Simons, "Liberation Theology: 2 Sides Polarized," *The New York Times*, (June 3, 1985), http://www.nytimes.com/1985/06/03/world/liberation-theology-2-sides-polarize.html; Joseph Cardinal Ratzinger, The Vatican, "Instructions on Certain Aspects of Liberation Theology," http://www.vatican.va/roman_curia/congregations/cfaith/documents/rc_con_cfaith_doc_19840806_theology-liberation_en.html; Nikolas Kozloff, "The Pope's Holy War Against Liberation Theology," *NACLA*, (no date given), http://nacla.org/news/popes-holy-war-against-liberation-theology.

4. Quoted by Manning Marable, "The Rainbow Coalition: Jesse Jackson and the Politics of Ethnicity," *Crosscurrents* 34, no. 1 (Spring 1984): 26; Timothy Charles Murphy, "The Influence of Socialism in Black and Womanist Theologies: Capitalism's Relationship as Source, Sin and Salvation," *Black Theology: An International Journal* 10, no. 1 (2012): 28–48; V.S. Vellem, "Black Theology of Liberation and the Economy of Life," *The Ecumenical Review* 67, no. 2 (July 2015): 177–186; Nancy J. Berneking and Pamela Carter Joern, eds. *Re-Membering and Re-Imagining* (Cleveland, OH: Pilgrim Press, 1995), xv; Barger, personal file notes, Minneapolis,

MN, April 16, 1998; "The Year's Top Stories: Political Christians, Christian Politics," *The Christian Century* (December 21–28, 1994): 1211–1213.

5. Joerg Rieger and Pui-lan Kwok, *Occupy Religion: Theology of the Multitude* (Lanlam, MD: Rowman & Littlefield, 2013); Rita Nakashima Brock, "What Has Occupy Got to Do with Feminist Liberation Theology," *Journal of Feminist Studies in Religion*, 29, no. 2 (Fall 2013): 169–172; Jeremy Varon, "Joining a Party For a More Powerful Left," *Tikkun Magazine* 29, no. 2 (Spring 2014): 38–42.

6. Alicia Garza, "Herstory of the #BlackLivesMatter Movement," http://blacklivesmatter.com/herstory/; Terrence L. Johnson, "Black Lives Matter and the Black Church," *Berkley Forum,* October 19, 2016, https://berkleycenter.georgetown.edu/forum/religion-and-black-lives-matter/responses/black-lives-matter-and-the-black-church; Josiah Ulysses Young, III, "Do Black Lives Matter to 'God'?" *Black Theology* 13, no. 3 (November 2015): 210–218.

7. Daniel H. Levine, "Assessing the Impact of Liberation Theology in Latin America," *The Review of Politics* 50, no. 2 (Spring 1988): 241–263, and "On the Premature Reports of the Death of Liberation Theology," *The Review of Politics* 57, no. 1 (Winter 1995): 105–131; Claudio de Oliveria Ribeiro, "Has Liberation Theology Died?" *The Ecumenical Review* 51, no. 3 (July 1999): 304–314.

8. Kate Bowler, *Blessed: A History of the American Prosperity Gospel* (New York: Oxford University Press, 2013).

9. José Casanova, *Public Religions in the Modern World* (Chicago, IL: University of Chicago Press, 1994), 6–10. The emergence of the conservative Tea Party Movement in 2009 displayed strong religiously motivated activism; see "The Tea Party and Religion," Pew Research Center, February 23, 2011, http://www.pewforum.org/2011/02/23/tea-party-and-religion/.

10. John Rawls, "The Idea of Public Reason Revisited," *The University of Chicago Law Review* 64, no. 3 (Summer 1997): 765–807. See original work, *Political Liberalism* (New York, NY: Columbia University Press, 1993).

11. Peter L. Berger "The Descularization of the World: A Global Overview," in *The Desecularization of the World: Resurgent Religion and World Politics,* ed. Peter L. Berger (Washington, DC: W.B. Eerdmans, 1999), 1–18.

12. Vyacheslav Karpov, "Desecularization: A Conceptual Framework," *Journal of Church and State* 52, no. 2 (July 2010): 232–270.

Bibliography

ARCHIVES CONSULTED

Gutiérrez, Gustavo. Personal Library. Instituto Bartolomé de las Casas, Lima, Perú.

Herzog, Frederick Papers. David M. Rubenstein Rare Book & Manuscript Library, Duke University, Durham, NC.

Ruether, Rosemary Radford Papers. Burke Library, Columbia University, New York, NY.

Shaull, Richard Papers. Princeton Theological Seminary, Princeton, NJ.

Theology in the Americas Conference Archives. Schomburg Center for Research in Black Culture, New York, NY.

PRIMARY SOURCES

"Catholic Church Warms to Liberation Theology as Founder Heads to Vatican." *Guardian* (May 11, 2015). https://www.theguardian.com/world/2015/may/11/vatican-new-chapter-liberation-theology-founder-gustavo-Gutiérrez.

"Religion: Male and Female Theology." *Time Magazine* (June 27, 1960): 76.

"Life in a Defatalized World." *Time Magazine* (April 2, 1965): 82.

"Catholics Reject Forman Demands; Episcopal Council Also Gives Manifesto a Cool Reply." *New York Times* (May 10, 1969): 1.

"Both Marx and Jesus." *Time Magazine* (June 5, 1972): 57.

"Jesus the Liberator." *Time Magazine* (September 1, 1975): 44.

"The Chicano Struggle." Chicano Reflection Group. In *Theology in the Americas*. Edited by Sergio Torres and John Eagleson, 207–209, Maryknoll, NY: Orbis Books, 1976.

"Obama Pastor's Theology: Destroy 'The White Enemy.'" *World Net Daily* (March 17, 2008). http://www.wnd.com/2008/03/59230/.

"Religion and Intellectuals." *Partisan Review* 37, no. 2 (February 1950): 103–105.

"The Year's Top Stories: Political Christians, Christian Politics." *Christian Century* (December 21–28, 1994): 1211–1213.

"The Tea Party and Religion." Pew Research Center (February 23, 2011). http://www.pewforum.org/2011/02/23/tea-party-and-religion/.

"Vatican Analyst: Pope Distances Himself from Liberation Theology." *Catholic News Agency* (September 17, 2013). http://www.catholicnewsagency.com/news/vatican-analyst-pope-distanced-himself-from-liberation-theology/.

"Women Exploring Theology at Grailville." Conference proceeding, Loveland, Ohio, Church Women United, New York, NY, June 18–25, 1972.

Addams, Jane. *Twenty Years at Hull-House*. New York, NY: Signet Classics, 1961.

Alberdi, Juan Bautista. "Foundation and Points of Departure for the Political Organization of the Republic of Argentina." In *Nineteenth-Century Nation Building and the Latin American Intellectual Tradition: A Reader*. Edited by Janet Burke and Ted Humphrey, 199–201. Indianapolis, IN: Hackett, 2007.

Alston, Wallace M., et al. "Whatever Happened to Theology?" *Christianity and Crisis* (May 12, 1975): 106–120.

Alves, Rubem A. "Protestantism in Latin America: Its Ideological Function and Utopian Possibilities." *Ecumenical Review* 22, no. 1 (1970): 1–15.

———. *A Theology of Human Hope*. New York, NY: Corpus Books, 1971.

———. "Christian Realism: Ideology of the Establishment." *Christianity and Crisis* (September 17, 1973): 173–175.

Ames, Edward Scribner Ames. "The Validity of the Idea of God." *Journal of Religion* 1, no. 5 (1921): 462–481.

Arendt, Hannah. *The Origins of Totalitarianism*. New York, NY: Harcourt, Brace, 1951.

———. *The Human Condition*. Chicago, IL: University of Chicago Press, 1958.

Arendt, Hannah, and Jerome Kohn. *Essays in Understanding: 1930–1954*. New York, NY: Schocken Books, 1994.

Arguedas, José María. *Todas Las Sangres*. Buenos Aires: Editorial Losada, 1968.

———. *Deep Rivers*. Austin, TX: University of Texas Press, 1978.

———. *Yawar Fiesta*. Austin, TX: University of Texas Press, 1985.

Assmann, Hugo. *Theology for a Nomad Church*. Maryknoll, NY: Orbis Books, 1975.

Ateek, Naim Stifan. *Justice, and Only Justice: A Palestinian Theology of Liberation*. Maryknoll, NY: Orbis Books, 1989.

Axelrod, Steven Gould, Thomas J. Travisano, and Camille Roman, eds. *The New Anthology of American Poetry*. New Brunswick, NJ: Rutgers University Press, 2003.

Baldwin, James. *The Fire Next Time*. New York, NY: Dial Press, 1963.

Baraka, Amiri. *Home: Social Essays*. New York, NY: Morrow, 1966.

———. *The Autobiography of LeRoi Jones*. New York, NY: Freundlich Books, 1984.

Baraka, Amiri, and William J. Harris. *The LeRoi Jones/Amiri Baraka Reader*. New York, NY: Thunder's Mouth Press, 2000.

Barth, Karl. *The Humanity of God*. Richmond, VA: John Knox Press, 1960.

Barth, Karl, Geoffrey W. Bromiley, and Dietrich Braun. *Ethics*. New York, NY: Seabury Press, 1981.

Barth, Karl, and Edwyn Clement Hoskyns. *The Epistle to the Romans*. London: Oxford University Press, 1968.

Baum, Gregory. "The Christian Left at Detroit." In *Theology in the Americas*. Edited by Sergio Torres and John Eagleson, 399–429. Maryknoll, NY: Orbis Books, 1976.

Beard, Mary Ritter. *Woman as Force in History: A Study in Traditions and Realities*. New York, NY: Persea Books, 1987.

Beckford, Robert. *Jesus Is Dread: Black Theology and Black Culture in Britain*. London: Darton, Longman & Todd, 1998.

Bellah, Robert Neelly. "Civil Religion in America." *Daedalus* 96, no. 1 (Winter 1967): 1–21.

———. *The Broken Covenant: American Civil Religion in a Time of Trial*. New York, NY: Seabury Press, 1975.

Bennett, John C. *The Radical Imperative: From Theology to Social Ethics*. Philadelphia, PA: Westminster Press, 1975.

———. "Fitting the Liberation Theme in our Theological Agenda." *Christianity and Crisis* (July 18, 1977): 164–169.

———. "The Geneva Conference of 1966 as a Climatic Event." *Ecumenical Review* 37, no. 1 (January 1985): 26–33.

Bentley, Sally, and Claire Randall. "The Spirit Moving: A New Approach to Theologizing." *Christianity and Crisis* (February 4, 1974): 3–7.

Berger, Peter L. *The Noise of Solemn Assemblies: Christian Commitment and the Religious Establishment in America*. Garden City, NY: Doubleday, 1961.

———. *The Sacred Canopy: Elements of a Sociological Theory of Religion*. New York, NY: Anchor Books, 1967.

———. "A Sociological View of the Secularization of Theology." *Journal for the Scientific Study of Religion* 6, no. 1 (Spring 1967): 3–16.

———. *The Desecularization of the World: Resurgent Religion and World Politics*. Washington, DC: Ethics and Public Policy Center, W. B. Eerdmans, 1999.

Berneking, Nancy J., and Pamela Carter Joern. *Re-Memebering and Re-Imagining*. Cleveland, OH: Pilgrim Press, 1995.

Bilbao, Francisco. "Chilean Sociability." In *Nineteenth-Century Nation Building and the Latin American Intellectual Tradition: A Reader*. Edited by Janet Burke and Ted Humphrey, 102–104. Indianapolis, IN: Hackett, 2007.

Bloch, Ernst. *The Principle of Hope*. Cambridge, MA: MIT Press, 1995.

———. *The Spirit of Utopia*. Stanford, CA: Stanford University Press, 2000.

Blondel, Maurice. *Action: Essay on a Critique of Life and a Science of Practice*. Notre Dame, IN: University of Notre Dame, 1984.

Bonhoeffer, Dietrich, John W. De Gruchy, and Isabel Best. *Letters and Papers from Prison*. Minneapolis, MN: Fortress Press, 2010.

Briggs, Kenneth A. "18 Christian Leaders Attack 'Debilitating' Secular Influences." *New York Times* (January 28, 1975): 30.

Brock, Rita Nakashima. "What Has Occupy Got to Do with Feminist Liberation Theology?" *Journal of Feminist Studies in Religion* 29, no. 2 (Fall 2013): 169–172.

Bucher, Glenn R. "Toward a Liberation Theology of the 'Oppressor.'" *Journal of the American Academy of Religion* 44, no. 3 (September 1976): 517–534.

Burke, Janet, and Ted Humphrey. *Nineteenth-Century Nation Building and the Latin American Intellectual Tradition: A Reader*. Indianapolis, IN: Hackett, 2007.

Bushnell, Horace. "Discourses on Christian Nurture." Massachusetts Sabbath School Society. http://catalog.hathitrust.org/api/volumes/oclc/8260134.html.

Câmara, Hélder. *Spiral of Violence*. London: Sheed and Ward, 1971.

Camilo, Torres. *Father Camilo Revolutionary Writings*. New York, NY: Harper & Row, 1969.

Camus, Albert. *The Rebel: An Essay on Man in Revolt*. New York, NY: Vintage Books, 1991.

Cardenal, Ernesto. *Salmos*. Buenos Aires: Ediciones C. Lohl, 1969.

———. *In Cuba*. New York, NY: New Directions, 1974.

———. *The Gospel in Solentiname*. Maryknoll, NY: Orbis Books, 1976.

Cardoso, Fernando Henrique, and Enzo Faletto. *Dependencia y desarrollo en América Latina; Ensayo de interpretación sociológica*. Mexico City: Siglo Veintiuno Editores, 1969.

Carey, John J. "Black Theology: An Appraisal of the Internal and External Issues." *Theological Studies* 33, no. 4 (December 1972): 684–697.

Carmichael, Stokely. "What We Want." *New York Review of Books* (September 22, 1966): 5–8.

———. *Stokely Speaks: Black Power Back to Pan-Africanism*. New York, NY: Random House, 1971.

Carmichael, Stokely, and Charles V. Hamilton. *Black Power: The Politics of Liberation in America*. New York, NY: Random House, 1967.

Carpentier, Alejo. *Explosion in a Cathedral*. Boston, MA: Little, Brown, 1963.

Casas, Bartolomé de las. *Brevísima relación de la destrucción de las Indias*. La Habana, Cuba: Ed. de Ciencias Sociales, 1977.

Case, Shirley Jackson. *The Christian Philosophy of History*. Chicago, IL: University of Chicago Press, 1943.

Channing, William Ellery. "Self-Culture." In *William Ellery Channing: Selected Writings*. Edited by David Robinson. New York, NY: Paulist Press, 1985.

Chodorow, Nancy. *The Reproduction of Mothering: Psychoanalysis and the Sociology of Gender*. Berkeley, CA: University of California Press, 1978.

Christ, Carol P. "The New Feminist Theology: A Review of the Literature." *Religious Studies Review* 3, no. 4 (1977): 203–212.

Christ, Carol P., and Judith Plaskow. *Womanspirit Rising: A Feminist Reader in Religion*. San Francisco: Harper & Row, 1979.

Consejo Episcopal Latinoamericano. *The Church in the Present-Day Transformation of Latin America in the Light of the Council. II. Conclusions.* Washington, DC: Division for Latin America, 1973.

Couch, Beatriz Melano. *La mujer y la Iglesia.* Buenos Aires, Argentina: El Escudo, 1973.

———. "Statement by Beatriz Melano Couch." In *Theology in the Americas.* Edited by Sergio Torres and John Eagleton, 374–376. Maryknoll, NY: Orbis Books, 1976.

Clark, J. Michael. *A Place to Start: Toward an Unapologetic Gay Liberation Theology.* Dallas, TX: Monument Press, 1989.

Cleage, Albert B. *The Black Messiah.* Kansas City, KS: Sheed and Ward, 1969.

Cleaver, Eldridge. *Soul on Ice.* New York, NY: McGraw-Hill, 1967.

Cleaver, Richard. *Know My Name: A Gay Liberation Theology.* Louisville, KY: Westminster/John Knox Press, 1995.

Coleman, John A. "Civil Religion." *Sociological Analysis* 31 (Summer 1970): 67–677.

———. "Civil Religion and Liberation Theology." In *Theology in the Americas.* Edited by Sergio Torres and John Eagleton, 113–138. Maryknoll, NY: Orbis Books, 1976.

Coleridge, Samuel Taylor. *The Complete Works of Samuel Taylor Coleridge. With an Introductory Essay Upon His Philosophical and Theological Opinions.* New York, NY: Harper & Brothers, 1863.

Coleridge, Samuel Taylor, and Henry Nelson Coleridge. *Confessions of an Inquiring Spirit, and Some Miscellaneous Pieces, Etc.* London: Edward Moxon, 1853.

Collins, Sheila D. *A Different Heaven and Earth: A Feminist Perspective on Religion.* Valley Forge, PA: Judson Press, 1974.

Comte, Auguste. *System of Positive Polity or Treatise on Sociology: Instituting the Religion of Humanity.* New York, NY: Franklin, 1973.

Cone, James H. "Christianity and Black Power." In *Is Anybody Listening to Black America?* Edited by C. Eric Lincoln. New York, NY: Seabury Press, 1968, 3–9.

———. *Black Theology and Black Power.* New York, NY: Seabury Press, 1969.

———. *A Black Theology of Liberation.* Philadelphia, PA: Lippincott, 1970.

———. "Christian Theology and the Afro-American Revolution." *Christian Century* (June 8, 1970): 123–125.

———. *The Spirituals and the Blues: An Interpretation.* New York, NY: Seabury Press, 1972.

———. *God of the Oppressed.* New York, NY: Seabury Press, 1975.

———. *My Soul Looks Back.* Nashville, TN: Abingdon, 1982.

———. *Martin & Malcolm & America: A Dream or a Nightmare.* Maryknoll, NY: Orbis Books, 1991.

———. "From Geneva to Sao Paulo: A Dialogue between Black Theology and Latin American Liberation Theology." In *Black Theology: A Documentary History* Volume II. Edited by James H. Cone and Gayraud S. Wilmore. Maryknoll, NY: Orbis Books, 1993, 371–387.

———. *For My People: Black Theology and the Black Church*. Maryknoll, NY: Orbis Books, 1994.

Cone, James H., and Gayraud S. Wilmore. *Black Theology: A Documentary History. Vol. I, 1966–1979*. Maryknoll, NY: Orbis Books, 1993.

———. *Black Theology: A Documentary History. Vol. II, 1980–1992*. Maryknoll, NY: Orbis Books, 1993.

Cox, Harvey Gallagher. *God's Revolution and Man's Responsibility*. Valley Forge, PA: Judson Press, 1965.

———. *The Secular City: Secularization and Urbanization in Theological Perspective*. New York, NY: Collier Books, 1990.

Crites, Stephen. "The Narrative Quality of Experience." *Journal of the American Academy of Religion* 39, no. 3 (September 1971): 291–311.

Cruse, Harold. *The Crisis of the Negro Intellectual*. New York, NY: Morrow, 1967.

———. *Rebellion or Revolution?* New York, NY: Morrow, 1968.

Cruz, Richard, and Mario T. Garcia. *Chicano Liberation Theology: The Writings and Documents of Richard Cruz and Católicos Por La Raza*. Dubuque, IA: Kendall/Hunt, 2010.

Daly, Mary. *Beyond God the Father: Toward a Philosophy of Women's Liberation*. Boston, MA: Beacon Press, 1973.

———. *Gyn/Ecology The Metaethics of Radical Feminism*. Boston, MA: Beacon Press, 1978.

———. *The Church and the Second Sex*. Boston, MA: Beacon Press, 1985.

de Beauvoir, Simone, and H.M. Parshley. *The Second Sex*. New York, NY: Alfred A. Knopf, 1993.

de Santa Ana, Julio. "The Influence of Bonhoeffer on the Theology of Liberation." *Ecumenical Review* 28, no. 2 (1976): 188–197.

Deloria, Vine. *God Is Red*. New York, NY: Grosset & Dunlap, 1973.

Dewey, John, and Thomas M. Alexander. *A Common Faith*. New Haven, CT: Yale University Press, 2013.

Douglass, Frederick, and David W. Blight. *Narrative of the Life of Frederick Douglas, an American Slave, Written by Himself*. New York, NY: Bedford Books of St. Martin's Press, 1993.

Du Bois, W.E.B. *Dusk of Dawn: An Essay Toward an Autobiography of a Race Concept*. New York, NY: Harcourt, Brace, 1940.

———. *Darkwater: Voices from within the Veil*. New York, NY: AMS Press, 1969.

———. *The Soul of Black Folk*. New York, NY: Penguin Books, 1996.

———. *The Negro Church: Report of a Social Study Made Under the Direction of Atlanta University; Together with the Proceedings of the Eighth Conference for the Study of the Negro Problems, Held at Atlanta University, May 26th, 1903*. Walnut Creek, CA: Altamira Press, 2003.

Durkheim, Emile. *The Elementary Forms of the Religious Life*. Oxford: Oxford University Press, 2001.

Edwards, Herbert O. "Black Theology and Liberation Theology." In *Theology in the Americas*. Edited by Sergio Torres and John Eagleson, 177–191. Maryhnoll, NY: Orbis Books, 1976.

Edwards, Jonathan, and John E. Smith. *Religious Affections*. New Haven, CT: Yale University Press, 1987.

Ellison, Ralph. *Invisible Man*. New York, NY: Modern Library/Random House, 1947.

Ely, Richard T. *Social Aspects of Christianity and Other Essays*. New York, NY: Thomas Y. Crowell, 1889. http://onlinebooks.library.upenn.edu/webbin/book/lookupid?key=ha010621321

Engels, Friedrich. *The Peasant War in Germany*. New York, NY: International Publishers, 2000.

Engels, Friedrich, and Lewis Henry Morgan. *The Origin of the Family, Private Property, and the State*. New York, NY: Pathfinder Press, 1972.

Equiano, Olaudah. *The Interesting Narrative and Other Writings*. London: Penguin, 2003.

Fanon, Frantz. *Black Skin, White Masks*. Los Angeles, CA: Braille Institute of America, 1967.

Fanon, Frantz, and Richard Philcox. *The Wretched of the Earth*. New York, NY: Grove Press, 2004.

Farrar, Stephan. "Liberation Theology Activist: Pope Francis is One of Us." *ChurchMilitant* (December 27, 2016). http://www.churchmilitant.com/news/article/liberation-theology-activist-pope-francis-is-one-of-us.

Feuerbach, Ludwig, and George Eliot. *The Essence of Christianity*. New York, NY: Cosimo, 2008.

Fiorenza, Elizabeth Schüssler. "Feminist Theology as a Critical Theology of Liberation." *Theological Studies* 36, no. 4 (December 1975): 605–626.

Flinders, Carol Lee. *At the Root of This Longing: Reconciling a Spiritual Hunger and a Feminist Thirst*. San Francisco, CA: HarperSanFrancisco, 1981.

Fontaine, W.T. "An Interpretation of Contemporary Negro Thought from the Standpoint of the Sociology of Knowledge." *Journal of Negro History* 25, no. 1 (1940): 6–13.

Forman, James. "The Black Manifesto." Archives of the Episcopal Church. http://www.episcopalarchives.org/Afro-Anglican_history/exhibit/specialgc/black_manifesto.php.

Freire, Paulo, and Myra Bergman Ramos. *Pedagogy of the Oppressed*. Harmondsworth, UK: Penguin, 1996.

Freire, Paulo, et al. "Black Theology and Latin American Liberation Theology." In *Black Theology: A Documentary History*. Edited by James H. Cone and Gayraud S. Wilmore, 404–408. Maryknoll, NY: Orbis Books, 1993.

Friedan, Betty. *The Feminine Mystique*. New York, NY: Dell Publishing, 1963.

Fuller, Margaret, and Larry J. Reynolds. *Woman in the Nineteenth Century: An Authoritative Text, Backgrounds, Criticism*. New York, NY: W.W. Norton, 1998.

Galeano, Eduardo. *Open Veins of Latin America: Five Centuries of the Pillage of a Continent*. Carlton North, AU: Scribe Publications, 2009.

García Márquez, Gabriel. *One Hundred Years of Solitude*. New York, NY: Harper & Row, 1970.

Garza, Alicia. "Herstory of the #BlackLivesMatter Movement." http://blacklivesmatter.com/herstory/.

George, Henry. *Progress and Poverty*. New York, NY: Cosimo, 2005.

Gilbert, Olive, Sojourner Truth, and Nell Irvin Painter. *Narrative of Sojourner Truth: A Bondswoman of Olden Time, with a History of Her Labors and Correspondence Drawn from Her Book of Life; Also, A Memorial Chapter*. New York, NY: Penguin Books, 1998.

Gilman, Charlotte Perkins. *Women and Economics: A Study of the Economic Relation between Men and Women as a Factor in Social Evolution*. New York, NY: Putnam, 1912.

———. *Herland*. Auckland: Floating Press, 1915. http://www.gutenberg.org/ebooks/32.

———. *His Religion and Hers: A Study of the Faith of our Fathers and the Work of our Mothers*. Westport, CT: Hyperion Press, 1976.

Gladden, Washington. *Social Salvation*. Cambridge, MA: Riverside Press, 1902.

Gogarten, Friedrich. *The Reality of Faith: The Problem of Subjectivism in Theology*. Philadelphia, PA: Westminster Press, 1959.

Goldstein, Valerie Saiving. "The Human Situation: A Feminine View." *Journal of Religion* 40, no. 2 (April 1960): 100–112.

Gore, Dayo F., Jeanne Theoharis, and Komozi Woodard. *Want to Start a Revolution?: Radical Women in the Black Freedom Struggle*. New York, NY: University Press, 2009.

Graham, David A. "Jeremiah Wright is Still Angry at Barack Obama." *Atlantic* (September 26, 2015). https://www.theatlantic.com/politics/archive/2015/09/what-ever-happened-to-jeremiah-wright/406522/.

Grant, Jacquelyn. "Black Theology and the Black Woman." In *Black Theology: A Documentary History*. Edited by James H. Cone and Gayroud S. Wilmore, 323–338. Maryknoll, NY: Orbis Books, 1983.

———. *White Women's Christ and Black Women's Jesus: Feminist Christology and Womanist Response*. Atlanta, GA: Scholars Press, 1989.

Grimké, Sarah Moore, and Elizabeth Ann Bartlett. *Letters on the Equality of the Sexes, and Other Essays*. New Haven, CT: Yale University Press, 1988.

Guevara, Ernesto, and David Deutschmann. *Che Guevara Reader: Writings by Ernesto Che Guevara on Guerrilla Strategy, Politics & Revolution*. New York, NY: Ocean Press, 1997.

Gutiérrez, Gustavo. *Teología de la liberación*. Lima: CEP, 1971.

———. *A Theology of Liberation*. Maryknoll, NY: Orbis Books, 1973.

———. "Two Theological Perspectives: Liberation Theology and Progressive Theology." In *The Emergent Gospel: Theology from the Underside of History: Papers from the Ecumenical*

Dialogue of Third World Theologians, Dar Es Salaam, August 5–12, 1976. Edited by Sergio Torres and Virginia Fabella, 227–255. Maryknoll, NY: Orbis Books, 1978.

———. *The Power of the Poor in History*. Maryknoll, NY: Orbis Books, 1983.

———. *On Job: God-Talk and the Suffering of the Innocent*. Maryknoll, NY: Orbis Books, 1987.

———. *A Theology of Liberation: History, Politics, and Salvation*. Maryknoll, NY: Orbis Books, 1988.

———. *Las Casas: In Search of the Poor of Jesus Christ*. Maryknoll, NY: Orbis Books, 1993.

Gutiérrez, Gustavo, and James B. Nickoloff. *Essential Writings*. Maryknoll, NY: Orbis Books, 1996.

Hacker, Helen Mayer. "Women as a Minority Group." *Social Forces* 30 (1951): 60–69. http://media.pfeiffer.edu/lridener/courses/womminor.html.

Hanisch, Carol. "The Personal is Political." In *Notes from the Second Year Women's Liberation, Major Writings of the Radical Feminists*. Edited by Shulamith Firestone and Anne Koedt, 76–77. New York, NY: Radical Feminism, 1970.

Harding, Vincent. "Black Power and the American Christ." *Christian Century*, no. 10 (January 4, 1967): 10–13.

———. "The Religion of Black Power." In *The Religious Situation: 1968: The First in a Series of Annual Volumes*. Edited by Donald R. Cutler, 3–38. Boston, MA: Beacon Press, 1968.

Harrison, Beverly. "Statement by Beverly Harrison." In *Theology in the Americas*. Edited by Sergio Torres and John Eagleton, 367–369. Maryknoll, NY: Orbis Books, 1976.

Hasset, John J., and Braulio Munoz. *Looking North: Writings from Spanish America on the US, 1800 to the Present*. Tuscon, AZ: University of Arizona Press, 2012.

Hayden, Casey, and Mary King. "A Kind of Memo." In *Personal Politics: The Roots of Women's Liberation in the Civil Rights Movement and the New Left*. Edited by Sarah M. Evans, 235–238. New York, NY: Vintage Books, 1979.

Heer, Jeet. "Conservatives to Pope Francis; Stick with Salvation. We'll Handle the Politics." *New Republic* (September 22, 2015). https://newrepublic.com/article/122889/pope-franciss-conservative-critics-just-dont-his-politics.

Hegel, Georg Wilhelm Friedrich, and Sibree J. Sibree. *The Philosophy of History*. New York, NY: Wiley, 1944.

Henry, Carl F.H. *God, Revelation, and Authority*. Waco, TX: Word Books, 1976.

———. *The Uneasy Conscience of Modern Fundamentalism*. Grand Rapids, MI: W. B. Eerdmans, 2003.

Herzog, Frederick. "The Political Gospel." *Christian Century* (November 18, 1970): 1380–1383.

———. *Liberation Theology: Liberation in the Light of the Fourth Gospel*. New York, NY: Seabury Press, 1972.

———. "Liberation Theology Begins at Home." *Christianity and Crisis* (May 13, 1974): 94–98.

———. "Introduction: On Liberating Liberation Theology." In *Theology for a Nomad Church*. by Hugo Assmann, 1–20. Maryknoll, NY: Orbis Books, 1975.

———. "Birth Pangs: Liberation Theology in North America." *Christian Century* (December 15, 1976): 1120–1122.

———. "Pre-Bicentennial U.S.A. in the Liberation Process." In *Theology in the Americas*. Edited by Sergio Torres and John Eagleson, 139–174. Maryknoll, NY: Orbis Books, 1976.

———. "God: Black or White." In *Theology from the Belly of the Whale: A Frederick Herzog Reader*. Edited by Joerg Rieger, 58–72. Harrisburg, PA: Trinity Press International, 1999.

———. "Theology of Liberation." In *Theology from the Belly of the Whale: A Frederick Herzog Reader*. Edited by Joerg Rieger, 80–90. Harrisburg, PA: Trinity Press International, 1999.

Hook, Sidney. "A Failure of Nerve." *Partisan Review* 10, no. 1 (1943): 1–23.

Horkheimer, Max, and Theodor W. Adorno. *Dialectic of Enlightenment*. New York, NY: Continuum, 2001.

Horney, Karen, and Harold Kelman. *Feminine Psychology*. New York, NY: W.W. Norton, 1973.

Isasi-Díaz, Ada María. *Mujerista Theology: A Theology for the Twenty-First Century*. Maryknoll, NY: Orbis Books, 1996.

Irudayaraj, Xavier. *Emerging Dalit Theology*. Madras, India: Jesuit Theological Secretariat, 1990.

James, William. *William James: Pragmatism and Other Writings*. New York, NY: Penguin Books, 2000.

———. *The Varieties of Religious Experience: A Study in Human Nature*. New York, NY: Modern Library, 2002.

Jasper, Karl, and Rudolf Bultmann. *Myth and Christianity: An Inquiry into the Possibility of Religion Without Myth*, New York, NY: Noonday Press, 1958.

Johnson, Terrence L. "Black Lives Matter and the Black Church." *Berkley Forum* (October 19, 2016). https://berkleycenter.georgetown.edu/forum/religion-and-black-lives-matter/responses/black-lives-matter-and-the-black-church.

Jones, Le Roi. "Cuba Libre." *Evergreen Review* (November–December 1960): 346–353.

Jones, William R. "Theodicy and Methodology in Black Theology: A Critique of Washington, Cone and Cleage." *Harvard Theological Review* 64, no. 4 (October 1971): 541–557.

———. *Is God a White Racist? A Preamble to Black Theology*. New York, NY: Anchor Press, 1973.

Kant, Immanuel. "An Answer to the Question: What is Enlightenment." In *What is Enlightenment?: Eighteenth-Century Answers and Twentieth-Century Questions*. Edited by James Schmidt, 58–64. Berkeley, CA: University of California Press, 1996.

Kant, Immanuel, Allen Wood, and George Giovanni. *Religion Within the Boundaries of Mere Reason and Other Writings*. Cambridge: Cambridge University Press, 1998.

Kant, Immanuel, and H.J. Paton. *Groundwork of the Metaphysic of Morals*. New York, NY: Harper & Row, 1964.

Ketteler, Wilhelm Emmanuel, and Rupert Ederer. *The Social Teachings of Wilhelm Emmanuel Von Ketteler: Bishop of Mainz (1811–1877)*. Washington, DC: University Press of America, 1981.

Kidd, Sue Monk. *The Dance of the Dissident Daughter: A Woman's Journey from Christian Tradition to the Sacred Feminine*. San Francisco, CA: HarperSanFrancisco, 1996.

Kierkegaard, Søren, and Howard V. Hong. *Concluding Unscientific Postscript to Philosophical Fragments*. Princeton, NJ: Princeton University Press, 1992.

King, Martin L. "Mas allay de Vietnam." [Beyond Vietnam] *Cristianismo y Sociedad* VI, no. 16–17 (1968): 42–44.

———. "Statement to the Press, August 20, 1965." Los Angeles, CA. http://www.thekingcenter.org/archive/document/mlk-press-statement-regarding-riots-los-angeles.

———. "My Dream." The King Center archive, *Chicago Defender* (December 19, 1966), 39. http://www.thekingcenter.org/archive/document/chicago-defender-my-dream#

———. "Letter from Birmingham Jail." The Martin Luther King, Jr. Research and Education Institute. http://www.thekingcenter.org/archive/document/letter-birmingham-city-jail-0

King, Martin Luther, and Clayborne Carson. *Stride Toward Freedom: The Montgomery Story*. Boston, MA: Beacon Press, 2010.

King, Martin Luther, Coretta Scott King, and Vincent Harding. *Where do we go from here: Chaos or Community?* Boston, MA: Beacon Press, 2010.

Kozloff, Nikolas. "The Pope's Holy War Against Liberation Theology." NACLA (no date given). http://nacla.org/news/popes-holy-war-against-liberation-theology.

Lacan, Jacques, Héloïse Fink, and Bruce Fink. *Ecrits: The First Complete Edition in English*. New York, NY: W.W. Norton, 2006.

Lame Chantre, Manuel Quintín. *Los pensamientos del indio que se educó dentro de las selvas colombianas*. Bogotá: Organización Nacional Indígena de Colombia, 1987.

Lastarria, Victorino, and R. Kelly Washbourne. *Literary Memoirs*. Oxford: Oxford University Press, 2000.

Leibniz, Gottfried Wilhelm, and Austin Farrer. *Theodicy: Essays on the Goodness of God, the Freedom of Man, and the Origin of Evil*. Eugene, OR: Wipf and Stock, 2001.

LeMone, Archie. "When Traditional Theology Meets Black and Liberation Theology." *Christianity and Crisis* (September 1973): 177–178.

Lerner, Gerda. *The Grimké Sisters from South Carolina: Rebels against Slavery*. Boston, MA: Houghton Mifflin, 1967.

Lester, Julius. "Review: The Black Experience in Religion." *Christianity and Crisis* 35 (March 31, 1975): 73–75.

Lincoln, C. Eric. *The Black Experience in Religion*. Garden City, NY: Anchor Press, 1974.

Locke, Alain, and Stanley Francis Helmore. *The New Negro*. New York, NY: A. and C. Boni, 1925. http://www.umass.edu/afroam/downloads/allen.newnegro.pdf.

Locke, John. *A Letter Concerning Toleration*. Buffalo, NY: Prometheus Books, 1990.
Locke, John, and John W. Yolton. *An Essay Concerning Human Understanding*. London: Dent, 1974.
Lubac, Henri de. *The Mystery of the Supernatural*. New York, NY: Crossroad, 1998.
Luther, Martin. *Treatise on Christian Liberty*. Philadelphia, PA: Fortress Press, 1957.
Macintosh, Douglas C. "Can Pragmatism Furnish a Philosophical Basis for Theology?" *Harvard Theological Review* 3, no. 1 (January 1910): 125–135.
———. *The Problem of Religious Knowledge*. New York, NY: Harper & Brothers, 1940.
Mannheim, Karl. *Diagnosis of our Time*. New York, NY: Oxford University Press, 1944.
Mannheim, Karl, Louis Wirth, and Edward Shils. *Ideology and Utopia: An Introduction to the Sociology of Knowledge*. New York, NY: Harcourt, Brace, 1949.
Marable, Manning. "The Rainbow Coalition: Jesse Jackson and the Politics of Ethnicity." *Crosscurrents* 34, no. 1 (Spring 1984): 21–42.
Marable, Manning, Nishani Frazier, and Campbell McMillian. *Freedom on My Mind: The Columbia Documentary History of the African American Experience*. New York, NY: Columbia University Press, 2003.
Marcuse, Herbert. *Eros and Civilization*. New York, NY: Vintage Books, 1955.
———. *Reason and Revolution: Hegel and the Rise of Social Theory*. Boston, MA: Beacon Press, 1960.
———. *An Essay on Liberation*. London: Allen Lane, 1969.
———. *One-Dimensional Man: Studies in the Ideology of Advanced Industrial Society*. Boston: Beacon Press, 1991.
Mariátegui, José Carlos *Seven Interpretive Essays on Peruvian Reality*. Austin, TX: University of Texas Press, 1990.
Mariátegui, José Carlos, and Michael Pearlman. *The Heroic and Creative Meaning of Socialism*. Atlantic Highlands, NJ: Humanities Press, 1996.
Maritain, Jacques. *The Range of Reason*. London: Geoffrey Bles, 1953. University of Notre Dame Jacques Maritain Center, http://maritain.nd.edu/jmc/etext/range14.htm.
———. *Reflections on America*. New York, NY: Charles Scribner's Sons, 1958.
———. *Integral Humanism: Temporal and Spiritual Problems of a New Christendom*. New York, NY: Charles Scribner's Sons, 1968.
Martí, José, Esther Louise Allen, and Roberto González Echevarría. *José Martí: Selected Writings*. New York, NY: Penguin Books, 2002.
Marx, Karl, Friedrich Engels, and C.J. Arthur. *The German Ideology*. New York, NY: International Publishers, 1972.
Marx, Karl, and Joseph J. O'Malley. *Critique of Hegel's Philosophy of Right*. Cambridge: Cambridge University Press, 1977.
Marx, Karl, and Friedrich Engels. *Capital: A Critique of Political Economy*. New York, NY: International Publishers, 1967.
Mathews, Shailer. *The Growth of the Idea of God*. New York, NY: Macmillan, 1931.

McFague, Sallie. *Speaking in Parables: A Study in Metaphor and Theology*. Philadelphia, PA: Fortress Press, 1975.

Mead, Margaret. *Male and Female: A Study of the Sexes in a Changing World*. New York, NY: HarperCollins, 2002.

———. *Sex and Temperament in Three Primitive Societies*. New York, NY: Perennial, 2008.

Mendieta, Eduardo, ed. *The Frankfurt School on Religion: Key Writings by the Major Thinkers*. New York, NY: Routledge, 2005.

Metz, John B. "Religion and Society in the Light of Political Theology." *Harvard Theological Review* 61, no. 4 (1968): 507–523.

———. *Theology of the World*. New York, NY: Herder and Herder, 1969.

Míguez Bonino, José. *Doing Theology in a Revolutionary Situation*. Philadelphia, PA: Fortress Press, 1975.

Millett, Kate. *Sexual Politics*. Garden City, NY: Doubleday, 1970.

Mills, C. Wright. *The Sociological Imagination*. New York, NY: Oxford University Press, 1959.

———. Listen, Yankee: The Cuban Case Against the United States." *Harper's Magazine* (December 1960): 31–37.

———. "Letter to the New Left." In *The Politics of Truth: Selected Writings of C. Wright Mills*. Edited by John H. Summers, 255–266. New York, NY: Oxford University Press, 2008.

———. "A Pagan Sermon to the Christian Clergy." In *The Politics of Truth: Selected Writings of C. Wright Mills*. Edited by John H. Summers, 163–172. New York, NY: Oxford University Press, 2008.

Miranda, José Porfirio. *Marx and the Bible: A Critique of the Philosophy of Oppression*. Maryknoll, NY: Orbis Books, 1974.

Moltmann, Jürgen. *The Crucified God: The Cross of Christ As the Foundation and Criticism of Christian Theology*. New York, NY: Harper & Row, 1974.

———. "An Open Letter to José Miquez Bonino." *Christianity and Crisis* 36 (March 29, 1976): 57–63.

———. *Theology of Hope: On the Ground and the Implications of a Christian Eschatology*. Minneapolis: Fortress Press, 1993.

Mora, José Maria Luis. "On Ecclesiastical Wealth." In *Nineteenth Century Nation Building and the Latin American Intellectual Tradition*. Edited by Janet Burke and Ted Humphreys. Indianapolis, IN: Hackett, 2007, 37–50.

Morgan, Robin. *Sisterhood is Powerful: An Anthology of Writings from the Women's Liberation Movement*. New York, NY: Random House, 1970.

Mott, Lucretia. "Not Christianity, but Priestcraft." In *Feminism: The Essential Historical Writings*. Edited by Miriam Schneir, 99–102. New York: Vintage Books, 1994.

Mumford, Lewis. *The City in History: Its Origins, Its Transformations, and Its Prospects*. New York: Harcourt, Brace & World, 1961.

Murray, Pauli. *Pauli Murray: The Autobiography of a Black Activist, Feminist, Lawyer, Priest, and Poet*. Knoxville, TN: University of Tennessee Press, 1989.

Myrdal, Gunnar. *An American Dilemma: The Negro Problem and Modern Democracy*. New York, NY; London: Harper & Brothers, 1944.

Nasaw, Daniel. "Controversial Comments Made by Rev. Jeremiah Wright." *Guardian* (March 18, 2008). http://www.theguardian.com/world/2008/mar/18/barackobama.uselections20083.

National Conference of Black Churchmen. "Black Power Statement, July 31, 1966." In *Afro-American Religious History: A Documentary Witness*. Edited by Milton C. Sernett, 555–566. Durham, N.C.: Duke University Press, 1985.

Neuhaus, Richard J. "Liberation Theology and the Captivities of Jesus." *Worldview* 16, no. 6 (June 1973): 41–48.

Neuhaus, Richard J., and Peter Berger. "The Hartford Declaration." *Theology Today* 32, no. 1 (April 1975): 94–97.

Niebuhr, Reinhold. *Beyond Tragedy: Essays on the Christian Interpretation of History*. London: Nisbet, 1937.

———. *Moral Man and Immoral Society: A Study in Ethics and Politics*. New York, NY: Charles Scribner's Sons, 1960.

Niebuhr, H. Richard. "The Irreligion of Communist and Capitalist." *Christian Century* 47 (October 29, 1930): 1306–1307.

———. *The Kingdom of God in America*. New York, NY: Harper, 1937.

———. *The Meaning of Revelation*. New York, NY: Macmillan, 1941.

———. *The Social Sources of Denominationalism*. Hamden, CT: Shoe String Press, 1954.

———. *Christ and Culture*. San Francisco, CA: HarperSanFrancisco, 2001.

Noble, S. "Under the Pope's 'Liberation Theology,' the Poor Suffer Most." *Independent Sentinel* (September 25, 2015). http://www.independentsentinel.com/under-the-popes-liberation-theology-the-poor-suffer-most/.

O'Connor, James T., and Conferencia General del Episcopado Latinoamericano. "Liberation: Towards a Theology for the Church in the World, According to the Second General Conference of Latin American Bishops at Medellin, 1968." *Officium Libri Catholici*, 1972.

Paine, Thomas. *The Age of Reason: Being an Investigation of True and Fabulous Theology*. New York, NY; London: G.P. Putnam's Sons, 1896. http://www.gutenberg.org/ebooks/3743.

———. *Common Sense (1776)*. Charlottesville, VA: University of Virginia Library, 1993. http://search.ebscohost.com/login.aspx?direct=true&scope=site&db=nlebk&db=nlabk&AN=2011049.

Pannenberg, Wolfhart, Rolf Rendtorff, Trutz Rendtorff, and Ulrich Wilkens. *Revelation as History*. New York, NY: Macmillan, 1968.

Paz, Octavio. *El Laberinto De La Soledad*. México City: Cuadernos Americanos, 1950.

Peirce, Charles Sanders, and Nathan Houser. *The Essential Peirce: Selected Philosophical Writings Vol. 2*. Bloomington, IN: Indiana University Press, 2001.

Phillips, Francis. "Pope Francis was all too familiar with Liberation Theology, that's why he opposed it." *Catholic Herald* (June 14, 2013). http://www.catholicherald.co.uk/commentandblogs/2013/06/14/pope-francis-was-all-too-familiar-with-liberation-theology-thats-why-he-opposed-it/.

Plaskow, Judith. *Sex, Sin, and Grace: Women's Experience and the Theologies of Reinhold Niebuhr and Paul Tillich*. Latham, MD: University Press of America, 1980.

Pope Francis. *Apostolic Exhortation Evangelii Gaudium*, Rome: The Vatican, 2013. http://w2.vatican.va/content/francesco/en/apost_exhortations/documents/papa-francesco_esortazione-ap_20131124_evangelii-gaudium.html.

Pope Leo XIII. *Rerum Novarum*. Rome: The Vatican, 1891. http://www.vatican.va/holy_father/leo_xiii/encyclicals/documents/hf_l-xiii_enc_15051891_rerum-novarum_en.html.

Pope Paul VI. *Gaudium Et Spes: Pastoral Constitution on the Church in the Modern World*. Rome: Second Vatican Council, November 7, 1965. http://www.vatican.va/archive/hist_councils/ii_vatican_council/documents/vat-ii_cons_19651207_gaudium-et-spes_en.html.

———. *Evangelii Nuntiandi*. Rome: The Vatican, 1975. http://www.vatican.va/holy_father/paul_vi/apost_exhortations/documents/hf_p-vi_exh_19751208_evangelii-nuntiandi_en.html.

Pope Pius X. *Pascendi Dominici Gregis: Encyclical of Pope Pius X on the Doctrine of the Modernist*. Rome: The Vatican, 1907. http://www.vatican.va/holy_father/pius_x/encyclicals/documents/hf_p-x_enc_19070908_pascendi-dominici-gregis_en.html.

Ramos, Samuel. *Profile of Man and Culture in Mexico*. Austin, TX: University of Texas Press, 1962.

Ransom, Reverdy C. *The Pilgrimage of Harriet Ransom's Son*. Nashville: Sunday School Union, 1949.

Ransom, Reverdy C., and Anthony B. Pinn. *Making the Gospel Plain: The Writings of Bishop Reverdy C. Ransom*. Harrisburg, PA: Trinity Press International, 1999.

Ratzinger, Cardinal Joseph. *Instructions on Christian Freedom and Liberation*. Washington, DC: Publishing and Promotion Services, United States Catholic Conference, 1986.

———. "Instructions of Certain Aspects of the 'Theology of Liberation.'" The Vatican (August 6, 1994). http://www.vatican.va/roman_curia/congregations/cfaith/documents/rc_con_cfaith_doc_19840806_theology-liberation_en.html.

Rauschenbusch, Walter. "The Problem of the Black Man." *American Missionary* 68, no. 3 (1914): 732.

———. *A Theology for the Social Gospel*. Memphis TN: General Books, 2010.

Rauschenbusch, Walter, Anthony Campolo, and Paul Rauschenbusch. *Christianity and the Social Crisis in the 21st Century: The Classic that Woke Up the Church*. San Francisco, CA: HarperSanFrancisco, 2008.

Richey, Russell E., and Donald G. Jones. *American Civil Religion*. New York, NY: Harper & Row, 1974.

Riesman, David. *The Lonely Crowd: A Study of the Changing American Character*. New Haven, CT: Yale University Press, 1950.

Ritschl, Albrecht, H.R. Mackintosh, and A.B. Macaulay. *The Christian Doctrine of Justification and Reconciliation: The Positive Development of the Doctrine*. Memphis, TN: General Books, 2010.

Roberts, J. Deotis. *Liberation and Reconciliation: A Black Theology*. Philadelphia, PA: Westminster Press, 1971.

———. *A Black Political Theology*. Philadelphia: Westminster Press, 1974.

———. *Bonhoeffer and King: Speaking Truth to Power*. Louisville, KY: Westminster/John Knox Press, 2005.

Robinson, John A.T. *Honest to God*. Philadelphia, PA: Westminster Press, 1963.

Rocca, Francis X. "Under Pope Francis, Liberation Theology comes of Age." *Catholic News Service* (September 13, 2013). http://www.catholicnews.com/services/englishnews/2013/under-pope-francis-liberation-theology-comes-of-age.cfm.

Rockefeller, Nelson A. *The Rockefeller Report on the Americas: The Official Report of a United States Presidential Mission for the Western Hemisphere*. Chicago, IL: Quadrangle Books, 1969.

Rodó, José Enrique. *Ariel*. Austin, TX: University of Texas Press, 1988.

Rollins, Sister Jeanne. "Liberation and the Native American." In *Theology in the Americas*. Edited by Sergio Torres and John Eagleson, 202. Maryknoll, NY: Orbis Books, 1976, 202–205.

Rossi, Alice. "Equality Between the Sexes: An Immodest Proposal." *Daedalus* 93, no. 2 (Spring 1964): 607.

Rousseau, Jean-Jacques. *The Social Contract*. Harmondsworth, UK: Penguin, 1968.

Rousseau, Jean-Jacques, and Maurice Cranston. *A Discourse on Inequality*. Harmondsworth, UK: Penguin Books, 1984.

Rousseau, Jean-Jacques, Christopher Kelly, and Allan David Bloom. *Emile, or, On Education: Includes Emile and Sophie, or, The Solitaries*. Hanover, NH: University Press of New England, 2010.

Ruether, Rosemary Radford. "Schism of Consciousness." *Commonweal* (May 1968): 330.

———. "Black Theology and the Black Church." *America* (June 14, 1969): 684–686.

———. *The Radical Kingdom: The Western Experience of Messianic Hope*. New York, NY: Harper & Row, 1970.

———. "Women's Liberation in Historical and Theological Perspective." *Soundings* 43, no. 4 (Winter 1970): 369.

———. *New Woman, New Earth: Sexist Ideologies and Human Liberation*. East Malvern: Dove Communications, 1970.

———. "The Black Theology of James Cone." *Catholic World* (October 1971): 18–20.

———. *Liberation Theology: Human Hope Confronts Christian History and American Power*. New York, NY: Paulist Press, 1972.

———. "Sexism and Theology of Liberation." *Christian Century* (December 1973): 1224–1229.

———. "Crisis in Sex and Race: Black Theology vs. Feminist Theology." *Christianity and Crisis* (April 15, 1974): 67–73.

———. *Religion and Sexism: Images of Woman in the Jewish and Christian Traditions*. New York, NY: Simon and Schuster, 1974.

———. "Letter of Rosemary Radford Ruether to Sergio Torres and the Planners of the Conference." In *Theology in the Americas*. Edited by Sergio Torres and John Eagleson, 84–85. Maryknoll, NY: Orbis Books, 1976.

———. *Sexism and God-Talk: Toward a Feminist Theology*. Boston: Beacon Press, 1983.

———. "Imago Dei, Christian Tradition, and Feminist Hermenutics." In *Images of God and Gender Models*. Edited by K.E. Borrsen, 267–290. Olso: Solum Forlag, 1991.

———. *Women and Redemption: A Theological History*. Minneapolis, MN: Fortress Press, 2012.

Russell, George. "Cover Stories Taming the Liberation Theologians." *Time Magazine* (June 24, 2001). http://content.time.com/time/magazine/article/0,9171,141037,00.html.

Russell, Letty M. *Human Liberation in a Feminist Perspective—A Theology*. Philadelphia, PA: Westminster Press, 1974.

———. "Theological Table-Talk." *Theology Today* 33, no. 2 (July 1975): 187.

Ruth, Sheila. "A Serious Look at Consciousness-Raising." *Social Theory and Practice* 2, no. 3 (Spring 1973): 289–300.

Sanders, Cheryl T., et al. "Roundtable Discussion: Christian Ethics and Theology in Womanist Perspective." *Journal of Feminist Studies in Religion* 5, no. 2 (Fall 1989): 83–112.

Sanders, Thomas G. "The Theology of Liberation: Christian Utopianism." *Christianity and Crisis* (September 17, 1973): 167–173.

Sarmiento, Domingo Faustino, and Kathleen Ross. *Facundo: Civilization and Barbarism*. Berkeley, CA: University of California Press, 2004.

Sartre, Jean-Paul, and George Joseph Becker. *Anti-Semite and Jew*. New York, NY: Schocken Books, 1948.

———. *Being and Nothingness: An Essay on Phenomenological Ontology*. New York, NY: Philosophical Library, 1956.

Sartre, Jean-Paul, and Léopold Sédar Senghor. *Black Orpheus*. New York, NY: French & European Publications, 2003.

Schleiermacher, Friedrich, and Horace L. Friess. *Schleiermacher's Soliloquies: An English Translation of the Monologen*. Eugene, OR: Wipf and Stock, 2002.

Schleiermacher, Friedrich, and John Oman. *On Religion: Speeches to its Cultural Despisers*. Louisville, KY: Westminster/John Knox Press, 1994.

Schlesinger, Arthur M. *The Vital Center: The Politics of Freedom*. New York, NY: Da Capo, 1988.

Schmitt, Carl. *Political Theology: Four Chapters on the Concept of Sovereignty*. Chicago, IL: University of Chicago Press, 2005.

Scudder, Vida Dutton. *Listener in Babel*. Boston, MA: Houghton Mifflin, 1903.

———. *Socialism and Character*. New York, NY: Houghton Mifflin, 1912.

Segundo, Juan Luis. "Christianity and Violence in Latin America." *Christianity and Crisis* (March 4, 1968): 31–34.

———. *Liberation of Theology*. Maryknoll, NY: Orbis Books, 1976.

Shaull, Richard. *Encounter with Revolution*. New York, NY: Association Press, 1955.

———. "The Revolutionary Challenge to Church and Theology." *Princeton Seminary Bulletin* 60, no. 1 (1966): 25–32.

———. Spiegel, Yorick. *Theologie der bürgerlichen Gesellschaft: Sozialphilosophie und Glaubenslehre bei Friedrich Schleiermacher* [Bourgeois and the Christian Religion: Problems of Accommodation in the Theology of Schleiermacher]. München: C. Kaiser, 1968.

Simons, Marlise. "Liberation Theology: 2 Sides Polarized." *New York Times* (June 3, 1985). http://www.nytimes.com/1985/06/03/world/liberation-theology-2-sides-polarize.html.

Smith, Adam. *The Wealth of Nations. Books 1–3*. Lexington, KY: Seven Treasures Publications, 2009.

Stanton, Elizabeth Cady. "The Slave's Appeal." Albany, NY: Weed, Parsons and Company, 1860. Anti-Slavery Depository, http://antislavery.eserver.org/tracts/stantonslavesappeal.

———. *The Woman's Bible*. Reprint edition. Salem, NH: Ayer, 1986.

Stanton, Elizabeth Cady, and Harriot Stanton Blatch. *Solitude of Self an Address before the United States Congressional Committee on the Judiciary, Monday, January 18, 1892*. New York, NY: National American Woman Suffrage Association, 1910. http://www.sscnet.ucla.edu/history/dubois/classes/995/98F/doc43.html.

Stark, Werner. *Social Theory and Christian Thought*. London: Routledge & Kegan Paul, 1958.

Stourton, Ed. "Is the Pope a Communist?" *British Broadcasting Company* (June 7, 2015). http://www.bbc.com/news/magazine-33024951.

Teilhard de Chardin, Pierre. *The Phenomenon of Man*. New York, NY: Harper, 1959.

Thompson, Clara, and M.P. Green, eds. *Interpersonal Psychoanalysis: The Selected Papers of Clara Thompson*. New York, NY: Basic Books, 1964.

Thurman, Howard. *The Negro Spiritual Speaks of Life and Death*. New York, NY: Harper, 1947.

Tillich, Paul. *The Courage to Be*. Welwyn, UK: James Nisbet, 1952.

———. *Dynamics of Faith*. New York, NY: Harper & Row, 1956.

———. *On the Boundary: An Autobiographical Sketch*. New York, NY: Charles Scribner's Sons, 1966.

Tillich, Paul, and James Luther Adams. *The Protestant Era*. Chicago, IL: University of Chicago Press, 1948.

Tillich, Paul, and F. Forrester Church. *The Essential Tillich*. Chicago, IL: University of Chicago Press, 1999.

Tillich, Paul, and Robert C. Kimball. *Theology of Culture*. New York, NY: Oxford University Press, 1959.

Torres, Sergio, and John Eagleson. *Theology in the Americas*. Maryknoll, NY: Orbis Books, 1976.

Townes, Emilie Maureen. *Womanist Justice, Womanist Hope*. Atlanta, GA: Scholars Press, 1993.

Tristan, Flora. *La Emancipación de la Mujer: O, El Testamento de la Patria*. Lima, Perú: Editorial P.T.C.M., 1948.

Troeltsch, Ernst. *The Social Teaching of the Christian Churches*. London: George Allen, 1931.

Trujillo, Alfonso Lopez. *Liberation or Revolution?* Huntington, IN: Our Sunday Visitor Inc., 1977.

Turner, Henry McNeal, and Edwin S. Redkey. *Respect Black: The Writings and Speeches of Henry McNeal Turner*. New York, NY: Arno Press, 1971.

Vallely, Paul. "Pope Embraces Liberation Theology." *Al Jazeera America* (September 22, 2015). http://america.aljazeera.com/articles/2015/9/22/pope-embraces-liberation-theology.html.

Varon, Jeremy. "Joining a Party for a More Powerful Left." *Tikkun Magazine* 29, no. 2 (Spring 2014): 38–42.

Vasconcelos, José, and Didier Tisdel Jaén. *The Cosmic Race: A Bilingual Edition*. Baltimore, MD: Johns Hopkins University Press, 1997.

Vekemans, Roger. *Caesar and God: The Priesthood and Politics*. Maryknoll, NY: Orbis Books, 1972.

———. *Teología de la liberación y cristianos por el socialismo*. Bogotá, Columbia: CEDIAL, 1976.

Verón, Eliseo. *Lenguaje y Comunicación Social*. Buenos Aires, Argentina: Nueva Visión, 1969.

Walker, Alice. *In Search of Our Mothers' Gardens: Womanist Prose*. San Diego, CA: Harcourt Brace Jovanovich, 1983.

Walker, David, and Peter P. Hinks. *David Walker's Appeal to the Coloured Citizens of the World*. University Park, PA: Pennsylvania State University Press, 2000.

Wallerstein, Immanuel. *The Modern World System Capitalist Agriculture and the Origins of the European World Economy in the Sixteenth Century*. New York, NY: Academic Press, 1974.

Ward, Lester Frank, 1841–1913. *Dynamic Sociology*. New York, NY: D. Appleton and Company, 1897. http://catalog.hathitrust.org/Record/009776846/.

Washington, Joseph R. *Black Religion: The Negro and Christianity in the United States*. Boston, MA: Beacon Press, 1964.

Weber, Max. *The Protestant Ethic and the Spirit of Capitalism*. New York, NY: Scribner, 1958.

———. "Three Forms of Theodicy." In *From Max Weber: Essays in Sociology*. Edited by Hans Heinrich Gerth. London: Routledge, 1991.

Wesley, John. *Explanatory Notes Upon the New Testament*. London: John Mason, 1831.

Williams, Delores S. *Sisters in the Wilderness: The Challenge of Womanist God-Talk.* Maryknoll, NY: Orbis Books, 1993.

———. "Womanist/Feminist Dialogue: Problems and Possibilities." *Journal of Feminist Studies in Religion* 9, no. 1/2 (Spring–Fall 1993): 67–73.

Williams, Maxine, and Pamela Williams. "Black Women's Liberation." *Militant* (July 3, 1970 and October 30, 1970). Documents from the Women's Liberation Movement archival collection, Duke University. http://library.duke.edu/rubenstein/scriptorium/wlm/blacklib/.

Williams, Robert F. *Negroes with Guns.* New York, NY: Marzani & Munsell, 1962.

Wilmore, Gayraud S. *Black Religion and Black Radicalism.* Garden City, NY: Doubleday, 1972.

———. "Ethnic Identities and Christian Theology." *Nexus* XVI, no. 1 (Winter 1972): 9–19.

Wittgenstein, Ludwig. *Philosophical Investigations.* Oxford: Basil Blackwell, 1953.

Wollstonecraft, Mary, and Carol Poston. *A Vindication on the Rights of Woman: An Authorative Text; Background; Criticism.* New York, NY: Norton, 1975.

Woodson, Carter Godwin. *The Mis-Education of the Negro.* Trenton, NJ: Africa World Press.

Wright, Richard. *The Color Curtain: A Report on the Bandung Conference.* Cleveland, OH: World, 1956.

———. *Black Power: A Record of Reactions in a Land of Pathos.* New York, NY: Harper Perennial, 1995.

X, Malcolm, and Alex Haley. *The Autobiography of Malcolm X.* New York, NY: Grove Press, 1965.

Yardley, Jim, and Simon Romero. "Pope's Focus on the Poor Revives Scorned Theology." *New York Times* (May 24, 2015): A1.

Young, Josiah Ulysses, III. "Do Black Lives Matter to God." *Black Theology* 13, no. 3 (November 2015): 210–218.

SECONDARY SOURCES

Abell, Aaron Ignatius. *American Catholicism and Social Action: A Search for Social Justice, 1865–1950.* Notre Dame, IN: University of Notre Dame Press, 1963.

Adams, Marilyn McCord. *Horrendous Evils and the Goodness of God.* Ithaca, NY: Cornell University Press, 1999.

Aguas, Raymond Bautista. "Relating Faith and Political Action: Utopia in the Theology of Gustavo Gutiérrez." Ph.D. dissertation, University of Notre Dame, 2007. In UMI Dissertation Publishing ProQuest.

Ahlstrom, Sydney E. "The Radical Turn in Theology and Ethics: Why it Occurred in the 1960s." *Annals of the American Academy of Political and Social Science* 387 (January 1970): 1–13.

———. *A Religious History of the American People*. New Haven, CT: Yale University Press, 1973.

Alcoff, Linda, and Eduardo Mendiata, eds. *Thinking from the Underside of History: Enrique Dussel's Philosophy of Liberation*. Lanham: Rowman & Littlefield, 2000.

Alonso, Carlos J. *The Spanish American Regional Novel: Modernity and Autochthony*. Cambridge; New York, NY: Cambridge University Press, 1990.

Anderson, Victor. "Pragmatic Theology and the Natural Sciences at the Intersection of Human Interest." *Zygon: Journal of Religion and Science* 37, no. 1 (March 2002).

Angell, Alan. "The Left in Latin America since *c.* 1920." In *Latin America Politics and Society Since 1930*. Edited by Leslie Bethell, 75–140. Cambridge: Cambridge University Press, 1998.

Aquino, Maria Pilar. "Latin American Feminist Theology." *Journal of Feminist Studies in Religion* 14, no. 1 (1998): 89–107.

Ardao, Arturo. "Assimilation and Transformation of Positivism in Latin America." *Journal of the History of Ideas* 24, no. 4 (October–December 1963): 515–522.

Armitage, David. *The Declaration of Independence: A Global History*. Cambridge, MA: Harvard University Press, 2007.

Armitage, David, and Jo Guldi, *The History Manifesto*. Cambridge, MA: Harvard University Press, 2007.

Arnold, Charles Harvey. *Near the Edge of Battle: A Short History of the Divinity School and the Chicago School of Theology, 1866–1966*. Chicago, IL: Divinity School Association, University of Chicago, 1966.

Ashley, Matthew J. "Johann Baptist Metz." In *The Blackwell Companion to Political Theology*. Edited by Peter Scott and William T. Cavanaugh, 241–255. Malden, MA: Blackwell, 2004.

Aubert, Roger, and David A. Boileau. *Catholic Social Teaching: An Historical Perspective*. Milwaukee, WI: Marquette University Press, 2003.

Baines, John M. *Revolution in Perú: Mariátegui and the Myth*. University, AL: Published for the Latin American Studies Program by the University of Alabama Press, 1972.

Baiton, Roland H. "Thomas Muntzer, Revolutionary Firebrand of the Reformation." *Sixteenth Century Journal* 13, no. 2 (1982): 3–16.

Barger, Lilian Calles. "'Pray to God, she will hear us.' Women Reimaging Religion and Politics in the 1970s." In *The Religious Left in Modern America: Doorkeepers of a Radical Faith*. Edited by Douglas Rossinow, Leilah Danielson, and Marian Mollin. New York, NY: Palgrave Macmillan, 2018.

Barth, Karl. *Protestant Theology in the Nineteenth Century: Its Background & History*. London: SCM Press, 1972.

Baumeister, Roy F. "How the Self Became a Problem: A Psychological Review of Historical Research." *Journal of Personality and Social Psychology* 52, no. 1 (1987): 163–176.

Bélanger, André-J. *The Ethics of Catholicism and the Consecration of the Intellectual*. Montreal: McGill-Queen's University Press, 1997.

Bender, Thomas. *Rethinking American History in a Global Age*. Berkeley, CA: University of California Press, 2007.

Bernard, L.L. "The Significance of Comte." *Social Forces* 21, no. 1 (October 1942–May 1943): 8–14.

Bernardi, Peter. "Social Modernism: The Case of the *Semaines Sociales*." In *Catholicism Contending with Modernity*. Edited by Darrell Jodock, 277–307. Cambridge: Cambridge University Press, 2000.

Bernardi, Peter J. *Maurice Blondel, Social Catholicism, & Action Française: The Clash Over the Church's Role in Society during the Modernist Era*. Washington, DC: Catholic University of America Press, 2009.

Bernauer, James William. *Amor Mundi: Explorations in the Faith and Thought of Hannah Arendt*. Boston, MA; Lancaster: M. Nijhoff, 1987.

Berryman, Phillip. *Liberation Theology: Essential Facts about the Revolutionary Movement in Latin America—and Beyond*. Philadelphia, PA: Temple University Press, 1987.

Berstein, Harry. "Some Inter-American Aspects of the Enlightenment." In *Latin America and the Enlightenment*. Edited by Arthur Preston Whitaker, 53–69. Ithaca, NY: Great Seal Books, 1961.

Bethell, Leslie. *Latin America: Politics and Society since 1930*. New York, NY: Cambridge University Press, 1998.

Betz, Joseph. "John Dewey and Paulo Freire." *Transactions of the Charles S. Peirce Society* 28, no. 1 (Winter 1992): 107–126.

Bidegain, Ana Maria. "From Catholic Action to Liberation Theology: The Historical Process of the Laity in Latin America in the Twentieth Century." The Helen Kellogg Institute for International Studies, 1985. http://kellogg.nd.edu/publications/workingpapers/WPS/048.pdf.

Blum, Edward J. *Reforging the White Republic: Race, Religion, and American Nationalism, 1865–1898*. Baton Rouge, LA: Louisiana State University Press, 2005.

———. *W.E.B. Du Bois, American Prophet*. Philadelphia, PA: University of Pennsylvania Press, 2007.

Boff, Leonardo, and Clodovis Boff. *Introducing Liberation Theology*. Maryknoll, NY: Orbis Books, 1987.

Bombogan, Dominador Jr. "Liberation Theology and Dependency Theory: Tracing a Relationship." *Hapag: A Journal of Interdisciplinary Theological Research* 1 (2004): 61–91.

Bouvard, Marguerite Guzman. *Revolutionizing Motherhood: The Mothers of the Plaza De Mayo*. Wilmington, DE: Scholarly Resources, 1994.

Bowler, Kate. *Blessed: A History of the American Prosperity Gospel*. New York, NY: Oxford University Press, 2013.

Bracey, John H., and August Meier. "Black Ideologies, Black Utopias: Afrocentricity in Historical Perspective." *Contributions in Black Studies* 12, no. 13 (1994): 111–116.

Bradstock, Andrew. *Faith in the Revolution: The Political Theologies of Müntzer and Winstanley*. London: SPCK, 1997.

Braude, Ann. "A Religious Feminist - Who Can Find Her? Historiographical Challenges from the National Organization for Women." *Journal of Religion* 84, no. 4 (2004): 555–572.

———. *Transforming the Faiths of our Fathers: Women Who Changed American Religion*. New York, NY: Palgrave Macmillan, 2004.

Braude, Ann, Jon Butler, and Harry S. Stout. *Women and American Religion*. New York, NY: Oxford University Press, 2000.

Breines, Wini. *The Trouble between Us: An Uneasy History of White and Black Women in the Feminist Movement*. Oxford; New York, NY: Oxford University Press, 2006.

Brekus, Catherine A. *The Religious History of American Women: Reimagining the Past*. Chapel Hill, NC: University of North Carolina Press, 2007.

Brewer, Stewart. *Borders and Bridges: A History of U.S.–Latin American Relations*. Westport, CN: Praeger Security International, 2006.

Brick, Howard. *Age of Contradiction: American Thought and Culture in the 1960s*. New York, NY: Twayne Publishers, 1998.

Briggs, Laura, Gladys McCormick, and J.T. Way. "Transnationalism: A Category of Analysis." *American Quarterly* 60, no. 3, Nation and Migration: Past and Future (September 2008): 625–648.

Brown, Robert McAfee. "Preface and a Conclusion." In *Theology in the Americas*. Edited by Sergio Torres and John Eagleson, xxvi. Maryknoll, NY: Orbis Books, 1976.

———. *Gustavo Gutiérrez*. Atlanta, GA: John Knox Press, 1980.

Bryne, James M. "Schleiermacher." In *Encyclopedia of Christianity,* edited by John Bowden. New York, NY: Oxford University Press, 2005.

Buck-Morss, Susan. *Hegel, Haiti and Universal History*. Pittsburgh, PA: University of Pittsburgh Press, 2009.

Buhle, Mari Jo. *Feminism and its Discontents: A Century of Struggle with Psychoanalysis*. Cambridge, MA: Harvard University Press, 1998.

Burns, E. Bradford. *The Poverty of Progress: Latin America in the Nineteenth Century*. Berkeley, CA: University of California Press, 1980.

Burrow, Rufus Jr. *James H. Cone and Black Liberation Theology*. Jefferson: McFarland, 1994.

———. "Enter Womanist Theology and Ethics." *Western Journal of Black Studies* 22, no. 1 (1998): 19–29.

———. *God and Human Responsibility: David Walker and Ethical Prophecy*. Macon, GA: Mercer University Press, 2003.

———. *God and Human Dignity: The Personalism, Theology, and Ethics of Martin Luther King, Jr*. Notre Dame, IN: University of Notre Dame Press, 2006.

Camp, Richard L. *The Papal Ideology of Social Reform. A Study in Historical Development 1878–1967*. Leiden, Netherlands: E.J. Brill, 1969.

Campbell, Leon G. "Ideology and Factionalism During the Great Rebellion, 1780–1782." In *Resistance, Rebellion, and Consciousness in the Andean Peasant World, 18th to 20th Centuries*. Edited by Steve J. Stern, 110–140. Madison, WI: University of Wisconsin Press, 1987.

Carnois, Bernard. *The Coherence of Kant's Doctrine of Freedom*. Chicago, IL: University of Chicago Press, 1987.

Carpenter, Joel A. *Revive Us Again: The Reawakening of American Fundamentalism*. New York, NY: Oxford University Press, 1997.

Carson, Clayborn. "Martin Luther King, Jr. and the African-American Social Gospel." In *African-American Christianity: Essays in History*. Edited by Paul E. Johnson, 159–178. Berkeley: University of California Press, 1994.

Carter, Heath W. *Union Made: Working People and the Rise of Social Christianity in Chicago*. New York, NY: Oxford University Press, 2015.

Carter, J. Kameron. *Race: A Theological Account*. Oxford: Oxford University Press, 2008.

Caruana, Louis. *Darwin and Catholicism: The Past and Present Dynamics of a Cultural Encounter*. New York, NY: T & T Clark, 2009.

Casanova, José. *Public Religions in the Modern World*. Chicago. IL: University of Chicago Press, 1994.

Cashdollar, Charles D. *The Transformation of Theology, 1830–1890: Positivism and Protestant Thought in Britain and America*. Princeton, NJ: Princeton University Press, 1989.

Cassirer, Ernst. *The Philosophy of the Enlightenment*. Princeton, NJ: Princeton University Press, 1951.

Castillo Cárdenas, Gonzalo, and Manuel Quintín Lame Chantre. *Liberation Theology from Below: The Life and Thought of Manuel Quintín Lame*. Maryknoll, NY: Orbis Books, 1987.

Cave, Alfred A. "Thomas More and the New World." *Albion* 23, no. 2 (March 1991): 209–229.

Chakarabarty, Dispesh. "Legacies of Bandung: Decolonisation and the Politics of Culture." *Economic and Political Weekly* 40, no. 46 (November 12–18, 2005): 4812–4818.

Chaney, Elsa M. "Old and New Feminists in Latin America: The Case of Perú and Chile." *Journal of Marriage and Family* 35, no. 2 (May 1973): 331–343.

Chapman, Mark D. *Ernst Troeltsch and Liberal Theology: Religion and Cultural Synthesis in Wilhelmine Germany*. Oxford: Oxford University Press, 2001.

Chappell, David L. *A Stone of Hope: Prophetic Religion and the Death of Jim Crow*. Chapel Hill, NC: University of North Carolina Press, 2004.

Chavarría, Jesús. *José Carlos Mariátegui and the Rise of Modern Perú, 1890–1930*. Albuquerque, NM: University of New Mexico Press, 1979.

Cherry, Conrad. *God's New Israel: Religious Interpretations of American Destiny*. Chapel Hill, NC: University of North Carolina Press, 1998.

Coleman, Frank M. *Hobbes and America: Exploring the Constitutional Foundations*. Toronto, Canada: University of Toronto Press, 1977.

Colletti, Lucio. *From Rousseau to Lenin: Studies in Ideology and Society*. New York, NY: Monthly Review Press, 1972.

Comblin, José. *The Church and the National Security State*. Maryknoll, NY: Orbis Books, 1979.

Cooper, John W. "Theilhard, Marx, and the Worldview of Prominent Liberation Theologians." *Calvin Theological Journal* 24, no. 2 (1989): 241–262.

Coronado, Jorge. *The Andes Imagined: Indigenismo, Society, and Modernity*. Pittsburgh, PA: University of Pittsburgh Press, 2009.

Cott, Nancy F. *The Grounding of Modern Feminism*. New Haven, CT: Yale University Press, 1987.

Crouter, Richard. *Friedrich Schleiermacher: Between Enlightenment and Romanticism*. New York, NY: Cambridge University Press, 2005.

Cullen, Daniel E. *Freedom in Rousseau's Political Philosophy*. DeKalb, IL: Northern Illinois University Press, 1993.

Culp, Mary Beth. "Religion in the Poetry of Langston Hughes." *Phylon* 48, no. 3 (1987): 240–245.

Curnow, Rohan M. "Which Preferential Option for the Poor? A History of the Doctrine's Bifurcation." *Modern Theology* 31, no. 1 (January 2015): 27–59.

Danielson, Leilah. *American Gandhi: A.J. Muste and the History of Radicalism in the Twentieth Century*. Philadelphia, PA: University of Pennsylvania Press, 2014.

Das, Robin R. "The Place of Werner Stark in American Sociology: A Study in Marginality." Order No. 3301435, Fordham University, 2008. In ProQuest, http://search.proquest.com/docview/304644782?accountid=7120.

Davaney, Sheila Greeve. *Pragmatic Historicism: A Theology for the Twenty-First Century*. Albany, NY: State University of New York, NY Press, 2000.

Davis, Angela Y. *Women, Race & Class*. New York, NY: Vintage Books, 1983.

Davis, David Brion. *The Problem of Slavery in the Age of Revolution, 1770–1823*. Ithaca, NY: Cornell University Press, 1975.

Davis, Harold Eugene. *Latin American Thought: A Historical Introduction*. New York, NY: Free Press, 1974.

Davis, Reginald F. *Frederick Douglass: A Precursor of Liberation Theology*. Macon, GA: Mercer University Press, 2005.

Davydova, Iria, and Wes Sharrock. "The Rise and Fall of the Fact/Value Distinction." *Sociological Review* 51, no. 3 (August, 2003): 357–375.

Dawson, Michael C. *Black Visions: The Roots of Contemporary African-American Political Ideologies*. Chicago, IL: University of Chicago Press, 2001.

DeCaro, Louis A. *Malcolm and the Cross: The Nation of Islam, Malcolm X, and Christianity*. New York, NY: New York, NY University Press, 1998.

De Juana, Alvaro. "Archbishop Romero had no interest in liberation theology, says secretary" *Catholic News Agency* (February 21, 2015), https://www.catholicnewsagency.com/news/archbishop-romero-had-no-interest-in-liberation-theology-says-secretary-79788.

Deegan, Mary Jo. *Jane Addams and the Men of the Chicago School, 1892–1918*. New Brunswick, NJ: Transaction Books, 1988.

Desanti, Dominque. "Flora Tristan: Rebel Daughter of the Revolution." In *Rebel Daughters: Women and the French Revolution*. Edited by Sara E. Melzer and Leslie Wahl Rabine, 273–288. New York, NY: Oxford University Press, 1993.

Dickerson, Dennis C. "African American Religious Intellectuals and the Theological Foundations of the Civil Rights Movement." *Church History* 74, no. 2 (2005): 217–235.

Diggins, John P. *The Promise of Pragmatism: Modernism and the Crisis of Knowledge and Authority*. Chicago, IL: University of Chicago Press, 1994.

Donos, Anto. "John Dewey in Spain and Spanish America." *International Philosophical Quarterly* 3, no. 163 (September 2001).

Dorn, Jacob Henry. *Washington Gladden: Prophet of the Social Gospel*. Columbus, OH: Ohio State University Press, 1967.

Dorr, Donal. *Option for the Poor: A Hundred Years of Vatican Social Teaching*. Maryknoll, NY: Orbis Books, 1983.

Dorrien, Gary J. *Reconstructing the Common Good: Theology and the Social Order*. Maryknoll, NY: Orbis Books, 1990.

———. *Soul in Society: The Making and Renewal of Social Christianity*. Minneapolis, MN: Fortress Press, 1995.

———. "Berger: Theology and Sociology." In *Peter Berger and the Study of Religion*. Edited by Linda Woodhead, 26–39. New York, NY: Routledge, 2001.

———. *The Making of American Liberal Theology: Imagining Progressive Religion 1805–1900*. Louisville, KY: Westminster/John Knox Press, 2001.

———. *Idealism, Realism, and Modernity, 1900–1950*. Louisville, KY: Westminster/John Knox Press, 2003.

———. *Making of American Liberal Theology: Crisis, Irony, and Postmodernity 1950–2005*. Louisville, KY: Westminster/John Knox Press, 2006.

———. *Social Ethics in the Making: Interpreting an American Tradition*. Malden, MA: Wiley-Blackwell, 2009.

———. *Kantian Reason and Hegelian Spirit: The Idealistic Logic of Modern Theology*. Chichester, West Sussex, UK: Wiley-Blackwell, 2015.

———. *The New Abolition: W.E.B. Du Bois and the Black Social Gospel*. New Haven, CT: Yale University Press, 2015.

Douglass-Chin, Richard J. *Preacher Woman Sings the Blues: The Autobiographies of Nineteenth-Century African American Evangelists*. Columbia, MO: University of Missouri Press, 2001.

DuBois, Ellen Carol. *Elizabeth Cady Stanton, Feminist as Thinker: A Reader in Documents and Essays*. New York, NY: New York University Press, 2007.

Dubois, Laurent. *Avengers of the New World: The Story of the Haitian Revolution*. Cambridge, MA: Belknap Press of Harvard University Press, 2004.

Dun, James Alexander. *Dangerous Neighbors: Making the Haitian Revolution in Early America*. Philadelphia, PA: University of Pennsylvania Press, 2016.

Dussel, Enrique D. *Filosofía de la liberación*. México: Editorial Edicol, 1977.

———. *A History of the Church in Latin America: Colonialism to Liberation (1492–1979)*. Grand Rapids, MI: W. B. Eerdmans, 1981.

Dussel, Enrique D., and Alejandro A. Vallega. *Ethics of Liberation in the Age of Globalization and Exclusion*. Durham, NC: Duke University Press, 2013.

Dyson, Michael Eric. *Making Malcolm: The Myth and Meaning of Malcolm X*. New York, NY: Oxford University Press, 1995.

Echols, Alice. *Daring to Be Bad: Radical Feminism in America, 1967–1975*. Minneapolis, MN: University of Minnesota Press, 1989.

Edwards, Kerry. "Sociological and Theological Method." In *Religion and the Sociology of Knowledge*. Edited by Barbara Hargrove, 79–97. New York, NY: Edwin Mellen Press, 1984.

Egan, Maureen L. "Evolutionary Theory in the Social Philosophy of Charlotte Perkins Gilman." *Hypatia* 4, no. 1 (1989): 102–119.

El-Beshti, Bashir M. "The Semiotics of Salvation: Malcolm X and the Autobiographical Self." *Journal of Negro History* 82, no. 4 (Autumn 1997): 359–367.

Elias, Edward. "Prophecy of Liberation: The Poetry of Ernesto Cardenal." In *Poetic Prophecy in Western Literature*. Edited by Jan Wojcik and Raymond-Jean Frontain, 174–185. London: Associated University Presses, 1984.

Eller, Cynthia. *The Myth of Matriarchal Prehistory: Why an Invented Past Won't Give Women a Future*. Boston, MA: Beacon Press, 2000.

Elrod, Eileen Razzari. "Moses and the Egyptian: Religious Authority in Olaudah Equiano's Interesting Narrative." *African American Review* 35, no. 3 (Autumn 2001): 409–425.

Elshtain, Jean Bethke. "Kant, Politics, & Persons: The Implications of His Moral Philosophy." *Polity* 14, no. 2 (Winter 1981): 205–221.

Escobar, J. Samuel. "Christian Base Communities: A Historical Perspective." *Transformations* 3, no. 3 (1986): 1–4.

———. "Religion and Social Change at the Grass Roots in Latin America." *Annals of the American Academy of Political and Social Science* (November 1997): 81–103.

Evans, Sara M. *Personal Politics: The Roots of Women's Liberation in the Civil Rights Movement and the New Left*. New York, NY: Vintage Books, 1979.

Faber, Samuel. *The Origins of the Cuban Revolution Reconsidered*. Chapel Hill, NC: University of North Carolina Press, 2006.

Faulkner, Carol. *Lucretia Mott's Heresy: Abolition and Women's Rights in Nineteenth-Century America*. Philadelphia, PA: University of Pennsylvania Press, 2011.

Fierro, Alfredo. *The Militant Gospel: A Critical Introduction to Political Theologies*. Maryknoll, NY: Orbis Books, 1977.

Findlay, James F. *Church People in the Struggle: The National Council of Churches and the Black Freedom Movement, 1950–1970*. New York, NY: Oxford University Press, 1993.

Fitzgerald, Paul J. "Faithful Sociology: Peter Berger's Religious Project." *Religious Studies Review* 27, no. 1 (January 2001): 10–17.

Fitzpatrick-Behrens, Susan Helen. *The Maryknoll Catholic Mission in Perú, 1943–1989: Transnational Faith and Transformation*. Notre Dame, IN: University of Notre Dame Press, 2012.

Flores, Ruben. *Backroads Pragmatists: Mexico's Melting Pot and Civil Rights in the United States*. Philadelphia, PA: University of Pennsylvania Press, 2014.

Foley, Barbara. *Spectres of 1919: Class and Nation in the Making of the New Negro*. Urbana, IL: University of Illinois Press, 2008.

Folks, Jeffrey J. "'Last Call to the West': Richard Wright's the Color Curtain." *South Atlantic Review* 59, no. 4 (1994): 77–88.

Foner, Eric. *The Story of American Freedom*. New York, NY: W.W. Norton, 1998.

Forsythe, Jennifer Marie. "La descolonización espiritual como practica multidisciplinaría en la obra de José Maria Arguedas." *Revista De Critica Literaria Latinoamericana* 36, no. 72 (December 2010): 217–231.

Foucault, Michel. *The Order of Things: An Archaeology of the Human Sciences*. New York, NY: Pantheon Books, 1971.

Fox, Richard W. "H. Richard Niebuhr's Divided Kingdom." *American Quarterly* 42, no. 1 (1990): 93–101.

Fox, Thomas C. "Liberation Theology Founder Dead at 70." *National Catholic Reporter* (February 2, 1996): 2.

Francisco, Grant D. Miller. "Rosemary Radford Ruether." In *Boston Collaborative Encyclopedia of Modern Western Theology*. Edited by Wesley Wildman, Boston University, 1990. http://people.bu.edu/wwildman/bce/.

Franco, Paul. *Hegel's Philosophy of Freedom*. New Haven, CT: Yale University Press, 1999.

Fraser, Steve, and Gary Gerstle *The Rise and Fall of the New Deal Order, 1930–1980*. Princeton, NJ: Princeton University Press, 1989.

Freedman, Estelle B. *No Turning Back: The History of Feminism and the Future of Women*. New York, NY: Ballantine, 2002.

Frei, Hans W. "Feuerbach and Theology." *Journal of the American Academy of Religion* 35, no. 3 (September 1967): 250–256.

Frey, Sylvia R. *Water from the Rock: Black Resistance in a Revolutionary Age*. Princeton, NJ: Princeton University Press, 1991.

———. "The American Revolution and the Creation of a Global African World." In *From Toussaint to Tupac: The Black International since the Age of Revolution*. Edited by Michael Oliver West, 47–71. Chapel Hill, NC: University of North Carolina Press, 2009.

Friesen, Abraham. "Thomas Muntzer in Marxist Thought." *Church History* 34 (1965): 306–327.

———. *Reformation and Utopia: The Marxist Interpretation of the Reformation and its Antecedents*. Wiesbaden: F. Steiner, 1974.

Frund, Arlette. "Phillis Wheatley, a Public Intellectual." In *Toward an Intellectual History of Black Women*. Edited by Mia Bay, et al., 35–51. Chapel Hill, NC: University of North Carolina Press, 2015.

García Canclini, Néstor. *Hybrid Cultures: Strategies for Entering and Leaving Modernity*. Minneapolis, MN: University of Minnesota Press, 1989.

Geary, Daniel. "Becoming International Again: C. Wright Mills and the Emergence of a Global New Left, 1956–1962." *Journal of American History* 95, no. 3 (December 2008): 710–736.

———. *Radical Ambition: C. Wright Mills, the Left, and American Social Thought*. Berkeley, CA: University of California Press, 2009.

Gehardt, Uta. "Margaret Mead's Male and Female Revisited." *International Sociology* 10, no. 2 (1995): 197–217.

Gerbi, Antonello. *The Dispute of the New World the History of a Polemic, 1750–1900*. Pittsburgh, PA: University of Pittsburgh Press, 2010.

Gibbons, Reginald. "Political Poetry and the Example of Ernesto Cardenal." *Critical Inquiry* 13, no. 3 (1987): 648–671.

Giddens, Steven Anthony. "Classical Social Theory and the Origins of Modern Sociology." *American Journal of Sociology* 81, no. 4 (January 1976): 703–729.

Gilbert, Sandra A., and Susan Guber. "'Fecundate! Discriminate!' Charlotte Perkins Gilman and the Theologizing of Maternity." In *Charlotte Perkins Gilman: Optimist Reformer*. Edited by Jill Rudd and Val Gough, 200–218. Iowa City, IA: University of Iowa Press, 1999.

Gill, Anthony J. "Rendering Unto Caesar? Religious Competition and Catholic Strategy in Latin America, 1962–1979." *American Journal of Political Science* 38, no. 2 (May 1994): 403–425.

Gill, Jill K. *Embattled Ecumenism: The National Council of Churches, the Vietnam War, and the Trials of the Protestant Left*. DeKalb, IL: NIU Press, 2011.

Gillespie, Michael Allen. *The Theological Origins of Modernity*. Chicago, IL: University of Chicago Press, 2008.

Gilman, Nils. *Mandarins of the Future: Modernization Theory in Cold War America*. Baltimore, MD: Johns Hopkins University Press, 2003.

Gilmore, Stephanie. *Feminist Coalitions: Historical Perspectives on Second-Wave Feminism in the United States*. Urbana, IL: University of Illinois Press, 2008.

Gilroy, Paul. *The Black Atlantic: Modernity and Double Consciousness*. Cambridge, MA: Harvard University Press, 1993.

Gleason, Philip, *Speaking of Diversity: Language and Ethnicity in Twentieth-Century America*. Baltimore, MD: Johns Hopkins University Press, 1992.

Goldberg, Michael. *Theology and Narrative: A Critical Introduction*. Nashville, TN: Abingdon, 1982.

Gosse, Van. *Where the Boys are: Cuba, Cold War America and the Making of a New Left*. New York, NY: Verso, 1993.

Gould, Jeffrey L. "Solidarity Under Siege: The Latin American Left, 1968." *American Historical Review* 114, no. 2 (April 2009): 348–375.

Grant, C. David. *God the Center of Value: Value Theory in the Theology of H. Richard Niebuhr.* Fort Worth, TX: Texas Christian University Press, 1984.

Green, Clifford. "Human Sociality and Christian Community." In *The Cambridge Companion to Dietrich Bonhoeffer.* Edited by John W. de Gruchy, 113–133. Cambridge: Cambridge University Press, 1999.

Greggs, Tom. "Religionless Christianity and the Political Implications of Theological Speech: What Bonhoeffer's Theology Yields to the World of Fundamantalism." *International Journal of Systematic Theology* 11, no. 3 (2009): 293–308.

Grenz, Stanley J., and Roger E. Olson. *20th Century Theology: God & the World in a Transitional Age.* Downers Grove, IL: InterVarsity Press, 1992.

Gronbeck-Tedesco, John A. "The Left in Transition: The Cuban Revolution in US Third World Politics." *Journal of Latin American Studies* 40, no. 4, Cuba: 50 Years of Revolution (November 2008): 651–673.

Gross, Rita M. *Feminism and Religion: An Introduction.* Boston, MA: Beacon Press, 1996.

Grumett, David. "Blondel, the Philosophy of Action and Liberation Theology." *Political Theology* 11, no. 4 (2010): 507–529.

Guétin, Nicole. *Religious Ideology in American Politics: A History.* Jefferson, NC: McFarland, 2009.

Hagopian, Frances. "Latin American Catholicism in an Age of Religious and Political Pluralism: A Framework for Analysis." *Comparative Politics* 40, no. 2 (January 2008): 149–168.

Hale, Charles A. *The Transformation of Liberalism in Late Nineteenth-Century Mexico.* Princeton, NJ: Princeton University Press, 1989.

Hall, Michael. "CALCAV And Religious Opposition to the Vietnam War." In *Give Peace a Chance: Exploring the Vietnam Antiwar Movement: Essays from the Charles DeBenedetti Memorial Conference.* Edited by Melvin Small and William D. Hoover, 35–52. Syracuse, NY: Syracuse University Press, 1992.

Hamilton, Brian. "Pope Francis and Liberation Theology." *Immanent Frame* (May 19, 2014). http://blogs.ssrc.org/tif/2014/05/09/pope-francis-and-liberation-theology/.

Harbeski, Raymond J. *God and War: American Civil Religion Since 1945* (New Brunswick, NJ: Rutgers University Press, 2012.

Harde, Roxanne. "Making of our Lives a Study: Feminist Theology and Women's Creative Writing." *Feminist Theology* 15, no. 1 (2006): 48–69.

Harp, Gillis J. "Lester Ward: Comtean Whig." *Historical Reflections* 15, no. 3 (Fall 1988): 523–542.

Hartch, Todd. *The Rebirth of Latin American Christianity.* New York, NY: Oxford University Press, 2014.

Hartman, Andrew. *A War for the Soul of America: A History of the Culture Wars*. Chicago, IL: University of Chicago Press, 2016.

Hatfield, Charles. "The Limits of 'Nuestra America.'" *Revista Hispanica Moderna* 63, no. 2 (2010): 193–202.

Haywood, Chanta M. *Prophesying Daughters: Black Women Preachers and the Word, 1823–1913*. Columbia, MO: University of Missouri Press, 2003.

Hebbethwaith, Pete. "Liberation Theology and the Roman Catholic Church." In *The Cambridge Companion to Liberation Theology*. Edited by Christopher Rowland, 179–198. Cambridge: Cambridge University Press, 1999.

Hellman, John. "The Humanism of Jacques Maritain." In *Understanding Maritain: Philosopher and Friend*. Edited by Deal Wyatt Hudson and Matthew J. Mancini, 117–124. Macon, GA: Mercer University Press, 1987.

Hetzel, Peter. *Jesus and Justice: Evangelicals, Race and American Politics*. New Haven, CT: Yale University Press, 2009.

Hewitt, Marsha Aileen. *From Theology to Social Theory: Juan Luis Segundo and the Theology of Liberation*. Bern: P. Lang, 1990.

Hick, John. *Evil and the God of Love*. New York, NY: Harper & Row, 1966.

Hill Collins, Patricia. *Black Feminist Thought: Knowledge, Consciousness, and the Politics of Empowerment*. New York, NY: Routledge, 2000.

Hinks, Peter P. *To Awaken My Afflicted Brethren: David Walker and the Problem of Antebellum Slave Resistance*. University Park, PA: Pennsylvania State University Press, 1997.

Hinson-Hasty, Elizabeth L. *Beyond the Social Maze: Exploring Vida Dutton Scudder's Theological Ethics*. New York, NY: T & T Clark, 2006.

Hogan, Linda. *From Women's Experience to Feminist Theology*. Sheffield: Sheffield Academic Press, 1995.

Holben, L.R. *All the Way to Heaven: A Theological Reflection on Dorothy Day, Peter Maurin and the Catholic Worker*. Eugene, OR: Wipf & Stock, 2010.

Holland, Joe. *Modern Catholic Social Teaching: The Popes Confront the Industrial Age, 1740–1958*. New York, NY: Paulist Press, 2003.

Hollinger, David A. "How Wide the Circle of the 'We'? American Intellectuals and the Problem of the Ethnos since World War II." *American Historical Review* 98, no. 2 (April 1993): 317.

Holstun, James. *A Rational Millennium: Puritan Utopias of Seventeenth-Century England and America*. New York, NY: Oxford University Press, 1987.

Hopkins, Charles Howard. *The Rise of the Social Gospel in American Protestantism, 1865–1915*. New Haven, CT: Yale University Press, 1940.

Hopkins, Dwight N., and Georg C.L. Cummings. *Cut Loose Your Stammering Tongue: Black Theology in the Slave Narratives*. Louisville, KY: Westminster/John Knox Press, 2003.

Horowitz, Irving Louis. *C. Wright Mills: An American Utopian*. New York, NY: Free Press, 1983.

Horsman, Reginal. *Race and Manifest Destiny: The Origins of American Racial Anglo-Saxonism*. Cambridge, MA: Harvard University Press, 2006.

Houlgate, Stephen. *Freedom, Truth and History: An Introduction to Hegel's Philosophy*. New York, NY: Routledge, 1991.

Howe, Daniel Walker. *Making the American Self: Jonathan Edwards to Abraham Lincoln*. New York, NY: Oxford University Press, 2009.

Huchison, William R. "The Americaness of the Social Gospel: An Inquiry into Comparative History." *Church History* 44, no. 3 (1975): 367–381.

Hulsether, Mark. *Building a Protestant Left: Christianity and Crisis Magazine, 1941–1993*. Knoxville, TN: University of Tennessee Press, 1999.

Hunsinger, George. *How to Read Karl Barth: The Shape of His Theology*. New York, NY: Oxford University Press, 1993.

Hunt, Mary E. "Women-Church: Feminist Concept, Religious Commitment, Women's Movement." *Journal of Feminist Studies in Religion* 25, no. 1 (Spring 2009): 85–98.

Hunt, Michael H. *Ideology and U.S. Foreign Policy*. New Haven, CT: Yale University Press, 1987.

Hutchison, William R. "The Americaness of the Social Gospel: An Inquiry into Comparative History." *Church History* 44, no. 3 (September 1975): 367–381.

———. *The Modernist Impulse in American Protestantism*. Durham, NC: Duke University Press, 1992.

Iggers, Georg G. *The Doctrine of Saint-Simon: An Exposition; First Year, 1828–1829*. Boston, MA: Beacon Press, 1958.

Inboden, William. *Religion and American Foreign Policy, 1945–1960: The Soul of Containment*. Cambridge: Cambridge University Press, 2008.

Israel, Jonathan I. *Radical Enlightenment: Philosophy and the Making of Modernity, 1650–1750*. New York, NY: Oxford University Press, 2001.

———. *A Revolution of the Mind: Radical Enlightenment and the Intellectual Origins of Modern Democracy*. Princeton, NJ: Princeton University Press, 2010.

———. *Democratic Enlightenment: Philosophy, Revolution, and Human Rights 1750–1790*. New York, NY: Oxford University Press, 2011.

Jackson, Thomas F. *From Civil Rights to Human Rights: Martin Luther King, Jr., and the Struggle for Economic Justice*. Philadelphia, PA: University of Pennsylvania Press, 2007.

James, C.L.R. *The Black Jacobins: Toussaint L'Ouverture and the San Domingo Revolution*. New York, NY: Vintage Books, 1963.

Jay, Martin. *The Dialectical Imagination: A History of the Frankfurt School and the Institute of Social Research, 1923–1950*. Boston, MA: Little, Brown, 1973.

Jennings, Willie James. *The Christian Imagination: Theology and the Origins of Race*. New Haven, CT: Yale University Press, 2010.

Jodock, Darrell. *Ritschl in Retrospect: History, Community, and Science*. Minneapolis, MN: Fortress Press, 1995.

———. *Catholicism Contending with Modernity: Roman Catholic Modernism and Anti-Modernism in Historical Context*. New York, NY: Cambridge University Press, 2000.

Johannsen, Robert Walter, Sam W. Haynes, and Christopher Morris, *Manifest Destiny and Empire: American Antebellum Expansionism*. College Station, TX: Published for the University of Texas at Arlington by Texas A&M University Press, 1997.

Johnson, Benton. "Continuity and Quest in the Work of Harvey Cox." *Sociological Analysis* 45, no. 2 (1984): 79–83

Jorrín, Miguel, and John D. Martz. *Latin-American Political Thought and Ideology*. Chapel Hill, NC: University of North Carolina Press, 1970.

Joseph, Peniel E. *The Black Power Movement: Rethinking the Civil Rights-Black Power Era*. New York, NY: Routledge, 2006.

Kahn, Jonathon Samuel. *Divine Discontent: The Religious Imagination of W.E.B. Du Bois*. New York, NY: Oxford University Press, 2009.

Kaminsky, Phyllis H. "Maurice Blondel: Spirituality in Praxis and Action." *Continuum* (Spring 1992): 72–92.

———. "Seeking Transcendence in the Modern World." In *Catholicism Contending with Modernity*. Edited by Jodock, Darrell, 115–141. Cambridge: Cambridge University Press, 2000.

Kantor, Harry. "Catholic political parties and mass politics in Latin America." In *Religion and Political Modernization*. Edited by Donalde Eugene Smith. New Haven, CT: Yale University Press, 1974, 210–221.

Karpov, Vyacheslav. "Desecularization: A Conceptual Framework." *Journal of Church and State* 52, no. 2 (July 2010): 232–270.

Kazin, Michael. *American Dreamers: How the Left Changed a Nation*. New York, NY: Alfred A. Knopf, 2011.

Kellner, Douglas. *Herbert Marcuse and the Crisis of Marxism*. Berkeley, CA: University of California Press, 1984.

———. "Ernst Bloch, Utopia, and Ideology Critique." Arlington, TX: University of Texas at Arlington. http://www.uta.edu/huma/illuminations/kell1.htm.

Kellner, Douglas, and Harry O'Hara. "Utopia and Marxism in Ernst Bloch." *New German Critique*, no. 9 (Autumn 1976): 11–34.

Kelly, Robin D.G. "'but a Local Phase of a World Problem': Black History's Global Vision, 1883–1950." *Journal of American History* 86, no. 3 (December 1999): 1045–1077.

Kern, Kathi. *Mrs. Stanton's Bible*. Ithaca, NY: Cornell University Press, 2001.

Kessler, Carol Farley. *Charlotte Perkins Gilman: Her Progress Towards Utopia with Selected Writings*. New York, NY: Syracuse University Press, 1994.

King, Richard H. *Race, Culture, and the Intellectuals: 1940–1970*. Baltimore, MD: Johns Hopkins University Press, 2004.

Kirwan, Michael. *Political Theology: An Introduction*. Minneapolis, MN: Fortress Press, 2009.

Klaiber, Jeffrey L. "Religion and Revolution in Perú: 1920–1945." *Americas* 31, no. 3 (1975): 289–312.

———. *Religion and Revolution in Perú, 1824–1976*. Notre Dame, IN: University of Notre Dame Press, 1977.

———. "The Catholic Lay Movement in Perú: 1867–1959." *Americas* 40, no. 2 (October 1983): 149–170.

———. "Prophets and Populist: Liberation Theology, 1968–1988." *Americas* 46, no. 1 (1989): 1–15.

———. *The Church, Dictatorships, and Democracy in Latin America*. Maryknoll, NY: Orbis Books, 1998.

Klemperer, Klemens von. "Beyond Luther? Dietrich Bonhoeffer and the Resistance to National Socialism." *Pro Ecclesia* 6, no. 2 (1997): 184–198.

Knasas, John F.X. "Aquinas and the Liberationist Critique of Maritain's New Christendom." *Speculative Quarterly Review* 52, no. 2 (1988): 247–267.

Knight, Franklin W. "Slavery in the Americas." In *A Companion to Latin American History*. Edited by Thomas H. Holloway, 146–161. Malden, MA; Oxford: Blackwell, 2008.

Knudsen, Jonathan B. "On Enlightenment for the Common Man." In *What is Enlightenment?: Eighteenth-Century Answers and Twentieth-Century Questions*. Edited by James Schmidt, 270–290. Berkeley, CA: University of California Press, 1996.

Kohn, Margaret, and Keally D. McBride. *Political Theories of Decolonization: Postcolonialism and the Problem of Foundations*. New York, NY: Oxford University Press, 2011.

Kruks, Sonia. *Retrieving Experience: Subjectivity and Recognition in Feminist Politics*. Ithaca, NY: Cornell University Press, 2001.

Laclau, Ernesto. *Emancipation(s)*. New York, NY: Verso, 1996.

Lacroix, Jean, *Maurice Blondel: An Introduction to the Man and His Philosophy*. New York, NY: Sheed and Ward, 1968.

Lahr, Angela M. *Millennial Dreams and Apocalyptic Nightmares: The Cold War Origins of Political Evangelicalism*. New York, NY: Oxford University Press, 2007.

Landsberger, Henry A., and Emanuel Jehuda De Kadt. *The Church and Social Change in Latin America*. Notre Dame, IN: University of Notre Dame Press, 1970.

Langley, Lester D. *America and the Americas: The United States in the Western Hemisphere*. Athens, GA: University of Georgia Press, 1989.

———. *The Americas in the Age of Revolution, 1750–1850*. New Haven, CT: Yale University Press, 1996.

Larrimore, Mark Joseph. *The Problem of Evil: A Reader*. Malden, MA: Blackwell, 2001.

Larson, Brooke. *Trials of Nation Making: Liberalism, Race and Ethnicity in the Andes, 1810–1910*. Cambridge: Cambridge University Press, 2004.

Lasso, Marixa. *Myths of Harmony: Race and Republicanism during the Age of Revolution, Colombia 1795–1831*. Pittsburgh, PA: University of Pittsburgh Press, 2007.

Lawrence, Joel. *Bonhoeffer: A Guide for the Perplexed*. London; New York, NY: T & T Clark, 2010.

Lehmann, David. "The Religious Field in Latin America: Autonomy and Fragmentation." In *Latin America 1810–2010: Dreams and Legacies*. Edited by Claude Auroi and Aline Heig, 419–455. London: Imperial College Press, 2012.

Lehmann, Paul L. "Karl Barth, Theologian of Permanent Revolution." *Union Seminary Quarterly Review* 28, no. 1 (Fall 1972): 68.

Lernoux, Penny. "The Latin American Church." *Latin American Research Review* 15, no. 2 (1980): 201–211.

Levine, Daniel H. "Assessing the Impacts of Liberation Theology in Latin America." *Review of Politics* 50, no. 2 (Spring 1988): 241–263.

———. "On the Premature Reports of the Death of Liberation Theology." *Review of Politics* 57, no. 1 (Winter 1995): 105–131.

Levine, Danile H., and Alexander W. Wilde. "The Catholic Church, 'Politics' and Violence: The Colombian Case." *Review of Politics* 39, no. 2 (April 1977): 220–249.

Levy, Ze'ev. "Utopia and Reality in the Philosophy of Ernst Bloch." *Utopian Studies* 1, no. 2 (1990): 3–12.

Lewis, David L. *When Harlem was in Vogue*. New York, NY: Knopf, 1981.

Lilla, Mark. *The Stillborn God: Religion, Politics, and the Modern West*. New York, NY: Knopf, 2007.

Lindley, Susan Hill. "'Neglected Voices' and 'Praxis' in the Social Gospel." *Journal of Religious Ethics* 18, no. 1 (1990): 75–102.

Livingston, James C., and Francis Schüssler Fiorenza. *Modern Christian Thought*. Minneapolis, MN: Fortress Press, 2006.

Lloyd, Brian. "Feminism, Utopian and Scientific: Charlotte Perkins Gilman and the Prison of the Familiar." *American Studies* 39, no. 1 (Spring 1998): 93–113.

Lovejoy, Arthur O. *The Great Chain of Being: A Study of the History of an Idea*. New Brunswick, NJ: Transaction Publishers, 2009.

Lovin, Robin W. *Reinhold Niebuhr and Christian Realism*. New York, NY: Cambridge University Press, 1995.

Loving, Gregory D. "Narrative and Power Toward a Theology for the Overdog." Order No. 9969457, Graduate Theological Union, 2000. In ProQuest Dissertations & Theses Full Text. http://search.proquest.com/docview/304622180?accountid=7120.

Löwy, Michael. "Communism and Religion." *Latin American Perspectives* 25, no. 4 (1998): 71–9.

———. "Socio-Religious Origins of Brazil's Landless Rural Workers Movement." *Monthly Review* 53, no. 2 (June 2001): 32–40.

Löwy, Michael, and Mariana Ortega Breña. "Communism and Religion: José Carlos Mariátegui's Revolutionary Mysticism." *Latin American Perspectives* 35, no. 2, Reassessing the History of Latin American Communism (March 2008): 71–79.

Löwy, Michael, and Penelope Duggan. "Marxism and Romanticism in the Work of José Carlos Mariátegui." *Latin American Perspectives* 25, no. 4 (1998): 76–88.

Löwy, Michael, and Michael Pearlman, eds. *Marxism in Latin America from 1909 to the Present: An Anthology* Atlantic Highlands, NJ: Humanities Press, 1992.

Luker, Ralph. *The Social Gospel in Black and White: American Racial Reform, 1885–1912*. Chapel Hill, NC: University of North Carolina Press, 1991.

Lukes, Steven. "The Meaning of Individualism." *Journal of the History of Ideas* 32, no. 1 (January–March 1971): 45–66.

Machen, J. Gresham. "Karl Barth and 'Theology of Crisis.'" *Westminster Theological Journal* 53 (1991): 197–207

Madsen, Deborah L. *American Exceptionalism*. Jackson, MS: University Press of Mississippi, 1998.

Mancini, Matthew J. "Maritain's Democratic Vision: 'You have no Bourgeois.'" In *Understanding Maritain: Philosopher and Friend*. Edited by Deal Wyatt Hudson and Matthew J. Mancini, 133–152. Macon, GA: Mercer University Press.

Marable, Manning. "The Rainbow Coalition: Jesse Jackson and the Politics of Ethnicity." *Crosscurrents* 34, no. 1 (Spring 1984): 21–42.

———. *W.E.B. DuBois, Black Radical Democrat*. Boston, MA: Twayne, 1986.

Marable, Manning, Nishani Frazier, and John Campbell McMillian. *Freedom on My Mind: The Columbia Documentary History of the African American Experience*. New York, NY: Columbia University Press, 2003.

Marsden, John Joseph. *Marxian and Christian Utopianism: Toward a Socialist Political Theology*. New York, NY: Monthly Review Press, 1991.

Martin, Leona S. "Nation Building, International Travel, and the Construction of the Nineteenth-Century Pan-Hispanic Women's Network." *Hispania* 87, no. 3 (September 2004): 439–446.

Martinez-Echazabal, Lourdes. "Mestizaje and the Discourse of National/Cultural Identity in Latin America, 1845–1959." *Latin American Perspectives* 25, no. 3, Race and National Identity in the Americas (May 1998): 21–42.

Massey, James A. "Feuerbach and Religious Individualism." *Journal of Religion* 56, no. 4 (1976): 366–381.

Matusow, Allen J. *The Unraveling of America: A History of Liberalism in the 1960s*. New York, NY: Harper & Row, 1984.

May, Henry F. *Protestant Churches and Industrial America*. New York, NY: Harper & Brothers, 1949.

———. *The Enlightenment in America*. New York, NY: Oxford University Press, 1976.

———. "Intellectual History and Religious History." In *New Directions in American Intellectual History*. Edited by John Higham and Paul K. Conkin, 105–115. Baltimore, MD: John Hopkins University Press, 1979.

Mazlish, Bruce. *A New Science: The Breakdown of Connections and the Birth of Sociology*. New York, NY: Oxford University Press, 1989.

McCann, Dennis. *Christian Realism and Liberation Theology: Practical Theologies in Creative Conflict*. Maryknoll, NY: Orbis Books, 1981.

McClay, Wilfred M. *The Masterless: Self & Society in Modern America*. Chapel Hill, NC: University of North Carolina Press, 1994.

McFarlane, Anthony. "Rebellions in Late Colonial Spanish America: A Comparative Perspective." *Bulletin of Latin American Research* 14, no. 3 (September 1995): 313–338.

McGovern, Arthur F. *Liberation Theology and Its Critics: Toward an Assessment*. Eugene, OR: Wipf & Stock, 2009.

McKanan, Dan. *Prophetic Encounters: Religion and the American Radical Tradition*. Boston, MA: Beacon Press, 2011.

McMahon, Robert J. *The Cold War in the Third World*. New York, NY: Oxford University Press, 2013.

McPherson, Alan L. *Yankee no!: Anti-Americanism in U.S.–Latin American Relations*. Cambridge, MA: Harvard University Press, 2003.

Meier, August. *Negro Thought in America, 1880–1915: Racial Ideologies in the Age of Booker T. Washington*. Ann Arbor, MI: University of Michigan Press, 1963.

Meier, Heinrich. *The Lesson of Carl Schmitt: Four Chapters on the Distinction between Political Theology and Political Philosophy*. Chicago, IL: University of Chicago Press, 1998.

Melzer, Authur M. "The Origins of the Counter-Enlightenment: Rousseau and the New Religion of Sincerity." *American Political Science Review* 90, no. 2 (June 1996): 344–360.

Mich, Marvin L. Krier. *Catholic Social Teaching and Movements*. Mystic, CT: Twenty-Third Publications, 2006.

Michaud, Derek, ed. "Juan Luis Segundo, 1925–1996." *Boston Collaborative Encyclopedia of Western Theology*. http://people.bu.edu/wwildman/bce/segundo.htm.

Mignolo, Walter. *The Idea of Latin America*. Malden, MA: Blackwell, 2005.

Milbank, John. *Theology and Social Theory: Beyond Secular Reason*. Cambridge, MA: Blackwell, 1994.

Miles, Rebekah. "Valerie Saiving: Reconsidered." *Journal of Feminist Studies in Religion* 28, no. 1 (2012): 79–86.

Miller, Marilyn Grace. *Rise and Fall of the Cosmic Race: The Cult of Mestizaje in Latin America*. Austin, TX: University of Texas Press, 2004.

Mondragón, Carlos. *Like Leaven in the Dough: Protestant Social Thought in Latin America, 1920–1950*. Madison: Fairleigh Dickinson University Press, 2010.

Montero, Oscar. *José Martí: An Introduction*. New York, NY: Palgrave Macmillan, 2004.

Moore, Laurence R. "Secularization: Religion and the Social Sciences." In *Between the Times: The Travail of the Protestant Establishment in America, 1900–1960*. Edited by William R. Hutchison, 233–252. New York, NY: Cambridge University Press, 1989.

Morello, Gustavo. *The Catholic Church and Argentina's Dirty War*. New York, NY: Oxford University Press, 2015.

Morris, Calvin S. *Reverdy C. Ransom: Black Advocate of the Social Gospel*. Lanham, MD: University Press of America, 1990.

Morrison, Ken. *Marx, Durkheim, Weber: Formations of Modern Social Thought*. London: Sage Publications, 2006.

Moyn, Samuel. *Christian Human Rights*. Philadelphia, PA: University of Pennsylvania Press, 2015.

Munck, Thomas. *The Enlightenment: A Comparative Social History, 1721–1794*. London: Oxford University Press, 2000.

Murena, Hector A. *El Pecado Original de America*. Buenos Aires: Fondo de Cultura Economica, 2006.

Murphy, Timothy Charles. "The Influence of Socialism in Black and Womanist Theologies: Capitalism's Relationship as Source, Sin and Salvation." *Black Theology: An International Journal* 10, no. 1 (2012): 28–48.

Nash, Gary B. *Race and Revolution*. Madison, WI: Madison House, 1990.

Nessan, Craig L. *Orthopraxis or Heresy: North American Response to Latin American Liberation Theology*. Altanta, GA: Scholars Press, 1989.

Nisbet, Robert A. *The Sociological Tradition*. New York, NY: Basic Books, 1966.

Noll, Mark A. *America's God: From Jonathan Edwards to Abraham Lincoln*. New York, NY: Oxford University Press, 2002.

———. *The Civil War as Theological Crisis*. Chapel Hill, NC: University of North Carolina Press, 2006.

Nubiola, Jaime. "The Reception of William James in Continental Europe." *European Journal of Pragmatism and American Philosophy* 3, no. 1 (2011): 73–85.

O'Brien, Thomas F. *Making the Americas: The United States and Latin America from the Age of Revolutions to the Era of Globalization*. Albuquerque, NM: University of New Mexico Press, 2007.

Okafor, Victor Oguejiofor. "A Reevaluation of African Education: Woodson Revisited." *Journal of Black Studies* 22, no. 4 (June 1992): 579–592.

Ozment, Steven E. *The Age of Reform (1250–1550): An Intellectual and Religious History of Late Medieval and Reformation Europe*. New Haven, CT: Yale University Press, 1980.

Pappas, Gregory Fernando. *Pragmatism in the Americas*. New York, NY: Fordham University Press, 2011.

Peden, Creighton. *Empirical Tradition in American Liberal Religious Thought, 1860–1960*. New York, NY: Peter Lang, 2010.

Pehl, Mattew. *The Making of Working-Class Religion*. Urbana, IL: University of Illinois Press, 2016.

Pellauer, Mary D. *Toward a Tradition of Feminist Theology: The Religious Social Thought of Elizabeth Cady Stanton, Susan B. Anthony, and Anna Howard Shaw*. Brooklyn, NY: Carlson, 1991.

Peña, Milagros. "The Sodalitium Vitae Movement in Perú: A Rewriting of Liberation Theology." *Sociological Analysis* 53, no. 2 (Summer 1992): 159–173.

Pérez-Bustillo, Camilo, and Karla V. Hernández Mares. *Human Rights, Hegemony, and Utopia in Latin America: Poverty, Forced Migration, and Resistance in Mexico and Colombia*. Leiden: Brill, 2016.

Perlstein, Daniel. "Teaching Freedom: SNCC and the Creation of the Mississippi Freedom Schools." *History of Education Quarterly* 30, no. 3 (Autumn 1990): 297–324.

Peterson, Carla L. *Doers of the Word: African-American Women Speakers and Writers in the North (1830–1880)*. New York, NY: Oxford University Press, 1995.

Piehl, Mel. *Breaking Bread: The Catholic Worker and the Origin of Catholic Radicalism in America*. Tuscaloosa, AL: University of Alabama Press, 2006.

Pilardi, Jo-Ann. "The Changing Critical Fortunes of the Second Sex." *History and Theory* 32, no. 1 (February 1993): 51–73.

Pinn, Anthony B. *Why, Lord?: Suffering and Evil in Black Theology*. New York, NY: Continuum, 1995.

———. *Moral Evil and Redemptive Suffering: A History of Theodicy in African-American Religious Thought*. Gainesville, FL: University Press of Florida, 2002.

Plantinga, Alvin C. *God, Freedom, and Evil*. Grand Rapids, MI: W. B. Eerdmans, 1983.

Pocock, J.G.A. *Barbarism and Religion*. New York, NY: Cambridge University Press, 1999.

Posada-Carbo, Eduardo. "Fiction as History: The Bananeras and Gabriel Garcia Marquez's One Hundred Years of Solitude." *Journal of Latin American Studies* 30, no. 2 (May 1998): 395–414.

Porterfield, Amanda. *Conceived in Doubt: Religion and Politics in the New American Nation*. Chicago, IL: University of Chicago Press, 2012.

Pottenger, John R. *The Political Theory of Liberation Theology: Toward a Reconvergence of Social Values and Social Science*. Albany, NY: State University of New York Press, 1989.

Prashad, Vijay. *The Darker Nations: A People's History of the Third World*. New York, NY: New Press, distributed by W.W. Norton, 2007.

Quijano, Aníbal, and Immanuel Wallestein. "Americanity as a Concept, Or the Americas in the World Sytem." *International Social Science Research* 134 (1992): 449–557.

Rabe, Stephen G. *The Killing Zone: The United States Wages Cold War in Latin America*. New York, NY: Oxford University Press, 2012.

Rama, Angel, and David L. Frye. *Writing Across Cultures: Narrative Transculturation in Latin America*. Durham, NC: Duke University Press, 2012.

Rama, Angel, and John Charles Chasteen. *The Lettered City*. Durham, NC: Duke University Press, 1996.

Rampersad, Arnold. *The Art and Imagination of W.E.B. Du Bois*. Cambridge, MA: Harvard University Press, 1976.

Randolph, Sheri M. "Women's Liberation or . . . Black Liberation." In *Want to Start a Revolution?: Radical Women in the Black Freedom Struggle*. Edited by Dayo F. Gore, Jeanne Theoharis, and Komozi Woodard, 223–247. New York, NY: University Press, 2009.

Raposa, Michael L. "Pragmatism, Democracy, and the Future of Catholic Theology." *American Journal of Theology and Philosophy* 30, no. 3 (September 2009): 288–302.

Rasmussen, Larry. "Bonhoeffer and the Antropocene." NGTT DEEL 55, Supplement 1 (2014): 941–954.

Raulet, Gerard. "Critique of Religion and Religion as Critique: The Secularized Hope of Ernst Bloch." *New German Critique*, no. 9 (Autumn 1976): 71–85.

Rawls, John. *Political Liberalism*. New York, NY: Columbia University Press, 1993.

———. "The Idea of Public Reason Revisited." *University of Chicago Law Review* 64, no. 3 (Summer 1997): 765–807.

Reardon, Bernard M.G. *Religion in the Age of Romanticism: Studies in Early Nineteenth Century Thought*. New York, NY: Cambridge University Press, 1985.

Reff, Daniel T. "The Jesuits Mission Frontier in Comparative Perspective." In *Contested Ground: Comparative Frontiers on the Northern and Southern Edges of the Spanish Empire*. Edited by Donna J. Guy and Thomas E. Sheridan, 16–31. Tucson. AZ: University of Arizona Press, 1998.

Reilly, Charles A. "Latin America's Religious Populist." In *Religion and Political Conflict in Latin America*. Edited by Daniel H. Levine, 42–57. Chapel Hill, NC: University of North Carolina Press, 1986.

Ribeiro, Claudio de Oliveira. "Has Liberation Theology Died?" *Ecumenical Review* 51, World Council of Churches, 1999.

Rich, Wilbur C. *The Politics of Minority Coalitions: Race, Ethnicity, and Shared Uncertainties*. Westport, CT: Praeger, 1996.

Rickford, Russell. *We Are an African People: Independent Education, Black Power and the Radical Imagination*. New York, NY: Oxford University Press, 2016.

Rideau, Émile. *The Thought of Teilhard De Chardin*. New York, NY: Harper & Row, 1967.

Rieger, Joerg, ed. *Theology from the Belly of the Whale: A Frederick Herzog Reader*. Harrisburg, PA: Trinity Press International, 1999.

Rieger, Joerg, and Pui-lan Kwok. *Occupy Religion: Theology of the Multitude*. Lanlam, MA: Rowman & Littlefield, 2013.

Robin, Corey. *The Reactionary Mind: Conservatism from Edmund Burke to Sarah Palin*. New York: Oxford University Press, 2013.

Rodgers, Daniel T. *Age of Fracture*. Cambridge, MA: Belknap Press of Harvard University Press, 2011.

Roland H. Bainton. "Thomas Muntzer Revolutionary Firebrand of the Reformation." *Sixteenth Century Journal* 13, no. 2 (Summer 1982): 3–16.

Romanell, Patrick. "Samuel Ramos on the Philosophy of Mexican Culture: Ortega and Unamuno in Mexico." *Latin American Research Review* 10, no. 3 (Autumn 1975): 81–101.

Rosen, Ruth. *The World Split Open: How the Modern Women's Movement Changed America*. New York, NY: Viking, 2000.

Rosenberg, Rosalind. *Beyond Separate Spheres: The Intellectual Roots of Modern Feminism*. New Haven, CT: Yale University Press, 1982.

———. *Changing the Subject: How the Women of Columbia Shaped the Way We Think about Sex and Politics*. New York, NY: Columbia University Press, 2004.

Rossi, Philip. "The Foundation of the Philosophical Concept of Autonomy by Kant and its Historical Consequences." In *The Ethics of Liberation—The Liberation of Ethics*. Edited by Dietmar Mieth and Jacques Pohier, 3–8. Edinburg: T&T Clark, 1984.

Rossinow, Douglas C. *The Politics of Authenticity: Liberalism, Christianity, and the New Left in America*. New York, NY: Columbia University Press, 1998.

———. "Letting Go: Revisiting the New Left's Demise." In *The New Left Revisited*. Edited by John McMillian and Paul Buhle, 241–256. Philadelphia, PA: Temple University Press, 2003.

Rowland, Christopher, and Mark Corner. *Liberating Exegesis: The Challenge of Liberation Theology to Biblical Studies*. Louisville, KY: Westminster/John Knox Press, 1989.

Ruiz, Ramon Eduardo. *Cuba: The Making of a Revolution*. New York, NY: W.W. Norton, 1970.

Salazar Bondy, Augusto. *Existe Una Filosofía De Nuestra América?* Mexico City: Siglo Veintiuno Editores, 1988.

Santiago-Vendrell, Angel Daniel. *Contextual Theology and Revolutionary Transformation in Latin America: The Missionology of M. Richard Shaull*. Eugene, OR: Pickwick Publications, 2010.

Savelle, Max. *Empires to Nations: Expansion in America, 1713–1824*. Minneapolis, MN: University of Minnesota Press, 1974.

Sawchuk, Kim. "The Cultural Apparatus: C. Wright Mills' Unfinished Work." *American Sociologist* 32, no. 1 (Spring 2001): 27–49.

Schall, James V. *Jacques Maritain: The Philosopher in Society*. Lanham, MD: Rowman & Littlefield, 1998.

Schoultz, Lars. *Beneath the United States: A History of U.S. Policy Toward Latin America*. Cambridge, MA: Harvard University Press, 1998.

Schutte, Ofelia. *Cultural Identity and Social Liberation in Latin American Thought*. SUNY Series in Latin American and Iberian Thought and Culture. Albany, NY: State University of New York, NY Press, 1993.

Schwaller, John Frederick. *The History of the Catholic Church in Latin America: From Conquest to Revolution and Beyond*. New York, NY: New York University Press, 2011.

Scott, David. *Conscripts of Modernity: The Tragedy of Colonial Enlightenment*. Durham, NC: Duke University Press, 2004.

Scott, Peter, and William T. Cavanaugh. *The Blackwell Companion to Political Theology*. Malden, MA: Blackwell, 2007.

Seidman, Steven. *Liberalism and the Origins of European Social Theory*. Berkeley, CA: University of California Press, 1983.

Selby, Peter. "Christianity in the World Come of Age." In *The Cambridge Companion to Dietrich Bonhoeffer*. Edited by John W. de Gruchy, 226–245. Cambridge: Cambridge University Press, 1999.

Shepard, John W. "The European Background of American Freedom." *Journal of Church and State* 50, no. 4 (Autumn 2008): 647–659.

Shil, Edward. "'Ideology and Utopia' by Karl Mannheim." *Daedalus* 103, no. 1 (1974): 83–89.

Shook, John R. "John Dewey and Edward Scribner Ames: Partners in Religious Naturalism." *American Journal of Theology and Philosophy* 8, no. 2 (May 2007): 178–207.

———. "Peirce's Pragmatic Theology and Stoic Religious Ethics." *Journal of Religious Ethics* 39, no. 2 (2011): 344–363.

Sigmund, Paul E. "Latin American Catholicism's Opening to the Left." *Review of Politics* 35, no. 1 (January 1973): 61–76.

Silverman, Maxim. *Frantz Fanon's Black Skin, White Masks: New Interdisciplinary Essays*. Manchester: Manchester University Press, 2005.

Singh, Nikhil Pal. *Black is a Country: Race and the Unfinished Struggle for Democracy*. Cambridge, MA: Harvard University Press, 2004.

Skemp, Sheila L. *First Lady of Letters: Judith Sargent Murray and the Struggle for Female Independence*. Philadelphia, PA: University of Pennsylvania Press, 2013.

Skrentny, John David. *The Minority Rights Revolution*. Cambridge, MA: Belknap Press of Harvard University Press, 2002.

Smith, Christian. *The Emergence of Liberation Theology: Radical Religion and Social Movement Theory*. Chicago, IL: University of Chicago Press, 1991.

———. "The Spirit and Democracy: Base Communities, Protestantism, and Democratization in Latin America." *Sociology of Religion* 55, no. 2 (Summer 1994): 119–143.

———. "'Las Casas' as Theological Counteroffensive: An Interpretation of Gustavo Gutiérrez's 'Las Casas: In Search of the Poor of Jesus Christ.'" *Journal for the Scientific Study of Religion* 41, no. 1 (March 2002): 69–73.

Smith, Donald Eugene, ed. "Patterns of Secularization in Latin America." In *Religion and Political Modernization*. New Haven, CT: Yale University Press, 1974.

Smith, Gary Scott. *The Search for Social Salvation: Social Christianity and America, 1880–1925*. Lanham, MD: Lexington Books, 2000.

Sobrevilla, David. "Transculturacion y heterogeneidad: Avatares de dos categorias literarias en American Latina." *Revista De Critica Literaria Latinoamericana* 27, no. 54 (July 2001): 21–33.

Sockness, Brent W. "Schleiermacher and the Ethics of Authencity: 'the Monologen of 1800.'" *Journal of Religious Ethics* 32, no. 3 (Winter 2004): 477–517.

Sorensen, Diana. *A Turbulent Decade Remembered: Scenes from the Latin American Sixties*. Stanford, CA: Stanford University Press, 2007.

Sorkin, David Jan. *The Religious Enlightenment: Protestants, Jews, and Catholics from London to Vienna*. Princeton, NJ: Princeton University Press, 2008.

Speer, James A. "The New Christian Right and its Parent Company: A Study in Political Contrasts." In *New Christian Politics*. Edited by David G. Bromley and Anson D. Shupe, 19–40. Macon, GA: Mercer, 1984.

Spiegel, Yorick. *Bourgeoisies and the Christian Religion: Problems of Accommodation in the Theology of Schleiermacher*. Munich: Chr. Kaiser Verlag, 1968.

Springer, Kimberly. *Living for the Revolution: Black Feminist Organizations, 1968–1980*. Durham, NC: Duke University Press, 2005.

Stansell, Christine. *The Feminist Promise: 1792 to the Present*. New York, NY: Modern Library, 2010.

Stavro, Elaine. "Rethinking Identity and Coalitional Politics, Insights from Simone De Beauvoir." *Canadian Journal of Political Science* 40, no. 2 (2007): 439–463.

Stehn, Alexander W. "Religious Binding of the Imperial Self." In *Pragmatism in the Americas*. Edited by Pappas, Gregory Fernando, 297–314. New York, NY: Fordham University Press, 2011.

Steigerwald, David. *The Sixties and the End of Modern America*. New York, NY: St. Martin's Press, 1995.

Stephanson, Anders. *Manifest Destiny: American Expansionism and the Empire of Right*. New York, NY: Hill and Wang, 1995.

Stern, Steve J. "The Age of Andean Insurrection, 1742–1782." In *Resistance, Rebellion, and Consciousness in the Andean Peasant World, 18th to 20th Centuries*. Edited by Steve J. Stern, 34–93. Madison, WI: University of Wisconsin Press, 1987.

Stevenson-Moessner, Jeanne. "Elizabeth Cady Stanton, Reformer to Revolutionary: A Theological Trajectory." *Journal of the Academy of Religion* 62, no. 3 (1994): 673–697.

Stone, Ronald H. "On the Boundary of Utopia and Politics." In *The Cambridge Companion to Paul Tillich*. Edited by Russell Re Manning, 208–220. Cambridge: Cambridge University Press, 2009.

Sturkey, William. "'I Want to Become a Part of History': Freedom Summer, Freedom Schools, and the Freedom News." *Journal of African American History* 95, no. 3–4 (Summer–Fall 2010): 348–368.

Sugrue, Thomas J. *The Origins of the Urban Crisis: Race and Inequality in Postwar Detroit*. Princeton, NJ: Princeton University Press, 1996.

Sutton, Matthew Avery. *Jerry Falwell and the Rise of the Religious Right: A Brief History with Documents*. Boston: Bedford/St. Martin's, 2013.

Swartz, David R. *Moral Minority: The Evangelical Left in an Age of Conservatism*. Philadelphia, PA: University of Pennsylvania Press, 2012.

Tarrant, Shira. *When Sex Became Gender*. New York, NY: Routledge, 2006.

Taylor, Barbara. "The Religious Foundations of Mary Wollstonecraft's Feminism." In *Cambridge Companion to Mary Wollstonecraft*. Edited by Claudia L. Johnson, 99–118. New York, NY: Cambridge University Press, 2002.

Taylor, Charles. *Sources of the Self: The Making of the Modern Identity.* Cambridge, MA: Harvard University Press, 1989.

Taylor, Charles, and Amy Gutmann. *Multiculturalism and "the Politics of Recognition": An Essay.* Princeton, NJ: Princeton University Press, 1992.

Thickstun, Margaret Olofson. "Writing the Spirit: Margaret Fell's Feminist Critique of Pauline Theology." *Journal of the Academy of Religion* 63, no. 2 (Summer 1995): 269.

Thompson, Kenneth W. "The Religious Transformation of Politics and the Political Transformation of Religion." *Review of Politics* 50, no. 4 (Autumn 1998): 545–560.

Thomson, Sinclair. *We Alone Will Rule: Native Andean Politics in the Age of Insurgency.* Madison, WI: University of Wisconsin Press, 2002.

Thurston, Michael. "Black Christ, Red Flag: Langston Hughes on Scottsboro." *College Literature* 22, no. 3 (October 1995): 30–49.

Tilman, Rick. *C. Wright Mills: A Native Radical and His American Intellectual Roots.* University Park, PA: Pennsylvania State University Press, 1984.

Tomlinson, B.R. "What was the Third World?" *Journal of Contemporary History* 38, no. 2 (April 2003): 307–321.

Trigo, Pedro, and Gustavo Gutiérrez. *Arguedas, Mito, Historia y Religión.* Lima: Centro de Estudios y Publicaciones, 1982.

Turner, Denys. *Marxism and Christianity.* Totowa, NJ: Barnes and Noble, 1983.

Tyson, Timothy B. "Robert F. Williams, 'Black Power' and the Roots of the African American Freedom Struggle." *Journal of American History* 85, no. 2 (September 1998): 540–570.

———. *Radio Free Dixie: Robert F. Williams and the Roots of Black Power.* Chapel Hill, NC: University of North Carolina Press, 1999.

Umansky, Lauri. *Motherhood Reconceived: Feminism and the Legacies of the Sixties.* New York, NY: New York University Press, 1996.

Valiente, O. Ernesto. "The Reception of Vatican II in Latin America." *Theological Studies* 32 (2012): 795–823.

Van Deburg, William L. *New Day in Babylon: The Black Power Movement and American Culture, 1965–1975.* Chicago, IL: University of Chicago Press, 1992.

———. *Modern Black Nationalism: From Marcus Garvey to Louis Farrakhan.* New York, NY: New York University Press, 1997.

Van Delden, Maarten, and Yvon Grenier. *Gunshots at the Fiesta: Literature and Politics in Latin America.* Nashville, TN: Vanderbilt University Press, 2009.

Vellem, V.S. "Black Theology of Liberation and the Economy of Life." *Ecumenical Review* 67, no. 2 (July 2015): 177–186.

Vial, Theodore. "Schleiermacher and the State." In *Cambridge Companion to Frederick Schleiermacher.* Edited by Jacqueline Marina, 269–286. Cambridge: Cambridge University Press, 2005.

Voekel, Pamela, and Michael Jo. "Vaya Con Dios: Religion and the Transnational History of the Americas." *History Compass* 5, no. 5 (2007): 1604–1639.

Walden, Daniel. "Dubois' Pan-Africanism, a Reconsideration." *Negro American Literature Forum* 8, no. 4 (Winter 1974): 260–262.

Walker, Charles F. *The Tupac Amaru Rebellion*. Cambridge: Belknap Press, 2014.

Walker Gogol, Eugene. *The Concept of Other in Latin American Liberation: Fusing Emancipatory Philosophic Thought and Social Revolt*. Oxford: Lexington Books, 2002.

Wall-Smith, Stephen B. "José Maria Arguedas: Godfather of Liberationism." *Christian Century* (November 18, 1987): 1034.

Walsham, Alexandra. "The Reformation and 'the Disenchantment of the World.'" *Historical Journal* 51, no. 2 (2008): 497–528.

Walzer, Michael. *Exodus and Revolution*. New York, NY: Basic Books, 1985.

Ward, Thomas. "From Sarmiento to Martí and Hostos: Extricating the Nation from Coloniality." *Revista Europea De Estudios Latinoamericanos y Del Caribe / European Review of Latin American and Caribbean Studies*, no. 83 (October 2007): 83–104.

Washington, Robert E. *The Ideologies of African American Literature: From the Harlem Renaissance to the Black Nationalist Revolt: A Sociology of Literature Perspective*. Lanham, MD: Rowman & Littlefield, 2001.

Waters, Kristin, and Carol B. Conaway. *Black Women's Intellectual Traditions: Speaking their Minds*. Burlington, VT: University Press of New England, 2007.

Welch, Claude. *Protestant Thought in the Nineteenth Century*. New Haven, CT: Yale University Press, 1972.

Wendt, Simon. "'They Finally Found Out that We Really Are Men': Violence, Non-Violence and Black Manhood in the Civil Rights Era." *Gender & History* 19, no. 3 (November 2007): 543–564.

West, Cornel. *Prophesy Deliverance!* Louisville, KY: Westminster/John Knox Press, 2002.

Whitaker, Arthur Preston. *The Western Hemisphere Idea: Its Rise and Decline*. Ithaca, NY: Cornell University Press, 1954.

———. *Latin America and the Enlightenment*. New York, NY: D. Appleton-Century, 1942.

White, Ronald C., and Charles Howard Hopkins. *The Social Gospel: Religion and Reform in Changing America*. Philadelphia: Temple University Press, 1976.

Wickberg, Daniel. "Intellectual History vs. the Social History of Intellectuals." *Rethinking History* 5, no. 3 (November 2001): 383–395.

———. "What is the History of Sensibilities? On Cultural Histories, Old and New." *American Historical Review* 112, no. 3 (June 2007): 661–684.

———. "In the Environment of Ideas: Arthur Lovejoy and the History of Ideas as a Form of Cultural History." *Modern Intellectual History* 11, no. 2 (2014): 439–464.

Wildiers, N.M. *An Introduction to Teilhard De Chardin*. New York, NY: Harper & Row, 1968.

Williams, Daniel K. *God's Own Party: The Making of the Christian Right*. Oxford: Oxford University Press, 2012.

Williams, George Huntston. *The Radical Reformation*. Philadelphia, PA: Westminster Press, 1962.

Williams, Reggie L. *Bonhoeffer's Black Jesus: Harlem Renaissance Theology and an Ethic of Resistance*. Waco, TX: Baylor University Press, 2014.

Williams, Rhonda Y. "Black Women and Black Power." *OAH Magazine of History* 22, no. 3 (2008): 59–71.

Wilsey, John D. *American Exceptionalism and Civil Religion: Reassessing the History of an Idea*. Downer Grove, IL: IVP Academic, 2015.

Wintz, Cary D. *Black Culture and the Harlem Renaissance*. Houston, TX: Rice University Press, 1988.

Woldring, H.E.S. *Karl Mannheim: The Development of His Thought: Philosophy, Sociology and Social Ethics, with a Detailed Biography*. New York, NY: St. Martin's Press, 1987.

Wood, Gordon S. *The Radicalism of the American Revolution*. New York, NY: Vintage Books, 1993.

Wood, Ralph C. "To the Unknown God: Peter Berger's Theology of Transcendence." *Perspectives in Religious Studies* 20, no. 2 (Summer 1993): 176–186.

Woodard, Komozi. *A Nation within a Nation: Amiri Baraka (LeRoi Jones) and Black Power Politics*. Chapel Hill, NC: University of North Carolina Press, 1999.

Woodhead, Linda, Paul Heelas, and David Martin. *Peter Berger and the Study of Religion*. New York, NY: Routledge, 2001.

Worrell, Mark P. "Authoritarianism, Critical Theory and Political Psychology: Past, Present, Future." *Social Thought and Research* 21, no. 1–2 (1998): 3–33.

Wright, Thomas C. *Latin America in the Era of the Cuban Revolution*. Westport, CT: Praeger, 2001.

———. *State Terrorism in Latin America: Chile, Argentina, and International Human Rights*. Lanham: Rowman & Littlefield, 2007.

Wuthnow, Robert. *The Restructuring of American Religion: Society and Faith since World War II*. Princeton, NJ: Princeton University Press, 1988.

Young, Alford A. Jr. and Donald R. Deskins Jr. "Early Traditions of African-American Sociological Thought." *Annual Review of Sociology* 27 (2001): 445–477.

Young, Cynthia Ann. *Soul Power: Culture, Radicalism, and the Making of a US Third World Left*. Durham, NC: Duke University Press, 2006.

Yount, David. *America's Spiritual Utopias: The Quest for Heaven on Earth*. Westport, CT: Praeger, 2008.

Zamir, Shamoon. *Dark Voices: W.E.B. Du Bois and American Thought, 1888–1903*. Chicago, IL: University of Chicago Press, 1995.

Zauderer, Naomi B. "Consumption, Production, and Reproduction in the Work of Charlotte Perkins Gilman." In *Charlotte Perkins Gilman: Optimist Reformer*. Edited by Rudd, Jill Rudd and Val Gough, 151–172. Iowa City, IA: University of Iowa Press, 1999.

Zea, Leopoldo. *The Latin-American Mind*. Norman, OK: University of Oklahoma Press, 1963.
———. *Positivism in Mexico*. Austin, TX: University of Texas Press, 1974.
———. *América Latina En Sus Ideas*. México, DF: Unesco, 1986.
———. "Identity: A Latin American Philosophical Problem." *Philosophical Forum* XX, no. 1–2 (Fall–Winter 1988–1989): 3–16.
Zepp, Ira G. *The Social Vision of Martin Luther King, Jr*. Brooklyn, NY: Carlson, 1989.
Zuckerman, Phil. "The Sociology of Religion of W.E.B. Du Bois." *Sociology of Religion* 63, no. 2 (July 2002): 239–253.
———. *The Social Theory of W.E.B. Dubois*. Thousand Oaks, CA: Pine Forge Press, 2004.

Index

abolitionism, 243
Acao Popular (Brazil), 146
Acción Democrática, 146
Addams, Jane, 159, 160
Adler, Alfred, 197
Adler, Mortimer, 137
affirmative action, 230
Ahlstrom, Sydney E., 254
Alberdi, Juan Bautista, 54, 56, 194
alienation, 4, 20, 33, 72, 73, 74, 90, 106, 132, 153, 154, 186, 188, 234, 242
Alinsky, Saul, 137
Allen, Richard, 169
Allende, Salvador, 222, 225, 250
Alliance for Progress, 146
Alson, Wallace M., Jr., 248
Alves, Rubem, 7, 30, 44, 73, 75, 80, 142, 144, 227, 277n5
   and Christian utopianism, 227, 228
   and transcendence, 71, 72
American Popular Revolutionary Alliance, 136
American Transcendentalism, 43
Anthony, Susan B., 242
anti-Semitism, 132, 140
anti-totalitarianism, 220
anti-war movement, 33, 304–5n4

Appeal for Theological Affirmation, An, 249–50
Aprista (Peru), 146
Arendt, Hannah, 121, 131, 132, 141, 221
Argentina's "Dirty War," 223
Arguedas, José Maria, 205, 206
assimilation, 117, 136, 188, 198, 206, 208, 209, 241
Assmann, Hugo, 200, 223, 237–38, 239
Augustine (Saint), 38, 88

Bachofen, Johann, 186
Baldwin, James, 15, 16, 209
Bandung Conference (1955), 193
Baraka, Imamu Amiri, 210, 211, 213
Barth, Karl, 20, 23, 46, 47, 95, 100, 123, 165, 225, 282–83n31
base ecclesial communities (BECs), 76, 198, 199, 203, 204, 223, 224, 251, 256, 257
Batista, Fulgencio, 24, 25, 198
Batten, Samuel Zane, 156
Baum, Gregory, 239
Beard, Mary Ritter, 177
Bellah, Robert, 242, 243
Beloved Community, 231
Benedict XVI (Pope), 257

Bennett, John C., 222, 225, 226
Berdyaev, Nikolai, 47
Berger, Peter, 186, 221, 247, 248, 249, 262
Berrigan, Daniel, 227
biblical text, 27, 190, 224, 240
    and absolutism, 43, 48, 113, 189
    and black theology, 20, 21, 23, 60, 78, 82, 103
    and feminism, 112, 113, 178, 185, 186, 190
    and liberation theology, 36, 102–3, 204
Bilbao, Francisco, 53, 195
biological determinism, 180
black Jesus, 18, 140–41, 215
Black Lives Matter (BLM), 258, 259
Black Manifesto (SNCC), 19, 20
black nationalism, 17–18, 80, 207, 208, 209–10, 211
Black Power, 15, 17, 24, 27, 63, 77, 80, 81, 82, 123, 168, 191, 210, 224
    and black manhood, 31, 83
    and self-identity, 211, 212
black social gospel, 140, 160, 161, 162, 167
black studies, 230
black theology, 104, 110, 214, 233, 237, 244, 245, 267n1
    and Black Power, 21, 22, 63, 191, 213, 230
    and liberation struggle, 3, 32, 75, 79, 119, 163, 169, 170, 204, 215, 230–31, 232
    and patriarchy, 33, 192, 213, 234, 245
    reconciliation, 278–79n28
    and white Christian tradition, 23, 103
Black Woman's Manifesto, 191
blackness, 212, 214, 230, 233, 244
Blackwell, Antoinette Brown, 178
Bliss, William D. P., 158
Bloch, Ernst, 39, 148
Blondel, Maurice, 29, 99, 134, 135, 147
Boff, Leonard, 257

Bonhoeffer, Dietrich, 140, 141, 142, 144, 145, 164, 170, 171
Bonino, José Miguez, 30, 72, 126, 142, 200, 220, 239
Braude, Ann, 181
Brazilian Landless Workers Movement, 256
Brightman, Edgar S., 167
Brown, Robert McAfee, 239, 246
Bryan, William Jennings, 157
Buber, Martin, 80–84
Budapest, Zsuzsanna E., 235
Bultman, Rudolf, 131
Burke, Edmund, 89
Bushnell, Horace, 45, 155

Caldera, Rafael, 137, 146
Callahan, Daniel, 164
Câmara, Hélder, 82
Campbell, Joseph, 186
Camus, Albert, 165
Camus, Albert, 73, 79, 80
capitalism, 14, 59, 107, 139
    and alienation, 25, 210
    as contributor to social ills, 45, 82, 111, 121, 123, 131, 138, 152, 155–56, 201, 242
    critiques of, 2, 47, 82, 122, 171, 175, 179, 230, 258
    and liberalism, 7, 28, 199, 201, 202–3
    and theology, 108, 111, 115, 139, 143, 145, 146, 158, 199, 227
Cardenal, Ernesto, 203, 204
Cardoso, F. H., 200
Carmichael, Stokely, 17, 22, 24, 77, 81, 82, 210
Carpentier, Alejo, 201
Casanova, José, 261
Catholic Action, 131, 132–33, 135–39, 146
Catholic Church, 1, 36, 37, 39, 40, 41–42, 45, 47, 53, 115, 197, 200–201, 228, 240, 241, 255, 261

and African Americans, 19, 59
attacks on liberation theology, 2–3, 99–100, 125, 134, 222, 223, 257
and capitalism/corporatism, 6, 91
and censorship, 2, 176
and Cuban Revolution, 25, 26
and feminism/feminist theology, 32, 183, 184
and indigenous peoples, 6, 31, 41, 54, 57–58, 63, 116, 136, 137, 146, 227
and neo-conservatism, 252, 253
and poverty, 27, 251
resistance to Marxism, 198, 251
and science, 52, 90, 91, 134
social action, 42, 46, 77, 131, 132–33, 135, 164–65, 211
support for liberation theology, 2–3, 8, 28, 29, 30, 37, 99–100, 147, 224, 225–26, 238, 257
see also Catholic Action; Catholic Worker Movement; Vatican II
Catholic Worker Movement, 136, 137, 304–5n4
Césaire, Aimé, 78
Channing, William, 45
Chardin, Pierre Teilhard de, 47, 125, 183
Chavez, Hugo, 257
Chavis, Benjamin F., 257
Chicago Divinity School, 93, 97, 179
Chicago Theological Seminary, 159, 178
Chicanos, 241, 243
Chodorow, Nancy, 180
Chopin, Kate, 190
Christ, Carol P., 235, 248
Christian democracy, 46, 133, 136, 138, 156
Christian Democrats, 26, 137, 146–47
Christian Faith and Life Community, 182
Christian humanism, 139
Christian idealism, 197
Christian realism, 152, 162, 163, 164, 166, 220, 221, 225, 228, 255

Christian socialism, 158
Christianity and Crisis, 220, 221, 222, 234, 248
church/state separation, 35, 38, 40–41, 48, 54, 116, 135, 241, 262
civil disobedience, 168, 221
civil religion, 106, 220, 239, 241, 242–43, 244, 246
Civil Rights Act (1964), 181
Civil Rights movement, 144, 148, 166, 168, 221, 243
Cleage, Albert B., 17–18, 215, 231
Cleaver, Eldridge, 212
Cold War, 7, 8, 13, 24, 122, 148, 152, 166, 221, 239
Coleman, John A., 242–43, 246
Coleridge, Samuel Taylor, 43
Collins, Sheila D., 184, 185, 186, 187, 190, 235, 239
colonialism/anti-colonialism, 64, 79, 115, 193, 195, 198, 201, 210
see also neo-colonialism
communism, 2, 7, 14, 27, 39, 40, 111, 116, 122, 135, 137, 139, 143, 162, 198, 199, 220, 223, 246, 250, 253
Comte, Auguste, 55, 90, 91
concientización, 203, 223
Cone, James, 3, 4, 36, 38, 40, 81, 93, 101, 153, 172, 224, 237, 238, 239, 278–79n28
black liberation theology, 20–23, 63, 72, 73, 75, 78–79, 80, 81, 85, 103, 104, 112, 119, 161, 163, 170, 213–14, 231–33
critiques of white Christianity, 48, 73, 110–11, 126–27, 163, 168, 169, 189, 230, 232–33, 244
theories on violence, 81, 82
and women's liberation, 31, 33, 187–88, 191, 234
Confessing Church movement, 140

consumerism, 2, 258
Cooper, Anna Julia, 191
Cott, Nancy, 175
Covey, Edward, 83
Cox, Harvey, 85, 164, 165, 166, 170, 171, 183
Crites, Stephen, 189
Crummell, Alexander, 207
Cruse, Harold, 210
Cuban revolution, 146, 198, 199, 201, 202, 210
Cullors, Patrisse, 258
cultural nationalism, 207, 210, 213. *See also* black nationalism

Daly, Mary, 4, 32–33, 64, 153, 183, 184, 187, 234, 235
Darwin, Charles, 94, 95, 131, 155
Davis, Reginald F., 78
Day, Dorothy, 136
de Beauvoir, Simone, 32, 175–76, 180, 182, 183
Death of God movement, 224, 293n29
decolonization, 18, 79, 204, 206, 210, 212
Delany, Martin, 207
dependency theory, 146, 199, 200, 202
Descartes, René, 138
Dewey, John, 76, 96, 97, 98, 99, 103, 121, 159
Dorrien, Gary, 158
Douglass, Frederick, 63, 78, 83, 118
Du Bois, W. E. B., 157, 160, 207–8, 209, 214, 231
dualism, 33, 48, 73, 74, 84, 86, 89, 96, 101, 107, 126, 138, 145, 162, 176, 184, 187–88, 245
Durkheim, Emile, 91, 108, 118, 165
Dussel, Enrique, 31, 64, 85, 204, 223, 239

Echeverría, Eseban, 53
economic justice, 40, 202

Ecumenical Association of Third World Theologians (EATWOT), 256
Ecumenical Movement for Human Rights, 223
ecumenicalism, 145, 146, 178, 220, 223, 239, 256
   and liberation theology, 4, 140, 141, 145, 228, 237
   among theologians, 30, 178, 239, 249
   and U.S. Civil Rights movement, 14, 15, 244
Eddy, Mary Baker, 186
Edwards, Herbert, 239, 244
Edwards, Jonathan, 48, 97
Ellison, Ralph, 209
Ellwood, Charles A., 154
Elshtain, Jean Berthke, 70
Ely, Richard, 154
Emerson, Ralph Waldo, 45
Engels, Friedrich, 39, 107, 113, 229
Equiano, Olaudah, 60
Erikson, Erik H., 181
essentialism, 180, 182, 187–88, 196, 209, 227
ethnic realism, 208
Eurocentrism, 195, 196
evangelical movement, 54, 59, 61, 77, 138, 254
   and social gospel, 156, 206, 304–5n4
   and spiritual conversion, 45, 154, 253
existentialism, 21, 32, 43, 44, 72, 74, 91, 114, 117, 132, 148, 152, 153, 175, 176, 207, 209, 212, 231

Faletto, Enzo, 200
Falwell, Jerry, 253, 254
Fanon, Frantz, 75, 78, 79, 83, 198, 212–13
Farmer, James, 254
feminist theology, 32, 34, 120, 126, 158, 180, 183, 186, 187, 192, 215, 235–36, 258, 267n13

and African American women, 191, 192
and the Bible, 113, 190
critiques of patriarchy, 64, 112, 234
and essentialism, 180, 187
and praxis, 175, 185
see also black theology: and patriarchy
Fensham, Florence, 178
Feuerbach, Ludwig, 25, 36, 93, 105, 106–7, 108, 110, 247
Fierro, Alfredo, 127
Finney, Charles, 45
Fiorenza, Elisabeth Schüssler, 64, 184–85, 235
Firestone, Shulamith, 176
Fisher, Albert Franklin, 140
folk religion, 41, 115
Fontaine, W. T., 112
Foote, Julia A. J., 62
Forman, James, 19
Foster, George Burman, 97
Fox, Margaret Fell, 64, 178
Francis (Pope), 1, 2, 257
Frankfurt School, 122, 148, 149, 185
Frazer, James G., 115
freedom, 3–4, 41, 42, 44, 48, 51, 52, 55, 56, 58, 59, 61, 65, 96, 105, 117, 121, 122, 123, 132, 135, 143, 151, 191, 229, 247
  for black people, 5, 7, 13–18, 20–22, 24, 30, 50, 57, 60–61, 72, 73, 74, 75, 77–80, 86, 112, 118, 123, 160, 167–70, 207–9, 212–13, 233
  and capitalism, 7, 139
  and democracy, 6–7, 109, 138
  as God's salvation, 70–71, 44, 54, 58, 59, 60, 69, 93, 106–7, 127, 16
  and liberation theology, 9, 10, 29, 64, 69, 74–75, 85–86, 148–50, 259
  as moral autonomy, 70, 73, 38, 89
  in the Third World, 7, 50, 57, 64, 123, 200, 206, 210
  for women, 5, 57, 62, 63, 74, 76, 83, 86, 119, 176, 182, 188
Frei, Eduardo, 137, 146
Freidan, Betty, 180
Freire, Paulo, 76–77, 84, 184, 237, 238, 278n17
Freud, Sigmund, 73, 121, 180, 181, 235
Fuller, Margaret, 187

Galeano, Eduardo, 201
García Márquez, Gabriel, 201
Garrison, William Lloyd, 154
Garvey, Marcus, 207
Garza, Alicia, 258
Geneva Conference (1966), 143, 144, 222
George, Henry, 155
Gilman, Charlotte Perkins, 171, 187, 190
Gladden, Washington, 131, 154–55, 157, 160
globalization, 260
God and Country (Peru), 252
God's co-suffering with humanity, 142, 282–83n31
God's transcendence, 5, 48, 71, 100, 228
Gogarten, Friedrich, 165
Goldenberg, Naomi R., 235
Goldstein, Valerie Saiving, 84, 178–81, 235
Gonin, Marcus, 134
gospel of prosperity, 261
Gramsci, Antonio, 29, 76
Grant, Jacquelyn, 191, 234
Great Awakening, 139
Great Mother, 183, 186, 190
Great Separation, 37–38, 40, 49, 262
Grimké, Angelina Emily, 186
Grimké, Sarah Moore, 186
Guevara, Ernesto "Che," 13, 24, 25, 26, 198, 200
Gutiérrez, Gustavo, 31, 34, 229, 239
  and Francis (Pope), 1, 2, 3

Gutiérrez, Gustavo (*cont.*)
   and liberation theology, 4, 5, 28–29, 30, 42, 47, 72, 73, 79, 85, 100, 102, 110, 150, 202, 204, 205–6, 226
   and Marxism, 93, 116, 125, 225
   and Maurice Blondel, 134, 135, 147
   and utopianism, 125, 126
   and worldliness, 147, 148, 149

Hacker, Helen Mayer, 177
Hall, G. Stanley, 154
Hamilton, Charles V., 17, 77, 210
Harding, Vincent, 18, 215
Harlem Renaissance, 208
Harrison, Beverly, 239, 245
Harvard Divinity School, 47, 178, 249
Harvey, Van A., 248
Hayden, Casey, 182
Hegel, G. W. F., 44, 51, 59, 79, 88, 89, 91, 94, 107, 109, 117, 194, 204, 212, 229
Henry, Carl F. H., 253
hermeneutics, 2, 20, 36, 77, 92, 102, 112, 157, 189, 258
Herron, George, 160
Herzog, Frederick, 23, 30, 48, 111, 224, 225, 239, 243, 244, 248
Hitler, Adolph, 145
holism, 138, 173
Holocaust, 23, 47, 148
Hook, Sidney, 121, 162
Horney, Karen, 180, 190
Hughes, Langston, 15–16, 208
Hulsether, Mark, 221, 222
humanism, 197, 202
Hurston, Zora Neale, 191, 208
Hutchinson, Anne, 64, 186

ideology, 49, 94, 101, 107, 108, 112, 114, 141, 226, 228, 240
   and anti-Semitism, 140
   and capitalism, 25
   and feminism, 112, 180–81
   and liberation theology, 37, 105, 106, 173, 204, 223, 224, 228, 242, 249, 263
   and Marxism, 48, 107, 108, 110
   and Nazism, 47
   as obscurer of reality, 9, 109, 126
   and racism, 5, 17, 23, 56, 61, 85, 111, 119, 140, 246
   and sexism, 33, 246
   and social control, 122, 124, 150, 249
   and utopianism, 124, 227
   and whiteness, 75, 110, 111, 158
immigration, 114, 131, 136, 139, 155, 177
imperialism, 115, 132, 137, 243, 248
   critiques of, 122, 179, 198, 229
   efforts against, 24, 215, 229
   and theology, 184, 228, 229
   of US, 3, 20, 29, 210, 222, 239
indigenous peoples, 5, 63, 196, 197, 204, 205, 227, 237
   freedom struggles, 7, 25, 50, 52, 55, 57, 62, 114–15, 116, 137, 257, 261
   political/social inclusion, 136, 146, 198
   subjugation of, 53, 54, 58, 195
   traditional beliefs, 6, 57, 229, 312n2
   and women, 31, 41, 62
individual's relationship to the social whole, 91, 119, 288n51
individualism, 7, 48, 73, 104, 107, 119, 139, 145, 146, 156, 158, 161, 189, 205, 208, 210, 226, 242
industrialization, 135, 199
Ingenieros, José, 136
institutional racism, 15, 20, 210
internal colonization, 210

Jackson, Jesse, 257
James, C. L. R., 58
James, E. O., 186

James, William, 96–97, 99, 117, 118, 141, 183
Jefferson, Thomas, 51, 54, 61, 242
Jews, 52, 54, 113, 141, 176, 177, 231
Jim Crow, 14, 15, 21, 22, 117, 118, 160, 167, 168, 176
jingoism, 242
John Paul II (Pope), 251
Johnson, Mordecai W., 167
Johnson, Terrence J., 258
Johnson, William H., 17
Jones, Absalom, 61, 231
Jones, LeRoi. *See* Baraka, Imamu Amiri
Jones, William R., 231–32, 233
Jung, Carl, 186, 197
just war theory, 221

Kant, Immanuel, 52, 71, 88, 148, 163, 229
  and categorical imperative, 72, 75
  and freedom, 69, 70, 73
  and rational faith, 42, 94, 95
Kaufman, Gordon, D., 249
Kennedy, Florynce "Flo," 191
Kierkegaard, Søren, 44, 277n5
King, Martin Luther, Jr., 14, 41, 79, 81, 111, 166, 167, 168, 221, 231, 233, 242, 254
King, Mary, 182
King, Richard H., 209
Kinsey, Alfred C., 176

L'Ouverture, Toussaint, 58
labor movement, 23, 25, 27, 118, 133, 136, 154, 157, 160, 162, 198, 199, 261
Lacan, Jacques, 212
Las Abejas Maya community, 257
Las Casas, Bartolomé de, 57, 204
Lastarria, José Victorino, 55, 195, 196
Latin American Bishops Conference (CELAM), 26, 27, 81, 93, 310n29

Lee, Jarena, 62
Leibniz, G. W., 231
Lemone, Archie, 237
Lenin, Vladimir, 86
Leo XIII (Pope), 45–46, 133
Lerner, Gerda, 177
Lessing, Doris, 190
Lester, Julius, 18, 230, 231
liberalism, 2, 7, 60, 89, 115, 135, 148, 212, 222
  critiques of, 7, 8, 14, 15, 56, 168, 230
  and religion, 2, 41, 45, 131, 133, 136, 137, 152, 201
  see also neoliberalism
liberation theology, 4, 8, 10, 31, 33, 34, 35, 63, 92, 132–33, 200, 204, 204, 206, 221–22, 223, 227, 237, 255, 256–57, 258, 260–61
  attacks on, 228, 236, 246, 249, 250, 251–53, 256
  and black freedom movement, 3, 23, 78, 103, 144, 215, 224, 259
  and Catholic Church, 1–2, 100, 133, 135, 136, 202, 225, 252
  and feminism, 9, 174, 178, 191, 192, 215
  and Marxism, 222, 223, 225, 243
  as political force, 5, 8, 37–38, 47, 49, 114, 153, 259, 263
  and pragmatism, 99, 150
  and Protestantism, 29, 140, 144–45, 253
  revolutionary inspirations, 4, 199
  and secularity, 173, 262
  and social gospel, 158, 163, 172, 226
  theoretical differences within, 219, 239, 240–41, 242
  this-world consciousness, 72, 132, 150
  and utopianism, 222, 243

liberation theology (*cont.*)
    see also Catholic Church: attacks on liberation theology; Catholic Church: support for liberation theology; Cone, James: black liberation theology; ecumenicalism: and liberation theology; freedom: and liberation theology; Gutiérrez, Gustavo: and liberation theology; poverty: and liberation theology; Protestantism: and liberation theology; salvation: and liberation theology; social justice: and liberation theology; Third World: and liberation theology; violence: and liberation theology; women: and liberation theology
Lilla, Mark, 38
Lincoln, C. Eric, 21, 230
Lippmann, Walter, 137
Locke, Alain, 208
Locke, John, 52, 53, 60, 73, 89
López Trujillo, Alfonso, 250, 251, 252
Lorin, Henri, 134
Lorscheiter, José Ivo, 257
Lotzer, Sebastian, 38
Lubac, Henri de, 147
Lugo, Fernando, 257
Luther, Martin, 38–40, 41, 88–89, 138, 225
Lutheranism, 39, 95, 142

Macintosh, Douglas C., 97, 98–99
magical realism, 201
Magisterium, 45, 99, 134
Malcolm X, 16–17, 20, 21, 161, 210, 211, 213
Manifest Destiny, 6, 158, 225, 240
Mannheim, Karl, 109, 110, 124
Marcuse, Herbert, 30, 73, 122–23, 143, 204

Mariategui, José Carlos, 204, 205
Maritain, Jacques, 42, 121, 131, 132–33, 135–39, 147, 202
Martí, José, 196, 198
Martin, Trayvon, 258
Marx, Karl, 48, 80, 88, 89, 94, 95, 105, 107, 155, 165, 229, 235, 244
Marxism, 1, 2, 39, 76, 107, 121, 122, 136, 142, 145, 146, 193, 199, 202, 225
    as antidote to oppression, 3, 26, 93, 124, 240
    and black freedom struggle, 103, 110–11, 117, 168, 209, 210, 212, 238
    in Cuba, 24, 25
    in Latin America, 108, 115, 229, 245
    and religion, 25, 108, 109, 110, 114, 116, 117, 124, 125, 136, 142, 143, 145, 148, 198, 222, 223, 235, 243, 251, 252, 253
masculinist theology, 21, 31, 32, 64, 170, 180, 183, 184–85, 192
Mather, Cotton, 48
Mathews, Shailer, 97, 98
Mays, Benjamin E., 167
McFague, Sallie, 189, 190
McKay, Claude, 208
Mead, George Herbert, 97, 111
Mead, Margaret, 177, 179–80, 181, 221, 234
Medellín bishops conference, 202, 203, 252
Melano Couch, Beatriz, 245
mestizaje, 194–95, 197, 205, 208
Metz, Johann Baptist, 47, 122, 148, 149, 164, 203, 229
Mignolo, Walter D., 198
Millett, Kate, 176
Mills, C. Wright, 94, 219–20, 238–39
modernism, 90–91, 99, 133, 134, 196–97, 220
modernity, 36, 45, 88, 91, 94, 121, 165, 179, 188, 194, 204, 206, 211
    and colonialism, 197, 198

and religion, 5, 9, 36, 71, 105, 133, 137–38, 139, 152, 166, 173, 196, 247, 248, 262
and secularism, 37, 149, 173, 195, 249, 261
modernization theory, 199
Moltmann, Jürgen, 30, 47, 122, 148–49, 164, 169, 203, 228–29
monotheism, 33, 176, 184, 235
Monroe Doctrine, 6, 240
motherhood, 74, 176, 180, 190, 234, 235
Mothers of the Plaza de Mayo, 223
Mott, Lucretia, 62, 64, 97, 119, 154
Mumford, Lewis, 165
Munger, Theodore T., 155
Müntzer, Thomas, 39–40, 123, 124
Murena, Hector A., 197
Murray, John Courtney, 136
Murray, Judith Sargent, 62
Murray, Pauli, 32, 181
Muste, A. J., 162
Myrdal, Gunnar, 209, 210

Nation of Islam, 16, 17, 211
National Committee of Black Churchmen, 213
National Council of Churches, 220, 239
National Organization for Women (NOW), 181
National Student Christian Federation, 164
Native Americans, 241, 243
neo-colonialism, 135, 201, 203, 204
neoliberalism, 258, 260, 261
Neo-Scholasticism, 133–34
Neuhaus, Richard J., 226, 227, 249
New Christendom, 137, 138
New Christian Right (U.S.), 252–54, 257, 261
New Left, 7, 40, 90, 123, 132, 144, 199
and anti-colonialism, 193, 222, 229–30

and Cuba, 24–25, 239
and feminism, 32, 181–82
New Theology, 155
Newman, Pamela, 191
Newton, Huey P., 210
Niagara Movement, 160
Niebuhr, H. Richard, 46, 100, 110–11, 189
Niebuhr, Reinhold, 48, 150, 220, 227
and black freedom movement, 161, 167
and Christian realism, 41, 81, 152, 163, 164, 235
and coercive power, 15, 19, 161–62
critiques of, 179, 180
private vs. public ethics, 100, 111, 161–62, 163, 167, 226
Nietzsche, Friedrich, 71, 72, 184
Nisbet, Robert A., 90
Noll, Mark, 98, 154
Novak, Michael, 226

Occupy Wall Street, 258, 259
Ogden, Schubert, 48
orthopraxis, 29, 93, 102–3, 250
Our Lady of Guadalupe, 240

pacifism, 82, 136, 220, 221
Paine, Thomas, 54, 60, 61
Pan-Americanism, 196
Pannenberg, Wolfhart, 47, 148
Parson, Elsie Clews, 177
Paul (Saint), 188
Paul VI (Pope), 251, 310n30
Paul, Nathaniel, 169
Peasants' War (Germany), 39
Peirce, Charles, 96, 98, 99
Pinn, Anthony B., 231
Pinochet, Augusto, 223
Pius X, 99, 133, 134
Pius XI, 135
Plaskow, Judith, 235
pluralism, 23, 26, 137, 146, 221, 236, 255

Porterfield, Amanda, 54
positivism, 56, 90–91, 92, 93, 99, 104, 135, 137, 196
poverty, 7, 29, 39, 40, 47, 64, 123, 143, 155–56, 160, 165, 166, 174, 199, 225, 226
    and black theology, 22, 23, 78, 84, 85, 111, 161, 168, 169, 233, 251
    and Catholic Church, 3, 25, 26, 77, 93, 133, 146, 202, 203, 257
    and Christian apathy toward, 43, 48, 78, 142, 154, 201, 204
    as detriment to faith, 39
    and exploitation, 75, 77, 81, 122, 138, 150, 198, 202
    and liberation theology, 1, 2, 5, 23, 30, 172, 199, 204, 205, 206, 227, 229, 255, 260–61
    structural roots of, 28, 93, 127, 146, 167, 203
    among women, 31
Powell, Adam Clayton, Sr., 140, 141, 161
Prado, Javier, 195
pragmatism, 97, 100, 101, 104, 140, 159, 228, 242, 253, 262
    and Catholicism, 99, 228
    in North America, 30, 96, 99, 197
    and scientific theology, 87, 98–99
praxis, 2, 29, 72, 77, 124, 125–26, 135, 145, 149, 169, 173, 175, 185, 202–3, 225, 229, 233, 240, 242, 246
Presbyterian Church (U.S.A.), 258
primitivism, 208
Protestant ISAL (Church and Society in Latin America), 30, 144, 145
Protestant Principle, 127, 153, 228
Protestantism, 27, 35, 44, 47, 52, 54, 99, 131, 153, 156, 157, 220–21, 268
    and black freedom movement, 4, 19, 230, 239
    and capitalism, 108, 109, 115, 145
    and Catholicism, 132, 134, 139–40, 223, 224, 226, 243
    and feminism, 32, 178, 183, 184, 185
    and individual liberty, 6, 60, 127, 139, 153, 206, 228
    in Latin America, 77, 136, 139–40, 144–45
    and liberalism, 41, 45, 201, 220, 221
    and liberation theology, 8, 29–30, 144, 154, 222, 224, 226, 253, 254, 255
    and political engagement, 140, 162
    and salvation, 88, 142
    and scripture, 36, 91, 142
    and the state, 37, 40, 42
    and US foreign policy, 221, 240
Puritanism, 241, 242

Quintín Lame, Manuel, 257, 312n2

Rainbow Coalition, 257
Rama, Angel, 205
Ramos, Samuel, 197
Ransom, Reverdy C., 160, 161, 231
rationalism, 36, 61, 116, 134, 247
Rauschenbusch, Walter, 131, 155–56, 157, 167, 226
Rawls, John, 262
Read, Joel, 181
Reagan, Ronald, 257
Reformation, 35–36, 37, 38, 39, 40, 49, 52, 62, 64, 88, 103, 173, 254
Re-Imagining Conferences, 258
religious quietism, 38, 170, 223, 232
Rich, Adrienne, 190
Ritschl, Albrecht, 94–95, 96, 97, 100, 156
Roberts, J. Deotis, 23, 239
    and black nationalism, 80, 81, 215
    and Christian social action, 81, 84, 170
    reconciliation theology, 80, 278–79n28
Rockefeller Report on the Americas, 222
Rodó, José Enrique, 197
Rollins, Jeanne, 241

Romero, Emilio, 115
Romero, Oscar, 257
Rossi, Alice, 177
Rossinow, Doug, 152
Rousseau, Jean-Jacques, 42, 53, 59, 69, 105, 106, 134, 138, 194, 229, 242
Ruether, Rosemary Radford, 4, 32, 33, 34, 40, 74, 83–84, 85, 163, 170–72, 184, 187–88, 192, 233–34, 239, 240–41, 243, 248, 249
Ruiz Garcia, Samuel, 257, 312n2
Rush, Benjamin, 54
Russell, Letty M., 178, 184, 250

Sacred Heart Seminary (Detroit), 239
Saint-Domingue, 58, 59
salvation, 2, 18, 69, 70–71, 72, 88, 92, 111, 142, 156, 169, 188
  as holistic freedom, 65, 76, 125, 251
  and the individual, 154, 155, 162, 170, 171, 253, 254
  and liberation theology, 28, 44, 69, 71–72, 73, 84, 116, 119, 127, 132, 138, 148, 149, 150, 227
  and political freedom, 60, 65, 74, 172, 259
  and the social, 156, 157, 160, 161, 169, 170, 172, 226
Sandanista revolution, 256
Sanders, Thomas, 227, 228
Santa Ana, Julio de, 142, 144–45
Santayana, George, 117
Sarmiento, Domingo F., 195
Sartre, Jean-Paul, 212
Schappeler, Christoph, 38
Schleiermacher, Friedrich, 43–44, 45, 46–47, 48, 71, 91, 94, 95, 98, 156, 192, 247
Schmitt, Carl, 49, 272n24
Scudder, Vida, 158, 159
secular humanism, 253

secularization theology, 95, 97, 98, 127, 132, 135, 136, 145, 147, 149, 151, 152, 154, 157, 164–65, 171, 221, 247–48, 250, 261–62, 293n29
Segundo, Juan Luis, 29, 47–48, 82, 86, 93–94, 102, 108–10, 252
Semaine sociale movement, 134
Sexton, Anne, 190
sexuality, 176, 186–87, 221, 253
Shakespeare, William, 197
Shaull, Richard, 30, 142–44, 145, 222, 250, 278n17
Shay's Rebellion, 243
situational ethics, 221
skepticism, 36, 52
slavery, 14, 21, 28, 40, 61, 75, 79, 81
  and Christianity, 15, 17, 19, 40–41, 43, 46, 54, 118, 231, 232
  and freedom, 53, 56, 58, 59, 60
  and literacy, 55, 78
  rebellion against, 22, 58, 59, 63
  relationship with masters, 111, 122, 154, 194, 211, 238
  and slave trade, 5, 57
  in US, 56, 60
  among women, 62, 83, 192
Smith, Adam, 53, 244
Smith, Christian, 267n13
social Christianity, 152, 159, 172
social democracy, 97, 144, 157, 161, 220
social gospel, 41, 45, 98, 131, 153–58, 163, 164, 206, 226, 240, 241, 243
social justice, 4, 108, 111, 157, 158
  and black churches, 258, 259
  and Catholic Church, 2, 134, 202
  and Christian gospel, 47, 140, 226
  in Latin America, 58, 115
  and liberation theology, 172, 243, 260–61
  role of modern state, 40, 139, 156

social sciences, 199, 242, 253, 262
    and affinity with theology, 88, 90, 92, 93, 94, 101, 102, 120, 154, 164, 247, 248
    and black theology, 93, 117, 119
    and Catholic Church, 26, 27, 91, 92, 239, 240
    and conflicts with theology, 87, 91, 92, 172, 248
    and feminism, 177, 178, 179
    and liberation theology, 86, 103, 200
    and Protestantism, 91, 92
socialism, 123, 155, 157, 240, 244, 250
    and Catholic Church, 136, 146
    critiques of, 28, 133, 154
    in Cuba, 26, 198–99
    and feminism, 120, 158, 171, 176, 182
    in Germany, 39, 47, 111, 121
    and labor movement, 45, 160
    in Latin America, 25, 114–15, 146, 204, 222, 227, 229, 240, 257
Society for the Defense of Tradition, Family, and Property (Chile), 252
Sodalitium Vitae (Peru), 252
Solentiname Community (Nicaragua), 203, 204
Somoza Garcia, Anastasio, 203, 204, 257
Sorel, Georges, 116
Southern Christian Leadership Conference, 166
Spencer, Herbert, 90
Spener, Philipp Jakob, 43
St. Simonians, 188
Stanton, Elizabeth Cady, 32, 64, 90, 112–13, 119, 178, 235
Starhawk, 235
Stark, Werner, 88
Steinem, Gloria, 185
Stern, Steve, 58
Stewart, Maria W., 154, 231
Strong, Josiah, 157

Student Christian Movement, 140, 142
Student Nonviolent Coordinating Committee (SNCC), 77, 181
Students for a Democratic Society (SDS), 181
subjectivity, 23, 44, 45, 112, 132, 187, 249
suffragettes, 177, 185

Taylor, Charles, 193
Taylor, Graham, 159
Teresa of Avila (Saint), 186
theodicy, 231, 232
Theology in the Americas conference (1975), 238–39, 247, 309n20
theonomy, 153
Third World, 30, 49, 79, 149, 193, 202, 204, 210, 211, 221, 222, 227, 228, 237, 238, 260
    and anti-colonialism, 4, 24–25, 27, 90, 122, 123, 148, 210, 259
    and development/modernization, 7, 29, 76
    and feminism, 191, 192, 215, 234
    and liberation theology, 165, 192, 215, 224, 256, 258
    and poverty, 26
    relations with US, 14, 17, 210, 222, 224, 239
Third World Women's Alliance, 191
this-world consciousness, 54, 60, 80, 119, 127, 132, 141, 152, 232, 259
Thompson, Clara, 180
Thompson, Helen, 177
Thurman, Howard, 167, 214
Tillich, Paul, 111, 113, 121, 122, 127, 152–53, 164, 215
Tolstoy, Leo, 155
Tometi, Opal, 258
Torre, Victor Raul de la, 136
Torres, Camillo, 26–27, 34, 82, 146, 203, 223, 239

Torres, Sergio, 223, 239
totalitarianism/anti-totalitarianism, 109, 121, 132, 138, 140, 220
Townes, Emilie Maureen, 191
transcendence, 5, 9, 43, 47, 48, 71–72, 100, 101, 132, 134–35, 141, 143, 145, 147, 149, 150, 153, 164, 171, 173, 175, 176, 187, 235, 247, 248, 249, 250
Trible, Phyllis, 235
Trigo, Pedro, 205
Trilling, Lionel, 179
Tristán, Flora, 62
Troeltsch, Ernst, 94, 95, 95–96, 97, 100
Truth, Sojourner, 62
Tufts, James, 97
Túpac Amaru, José Gabriel, II, 57, 58, 115
Turner, Henry McNeal, 18, 207
Turner, Nat, 169

U.S. Catholic Conference, 239
Union Theological Seminary, 22, 140, 152, 179, 220, 244, 245
United Front (Colombia), 27, 146
United Methodist Women, 181
Universal Declaration of Human Rights (1948), 137
urbanization, 131, 135, 139, 227, 243, 246; Marx's critique of, 228
Ureña, Pedro Henríquez, 197

Vallejo, Cesar, 204
Vasconcelos, José, 136, 197
Vatican II, 4, 26, 27, 29, 32, 46, 133, 148, 165, 183, 201–2
Vekemans, Roger, 250, 251
Verón, Eliseo, 94
Vietnam War, 18, 221
violence, 16, 39, 160, 201, 202, 209, 210, 223, 252, 258
  and Black Power, 18, 21, 23
  and liberation theology, 3, 73, 77, 81–83, 222, 251
  as means of social change, 52, 59, 79–80, 94, 135, 144, 161–62, 225
  versus nonviolence, 15, 18, 21, 39, 52, 73, 79–83, 135, 144, 161–62, 202, 209, 222, 225, 230, 251
von Drey, Sebastian Johann, 45, 91
von Ketteler, Wilhelm Emmanuel, 133

Walker, Alice, 191
Walker, David, 61, 63, 77, 118, 231
Ward, Lester F., 91, 119
Washington, Booker T., 160
Weber, Max, 90, 91, 96, 108, 109, 117, 121
Wells, Ida B., 160, 191
Wesley, John, 43
West, Cornel, 9, 104
Whitehead, Alfred North, 179
whiteness, 110, 111, 118, 212, 233
Will, George, 2
will of God, 36, 37, 62, 63, 77, 79, 103, 141
Williams, Delores S., 191
Williams, Maxine, 191
Williams, Preston, 239
Williams, Reggie L., 140
Williams, Robert F., 24, 82
Wilmore, Gayraud S., 20, 23, 168, 206, 207, 215
Winthrop, John, 242
Wittgenstein, Ludwig, 189
Wollstonecraft, Mary, 59, 61–62
womanist, 191
Women and Religion Task Force, 181
women, 13, 50, 52, 54, 55, 56, 60, 69, 113, 114, 152, 178–79
  black women, 34, 61, 83, 160, 191
  ecclesiastical leadership, 178, 181, 192
  elite white women, 57, 61, 174
  and liberation theology, 3, 4, 5, 31–32, 84, 112, 114, 163, 170–73, 174–75, 183–92

women (*cont.*)
  marginalization of, 7, 34, 40, 174
  and social Christianity, 158, 159
  and traditional Christianity, 33, 41, 183
  women's movement, 59, 62, 63, 74, 76, 83, 86, 112, 118–20, 126, 175–82
women's history, 64, 174, 177, 190
Women's International Terrorist Conspiracy from Hell (WITCH), 188
women's studies, 230
Women's Trade Union League, 158
Woodson, Carter G., 77, 79
World Council of Churches (WCC), 142–43, 220, 221, 237, 258
Wright, Jeremiah, 3
Wright, Richard, 193, 209
Wuthnow, Robert, 221

Zapatistas, 257
Zea, Leopoldo, 194